THE AMERICAN GI
IN EUROPE IN WORLD WAR II

THE AMERICAN GI IN EUROPE IN WORLD WAR II

THE MARCH TO D-DAY

J.E. KAUFMANN
AND H. W. KAUFMANN

STACKPOLE
BOOKS

Published by
STACKPOLE BOOKS
5067 Ritter Road
Mechanicsburg, PA 17055
www.stackpolebooks.com

Printed in the United States of America

10 9 8 7 6 5 4 3 2 1

Library of Congress Cataloging-in-Publication Data

Kaufmann, J. E.
The American GI in Europe in World War II : the march to D-Day / J.E. Kaufmann and H.W. Kaufmann.
p. cm.
Includes bibliographical references and index.
ISBN 978-0-8117-0449-6 — ISBN 978-0-8117-0454-0 — ISBN 978-0-8117-0526-4 1. World War, 1939–1945—Campaigns—Western Front. 2. World War, 1939–1945—United States. 3. United States. Army—History—World War, 1939–1945. 4. World War, 1939–1945—Personal narratives, American. 5. United States—Army—Biography. I. Kaufmann, H. W. II. Title.
D769.K34 2009
940.54'1273092—dc22
[B]

2008046869

CONTENTS

INTRODUCTION

This first book—*The March to D-Day*—in our three-volume series on the American GI in Europe in World War II provides the background to the United States' entry into the war, the training of the troops, and their shipment to Europe; it also details the North African and Mediterranean campaigns through the first half of 1944. The second volume covers the preparations for Operation Overlord and the landings in Normandy on D-Day, June 6, 1944. The final installment continues with operations in Normandy after D-Day, the Brittany campaign, and the invasion of southern France.

The objective of this series is not to compile a history of individual units of the U.S. armed forces or thoroughly examine the campaigns in which they took part during the war in Europe. We included only enough historical information to provide background and context for veterans' accounts. We thought it would be interesting to follow some of these American veterans from the time of their induction and training to their participation in the invasions of Normandy and the French Riviera during the summer of 1944. We also thought it important to shine the spotlight not only on combat veterans, but also on the men who made it all possible by operating the rear echelons and supporting the troops in the front lines.

This series presents a small sampling of the experiences of American veterans in World War II and makes no claim of being a comprehensive compendium of the war. Some units, such as the airborne, are represented to a greater extent than others. This is not because we feel that their role was more important, but because more paratroopers and glidermen came forward to share their experiences with us than other troops did. The same is true of the larger number of accounts from coast guardsmen than from members of the navy.

Instead of covering the battles in the European theater of operations, as others have done, we follow the veterans from the time of their induction and training in the United States, across the Atlantic to Great Britain, and on to Normandy or South France, as the case may be. Some of the accounts in this series have already appeared in other books, which we recommend also reading to get a better understanding of the events.

It should also be pointed out that many of these accounts were compiled forty-five years or more after the events and at least some of the narrators may have been influenced by what they read or heard during the intervening years. Discrepancies may occur on such topics as the length of the rope, the amount of ammunition carried by the paratroopers, or the nomenclature of the weapons they used. Some of the veterans' comments and opinions may be questionable, but that does not mean their information is wrong; in many cases, the details cannot be verified. The reader should be aware of this and use his or her own judgment about whether to accept the questionable comments as fact.

Exaggeration and distortion are always a problem, but we have done our best to remove obvious problems and accounts that were clearly fabrications. For instance, we did not complete one veteran's interview after he claimed that he had volunteered for a secret mission to France while he was training in England. He admitted that he did not speak French and had no special skills beyond basic training to qualify him for such a mission. No facts disclosed by the man could be taken seriously, and the interview was terminated.

One veteran claimed that he took part in a special mission in Normandy on June 3, 1944, to mark the drop zones for the airborne Pathfinders. He showed us a Silver Star that he claimed to have received for this mission, but he was unable to produce a copy of the accompanying certificate to confirm his rather farfetched story. More than ten years later, in *U.S. Airborne Divisions in the ETO*, Steven Zaloga briefly mentioned the June 3 mission, and while this veteran's account appeared in a recent book published in Belgium, his description of the operation had changed. We decided to reexamine his account and requested a copy of his records from the military records center at St. Louis, where most World War II files were destroyed in a fire in the 1970s. His records indicated that he was in the U.S. until late summer 1944 and that he first participated in combat in September 1944. We could not find corroboration of his account of the mission in Normandy, but his military record closely followed his account of what he actually did after that date. It is difficult to explain why this man would fabricate such a fact since his military career did not lack luster; indeed, he received a Bronze Star for his role in Operation Market Garden.

Another veteran, a Texan named Charles Bell, was willing to talk about his more mundane activities in the army. According to his records, he had been awarded both the Silver and Bronze Stars with Oak Leaf Clusters for each. When asked for details, he simply proffered the accompanying certificates, unwilling to appear boastful. We have included the contents of these certificates in the text.

These are some of the problems encountered when interviewing and attempting to substantiate the accounts of veterans. It must be hoped that the more witnesses and accounts there are, the greater the chance of achieving accuracy. It is our hope that the veterans' accounts in these volumes will enrich the body of information concerning these momentous events in world history.

CHAPTER 1

Background, 1939–41

The Japanese air assault on Pearl Harbor early on the morning of December 7, 1941, catapulted the United States into World War II. Shortly afterward, Hitler declared war on the United States in support of his Japanese ally. Months earlier, President Franklin D. Roosevelt and Prime Minister Winston Churchill had agreed that when the United States finally entered the war, the Allies would give the liberation of Europe first priority. They also concluded that after the summer of 1940, when France fell, the only way back onto the continent would be through an invasion of Italy or France.

After the surrender of France in 1940, the American public had remained divided on becoming involved in another foreign war. Nonetheless, the U.S. military establishment had continued to plan for a conflict by sending military attachés to observe and report on their potential enemies' war preparations. On July 10, 1940, the army responded to the fall of France by establishing the Armored Force under the leadership of Brig. Gen. Adna R. Chaffee. Chaffee's new force was pitiful compared with the German war machine. It numbered a mere 8,000 men and 393 light tanks, while the Germans had more than 2,000 tanks by this time. When America finally entered the war, the Armored Force was hard-pressed to prepare and train its men and obtain modern armored vehicles.

In 1940, the American army was smaller than most European armies. The Germans began the summer of that year with about 150 divisions and the French, before their defeat, with about 90, whereas the U.S. Army had about a dozen. Roosevelt nonetheless remained undaunted. In a radio broadcast on May 26, 1940, he proclaimed that the armed forces were "at peak for peacetime service" and vowed, "We shall rebuild them swiftly, as the methods of warfare swiftly change." On May 29, he appealed to Congress to increase defense spending to include 3,000 new aircraft and up to 2,000 new tanks. At the end of July, the president requested the call-up of National Guard units for active service. The 9th Infantry Division formed in August 1940, giving the U.S. Army twelve infantry divisions and two armored divisions. On August 27, 1940, Congress authorized Roosevelt to activate reserve components for twelve months. Thus began the induction of the first National Guard divisions into national service for a year of training. By December 1941, the remaining National Guard divisions went into federal service, raising the army's strength to thirty-three divisions, including two armored and two cavalry.[1]

During that same summer, Congress passed the Naval Expansion Act, sometimes referred to as the Two-Ocean Navy Act, and Roosevelt signed it on July 19, 1940. The act called for the construction of warships, naval aircraft, and auxiliary shipping to prepare the country for war.

Back on August 31, 1939, Roosevelt appointed Gen. George C. Marshall as the new army chief of staff. Marshall would remain in that position until the end of the war. He became so indispensable to the president that he had to give up his hopes of leading the invasion forces into France, contenting himself to guide the U.S. armed forces through the war.

Paths to Glory

Larry Eugene Knecht, who grew up in Chicago during the darkest years of the Great Depression, traveled south looking for work when he turned twenty. Good jobs were still scarce, however, and in desperation, he decided to check out what the army had to offer. The recruiter assured him that he was exactly what the army was looking for: an athlete with the potential to become a great warrior. He would receive the royal treatment and get promoted to corporal in no time at all. Pleased with these prospects, Knecht signed up on September 24, 1934, and began his service with the 29th Infantry at Fort Benning, Georgia. It did not take long for disillusionment to set in. Army life for athletes was the same as for everyone else, and promotions were hard to come by.

After transferring from one unit to another, Larry Knecht was pleased to end up on the Georgia coast at Fort Screven. It was a veritable island paradise, with sandy beaches and a mild climate, land was very popular in the 1930s. Although most units had reveille at 5 A.M., his did not rise until 6 A.M. Fort Screven was a turn-of-the-century coastal fortification strung along the beach and the swampy terrain behind the island. Knecht served in the 4th Company (the machine-gun company), 1st Battalion, 8th Infantry. In June 1940, his sojourn at this posh outpost on the beach came to an end, as the 8th Infantry—with headquarters and its 2nd Battalion at Fort Moultrie, South Carolina—relocated to Fort Benning to join the 4th Infantry Division. At Fort Benning, the 3rd Battalion was

1. Between September and December 1940, the following nine National Guard infantry divisions were inducted: 27th, 30th, 31st, 35th, 36th, 37th, 41st, 44th, and 45th. The 26th, 28th, 29th, 33rd, 34th, 38th, 40th, and 43rd National Guard Divisions followed between January and March 1941, followed by the 32nd in October. The other infantry divisions were regular army formations (several reactivated): 1st, 2nd, 3rd, 4th, 5th, 6th, 7th, 8th, 9th, 24th, and 25th.

Early-model B-17s over New York, 1938. W. OSTROWSKA

reactivated, and the regiment was brought up to strength.

When activated in June 1940, the 4th Division consisted of three regiments: the 22nd, 8th, and 29th Infantry, the last of which had been training troops at Fort Benning for many years. In 1941, the 29th was sent back to the Infantry School at Fort Benning and replaced by the 12th Infantry. "We had men who had been corporals for ten to twelve years," Knecht recalls, "while we lost many of our men to OCS [Officer Candidate School] in the next few years, who eventually became officers in other units."

That summer, the newly activated 4th Infantry Division became a motorized division, along with the 6th, 7th, and 8th Infantry Divisions, remaining such until 1943. During that time, Knecht had also moved through the ranks, becoming a chief warrant officer (CWO) in the 8th Infantry, 4th Division, in 1944. He knew most of the men who passed through the regiment.

Charles L. Jackson, who completed high school during the height of the Depression, participated in the Citizens Military Training Camps (CMTC) program held during the summer and decided to become an army officer. After five semesters of college, he received an appointment to West Point, graduating on June 14, 1938. Lieutenant Jackson then reported to the 29th Infantry at Fort Benning's Infantry Training Center. In the summer of 1941, he transferred to the 12th Infantry at Fort Dix, New Jersey, just as the regiment was readying to ship out to Trinidad. President Roosevelt had just given fifty old destroyers to the British in exchange for bases in the Caribbean, and Jackson's regiment was getting ready for tropical duty. The move was canceled, however, and Jackson returned to Fort Benning with the 4th Division when the 12th Infantry replaced the 29th. Like Larry Knecht, the newly promoted Captain Jackson remained with the 4th Division through the Normandy campaign and eventually reached the rank of lieutenant colonel. He commanded the 1st Battalion of the 12th Infantry during the invasion.

In 1935, the Great Depression still held the nation in its grip, and jobs were scarce, especially for teenagers like Thomas Cortright, who lived in Aurora, a small town nestled in the farmlands of Illinois to the west of Chicago's towering skyscrapers. Casting about for a source of extra cash, Cortright hit upon the notion of joining the Illinois National Guard. He would not only get paid for attending the weekend meetings, but also get to wear a uniform and play soldier, an idea that had great appeal for a young man still wet behind the ears. The only obstacle that stood between him and his aspirations was his age. Undaunted by such a trifling thing, he subtracted one year from his date of birth and signed up on May 28, 1935. Evidently, the National Guard recruiters were too pressed for manpower to scrutinize the records. Cortright describes his experience:

> I was seventeen years of age. I lied a year and went into the Illinois National Guard, Company D, 129th Infantry Regiment. I was assigned to a machine-gun company, and I was number ten man. There were ten men, and the number nine and ten were the mule leaders, except we had no mules to lead. Instead, we had two little two-wheeled trailer affairs with a Browning .30-caliber water-cooled machine gun mounted on it and designed to fire from. The number nine and ten men therefore became the pullers of the cart.
>
> A year later I became a corporal, and in another year I was a sergeant. It was about that time that the training intensified, and we were going to drill at the armory twice a week and NCO School another night of the week. Every other weekend was spent in training of some kind, such as marksmanship in some gravel pit range or in the armory basement range in conjunction with other National Guard machine-gun companies, or making a mock attack on some outlying farm building. Then there was summer camp for two weeks. Usually we went to Camp Grant near Rockford, Illinois, but with the expanded training, we went to Camp McCoy, Wisconsin, one year, and another to maneuvers near Pearl, Michigan, for four weeks. This last one was after they reorganized the army into triangular divisions in 1940,[2] and our company became a heavy-weapons company. That meant that we had three machine-gun platoons and one mortar platoon, of which I was the sergeant. In that capacity, I went to a training school in Skokie, Illinois, where we all did various things, including firing the Stokes 3-inch mortar. I proved very adept at this and received an overall rating of 98.5, along with a cup for the highest achievement ever at this camp.

Sergeant Cortright left his regiment for OCS, after which he was assigned as the executive officer of an infantry company of the 22nd Infantry, 4th Division.

Another thrill-seeking teenager, Marcel Galen Swank of Rosemount, Minnesota, turned sixteen on December 17, 1938, and enlisted within three days in the 135th Infantry Regiment of the 34th Division, Minnesota National Guard. In many states, sixteen- and seventeen-year-olds apparently could join the National Guard with parental permission. Swank, who was hoping for a life of derring-do in the military, later left the 135th to join a new elite unit that offered the challenge he was seeking, thus becoming one of the first army Rangers. Ranger Sergeant Swank was one of a handful of American soldiers to land in France in 1942, when he took part in the Dieppe raid.

Arnold Delmonico, whose fascination with photography and interest in aircraft led him to enlist in the Army Air Corps on December 23, 1939, left his native Connecticut for Langley Field, Virginia, where he completed a month of basic training.

> I was assigned to the 21st Recon Squadron, after leaving Langley, which was on maneuvers in Miami, Florida. We lived there in quarters, which consisted of sixteen-by-sixteen pyramidal tents that were located on the site of the present international airport.
>
> The mission of the 21st Recon was to fly patrols up and down the coast of Florida as far north as Georgia and down beyond

2. In the late 1930s, the army began changing the structure of its divisions to a triangular configuration. The 2nd Infantry Division was the first to undergo this change and was followed by the remaining regular divisions in 1940 and by National Guard and reserves in 1941. Before this, the divisions were square, consisting of two brigades of two regiments each. The triangular formation eliminated the brigades and maintained three instead of four regiments. The preexisting fourth regiment usually was used to form a new division.

> Cuba. The purpose was to identify ships in the waters off the coast of the U.S. Any unidentified ship was to be photographed and recorded. On many of those flights, we spotted and located German freighters and tankers in these waters. A couple of times we spotted German U-boats.

Private Delmonico flew on these patrols up and down the East Coast until August 1940. He photographed ships from a Douglas B-18 bomber with a K-3B hand-held camera that produced large eight-by-ten negatives. At the time, the B-18 was the workhorse of most bomber units, until it was replaced by the new B-17 Flying Fortress. The unarmed recon aircraft in which Delmonico flew carried only a crew of five: pilot, copilot, navigator, radioman, and photographer.

> I believe there were four others in the unit who did the same job as me. Patrols went up everyday, generally two aircraft each morning; one would take the southern route and one the northern route. On their return, there would be two more aircraft that would go up for the afternoon, with one cameraman on each aircraft.
>
> On occasion, when finding some of these unidentified ships that mounted guns in the rear, the crew would uncover them as soon as they saw us coming. After removing the tarpaulins, they would track us with them. They never did fire at us. These ships flew no flags and didn't have any outward signs of identification such as a name painted on the hull.
>
> We spotted U-boats occasionally. One of the U-boats was hit by an English warship and was crippled. They finally managed to get up the Indian River in Florida until they made repairs and then scampered away. I photographed that one. I don't know if it got away, because the British may have been waiting for it. I believe this was sometime during the spring of 1940.

In August 1940, Arnold Delmonico attended a photo school in Denver, where he served as an instructor after graduation, eventually reaching the rank of technical sergeant. From there, he was sent as a cadet to the photo commander's course at Yale University. Once he completed the course in 1943, he was commissioned as a lieutenant and assigned to Yale as an instructor. In early 1944, he received his final assignment: the Photographic Section of the 490th Bomb Group. Soon he took part in B-24 and B-17 missions over German-occupied Europe, and he flew over Normandy on D-Day.

David E. Thomas graduated from medical school in 1937 and joined the army in 1939 with a reserve commission and the rank of lieutenant. During the summer of 1939, he went to Fort Hays, Kansas, to take the competitive exam for an appointment as a regular army officer. After passing the exam, he was assigned to the hospital at Fort Devens, Massachusetts, where the medical staff included four other officers in November 1939. The following spring, Thomas attended the Medical Field Service School, at that time located at Carlisle Barracks, Pennsylvania, where the personnel did much "shooting and saluting." After five weeks of training, the Carlisle Barracks students went on a motor march to Camp Polk for the Louisiana maneuvers of 1940.

> I was assigned as a surgeon with an infantry unit of the 1st Infantry Division. When I reported, they didn't have a doctor, but they had a medical detachment. It was a goddamn mess if I ever saw one. They had not even dug a slit trench, and there were turds all over the place. The first thing I made them do was dig a slit trench, and then go around and scratch up all the turds they left here and there.

It is a swampy area, and at that time, Polk was a lot of cut-over pineland, badly eroded, and with a lot of Razorback hogs running around. The army was awfully green at the time. They dug garbage sumps, and they would fill them full before they would cover them over. Every now and then, a hog fell in and drowned.

This first time I was down there, they were really playing games. They had sticks for guns. That was the time they had the expression "OHIO." It was a song of the original draftees who were drafted for a year, and they were afraid they would be extended for over a year. The slogan was "Over the hill in October." When this maneuver was over, we were all gathered together, and we were camped in big tents on the side of a hill. This big rain came, and you had to stay in your cot because the water was flowing right through the tent.

When he returned to Carlisle Barracks, Lieutenant Thomas graduated and reported to Fort Devens, only to learn that he had been assigned to the newly created Armored Corps at Fort Knox, Kentucky. He describes life as a military surgeon there.

Fort Knox was an established post and real nice. There wasn't any living for junior officers. I left my wife and kid at home until I got a little place outside of town. I had to buy the chickens from the guy to get the place, and the rent was $40 a month. We had kerosene stoves in the living rooms and a bucket-a-day coal-fed water heater in the kitchen. They had to have a corps surgeon, so they picked me, and I was never occupied. I spent my time shooting pool. Medical officers were wasted in these higher headquarters; they weren't doing any medicine, just doing paperwork. I was the surgeon of the 1st Armored Corps Provisional. It was a "chicken colonel" spot, and I was a first lieutenant. I didn't know what I was supposed to do, but later in the war, I found they didn't do much of anything.

Parade in Washington, DC, late 1930s. W. OSTROWSKA

Patton was a brigadier and Scott [Charles Scott, the first commanding officer of the 2nd Armored Division] was older. I remember Georgie Patton commanded the 2nd Armored, and my boss, Col. Robert Duenner, took me, and we drove down to Fort Benning to make a medical inspection of the 2nd Armored Division. It was an interesting trip down there. We didn't have any fancy highways. For instance, we had to cross the Cumberland River on one of these barges that crossed back and forth. It was a ferry driven by the current and attached to a cable; turn it downstream to go one way and upstream to go the other. When we got there and inspected the camp, we found the water supply was just a couple inches beneath the soil. They just had had a good hard freeze, and the damn division area was covered with geysers from where the pipes cracked. Colonel Duenner looked things over and told General Patton about what he observed with all this water, and Patton asked him what to do about it. Old Bob Duenner didn't know what to tell him.

At Fort Knox once, a sergeant from the office and I took a guy who was being committed to a mental hospital by train to New Orleans. We took him to the hospital, and they offered us a cup of coffee. It was so thick you could almost cut it; it was full of chicory. They gave me the cup of coffee, I tasted it, and I thought, "Christ, one of the patients must have made this!"

Thomas spent almost a year with the new Armored Corps, but it turned out to be one of the most boring assignments of his career. One day, he came across a notice calling for volunteers for the newly forming airborne forces. Eager to escape the tedium of his post, he sent in an application. The answer came back quickly: He was accepted. He wasted no time in packing his bags and shaking the dust of Fort Knox off his boots.

In 1940, Capt. Stanhope B. Mason returned from duty in the Orient to take a position as a battalion commander in the 5th Infantry Division. He joined the division when it assembled at Camp Custer, Michigan, late in the year. He had served for three years in Hawaii and two in the Philippines. Because of his staff experience in the Far East, he was promoted to major and assigned as an assistant to the G-3 of the 1st Infantry Division at Fort Devens for planning an amphibious operation against Martinique.

Stanley Stypulkowski enlisted in the army in New York City shortly after the Germans conquered Poland. He was stationed at Fort Jay on Governor's Island in New York City and assigned to the antitank company of the 16th Infantry, 1st Division. But Stypulkowski did not stay in his native New York for long. In November 1939, the 16th Infantry moved south in a truck convoy and encamped with the rest of the division at Fort Benning. "We built what was known as a tent city and lived in pyramidal tents," says Stypulkowski, "and were stationed there for several months as we conducted field maneuvers." The tents he refers to were the pyramidal M-1934 tents designed for eight men; the larger squad tents that could accommodate twelve men were not developed until 1942. Before the onset of summer, the whole division moved out for the Louisiana maneuvers of May 1940. The hot and steamy climate of Louisiana was quite an experience for the New Yorker but prepared him well for the hardships of war. Stypulkowski remained with the "Big Red One" through Africa and Italy, leaving it only when carried off the beaches of Normandy on a stretcher.

Sam Zittrer, who enlisted when the German Army began its assault on the West, on May 10, 1940, reported to the 18th Infantry at Fort Hamilton, New York, just as the regiment was returning from the Louisiana maneuvers with the 1st Division. "I got my basic training there," he recalls, "and after about four months of being in Fort Hamilton, Brooklyn, we went to upstate New York to participate in maneuvers in 1940. After the completion of those maneuvers, we returned to Fort Hamilton." Like Private Stypulkowski, Private Zittrer remained with the 1st Division until he too was wounded in the Normandy landings, but he eventually returned to duty.

Clyde D. Strosnider struggled to help his parents support their large family during the Depression years.

> I was a farmhand as a child. In Maryland, I did farm work, picked tomatoes for 10 cents a bushel. I worked on a golf course, 50 cents for eighteen holes, carrying two or three bags at a time. During this time, the Civilian Conservation Corps (CCC) looked inviting. So a group of my friends and I joined at age sixteen in 1938. I stayed there for one and a half years. During that time, I thought the army offered more opportunities.

So Strosnider went to the local recruiting office in 1940, hoping to get an assignment to an army hospital in Honolulu. There were no openings in Hawaii, however, so he accepted an assignment to the 26th Infantry Regiment in Plattsburg Barracks, New York. At the time, the 1st Division was converting from a square division with four regiments—the 16th, 18th, 26th, and 28th—to a triangular division, with the 28th becoming part of the 8th Division in June 1940. Strosnider trained as a rifleman and served with Company I from the time he joined up through the campaigns of Africa, Italy, and Normandy. He was not transferred to another company until the Battle of the Bulge.

Walter Condon joined the 181st Infantry Regiment of the 26th National Guard Division (Massachusetts) in November 1937. His first assignment was with the howitzer company. He also trained with 81-millimeter mortars and 37-millimeter antitank guns at Camp Edwards on Cape Cod, Fort Devens, and Pine Camp in New York. His memories of this period remain quite vivid.

> We trained with the Springfield rifles, but later in 1939, we were issued the first 1,000 M-1 Garand rifles. They were issued by locker numbers, so since I had locker number 52, I received rifle number 52. We took them down to the rifle range, which is now only about 1,000 yards from my present home and is now the property of the Worcester Police Department in Shrewsbury. We tested them and found all 1,000 of them were defective. They would jam between the seventh and eighth rounds. This was quickly corrected with the production of a new sear that had a beveled back edge instead of straight back edge.[3]
>
> In 1939, they had selected some of us to send to the Intelligence School at Fort Devens for a three-month period. My experience as a radio ham helped in my selection. There I worked on coding and decoding messages. I was transferred to the Headquarters Company at that time because the division had been triangularized. I was in the regimental headquarters and was put on the radio and given a promotion. The army was just getting into placing radios in our trucks. We had them at Camp Drumund[4] and that included a big, heavy portable set with a battery that could get a signal out to five to ten miles. It was one of the first army radios. It is amazing that when I entered the army in 1942 and joined the 29th Division, they never took advantage of my experience.

Eventually reaching the rank of technical sergeant, Condon served as a combat engineer throughout the war in the 29th Division and took part in the Normandy invasion.

---

3. The Garand M-1 was designed by John C. Garand, a Canadian weapon designer working at the Springfield Arsenal in the early 1930s. The army adopted it and in January 1936 began production of this rifle, but it was not available in sufficient numbers to issue to all the troops until 1943. Early in World War II, the marines chose to retain the Springfield bolt-action rifle, but that changed after the Guadalcanal campaign.
4. No records indicate the existence of a Camp Drumund or Drummund in 1939 or thereafter. It is not clear what camp Condon is referring to, although Pine Camp in upper New York was renamed Camp Drum during the Korean War.

Preparations for War

The ranks of the National Guard began to swell during 1940 and early 1941, but most units were not even close to full strength, although they had a surplus of unqualified and unfit officers. The units finally filled out after induction into national service brought an infusion of draftees. In the meantime, the officers were whittled down to the most capable and fittest.

In September 1940, William H. Lewis, a strapping nineteen-year-old from Wichita Falls, Texas, visited the local National Guard unit, the 142nd Infantry Regiment of the 36th Division, where one of the division's artillery officers pressed him to join up. Lewis, however, less fascinated with the big cannons of the artillery unit than the machine guns of the heavy-weapons company of the infantry regiment, opted for the latter. He never regretted that decision, since the artillery unit he had spurned was dispatched to the Far East in early 1942, and its survivors ended up in Japanese prison camps in Southeast Asia.

William Lewis joined up for the adventure, extra income, and limited obligation of one year of service. He got a little more than he expected when the division was inducted on November 25, 1940.

> In December, we moved into Camp Bowie, which was near Brownwood, Texas. It was situated at the edge of the hill country and was pretty flat. There was nothing there when we arrived but a pasture. We laid out the roads and set up the camp, which consisted mainly of a tent city with pyramidal tents and some permanent structures such as the mess hall, latrines, and a few other buildings. The tent carpenters used green wood for the floors, which were set about two to three feet above the ground. In our tents, we had a stove in the center, which used natural gas. When it was warm out, we could roll up the side flaps of the tents to catch the breeze.

In late summer, the division moved off to take part in the Louisiana maneuvers of August and September.

> We were there for about three months. The towns of Mansfield, Many, and De Ridder were nearby, and the terrain had some small hills but was relatively flat, with pine tree forests and some swampy areas. In some places, the snakes, yellow jackets, and mosquitoes were a real problem. But boy, was it ever hot and humid! When you marched down the side of those dirt roads, the vehicles would come along kicking up a cloud of dust that would cover you and add to the misery.
>
> The 45th Division was there, and also a cavalry regiment. They were complaining that the horses were not doing well. Maybe it was the water. We were dressed in our blue denim uniforms with the floppy hats, and we also had our old English-style helmets. They were sure difficult to wear. We had referees and were part of the blue army in these games. Occasionally we saw some small tanks. Small single-engine aircraft would fly over, and sometimes they dropped bags of flour to simulate bombs. It was really some exercise, and I guess good training, because after these maneuvers you were ready for anything.
>
> While we were there, a big storm hit; I think it was a hurricane. They warned us to dig ample drainage for our tents before the storm hit. When it came, everything got drenched, and you had to take cover where you could find it. When the operations were over, we departed just as we had arrived: by truck. When we crossed back into Texas, we stopped at the town of Mexia, which was "wet." Boy did the booze flow in the streets that night!

After they returned to Camp Bowie, Lewis and his comrades were sent to Fort Sill to attend the Infantry-Artillery Coordination School. They returned to Camp Bowie just before December 7, 1941. The next year would take PFC William Lewis away from his beloved Texas Division. Eventually, he landed on Omaha Beach on June 6, 1944, as a member of another National Guard unit, the 29th Division.

After John B. Ellery graduated from high school in 1938, he left his native Wisconsin in search of adventure.

> I graduated from high school in 1938, and received an appointment as a U.S. Merchant Marine cadet. For about two years, I served on the fringes of the war in Europe. The merchant marine operated on a quasi war basis following the proclamation of national emergency issued by President Roosevelt on September 8, 1939. I was subsequently awarded the Merchant Marine Defense Bar. Although I enjoyed the merchant marine and took pride in my service, I decided that I wanted more excitement than a cargo ship could provide. Unfortunately, the merchant marine branch of the U.S. Naval Reserve was not much interested in my desire to volunteer for submarine school or destroyer duty. Of course, it must be remembered that the naval reserve was not called up until June 1941.
>
> In January 1941, I heard that the army was going to commission some minelayers at Governor's Island in New York Harbor. I immediately went to Fort Jay and was told that with my maritime experience, I would have no problem becoming a second mate on an army mine planter. On January 14, I enlisted in the regular army, and after a brief stay at Fort Jay, I was on my way.

John Ellery was on his way indeed, but not for sea duty. Instead, he was stationed first at Fort Wadsworth, then at Fort Devens, and finally at Fort Benning. He became a member of the 16th Infantry Regiment, 1st Division. "Along the way," he says, "I discovered that I liked the infantry, and I became a soldier. The training and experience proved to be tough, thorough, and I believe, effective."

In 1941, he took part in his first amphibious landings in Buzzards Bay, Massachusetts. Later in the year, he participated in further amphibious operations in the Carolina maneuvers. He was promoted to staff sergeant and served with the 16th Infantry in Africa, Italy, and Normandy.

Dale K. Kearnes from Pittsburg, Kansas, realizing that he would eventually be called up anyway, volunteered in February 1941. He filled the ranks of a newly federalized National Guard division which represented Nebraska, Missouri, and his home state of Kansas. "They sent me to

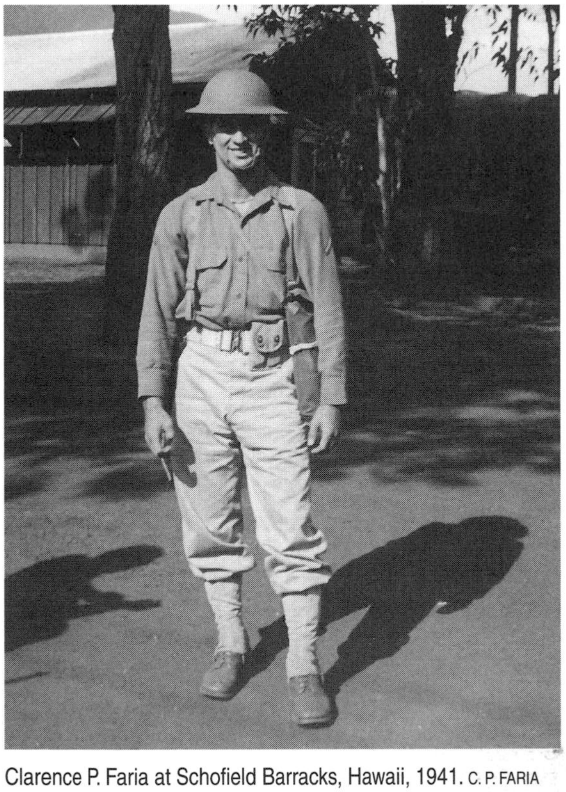

Clarence P. Faria at Schofield Barracks, Hawaii, 1941. C. P. FARIA

Leavenworth, Kansas, for a couple of days and then down to Little Rock, Arkansas, where the 35th Division was stationed. At the end of the year, we were getting ready for Christmas vacation after having completed the Louisiana maneuvers." His tour of duty would take much longer than he had anticipated. "I went in for a year to get it over with and came back four years, eight months, and eleven days later."

Like many of his contemporaries, James Montgomery Crutchfield, already twenty-seven years old, was determined to do his patriotic duty. He thought, however, that his low draft number guaranteed that he would not be called up, especially since no one in his county had been. So he dropped out of Northwest State University in Alva, Oklahoma, and volunteered for the army on February 2, 1941. He was sent for his physical to Oklahoma City, where a large number of men were being processed.

The induction exam, which was tough and thorough, included a psychological test. During this phase of the test, the inductee talked to a psychiatrist in a small partitioned area that provided little privacy, surrounded as it was by the men awaiting their turn to be interviewed. While Crutchfield waited, a country boy with scant education entered the psychiatrist's cubicle. After a few questions, the doctor asked him, "What is the difference between an elephant and a book?" Baffled, the young man replied in a countrified dialect that he didn't know. That concluded his test; the man was rejected. When his turn came, Crutchfield gave his answers with care for fear of being rejected. The doctor's questions seemed mostly to center on Crutchfield's feelings toward the opposite sex. Apparently he gave the answers the doctor was looking for, because he was inducted.

From Oklahoma City, Crutchfield went to Fort Sill, Oklahoma, where he cooled his heels for a good number of days waiting for a newly formed enlisted men's survey school to open. He was in the first class to graduate from the school, having learned the skills necessary to lay gun batteries and perform other artillery operations. At this time, instead of undergoing basic training, the recruits were trained in their assigned units. The school imparted only some of the basics a soldier needed to function in a military environment.

After completing his schooling, Crutchfield was assigned to the 57th Field Artillery Battalion, which had formed in June 1941 at Fort Ord, California. When he arrived at the 57th, he was promoted to private first class and eleven days later to corporal, because he was taking the slot of a noncommissioned officer and the unit commander did not believe in skipping ranks in promotions. Before the end of the year, Crutchfield reached the rank of sergeant. In early 1942, after he met all the qualifications, he was sent to Officers Candidate School.

While the war broke out in Europe during America's official isolation, John Robert Slaughter had no difficulty making up his mind about joining the military.

> My decision to join the National Guard was not entirely patriotic. My family needed extra income, and I had become impatient in my quest for manhood. The nation had been in the throes of the Great Depression, and my family was struggling to make ends meet.
>
> Propaganda films were very popular, especially with impressionable schoolboys. *For Whom the Bell Tolls, Sergeant York, A Yank in the RAF,* and *Hell Below* were some of the many films depicting heroism and glorifying war on the silver screen. World War I songs filled the airwaves. They were intended to induce jingoistic patriotism, and in my case, they succeeded.

Slaughter, following in the footsteps of many young men before him, joined the ranks of the National Guard.

A National Guardsman's Active Duty with the 29th "Blue and Gray" Division in 1941

John Slaughter, who was in the 29th Division when it was inducted into national service on February 3, 1941, has vivid memories of his first year of service.

Company D and the other Roanoke Guard companies reported to the American Legion Auditorium, which then was near the Norfolk and Western passenger depot in downtown Roanoke and across the street from Hotel Roanoke. We slept on cots set up in rows on the floor of the arena. There was hardly room to walk. We marched across the railroad tracks and up Jefferson Street to the Manhattan Restaurant for our meals. This was the beginning of almost five years of Spartan military living for some of us.

Before departing Roanoke, a military send-off was given by some of our predecessors of the Virginia National Guard and veterans of the First World War and with the blessings of the city of Roanoke. A parade culminated in front of the courthouse on Campbell Avenue. [An article in the hometown newspaper reported that "because of freezing temperatures and a stiff wind, only hundreds of spectators were downtown to see the parade, where thousands might have been."] A proclamation by Post #64, 29th Division Association, was read by the mayor.

On February 13, after ten days of encampment on the Legion Auditorium floor, we boarded an N&W passenger train and steamed north to our new careers. The destination was Fort Meade, Maryland, a sprawling military reservation situated between Washington, D.C., and Baltimore.

As we piled off the train and marched the short distance to our new homes, some of which were still under construction, my thoughts turned to how strange this place was. It was the first time I had ever spent a night away from home.

Our new barracks were elongated, unpainted yellow pine clapboard buildings two and a half stories high. The streets were unpaved, and there was not a blade of greenery anywhere.

Each company had an orderly room and a mess hall, but Company D had three two-and-a-half-story buildings that housed noncommissioned officers and privates. The main dormitories had two rows of twenty cots each, with the feet of the cots facing the middle aisle. A footlocker was at the foot of each bed. Each bed had two white sheets, a pillow with white pillowcase, and two woolen olive drab blankets. At each end of the dorm were two small private rooms, two sergeants to each room. Leading into the barracks from the backdoor and turning to the right and down about four steps was the washroom. Facing you were about eight or ten washbasins with mirrors above each. Turning left, there were shower stalls with an alum-water footbath. Following on around, there were commodes and urinals. Outside were a mess hall and kitchen and a smaller building that housed the orderly room. Capt. L. Eugene Meeks and 1st

continued

A National Guardsman's Active Duty *continued*

Sgt. George W. Boyd worked out of this office. Captain Stinnett had failed the physical, and reluctantly, he was sent home.

The company clerk, Cpl. Joseph M. Young, also worked in the orderly room. He worked under the first sergeant, keeping records of payroll, sicknesses, AWOLs, promotions, and the like.

Adjoining the orderly room was the supply room. Here the supply sergeant, Arthur Joseph Lancaster, issued clothing and equipment to the men and kept inventory of what was given out. If equipment was lost or stolen, the man could expect its cost to be withheld from his next paycheck.

Lancaster was not very articulate. Standing in formation one day, he tried to explain that three sheets would be issued and how each man would rotate them so that the top sheet could be turned in for washing each morning. His instructions: "Put the top sheet on the bottom sheet, and bottom sheet goes over the top sheet, and the third sheet on the . . . Oh hell, you know what I mean!"

New uniforms were issued; new weapons soaked in Cosmoline, unpacked, and cleaned; physicals given; and all kinds of immunization shots administered. A different way of life was apparent to the newcomers. Discipline was something foreign to some of us, and we soon learned rule infractions were not tolerated.

We "buck privates" learned to march in step, do manual-of-arms drills, make beds the military way, keep the area policed, keep uniforms cleaned and pressed, take care of personal hygiene, do weapon drills, memorize the general orders of guard duty and recite them upon command, salute and say "sir" to officers. Some of the older men had spent years in the National Guard and were comfortable in this new setting. Those of us new and awkward in this strange environment were constantly being embarrassed.

Capt. Walter O. Schilling of Roanoke demanded compliance to rules and regulations. The captain, not a large man, was wiry and tough. He threatened to take his bars off and step behind the barracks with any malcontent.

Cpl. Kurnel Major Hartman, a 200-pound redhead, was having trouble with one of the men in his squad. He marched the troublemaker to the captain's office. In his high-pitched, squeaky voice, Hartman said, "Capun, sir, Private Stevens won't do a thing I asked him to do." Schilling said, "God damn it corporal, how much do you weigh?" Hartman answered, "About 200, sir!" The captain said, "Now how much does Stevens weigh, corporal?" Red replied, "About 150, sir!" Schilling then said, "Get the hell out of here!"

S.Sgt. John B. "Bubbles" Sink was the mess sergeant. He was in charge of the kitchen and supervised the cooks and kitchen police (KP). Nothing seemed to worry the sergeant. Often the men complained about the quantity or the quality of the food. Someone once complained about rocks in the beans. Sink put his finger over his mouth: "Sh-h-h, don't let

A National Guardsman's Active Duty ***continued***

anyone hear; everyone will want them in theirs."

The first draftees assigned to the company arrived in the early spring of 1941. These men were from southwest Virginia, eastern Tennessee, and western Kentucky. They had been farmers, coal miners, factory workers, and recent high school students.

Curtis Moore, a Salem, Virginia, native, recalls his first impression of army life. His group of raw recruits marched into the Company D area, and one of the first things they saw was Pvt. Johnny Steele digging a 4-by-4-by-4 hole using a pick and shovel. Sgt. M. R. Patterson was standing over Steele, baseball bat in hand, supervising the construction of this square hole.

That scene was never forgotten by those nervous new arrivals. Steele, perspiring profusely, was armpit deep in the cavity, throwing dirt into a huge pile. The sergeant measured the dimensions of the hole, making sure the walls were straight. When the hole was completed to the sergeant's satisfaction, the private was ordered to shovel the dirt back into the hole.

A few weeks later, a second group of selectees was integrated into the company. These men were from north of the Mason-Dixon line—Pennsylvania and Maryland. Some were of different ethnicities—Polish and Italian. These "foreigners" brought with them some of their customs and strange manners of speech. They were amused at the thick-tongued drawl of the mountaineers from Appalachia: "Yawl cum ovah, ya heah." And the southern "rednecks" had to strain their ears to understand the "Geez goiz, I'm from Sout' Philly." It wasn't long until the Yankees were saying "yawl come" with thick tongues and the southerners were imitating their new buddies with "Croist kid, deal the ciads!"

Some of the older men left the company and were discharged; others qualified for Officers Candidate School. The recently drafted men not only filled the gap, but soon swelled the rank to near full strength. L. Eugene Meeks was promoted to captain. First Sergeant Boyd left the company as an officer, and James H. "Rudy" Obenshain was promoted to first sergeant. Meeks was promoted to major, and Schilling became company commander.

Some of us were selected to teach basic training to a third group of recruits, which were true Yankees from New England. Upon completion of thirteen weeks of training, the cadre and the graduates joined the regiment at A. P. Hill Military Reservation near Fredericksburg, Virginia. The mode of travel was by foot, carrying weapons and full field packs.

The 29th engaged in maneuvers at A. P. Hill and then were sent to the Carolinas. We had almost completed our obligation of a year's training. It was the end of 1941, and the first battalion was bivouacked in woods near South Hill, Virginia. We were on our way back to Fort Meade, and our discharges were waiting.

continued

A National Guardsman's Active Duty *continued*

Needless to say, the men of the 29th Division were not discharged after the Japanese attack on the Hawaii in December 1941. Slaughter noticed a change in the relations between the American public and men in uniform after that fateful day. Before Pearl Harbor, soldiers were treated like pariahs in many communities across America. A courthouse lawn in North Carolina had sported a sign reading, "Dogs and Soldiers Keep off the Grass!" Many restaurants had refused admittance to soldiers, blacks, and dogs, and sometimes public restrooms had been off-limits to soldiers. Often merchants overcharged or downright cheated men in uniform. But after the attack on Pearl Harbor, the American public embraced uniformed men with warmth and enthusiasm, and the film industry lionized them.

One of my neighborhood buddies, Medron R. "Pat" Patterson, came by the house one night on his way to National Guard drill. He was all decked out in an immaculate uniform with brass insignias shining. He had already made corporal and explained that with each promotion came more pay.

He was a well-built lad and very impressive looking in his olive drab wool dress uniform. I secretly admired his military demeanor and inquired as to how I might join the National Guard. He assured me Capt. William Stinnett was looking for good men for his heavy-weapons company. He didn't say the captain was looking for naive young boys.

The captain did question my decision but said that if my parents signed for me, he would consider the request. I had been told that the guard was to be activated into federal service for a year's training, and I decided then and there that the year would do me good. Afterward I would finish my education.

My parents had a fit. They tried to explain that I should finish school. When they saw my determination, they signed. I promised I would send at least half of my $30 a month to help with household expenses.

John Slaughter's sixteenth birthday on February 3, 1941, was quite memorable. It was the day the president issued Executive Order No. 8633, calling up his Virginia National Guard unit for a year of service with the remainder of the 29th Infantry Division, of which it was part.

By March 1941, Thomas Cortright had reached the rank of first sergeant in the 129th Infantry of the Illinois National Guard, and he was rather proud of his achievement. "On March 5, 1941, when we were inducted into Federal Service," recalls Cortright, "my pay was $72 a month plus a quarters allowance of about $22. Shortly thereafter, it was raised to $96 and $30 respectively."

Cortright's regiment was assigned to the 33rd Division and moved to Camp Forrest, Tennessee, later that month. The regiment was delayed for a few weeks, according to Cortright, because Camp Forrest was not yet ready to receive it. The unit had to stay in the armory for two weeks before shipping out. Finally, Cortright's regiment boarded the train, leaving the prairies of the Midwest for the hills and woodlands of Tennessee.

Calling Up the Reserves

The following is the account of Harold A. Shebeck, a reservist who was living in Wisconsin when he was called to the colors.

My first experience in army life came in 1934 and 1935, when, for one month each summer, I was a student at the Citizens Military Training Camp (CMTC) at Fort Snelling, Minnesota. The CMTC provided military training for one month each summer during the 1930s at various camps around the country for young men ages seventeen to twenty-one. Military training was held in the mornings, which consisted of practically everything that basic trainees get in the army today. The afternoons were devoted to sports and athletics, but we did have retreat parades about 5 P.M. a couple of afternoons each week. Throngs of spectators from Minneapolis and St. Paul would come out to watch these colorful spectacles. The total program consisted of four months' training called the Basic Red, White, and Blue course, over four summers, after which it was possible to get a commission as a second lieutenant in the army reserve by taking a few correspondence courses, passing a final examination, and appearing before a board.

There were very few officers in World War II, however, who obtained their commissions via the CMTC. Most men seemed to attend only one or two summers or, if they finished the four summer camps, never tried for a commission. No pay was involved, but we got our transportation provided. The program went out of existence with the advent of World War II.

I attended Ripon College in Wisconsin, majoring in education and history. The school had an outstanding ROTC Department. I attended the compulsory six-week summer camp for advanced ROTC students at Camp Custer, Michigan, in 1936. It was here we began to learn the school of the soldier, squad, platoon, and company, as well as all of the basic military ingredients preparing us for leadership roles upon our graduation a year later. That summer, there were ROTC cadets from other northern universities as well as several midwestern military academies. Upon graduation in 1937, I was commissioned as a second lieutenant, infantry, in the army reserve.

After graduation, I obtained a position as a high school coach, principal, and social studies teacher at Bison, South Dakota, where the entire high school enrollment was 76 in a town of 276 people. I remained in this school system until 1940, and during the school year of 1940–41, I attended Washington University in St. Louis, where I studied vocational rehabilitation.

On September 24, 1941, I was called to extended active duty and sent as a student to the rifle and heavy weapons course at the Infantry School at Fort Benning, Georgia.

"On our arrival, we found we had to finish the dayroom, provide some type of laundry equipment, and build miles of wood cleat sidewalks." In August and September 1941, Sergeant Cortright took part in the massive maneuvers in the sweltering lowlands of Louisiana and Arkansas. This was good training for the 129th Infantry, which departed for the Pacific in the late summer of 1942. Cortright, however, ended up in the European theater of war.

Kenneth Kitchner Jarvis, from Alhambra, California, served in the National Guard through most of the Depression years and was already a staff sergeant at the age of twenty-six, when the 40th Division was inducted on March 3, 1941. He was an assistant to the sergeant major in the Adjutant General's Office.

> We formed in the Armory Building in Exposition Park next to the Los Angeles Coliseum and boarded the train right outside and went up to Camp Louis Obispo. After several months, I was offered a job as first sergeant of a rifle company. Then came the big decision: Do I take the job or stay where I am, where I was next in line for the sergeant major's job, which was a master sergeant, one more stripe? But how long would that take? I took the job as first sergeant.
>
> I had the honor of waking up the company every morning. Once in a while, I would have to turn over a bed to shake the man out. I had to assign all of the duties (KP, latrine, etc.) and see to it that we were ready for all formations. I issued the passes and also had to keep the company commander happy. I enjoyed this job and think I did a pretty good job of it, but then we were sent to Fort Lewis, Washington, for field maneuvers.
>
> It rained most of the time, and when it didn't rain, the water dripped down from the trees. We were in maneuvers and couldn't leave the cover of the trees for fear of being spotted by the Air Corps spotters. We remained wet continuously and couldn't take advantage of the sun when it did shine. The result was that many men went to the hospital with the flu, and I was one of them.

While he was recovering in the hospital, Jarvis was replaced as first sergeant and lost two stripes, being demoted to buck sergeant (three stripes). That fall, Jarvis went with a group of his high school buddies, all members of the "Bachelors Club," to Catalina Island for the weekend. But this did not work out as planned either, because he met a girl and fell in love, which precluded his continued membership in the club.

Jarvis later rose once again to the rank of staff sergeant and became the platoon sergeant. Finally, he was moved to the Intelligence Section (G-2) of the division, promoted to master sergeant, and sent to OCS, never to return to the 40th Division.

William L. Conrad was sworn in when National Guard units were being inducted into federal service.

> On March 13, 1941, we were examined in Toledo, Ohio, and placed as fit for service. After the examination, we boarded trains for Fort Thomas, Kentucky, where we were inducted into service and given army clothes. Within a few days, we were again put on trains and shipped to Texas, where we were separated and sent to various training centers. I was sent to Camp Wolters at Mineral Wells, Texas, about fifty miles from Fort Worth. [Wolters was one of several new camps that operated as infantry replacement centers for the expansion of the army.]
>
> We were the first personnel in the camp, and we had to complete the barracks, put in steps and sidewalks. The rifles we received were packed in Cosmoline, and it took two

> days to clean them out and make them ready to pass inspection. We did our basic training and had a taste of what a rifle platoon had to do. After about four months of basic training, we again boarded trains and were shipped to Fort Benning, Georgia. There we were picked up by an army truck and taken to our company, where we were assigned to our barracks in the Harmony Church area of the camp. After orientation, we began our training. In the fall of 1941, we went on maneuvers in Louisiana.

Private Conrad, assigned to the 8th Infantry, 4th Division, arrived in Louisiana in August 1941. Even though he had already experienced the humid heat of the South during his sojourn in Georgia, the young Ohioan found the wetlands of Louisiana quite enervating. But an accident at home required his return to the family fold, delivering him from the southern summer. His reprieve was of short duration, however, for he was recalled to active duty when war was declared on December 8, 1941.

Robert J. Hahlen, another northerner, volunteered for military service in the Air Corps. After being sworn in in his home state of Wisconsin on March 16, 1941, he was sent south to Pine Bluff, Arkansas, where there was "a brand new primary school for flying cadets in those days. We were the first class in there; I was in class 41 H. When we arrived on about March 19, it rained, and continued to do so for the rest of the month, so we didn't do any flying. They were still working on the airfield trying to get it scraped out."

Hahlen learned to fly in the PT-19, a large two-seater, single-wing aircraft. After preflight and primary flying school, he transferred to the basic flying school at Randolph Field, on the outskirts of San Antonio. After he and his fellow pilots-in-training completed their instruction at Randolph Field, they were stationed at Kelly Field, on the other side of San Antonio. Here they underwent advanced training and flew the AT-6, a single-engine aircraft, and a twin-engine trainer aircraft. "We were the last class in the old wooden barracks from World War I. After our class, they built new ones."

Kelly Field, like most of the bases and camps throughout the United States, was gearing up for the war the nation was about to join. The men who were called up during the first half of 1941 witnessed firsthand the modernization of the U.S. military. While they were in training, the blue denims, M-17 and M-26 English bedpan-style steel helmets, and .03 Springfield rifles were finally phased out. These men also witnessed the genesis of the U.S. Army Air Corps, whose standards were being established for the first time.

Robert Hahlen graduated on October 31, 1941. He was given the rank of second lieutenant and assigned to the 38th Bomb Group Medium, a B-26 unit, which had been organized on the East Coast sometime before Hahlen's graduation.

> On December 6, I was put in the hospital in Jackson, Mississippi, where the 38th was stationed. I had a collapsed lung. I think I was the first person in the air force with a collapsed lung, because they didn't know what to do with me. They left me in a bed for two weeks and didn't do a thing with me. Then they grounded me, so I wasn't much good to the combat group, so they transferred me. After that, the 38th Bomb Group went to the West Coast and then to Australia.

Thus because of this fluke malady, Hahlen ended up taking part in operations supporting the invasion of France.

CHAPTER 2

America at War

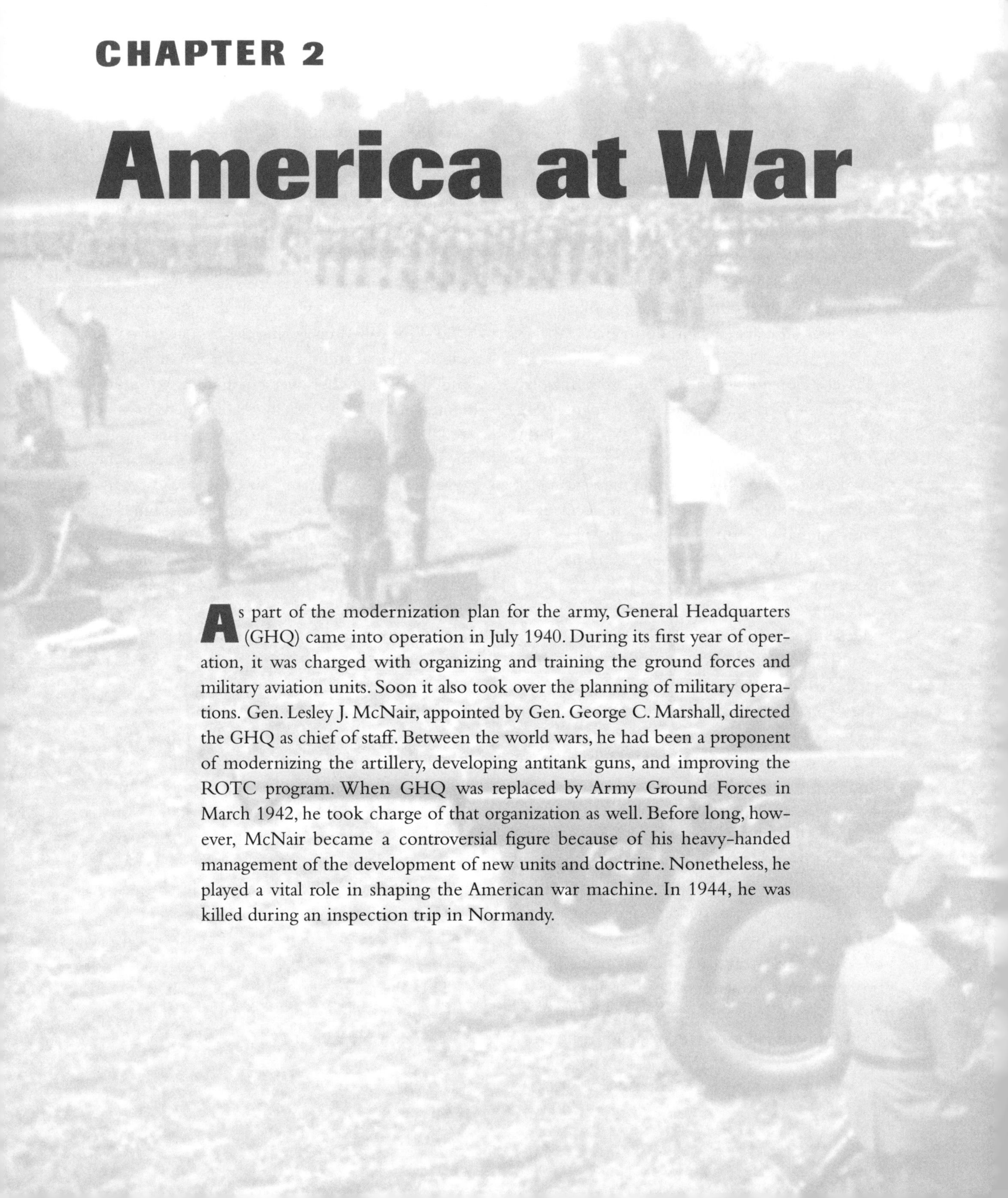

As part of the modernization plan for the army, General Headquarters (GHQ) came into operation in July 1940. During its first year of operation, it was charged with organizing and training the ground forces and military aviation units. Soon it also took over the planning of military operations. Gen. Lesley J. McNair, appointed by Gen. George C. Marshall, directed the GHQ as chief of staff. Between the world wars, he had been a proponent of modernizing the artillery, developing antitank guns, and improving the ROTC program. When GHQ was replaced by Army Ground Forces in March 1942, he took charge of that organization as well. Before long, however, McNair became a controversial figure because of his heavy-handed management of the development of new units and doctrine. Nonetheless, he played a vital role in shaping the American war machine. In 1944, he was killed during an inspection trip in Normandy.

During the interwar years, the American military had lagged behind in the field of armored warfare. Rising stars such as Dwight D. Eisenhower, Douglas MacArthur, and Adna Chaffee contributed their ideas to the development and use of mechanized and tank units.[1] Although some prewar authors crowed that the United States had developed superior armored vehicles and tactics by 1939, the reality was much less rosy. American tanks, despite their superior suspension systems and engines, were undergunned, and the army did not form its first armored divisions until 1940.[2] In fact, much of the supporting artillery was either old, like the French 155-millimeter guns from the last war, or ineffective, like the 37-millimeter guns used in tanks and antitank units. Only the ability of American industry to produce a large quantity of vehicles and weapons of relatively good overall quality compensated for the lack of individual superiority of some American weapons.

The Douglas B-18

The Army Air Corps selected the Douglas B-18 as a twin-engine bomber in the mid-1930s. It was developed as a long-range bomber from the commercial DC-2 passenger transport. The army purchased several DC-2s, which it designated C-32, for use as transports in 1936. It also also acquired some DC-3 commercial passenger aircraft on the eve of the war. Like the B-18, the DC-3 was derived from the DC-2, and by early 1942, a military version, the C-47 transport, was built. Despite modifications, the B-18 had a top speed of only 217 miles per hour, slow for a bomber, so it was replaced by new multi-engine Boeing B-17 bombers in the late 1930s. Since the C-47 was slightly faster and had a larger carrying capacity than the B-18, it soon replaced the obsolete bomber as a troop carrier and also served as a cargo transport. For more information, see *U.S. Bombers* by Lloyd S. Jones.

Sky Troopers

The participation of German paratroopers in the spring–summer campaign of 1940 sowed dismay among their possible opponents and caused an immediate reaction. Lt. Col. William C. Lee paved the way for the creation of an American airborne force with volunteers from the 29th Infantry Regiment. He formed the Test Platoon in the summer of 1940 by order of the War Department. Lee's volunteers traveled by air to Highstown, New Jersey, to train for a week on 250-foot towers like one the lieutenant colonel had observed at the 1940 New York World's Fair.[3] Later, two towers were purchased and installed on the grounds of Fort Benning for the first parachute school for American airborne troops. On August 16, the first members of the Test Platoon made their maiden parachute jumps from Douglas B-18 twin-engine bombers. This feat was followed by a mass jump at the end of the month. Soon the call

1. Eisenhower was sent on a cross-country trip after the war to see how practical land routes were for motorized units without using railroads. He only proved that the nation's road network was not adequate, and it took him many weeks to cross the country. MacArthur rose to the position of chief of staff and helped shape the army during the 1930s, although he doubted the value of the tank; he wanted light and fast tanks to fulfill the mission of the cavalry as a long-range raiding force. Chaffee was involved with the development of armored units.
2. For much of the interwar period, the army gave control of tanks to the infantry and allowed the cavalry to have armored cars. Many of those combat cars turned out to be light tanks mounting nothing heavier than .50-caliber machine guns. The cavalry generals had no desire for the larger and slower medium tanks. The role of tanks was changed in 1940 with the formation of the Armored Corps.
3. The World's Fair held in New York opened in April 1939, just a few months before the war began, and did not close until October 1940. Retired navy commander James H. Strong, who had studied Russian training methods and saw their wooden towers, built his first steel towers at Highstown and then another set for the military after Lee saw the 262-foot tower at the World's Fair.

American Armored Divisions

The efforts of Gen. Adna Chaffee resulted in the formation in the summer of 1940 of the Armored Force, with the first two armored divisions: the 1st Armored Division at Fort Knox and the 2nd Armored Division at Fort Benning. Col. George S. Patton Jr. served as an armored brigade commander in Gen. Charles L. Scott's 2nd Armored Division. Scott replaced Adna Chaffee as commander of the corps in December 1940. (Chaffee died of cancer in 1941.) Cadres from these two divisions helped form the 3rd and 4th Armored Divisions in April 1941, and in October, the 5th Armored Division was formed.

Although they were impressive on paper, these divisions had only light M2A4 tanks with 37-millimeter guns and awaited the arrival of new medium tanks in 1941. The light M3 Stuart tank replaced the M2A4 in 1941 but was armed with the same weapon. The new but awkward medium M3 Lee/Grant tanks became available in 1941.[4]

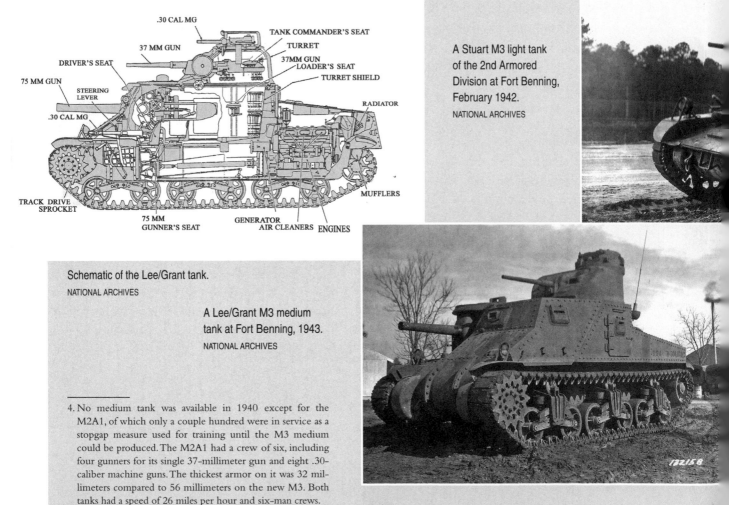

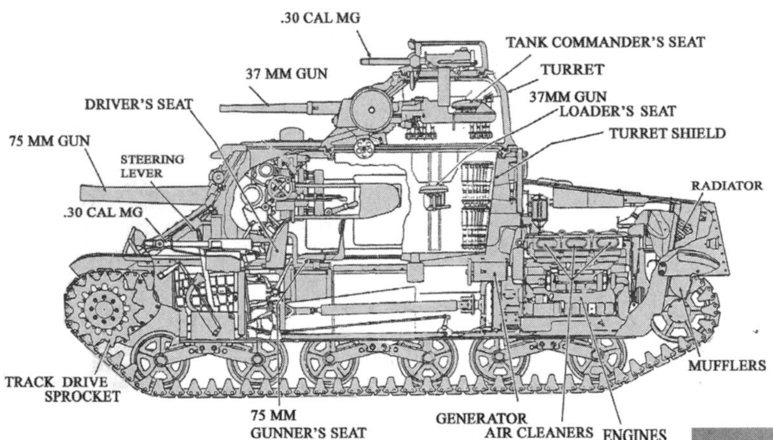

Schematic of the Lee/Grant tank.
NATIONAL ARCHIVES

A Stuart M3 light tank of the 2nd Armored Division at Fort Benning, February 1942.
NATIONAL ARCHIVES

A Lee/Grant M3 medium tank at Fort Benning, 1943.
NATIONAL ARCHIVES

4. No medium tank was available in 1940 except for the M2A1, of which only a couple hundred were in service as a stopgap measure used for training until the M3 medium could be produced. The M2A1 had a crew of six, including four gunners for its single 37-millimeter gun and eight .30-caliber machine guns. The thickest armor on it was 32 millimeters compared to 56 millimeters on the new M3. Both tanks had a speed of 26 miles per hour and six-man crews.

American Armored Divisions *continued*

The turret was armed with a 37-millimeter gun, but the tank included a sponson-mounted 75-millimeter gun on the right side of the hull, with only 15 degrees of traverse. The introduction of gyrostabilizers for both guns allowed this tank to fire on the move, a definite advantage over past armored vehicles, according to Christopher Chant's *World Encyclopedia of the Tank*. The Americans had not yet developed a turret for such a large weapon, but they soon would. The medium M4 Sherman tank, with a turret-mounted 75-millimeter gun, began replacing the medium M3 during the latter part of 1942 and served as the main battle tank for American forces by 1943. Like the M3, the M4 had a reliable engine but also a high profile, and it lacked sufficient armor and firepower to match the newest German tanks, the Panzer V Panther and Panzer VI Tiger of 1943.

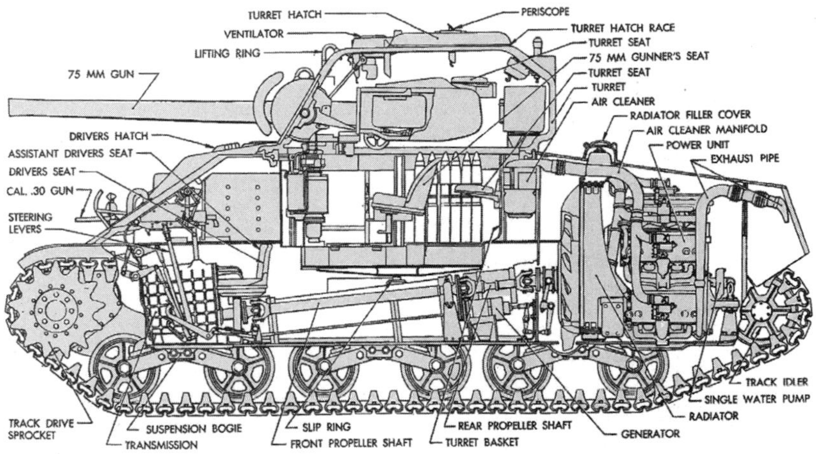

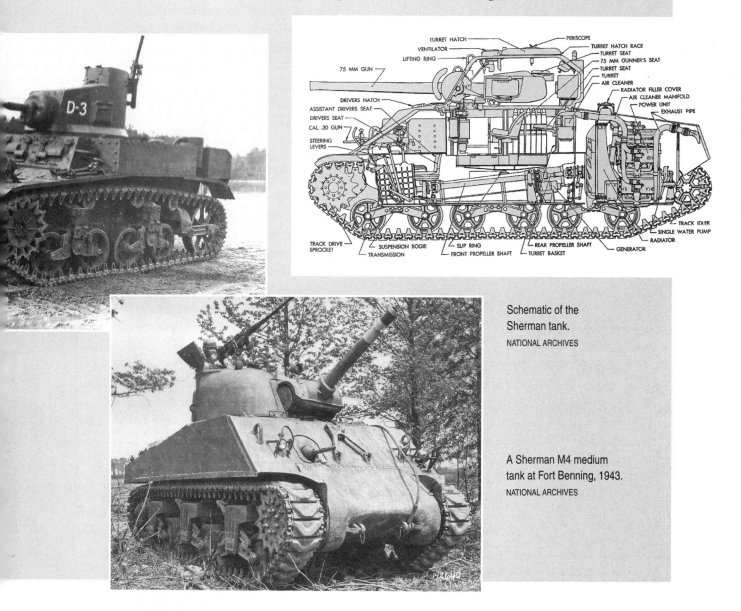

Schematic of the Sherman tank.
NATIONAL ARCHIVES

A Sherman M4 medium tank at Fort Benning, 1943.
NATIONAL ARCHIVES

Airborne Doctor

To 1st Lt. David Thomas, his assignment to the newly formed Armored Force was not much of a challenge.

When they formed an experimental thing called the I Armored Corps, they looked around for the least occupied medical officer, so I got the job and became a corps surgeon sitting in a "chicken colonel" slot. I was the assistant to the surgeon of the Armored Force; he didn't do anything, and I helped him! The only trouble was that there wasn't anything to do there either. I was passing the time away reading the *Army and Navy Journal,* and here was an article that said that they were looking for a regular army medical officer to join the paratroops. [At that time, doctors were given the rank of only first lieutenant when they were commissioned.] So I put in for it, and two weeks later, I thought I'd better run this by my wife. I told her there was a great opportunity for me to put in for becoming a parachutist, because they were looking for a regular army doctor to do it, and there was an extra $100 a month in it. She said, "100 bucks! Go for it!" My orders came through in August 1941, and I reported to Fort Benning, Georgia. My initial assignment was battalion surgeon of the 503rd Parachute Infantry Battalion. [This battalion was newly activated.]

I attended jump school and graduated in Group Parachute School Number 8. We qualified in the DC-3, the civilian version of the C-47, and I received my wings on November 8, 1941, just before Pearl Harbor. From the 503rd, I went to the newly formed Provisional Parachute Group, which was commanded by Col. Bill Lee, the "Father of the Airborne" [later first commander of the 101st Airborne Division], and was group surgeon for about six months. Again, as always, there was not much to do in higher headquarters.

From there, I spent a stint as regimental surgeon of the 502nd Parachute Infantry Regiment, which was newly formed in the Alabama Training Area [in early 1942]. The 502nd was the first outfit over there, and they hadn't paved the roads yet. The jeeps were getting mired down. That was at the time the army was getting out of the horse business, and there were a lot of spare horses around. They rounded up a bunch of these horses and shipped them over to the 502nd. We took a lieutenant who had been a cavalry officer and had switched to the infantry to get in the airborne, and he became the riding master. All the officers had to learn to ride to get to the training area. This was across the Chattahoochee River from Fort Benning.

Thankfully, in the summer of 1942, I was sent to England for six weeks to go through the British parachute-training course. We flew over in a group, which included Bill Ryder, who had led the Test Platoon in 1940, and about four other officers, on an American Export Airlines flying boat in July 1942. We went to our various areas of expertise. I spent my time with the 16th Field

Airborne Doctor ***continued***

Ambulance, which corresponded to a medical battalion in the American army.

While I was in England, I jumped from a platform suspended from a barrage balloon. This was part of the training of the British airborne. They would run the barrage balloon up 600 feet, to which they had attached a platform with a hole in it, which was a mockup of a Whitley bomber, and they put you through the drill of going through at rigid attention. This was static line jumping, but you had no slipstream to inflate your chutes, and you would fall a hell of a ways before your chute opened. It was quite a thrill. I asked a guy, "Has anybody ever gotten killed because of it not opening before you hit the ground?" He said, "We had a few, old chap, but you know that is the luck of the game." They carried no reserve chute.

I also jumped from the Whitley, an orange-crate-and-canvas bomber. They took out the dorsal turret, which left a big hole in the bottom of the plane, and when you jumped, you sat on the floor of the aircraft transversely. We had numbers one through ten, as I recall, with the evens on one side and odds on the other. When it was time to jump, number one would swing into the empty turret and hang his butt on the edge of the hole. When the light turned green, he would exit in a position of rigid military attention, with his back tilted way back, because if he didn't, he would bump his nose on the other side. That is why there are so many snub-nosed old British paratroopers! When one cleared, number two would swing in and continue the drill.

After studying the British landing technique, Thomas, now a captain, concluded that it was more efficient than the American style.

Originally, we were taught that when we landed, our feet should be apart about the width of our hips, and we were supposed to do either a right front tumble, a left front tumble, a right rear tumble, or a left rear tumble. This was just too damned complicated to teach the average soldier. Over in England, they were landing with knees and ankles together, and when they hit the ground, they just did whatever physics and the wind did to them. They tucked their elbows into their sides and just sort of went whichever way they went. It cut down a lot on fractured ankles. That is what we picked up from the British, primarily me, because that was my main interest in going through their training—to find out what they used that we could use in ours. That has been standard ever since then.

Captain Thomas and his companions returned to America on a Pan Am Clipper, a commercial seaplane, still a hazardous trip in those days. Armed with the knowledge gleaned from the British, Dave Thomas made recommendations that would prevent unnecessary fractures and broken legs during combat jumps in Europe and the Pacific.

for more volunteers went out, and the American airborne troops began to expand rapidly.

On September 16, 1940, the Adjutant General's Office authorized the creation of the 1st Parachute Battalion at Fort Benning. Lee's Test Platoon was incorporated into the new unit, which became the 501st Parachute Battalion on October 2, expanding into the 501st Parachute Infantry Regiment in February 1942. The War Department activated the 502nd Parachute Battalion in July 1941 and enlarged it into a regiment at the same time as the 501st. The expansion order also called for the creation of additional parachute regiments. The new regiments formed in the summer of 1942, and the first two airborne divisions, the 82nd and 101st, came into being in August 1942.

The first glider units came into existence in July 1941, in response to the German air landings on Crete. When the first glider regiments formed in March 1942, they practiced without gliders for many months, because they had no suitable aircraft. Unfortunately, the glider units failed to capture young men's imagination and attracted few volunteers. As a result, most of the men that made up their contingent were transferred into them willy-nilly to undergo the special training required.

Maneuvers

By the close of 1941, the creation and expansion of the new specialized units were well under way. The army had also started activating and training additional divisions, including the National Guard, using draftees to fill out the ranks. The training of these units and testing of new tactics took place in large-scale operations at the Louisiana, Carolina, and Tennessee maneuver areas. The new Desert Training Center was established in California. Training for amphibious operations was carried out along the coasts of Virginia, Massachusetts, Florida, and Washington and involved division-size units, including the 1st and 3rd Infantry Divisions. There were also many smaller maneuvers. Whereas the troops had been poorly equipped during the maneuvers held in 1939 and 1940, now they lacked neither equipment nor ammunition.[5]

The largest maneuvers, which took place in Louisiana in August 1941, involved up to sixteen divisions, including two armored and several brigades and regiments of horse cavalry. The Louisiana maneuver area included most of western Louisiana between Lake Charles in the south and Mansfield in the north and the territory between the Sabine and Red Rivers. By September, more than 400,000 troops of the 2nd and 3rd Armies were involved. Gen. Henry "Hap" Arnold, commander of the newly formed Army Air Forces, also dispatched several air groups to participate in the Louisiana maneuvers in September. For the first time since the Great War, commanders were able to operate divisions and corps, as well as plan for and experience the types of combat and logistical problems that would confront them. A number of the divisions engaged in these maneuvers, including the 1st, 4th, 8th, and 29th, later took part in the Normandy campaign.

The environment of the maneuver area contributed to the misery of the foot soldiers with bayous in some areas adding to the discomfort of the region's hot, muggy summers. While the soldiers traipsed through the wet woodlands, they sweated profusely, causing their clothing to stick to their bodies, and they were often harassed by mosquitoes. As the sun went down, the slight drop in temperature offered some relief, until the mosquitoes arrived in force and made matters even more unpleasant. Those who were not in

5. The Louisiana maneuvers of May 1940 included units of the new Armored Force. Several regiments or brigades of armor and horse cavalry and the 1st Infantry Division took part. The maneuvers demonstrated the advantages of armor over horse cavalry units. In the Tennessee maneuvers of 1941, Patton led the 2nd Armored Brigade and demonstrated how armored units could effectively breach defensive lines and isolate units.

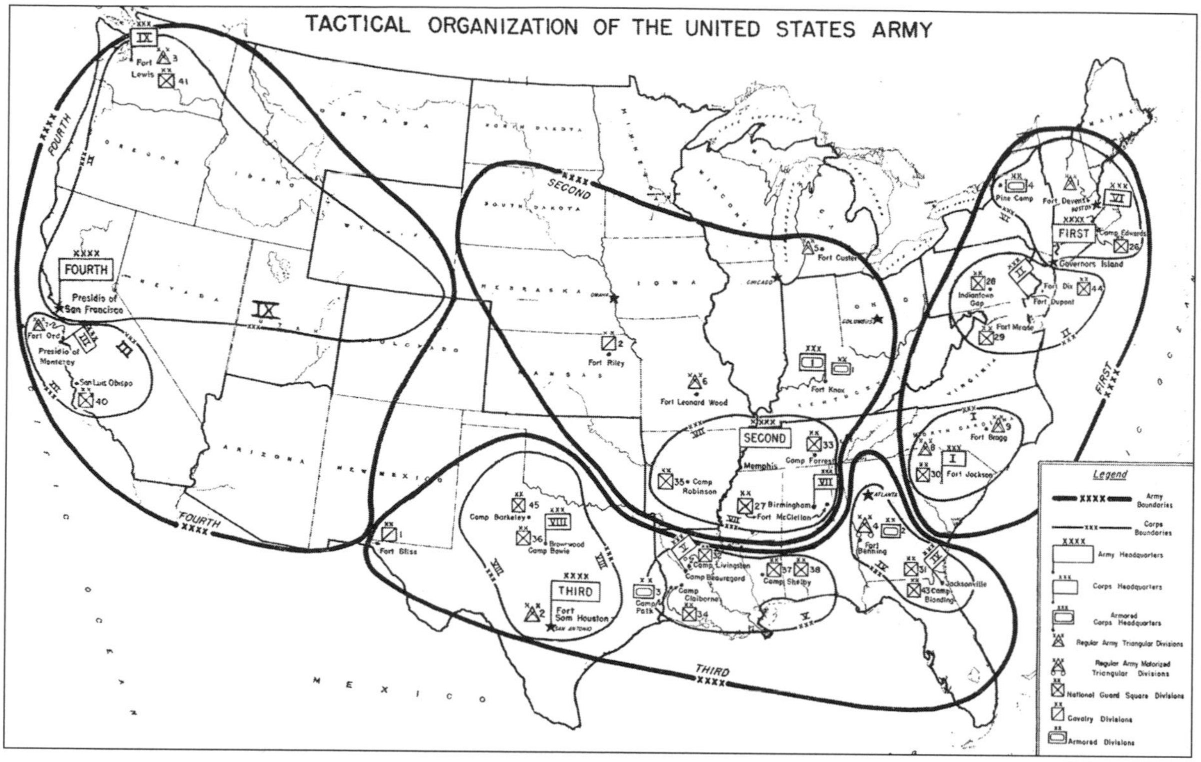

Location of major army units (Regular and National Guard) in 1941. BIENNIAL REPORT 1939 TO 1941

the marching columns or on patrols needed to be alert for a variety of poisonous snakes that inhabited the region. For many southerners, it was no big deal, but for some of the northerners or city slickers, it was a new and trying experience.

After watching all the maneuvers, General McNair concluded that the troops were poorly prepared against air operations. On the other hand, he was duly impressed with the operation of the antitank units. According to the official publication *Organization of Ground Combat Troops,* by Kent Greenfield et al., despite being poorly armed, they knocked out 91 percent of the 983 tanks, essentially eliminating the 1st Armored Division in the Carolina maneuvers. Patton's armored units also had a habit of taking losses, which drew some criticism. Col. Dwight Eisenhower was impressed with the use of light aircraft for artillery observation and liaison and urged their adoption for military operations.

The 29th Division, which would later spearhead the assault into Normandy, took part in the Carolina maneuvers of October and November 1941. The training of this division was typical for the National Guard units that were activated in February 1941. On induction, the division was only at half strength, numbering four regiments of infantry, which were awaiting the arrival of newly drafted personnel. Regiment-size units were stationed at various military reservations for training, and many of their officers were sent to different posts for additional instruction to bring them up-to-date on new developments in warfare, according to Joseph Ewing in *29 Let's Go.*

On its way to the Carolina maneuvers, the 29th Division stopped over for training at Camp A. P. Hill, a post that included a variety of environments ranging from piney woods to swamps. It was only slightly less unpleasant than the Carolinas. Later, the division trucked to Fort Bragg, North Carolina, where it participated in the exercises. The warm, humid climate provided an excellent testing ground for men and equipment alike. During these maneuvers, the troops learned

Infantry training in the late 1930s. JOHN A. ALLISON

to adapt not only to the new standards imposed by mobile warfare, but also to extreme environmental conditions.

Herman F. Byram, who had volunteered for the army in September 1934, served in the 17th Infantry Regiment at Fort Cook, Nebraska, until 1939. (The 17th later became part of the 7th Division, which went to the Pacific.) From here, Byram was transferred to the cadre of Ouachita College in Arkadelphia, Arkansas, and served there until late 1942, when he was selected for Officer Candidate School. He took part in the Louisiana maneuvers, but only in an administrative capacity. His job was to clean up after the troops. The operations area encompassed a few hundred square miles of mostly privately owned property. The soldiers who crossed open fields usually tramped through farmers' crops and damaged them, as well as other property. Byram's job was to ensure that suitable restitution was made to the civilian population. Similar problems also arose during training operations in England, where the American army followed the same procedures.

> The colonel told me that Sergeant Taylor and I were going down to Arkansas to set up a claims board. I said I was to go on leave, and he said it made no difference and that my leave was canceled. We were there most of a month with this claims board. The army had to get permission from all the landowners to maneuver on their property, and we had to mark it on a map. We would mark it a different color if the farmer didn't want them on the land.
>
> Anyone with damage done would come in to us, and we would process the claims. One claim was from a blind farmer who had a watermelon patch. The GIs got in there while the watermelons were green and just beginning to turn pink. They would slice them in half and throw them in his well. That came to us, and all the members of that unit had to pay for his watermelons. Every watermelon destroyed in Louisiana turned out to be a seed watermelon, and that was $5 apiece. You could buy a 50-pound watermelon anywhere for 50 cents. Every watermelon that went down that farmer's well became a seed melon!

Amphibious Training

Specialized training for amphibious operations began in 1940 and was constantly plagued by lack of equipment. Although three task forces were created, only Task Force 1 (TF 1), operating in the Caribbean, was given the mission of assaulting a defended coastline. The 1st Division was assigned to TF 1 in November 1940 because of its previous training. According to *Organization of Ground Combat Troops,* only 10 percent of its personnel participated in the first amphibious operation and 20 percent in the second.

On the West Coast, the 2nd Marine Division practiced landings in the San Diego area, and the 3rd Division conducted its exercises in the Puget Sound. A major operation in Hawaii was planned for early 1942 but was called off at the outbreak of war.

Maj. S. B. Mason had been transferred from the 5th Division to the 1st on the recommendation of Brig. Gen. James Garrish Ord, with whom he had worked in the Philippines.[6] Mason worked on plans for further training in sea assaults with Ord as part of the Carib Force staff, and this included plans for amphibious operation against Martinique in the Caribbean, which had been canceled prior to the Carolina maneuvers in 1941.

> During the planning for the operation in Martinique, I was an assistant in the G-3 Section of Ord Force and was at that time an expert—or becoming expert—in small boat landings. Up to that time, we had nothing but sea craft from lifeboats of the big ships. I worked entirely on the subject in the operations section of the Ord Force and became what might be called an expert. The 1st Division had previously had some experience in landing operations practice, but very little, and without Higgins boats. My joining the 1st Division was an advantage not only to me, but to the division to have an individual in there who had taken the army's point of view on what to do with a landing. Up to that time, it was the navy's mission to land the marines on the beach, and their means of loading them onto small craft and getting onto the beach was a matter of getting the maximum number of men in the landing. The navy had *FTP 167,* which took care of landing operations, so I immediately started in and devised a method of breaking it down into the integral units so they could fight when they got to the beaches.[7]

The 1st Division, with the 1st Marine Raider Battalion and the 70th Tank Battalion, sailed for Martinique on January 9, 1942. According to an account in Marvin Jensen's *Strike Swiftly,* one of the ships in the convoy was torpedoed by a U-boat, and eventually the operation was canceled.

The division continued amphibious training at New River, North Carolina, during August 1941. The troopship *Hunter Liggett* served as the division's headquarters for these operations and the first ramped landing craft began to appear.[8] During the next year, Major Mason's contribution appears to have included the dividing up of the infantry battalion companies into six or seven sections, since the landing craft could not accommodate a full platoon, and possibly the combat loading of ships. When the landings in North Africa took place and thereafter, these methods continued to be used.

According to *Organization of Ground Combat Troops,* Gen. Holland Smith, G-5 of GHQ, considered the amphibious operations of the 1st Division to be a failure:

> The late change of locale, though justified by the submarine menace, made adequate preparation impossible, with the result that the "excellent plans" of the 1st Division miscarried; the Navy failed to provide suitable transports or adequate combatant vessels and aircraft; combatant vessels had not practiced shore bombardment in the

6. James Garrish Ord, born in 1886, is often confused with Maj. James Ord, another West Point graduate, who was a friend of Eisenhower's and died in the Philippines in an air crash in 1938. J. G. Ord became a brigadier in 1940 and was assigned to the 1st Division. In 1942, he was promoted to major general and given a high-level staff assignment in Washington.

7. *Fleet Training Publication 167 for Landing Operations Doctrine,* or *FTP 167,* with some modifications in 1942 and 1943, remained the basic army and navy guide. It is not known to what extent Mason may have effected any changes in procedure.

8. Built in 1922 as the 14,200-ton liner *Pan America,* the ship was taken over by the army and renamed the *Hunter Liggett* in February 1939. The navy took it over in June 1941 and designated it as AP-27 (later APA-14). In 1939, the navy had only a single troop transport for the marines, the 10,000-ton *Henderson* (AP-1), built in 1917 and capable of carrying 2,200 troops.

past year; naval aircraft were untrained for cooperation with ground troops; and the Navy failed to land troops on designated beaches.

Naturally, General Smith blamed the navy for the problems and not the 1st Division planners. Nonetheless, on Smith's recommendations, these operations produced two positive outcomes: the unification of landing operations under one commander, and the creation of the Army Amphibious Training Center in June 1942. The 70th Tank Battalion was ordered to continue further amphibious training operations. Its cadre came from the 67th Armored Regiment, one of the first tank units of the new Armored Force in 1940. The 70th would eventually participate in operations in North Africa and Sicily and spearhead the landings on Utah Beach in 1944 with tanks specially outfitted for amphibious operations.

Major Mason participated in the Louisiana and Carolina maneuvers with the 1st Division. The units were still not fully equipped, and the maneuvers of 1940 revealed the shortage of equipment. Broomsticks were used as machine guns, and trucks were painted with the word "Tank." An old M2 tank with two turrets mounting machine guns sported a sign proclaiming it to be a new M3 tank, which was not yet available. The situation greatly improved in 1941, however, even though shortages continued. The 1st Division returned from Carolina maneuvers at the beginning of December 1940 to continue regular training.

Hyatt W. Moser, who joined the army in November 1940 as a volunteer, was sent from his home state of North Carolina to Atlanta, where he joined and trained with the 62nd Signal Battalion. In 1941, he was assigned as a radio operator to one of the battery units that took part in the Louisiana and Carolina maneuvers. Shortly before Pearl Harbor was attacked, the 62nd moved to Camp Blanding, Florida. Soon after Pearl Harbor, Moser was transferred with a select group to Quantico, Virginia, to join the Atlantic Fleet Amphibious Corps.

The unit I was assigned to was the 71st Signal Company, which was composed of all army personnel. The school was run by the marines, but naval personnel were also present. We had amphibious training for the army units, and we went on practice invasions of Cove Point, Maryland. The 1st Division was one of the units, and others came and made practice landings at Cove Point and Chesapeake Bay. We ran that for some time. One of my jobs was operating navy signal lamps, which sent Morse code by signal light. One of my duties was to challenge all ships entering Chesapeake Bay, get their call signs and identify them, then radio Washington and inform them what ship it was. During that period of time, they decided to discontinue this Amphibious Corps, and they also conceived the Amphibious Engineers, who were trained to do similar jobs, since they must have decided the European theater would be an army operation. A select group of us from the 71st Signal Company was transferred to form two new units at Camp Edwards, Massachusetts.

These two new units were the 286th and 278th Joint Assault Signal Companies. At Camp Edwards, Moser's unit merged with others to form the future 1st Engineer Special Brigade, which distinguished itself in several invasions, including Normandy.

Frank F. Andrews, who enlisted in 1940 when he lived in North Dakota, was assigned to the 7th Infantry Regiment of the 3rd Division on the West Coast.

I spent my entire five years in service with the 3rd Infantry Division shortly after arriving on the West Coast. I entered the service

ROTC formation at Purdue University. W. OSTROWSKA

after I turned eighteen at Fort Snelling, Minnesota, which was a big base. I was there only a few days and shipped to Vancouver, Washington. We were just across the river from Portland. It was July 1940 when I arrived, and we were there for about six months and moved up to Fort Lewis into some of the new buildings they just built.

Vancouver had the old permanent brick structures that had been there for a long time, before any of those wooden barracks were built. Practically all the other camps were two- or three-story buildings. The old Farragut Naval Base was not there before World War II and was built to monstrous size during the war. Several years after the war, they sold the buildings, and now it is a park.

The 7th Infantry moved from Vancouver Barracks to Fort Lewis to join the 15th Infantry of the 3rd Division in February 1941. Lt. Col. Dwight D. Eisenhower, who had served in the 15th Infantry since the beginning of 1940, participated in the large-scale maneuvers in California. Shortly after that, he was promoted to chief of staff of the 3rd Division, and in March 1941, he was placed in the IX Corps headquarters (3rd and 41st Divisions). The division's 30th Infantry Regiment left the Presidio in California in March 1941 to join the remainder of the division in the north.

We made our first efforts at amphibious training in 1941. We would sail out of Olympia and attack McNeil Island, the prison island, in Puget Sound. I remember going out there several times and the fog was so thick that we would spend all day milling around; and when the lights came on at night, we would find our way back to Olympia, and that would be the extent of the maneuver for the day. It was a rough place to try to work.

At that time, those small boats we used in training were called Higgins boats. I don't know who Higgins was or who manufactured them, but all they were small plywood boats with diesel engines. I never did see one for some time with a ramp on. Ours had a blunt nose and you went out over the top.[9]

They did not have regular camps for basic training when I arrived. It was the middle of 1941 when the first few guys from each company left and transferred to regular training camps. We went in small numbers to the company we were going to be assigned to, and one of the platoon sergeants would have ten or twenty men to give basic training.

It was all done in the company and not regular training camps. My training was with the machine gun in a heavy-weapons company. I never did get into mortars, so I didn't have varied experience. I was trained on the .30-caliber MG. They used them like in World War I. You would sandbag them down, and everything was for accuracy.

In the spring of 1942, we went down to San Diego Harbor, and the 3rd Infantry Division and the newly activated 2nd Marine Division took their amphibious training together, attacking North Island. We spent the rest of the summer at Fort Ord, California.

Harold J. Taylor was drafted while the 3rd Division participated in IX Corps maneuvers in California in the early part of the summer of 1941.

On June 17, 1941, I, along with a group of other draftees, was bused to Fort Benjamin Harrison in Indianapolis for my physical and induction into the army. Those that passed were put on a troop train and taken to Camp Roberts, California. On our arrival, I was singled out, as were some of the others, to be schooled in communications as well as all areas of infantry training. I was schooled in receiving and sending Morse code and voice communications with the equipment of the day. Our infantry training consisted of long marches, running obstacle courses, daily target practice with 03 [Springfield bolt-action] and M-1 rifles, and grenade handling. After three months of basic training, the men were split up and then shipped off to units around the country.

It so happened that I was sent to the 15th Infantry HQ of the 3rd Infantry Division located in Fort Lewis, fifteen miles south of Tacoma. On my arrival at the 15th Infantry Regiment, I was put into communications, where my schooling continued. Regular field maneuvers gave us a chance to put in practice what we learned. It was still the fall of 1941 when the 3rd Division's status was changed from regular infantry to amphibious infantry for making landings on enemy soil. Our initial training began in Puget Sound north of Tacoma.

Taylor also took part in the amphibious training exercises in California in 1942. Long before Taylor and Frank Andrews joined the 3rd Division, Verl Loris Pendleton from Missouri had enlisted at St. Joseph, on October 12, 1939. The area was still feeling the effects of the Great Depression, and the only work he could find was for 50 cents a day as a farmhand. He went to the local recruiter, believing he could do better in

9. The Higgins boat was an LCP, adopted in November 1940 by the navy, and it was still in service during the landings in Guadalcanal and North Africa. The LCP was replaced with LCVPs with front ramps toward the end of 1942. Jack Higgins, the New Orleans boat builder, developed the LCP(R) with a ramp in mid-1941 based on reports of similar Japanese landing craft with bows. He designed the LCVP shortly after that. See Norman Friedman's *U.S. Amphibious Ships and Craft* for more information.

the army, and in mid-October, he was on an army bus that took him and other new recruits to Fort Leavenworth, Kansas. After receiving uniforms, some other gear, and a few basic instructions, Pendleton was on a train to Vancouver Barracks in Washington, where he was assigned to Company A, 1st Battalion, 7th Infantry. Along with new recruits from other companies, he was given a form of basic training by NCOs from the 3rd Division, which included practice at the rifle range in the town of Bonneville, several miles farther up the Columbia River. During 1940, the 1st Battalion, 7th Infantry, organized a message center, taking men from each company. Pendleton's friend Frank Andrews from Company D joined him in the message center.

For the amphibious training of 1941, Pendleton was detached with about thirty-five to forty others from the division's regiments and sent to Fort Ord, where the men found nothing but tents for accommodations. They brought with them the twenty early Higgins boats on which they had been training and formed a boat detachment under the direction of the navy. Some of those men were mechanics; others, like Pendleton, were used to pilot the boats, something he had not done during the training in the Puget Sound. The division arrived several weeks later, in 1942, to begin new amphibious exercises in Monterrey Bay, where Fort Ord had frontage. Corporal Pendleton and the others had operated the landing craft in the Puget Sound, but now the navy was in charge and put the men in navy uniforms, which they wore during the landings. The waters in the bay were often choppy and rough, and strong winds made it difficult to stay on course. Pendleton and his group would pilot their craft out into the bay, and then troops from the division would begin climbing down rope ladders from navy ships onto their landing craft. On one exercise, the sailors from the navy piloted half the landing craft available. By the time they reached shore, the navy had wrecked all of theirs, but Pendleton and his fellow soldiers in navy uniforms had lost only one.

Before the end of the summer of 1942, the 9th Division was trained with the 1st Division in the Atlantic for amphibious operations. The 1st and 3rd Infantry Divisions later formed the spearheads of the amphibious force for European operations, because the marine divisions were destined for the Pacific.

We Are at War

Shortly after they attacked Pearl Harbor on December 7, 1941, the Japanese declared war on the United States, which retaliated with its own declaration of war. Hitler immediately declared war on the United States in support of his Axis ally. The American army was still months away from being ready to go on the offensive. The Army Air Force was equally unprepared. Although it had acquired some combat experience on escort duties in Atlantic waters, the U.S. Navy also had to work out numerous problems before it could take the initiative. It was ready to do so before the army, however. Until early 1942, the men already in uniform and those about to be drafted had no idea whether they were bound for the European or Pacific theater of operations.

John Slaughter's 29th National Guard Division had just completed the Carolina maneuvers, and its year of federal service was about to expire in a couple months.

> The 1st Battalion was bivouacked in woods near South Boston, Virginia. We were on our way back to Fort Meade, and our discharges were waiting. It was a chilly night, and the 1st Platoon was huddled around a blazing campfire. Some of the men were playing cards; others were just watching the blaze. I was lying on a blanket on the ground, almost asleep. It was Sunday, December 7, and some of the company had gone into town.

The USS *Shaw* explodes at Pearl Harbor, December 7, 1941. NATIONAL ARCHIVES

> Sgt. Bill Hurd came running into the area screaming, "The Japs have bombed Pearl Harbor!" Some of us said, "Shut up, Bill! We're trying to sleep!" Hurd exclaimed, "I swear it's the truth!" Verification soon came from radios. Anger and frustration overcame us at the thought of such a cowardly act, and soon the realization came that we were not going home after all. Discharges were frozen, and the song "I'll Be Back in a Year, Little Darling," changed to the phrase "in for the duration."

After the declaration of war and their return to Fort Meade, many of the men in Slaughter's unit received Christmas furloughs. The 115th Infantry was set to guard key defense installations and lines of communication in Pennsylvania and Virginia as far west as Pittsburgh, as far east as Philadelphia, and as far south as Richmond. The 175th Infantry remained in training until it relieved the 116th Infantry, which patrolled and defended part of the Chesapeake Bay and the Atlantic coast as far south as Cape Hatteras, as described in Joseph Ewing's *29 Let's Go!*

In mid-January 1942, the 116th Infantry took part in the Atlantic Task Force amphibious exercises, which were severely restricted because of the threat of U-boats. After that short training phase, the division got its first wartime assignment. The men in John Slaughter's unit were issued live ammunition in early 1942.

> On one of the coldest nights of the year, the outfit loaded onto trucks and shipped out to Camp Pendleton, near Norfolk, Virginia.[10] With the temperature at 9 degrees, sitting in the back of a 2½-ton Army truck,

10. Camp Pendleton was created in 1912 in a then-remote area at Virginia Beach for use mainly by the National Guard as a rifle range.

> with only canvas covering the riding area, quickly became a shivering experience. All I could think about as we highballed down the highway was getting under a hot shower in those steam-heated barracks at Pendleton. With little sleep, in the darkness of early morning, we pulled into a wooded area. There were about three inches of snow, and the ground was frozen solid. Someone up front yelled, "Detruck! Pitch tents!" I couldn't believe they were asking us to sleep on the ground in this frozen pine forest.
>
> We were awakened the next morning, loaded on weapon carriers, and driven east for the shore. We were to protect the coast from the invading 1st Marine Division, who were the "enemy." They were to make an amphibious assault landing near Virginia Beach. Digging gun emplacements in the frozen ground wasn't easy, but wading ashore from landing craft through the icy surf was even worse. Some of those poor "leathernecks" became paralyzed when they hit the icy water and had to be rescued.
>
> Our assignment after that exercise was the wartime patrolling of Eastern Shore, Maryland. We stayed in CCC barracks near Andover and patrolled the shoreline day and night in jeeps armed with machine guns and live ammunition.

The 1st Division had just returned to Fort Devens from the Carolina maneuvers when the Japanese hit Pearl Harbor. "All leaves were canceled," recalls Clyde Strosnider.

> There were radio announcements; public address systems, train stations, and theaters all were interrupted, telling all troops to return to base headquarters. Thereafter, we took boat landings on Virginia Beach; they took boat landings on the Sandwich Islands off of Cape Cod. The base was put on a wartime footing. No lights at nighttime; we were confined to camp. The patrolling of the camp and guard duty was all done under cover of darkness. We had orders to shoot anyone disobeying our orders to halt.
>
> To test these orders, my OD (officer of the day) came at me in an unmarked car into the motor pool where I was patrolling. Under cover of darkness, he came at me, ignoring my orders to halt. So I went down on one knee and brought my rifle into firing position, because I figured this was the real thing, and when I came into firing position, he came to a full stop.

Tom Cortright's National Guard unit had also recently returned from the Louisiana maneuvers to its post at Camp Forrest, when it got news of the surprise attack in the Pacific.

> We hardly settled in after that when December 7 was upon us. We moved out on December 8 on a perceived plan to protect war industries. Our company was divided up among three small towns in Tennessee. I have forgotten the other names, but I was in Lebanon with the company HQ and one of the platoons. We took over the fire station in the center of town for the headquarters and billeting. Our mission was to guard the blanket factory. After about two weeks, somebody high up in the army decided there would not be any sabotage, and we went out to a camp in Nashville, Tennessee, for a week or so, and then back to Camp Forrest.

M. Sgt. Kenneth Jarvis left the 40th National Guard Division for OCS at Fort Benning. After completing the three-month course, he was promoted to second lieutenant and returned to California, where he was assigned to the 35th

President Franklin Roosevelt signs the declaration of war on Japan, December 8, 1941. NATIONAL ARCHIVES

Division. The 35th relieved the 40th Division in February 1942, when the latter went to Fort Lewis in preparation for an assignment to the Pacific.

> I was assigned as a platoon leader in an infantry company. My assignment was to guard the coastline from San Pedro to Redondo Beach, California. We were reinforced with a few army-trained guard dogs. About all we could have accomplished would have been to sound an alarm. It kept me busy driving back and forth, checking in with my men along the line. We had a lot of rumors of Jap submarines along the coast but that was about it.

While Jarvis was attending OCS, the 35th National Guard Division returned from the Louisiana maneuvers in October 1941 and moved to California. Dale Kearnes was in the division's 130th Field Artillery Battalion at the time.

> At the end of the year, we were getting ready for Christmas vacation. I was in the 130th Field Artillery, and they had a shortwave radio. On Sunday, a message came in about the Pearl Harbor attack. Our division was already on trains and going to the West Coast. We wound up at Fort Ord. Then we went down to San Louis Obispo, and during Christmas, we had turkey in our mess kits out in the rain, because they cleared the barracks because they thought the Japs might come in. In a month or so, the Japs put a shell in north of Santa Barbara at the oil fields, and they took the whole division down as coast guards.

Murray S. Pulver, who later wrote a memoir about his experiences called *The Longest Year,* joined the New York National Guard the day before it moved south for training in Alabama in October 1939. Two years later, he made sergeant, and he took leave to make the final arrangements for his marriage, which was to take place on December 11, 1941. On December 8, however, the 27th National Guard Division from New York departed for California, where it took up defensive positions, and Pulver had to change his marriage plans. He finally tied the knot in California in February. His honeymoon was short-lived, however, because the division departed for Hawaii in April 1942 to defend Maui. By the end of the year, Pulver was sent back to the continental United States for OCS and eventually ended up with the 30th Division in Normandy.

Charles Scheffel of Enid, Oklahoma, was beginning his junior year when the draft was restored in 1940. Even though the last two years of ROTC, the advanced courses, were not required, he signed up because he needed the money. At the time of Japan's attack on Pearl Harbor, he still had one semester left. He married during that last semester in the spring. About that time, a colonel from Washington tried to persuade him to join the Finance Corps, but Scheffel opted to stay with the infantry. After graduation, he was commissioned and reported to Fort Sill for his active-duty physical at the beginning of June 1942. The next day, he was on a packed train for an eight-hour ride to Camp Robinson, near Little Rock.

> I was assigned to the 15th Training Regiment, Branch Immaterial Replacement Training Center (BIRTC). "Immaterial" means that we would be training new draftees into the army not for any particular branch of service, but just general training. After eight weeks, they would be assigned to a particular branch or be kept in the infantry.
>
> I was assigned as a platoon leader with three squads totaling forty draftees. The NCOs were older men serving as cadre. I would stand back if we were involved in something in which my own experience was lacking. Our company was mostly from the Chicago area; about half of them could read and write. That's why they were sent on to the infantry.
>
> Each officer had a small wooden hut just large enough for a cot with pull-up shutters over screens.
>
> My instruction included bayonet training and hand-to-hand combat because of my athletic abilities. Officers wore a campaign hat with a wide brim during training. I taught map reading and the use of the compass, but the toughest part was the full-field-pack twenty-five-mile marches over the rugged terrain of the camp. It covered an area of the pine-clad Ozark hills on the north side of the Arkansas River. We would have one night problem a week. Chiggers were the biggest bother, and we sprinkled powdered sulfur inside our leggings and GI heavy field shoes.
>
> On September 18, 1942, I had a physical exam for overseas service, and on the nineteenth, I got word that the shipment of about twenty second lieutenants would be leaving on October 2 for Camp Kilmer. September 22, 1942, we were issued combat equipment.

On October 2, 1942, Scheffel's troop car was attached to a civilian train, and his wife purchased a ticket for the same train. As a result, he spent most of the remainder of the trip in the passenger car with his wife. His troop car was hooked up to another train in Memphis and Washington, D.C., where they repeated the process. When the last train, traveling to New York City, reached New Brunswick, New Jersey, his car was unloaded, and he and the other soldiers were trucked to Camp Kilmer. Scheffel arranged to meet his wife at the Piccadilly Hotel in New York the next day. Once he arrived at Camp Kilmer, however, he was told they were sealed in and would be soon embarking, and he received his immunizations and a weapon. He paid an enlisted man to send a telegram to his wife to let her know he would not be able to meet her. It was five months before her first letter reached him in Algeria, and he did not see her again until November 1944.

At Camp Kilmer, Scheffel waited with Lt. Ozell Smoot, who had been with him at Camp Robinson. "Ozell was a full-blooded Creek Indian from Oklahoma City. He had been drafted in 1940, making sergeant, and then went to OCS at Fort Benning. We became good friends. He later became a captain and company commander in the 1st Division and was killed at Aachen in late 1944."

Soon they were taken by truck down to the river, where they boarded a ferry that carried them across to the *Queen Elizabeth*. The ship departed on October 9, 1942, also carrying half of the 29th Division. After they docked in Scotland on October 11, they went by train to Litchfield,

England, and became part of a group of about 200 replacements, with Scheffel in charge and Smoot acting as his executive officer (XO). About two weeks later, they were on a British ship on the way to North Africa as replacements.[11]

Carl J. Strom of Grand Rapids was in his first year of college at the time of the Japanese attack on Pearl Harbor. After he concluded that he would not have time to finish college before he was drafted, he decided to get married without delay. Thus he got married in April 1942 and was inducted in August.

> I was sent to Camp Wheeler, Georgia, for three months of basic training. This was, to us civilians, a tough experience: up at about 5 A.M. each morning with calisthenics, a short breakfast, and then training all day and often into the evening with ten-minute breaks each hour, and lunch and dinner. We learned not only to drill, which my high school ROTC and four summers of CMTC at Fort Custer made easy for me, but how to use our new M1 Garand rifle, and we were trained on light and heavy machine guns, 60- and 81-millimeter mortars, including breakdown and maintenance. In addition, we had bayonet fighting, hand-to-hand combat, and much more. We were soon going on twenty-five mile hikes with full forty-pound packs and camping out overnight. We learned how to dig defensive positions, camouflage them, and use gas masks. It was indeed stressful, and for a few men, especially trying. We said they were "wearing us down to build us up again!" At the end of our thirteen weeks, we were in much better physical shape than when we started. Several weeks into basic training, we were advised that anyone wishing to apply for OCS could make an application. We would first attend a six-week NCO School. I applied and was accepted.
>
> NCO School was easier than basic training, as we were in better shape to begin with, and we knew all about our weapons and how to handle individual situations. Training was on handling infantry squads and platoons in combat. We were given instructions on directing men in combat, placing of riflemen, machine guns, and mortars in attack and defense. I completed the course without difficulty and was ordered to report to OCS at Fort Benning.
>
> OCS was a very intensive and rigorous thirteen-week school to prepare men for command. The first week was spent in very thorough physical examinations and orientation. We were assigned to 200-man companies; those who passed the course and graduated were to be assigned to infantry divisions. We began with field training in the methods of command of units and courses in tactics, efficient use of weapons, and requirement of positions in the line of command. On graduation, I received my second lieutenant bars and a welcome ten-day leave home to see my wife.
>
> My first assignment was to Basic Infantry Replacement Training Center at Camp Robinson, Arkansas. Here I commanded a platoon of men who had completed their basic training and were being held for assignment to infantry divisions. I was there about two months, after which I was assigned to the 35th Infantry Division at Camp Rucker,

11. Scheffel is not clear about what happened at Litchfield. In his account, he indicates that a Colonel Bacon arrived and informed them they were designated Company C, Provision Replacement Group on October 14. In his book *Crack! and Thump,* written sixteen years after his account for us, he indicates they received British equipment and training. His coauthor, Barry Basden, found that Scheffel and the other GIs with him were part of an experiment and had been sent to the England to be attached to a British unit. If this were the case, they were not sent as replacements to North Africa, but as an American company in what was probably a British brigade.

Replacement Training Centers and Officer Candidate Schools

The following centers were set up to accommodate the rapidly expanding army, and especially for those branches that relied heavily on specialists:

- The Infantry School at Fort Benning (GA) existed since October 1918. An OCS was opened in July 1941. In March 1941, Infantry Replacement Training Centers opened at Camp Croft (SC), Camp Wheeler (GA), Camp Wolters (TX), and Camp Roberts (CA). Four others opened later, at Camp Fanin (TX), Fort McClellan (AL), Camp Blanding (FL), and Camp Croft (SC).
- The Field Artillery School was established in April 1919 at Fort Sill. The OCS opened in July 1941. Replacement Training Centers opened at Fort Sill (OK), Fort Bragg (NC), and Camp Roberts (CA) in March 1941.
- The Coast Artillery School, established in 1824, was at Fort Monroe. In July 1941, the OCS opened, but it was moved to Camp Davis (NC). The Antiaircraft Artillery School, splitting off from the Coast Artillery School, opened at Camp Davis in March 1942. Replacement Training Centers opened in March 1941 at Fort Eustis (VA) (for antiaircraft), Fort Bliss (TX), and Camp McQuade (CA). Camp Wallace (TX) and Callan (CA) became Antiaircraft Artillery Centers.
- The Cavalry School at Fort Riley (KS) existed since 1919. The Replacement Training Center opened there in March 1941 and the OCS in July 1941.
- The Armored Force School was created in September 1940 at Fort Knox (KY) and established an OCS in July 1941. The Replacement Training Center was part of the Armored Force School.
- In 1942, a Tank Destroyer School and Replacement Training Center went into operation at Camp Hood (TX).
- Air Corps Replacement Training Centers were at Atlantic City (NJ), Miami (FL), Keesler Field (MS), Gulfport (MS), Jefferson Barracks (MO), Lincoln (NE), Amarillo (TX), Sheppard Field (TX), Kearns Field (UT), and Fresno (CA).

Other Replacement Training Centers also opened in 1941:

- Engineer at Fort Belvoir (VA) and Fort Leonard Wood (MO). (Camp Abbott (OR) opened in 1943.)
- Signal at Fort Monmouth (NJ) and Camp Kohler (CA).
- Medical at Camp Lee (VA), Camp Grant (IL), Camp Robinson (AR), Camp Barkeley (TX), and Greensboro (NC).
- Ordnance at Aberdeen Proving Ground (MD).
- Quartermaster at Fort Lee (VA), Fort Warren (WY)

Other Officer Candidate Schools were established in 1941 as well:

- Engineer at Fort Belvoir (VA).
- Signal at Fort Monmouth (NJ).
- Medical administrative at Carlisle Barracks (PA).
- Ordnance at Aberdeen Proving Ground (MD).
- Quartermaster at Fort Lee (VA).

After 1941, replacement training centers for the Transportation Corps went into operation at New Orleans (LA), for the military police at Fort Custer (MI), for the Chemical Corps at Camp Sibert (AL), and for finance at Fort Benjamin Harrison (IL).

> Alabama. Here two brand new second lieutenants, such as myself, were assigned to each platoon, and we took turns commanding the platoon. An Oklahoma National Guard division had been transferred to new infantry divisions being formed. Regular army and National Guard units usually lost the majority of their experienced officers and noncoms to cadre for new divisions being formed, made up largely of draftees. After a few weeks with the 35th, I received orders to report to Fort Meade, Maryland, for shipment overseas. After a brief stay, I was sent to Camp Patrick Henry near Newport News, Virginia, where on October 5, 1943, I boarded a Liberty ship.

Col. Dwight D. Eisenhower was serving as General Krueger's chief of staff at Fort Sam Houston in San Antonio, Texas, when the Japanese struck. The first five days of the war were frantic for him. Men and equipment were loaded onto whatever railcars were available and rushed to defend the West Coast. Orders were sent to protect the Mexican border against spies. The sense of urgency sent normal procedures by the board. On December 12, Eisenhower was instructed to report to the War Department. After that, he swiftly moved up the command echelons, so that before the end of the next year, he was in charge of the most important operational forces in the European-African theaters.

From Iceland to the Philippines, the picture was the same: Soldiers still wearing World War I–era "bedpan" helmets and armed with bolt-action Springfield rifles guarded the coastlines and important installations. Few units were well equipped; virtually all needed to be reequipped and brought up to strength. For many days, the defense of hundreds of miles of the West Coast depended entirely on a few army divisions.

The fighter aircraft of the Army Air Force were in most cases outmatched by their Japanese and German opponents. The German tanks were superior to the majority of American tanks in service, and many units remained underequipped, even though most of 1941 had been spent mobilizing and modernizing the armed forces of the United States.

State of the Military in 1941

As part of the plan for mobilization, the army command decided in 1940 to create Replacement Training Centers to give new recruits some basic training before they were sent to active units. These centers were activated in the spring of 1941. Not enough were created to meet the demand that year, however, and thus many recruits joined units without basic training and had to learn on the job. After April 1941, most recruits received a thirteen-week basic training course at the centers. More specialized schools, such as Infantry, Artillery, and Armored Schools, provided additional training, as did Officer Candidate Schools, which transformed enlisted men into commissioned "ninety-day wonder" officers.

By the end of the year, eighteen National Guard divisions completed training after activation and received additional men from the new Replacement Training Centers. According to an article by S. L. A. Marshall titled "How the Army Is Organized," these divisions were preparing to convert from the square divisional organization, with four regiments in two brigades to the three-regiment triangular organization, which had already been adopted by the regular divisions in 1939.

In the rapidly expanding armored force, 50 percent of the personnel had to consist of trained technicians. To meet this demand, an armored school was established at Fort Knox. By the end of 1941, it graduated 25,000 specialists. Additionally, 35 percent of the army's contingent needed to have special skills, and General Marshall set up other specialized schools to train them.

While army installations expanded, the navy also prepared for war. Navy training schools prepared new recruits at Newport, Rhode Island; Great Lakes, Illinois; and San Diego. In addition, as with the army, specialty schools provided advance training.

The Naval Academy at Annapolis, Maryland, and the Military Academy at West Point, New York, produced a highly skilled officer corps, but both services had to rely heavily on the ROTC and OCS to fill the commissioned ranks. Planners who set goals of 2 million to 4 million servicemembers early in the war found later that the U.S. armed forces could swell to more than 10 million reasonably well-trained and well-armed men.

CHAPTER 3

The Road to North Africa, 1941–42

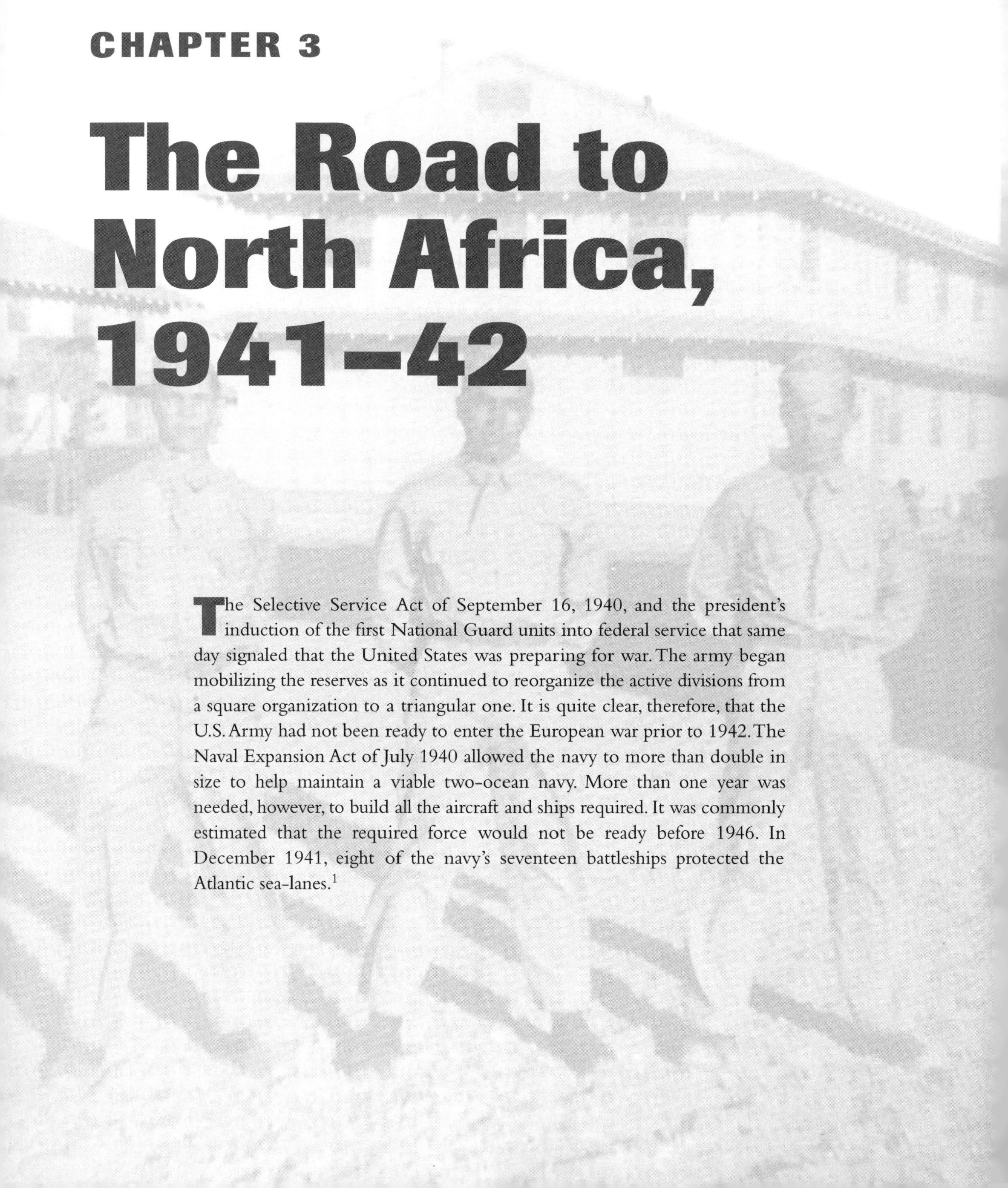

The Selective Service Act of September 16, 1940, and the president's induction of the first National Guard units into federal service that same day signaled that the United States was preparing for war. The army began mobilizing the reserves as it continued to reorganize the active divisions from a square organization to a triangular one. It is quite clear, therefore, that the U.S. Army had not been ready to enter the European war prior to 1942. The Naval Expansion Act of July 1940 allowed the navy to more than double in size to help maintain a viable two-ocean navy. More than one year was needed, however, to build all the aircraft and ships required. It was commonly estimated that the required force would not be ready before 1946. In December 1941, eight of the navy's seventeen battleships protected the Atlantic sea-lanes.[1]

As the war took one bad turn after another for the Allies, Britain was left to stand alone against the Axis powers. In the fall of 1940, President Roosevelt negotiated to exchange fifty old American destroyers for bases in British territory. On December 29, 1940, the president told the nation during a "fireside chat" that the United States would serve as an "Arsenal of Democracy." In March 1941, he got Congress to pass the Lend-Lease Act to help keep Britain afloat by providing it with the war materials it needed to survive, according to Sherman Pratt's *Autobahn to Berchtesgaden*.

Early in 1941, British military planners joined their counterparts in Washington, D.C., and concluded that once America entered the war, the first objective would be the defeat of the European Axis powers. American military planners formulated their strategies based on that decision. U.S. troops landed in Newfoundland on January 29, 1941. As American and Canadian representatives worked closely to coordinate the defense of the continent in 1941, the United States took over responsibility for Greenland's defense in March in spite of protests from the Danish government. The United States Coast Guard and the army landed in Greenland on June 30, preventing the Germans from setting up meteorological stations on the island. On May 16, Iceland proclaimed its independence from Denmark, and it allowed the U.S. 6th Marines to land on its territory on July 7 to replace the British and Canadian troops on the island. American troops also disembarked in Bermuda on April 20, Trinidad on May 5, and British Guiana on July 20, expanding the American defensive perimeter on the Atlantic frontier. Additional units landed on St. Lucia on August 4, Antigua on October 2, Jamaica on November 21, and Surinam on December 3. In August 1941, as the United States continued to bolster its continental defenses, President Roosevelt sailed for Newfoundland aboard the cruiser *Augusta* to meet with Winston Churchill, who arrived aboard the battleship *Prince of Wales*. Their meeting resulted in the Atlantic Charter.

America on the Road to War

In the spring of 1941, the Germans expanded the war zone as far west as Iceland and the Denmark Straits. Grand Adm. Erich Raeder, commander in chief of the German Navy, wanted to treat American ships in the war zone like the other neutrals—in other words, as subject to attack. He insisted that Germany was not obligated to respect the Pan-American neutrality zone or the limit of 300 miles from the North American coast. Hitler considered limiting the zone to 3 miles. Raeder also advised Hitler that French Northwest Africa must be secured to protect it from American intervention.

The first serious incident in the Atlantic took place on May 21, 1941. According to the U-boat commander, the American merchant ship *Robin Moor* was not marked as a neutral and its flag was unrecognizable. After stopping and inspecting the ship, the Germans claimed that it carried contraband and ordered the crew to abandon it before they sank it. A month later, on June 19, U.S. warships escorted convoys carrying lend-lease supplies as far as Iceland. The next day, *U-203* launched an unsuccessful attack on the American battleship *Texas*. Foul weather and the warship's zigzag course foiled the underwater attack.

On September 4, 1941, the USS *Greer*, a destroyer on a mail run to Iceland, escaped

1. During 1941, the navy had sixteen battleships and eleven aircraft carriers under construction, plus numerous other . warships, from heavy cruisers to destroyers and smaller types. Four of those new battleships came into service during 1942, but only one of the new carriers, and that was at the end of the year. Six more battleships came into service during 1943.

Army Expansion

In 1941, Gen. George C. Marshall, chief of staff of the U.S. Army, reported in his biennial report to the secretary of war that as of July 1, 1939, the army's personnel were scattered over 130 posts, camps, and other installations, and there was practically no field army within the continental United States. In addition, he complained, the army lacked motor transport and corps troops and had few special troop units. "As an army we were ineffective," he wrote, and the country was reduced "to the status of that of a third-rate power."

	Men	Army	Divisions	Army Air Forces	Aircraft delivered	Air groups
July 1939	174,000 (210,000)[a]			24,700, incl. 300 new pilots (1,200 pilots)[c]	(5,500)[a]	15 (62 squadrons)
September 1939	(227,000)[a] (235,000) NG[a]		5	26,000	800 1st line	
December 1939					2,500 (1,270 cbt)	
Summer 1940	(375,000)[a]			57,100	(36,500)[a]	(54)[a]
September 1940	(500,000)[a] (270,000) NG[a] (630,000) S[a]		8 Inf 1 Arm 1 Cav 18 NG	75,000 (12,000 pilots)[c]		
Spring 1941				(30,000 pilots)[c] (100,000 mechanics)[a]		
July 1941	1,400,000	456,000 = 29 Inf 43,000 = 4 Arm 308,000 = 215 Rgt 46,000 = HD 120,000 = Overseas 160,000 = Service 100,000 = Training		167,000	12,000	(209 squadrons)
December 1941	1,638,000	4,602,000 (incl. reserves)	14 Inf 2 Arm 1 Cav[d]	354,100	12,300 (4,000 cbt) (37,500)[a]	67[b]
December 1942	5,400,000		73 (100)[e]	1,597,000	33,000 (11,000 cbt)	
July 1943	6,900,000			2,000,000	85,900 (20,000 cbt)	136 (269 in December)
March 1945	8,157,300	5,522,00	89	2,290,500	July 1940 to August 1945 63,000 (31,300 cbt)	(243 in February)

Notes: NG = National Guard; S = selectees; Inf = infantry; Arm = armored; Cav = cavalry; Rgt = regiments; HD = harbor defense; Overseas = men in overseas garrisons; Service = branches such as signal, engineers, or quartermaster; Training = selectees (draftees) in training (from 100,000 to 200,000). "Aircraft delivered " includes training aircraft; those listed in parentheses with "cbt" represent the approximate number of combat aircraft of all types. Numbers rounded off and some are estimates.

[a] Authorized.

[b] Many only had cadre and lacked aircraft.

[c] Planner intended to train this many pilots for the year.

[d] Only these 17 divisions, of 34 divisions in the army, were ready for combat.

[e] Only 89 mobilized by March 1945.

Army Expansion *continued*

U.S. Army, August 1941

ARMIES	CORPS	DIVISIONS		
		Regular	National Guard	Reserve[g]
First	I	1st	26th, 43rd	76th, 95th, 97th
	II		27th, 44th	77th, 78th, 98th
	III		28th, 29th	80th, 99th
Second	V	5th	37th, 38th	83rd, 84th, 100th
	VI	6th	32nd, 33rd	85th, 86th, 101st
Third	IV	4th, 8th, 9th	30th, 31st	81st, 82nd, 87th
	VIII	1st Cavalry, 2nd	36th, 45th	90th, 95th, 103rd
Fourth	VII	2nd Cavalry	34th, 35th	88th, 89th, 102nd
	IX	3rd, 7th	40th, 41st	91st, 96th, 104th
Hawaii		24th, 25th		
Philippine Islands		Philippine		
	I Armored	1st, 2nd, 3rd, 4th Armored[f]		

[f] The 5th Armored Division was activated in the fall of 1941.
[g] None of the Reserve divisions were activated before 1942.

unscathed from a confrontation with *U-652* by keeping the submarine at bay with depth charges. On September 11, Roosevelt, declaring these attacks to be acts of piracy, ordered all ships to shoot on sight when operating in the American defensive zone. Hitler commanded Raeder's underwater raiders to stay away from American ships. Despite this order, on October 17, a U-boat attacked a convoy southwest of Iceland, hitting the destroyer USS *Kearney* with a torpedo and killing eleven sailors, the first American military casualties of a war the United States had yet to enter. Shortly afterward, on October 31, the destroyer USS *Reuben James* was torpedoed and sunk west of Iceland, and ninety-six men were lost. The escalating threat forced the U.S. Navy to escort troop convoys from Halifax, Canada. On November 10, 1941, Roosevelt persuaded Congress to approve a measure allowing the arming of merchantmen.

Despite the attacks on American shipping, Great Britain's precarious situation, and the possible collapse of the Soviet Union, invaded on June 22, 1941, the American public continued to oppose U.S. involvement in the war. On November 5, 1941, a poll conducted by the American Institute of Public Opinion revealed that 63 percent of Americans were against and 26 percent were for Congress declaring war on Germany. In September, America's pioneer aviator and national hero Charles Lindbergh still pushed the "America First" campaign, claiming that "the British, the Jewish, and the Roosevelt administration were the three most important groups . . . pressing this country towards war."[2]

2. In the speech in which Lindbergh made this comment, he claimed that he "admired the Jewish race" and did not intend his words to mean that he was anti-Semitic. Nevertheless, his comment reveals a deep-rooted anti-Semitism, typical of a time when prejudice against minority groups and non-Christian religions was rife in the United States.

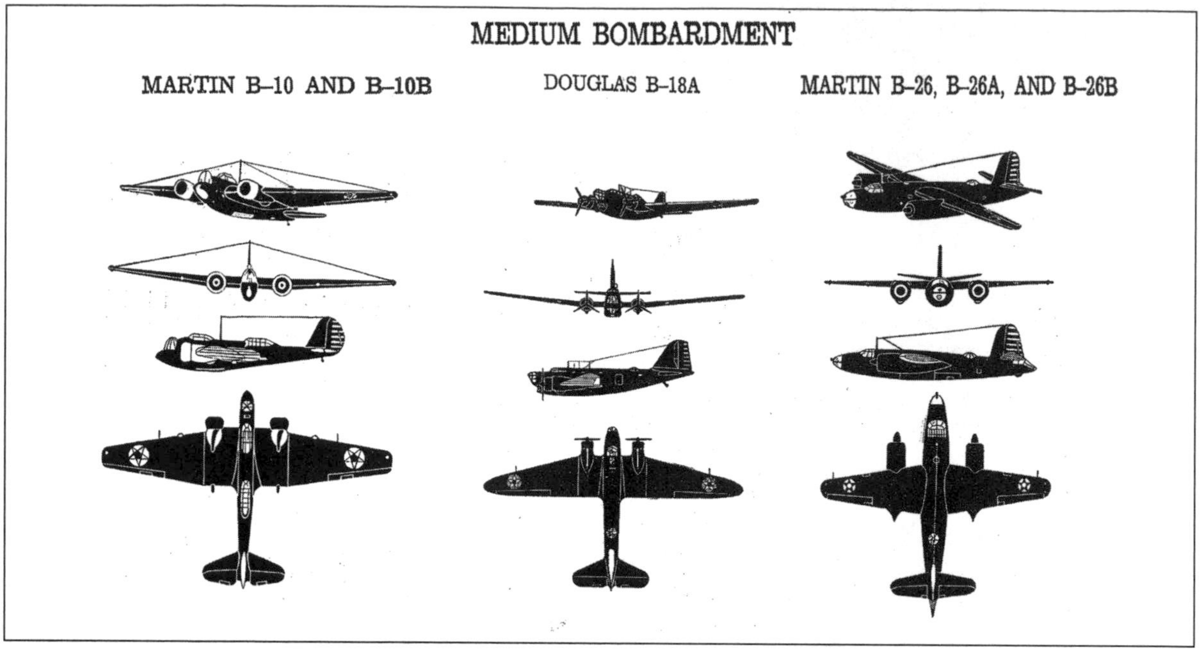

On July 9, 1941, Franz Halder, German Army chief of staff, recorded in his diary that according to intelligence estimates, the U.S. Army numbered merely six infantry, two armored, and two cavalry divisions. General Halder, like most of his compatriots, underestimated not only America's strength, but also its potential. In August 1941, the U.S. Army, including its reserve and National Guard components, numbered twenty-nine infantry, four armored, and two cavalry divisions, plus a tactical air force of about 200 squadrons. By the time war broke out, it had acquired one additional armored and one infantry division.

Before the summer of 1942, fortune did not seem to smile upon the Allies in this Second World War. When the United States finally entered the war, the German Army was engaged in a final push against Moscow, and the campaign between Great Britain and the Axis powers in North Africa was still seesawing between the two opponents. For almost six months after the attack on Pearl Harbor, the Japanese advance against America and its new allies seemed to be irresistible.

On January 26, 1942, elements of the 34th Division landed in Northern Ireland, spearheading the presence of the U.S. Army in Europe. In the spring of 1942, the 5th Infantry Division arrived in New York City, where it embarked in April for a year of duty in Iceland. The 1st Armored Division deployed in Northern Ireland in May and went on to England in October. After further training exercises in the southeastern United States, the 1st Infantry Division sailed from New York City in August 1942 to set up camp at Tidworth Barracks in southern England. By the end of that summer, the American expeditionary force in Great Britain consisted of three infantry divisions and one armored. They faced dozens of German divisions in northwest Europe. But several other divisions were getting ready to ship out across the Atlantic at the end of the summer.

The U.S. Army Air Forces

The U.S. Army Air Corps became the U.S. Army Air Forces (AAF) on June 20, 1941. Its Combat Command, which conducted air operations, replaced the GHQ Air Force and the Air Corps. Unlike the Army Ground Forces, the Army Air Forces attracted sufficient numbers of volunteers and expanded rapidly. In April 1939, Roosevelt

Air Force Units

American air units were divided into groups and squadrons as follows:

- A heavy bomber group included a group headquarters of about 75 men and four squadrons each with about 400 men and 12 bomber aircraft, for a total of about 294 officers and 1,497 enlisted men.
- A medium bomber group was organized the same way, except that each squadron had less than 400 men and 16 aircraft.
- a fighter or fighter bomber group included a group headquarters and three squadrons each with about 400 men and 25 aircraft, for a total of about 145 officers and 805 enlisted men. A P-38 (twin-engine fighter) group numbered 892 enlisted men.

Any number of groups came under an air force command in a theater of operations. The groups could be organized into fighter, bomber, and troop carrier commands. A bomber command with a large number of groups was subdivided into divisions, which were further subdivided into wings.

Group	Aircraft	Number of aircraft/aircrew	Crew size	Total personnel
Heavy bomber	B-17/B-24	72/96	9–11	2,261
Medium bomber	B-25/B-26	96/96	5–6	1,759
Light bomber	A-20/A-26	96/96	3–4	1,304
Fighter	P-47/P-51	111–126/126	1	994[a]
Troop carrier	C-47	80–110/128	4–5	1,837
Squadron				
Tactical recon	F-6/P-39/P-40 L-4/L-5	27/23	1	233
Photo recon	F-5	24/21	1	347

[a] A P-38 group had 1,081 men.

signed the National Defense Act of 1940, which funded the building of 6,000 aircraft. The selection of the B-17 four-engine heavy bomber prior to the war gave the air force an efficient offensive weapon for strategic bombing. Additional, more effective fighters and bombers gradually replaced the aircraft of the U.S. air fleet of the 1930s. Although America managed to outproduce Germany by December 1941, its 9,000 pilots still had only about 1,000 first-line combat aircraft at their disposal. By that time, the AAF numbered sixty-five air groups, whose personnel represented the nucleus of the much larger future force. At the time, many of its airmen were still in training.

In September 1939, the bomber force had included only twenty-three B-17s, but by December 7, 1941, it numbered fifty-eight, which formed part of the thirteen largely incomplete heavy bomber groups. In addition, about thirty of the air groups included fighter units made up mostly of P-39s, which were still considered adequate in 1942. Older aircraft were replaced as quickly as possible, however, while newer ones went into production.

American Bombers and Fighters

The B-17E, which was an improvement over earlier models, included a tail gun position with an upper and lower gun turret. Although some important changes were incorporated in the engines and the design of the B-17F, its appearance was similar to the E model. Unfortunately, production output did not get this model into Europe in sufficient numbers until 1943.

Data for Two Types of B-17 Bombers

	B-17E	B-17F
Maximum speed	317 mph	299 mph
Service ceiling	36,000 feet	37,500 feet
Bomb load	4,000 pounds	6,000 pounds
Armament	9 x .50-cal MG	11 x .50-cal MG
Crew	10	10

The final version, the B-17G, which went into service in 1943, included a remote-controlled chin turret. Some improvements were also made in the engines.

The B-24 heavy bomber was overshadowed by the B-17 but in some respects offered more advantages, even though it was more difficult to fly. Except for armament, few changes were made in most of the models. Once again, the army air corps did not receive enough B-24s until 1942. The H was given a nose turret. The J, whose performance was similar to that of the H, sported further modifications. The Americans sold a number of B-24s to the British, who nicknamed this model the "Liberator."

Data for Two Types of B-24 Bombers

	B-24D	B-24H
Maximum speed	303 mph	290 mph
Service ceiling	32,000 feet	28,000 feet
Bomb load	5,000-8,000 pounds	
Armament	11 x .50-cal MG	10 x .50-cal MG
Crew	10	10

Between 1940 and 1942, the two main American fighters were the P-39D Aircobra and P-40E Kittyhawk, both of which reached speeds of 335 miles per hour and had a ceiling of 29,000 feet. They were armed with .50-caliber machine guns, but some Aircobras had 37-millimeter guns. The twin-engine P-38 Lightning was suited for bomber escort and recon duty. By 1943, the P-47 Thunderbolt and P-51 Mustang fighters were delivered in sufficient numbers to form enough fighter squadrons to protect the bomber force.

ASK RICHARD BONG

Data for Fighter Aircraft

	P-38	P-47B	P-51B
Maximum speed	374 mph	429 mph	440 mph
Maximum range	1425 miles	1100 miles	2200 miles
Ceiling	30,000 feet	42,000 feet	42,000 feet
Armament	1 x 20m & 4 x .50-cal MG	6 or 8 x .50-cal MG	4 x .50-cal MG

The most remarkable feature of the Thunderbolt fighter and Flying Fortress was their ability to take severe punishment and remain in the air.

Between 1940 and 1942, American fighter aircraft were outclassed by German fighters, so the U.S. squadrons in Great Britain had to use British Hurricanes and Spitfires to match the Germans. The twin-engine P-38 Lightning was not ready until later in 1942, and the redoubtable P-47 Thunderbolt did not make an appearance until even later.

On January 28, 1942, the AAF activated the 8th Air Force at Savannah. In February, an advance party consisting of Gen. Ira C. Eaker and a few officers landed in England. On May 11, the 8th Air Force, under the command of Lt. Gen. Carl Spaatz, disembarked in England from a troopship. The planners had proposed building up the strength of the 8th Air Force to sixty combat groups totaling approximately 3,500 aircraft by April 1943. In June 1942, the aircraft for the 8th Air Force began to fly across the North Atlantic. The first flight landed in England on July 1. The first leg of the North Atlantic route took the planes from Maine, over Canada, Greenland, and Iceland, to Northern Ireland. The second leg took them from Ireland to England. By the late summer of 1942, the 8th Air Force consisted of the 1st and 31st Fighter, 60th Transport, and 97th Heavy Bomber Groups. It grew to include eight fighter, ten bombardment, three transport, and one reconnaissance group by the end of the year. The first bombing mission of the 8th Air Force was an unsuccessful low-level raid involving six A-20s of the 15th Bombardment Squadron that took place on July 4, 1942. The first bombing missions began on July 12. The Americans preferred to send heavy bomber squadrons on high-altitude daytime bombings, trading security for greater accuracy. The British, on the other hand, continued with their nighttime missions, sacrificing accuracy for fewer aircraft losses.

In the late summer of 1942, the 8th Air Force had expanded to include 150 B-17s, 12 A-20s, 150 Spitfires, and 75 P-38s in 3 fighter groups totaling about 400 aircraft. Three new fighter groups and six additional bomber groups formed up in the fall, but most of these units were not fully operational, because they were still inexperienced. The 97th and 301st Bomber Groups, two of the most experienced units of the 8th Air Force, plus three veteran fighter groups were assigned to the North African campaign.

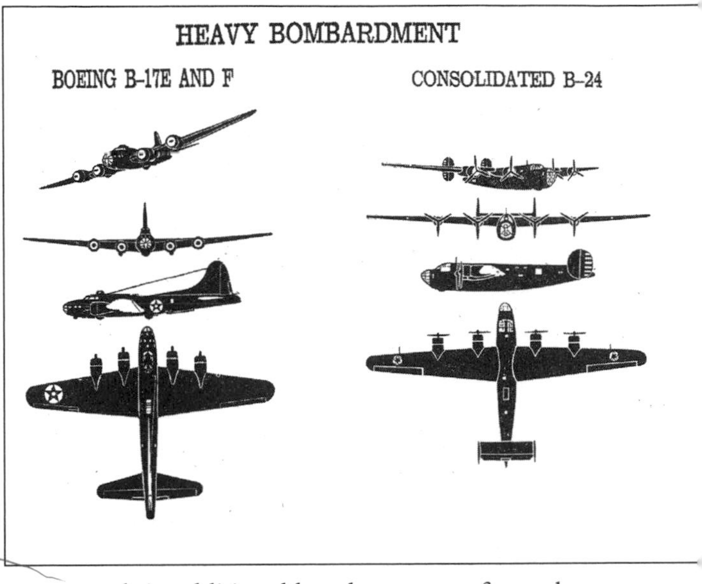

Allied Plans for 1942

When the war began, fewer than a dozen army divisions were fully armed and ready for combat, but in 1942, the American armed forces rapidly increased in strength as they received deliveries of new equipment every month. The AAF grew in tandem with the rest of the army. In the second half of the year, it established the 8th Air Force in England and sent several squadrons to Egypt to form the Middle East Air Force, later renamed the 9th Air Force. The navy was in relatively good shape. Most of the battleships damaged at Pearl Harbor had sunk in shallow waters, and all but two were beyond repair. Most of the ships were refloated, repaired, and put back in action by 1943—in less time than it would have taken to build a new battleship.

Until the fall of 1942, many army units had gone to the Pacific, where the navy concentrated its efforts until it stopped the Japanese juggernaut at Midway in the summer, weeks after the fall of the Philippines and the largest surrender of America troops during the war. The first American offensive took place in August, when the marines, later followed by the army, landed on Guadalcanal. The campaign lasted half a year, drawing in major ground, air, and naval forces of both the United States and Japan.

Only 2,500 of the 8,000 troops intended for Iceland and 4,100 of the 16,000 planned for Northern Ireland actually embarked on January 15, 1942, while 21,000 soldiers went to the Southwest Pacific. By mid-March 1942, of the 132,000 army troops sent overseas, only 20,000 were in Iceland and Northern Ireland. General Eisenhower, as chief of the War Department Operations Office for the Pacific, demonstrated his skills as a strategist and logistician when he strongly recommended that the movement of reinforcements take priority over all planned operations in the Atlantic. He considered this move as only a temporary option, however. Impressed by his skills, General Marshall appointed him commander of the American armed forces in the European theater in June 1942.[3]

Although the British had hoped to establish a foothold in Northwest Europe as soon as possible, the American army was not able to expand rapidly enough to provide the required divisions in 1942. The battle of the Atlantic reached a climax that year, and by mid-1943, the Allies had the situation under control. Joseph Stalin, the Soviet leader, demanded that his allies open a second front in Europe. But the Americans, who still had to train and build up their new divisions while supplying Lend-Lease materials to the British as well as the Soviets and containing the Japanese threat, were not ready to go.

On January 9, 1942, the Americans established the Joint Chiefs of Staffs, in order to deal with the British on equal terms. Gen. George C. Marshall was appointed chief of staff for the army, Gen. Henry H. Arnold for the air, and Adm. Ernest J. King for the navy. The British and Americans finally agreed on a ground campaign involving a landing in French Northwest Africa. A joint committee calculated that only 25,000 troops could be transported across the Atlantic in mid-January 1942, because shipping had to maintain other American military forces already overseas. The troop capacity would increase to 35,000 by April. A North African operation would delay any other major troop movement across the Atlantic for at least three months. Thus, after reconsidering their plans and scrapping one for a 1942 landing in France, in July the joint committee agreed on the North African invasion, code-named Gymnast, which would take place late in the year.

While serving in the War Plans Division in February 1942, Eisenhower had considered obtaining suitable craft to land army units on hostile shores in all theaters of operation. But the navy, which was in charge of the construction of these vessels, refused to provide the crews for them, fearing a drain on its manpower. Naval officials did not want to be forced to accept draftees to fill the resultant shortages. "The Navy was thinking only in terms of restoring the fleet," wrote Eisenhower years later. "They were not particularly interested in landing craft for future offensives. But if we didn't start building we would never attack."

Finally, in April 1942, after a conference in the White House, a plan emerged to build 8,200 craft of all types, including 6,700 to carry small tanks and vehicles. It was hoped that 2,500, including 2,000 for tanks and vehicles, would be ready in

3. Marshall had assigned Eisenhower to the War Plans Division (WPD) section for the Pacific in December 1941. When the army was reorganized on March 9, 1942, the WPD was redesignated as the Operations Division (OPD), which Eisenhower headed between February and June 1942.

Landing Craft

The British developed the landing craft, tank (LCT), in October 1940. Dissatisfied, Winston Churchill ordered a vessel with oceangoing capability. The result was the landing ship, tank (LST), built by companies in the United States and Canada. The British Admiralty further improved the design, which went into production in the United States in February 1942. In addition, the landing ship, infantry (LSI), was developed to transport troops.

In 1940 and 1941, American units practiced amphibious landings on both coasts using small craft unsuitable for moving heavy equipment and vehicles from the ships to the beaches. The first Higgins boats had no ramps and the troops were required to jump over the side.

In the United States, the construction of LSTs and LCTs began in May 1942. In addition, the British requested a larger infantry landing craft, which led to the development of the landing craft, infantry (LCI). All these craft were shallow-draft vessels that could bring their cargoes right up to the beach, and most included ramps in the bow, although the LCI carried small foot ramps along its bow instead. The large seagoing LST included an elevator to lower vehicles from the upper to the lower deck, where a special bow door dropped to serve as a ramp to the beach. These LSTs usually carried two or more landing craft, vehicles and personnel, (LCVPs) on davits.

By the end of the war, 27 LSDs and more than 1,150 LSTs, 550 LSMs (of which 50 were armed and carried rocket projectors), 650 LCT(5)s, and 960 LCI(L)s were built, as well as thousands of the smaller types of landing craft.

American and British Landing Vessels

Type of vessel	Designation[a]	Length	Capacity	Armament
Landing craft, mechanized	LCM(3)	50'	1 tank or 60 troops	2 x .50-cal MG
Landing craft, mechanized	LCM(6)	56'	1 tank or 120 troops	2 x .50-cal MG
Landing craft, tank	LCT(1)	152'	3 medium or 6 light tanks	2 x 2-pounders
Landing craft, tank	LCT(2)	160'	Same as LCT(1)	2 x 2-pounders or 2 x 20mm
Landing craft, tank	LCT(5)	117.5'	4 or 5 medium tanks	2 x 20mm
Landing craft, tank	LCT(6)	120'	4 medium or 3 heavy tanks	2 x 20mm
Landing craft, infantry (small)	LCI(S)	105'	102 troops	4 x 20mm
Landing craft, infantry (large)	LCI(L)	158.5'	205 troops	5 x 20mm
Landing craft, vehicles and personnel	LCVP	36'	36 troops	2 x .30-cal MG
Landing craft, assault	LCA[b]	41.6'	35 troops	2 x Lewis guns
Landing ship, medium	LSM	203.6'	5 medium or 3 heavy tanks or LVTs or 9 DUKWs[c] & 54 troops	
Land ship, tank	LST(2)	327'	6 LCVPs and 70 trucks or 39 light or 20 medium tanks or 22 DUKWS and up to 250 troops[d]	7 x 40mm 12 x 20mm (varied)
Landing ship, dock	LSD	458'	2 or 3 LCTs or 14 LCMs or 47 DUKWs and 240 troops	1 x 5" gun, 2 x twin 40mm, 2 x quad 40mm & 16 x 20mm

[a] Not all models listed.
[b] British type.
[c] A DUKW was an amphibious vehicle.
[d] Numbers of troops could be increased for short distances.

LCI 320. WARREN C. HOTARD

time for a landing in France in 1942 called Sledgehammer. The British, however, believing that many more landing craft would be necessary for a cross-channel attack, persuaded Roosevelt in May to build larger oceangoing craft such as LSTs. As it turned out, only 10 percent of the total number of landing craft required for Sledgehammer arrived in Great Britain by September.

Operation Torch, the invasion of North Africa in November 1942, was carried out with the equipment that would have been available for a cross-channel attack that same autumn. This invasion initially involved 65,000 soldiers and consisted of three task forces that landed at widely separated points in Morocco and Algeria. The Western Task Force included twenty-two transports loaded with troops, tanks, and equipment that set off from the United States. The other two task forces came from Great Britain. The Central Task Force included three LSTs and fifteen LSIs.[4] The Eastern Task Force numbered four transports and eleven LSIs. The size of Operation Torch, which supplanted American plans to invade Europe in 1942, indicates that an attempt to attack the defended European coastline at that time would have met with disaster.

U.S. Army Reorganization

In February 1942, the U.S. Army underwent a major reorganization that replaced the GHQ with the new Army Ground Forces. General McNair took command of this new organization at the War College in Washington, D.C. This gave him control of all ground troops in the United States, where the emphasis was on training, doctrine, and the operation of replacement training centers. The Army Air Forces and Army Service Forces were separate commands.

American infantrymen were better equipped than most of the other Allied soldiers. The .30-caliber M-1 rifle, a semiautomatic weapon, replaced most of the old bolt-action Springfield rifles in 1942.[5] Although slightly bulkier than most rifles, it proved to be one of the best rifles in service. The M-1918 Browning automatic rifle (BAR) was a very efficient weapon, providing much of the squad's firepower. The M-1917 water-cooled Browning and M-1919 air-cooled machine guns served as the companies heavy weapons. All these weapons used .30-caliber ammunition. Infantry units also had heavy .50-caliber machine guns, small M-3 submachine guns, and .45-caliber pistols. Other weapons such

4. LSIs were British transports designed to carry troops and landing craft—usually British LCAs (landing craft, assault). They came in large and small types but in many ways were similar to American amphibious troop transports.

5. The old 1903 Springfield (the 03) continued in use with the marines in 1942. They switched to the M-1 after the Guadalcanal campaign. The army retained the 03 for use as a sniper weapon with a scope added, since it had greater accuracy than the M-1.

as the 60- and 81-millimeter mortars were found at company and battalion levels. All these weapons were adequate, even though some were not as efficient as the German models. This armament had become standard for most infantry units by 1940, and remained so throughout the war. The American infantry trained with these weapons and used them in combat. The only significant change came when the 57-millimeter antitank gun replaced the ineffective 37-millimeter. The rocket launcher antitank weapon, or Bazooka, was introduced so quickly in 1942 that the first units going into combat in North Africa had no training with it. In fact, these weapons were issued to them as they embarked on their journey.

Each platoon was equipped with a battery-powered SCR-536 handie-talkie, the smallest radio the army had, which weighed 5 pounds and had a range of about a mile. After the war, many referred to these devices as walkie-talkies, but the handie-talkie was a larger portable radio. Company and battalion commanders had at their disposal SCR-300 radios that weighed 32 or 38 pounds, depending on the type of battery, and a range of three miles or more. According to War Department Technical Manual TM 11-242, published in February 1945, "It is primarily intended as a *walkie-talkie* for foot combat troops." The SCR-300 replaced the first walkie-talkies, the SCR-194 and SCR-195, after the invasion of North Africa. It was also carried in a one-man pack, but its transmissions were easily masked. The SCR-284 was used at the regimental level. It weighed 110 pounds dismounted and 250 pounds complete and had a range of about twenty-five miles. It was later replaced with the SCR-694, which had a much greater range. These portable radios became standard equipment in early 1943, along with heavier long-range radios. Telephones with their cables and messengers remained in use as well.

The American M3 Grant and later M4 Sherman tanks had only a slight advantage over the British tanks, which proved inferior to most of the newer German models of 1942. The American tanks were able to stand up to the German Panzer III and IV tanks, but not to the Panzer VI Tiger, which did not appear in the west until the later stages of the North African campaign.[6] Production of the Sherman tank got in full swing during the summer of 1942. American medium-tank battalions soon began to receive their first M4s, but by the fall of 1942, many units still had not replaced their M3s. Thus during Operation Torch, the invasion of North Africa, the American armored units were not yet fully equipped with M4 Sherman tanks. The 2nd Armored Division's new M4 tanks and M7 105-millimeter self-propelled howitzers had been transferred to the British in the summer of 1942. The 1st Armored Division arrived in the United Kingdom with M3 Grant tanks. During Operation Torch, the battalions of the 1st Armored Division and the detachment from the 2nd Armored Division had a mixture of light Stuart and medium Grant and Sherman tanks. In February 1943, a GHQ tank battalion arrived with M3s. At the same time, the 1st Armored Division was calling for 120 M4 tanks, including 54 from the British, to replace its losses in Tunisia. Although production of the Sherman was well under way by the summer of 1942, sufficient units were not available until 1943.

6. During the summer of 1942, the British used the American M-5 Stuart light tank and M-3 Grant/Lee against the Germans in North Africa. They had ordered a model of the M-3 with a turret that did not mount the MG cupola, which enlarged the silhouette of the vehicle. This medium tank mounted a small 37-millimeter gun in its turret, but the sponson mounted its main weapon, a 75-millimeter gun, which was able to challenge German armor in North Africa. The tank was effective only when the enemy appeared in the limited field of fire of the 75-millimeter gun and had to maneuver to get the gun into firing position. The M-5 Stuart tank was light and fast, and like the Grant, it was mechanically reliable. Its small 37-millimeter gun was no match for most German armor, however.

CHAPTER 4

Invasion Practice, 1942

In the course of Operation Jubilee, which began on August 18, 1942, the 2nd Canadian Infantry Division and supporting British troops landed at Dieppe, France. It was one of the largest amphibious raids staged by the Allies up to that time. The British claimed that it was successful and it provided the Allies with invaluable lessons for the upcoming invasion of North Africa. According to an official British history of 1943, the Germans "realized that their enemies were able to stage with success a landing on a scale heavy enough to make a still larger combined operation a practical proposition."

In fact, the Dieppe raid was a disaster. The landing took place on a section of coastline backed for most of its length by cliffs that were not scalable by an assaulting force at many points. In addition, of the few exits from the beach, one led right through the city of Dieppe. The 2nd Canadian Division disembarked on the beaches of Dieppe and farther west, at Pourville, where there was another exit inland. British commandos, who landed on both flanks, were more successful because they arrived first. One of their primary missions was to take out coastal batteries of 5.9-inch guns, which they partially achieved. The main Canadian force, however, which landed on the beaches of Dieppe with a couple dozen Churchill tanks, was mowed down, its wooden landing craft shot to pieces. Additionally, the air battle was not the unqualified success the Allies claimed it to be, especially since the British accidentally shot down a number of their own aircraft.

Nevertheless, the Allies were able to draw many lessons from this raid before they embarked on Operation Torch several weeks later. The debacle had given them a clearer understanding of the difficulties faced by amphibious forces when they attacked shores held by the Axis powers. It had become clear, for instance, that they needed to back any major landing operation with a bombardment force of battleships and heavy cruisers, as well as coordinate with and identify friendly aircraft. The most important lesson, however, was that trying to take a well-defended port by direct assault was too risky. Dieppe held special significance for the U.S. Army, because it was the first time American troops landed in France during the war. Indeed, a small group of newly organized American Rangers made it ashore with the Canadians and British and, unfortunately, also suffered casualties.

Birth of the Rangers

In mid-May 1942, Dwight Eisenhower attached Col. Lucian K. Truscott to the staff of the British Combined Operations to study their methods, including planning, organization, preparation, and conduct of combined operations. Truscott's mission was to keep the War Department informed on developments in training, technique, and equipment. On May 26, Truscott sent proposals to General Marshall recommending the creation of an American unit similar to the British commando units. Marshall accepted his recommendations and issued the authorization on May 28.

At the time, there were only two American divisions in Great Britain: the 34th Infantry and 1st Armored. Although the commander of the 1st was concerned about the loss of trained men, he cooperated when the call for volunteers went out.

The volunteers were organized into a battalion-size force of six companies, with three officers and sixty-three men each, and a headquarters company with eight officers and sixty-nine men. William Darby was appointed to command this new unit and carefully selected his volunteers, of whom 60 percent came from the 34th Infantry, 30 percent from the 1st Armored, and 10 percent from the Engineer, Signal, and Quartermaster Corps. Truscott decided to name this unit the Rangers, giving it a distinctly American identity.

American Rangers in the Dieppe Raid

A group of fifty Rangers—six officers and forty-four enlisted men—took part in the Dieppe operation on August 18, 1942. Forty went in with No. 3 Commando on the left flank. This attack failed, and only four Rangers made it ashore, because most of the landing craft were forced to turn away. A few Rangers attached to No. 4 Commando landed on the right flank. The remaining few Rangers went in with the Canadian division and fared worse than their comrades did.

Of the Rangers who managed to go ashore with No. 3 Commando, Ranger Lt. Edwin Loustalot was killed, and Sgt. Albert Jacobsen, PFC Walt Bresnahan, and PFC Edwin Furru were captured. Even before it reached the shore, No. 3 Commando was attacked by E-boats as it crossed the English Channel, and several Rangers in this group were wounded at sea.

The four Rangers with No. 4 Commando on the right flank fared better. Ranger Cpl. Franklin Koons was the first American soldier to kill a German in combat, and he received the British Military Medal and the U.S. Silver Star.

At about 5:20 A.M., about two hours after the commandos had landed on the flanks, Ranger Lt.

Joseph Randall, assigned to the Canadian Royal Hamilton Light Infantry, went ashore on White Beach, and T/4 Howard Henry, with the Essex Scottish, made it to Red Beach. Both soldiers were killed, and the Canadian units to which they were attached took casualties amounting to 85 percent of their strength. Finally, Ranger Sgts. Marcel G. Swank and Lloyd N. Church went ashore with the Cameron Highlanders of Canada on Green Beach at Pourville. Both men were wounded during the withdrawal, and the Germans captured the seriously wounded Church. Swank ran into the surf and swam out to a landing craft in the late morning. That day at Dieppe was an unmitigated disaster for both the Canadians and the American Rangers. The surviving Rangers returned to England to form a small experienced cadre for the 1st Ranger Battalion and the upcoming invasion of French North Africa.

The day Sgt. Marcel Swank crossed the Channel to Dieppe with the 2nd Canadian Division in August 1942, he was nineteen years old. He had joined the National Guard in December 1938 and gone on active duty when the 34th Division was federalized in February 1941. His unit moved from his hometown in Minnesota to Camp Claiborne, Louisiana, where it participated in the Louisiana maneuvers most of the summer. In May 1942, it disembarked in Northern Ireland, just in time for Swank to volunteer for the newly forming Rangers. He then trained for two months at the British Commando Depot (School) at Achnacarry, Scotland, where he practiced assault landings and learned to use German, British, French, and Italian automatic weapons.

Sergeant Swank was one of a select group of fifty Rangers to participate in the Dieppe raid. The night before the raid, he and the men of Canadian unit to which he was attached were informed of their mission. "In fact, during the entire action, I was uncertain as to where I was," recalls Swank, which is not surprising, since the men were given very little information. The crossing on that ill-fated day is clearly etched in Swank's memory.

> The Queen's Own Cameron Highlanders of Canada, 2nd Canadian Division, sailed from Newhaven, England, at approximately 2000 hours on August 18, 1942, in plywood R-boats. Each craft carried twenty to twenty-five men. They sailed all night, as part of a larger flotilla, the sixty miles to the coast of France. Attached to the Camerons were two Americans: Sgt. Lloyd N. Church and myself, Marcel G. Swank. We were aboard the same craft.
>
> At approximately 0525 hours, the Camerons were at sea about 1,000 yards off Pourville (Green Beach), France. The beach was about 800 yards long and lies some two kilometers to the west of the primary objective, the port of Dieppe. The landing craft began their run for the beach in a sweeping line some 400 to 450 yards wide, following the South Saskatchewan Regiment, which had landed at 0450 hours. The South Saskatchewan Regiment landing had been a surprise to the Germans; however, they failed to overcome the beach defenses. It was now daylight, and the German shore batteries opened fire on the British destroyers supporting the landing. German automatic-weapons fire began playing into the line of landing craft, and mortar explosions appeared along the waterline.
>
> As we made for the beach, I heard a sound distinct from that of the gunfire and engines. I knew what it was, but I couldn't believe it. I thought this only happened in movies. I looked to my right, and there on the small forward deck of the craft next to me stood a piper. He looked like a figurehead in the gray dawn and was playing "One Hundred Pipers." In the great tradi-

tion of the Scots, he was telling the world that the Camerons were coming. To this day, it is my proudest boast that I went into battle with bagpipers playing. It remains the most magnificent moment of my life. I've never been so ready to die.

The landing (approximately 0535) went quite well; however, the withdrawal (approximately 1145) was a disaster. The piper, Cpl. Alex Graham, was wounded and captured. Sergeant Church received a head wound on the beach during the withdrawal. He was captured and returned home after the war; however, he never recovered from the wound. After numerous operations and comatose episodes, he died on November 11, 1950, at the Des Moines Veterans Hospital.

In September 1979, I met Alex Graham in Dieppe. I told him of my great admiration for his courage at Pourville. After my return to the States, he sent me a bagpipe in the Cameron tartan.

Swank evaded capture by running into the sea and swimming toward the Allied vessels. He managed to reach a passing landing craft and was hauled onboard by the crew. At about noon, he transferred to the British destroyer HMS *Calpe,* where he was joined by Ranger Sergeant Kenyon. The other American had been attached to the Royal Regiment of Canada, which had landed on Blue Beach at Puits. Although Kenyon's landing craft had tried to land three times, the enemy had driven it off each time. Finally, German fighters had strafed the invasion craft, hitting Kenyon while he was attending to the Canadian wounded. The Royal Regiment of Canada suffered 95 percent casualties.

On his return to England, Sergeant Swank was taken to the 1st Canadian General Hospital near Bramshot, where he was treated royally by the military and civilian personnel alike. Later, Swank went into the Mediterranean with the 1st Rangers and was promoted to second lieutenant after the campaigns of North Africa and Italy.

Ranger S. Sgt. Gino Mercuriali also recalls participating in the raid. In June 1938, he had joined the 34th Division of the National Guard, like Marcel Swank, and had gone to Northern Ireland with the division.

My company was located at Castle Rock, Northern Ireland. Another sergeant and I often talked about the exploits of the commandos and expressed the idea of liking to be in such a unit. The hit-and-run tactics with the out-of-combat time in between raids appealed to us. So when the news of such an American unit came out, asking for volunteers, I jumped on it, but the other sergeant did not volunteer. At least three others did join: Ernest Stark, Don Earwood, and Woodrow Bock. My name was not forwarded, so I inquired as to why not, and was told that I was slated for a return to the U.S. to attend OCS. (The other sergeant must have known he was included on this list.) I protested and went to Captain Murray, our battalion commander, and he assured me I would be given that chance. Away I went for the interview, and I was accepted.

We underwent special training at Achnacarry, Scotland. Ours was a unit that did not burden itself with the standard army pack; much of the time, we carried rations and a raincoat and little else. We wore the British commando shoe with its tire-tread design and cut our leggings short to prevent calf muscle cramp. Even though I trained with the submachine gun and, as a sergeant, could carry the weapon, I opted for the M-1, as I didn't trust the submachine gun, since it was too likely to jam.

A ranger company consisted of about seventy-five men, and six men from each company were chosen to train with a

British commando company. As I look back, while we were somewhat in awe of these veterans, and were friendly with them, I don't believe we established any personal rapport that we well may have done—probably due to our tenuous state in their unit and our desire to spend our free time in a free-spirited way, as you may well imagine. We were housed in an empty house, laying out our blankets on the bare floor, and ate many additional meals in town, as the British ration was not to our liking. I confronted the company commander for the lack of utensil cleaning, and he did make provisions for us by adding a garbage pail (you were supposed to eat it all) and a tub of hot water for cleaning our utensils. Still, we liked the people very much and understood their ways to a degree.

Our training here was much like that of Achnacarry, with more emphasis, I assume, on the British purpose to learn about the Americans' staying power, as much of the training included long, enduring marches. We also learned to use a 20-millimeter gun from the hip, using a rope sling.

Before we were picked for this assignment, there had been a few people picked from the Rangers for this special raid. We did not know that at the time, but later, we learned that they returned to our unit while in Scotland because the raid had been postponed.

I went to the guard house with someone and talked to a Canadian that told me he was accused of talking about the upcoming event. We did know we were there for some type of mission and were, sometime during our stay, briefed and trained by making landings on the Isle of Wight. One significant lesson we learned was not to hang grenades from our belts. We were to study the terrain from a mock-up of the coastline and supposedly precise gun locations, etc., just as we did later for the Algerian invasion.

Our company, and I assume most, if not all, were loaded into a landing craft, not a LCP as we know them, but a boat with a "red wing engine" housed in the center and a ramp around the sides, which provided a place to sit. You might also crawl under, but I don't recall that anyone did. We experienced the E-boat's attack but fortunately did not lose any personnel in our craft as far as I know. The flaming "onions" from their guns were a sight to behold, as they appeared to be aimed to hit between the eyes. We had to evacuate our craft for another one. I don't believe I ever knew how it had become empty, but this was a blessing, as we would be sitting ducks, if not already so.

Our evasive action threw our timing out, so we were directed to congregate with the mother ship in the Dieppe Harbor. This was an experience not unlike World War I, as far as the combat airplanes were concerned. Numerous parachutings were observed, and many times it could not be determined who was who. Some of these planes and pilots were American. Of course, we were within shelling distance from land and could see the Bofors and pom-poms being fired from the ship's deck and the tanks trying to make their landing in the harbor area. Yet we were relatively safe, surely not envious of the Canadian troops trying to get to shore. It was truly a sad sight. On this occasion, as with later ones, my composure, I would say, was very good. I always seemed to be engaged enough that things weren't so scary as they were happening, but sometime later, when recalled, they scared you out of your pants.

After returning to our base in England, Sergeant Kavanaugh and I went to a place much like our USO. We were asked the question, "What do you think of the raid?" We were surprised to learn of the news of the raid in the U.S. newspapers, since it would have you think it was an American operation! The British didn't much appreciate this.

Mercuriali's photo appeared in the July 31, 1944, issue of *Life* magazine and on the cover of the book *Life Goes to War.*

Although the 1st Rangers did not return to France, the unit's experiences at Dieppe and in North Africa showed the Allied military planners the capabilities of elite troops. In 1942, after only two months of training, the Rangers were definitely a cut above a regular infantry unit, even though they were still green troops like the rest of the American forces in Great Britain.

On to Africa: Operation Torch

The first major amphibious invasion carried out by American forces took place in North Africa on November 8, 1942, only a few months after the marines stormed ashore on the Pacific island of Guadalcanal. The decision to invade North Africa was made late in the summer, after the feasibility of invading France had been ruled out for at least another year. The scale of the operation in relation to the invasion beaches was massive, even though the number of forces committed was small compared with those that would participate in the Normandy operation a little more than a year and a half later. Three task forces ferried the invasion troops to widely separated landing areas. In some cases, the landing areas for the individual task forces were also widely scattered. Only the 1st and 3rd Infantry Divisions had a significant amount of practice in amphibious operations, but it was not enough. The experience in landing procedures the 9th Division and armored units had acquired during their summer off the Virginia coast was even more limited. Some of the American units, such as the 168th Infantry of the 34th Division, had received amphibious training in Scotland in October 1942. This regiment took part in the initial landings, but other units of the 34th arrived later.

The invasion force also included the 1st Ranger Battalion, British 78th Division, commandos, and naval units that joined the operation against Algiers. More than 100,000 troops sailed from America and the British Isles for this operation. The 34,000-man Western Task Force, which included the 3rd Infantry, 9th Infantry, and 2nd Armored Divisions, sailing from the United States, was to strike at three sites in Morocco and was divided into three attack groups. The Center and Eastern Task Forces, sailing from Great Britain, included the 1st Infantry, 34th Infantry, 78th British Infantry, and 1st Armored Divisions, plus a regiment of the 9th Division. The 39,000-man Center Task Force targeted Oran, while the 33,000-man Eastern Task Force was to land at Algiers. The 9th Division's 39th Infantry joined the Eastern Task Force to land with elements of the 34th Division and the British. The attack on the Moroccan coast was thus an American affair, whereas the force that assaulted the Algerian coast included British and American troops. The British contingent, except for commandos, was held back, however, because it was feared that the French would be more likely to oppose a British landing.[1] Gen. George Patton led the Western Task Force, Gen. Lloyd Fredendall commanded the Center Task Force, and Gen. Charles W. Ryder was in charge of the Eastern Task Force.

1. The animosity of the French authorities in Africa toward the British stemmed from two 1940 events: the British attempts to sink their fleet in North Africa after the surrender of France that summer and Charles de Gaulle's British-sponsored attempt to take Dakar in West Africa in September. The Americans, who had traded with Vichy France, were theoretically neutral and were looked on with more favor by the French authorities. In addition, Roosevelt sponsored General Giraud as a rival to De Gaulle to head the Free French forces. Giraud's role ended sometime after the conquest of North Africa.

The entire operation consisted of three main landing areas in Morocco and two in Algeria. For Morocco, the 3rd Division was the main force, and it concentrated on landing at Fedala and taking Casablanca. In Algeria, the main force was the 1st Division, landing at Oran. A strong mixed force landed at Algiers, to be followed by the British 78th Division. The 9th Division had limited objectives, which included creating three widely separated beachheads—two in Morocco (one far to the north of the 3rd Division and one far to the south) and one in Algeria at Algiers—needed because ports were the immediate targets for bringing in supplies and heavy equipment. New landing craft and strategies would make this the last invasion of this type in the European–African theater, however.

The invasion of North Africa, which was quickly planned, was considered a necessary action because the Americans and British did not have the capability of opening a second front on the scale they had promised Joseph Stalin, the Soviet leader, anywhere else. Timing for this operation was limited; it had to be launched early in November, or winter weather could seriously hinder amphibious operations for several months. Although the window of opportunity was very short and the troops lacked adequate training, the Allies undertook the operation hoping that after secret parlays with their leaders, the French troops in North Africa would offer only token resistance. On November 2, the Western Task Force was moving in the direction of Dakar to confuse the French and Axis forces. At the same time, the Allies tried to convince the enemy the objective of the other two task forces was Malta. The command post for General Eisenhower, the commander in chief of the operation, was Gibraltar, whose airfield facilities were crammed with aircraft that would fly into North Africa once airfields there were secured.

Before he departed for North Africa, Gen. Lucian Truscott, one of the American commanders, took part in a practice landing in the Chesapeake Bay in October. To his disappointment, the exercise was a flop, because the navy had been unwilling to commit its landing craft to the rehearsals for fear of damaging their propellers. Truscott complained to Patton, who replied, "Dammit, Lucian, I've already had enough trouble getting the Navy to agree to undertake this operation. All I want is to get them to sea and take us to Africa. Don't you do a damn thing that will upset them in any way!" Undeterred, Truscott met with Adm. H. Kent Hewitt, commander of the naval forces, who turned out to be quite open to his suggestions. The training exercises were allowed to proceed as planned for the benefit of the troops and sailors. Although the soldiers needed further amphibious training when they sailed for North Africa, they were not totally unprepared. Patton, realizing that his task force would land on the difficult Atlantic beaches of Morocco, hoped that the French would not put up much of a fight.

Never before had the navy "landed an army at the planned time and place," said General Patton, telling them, "If you land us anywhere within fifty miles" of the objective, then "I'll go ahead and win."

The landings took place before dawn, and as expected, the troops ran into difficulties. Loading took longer than anticipated, so the landings were delayed; some ships did not hold their stations; and a number of landing craft got hung up on rocks and were damaged on landing. The French offered resistance in some places. In Morocco, the defending forces consisted of 55,000 French troops, including elements of the Foreign Legion and native units; 120 to 160 obsolete tanks; and about 80 armored cars. In addition, elements of the French fleet, including the battleship *Jean Bart,* and more than 150 first-line aircraft posed a distinct threat to the invading force. In Algeria, the French had 50,000 troops, about 110 obsolete tanks, and some armored cars.

Despite all the problems, however, the invasion succeeded. The troops got their feet wet, and they and the navy gained real experience that helped in the planning of future operations, which might have ended in disaster without having first made these landings. This was General Eisenhower's first major operation as overall commander.

The Landings at Fedala

The landings at Fedala are a textbook example of an attack on a defended port and its attendant problems. The details here have been drawn from Brig. Gen. Arthur Wilson's "Report of Operations in North Africa," dated December 12, 1942. The 3rd Infantry Division, in the center assault group of Patton's Western Task Force, made the key landing at Fedala, which was intended as a jumping-off point for taking Casablanca and was probably one of the riskiest landings of Operation Torch.

The planners had found a mile of open sand beaches that seemed ideal for an amphibious landing that would stretch from the sea jetty of the port of Fedala eastward for about two miles. They were separated by rocky coastline and located between Cape Fedala, where a battery of two 75-millimeter guns overlooked the beaches, and Point Blondin, where a battery of four 138-millimeter guns at Fort Dupont stood guard. Another beach to the west of the town of Fedala was selected for landing of the 3rd Recon Troop, to eliminate the threat of the guns on Cape Fedala; however, the unit had to pass by the muzzles of a battery of four 90-millimeter guns at the base of the peninsula where the cape was. The beaches were denoted as Red, Yellow, and Blue Beaches.

The regiments of the division were formed into landing teams (LTs). The 1st and 2nd Battalions of the 7th Infantry, LT 1 and LT 2, were to land on Red 2 (adjacent to the town of Fedala) and Red 3. LT 1 was to clear the beach, move into the town, take the port facilities, and clear the coastal batteries with the assistance of the 3rd Recon, which was to land west of the town on Yellow Beach. LT 2 was to land on its left, move inland for a mile, turn to the southwest, and move to isolate the town. The 30th Infantry, which consisted of two similar landing teams, was to land on Blue 1 and Blue 2, which was inside a river mouth between Blue 1 and Point Blondin. The 30th's LT 1 was to advance five miles inland to the heights and secure the beachhead, and LT 2 was to cross the river, capture the bridges, and take the battery at Point Blondin. The third landing teams of both regiments were scheduled to arrive an hour to an hour and a half later on the Red Beaches. The 15th Infantry, 2nd Battalion of the 20th Engineers and the 1st Battalion of the 67th Armored Regiment (1st Armored Division) formed the floating reserve at sea.

The plan was workable only if the French did not resist and conditions were ideal, still leaving many obstacles to overcome. The fleet that set off from America had to cross the U-boat-infested waters of the Atlantic without suffering significant losses.[2] Fortunately, it encountered no major problems, although weather reports indicated that on November 7, it might be difficult to bring in the paratroopers. Just before D-Day, the convoy, led by the heavy cruiser *Augusta,* turned toward Dakar to mislead the French. After swinging back on course, the Western Task Force broke into its three assault groups, heading for their assigned targets. A message from the overall commander, General Eisenhower, stressed that "every effort was to be made to effect a peaceful landing and a general offensive was not to be started as a result of some isolated hostile act."

2. The 8,500-ton *Thomas Stone* was launched in 1941 as the liner *President Van Buren* and taken over by the navy in January 1942, and then converted into troopships (AP 59, later APA 29). While carrying the 2nd Battalion, 39th Infantry, the ship was torpedoed after passing the Straits of Gibraltar on November 7. It was not sunk but was unable to take part in the landings. The ship was towed to Algiers, where it was badly damaged in an air raid on the night of November 24-25 and scrapped over a year later.

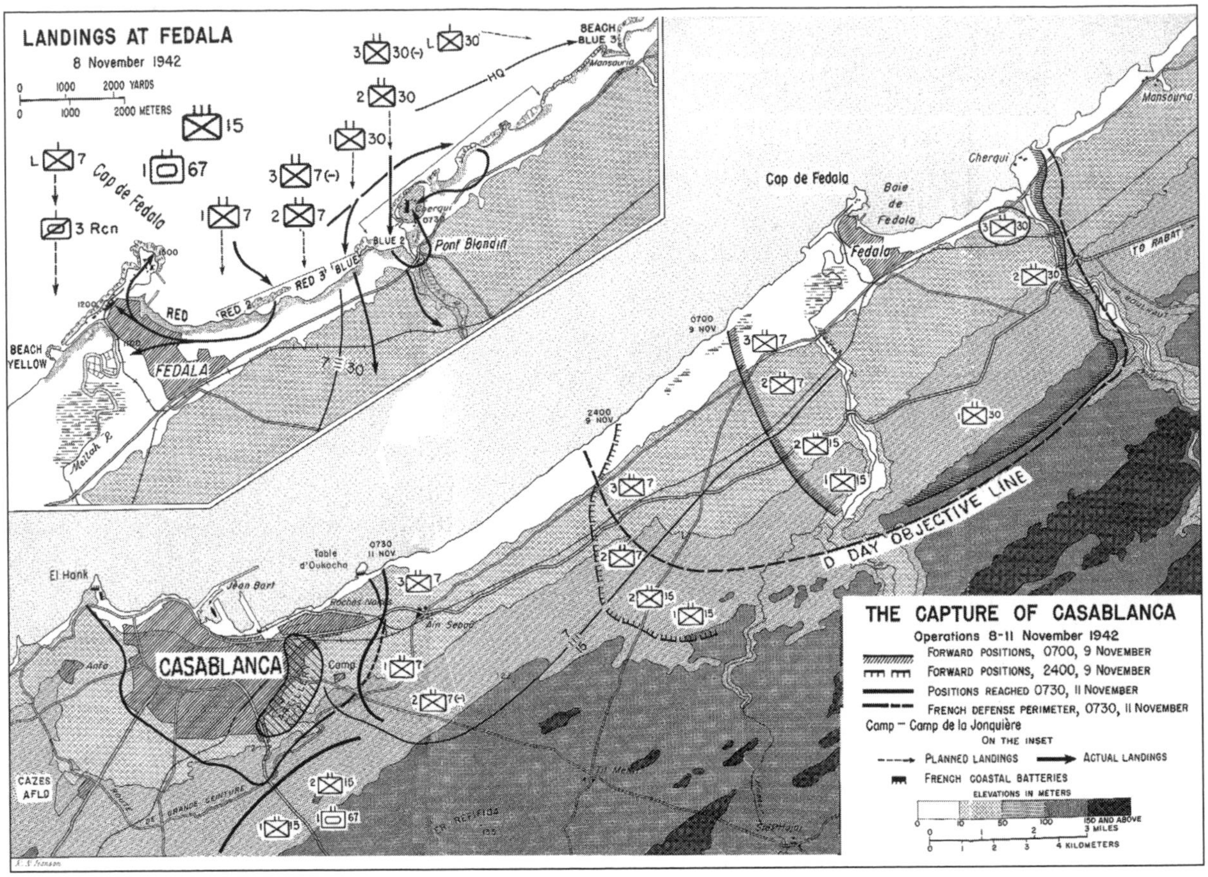

Landings at Fedala, Morocco

At first everything went according to the intricate plan. Shortly before midnight, as the convoys approached the African coast under the cover of night, a broadcast from Washington announced the landings. The navy easily found its assigned position with the help of the lighthouses and lights of the towns, which remained on until the French realized that something was afoot. Negotiations with the French authorities in Africa had not yet been finalized, so the chances for a peaceful landing rapidly evaporated.

Soon the complex Fedala invasion plan began to unravel. The troop transports failed to reach the transport area on time, and H-hour was moved back from 4 to 4:30 A.M., and finally to 4:45. At about 1 A.M., the first landing craft were lowered, but on some of the ships, the sailors did not have enough experience in lowering the vessels and handling boarding operations. Problems continued to mount when the ships did not reach the transport area in the same formation in which they had sailed for the last fourteen days. In the darkness, the coxswains of the landing craft who were assigned to pick up their combat loads from other ships were unable to find their assigned vessels, and they cruised between transports calling out their identities on megaphones.

As the shore lights went out, thanks to the early warning, several of the landing craft that had to find their away ashore in total darkness got lost. One group of four boats carrying an MP detachment stumbled into Casablanca Harbor by accident and ran afoul of a French destroyer. Other, luckier groups identified the lighthouse at Casablanca and turned back to the transport area. The 3rd Recon, with silencers on the motors of its rubber landing craft, was slated to go ashore at Yellow Beach and move quickly against the batteries at Cape Fedala. Unfortunately, it was unable to land.

The 7th Infantry's LT 1, which was already an hour late when its troops hit the beach at 5 a.m., landed on Red 3 instead of Red 2. The French flooded the area with their searchlights, a definite sign of trouble, as the searchlights were to be pointed vertically skyward to indicate that they would not resist. Patrol boats took out the lights, but then losses to landing craft began to mount as they hit reefs or made bad landings in the darkness.

At least the weather favored the invaders; it turned out to be the calmest day in more than sixty years for that time of year. As the sun peeked over the horizon, the French batteries at Point Blondin and Fedala swept the beaches with their fire. At other points, the *rat-tat-tat* of French machine guns rent the air. The light cruiser *Brooklyn* engaged the French 138-millimeter battery at 6:17 A.M. LT 2, possibly confused by the fact that LT 1 had landed on the other team's designated beach, landed on Blue 3, about two miles to the northeast of Point Blondin. LT 1 moved on its objectives, forcing the surrender of a company of Senegalese soldiers who had no interest in resisting. By 6:30 A.M., it reached Fedala and captured members of the German Armistice Commission with a wealth of documents concerning the infrastructure of the region.

During the naval bombardment, one of the oil tanks was hit, although the planners had warned against targeting the tanks lest this light up the entire area. But luckily their fears were unfounded, because instead of erupting into bright flames, the tank belched out a thick cloud of black smoke that hid the invasion fleet from view. The expedition of LT 1 was not an unmitigated success, however. The destroyers that had silenced the French 90-millimeter battery failed to suppress the 75-millimeter gun battery, which continued to shell the beaches. Friendly naval fire also hit the town, killing some GIs. By 9 A.M., LT 1 had to take both batteries by force with the help of the 3rd Recon, which had landed on a Red Beach later that morning.

LT 2 of the 30th Infantry landed at the mouth of the wadi as intended, but some of its boats shattered on the shoals. It was joined by LT 2 of the 7th Infantry, which had landed on the wrong beach and found itself north of the battery. Together the two landing teams took the objective. LT 1 from the 30th set up defensive positions, while the 7th Infantry set out southward toward its intended objective.

Not long after the 30th Infantry had set up its defensive positions, a distant clanking shattered the silence to the north and east and grew in volume as about twenty old Renault tanks appeared on the horizon. The 30th made short shrift of the antiquated tank force.

The men of the 15th Infantry crowded the decks for hours to watch the action onshore while landing craft milled around. Earlier in the morning, Captain Emmett, the naval commander, had suspended the troop landings as long as the French 75-millimeter battery fired on the beaches. Finally, at 11 A.M., the troops still onboard ship were ordered to land. General Patton, who followed the progress of the other operations, ordered the remaining troops and engineers ashore at 4 P.M. Beginning in the late morning, French aircraft from Casablanca sporadically bombed and strafed the beachhead, but they were unable to break through the fighters from the carriers that protected the transports. Besides the sniping that went on throughout the day, the American troops on the beachhead faced no further organized resistance.

The landings took their toll on the American invasion force. About 125 boats were beached on the Red Beaches and more than 75 on the Blue Beaches and could not be recovered. The troops onshore had no means of transportation until the port of Fedala was put into operation. By evening, the 15th Infantry moved up along-

Report on Operation Torch

The summer before the invasion of North Africa, Lt. Col. Stanhope B. Mason had sailed for England onboard the *Queen Elizabeth*. The 1st Division followed him in August on the *Queen Mary* and assembled at Tidwell Barracks near Salisbury.[3] Mason was sent to London, where he was involved in working out the plans for the landings at Oran with Gen. Terry Allen, the division commander at Norfolk House.[4] Mason gave an account of Operation Torch in a G-3 Report issued on November 24, 1942:

> On September 4, 1942, the division received the mission of landing on beaches X and Y and capturing the ports of Arzew and Oran and their port facilities.
>
> Planning was completed by October 15 in London and then the HQ was moved to *Reina del Pacifico*. Combat teams moved from Tidworth Barracks to Glasgow to practice amphibious training during September.
>
> Equipment moved to ports of embarkation on October 7 and personnel on October 12. All personnel loaded on ships by October 16. A landing exercise took place on October 18-19.
>
> The division embarked on seven troop ships and nine cargo ships in the Clyde on October 26 and passed Straits of Gibraltar on November 6.
>
> 1st Ranger Battalion attached to 1st Division and landed two companies at Arzew and captured the seacoast defenses.
>
> Oran fell on 15 November and 1st Engineer Battalion secured the dock area then.
>
> Division lost 9 officers and 85 EM and had 4 officers 65 EM seriously wounded. Plus 7 EM missing in action and 66 EM missing.

3. Mason may have confused the ship he was on and may have actually sailed with the division instead of being sent ahead of them.
4. Mason became chief of staff for the 1st Division at the beginning of January 1943 and held that position until General Huebner moved to V Corps just before the Ardennes Offensive in December 1944. Early in 1943, the division headquarters moved from Oran to Tunisia.

side the 7th in preparation for their march on Casablanca. The next day, November 9, they moved off at 7:30 A.M. That morning, the weather took a turn for the worse. The sea, which had been calm the previous day, lashed the coast with four- to six-foot-high waves. The landing craft experienced more difficulties reaching the Red Beaches, and almost half of them smashed against the shoals. As a result, all unloading for the invasion force moved into the port, but the operation was slow because the channel could handle only one ship at a time entering at high tide. The first ship docked at 2 P.M. and began unloading. The army engineers and sailors had to rely on a great deal of improvisation to run the harbor. The armored battalion began disembarking that evening. On November 10, the two regiments of the 3rd Division and the armored battalion moved against Casablanca, and a cease-fire went into effect the next day.

The success of the Fedala landings can be attributed mostly to the lack of motivation on the part of the French—except for the artillerymen at the coastal batteries—to offer serious resistance.

Mason made the following recommendations to modify his own previous planning:

Assault Ships to be combat loaded. [In some cases, vehicles and crews were on different ships, and ships could not unload certain supplies and equipment when needed.]

That personnel and vehicle landing craft be balanced so troops land with their heavy equipment.

Tactically the ideal landing formation is Combat Teams abreast each in column of battalions.

Any preliminary practice before the operation should be with sufficient time so damaged equipment can be repaired or replaced. [Practice took up to a week before embarkation.]

Planning must be complete and detailed and all orders issued before sailing. Secrecy must be maintained but individuals in command or on staffs must know plans and have time to study them.

The key to success for *Operation Torch* was army and navy staffs working together in London throughout the whole planning stage.

The 1st Division en Route to North Africa

Lt. Charles M. Hangsterfer from Philadelphia entered the army as an ROTC graduate from Gettysburg College at age twenty-two in 1940. "I went on active duty in 1940," he says, because "prospects to get a job were poor, and my grades were not high enough in college to get into law school." Hangsterfer served with the 16th Infantry, 1st Division, at Fort Jay and took part in amphibious training in Puerto Rico, North Carolina, and Virginia. He arrived with the advanced detachment of the division early in July 1942.

I left the U.S. in late June 1942 from New York on a British ship named *Malojia* and arrived in Liverpool in approximately fourteen days. I was in charge of a 5-inch gun crew and 20-millimeter antiaircraft guns.[5] Although infantry, we did learn how to fire the guns, but not at the enemy. There were no problems from the enemy on the way across the Atlantic. For the men, it was an experience in getting used to British food and sleeping quarters aboard ship.

Hangsterfer took part in the invasion of North Africa and remained with the division through all of its seaborne invasions, serving as the regimental communications officer during Operation Torch.

T. Sgt. Theodore George Aufort, who also served in the 16th Infantry, was with the division when it sailed from New York on the *Queen Mary.* The ship made a zigzag every eight minutes as it plowed its way through the North Atlantic on a five-day crossing. After disembarking at Grenock, Scotland, the troops boarded trains that took them through the night to their new home at Tidworth Barracks. Aufort recalls: "In Scotland, we did some invasion training and boarded ships. The *Moro Castle,* sister ship of the *Warwick Castle,* took us past the Rock of Gibraltar and into the Mediterranean Sea, and then we invaded North Africa on November 8, 1942."

The 1st Ranger Battalion, which landed before the 16th and 18th Infantry combat teams, was to clear the port of Arzew. Ranger Sgt. Gino Mercuriali, who had participated in the Dieppe raid months before, was with Company D when it boarded HMS *Royal Ulsterman* with Company C in Scotland in mid-October 1942.

The battalion's mission was to clear two French forts dominating the harbor on the right

5. *Malojia* was a 21,000-ton British P&O liner built in 1923. It was taken over by the government during the war as a troopship armed with eight 6-inch and two 3-inch guns. Either the information is wrong about the 6-inch guns, or Hangsterfer was assigned to one of those instead of a 5-inch gun. On a BBC history website, one British soldier claimed it carried 4,000 troops to India, but he also listed the ship as 30,000 tons.

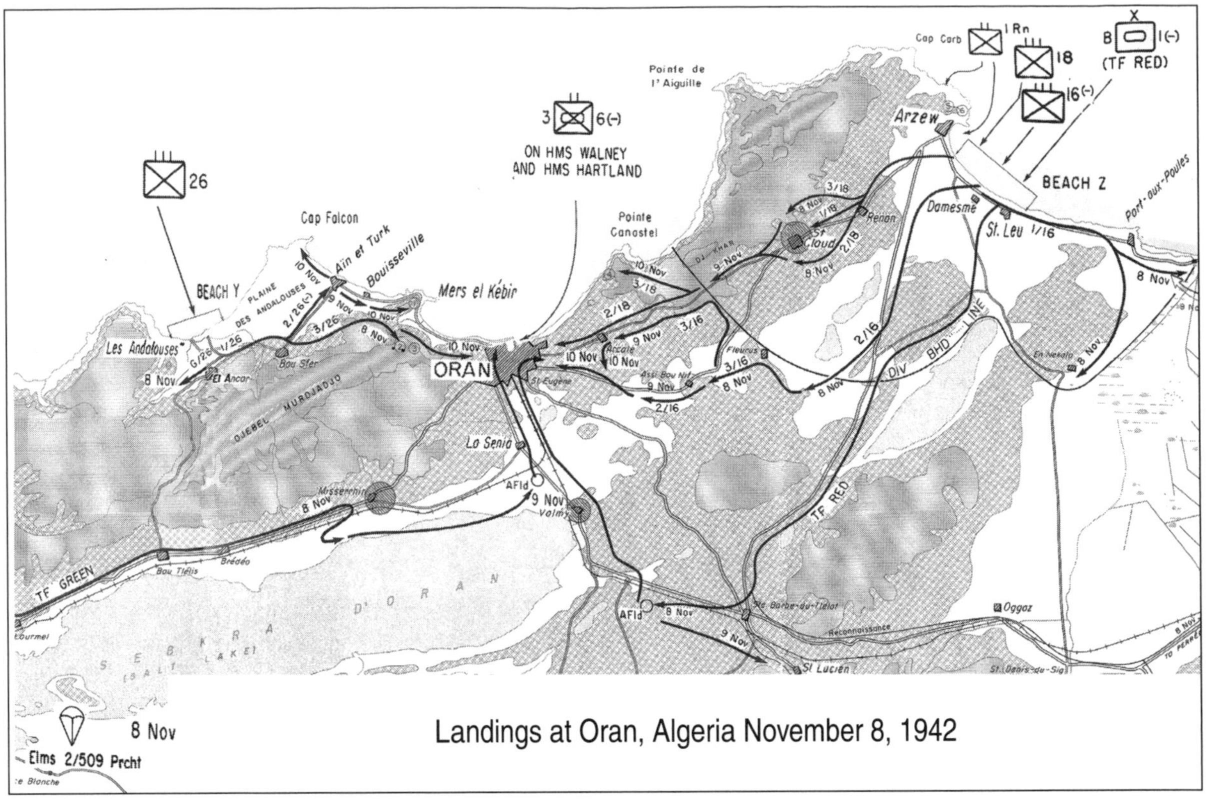

Landings at Oran, Algeria November 8, 1942

flank of the invasion area. Ranger Companies A and B landed after 1 *a.m.* and took the lower fort in the harbor. At 2:15 *a.m.*, when they signaled their success with a flare, the remaining four companies, including Mercuriali's Company D, began landing. Company D, which served as an 81-millimeter mortar company, used two-wheel carts to tow these heavy weapons and their ammunition in support of the assault on Fort du Nord. The fort was actually a battery of four 105-millimeter guns on the heights above the harbor. Mercuriali describes his company's landing:

> As I recall, from our landing site in the LCPs, the distance on the roadway along the coast was five miles, and we knew details such as the number of telephone poles along the route. While aboard ship, we practiced the unloading of mortar ammo from the ship's hold, which meant transporting the shells from the main deck area to the upper deck, from which we would load into the assault craft. Rather than carry the ammo up the steps, we elected to place someone on the landing craft and relay the shells by tossing them up one by one.
>
> Our particular landing site was a short beach of maybe fifteen feet depth and an almost upright sea bank of possibly near fifteen feet. Our intelligence did not consider this an obstacle, although we were using machine-gun carts to transport the 81-millimeter mortar and ammo. When we landed, I had the men cut the ties of the ammo and mortar, hand each item up the bank, reload the carts, and go off on our way.
>
> Under cover of dark, we made our destination on schedule and placed our mortar fire on the target by the second round, thus assuring the assault forces their success. Damn, those guys were good!
>
> This was the last time we were used as a mortar company. This operation was over in a matter of a few hours. Celebration con-

> sisted of shooting holes in the wine kegs on the docks that other companies assaulted and drinking from our helmets.

The Rangers took Fort du Nord, captured 300 prisoners, and secured the port of Arzew by shortly after 4 A.M. During the day, after the 18th Infantry of the 1st Division landed and took the main road through the hills to Oran, the French Foreign Legion put up a spirited resistance in the fortified village of St. Cloud, less than halfway to Oran, stopping the 18th's advance. Ranger Company C moved forward and attacked the next day, taking heavy losses. Meanwhile, Company D "took up bivouac in some deserted buildings and some type of oil company grounds," recalls Mercuriali. "I managed to exchange a battery to get the French Renault car operating, but I didn't have it long, as Darby commandeered it as his own."

The infantry, led by General Allen, landed in the bay southeast of the town, while the Rangers secured Arzew. The 18th Infantry's assault craft emerged out of a heavy smokescreen laid out by the British and moved on Arzew within a few hours, meeting some resistance. The 16th Infantry regimental combat team encountered no opposition. For Aufort, the experience was heartening. "The British took us ashore on their small infantry landing barges. Our objective was the city of Oran, which we took in three or four days. We fought the Vichy French, but their hearts weren't in it." Still, "we lost quite a few men."

The medium M3 tanks of Combat Command B (CCB), 1st Armored Division, came ashore on prototypes of the LSTs, which had been used in the shallows of Lake Maracaibo, Venezuela. The assistant division commander, Brig. Gen. Theodore Roosevelt, led the 26th Infantry combat team ashore west of Oran with elements of CCB. The 1st Division performed well during the operation and secured Oran on November 9. The 34th Division was even more successful at Algiers, which surrendered the same day. The navy's attempts to enter the harbors of Oran and Algiers during the beach landings failed, however.

The 3rd and 9th Divisions in the Assault

The 3rd Infantry Division's trek to the war theater was long and arduous. First it had to cross the United States by train from Fort Ord in California to Camp Pickett in Virginia. Then it had to undergo some hurried last-minute amphibious training before it embarked. Neither the 3rd nor the 9th Division received any additional training at sea. According to Pvt. Harold Taylor, the 3rd Division's cross-country trip was quite unforgettable.

> A cadre left several days ahead of the division to prepare for our arrival. Our movement from Fort Ord to Camp Pickett was initiated on September 6, 1942. I was a member of the cadre unit. I was assigned to ride the caboose of the advance troop train. It was an experience I will never forget.
>
> I had been on troop trains before, but not in the caboose. En route, we stopped off in the Dallas, Texas, area to take on coal and water. The caboose being the last car of the troop train, of course, it extended beyond the train's service area. It so happened a section gang was repairing some track in the vicinity of the caboose, so I stepped off to have a little dialogue with them. The train started moving ever so slowly, and it appeared it was just moving up. As it gained momentum, I found myself running to catch up with it. I grabbed the vertical bar at the rear of the caboose and swung myself around to the left so as to plant my feet on the first step, after which I made my way up to the top platform. After I regained my composure, I sat back and relaxed as we

rolled on toward Virginia. We arrived a few days later. The division's troop trains left California on September 14 and arrived on September 20, 1942.

Camp Pickett was a relatively new post, and most of the sidewalks had not been put in yet. It was the staging area for the 3rd Division, and we remained there only about a month, from the end of September to the end of October.

Numerous trips were made by truck to Norfolk, Virginia. In preparation for overseas combat, we practiced loading and landings out on the Chesapeake Bay and at Norfolk, Virginia, in what was known as Operation Quick.

Cpl. Verl Pendleton and the ad hoc boat detachment left Fort Ord after the main body of the division. When the train that carried them stopped in Kansas City, he was tempted to get off and make a quick detour to his home. After he arrived at Camp Pickett, he asked his first sergeant, Cole Miller, for a furlough to see his family, since he had not been home for almost two years and knew he would be shipping out. He was denied leave, however, so he went AWOL for thirteen days, returning to St. Joseph to say good-bye to his family and get married. When he rejoined his unit, retribution for his act of insubordination was quick and severe: He was demoted from corporal to buck private. His captain asked him why he had gone AWOL instead of participating in additional amphibious training off the coast of Maryland with the regiment, and Pendleton confessed that he had wanted to see his family before he went to war. His division soon boarded for its journey across the ocean.

In the early morning of October 23, 1942, our movement to Norfolk was initiated, and our segment of the division went aboard the *Elizabeth C. Stanton,* apparently a converted cargo ship.[6]

I don't remember the number of troops that went aboard the ship, but I am sure a couple thousand. Other ships in the harbor were being loaded with men and equipment just as we were. In our second day out into the Atlantic, we were told where we were going, where we were going to land, and what our objective was. Our objective was Casablanca, and we were to land at Fedala ten miles north of Casablanca and would remove any resistance in and around Casablanca. We were told en route to our objective that we would be joined by other convoys from New York and England to form a convoy of 850 ships. [The convoys from England did not join them.] Since our objective was Casablanca, the rest of the convoy would be deployed along the north coast of Africa and the Mediterranean and wipe out resistance at Oran and other ports east.

There was little opportunity for training at sea, and the unit commanders who were assigned their objectives had only a few days to formulate their own plans. The soldiers received one of the first country information booklets to be published by the government, with information about the French colony they were about to invade. Later editions, such as the booklet for France, also included stronger injunctions about sexual relations with the locals.

The 3rd and 9th Infantry and 2nd Armored Divisions set sail for their objectives, accompanied by escort and fire-support vessels, the aircraft

6. Actually, the 8,000-ton *Elizabeth C. Stanton* was launched in December 1939 as the *Sea Star* and was transferred to the navy in September 1942, when it was converted into a troopship (AP-69) shortly before loading troops for the invasion of North Africa. The ship had the capacity for more than 1,800 troops.

carrier *Ranger,* and four of the new escort carriers. The crews of the escort carriers were barely trained, and their pilots lacked the carrier training necessary to begin preinvasion air operations. The *Ranger* had been on U-boat patrols in the Atlantic during the previous year, but its main problem was a short deck. "In heavy Atlantic water, it would be covered by green water at times, and the tin cans [destroyers] would disappear," recalls David Lee "Tex" Hill, who served as a dive-bomber pilot on the *Ranger* before the United States entered the war.[7] This was one of the reasons why the invasion had to be undertaken before mid-November.

When the Western Task Force assembled off Morocco, the 3rd Division and one tank battalion from the 2nd Armored Division had the key task of landing at Fedala, advancing to the southwest, and taking Casablanca. This was probably the riskiest of the landings, because the assault troops were to land in a bay defended by a French coastal defense battery on each side. The main difficulty turned out to be shallow shoals near the beaches, which resulted in the loss of a substantial number of landing craft. These vessels consisted of old rampless Higgins boats, the LCP(L), and a new version with ramps, the LCP(R). Cpl. Frank Andrews of the 1st Battalion, 7th Infantry, was among the first to come ashore on Red Beach, where his battalion landed instead of its designated site. He was on the same type of Higgins boat as the one on which he had trained in the Puget Sound.

> Going over the side of the big transport into what we called the old Higgins boat—no ramp, blunt nose—we moved in a column on both sides of it, usually loaded pretty heavy. You went to the front, leaned forward with your belly on side of the thing, bowed, and just rode and hung on and hoped you landed on your feet. The landing in North Africa took us out in the open ocean, where the swells are pretty big, and you have to time yourself and wait until a swell has hit and the boat is stable for a second, so that you can get your feet under you and run and get away from it. I have seen cases where somebody jumped at the wrong time and found himself standing out in the water while the boat was another fifty feet in toward shore. It was a different story before we were equipped with good landing craft.
>
> First, we loaded and put out to sea and hit some beaches in Maryland, and came back by train to Camp Pickett. The second time we put to sea, we joined ships from other ports, a lot of ships, and took a zigzag course across North Atlantic, which was about the roughest ride I ever had. We joined still more convoys and headed south to the North African invasion and landed north of Casablanca.
>
> Fedala is the town about thirty miles north of Casablanca with good beaches that they no doubt had in mind when they picked it. The 7th and 15th Infantry hit the beach, and we headed south to Casablanca. The 30th Infantry hit the opposite way and set up roadblocks to keep the French from coming in behind us. The idea was to capture the docks to bring in the supplies.
>
> When we went overseas, I was a corporal, and a lieutenant was in charge of our small recon group in the battalion. The lieutenant took practically the whole squad, with the job of infiltrating into town and capturing the communication radio and telephone building in Fedala. My job was to get to the edge of town with a bunch of

7. In 1941, Hill joined the American Volunteer Group and served with the "Flying Tigers" in the Far East, where he achieved fame. In the summer of 1942, he became a member of the AAF.

colored flares and equipment for signaling the navy for controlling their firepower. I had to contact the battalion commander and, from the edge of town, signal for what firepower we needed, because that was the only artillery we had at the time.[8]

Our units brought the old pack 75-millimeter guns in addition to our mortars. The bazookas were a new secret weapon just issued on the ships and had never been seen before.[9] It was a different story than a year later for weaponry. I remember the light tanks going by with their 37-millimeter cannons. I was in this patrol group all the way through the African and Sicilian campaigns.

Verl Pendleton found the troopship a little too crowded for his tastes and did not like standing in the long chow lines. He and a friend gained access to a supply of chocolate and canned pineapple, and for most of the trip, that is what they ate. As a result, years later, he still had no fondness for either item. When the sea voyage finally ended, as he made his first landing in enemy territory at Fedala, he reports that the landing craft dumped him off in water over his head.

Harold Taylor recalls his experience with the 15th Infantry, 3rd Division. The 15th formed part of the floating reserve and did not land until several hours after the other two regiments.

Under the cover of darkness on a starlit night on November 8, 1942, we slipped within five miles of our landing area. Standing on deck, I could see the silhouette of many of our ships in the convoy. For a moment, everything seemed so quiet and motionless. Perspiration developed on my forehead as a chain of rope ladders were dropped down the side of the ship. Down in the water below was the sound of idling engines of Higgins boats. There was no such thing as regular landing craft in the early stages of the war. After this, we put into practice what we had learned in our many months of training. We had no heavy equipment we could rely on, because the heavy equipment had to be ferried in after the beachhead was established. After three days of hostilities, fighting ceased, with only occasional sniper fire present.

Pvt. Robert M. Gehlhoff from Florence, Wisconsin, was drafted in September 1941 and also assigned to the 3rd Division. He served in the 3rd Battalion, 15th Infantry.

In October 1942, we left Camp Pickett with an eighty-ship armada. For the several-week trip, we were left pretty much on our own—reading, sleeping, and eating—with an occasional exercise drill over and under the obstacles onboard ship. We ate well.

During a blustering storm, the ship rose and fell, rolling from side to side. Waves crashed over the deck. We were all ordered below deck, where the listing from side to side seemed worse than ever. Every time the ship tilted to one side, all wondered if it would right itself again or tip over. This was a troopship, so there was tier after tier of bunks, close together and six high. As the ship tipped and dipped, one whole row of bunks became loose at the top of the overhead mooring. As the ship righted itself, this one whole tier of bunks didn't, crashing flat on the floor. All the soldiers in that row of

8. Fire support for the center attack group came from the heavy cruiser *Augusta,* a light cruiser, and several destroyers. On November 8, these ships were diverted to intercept French ships departing from Casablanca after the new battleship *Massachusetts* and two heavy cruisers had neutralized the French battleship *Jean Bart.*

9. The troops received the bazookas with instructions for their use onboard ship, but they were not allowed to fire any practice rounds during the voyage. At the time, the bazookas were called "rocket guns."

bunks thought the ship had capsized. For a few moments, there was a lot of screaming and hollering—especially from those riding the top bunks.

I was a scout in Company I during the African campaign and then transferred to the battalion HQ S-2 section. There were usually six to eight in this section. We operated with carbines, binoculars, telephones, and a radio. We were the eyes and ears of the battalion and operated in the battalion sector, with duties that included patrols, prisoner interrogation, and manning observation posts.

While the 3rd Division went after its objectives with relatively little trouble, the 9th was widely scattered and thus had more difficulty accomplishing its mission. Some of its elements landed at distant points to the north and south, taking Port Lyautey and Safi. The French put up token resistance before they laid down their arms, and after taking control of Morocco and Algeria, the Allies pushed on into Tunisia. None of this could have been accomplished without the follow-up support units that took up the rear lines, maintaining communications and logistical support for the forces moving into Tunisia.

Role of the Air Forces in the Invasion

Naval aircraft and the Army Air Forces also played a key role in the invasion of North Africa. Planes from the aircraft carriers provided support for the invasion forces over the Moroccan beaches until army air bases could be established on land. Spitfires flown by the AAF, backed by the British navy and RAF, flew out of Gibraltar to support the Algerian landings.

In addition to the planes that flew combat and support missions, reconnaissance planes also served in the campaign by gathering intelligence.

Enlisted Pilots

Ray Welty was a member of an unusual group of volunteers for pilot training. He had served in the New Mexico National Guard since July 10, 1938. His unit, the 158th Field Artillery, was federalized in January 1941, when it became the 104th Anti-Tank Battalion at Fort Sam Houston.[10] At the time, Welty was a staff sergeant communications chief. In August 1942, he transferred to the Army Air Corps and moved across San Antonio to Brooks Air Field. As an aviation mechanic, he became the crew chief for the base commander. After the attack on Pearl Harbor, his unit was sent to fly patrols off Panama for ten days. On their return to Texas in August 1942, Welty was sent to flight school at Tulsa, Oklahoma, to train as one of the "flying sergeants." This program was founded to produce a larger number of pilots by training NCOs that showed potential, but it lasted only until the end of the year. Welty washed out of the program.[11]

Many of the first class of 1942 went to North Africa with the 82nd Fighter Group and flew P-38s in combat. Other graduates flew other types of aircraft, and when the program ended, many of the "flying sergeants" became flight officers. One of them later became famous as a postwar test pilot—Chuck Yeager.

10. The 158th Field Artillery was from the Oklahoma National Guard and was not converted. The 104th Infantry Anti-Tank Battalion was from the New Mexico National Guard. It formed in January 1941 at Santa Fe and was sent to California, not Texas. The veteran's memories were a bit confused on details, but his records show he entered the unit in Santa Fe, New Mexico.

11. In 1943, he attended glider maintenance school. He then went into training as a glider pilot until April 1944, too late to arrive in time for D-Day. He did take part in the glider landings of Operation Market Garden and received the Air Medal for that operation.

The 3rd Photo Recon Group flew several types of P-38s that mounted cameras instead of guns. Lt. Thomas W. Barfoot from Trinidad, Colorado, was one the pilots flying these unarmed aircraft. He had volunteered for the service at age twenty-two on December 11, 1941.

> I started as a second lieutenant P-38 pilot. We went from Colorado Springs to New York, where we boarded a transport ship that was manned by Vietnamese—or Oriental, anyway. The whole squadron boarded, and we joined a huge convoy and ended up in Glasgow in the fall of 1942—I think we left in October. The aircraft were shipped in pieces by boat and ended up in Blackpool, England, where they were assembled by specialists from Lockheed as well as military personnel. The aircraft were put in flying condition, and the pilots were taken from Moesworth to Blackpool to test-hop the airplanes. We were then instructed to proceed to Lands End, England. We left Lands End just a few days after the invasion of North Africa and flew from there to Oran, North Africa, which was a seven-hour-and-twenty-minute flight, being escorted by a B-26. No preparations for us landing in North Africa, I can assure you.
>
> We landed when it was very dark, and we had two cross-runways, no lights and no control tower, and it was land as you can when you can. Of course, we had some airplanes that landed in one direction and some that landed in the other. It was hectic, but no one was hurt or injured. We landed in the dark with no facilities there whatsoever—housing, messing, or what have you. We went into town to find a hotel that was nonexistent at that time, so we spent the night sleeping on tables in a restaurant. On our trip to and from Oran to the airstrip, we could hear and see sniper fire by those Frenchmen that hadn't given up. We took off from there and went on into Maison Blanc, Algiers.[12]
>
> We flew our missions there, and from that point on, I was made operations officer of the 12th Photo Squadron. I transferred to the 5th Photo Squadron and flew missions with that organization, and then subsequent to that was made group operations officer. Subsequent to that, I was made group commander.

The Advance into Tunisia

On November 11, 1942, a cease-fire took effect, and before long, many French units and their leaders joined the Allied cause. An infantry and an armored division of the British 1st Army, supported by smaller American units, advanced into Tunisia during November, but the Axis forces remained firmly in control through December. The distance between Algiers and Tunisia was 400 miles, and the American divisions had to reorganize and receive logistical support before they could move on. Thus the American force was not ready to go until January 1943. Even then, the supply lines were poor and were unable to maintain the advance of all the American divisions in Africa, so only one of the two armored divisions was able to take part in the campaign initially. This logistical shortfall, combined with the defeat at Kasserine Pass in February, forced the Allies to institute changes in command and tactics.

The 1st and 3rd Divisions set up camps in Algeria and engaged in additional training before they moved into Tunisia. "We were fortunate enough to spend that winter pulling guard duty on the Spanish Moroccan border," says Frank Andrews of the 3rd Division, "and missed a good portion of the fighting in Tunisia. We arrived

12. Maison Blanc was a major airbase outside of Algiers. It was quickly put into use by the Allies after the Torch landings.

in the spring and spent a little time outside of Tunis." In the meantime, the logistical lines were set up and maintained.

Replacements arrived soon after the landings. Lt. Charles Scheffel was on the converted British liner *Scythia,* carrying mostly British troops and his group of replacements from England.[13] On November 8, 1942, the captain announced the invasion of North Africa, but they remained at sea until mid-November, when they passed through the Straits of Gibraltar. Scheffel and most of the others lined the deck looking at the lights of Algeciras, Spain, and Tangiers on the African side, while only the silhouette of Gibraltar stood out in the blacked-out British colony. As the convoy neared Algeria, they came under aerial attack, and a torpedo scored a hit on the ship. [14]

> The "abandon ship" was sounded, and men scrambled to their stations. As we assembled at our abandon ship station, an announcement came over the ship's system that the order had been rescinded and to stand fast. The captain said we had been hit in the number-one hold area, forward near the bow, and that flooding of the ship had been stopped. Tracers and shells exploded at night. Corporal Burke had been hit in the leg. His wound did not appear serious. One of the medics and myself helped him down to the ship's infirmary to be treated. One or two other wounded men were there. They unwrapped his leggings and found a bullet was protruding from his leg. It came from either an enemy machine gun or a spent round from one of our own convoy weapons.
>
> That morning, we limped through the breakwater of Algiers Harbor.

After reaching port, Scheffel led his company ashore. As he and his men moved up the road from the wharf, German bombers arrived overhead. "Fragments from AA shells that exploded overhead were falling all over the area that sounded like hail," says Scheffel. He stopped to pick up a jagged piece about an inch long and dropped it quickly after burning his fingers on it.[15]

A day or so later, a captain from the 39th Infantry directed him to split his group and send half of it to the 1st Division. Lt. Ozell Smoot took those men over to the 1st Division, while Scheffel's group was fed into the 9th Division. Scheffel was assigned as a platoon leader in the 39th, and in 1943, he took part in the campaigns in Tunisia and Sicily, where he saw extensive combat. His first action took place at El Guettar, Tunisia, in March.

Capt. David D. Moore of Trenton, Missouri, who had joined the army at age twenty-two in 1936, led Company A, 361st Quartermaster (QM) Battalion, one of the support units that took part in the invasion, which later converted into the 478th Amphibian Truck Company. Moore joined the company on June 21, 1942, and took command of it when it transferred into the 1st Engineer Amphibian Brigade. In early July, the company sailed aboard the SS *Wakefield* (former SS *Manhattan*) for Belfast, where the battalion began training at Carrickergusn. In the

13. The 20,000-ton passenger ship *Scythia* had a capacity for 2,200, so as a troopship, it probably could easily carry more than 3,000 troops. In *Crack! and Thump,* Scheffel indicates that his company was attached to the British unit carried on the ship.

14. Scheffel has November 16 as the date they entered the straits. Data on the *Scythia* is conflicting, with various sources giving the dates of November 21 and 23 for when it was attacked.

15. Scheffel explains in *Crack! and Thunder* that upon landing, he moved through the town and set his men up in a tunnel while under orders from the British. It was not until a day or so later that he met an officer from the 39th Infantry after a British brigadier gave him permission to take his men to join American forces.

Effects of Naval Gunfire against Coastal Artillery

The force that attacked Fedala included a cruiser and destroyers that bombarded the coastal artillery. The 75-millimeter gun battery at Point Fedala posed the greatest threat when it put the invasion beaches under fire. Although the destroyers targeted the position, only one gun tube was lightly damaged by a shell fragment; however, the gun was still able to fire at short distances at the time the Allied ground troops captured it. The nearby 90-millimeter battery of four guns remained intact. At Point Blondin, the four 138-millimeter guns, with a range of 18,045 meters, presented a serious threat to the transports until they were taken on by a cruiser. The recoil mechanism of one of the guns was damaged, but the weapon remained serviceable.

meantime, 1st Lt. Herrel K. Powell, from Moore's company, took a detachment of about seventy-five men from the battalion to a U.S. naval base at Roseneath, Scotland, where he proceeded to round up equipment and supplies for the battalion that had been delivered to various ports in the area. The battalion joined Powell and his men at Roseneath in mid-October, in time to move to Liverpool and board the SS *Otranto* as a follow-up group for the invasion. Moore recalls his company's experiences:

> My company was the only battalion company that was combat-loaded. It was scheduled to go on detached service with the II Corps to handle their gasoline supply. [Company A was formerly the 201st Gasoline Company.] However, the SS *Otranto* developed engine trouble and was not able to keep up with the convoy. It managed to limp into Gibraltar. While under repair there, an Italian two-man sub attempted to place a mine on its hull. All the troops remained at general quarters while divers went over the hull. Luckily, the crew of the sub had been knocked off by the random depth charges used to protect the harbor of Gibraltar before they could place the mines. [This action may have taken place on December 7.]
>
> Due to our delay at Gibraltar, Brigadier General Wolfe, our brigade commander, also the ranking officer in the Mediterranean Base Section, had ordered a gasoline supply company that was scheduled to handle the base operations to Tunisia with the II Corps. Thus, my company handled the gasoline supply operations in the Base Section. The largest detachment was located in Oran, under the command of Lt. Powell. Another was in charge of a motor gasoline and diesel dump near Arzew, under the command of 2nd Lieutenant Charles Nilsson, Jr. A transshipment depot was located at Paragoux to handle transfers between the narrow-gauge rail line from Arzew and the main line between Oran and Algiers. One of my sergeants was in charge of this detachment. I was located at battalion HQ at Fort de Sud on the coast just east of Arzew and maintained active control of an aviation gasoline dump while maintaining liaison and overall command of the detachments. All of these detachments used French and Arab crews to handle the unloading of Liberty ships and the transfer of gasoline supplies to coastal steamer and railcars for shipment to other terminals.

During this same time, Company C, Capt. Lester Kennedy commanding, performed its normal function as a truck company, handling the movement of supplies between various ports and dumps in Algeria. Company B, which was a medium maintenance company, was redesignated as the 3497th Ordnance (Medium Maintenance) Company.

Shortly after the departure of Brigadier General Wolfe to AFHQ, and before it was reorganized as the 1st Engineer Special Brigade and assigned to I Armored Corps Reinforced (which became the 7th Army on the invasion of Sicily), Col. Eugene M. Caffee transferred from the 20th Engineer Regiment to assume command of the brigade at that time.

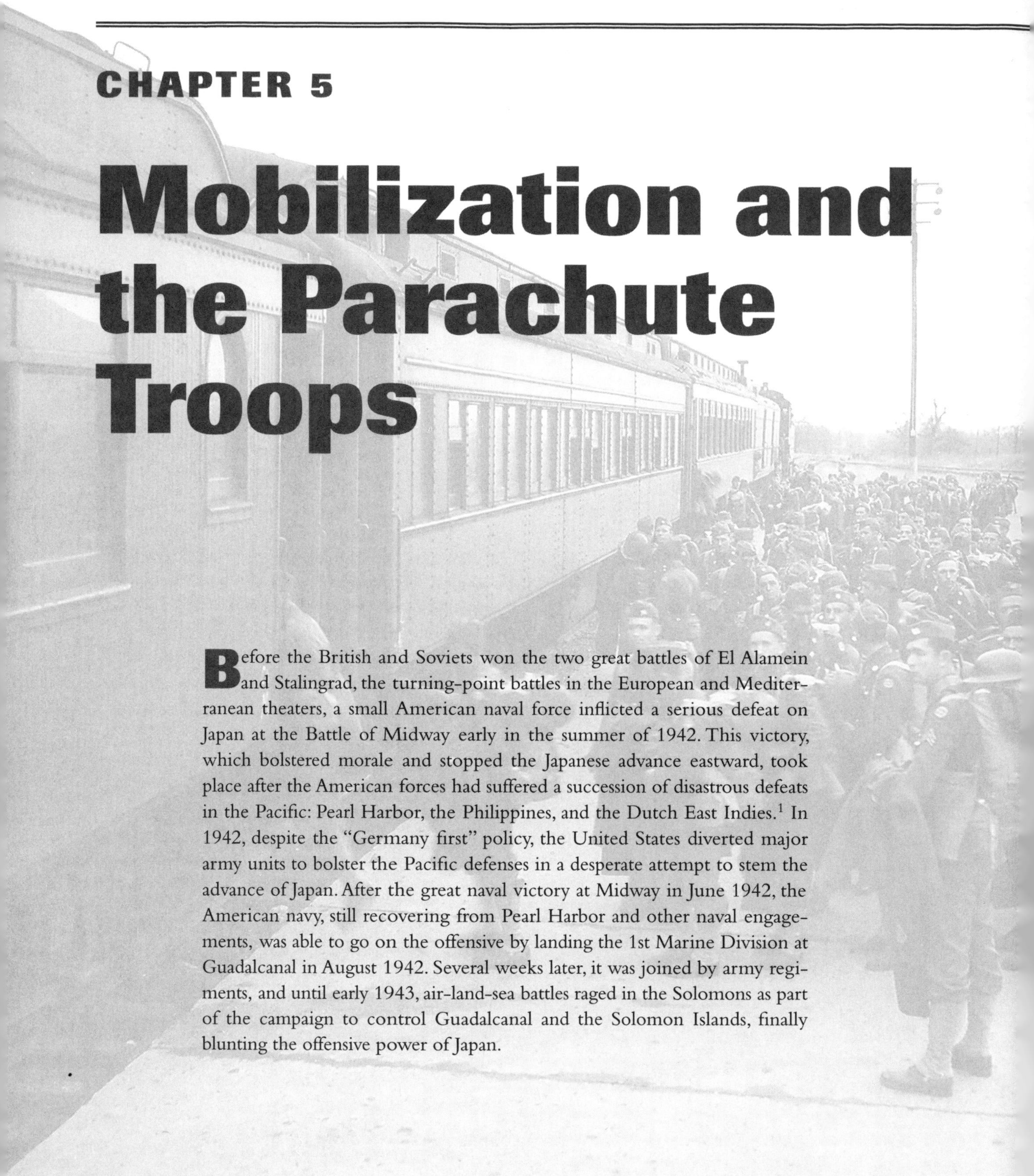

CHAPTER 5

Mobilization and the Parachute Troops

Before the British and Soviets won the two great battles of El Alamein and Stalingrad, the turning-point battles in the European and Mediterranean theaters, a small American naval force inflicted a serious defeat on Japan at the Battle of Midway early in the summer of 1942. This victory, which bolstered morale and stopped the Japanese advance eastward, took place after the American forces had suffered a succession of disastrous defeats in the Pacific: Pearl Harbor, the Philippines, and the Dutch East Indies.[1] In 1942, despite the "Germany first" policy, the United States diverted major army units to bolster the Pacific defenses in a desperate attempt to stem the advance of Japan. After the great naval victory at Midway in June 1942, the American navy, still recovering from Pearl Harbor and other naval engagements, was able to go on the offensive by landing the 1st Marine Division at Guadalcanal in August 1942. Several weeks later, it was joined by army regiments, and until early 1943, air-land-sea battles raged in the Solomons as part of the campaign to control Guadalcanal and the Solomon Islands, finally blunting the offensive power of Japan.

The army mobilized as rapidly as possible throughout 1942. Many of the first units to be trained, including National Guard and reserve units augmented with draftees, were dispatched to the Pacific or trained for the North African invasion. Only a few Regular army units, such as the 2nd and 4th Infantry Divisions, remained in the United States. In 1942, the combat-ready American armed forces were not yet large enough for massive operations, especially amphibious ones.

Meanwhile, many men enlisted, while others were drafted by the tens of thousands. So many men were available in 1942 that they could not all be processed. Many who volunteered for the Army Air Corps were given a quick physical and put on reserve for many months before they were called up for active duty. But the servicemen who went overseas in 1942 did not enjoy the same advantages as the enlistees of 1943. They were the pioneers who forged the American combat tactics and strategy that eventually benefited later inductees.

Recruitment, Training, and Expansion

Between the time the draft began and the end of 1942, the armed forces rejected a large number of men who might well have been accepted in most foreign armies. According to Paul de Kruif, who analyzed the problem in a 1942 article titled "How Can the Nation Strengthen Its Health?" 50 out of every 100 men inducted were rejected in 1941. Dental problems of a serious nature accounted for 10 percent of the rejections, poor vision for 6 percent, heart disease for 5 percent, impaired hearing for 3 percent, venereal disease for 1 percent, and a variety of ailments ranging from "feeble mindedness" to fallen arches for 25 percent. De Kruif attributed these problems to the shocking living conditions that prevailed in many parts of the United States, about which the public did not want to know. Among the many illnesses that plagued Americans early in the war, De Kruif reported that pneumonia was the number-one killer in the early 1940s. The spread of this disease was finally checked by the development of sulfa drugs during the war. Syphilis was a serious problem, and tuberculosis had reappeared, for which, thankfully, new treatment methods had been developed. These health issues sapped America's strength during the first year of the war, however, as a large number of inductees failed to pass their physicals. Disease control was important not only to run an effective army, but also to maintain a healthy and productive workforce. Nevertheless, these public-health issues did not prevent the United States from assembling its largest army of the twentieth century or equipping it properly. To some extent, the massive mobilization of the country also helped improve the overall medical welfare of the nation.

The peacetime method of training men in their assigned units turned out to be inadequate when the time came to supply units with replacements, so new measures had to be implemented in 1941. By 1942, training centers for new recruits and draftees turned out a large pool of replacements ready to take on their duties in their assigned units. In March 1942, the Army Ground Forces (AGF) replaced the General Headquarters (GHQ). In addition, several new commands were organized, including the Armored Force, Antiaircraft Command, Airborne Command (later Center), Replacement and School Command, Desert Training Command, Amphibious Training Command, and Mountain Training Center. Army training camps set up early in 1941 included Infantry Replacement Training Centers, a Cavalry

1. Eight battleships were at Pearl Harbor on December 7, 1941, and all were sunk or damaged. Only five were repaired and put back in service during the war. The other eight American battleships were in the Atlantic or refitting, with none being available for the battle of Midway. The invasion force that arrived at Guadalcanal on August 7, 1942, included one battleship with several cruisers and destroyers.

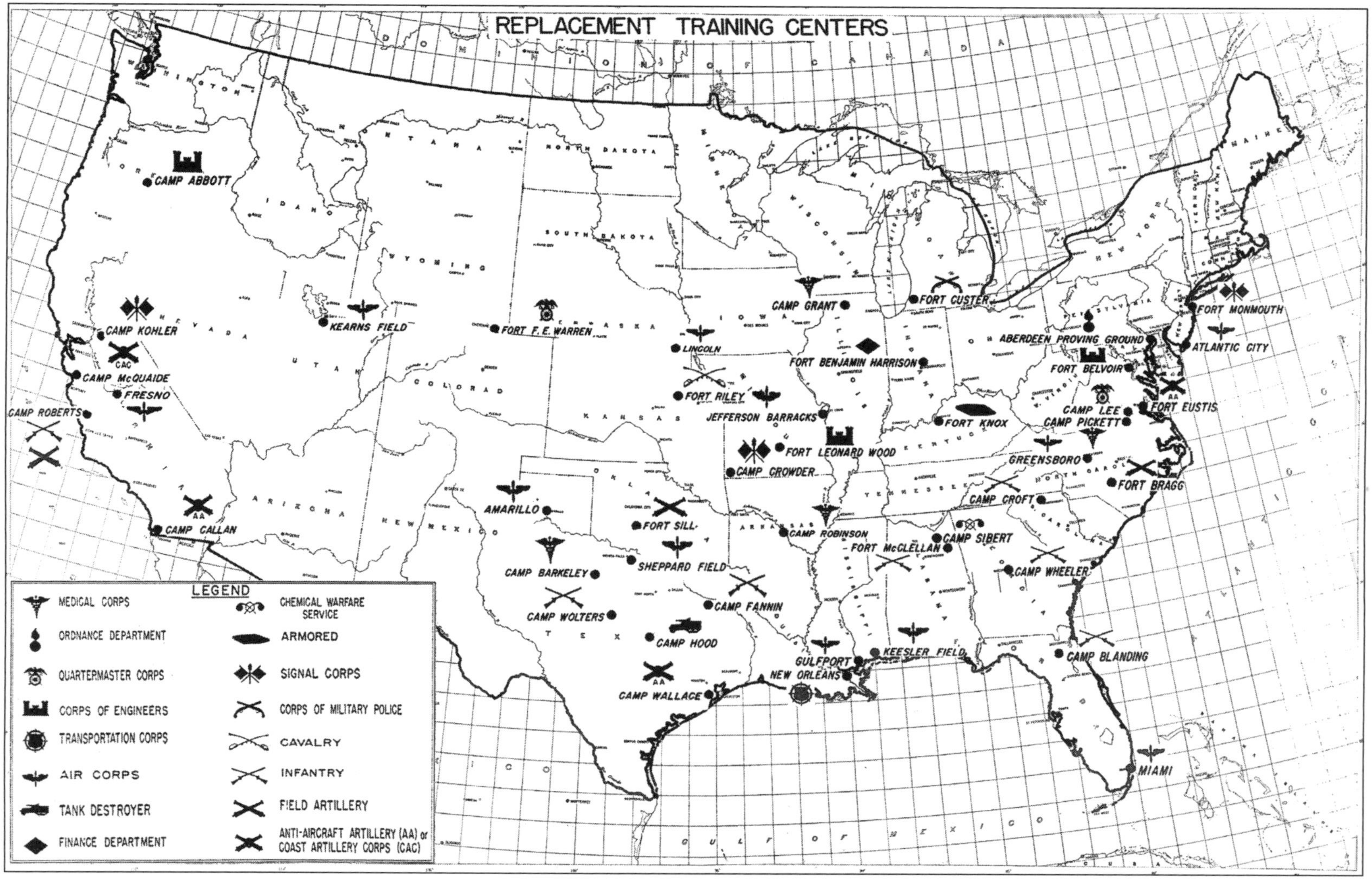

Branch Training Centers (13 weeks of Basic Training) 1942 to 1943. BIENNIAL REPORT OF THE CHIEF OF STAFF

Replacement Training Center, Artillery Replacement Centers, and Officer Candidate Schools (OCS). Additional Infantry Replacement Training Centers opened in 1943 at four other army camps. Other training centers were established for the various branches, such as the engineers at Fort Belvoir, Virginia, and Fort Leonard Wood, Missouri. Other centers opened later in the war.

The army also set up Replacement Training Centers overseas, where troops trained in the United States but not assigned to any unit were quartered until they were sent as replacements to units that had taken casualties. Soldiers who recovered from their wounds were usually sent to new units instead of being sent back to their old ones, although many soldiers recovering from minor wounds went AWOL from the replacement centers to go back to their old units. Airborne troopers able to return to duty generally went back to their units whenever possible. Enlisted men promoted to officer rank tended to move to different units.

Airborne Training

Following the attack on Pearl Harbor, many Americans rushed to join the armed forces. Although the majority of these volunteers opted for the more traditional branches of the army, a smaller number of more adventurous spirits preferred to enlist in the new and more glamorous specialized units. Such was the case for Ray Byron Hood, the teenage son of a west Texas teacher who avidly followed the course of the war on the family radio. In 1940, shortly after Ray graduated from high school at age sixteen, his father got a more promising position, and the family moved to Big Spring, Texas. Underemployed and bored in his new surroundings, young Ray soon rebelled against his parents' strict rules, becoming a "young jackass," as he ruefully admits. One Saturday at the theater, the movie *Parachute Battalion* starring Edmond O'Brien and Harry Carey, aroused his enthusiasm. "Jumping out of airplanes seemed ideal," he concluded starry-eyed, as it would be "romantic enough to impress girls and show my parents that I was a true adult."

Unbeknownst to his parents, he decided to go to Odessa, about sixty miles away. With a mere $8 in his pocket, he lived on a diet of Royal Crown Cola and peanuts until his money ran out. At the recruiting office in Odessa, he found out that he could not enlist without his parents' permission, because he was still underage. Undaunted, he forged his father's signature on the recruitment papers giving him permission to enlist and tricked a notary public into notarizing the document. On July 15, 1942, he happily boarded a bus for Lubbock, Texas, where he was sworn in and sent on to the reception center at Fort Sill. He stayed there for about a week to get basic instructions, inoculations, and uniforms. He also received "the first of a long series of ear-bangings concerning the Articles of War, and tasteful home movies warning of the perils of VD: "But sir, she looked clean!"

His next destination was Camp Roberts in California. After crossing the Great Plains and the Rocky Mountains, his train rolled into San Luis Obispo, the nearest town to the army training camp. At the camp, Hood was assigned to the 3rd Platoon, A Company, 86th Infantry Training Battalion. Although he had volunteered for the parachute troops, he had to undergo basic training first.[2]

The battalion's companies consisted of three platoons of four squads, each comprising about twelve men Of these, eleven were issued bolt-action 1903 Springfield rifles and one a 16-pound Browning automatic rifle (BAR). "Since I

2. At about this time, other volunteer paratroopers were sent to Camp Toccoa, Georgia, for their basic training with the regiments in which they would serve. Next, they went to Fort Benning for parachute training.

only weighed 130 pounds," says Hood, "I was—for my sins—given the BAR." The standard rifle issued to the recruits was the old bolt-action Springfield, because the M-1 semiautomatic rifles were in short supply. The trainees did not see an M-1 until their thirteen weeks of training neared completion.

The man in charge of Hood's platoon was Sergeant Schmidt, a professional soldier who was part of the battalion's cadre. He was, according to Hood, a very strict but fair and outstanding teacher who really knew his trade. "He was quite aloof, in an understated way, and he had the knack of making us want to please him." Schmidt was typical of the older sergeants who helped shape the citizen army. Hood's first sergeant was also a colorful character.

> The first sergeant was a swarthy snarl of profanity very aptly named Wolfe. He had an explosive temper, and on two occasions, I saw him literally jump up and down on his fatigue hat. He had been in the army longer than I had been alive, and he considered all recruits to be unwelcome intruders bent on disrupting an otherwise orderly and reasoned existence. He never, never spoke to the assembled company without prefacing his remarks with "You dumb bastards" or "You simple sons of bitches." I considered him a fearsome creature, and it was quite some time before it dawned on me that he was a very funny man. He mangled the language handily, spoke of Hitler as "Hilter," and warned us of the "consulquenches" of not using our water "purlification" tablets.

The company commander, a Regular army captain, seemed to be mostly concerned with the proper pronunciation of his name. He opened his welcome speech with "I am Captain Niblock. That's pronounced Nib-lock. It isn't Niblick, and it isn't Nibble-dick, but Niblock."

Since the 86th Infantry Training Battalion was an antitank outfit, the company was instructed in the care and firing of the 37-millimeter antitank gun, mounted on wheels and pulled by 4-by-4 prime movers or teams of sweating recruits, recalls Hood. "It weighed 947 pounds and, though we didn't know at the time, was already obsolete."

The men in Hood's basic-training platoon were a mixture of volunteers and draftees, mainly from Texas and Oklahoma. Most of them were eventually assigned to the 36th Infantry Division, a Texas National Guard unit. Some of Hood's comrades in arms were quite dejected about being in the army, especially the man in the next bunk, whose name was Holman. He was about forty years old, and to Hood, he seemed quite ancient. He also amazed Hood by spending hours each night writing long letters to his wife in Amarillo. "He was always cross and grouchy, a real complainer, and I considered him a sorehead who didn't know a good thing when he found it, because I was having a hell of a good time." Years later, much older and wiser, Hood realized that his youthful enthusiasm must have grated on the nerves of some of the older draftees.

Hood took to the training like a duck to water. Unlike many of his peers, he was in top physical condition. Hood attributes it to work I had done to earn spending money: chopping wood, shoveling sand and gravel for country road crews, and manhandling bales of cotton at a gin-and-compress." His skill hunting rabbits and squirrels with a .22 rifle had prepared him for the army, as had his experience as a Boy Scout in a troop with a very knowledgeable scoutmaster.

At the time, Camp Roberts had the largest macadamized parade ground in the world, at a mile long and a quarter mile wide. Almost every day, the trainees stood retreat in massed battalions, facing into the westering sun. "The rifles and helmets made a nice metallic clatter hitting the asphalt when sun-stunned recruits fainted," says Hood, "while ambulances waited at the rear of the formations to haul away the malingerers and the heat-stricken."

The junior officers were almost as green as the recruits, although the trainees were not aware of it. The platoon leaders were second lieutenants who had recently completed OCS and trained with the enlisted men for a brief period. According to Hood, the NCOs provided the actual instruction and seemed to run the platoon, whereas Captain Niblock and the other officers seldom made an appearance. "Officers did conduct the lectures on military courtesy and VD avoidance, but I think the second lieutenants were learners also. I was then, and still am, impressed with the efficiency and conscientiousness of the sergeants and corporals. They were all, with the exception of First Sergeant Wolfe, very patient men."

A small number of trainees did not fit into the army. In Hood's platoon, one man regularly peed in his bed, inciting the ire of First Sergeant Wolfe, who bellowed more than once, "Ewer, you dumb son of a bitch, did you piss in your bunk again? Bring your goddamn mattress out and throw it over the goddamn clothesline. Your goddamn name oughta be 'urine' instead of Ewer, you dumb son of a bitch."

Gambling was a popular pastime among the men in their free time. At night, the recreation room located in the center of the battalion quadrangle was, according to Hood, a sort of "bush league Monte Carlo," where blackjack, poker, and craps were the main forms of recreation. Several of the more experienced and street-smart recruits ran blackjack tables, and Hood saw some big money exchanging hands in the poker and crap games. In his first poker game, Hood won $15 and decided, with his typical youthful enthusiasm, that he had found his calling, but when Lady Luck stopped smiling on him, he reconsidered his decision.

Although Camp Roberts was like a frying pan in the summer, Hood, who had spent his short life in west Texas, was conditioned to the heat and did not suffer from it. The training included a lot of hiking and required brute strength to maneuver the 37-millimeter guns through the sand. Not until almost the end of the training cycle were a few selected men, including Hood, allowed to fire a single round each from the antitank gun.

During his basic training, Hood obtained only one pass. On a Saturday afternoon, he and two other soldiers went to Paso Robles, where they purchased service hats and garrison belts. "We looked around rather desperately for something else to buy, but we really didn't need anything, except feminine companionship. Not hookers," Hood assures, "because I was far too naive to consider such a thing, even had the opportunity been there." They wandered around town, ate hamburgers and drank malted milk, and finally went to a movie, things they could have done without leaving the base. When he was eventually transferred to Fort Benning, he had to get rid of his new service cap, because paratroopers did not wear them.

In April 1941, twenty-four-year-old Carlos C. Ogden from Paris, Illinois, was drafted and sent for his basic training to Camp Croft, South Carolina. He joined the federalized 28th Division of the Pennsylvania National Guard that same year. In January 1942, he was promoted to corporal, and when his division reached Camp Livingston, Louisiana, he was selected to serve as cadre for training new troops. Ogden, a graduate of Illinois State Teachers' College, had leadership abilities that soon brought him to the attention of his superiors, who sent him to OCS in August. He was commissioned on November 11, 1942.

Shortly after Ray Hood finished his basic training and left Camp Roberts, Ogden transferred there to train the new recruits. Ogden was by no means one of those "ninety-day wonders" for whom Hood felt nothing but contempt because they were seldom seen by the trainees. He was a well-seasoned soldier who took his job of training the troops very seriously. While he was at Camp Roberts, Lieutenant Ogden met a young lady from nearby San Luis Obispo, whom he married after a brief courtship. The following September, he was promoted to first lieutenant, and about a year after that, he was appointed to the 79th Division at Camp Laguna, Arizona. Eventually he ended up in Normandy, where he was awarded the Medal of Honor for action above and beyond the call of duty.

In the fall, Ray Hood, like tens of thousands of other soldiers, was once more on a troop train bound for his next assignment, the Parachute School at Fort. Benning. During the war, the only practical way to cover the long distances across the United States was by train, as air travel was still in its infancy and was reserved for the moneyed class.

On the eastward journey, the train pulled into Big Spring, but no one was allowed off. "I did have my head out the window," says Hood, "hoping that I would see someone I knew and thus get a message to my parents, but no such luck." Before long, the train pulled out of the station, and Hood watched his hometown disappear in the distance. He would return home one more time before going overseas.

Even before they crossed the Mississippi, hot, humid air swirled into the packed passenger cars through the open windows of the train, which was not air-conditioned. Hood was fortunate to have to share a compartment with only two other soldiers, which allowed them to travel in relative comfort. The trip took about three days. Although liquor was forbidden on the troop trains, "the porters on the train sold a lot of whiskey—ten bucks per pint, with lots and lots of customers." The soldiers idled away their time in the same way they had at Camp Roberts, playing craps and poker, and fighting occasionally. If any officers traveled with them, Hood did not see them, but a group of NCOs maintained some semblance of order. Because the facilities were limited, the soldiers ate only two meals a day, which consisted of lunch meat and cheese sandwiches, apples or oranges, and coffee in the morning or cold tea without ice in the afternoon. Hood suspected that the porters made huge profits. "These guys, 'real patriots,' besides the whiskey, sold us sandwiches and soft drinks, fruit and cookies, and magazines and newspapers—all at inflated prices."

> Finally, after many days, the train arrived at its destination. One of the more unpleasant facets of a troop train ride was the inability to stay clean. There was no hot water, the cold water ran in a trickle, and the soap wouldn't lather. This trip took place in October 1942, and by the time we arrived in Georgia, we were a sweaty, smelly bunch, tired and ill-tempered, with some dandy hangovers evident. The floor of the train was littered with orange peels, apple cores, banana peels, bread crusts, paper, discarded trash of all kinds, really ignored by the bootlegging porters. Getting off that rattler was a real relief!

Robert A. Flory was another youngster who, like Ray Hood, had dreamed of achieving glory on the battlefield. He grew up in the rural Midwest and graduated from high school in Anderson, Indiana, in April 1942. Although he was a little older than Hood, he was no less eager to embark upon a grand adventure.

While Hood was finishing his training at Camp Roberts in September 1942, Flory and two of his boyhood friends enlisted in the U.S. Army. He too had lied about his age because he was only seventeen and his father refused to sign a release. The three young men entered service at Fort Benjamin Harrison, Indiana. Flory signed up for cadet pilot training, but after three days of KP, he returned to his barracks downhearted. His sergeant told him that the waiting list for pilots was so long that it might be months before he would be accepted into training. "That's when he started extolling the virtues of the U.S. Army Parachute Troops—$50 extra per month for jump pay, special uniforms, no guard duty, no KP, and many other lies," says Flory. The next day, he boarded a train headed for Camp Toccoa in northern Georgia. The training for the would-be paratroopers was very rigorous.

> Every morning before breakfast, with jump boots and shorts, we had to run up Mount Currahee [rising about 1,000 feet above the level of the camp] and back—3 miles. If you couldn't make the line, you were sent to the line infantry and couldn't go to Airborne School. Training included the obstacle course, firing weapons, bayonet training, etc. We had a tower at Camp Toccoa, which was about 30 feet high where you jumped and rode down the cable. I was watching other fellows jump ahead of me; all I could see was that $50 a month coming up. It was an exhilarating feeling. After thirteen weeks of the most rigorous basic training ever devised, we ended up in Fort Benning, Georgia.

The actual parachute training began at Fort Benning, where the soldiers went through four stages of jump school that lasted one week each. Stage A involved physical training; stage B, practicing jumps at ground level and from the 34-foot tower; stage C, jumping from the 250-foot towers (including at night); and stage D, making five jumps from a C-47.[3] The training during the four stages was grueling and meticulous.

> During the four stages of jump school at Fort Benning in November 1942, we jumped out of the towers to learn how to land. While hanging suspended from a harness, a drill sergeant taught you how to steer your parachute, which I never could do. Then you go to this 250-foot tower with the parachutes, they pull you up to the top, and you are released while the drill sergeant watches how you fall and land. They also had a wind machine, where you are on the ground laying on your stomach, and they start it up, and it inflates your chute and starts dragging you. That is where you learn to get out of your harness and deflate your chute.

Some of the early training structures, built at Fort Benning were copied from a German airborne training manual and proved to be quite daunting for the recruits. One was used for only a short period of time, and Flory happened to be among the men who trained with it.

> This tower would terrify anybody. You lay on your stomach, they fastened a harness around the middle of your back, and they hauled you to the top. On the signal from the drill sergeant down there, you are supposed to pull a ripcord as you start falling, you change hands with that ripcord, and as

3. The training during these stages appears to have changed from 1942 through 1943. Some claim that no night jumps from the 250-foot tower were made. In regard to the five qualifying jumps in the final stage, a few have claimed that the final jump was at night, but the majority state that all five were daytime jumps. Even the type of towers used changed. One type Flory mentions in his description, where the individual dropped 20 feet straight down in a horizontal position, was in use for only a short time. Most of the records at Fort Benning were destroyed in a postwar fire, so there is no official source noting all the changes that took place in training during the war.

> you fall about 20 feet, you are snapped up. It is a hell of a shock, and if you drop that ripcord, you snap back up and do it again. And naturally, I dropped that damn ripcord, so I had to go back, and the second time I made sure I had that ripcord.

Although Flory did not think the 34-foot tower in stage B particularly daunting, Gerard Devlin says in *Paratrooper* that it was the most difficult obstacle for the volunteers, most of whom failed to complete their training at this stage and returned to regular infantry units.

During stage D, every soldier had to pack his own parachute, a process that was branded in Flory's memory.

> I went down to the packing sheds in the evening and drew a chute to pack. On my third jump, my first sergeant told me that when I got back to the barracks, I was going on guard duty. I was in no hurry to get back; consequently, everybody had packed their chutes and left, and he got a little irritated at me. He said to get out of the way and he would pack the parachute for me. It was a brand new parachute. He packed it and I went on guard duty. The next morning, we drew our chutes. We drew a reserve also, which we didn't pack; the riggers did that. Getting ready to enplane, we were standing alongside when the jumpmaster came along and inspected us. I know I was set up. Standing at attention, he said to me, "Soldier, did you check that reserve?" I replied, "Yes, sir!" and he said, "Are you sure?" "Yes, sir!" I snapped. He reached out and pulled my ripcord; the thing was full of sawdust. These are the things they did to try to make you refuse to jump. He sent me back to draw another reserve. Believe me, when I put it on, I was checking those flaps to see if there was nylon in there.
>
> We went ahead and made our five jumps and had a ceremony, and the wings were pinned on us at the end of November or early December 1942. Not a single man of that regiment refused to jump.

After completing jump school, Flory and his fellow paratroopers from the 506th Parachute Infantry were given a furlough. When they returned, the unit moved to the other side of the Chattahoochee River, into Alabama across from Fort Benning, where they made their sixth jump, the first one with weapons. Next, the regiment moved to Camp Mackall.

Ray Hood, Robert Flory, and thousands of their comrades went through airborne training when it was still in its infancy. At the time, most of the standard training techniques were still being developed and tested. In mid-1942, before Hood and Flory began their training, the newly formed Airborne Command was preparing to expand its airborne battalions and form divisions, driving up the demand for recruits. The Airborne Command decided to center its post-basic-training recruitment efforts in places like Camp Roberts.

As soon as he arrived at Fort Benning, Ray Hood was assigned to Company R, a training company in the Student Training Regiment at Fort Benning. Like Flory before him, he was unimpressed by the quarters in the area by Lawson Field called the "Frying Pan" because it was exposed to the sweltering summer heat with no protection from the sun. The first three weeks of Hood's stay were devoted to parachute packing and physical conditioning, which included hand-to-hand combat, "familiarly known as grab-ass." Each of the classes, conducted by young sergeants in top physical condition, lasted about four hours a day. Hood's memories of Fort Benning are associated with the treatment he and his comrades received from the cadre.

> It was not at all unusual for several sergeants to return from pass at 2 A.M. and roust out the men for a little extra physical effort. One favorite was a night run around Lawson Field, which was seven miles. Awash in beer, carrying flashlights, the sergeants were our enthusiastic escorts. I think those bozos could have run for a week without noticing it, and the pace was considerably faster than a jog.
>
> Another peril of passage was the "Tarzan Test," which is funny as hell now and was funny to me even then, but not every victim will agree. With their flashlights and ever-present army whistles, they would shove us into some kind of military formation in the Georgia dark, then make the announcement: "We gonna play Tarzan. Yep, we gonna give you guys the Tarzan Test. We gonna turn off the flashlights, and I'm gonna blow this whistle for ten seconds. And when I get through blowing this whistle, we gonna turn on the flashlights again. I don't wanta see nobody's ass on the ground. You gonna climb trees. I don't give a good goddamn how big or how little your personal tree is, you gonna climb that son of a bitch, you hear me? Climb that son of a bitch, I said! Evah damn one a you guys bettah climb a goddamn tree, or I personally will be real pissed off, and you don't wanta piss me off."
>
> Darkness. The sound of running feet. Curses. More curses.
>
> Then the flashlights would be turned back on to reveal a ludicrous sight: The pine trees, ranging in size from saplings to those more than a foot in diameter, weren't easy to climb, since the lowest limbs were eight or ten feet off the ground. Flashlights would reveal two or three men desperately clinging to a small sapling, which was bent over from their weight. The real wise guys would wait until time for the flashlights to be turned on, then put arms and legs around a pine tree, feet some six inches off the ground. The catch here was the fact that each Tarzan had to stay off the ground until given the beered-up sergeant's permission to return to earth—permission which was always slow in coming.

The sergeants sometimes had to walk away to keep their laughter from erupting in front of the soldiers.

Officers, ranging in rank from second lieutenants to majors went through jump school with Hood and his comrades. The physical training they underwent became the signature training for the airborne.

> Grab-ass took place in large sawdust pits, approximately 30 yards square, and the sergeants delighted in harassing these officers. These sergeants were, to a man, pleasantly sadistic in manner and delighted in ordering the performance of 25 to 50 extra push-ups or 200 side-straddle hops for the slightest lapse of decorum. Folded arms, hands on hips, hands in pockets—these were all felonies and resulted in quivering muscles and burning lungs. I promise you that you can do a damned sight more push-ups than you ever dreamed you could do, and you can duck-walk a mile further than you ever considered possible. They were persuasive men.
>
> They took an obvious delight in harassing the officers and made no effort to hide the fact. Really sarcastic and insulting remarks were followed by a deliberately delayed "sir." I remember some of these remarks very clearly, because they shocked

> me: "That forearm smash wouldn't knock a sick whore off a piss-pot. I got a kid sister could kick your ass, (delay) sir." "Don't you understand words with more than one goddamn syllable . . . sir?"

Most of the officers remained poker-faced, recalls Hood, who concludes that this type of mixed training forged strong bonds between the airborne officers and the men they would eventually command, because they had all survived the same training together. Another aspect of paratrooper training was that the soldiers were required to go everywhere at a very fast double time, a practice that remained in effect for many years.

The parachute-packing classes were held in a large hangar near Lawson Field, the Army Air Corps facility at Fort Benning. The hangar was filled with rows of polished hardwood tables about fifteen feet long and two and a half feet wide. For Hood, the parachute packing was not too difficult, but it was time-consuming, each step requiring extreme care. The nylon was very slippery and hard to manage, and the proper folding of the chutes was a tricky operation.

During stage B, Hood also experienced the 20- and 34-foot towers, which he claims scared him more than anything else the school had to offer. "The jumper's harness was attached to a steel cable that ran at a slant by each tower. Jumping off the 34-foot tower, he would fall about 15 feet, then slide down the cable to a sawdust pile. Those towers absolutely scared the hell out of me. Jumping from a plane was much easier, though I certainly don't know why."

Many men washed out that week, a fact that puzzled young Hood. The 34-foot tower did not look all that imposing. From ground level, he watched his fellow soldiers filing up the stairs of the tower, coming out the door on top, and sliding down the line to the pit. It seemed simple enough. When his turn came to step up to the doorway, he realized that the slide was not as simple as it had seemed from down below. In fact, he had to hurtle toward the ground for a dozen feet or more before his line played out, breaking his fall with a tremendous jolt. Only then did he slide gently to the ground. This process was quite a shock for the would-be paratroopers, especially if they had not fastened their harnesses properly. A misplaced harness was likely to inflict an excruciating jolt of pain around the crotch area of the careless paratrooper. Many of the troopers who survived the jolt and went on to become paratroopers claimed that no actual jump was ever so painful. For a few fortunate men, the first training jump was totally unmemorable. Be that as it may, the paratrooper's overall training was an unforgettable experience.

During stage C, Ray Hood and his comrades packed chutes under close supervision for the students in stage D. A small sewn-in pocket on the pack frame of each parachute held a white card, called the Rigger's Report, or Double R, on which was written the date the parachute was inspected and packed and the name, rank, and army serial number (ASN) of the man who packed it. In stage C, the trainees also were introduced to the 250-foot towers. The jumper put on a parachute harness. His chute was deployed on a large hoop attached to one of the four tower arms by a long cable. Next, the jumper was lifted almost to the top and ordered by loudspeaker to drop a small piece of paper in order to determine wind direction. If the wind was blowing from a safe direction, the jumper was lifted the remaining few feet to the top and released by a controller at ground level. Hood saw a man blown into the tower only once. One of the ambulances standing by during the training session carried the badly injured trooper away.

The would-be paratroopers were issued jump boots when they arrived at the school, but they were not permitted to "blouse" their pants until

Parachute School

After the United States entered the war, the War Department ordered the formation of four parachute regiments. Two battalions were quickly expanded into regiments, but the remaining two regiments were not activated until May 1942. On March 23, 1942, the Airborne Command, which replaced the Provisional Parachute Group, was activated at Fort Benning under Col. William C. Lee. In April, the command was moved to Fort Bragg, North Carolina.

The plans for Operation Bolero, which would be the buildup for a landing in northern France called Operation Roundup, led General McNair to believe that an airborne division would be needed for the invasion of Europe. By August 1942, he and his superiors decided to form two airborne divisions: the 82nd and 101st. Eventually force of five such divisions was created. Each airborne division was to include one parachute infantry regiment with 1,958 men and two glider regiments with 1,605 men each, instead of the normal 3,000 men of an infantry regiment.

Gen. William Lee, who eventually became known as the "Father of the Airborne," went on to command the 101st and was replaced by his chief of staff, Gen. Eldridge C. Chapman, as commander of the Airborne Command in August 1942. Neither of these pioneers of America's airborne elite had graduated from West Point.

The Parachute School was activated in May 1942. Within a few months, several new regiments were formed. The standards for the selection of recruits, set in January 1942, were very specific, as indicated by the following document:

a. Volunteer for parachute duty.
b. Alert, active, supple, with firm muscles, and sound limbs; capable of development into an aggressive individual fighter, with great endurance.
c. Age—20 to 30 inclusive.
d. Physically qualified:
    1) Weight—maximum not to exceed 185 pounds
    2) Vision—minimum visual acuity of 20-40, each eye.
e. Every volunteer must sign the following statement:

I, (name of soldier) hereby volunteer for duty with parachute troops. I understand fully that in performance of such duty, I will be required to jump from an airplane and land via parachute.

Signature of Soldier

they jumped during stage D, their last week of training. Hood began stage D a week or two ahead of Flory, during Thanksgiving week of 1942. He was a member of class 43 at the time. The jump, which was scheduled for the Monday before the holiday, was canceled because it rained. Quite a few men had quit that morning. Since Thursday was Thanksgiving, Hood's class had only three days to complete their jumps that week. The final jump was an unforgettable experience for Hood.

> I was scared, but not as much as I'd anticipated. I was primarily concerned with performing in an adult manner and not disgracing myself by stumbling or otherwise interfering with the speedy exit from the plane. I spent a lot of time fretting about being a grown man, which must indicate that I wasn't. I performed adequately; the parachute opened as the sergeants promised it would. A real piece of cake! I was elated. We made our five jumps in three days. I believe that our initial five jumps were made from an altitude of 1,200 feet.

When he received his jump wings, Ray Hood was elated and bursting with pride. He was immediately assigned to the Communications School at Fort Benning for four more weeks of training. At the school, he learned to use the SCR-536 and SCR-300 radios. Hood considered the SCR-300 the workhorse of the infantry. Hood learned the Morse code and was able to send and receive fifteen words per minute. The course also included wire splicing, switchboard operation, and radio and telephone voice procedure, using several letters combined. More than any other means of communication, the new radios were essential for airborne units, as field telephones were impractical for troops that operated in isolated conditions. Thus the radioman was vital so that the airborne unit could maintain contact during combat operations.

Howard "Bud" Houser had served in the Kansas National Guard between 1931 and 1936. In May 1942, he received his draft notice and reported to Camp Roberts, where he was assigned to administrative work because of his civilian experience. Houser had not been looking for an easy way out of military duty. Earlier in the year, he had volunteered for the marines with his nephew, but he had been rejected for service in both the marines and the navy because of a previous foot injury. Weary of his administrative duties at Camp Roberts, Houser volunteered when a recruiting team for parachutists arrived at the post, at about the same time Ray Hood was going through basic training at the camp. The recruiters did not seem overly concerned about his foot, and within a few months, Houser became a paratrooper.

> I happened to be at Fort Benning when the 82nd Airborne came in as a division for their training. I remember several incidents that are now funny but were not then, the men who washed out—who refused to go up the [34-foot tower] and to jump off—and others who could not do the extreme training. One time we were watching a jump, and this one man—his chute did not open—hit the runway, and that sobered up a lot of the fellows.

Houser's description of a post-training jump with his 502nd Parachute Infantry Regiment (PIR) indicates that he went through the jump training ahead of Hood and Flory. After the men in his group received their wings on the fifth jump, they made a sixth jump in full combat gear.

> We knew we had a man in there who was always scared to go out the door. The company commander told me, since I was his company clerk, to get behind that man, and "if he fails to go out, he goes out with you." He reached for the door and said he wasn't going to go, so I grabbed ahold of him and we both went together. That's when I fell and my parachute got wrapped up with one of the shroud lines. And I was coming down headfirst with my chute half open, just as I was going to pull my ripcord because I knew I was close to the ground, my momentum was too great.

> I assembled my weapon and started to get up to run over to the assembly point and fell flat on the ground, and I heard somebody laughing. Here were a couple of medics standing over me ready to carry me. I spent Thanksgiving and Christmas in the hospital.

Many of the volunteer paratroopers had a variety of backgrounds. Some, like Hood and Flory, were raw recruits. Others, like Houser, already in their mid- or late twenties, had served previously. Others still had seen service in various branches of the army before they joined the parachute units. PFC William Gammon, for instance, joined the military in August 1938. He trained and served with the 18th Field Artillery at Fort Sill, Oklahoma. (Between the world wars, the new recruits usually were trained in their assigned unit, where they got on-the-job training.) In 1941, he transferred to the 19th Engineers at Fort Ord in the scenic area of Monterey, California, where he remained for five months. Finally, in November 1941, he left the army, but his stint as a civilian was short-lived. He was drafted into the army on May 18, 1942, because he failed to join the reserve pool. This time, he reported at the Presidio to draw his uniforms and went on to Camp Roberts for basic training.[4] He decided to join the parachute troops after seeing a glamorous recruiting poster that promised adventure and excitement.

The paratrooper recruiting team at Camp Roberts watched Gammon do push-ups, run, and tumble, a routine required of all would-be paratroopers. Even though he had some problems with the tumbling, he was accepted. He found the basic training at Camp Roberts barely challenging because of his previous experience, so Gammon ran the obstacle course after the daily drill to prepare for his airborne training. After he shipped east to the parachute training facility, he went through the same training as the others before he suffered his first mishap during stage D. "We made our first jump at 1,500 feet, and it wasn't too bad. But after the second jump, we were walking up the hill when an airplane went over and a guy's chute didn't open. He plummeted right into the ground, so the third jump was a little rough."

After he completed his jumps, Gammon attended the radio communications school, where he made two more jumps before he joined the 377th Field Artillery Battalion of the 101st Airborne (A/B) Division, at Fort Bragg.

The new parachute units also had to include professionals. One was Capt. David Thomas, who, after returning from a tour of airborne training facilities in England, reported to the 505th PIR, where he was the regimental surgeon. Before this, he had served in the 503rd Battalion with a senior captain, James Gavin. Thomas had been promoted to captain in the 503rd Battalion at the same time as Gavin during the summer of 1941. By the time Thomas reported to the 505th PIR late the next summer, Gavin had reached the rank of major and commanded the regiment, and he achieved the rank of full colonel within a year. Thomas, who had a great deal of admiration for him, said that Gavin was the finest soldier he had ever known.

Jack R. Isaacs, another volunteer for parachute training, enlisted at Fort Riley, Kansas, in October 1940 at the age of seventeen, after graduating from high school. (His birthday is listed on military records as having been in 1921 but elsewhere as October 1922.) He served as a rifleman with the 17th Infantry, 7th Division, at Fort Ord, California, and as a mortar man in the 15th Infantry of the 3rd Division at Fort Lewis, Wash-

4. It is not clear why the army sent Gammon through basic training, since he had already been trained. He began his training at Camp Roberts almost two months before Ray Hood arrived and while Houser was still stationed there.

ington, where he was promoted to sergeant. He took part in the practice amphibious landings on the West Coast at McNiel Island, Washington, with the 3rd Division. By this time, training had become monotonous duty.

In the spring of 1942, Isaacs was recommended for OCS. He attended OCS Class 36 and graduated on July 17, attaining the rank of second lieutenant at age nineteen. Shortly after that, he was accepted for parachute training, and after five weeks, he earned his wings—ahead of Hood, Flory, and Houser. Next, he attended the Army Demolitions School at Fort Benning, after which he was assigned to Company G, 505th PIR, 82nd Airborne Division. Since he was the youngest and most junior lieutenant in the company, he was assigned as assistant leader of the 3rd Platoon. His regiment's training routine included additional parachute jumps, instruction, and exercises involving infantry tactics. The physical training was intense to keep the men in top condition in preparation for overseas combat.

On January 19, 1943, Jack Isaacs married his high school sweetheart, Evelyn Snoddy from Birmingham, Kansas. The brief ceremony took place near Fort Benning in Columbus, Georgia. In February 1943, the regiment moved to Fort Bragg, North Carolina, and became part of the newly formed 82nd Airborne Division. Young Isaacs was promoted to first lieutenant and became the platoon leader of the 3rd Platoon. Not long after that, Isaacs's division embarked for North Africa and he had to part from his bride.

The selection of volunteers for the paratroopers was to be done at reception centers and replacement centers, but the problems soon multiplied. Apparently the screeners accepted men who were overage and had poor vision or a faulty bone structure. In addition, many volunteers did not fully understand that they would be expected to jump from an airplane in flight. Many were just looking for alternative duty to delay their inevitable departure, while others thought only of the extra $50 a month they would be making. Few had a clear idea of what was expected of them. Thus training accidents were not uncommon, according to Dr. David Thomas.

> I was working the jump field at Benning one time when we had a strange occurrence. This was the fourth jump of the five required for qualification for this particular class. This one guy clears the aircraft, and another guy is real anxious and is practically riding his back. What happens is that the first guy's chute opens, and the second guy goes through his suspension lines and his chute opens. What happens is that you wind up with an open parachute, suspension lines, a parachutist wrapped up in the second man's canopy, more suspension lines, and another parachutist at the end of those suspension lines. Number one man has his chute open, and number two doesn't have his open. So two guys come down rapidly. The first fellow hits, going at a pretty good speed, and knocks himself out. The second fellow, when he gets the weight off of him, makes a normal landing. So I give this guy some smelling salts and slap him a couple of times, and he comes to and says, "That's all, that's all; I am not going to do any more of that." So I am selling him a con job. I say, "Look fellow, what happened to you is a 50,000-to-1 shot, and there is no possible way that can happen again to you. Tell you what I am going to do: I am going to take you back to the hangar and I am going to get you on another aircraft, and you are going to jump again and be the first man to qualify in your class." I just about got the guy sold on this scenario when in comes a fellow who did just what I described hap-

pened to this guy, and he bounced about three feet and must have broken every bone in his body, and this kid says, "That's it; no more." I didn't argue with him anymore.

Frightening accidents and tough training led many of the would-be paratroopers to quit sooner or later. It was clear that changes had to be made. Thus on May 25, 1942, on orders from the secretary of war, the commanders of Replacement Training Centers at Camps Walters, Roberts, Croft, and Wheeler selected 105 physically fit volunteers during training for transfer to Fort Benning. The age requirement changed to encompass eighteen- to thirty-two-year-olds.

In 1942, prospects of creating two fully manned airborne divisions appeared to be good, since the number of volunteers was adequate. The activation of the 82nd and 101st Airborne was accomplished by October, but neither division was ready for the North African invasion. A special task force consisting of the 509th Parachute Infantry Battalion did take part in Operation Torch, however.[5] Many of the volunteers who joined the 82nd Airborne Division in 1942 were sent to North Africa for operations in the Mediterranean in the summer of 1943. The men of the 101st, on the other hand, continued to train while they waited for their "Rendezvous with Destiny," as General Lee poetically called it.

5. The 509th was originally the 504th Parachute Battalion and then formed part of the 503rd Parachute Infantry Regiment. It arrived in Great Britain aboard the *Queen Mary* in June 1942.

CHAPTER 6

Formation of the Airborne Divisions

Lt. Harold Shebeck, one of the first members of the 82nd Airborne Division, graduated from the Infantry School at Fort Benning on December 21, 1941. The next day he married a fellow teacher from South Dakota whom he had met before he joined the army. Because of the attack on Pearl Harbor two weeks earlier, he was unable to get leave to get married, so, he says, "while a cab waited to take us to the railroad station, we were married in a Lutheran minister's parsonage in Columbus, Georgia." They spent their wedding night on a train bound for Camp Wolters, Texas, where they arrived on the afternoon of December 24. When Shebeck assumed command of Company B, 61st Infantry Training Battalion, the unit was undergoing basic training and consisted of 252 men and only two other officers, both of them lieutenants. Shebeck had no difficulty meeting his responsibilities, thanks to his recent training at the Infantry School.

Shebeck was given the days of Christmas Eve and Christmas off, probably, he surmises, because the battalion commander felt sympathy for him upon learning that he had been married for only two days. "My wife and I spent that Christmas evening 1941 sitting on the mezzanine of the Baker Hotel in nearby Mineral Wells, listening to the music of Jack Amlung and his band playing in the lobby. My thoughts were far away that evening, as I wondered what the future had in store for me."

The draft in America was now in full swing, and Infantry Training Centers opened all over the country. New infantry divisions were activated as the inducted men completed their basic training. Officers and NCOs were transferred out of these training centers to provide the cadres for the new divisions. Some officers came directly from the Infantry School, while others, like Shebeck, were called to active duty from civilian life.

> So it came about that I received orders to report to the 82nd Infantry Division, which was being activated at Camp Claiborne, Louisiana, on March 25. The 82nd had a long and proud history from World War I. Numbered among its former members were Sgt. Alvin York and Gen. Jonathan Wainwright, who had been chief of staff.[1] Now Wainwright, on Corregidor, was in a different war. The newly named commander of the 82nd was Maj. Gen. Omar Bradley, who had handed me my diploma just three months before, when he was commandant of the Infantry School. Brig. Gen. Matthew Ridgway was assistant division commander, and Col. George Pope was chief of staff. I was assigned to the special staff of the division as special services officer, which at that time seemed to be under the G-1 Section.

During the next three weeks, the staff of the 82nd Airborne worked very hard on planning, training, and resolving a host of inevitable problems as it awaited the arrival of 15,000 men from all over the country. "When the first troop trains arrived on March 25, 1942, the date the division was activated (the cadre, including myself, had arrived on March 3), how bewildered and apprehensive many of the men looked," Shebeck recalls. Two division bands were on hand to cheer the men, who were immediately served warm food on General Bradley's orders. Most of the new arrivals were assigned to rifle companies, but hundreds of more specialized technical positions still needed to be filled. The classification officer in the G-1 Section scoured personnel records night and day to identify individuals with the experience necessary to fill these positions. As the special services officer, Shebeck was responsible for the administration of the athletic and recreational activities in the division. His duties included handling arrangements for the USO shows.

In late May 1942, Shebeck was sent for a four-week course at Fort Meade, Maryland, which involved "survivor warfare tactics" and hand-to-hand combat. There he met a major in his early fifties who had taught physical education at Columbia University in civilian life. "He was only about five feet, six inches tall and weighed about 130 pounds, but he could pin 200-pound officers half his age," says Shebeck. The major taught Shebeck and his classmates deadly tricks, such as strangling a person using only two fingers. Midway through the course, they learned that "in the previous classes there were so many student officers who had returned to their units injured from the 'instruction' received from our major that he had been ordered to let up on some of his methods." Even though Shebeck was dazzled by the major's skill and instruction, he was quite relieved to return to the 82nd in one piece.

General Bradley commended his chief of staff, Lt. Col. George van W. Pope, for having pulled together an exceptional officer cadre for the division. The 82nd Infantry Division was whipped into shape by the end of June. Later that month, Bradley was transferred to the 28th Infantry

1. Alvin York was awarded the Medal of Honor for action behind enemy lines in the Argonne in 1918. When the officers and NCOs on his patrol were killed or wounded, he took command of his unit. Eventually, he captured more than 100 German soldiers and was instrumental in pressuring the German commander of the sector to withdraw his forces.

The Creation of Specialized Airborne Units

Lt. X. B. Cox Jr. joined the 82nd Division as it was shaping up at Camp Claiborne. This ROTC graduate of Texas A&M was called to active duty in June 1941 and assigned to the 23rd Infantry of the 2nd Infantry Division, stationed at Fort Sam Houston, Texas, before he became part of the cadre that helped form the 82nd Infantry Division. In January 1942, he was sent to Fort Benning on a two-month training assignment. On his arrival at Camp Claiborne, he was promoted to captain and appointed executive officer (XO) in an infantry battalion that had received an allocation of draftees from Ohio, Kentucky, and Indiana. When the division reorganized into an airborne division and split to create the 101st A/B Division, Cox was assigned to the newly formed 81st Antiaircraft (AA) Battalion of the 101st A/B Division. The parachute units required specialized units like the 81st, which was to have an antiaircraft and antitank role.

The 81st AA Battalion was formed on September 4, 1942, from personnel of the 1st Battalion, 327th Infantry. Initially, Cox's Company B was transferred to the 401st Glider Infantry Regiment, while Companies A, C, and D of the 1st Battalion transferred to the 2nd and 3rd Battalions and were redesignated as Companies F, K, and L. Later, the 3rd Battalion of the 401st, without Company K, transferred to the 81st and became Batteries C, commanded by Capt. Robert Kim, and F, under Capt. George Brown. Captain Cox's Company B, under the command of Capt. A. G. Bemired, became Battery B of the AA Battalion. The battalion's commanding officer served on the division staff as both the antitank and antiaircraft officer, since his unit had a dual function. All of the battalion's officers and soldiers were infantrymen and needed training for their new assignment. In fact, none of the men had qualified as paratroopers or glider men.

The 81st AA Battalion also received the 1st and 2nd Platoons of the 327th Glider Infantry Regiment, which was led by Capt. John R. Bacon and became Battery A. Also from the 327th came Heavy Weapons Companies H and E, which became Batteries D, commanded by 1st Lt. Francis Chambers, and E, under

Division, which was stationed across the Red River from the 82nd and was having difficulties. One of the problems it faced was that many of its ablest NCOs had been sent to OCS. In addition, several of its officers had volunteered for the Army Air Corps, leaving the unit rudderless. Undaunted, General Bradley got things in order, bringing the 28th to the same level of efficiency as the 82nd. Meanwhile, General Ridgway took command of the 82nd, and Col. Maxwell Taylor became his chief of staff, while Colonel Pope went with General Bradley. Shebeck was sorry to see Bradley leave:

"The Doughboy's General" had a good down-to-earth approach to things. He had a rather quiet, fatherly manner, and unlike a lot of West Pointers, he seemed to look more favorably on reserve officers.

The training of the 82nd continued, and on August 15, 1942, the first two airborne divisions came into being. Our division was split to form the 82nd and 101st Airborne Divisions. About this time, I was promoted to captain. There was a lot of shuffling of personnel, and we lost an infantry regiment to the 101st and acquired the 504th Para-

The Creation of Specialized Airborne Units *continued*

Capt. Ralph Hewitt. HQ Company of the 1st Battalion, 327th Glider Regiment, had been the Headquarters Detachment of the 3rd Battalion of the 401st Glider Infantry and was transferred to the antiaircraft battalion as the Headquarters Detachment under Capt. Edward McGraf. The battalion commander, Captain Cox, and other staff officers belonged to the Headquarters Detachment. Finally, the Medical Detachment, under Capt. Robert Orbey, was created from personnel from the 327th and 401st Infantry.

Thus, in September 1942, the completed battalion consisted of three batteries of antitank guns, A, B, and C; three batteries of antiaircraft guns, the D, E, and F; Headquarters Detachment; and the Medical Detachment. Each of these batteries numbered five officers and seventy-one men. The Headquarters Detachment included three officers and twenty-six men, and the Medical Detachment had one officer and twenty-three men. The unit was maintained at 5 percent overstrength.

Each antitank battery was equipped with eight 37-millimeter antitank guns, and each antiaircraft battery with twelve .50-caliber air-cooled machine guns.[2] Each battery included the necessary number of jeeps and trailers. The machine guns were also outfitted with ground mounts to support the infantry.

In October 1942, the 81st Airborne AA Battalion transferred to Fort Bragg after its men were trained as glider men, although they received only ground training, because the gliders were not yet available. According to Cox, they "carried on a strong training program," with "unit drills, physical training, weapons training and firing, glider loading, and flights." Furthermore, "much of the training was performed away from Fort Bragg, such as Camp Davis for antiaircraft firing, Laurenberg-Maxton Air Base, and Camp McCall for glider training."

2. Later in the war, the 37-millimeter guns were replaced with 57-millimeter AT guns, and later still, with a British 6-pounder (57-millimeter) gun, which worked more effectively with gliders.

chute Regiment, which arrived from Fort Benning. Originally the plan was for two glider regiments and one parachute regiment in the division, but eventually this was reversed.

The Airborne Divisions Prepare for War

After it was converted into an airborne division in August 1942, the 82nd moved from Camp Claiborne, Louisiana, to Fort Bragg, North Carolina, in early October. The division had only a few months to receive and train its new units, which included two parachute regiments. The 82nd had been activated in the spring of 1942 with three infantry regiments—the 325th, 326th, and 327th—all of which were designated as glider units in August. By October, the 82nd "All American" Airborne Division retained only the 325th Glider Infantry Regiment. In August, the 326th was used to form the new 101st A/B Division; in October, the 327th was removed from the 82nd Division, and in 1943, it became part of the 13th A/B Division. When it set out for North Africa in April 1943, the 82nd A/B Division had had less

A 225-foot tower at Fort Benning. NATIONAL ARCHIVES

than one year to reorganize and prepare, too little time to be fully effective. The only major field operations in which it had participated before going into action were the Tennessee maneuvers.

When Harold Shebeck joined the 82nd Division, it was located at Camp Claiborne near the town of Alexandria. Also nearby were Camp Livingston, Camp Beauregard, Fort Polk, and Esler Air Base, all of which swelled the population of the area, and Shebeck describes the city as "a veritable bedlam, with thousands of servicemen packing the streets every evening." In September 1942, the newly formed 101st A/B Division left Camp Claiborne for Fort Bragg, where it was joined by the 82nd A/B Division in October. Many of the 101st's future paratroopers, Ray Hood and Robert Flory among them, were converging on Fort Benning for their parachute training at that time. The men and officers of the two divisions, which were changing into airborne formations, had to decide whether to undergo airborne training or be transferred to other units. Those who were not assigned to parachute units had the choice of going to parachute training or becoming glider men.

In November 1942, a glider base was established at Laurinburg-Maxton, North Carolina, and the newly developed CG-4 cargo glider was tested at Wright Field, Ohio. A small number of CG-4 gliders were dispatched to North Carolina for training purposes. As the 82nd and the 101st A/B Divisions began training in earnest, a special airborne training site with drop zones for parachutists and landing zones for gliders was prepared about forty miles from Fort Bragg. After the 82nd shipped out, the newly activated 13th A/B Division took its place at Fort Bragg. The 11th and later the 17th A/B Divisions were formed at Camp Mackall, a new camp that officially opened in April 1943 and was named in honor of the first paratrooper killed in the North African invasion of 1942.

North Carolina was not the final choice for an airborne training site. In November 1942, rumor spread that the 82nd A/B Division would move to the wide-open spaces of Alliance Air Base in Nebraska. Captain Shebeck was one of eight staff officers selected to accompany Gen. Joseph Swing, commander of the division artillery, on a two-day trip to the Nebraska site. Bad weather interrupted their visit, causing their twin-engine C-47 transport to stop over at Kansas City. The group landed at Alliance late the next morning and departed the morning after their inspection, returning to Fort Bragg in the evening. After that visit, it was decided not to move the division to Nebraska.

After the return of the exploratory group, Colonel Cutler of the 326th Glider Infantry Regiment was informed that his unit was transferring out of the 82nd A/B and was to be replaced by the 505th PIR.[3] The 326th departed for Alliance early in 1943 and did not return to Fort Bragg until the end of the year. Later, General Swing took over the newly formed 11th A/B Division at Camp Mackall.

Not long after he arrived at Fort Bragg, Captain Shebeck met Col. Maxwell Taylor, who had serious doubts about the physical condition of the division staff officers and their ability to meet the demands placed on this highly specialized unit. Taylor decided to make his staff officers get into shape by ordering them to make a fourteen-mile hike. Shebeck laid out the course around Fort Bragg, which began and ended at division headquarters. After the colonel approved the route, Shebeck asked the G-2 to make several copies of the memo he sent to the officers.

> Colonel Taylor instructed me and the assistant division finance officer to accompany him on the first hike the next day. A roster of all division staff officers would be set up on a schedule to be involved in this training. I was twenty-six years old at the time and in excellent physical condition, and I knew that Taylor was forty-two and in the same condition. I figured I should be able to keep up with him because of the age difference, if nothing else. The three of us started out after lunch that day, and the first mile or two we walked together, discussing subjects of mutual interest. After three or four miles, Taylor was a couple hundred yards ahead of the other officers and myself, and after six or seven miles, he was out of sight. We arrived at the mess hall at about 5 o'clock. I spied Taylor and General Ridgway eating at a back table. As I came up to talk to them, Taylor smiled and asked if we had just gotten back. He had completed his hike about an hour earlier.

A paratrooper hung up in a tree during training at Fort Benning.
NATIONAL ARCHIVES

Captain Shebeck still had to decide whether to become a paratrooper. Most of the division's staff had already qualified, and all staff members were

3. This gave the airborne division the new standard of two parachute infantry regiments and one glider regiment instead of one parachute infantry regiments and two glider regiments. In October 1942, the two airborne divisions made these changes, and by 1943, it was standard for the table of organization.

"encouraged" to make at least one jump. Shebeck jumped with three other staff members at Andy's Field, an area adjacent to Pope Field, where training drops were made. He had heard from veteran jumpers that the first jump was the easiest, and it turned out to be true. After about an hour of instruction, which was mainly on how to land, Shebeck made his jump without a hitch. After that, however, he opted to become a glider man.

The Glider Men

The number of gliders available for practice and training increased between 1942 and 1943. Inevitably, some of these aircraft were lost in training because of inexperienced pilots. Careless soldiers also inflicted damage by allowing their rifle butts to break through the gliders' fabric skin. As a result, says Captain Shebeck, the 82nd rarely had more than twenty gliders fit for training at any one time.

> During the fall and winter of 1942–43, our glider regiment did the best it could with the available aircraft. Most of our training seemed to be loading and unloading the aircraft. Sometime during February 1943, the 325th Glider Regiment went to Maxton for about two or three weeks at Camp Mackall, which had an air base with suitable facilities for glider training. It was at Camp Mackall that I took my one and only glider flight before the Normandy invasion. If my memory serves me correctly, we flew down to Florence, South Carolina, and back. We had only one glider flight while training from August 1942, when the division became an airborne division, until June 1944, indicating that there must have been some kind of shortage of gliders for training.

Joe Brown Gault, another young officer of the 82nd, had received his commission in June 1941 when he graduated from Texas A&M. That summer, he reported to Camp Wolters as an infantry training officer, and in early 1942, he was assigned to the 82nd Division at Camp Claiborne. In mid-August, when the division was redesignated as an airborne division, Gault was assigned to the 325th Glider Infantry. "No, we didn't volunteer for gliders," he says. "They assembled us one day, and they told us the whole division was airborne." A good number of the men in his unit decided that parachuting was more glamorous than gliding and opted to join the parachute regiments. Lieutenant Gault's men didn't see a glider at Fort Bragg for many months. Gault had the highest admiration for his company commander, Capt. Bennie A. Zinn, another Texas A&M graduate who had been called up from his teaching job.

> The leadership of Captain Zinn began at Camp Claiborne, and let me tell you, never has there been a greater instructor to both officers and men. I watched him set 200 men down in the midday heat of Louisiana and hold them spellbound. I remember the period on latrine. He used Lieutenants Greene and myself to demonstrate. The men [of Company F] went wild and needed no further instruction on the use of a latrine.

All the other company officers were reservists with very little experience. Some of them were eventually detached for cadre duty and replaced with even newer reservists. When the division reached Fort Bragg, many of the Company F officers, including Captain Zinn and later Lieutenant Gault, were transferred to other units in the division. During the time Lieutenant Gault was with the company, his men had to scratch out the outline of a glider fuselage in the dirt and use that for training. "Most of the training was in old army infantry tactics," Gault recalls, "and every so often, we marked off an eight-by-twelve

Shock harness used for only a short time for paratrooper training in 1942. NATIONAL ARCHIVES

area and designated a door. We glider men loaded through this door and squatted opposite each other, then unloaded and fanned out into simulated combat. But no worry, we had seen stick bayonets and wooden machine guns. The men took it with a dry grin and went on training."

In early 1942, Company F, 2nd Battalion, 325th Glider Infantry, was a standard infantry company numbering about 200 men, divided into four numbered platoons commanded by lieutenants. It was led by Captain Zinn with 1st Lt. C. R. Rucher as the XO. It was reorganized when it was designated as a glider infantry. Its contingent was reduced to about 150 men, and one of its rifle platoons was eliminated. The 1st and 2nd Platoons were supported by the 3rd Platoon, which became the weapons platoon and was assigned .30-caliber machine guns and 60-millimeter mortars. The 325th Glider Regiment, like many similar units, consisted of only two battalions, while the parachute regiments consisted of the standard three.

The day of the long-anticipated glider ride dawned bright and clear. The men of the 325th eagerly piled up on trucks for the short ride from Fort Bragg to Pope Field to see if all their training had borne fruit. Lieutenant Gault and his men got their first close-up look at a real-life glider. A group of thirteen men was selected for the first glider ride. Their first experience with a real glider was somewhat of a letdown for most, because they went up and came back down, and that was it for the rest of the day. After their introduction to gliders, the men of the 325th went back to drawing rectangles in the dirt.

The 82nd Airborne Division had only a few months of training before it departed for North Africa in April 1943. Lieutenant Gault and his men did two more practice exercises with gliders in the weeks preceding their embarkation.

The Glider Regiment, 1942–44

The organization of a standard glider regiment was not changed until after the invasion of Normandy. Until that time, it included a regimental headquarters and headquarters company, a service company, and two rifle battalions.

The regimental headquarters and headquarters company included the regimental staff, a communications section for each battalion, and antitank platoon with eight 37-millimeter guns and several 2.36-inch rocket launchers; an intelligence and reconnaissance platoon, a personnel records section, and a headquarters section of the medical detachment, with 3 officers and 18 men. The regimental staff had 8 officers, including a CO, XO, S-1, S-2, S-3, and S-4, and 1 warrant officer. The headquarters company, not including the headquarters section of the medical detachment, had 5 officers, 1 warrant officer, and 130 enlisted men.

The service company included a supply section, a motor section, and special services. It had a total of 6 officers, 3 warrant officers, and 84 enlisted men, with three .50-caliber antiaircraft machine guns and ten 2.36-inch rocket launchers.

The two rifle battalions, the 1st and 2nd, each contained 27 officers, 1 warrant officer, and 630 enlisted men and were organized with a headquarters and headquarters company, battalion staff, a mortar platoon with six 81-millimeter mortars, a heavy machine-gun platoon with four .30-caliber machine guns, an intelligence section, a supply section, and a medical section of medical detachment with 2 officers and 24 enlisted men. Each battalion also had three rifle companies—A, B and C in the 1st Battalion and E, F, and G in the 2nd. (Heavy Weapons Companies D and H were not added until after Normandy.) Each rifle company included two rifle platoons and one weapons platoon. A rifle platoon consisted of two rifle squads and one weapons squad. Each rifle squad had one BAR and one 2.36-inch rocket launcher, and the weapons squad had one 60-millimeter mortar, one BAR, and one 2.36-inch rocket launcher. The weapons platoon had two squads, each with one 60-millimeter mortar, one light .30-caliber machine gun, and one 2.36-inch rocket launcher.

The glider battalion had 22 officers and 621 enlisted men, with 5 officers and 150 men per rifle company, according to Army Manual T/O 7-51, 5 September 1942.

During the largest exercise, held in South Carolina, the men were fed en route before they boarded the gliders.

> They carried us in very low, up and down, and many men became airsick. They took off their helmets and upchucked into them. We had a gung-ho lieutenant who upchucked and then swallowed it to keep the men from knowing he was sick. We were to perform a problem on landing, but all the men could do was rush out and fall on the ground. A funny thing, though: I saw no vomiting on the way to France or Holland. Most glider rides were smooth except if you got in the prop wash. Wind noise was loud, but once we were cut loose, it was quiet as a mouse. We were usually in short

field packs, with no camping equipment, and most were riflemen.

Clinton Elmer Riddle, who completed high school in 1941, was training for a job in the aircraft industry when the war broke out, and he decided to enlist in the navy. When he returned to his home in the hills of eastern Tennessee, however, his mother pleaded with him to change his mind. But to his mother's consternation, he was drafted on December 10, 1942. After completing six weeks of basic training at Camp Wheeler, he spent another six weeks at Clerk School. A week after he finished the training, he was transferred to Fort Bragg, where he was assigned to a glider unit in the 82nd A/B Division. He received little glider training, as he was with the 82nd for little more than a month before the unit shipped out to North Africa in April 1943. The regiment entrained at Fort Bragg on April 14 for New York, and then departed from there on a transport on April 27.

Harold Eugene Owens was a regular who ended up in the 325th Glider Infantry. Unlike most of his comrades, he was not dismayed by his fate, because he had been looking for adventure well before the United States entered the war. He had left school during the Depression in 1939, joined the Civilian Conservation Corps (CCC) in his native West Virginia, and returned home a year later. When the dark clouds of war gathered on the horizon, his father advised him to join the service and try to rise through the ranks as much possible before the nation became involved. Owens was only sixteen years old at the time and needed his father's permission to enlist, so father and son went together to Charleston, where the teen enlisted. He was sworn in on August 28, 1940, and sent to Fort Thomas, Kentucky, to join the 5th Infantry Division. Shortly after that, he was transferred to Fort Bragg and assigned to Company K, 3rd Battalion, of the newly activated 39th Infantry of the 9th Infantry Division. He went through basic training in Company K for only two weeks.

In those days, the army had a shortage of weapons, so one company would have the weapons one week, and the next company would get them the next. I was assigned to a 60-millimeter mortar section, but I was in the army six months before I saw a 60-millimeter mortar.

We lived in tents at Fort Bragg. In the summer time, we went down to the lake to bathe, but in the winter, we likely would have frozen to death. They had a shower there, but it was awfully cold. We stayed there in tents till January, and then they moved us to the main post, where they had wooden barracks, the new two-story type.

Owens's regiment remained in garrison until the fall of 1941, when the division took part in the Carolina maneuvers as weather permitted. The unit returned to Fort Bragg in December. After the attack on Pearl Harbor, some of detachments from the division were sent on guard duty. "The 39th Infantry was sent to guard the shipyards at Wilmington while my battalion went up into the hills around Hickory, North Carolina, around the Catawba River to guard the power dams and the causeways across them," recalls Owens. The 3rd Battalion remained in that location for about six weeks, until it was relieved by the home guard, at which time it returned to Fort Bragg.

In the meantime, the division received additional draftees, mainly from the eastern states. Most of the brighter recruits were sent to OCS. In February 1942, Owens, by now a corporal and the leader of a 60-millimeter mortar squad, was sent to Camp Claiborne as part of the cadre that would organize and train the 82nd Infantry Division. He was promoted to a three-stripe buck sergeant, the lowest-ranking type of sergeant, for this assignment.

Paratrooper training at Fort Benning.

At Camp Claiborne, he was assigned to Company A, 325th Infantry. While he was in Louisiana, Sergeant Owens was assigned to the honor guard that welcomed Alvin York, who had come to visit his old division. When the 82nd became an airborne division, it retained the 325th Infantry and, for a few months, the 326th. When he reached Fort Bragg, Owens discovered that his old division, the 9th, had moved out, and the 2nd Armored Division was now in the area. The armored troops took over their bivouac, and the 82nd Airborne Division moved into the old quarters of the 9th Division.

At Fort Bragg, Owens's unit learned to use parachutes, but it did not see any gliders until early 1943. In December 1942, before the gliders arrived, Owens was sent to Camp Forrest, Tennessee, for Ranger training.

I went through the Second Army Ranger School. We were allowed five demerits before they kicked us out of the school, and then your commanding officer had to write Gen. Ben Lear and explain why he sent such an individual to the school. If an officer were thrown out of the school, his commanding officer had to report to the general in person. We didn't lose any enlisted men, but we did lose about three officers. It was about the worst ordeal I went through in my life, and I haven't seen anything like it since. Even the worst of combat didn't compare to that school. Amazing as it may seem, on the way back home from the war, I met a lot of fellows who went through the training with me, and I believe it must have helped us survive.

After finishing Ranger School, Owens returned to the division to help train the men in his unit in Ranger tactics. Not long after that, Owens's unit was taken by truck to Laurinburg

The Gliders

The mainstay of the American glider fleet was the Waco CG-4A. It consisted of a steel frame covered with canvas and accommodated two pilots and thirteen men. Because of a shortage of pilots, however, the copilot was more often than not an infantryman. The craft was also able to carry a payload of 3,800 pounds instead of troops, which amounted to a jeep or a 75-millimeter gun and three soldiers. The nose of the glider, which included the pilot's compartment, was lifted upward to remove the payload, whereas the troops exited from side doors.

The pilot had few navigational instruments: a compass, an altimeter, and an airspeed indicator. He communicated with the tow aircraft by means of a phone line wrapped around the tow cable. The first glider was tested in June 1942. The craft went into production not long afterward. About 1,000 Waco CG-4As were supplied to the British, who gave them the name of Hadrian.

During the Normandy invasion, many of the Americans troops flew in on the British Horsa gliders. The American glider men disliked this aircraft, because it was made of plywood and cracked easily on landing in rough fields. The British instructed the troops to put their arms around the soldiers on each side of them and lift their feet before landing to prevent them from falling out if the fragile floors shattered. In addition, the Horsa did not have the ability to stay airborne for as long as the CG-4A once it was released, thus allowing less time for the pilot to select his landing site. The British glider had a larger capacity, however, and could carry up to twenty-eight soldiers in addition to the two pilots.

The American forces used the C-47 as the main tow plane for these gliders. It reached a maximum speed of 270 miles per hour—more than enough for the CG-4A, which was designed to fly at 125 miles per hour, and for the Horsa, which reached about 180.

Air Base in South Carolina for its first glider flight—an unforgettable experience.

> They loaded us in one glider, pulled us up on the runway, then pulled another glider up alongside, where it rammed into ours, and we had to get out and get into another. We were in and out of three or four gliders before we finally got to take off. When we did take off, we went down the runway and we became airborne, but our tow plane was still on the ground. We are flying, and all of a sudden, I see the pilot reach up, slap something up there, and shucks, here we are right back on the ground again, with dust flying all over as we land on the skids. They came back out, put us on trucks, took us over to another glider, and finally we took off on the nicest flight I ever had in my life. It was a beautiful day, nice and sunny.

The aircraft carried thirteen infantrymen, a few ammunition carts, the pilot, and the copilot. According to Sergeant Owens, his unit's training with CG-4 gliders consisted of only a few brief flights around the airfield. During these sessions, the glider men also learned how to tie the cargo, what to do during the flight, and how to proceed once they landed.

Shortly after the training sessions, to his surprise, Sergeant Owens was selected once again as cadre for the new 11th A/B Divi-

Mock-up for teaching paratroopers how to exit aircraft. NATIONAL ARCHIVES

sion. He knew that something important was brewing, because he had recently taken his shoes to the cobbler's, but before he had a chance to retrieve them, he received a brand new pair. He had also heard on the grapevine that the 82nd would be shipped overseas. "Sure enough," recalls Owens, "they pulled us out and took us back to Bragg, where we packed our gear and were put on a train that took us to Camp Edwards, Massachusetts, in April 1943."

The 101st and 82nd A/B Division had a similar experience. Before leaving Camp Claiborne, their troops trained as glider men. The parachute regiments did not join the two divisions until they reached Fort Bragg. After moving to North Carolina, Captain Cox and his antiaircraft battalion continued an intense training program consisting of unit drills, physical training, weapons training and firing, glider loading, and flights. Much of the training was done away from Fort Bragg, in places like Camp Davis for antiaircraft firing and Laurinburg-Maxton Air Base and Camp Mackall, North Carolina, for glider training. Next, Cox's unit participated in the second Army maneuvers in Tennessee.

The glider men, like the paratroopers, trained for action behind enemy lines, and operating in an isolated position with light weapons only. The difference between the glider and the parachute units was that the glider troop squads were expected to land in their target area intact if they survived the landing, whereas paratroop squads ran the risk of being widely scattered. Whether they reached the landing zone by parachute or glider, the airborne troops faced a high-risk situation when they operated behind enemy lines.

During World War II, paratroopers and glider men alike had little control over their destiny once they were airborne. The paratroopers were practically helpless while they floated down into hostile territory, especially if they missed their drop zone. The glider men, on the other hand, were trapped in a vulnerable, lightweight, and difficult-to-control aircraft until they landed. The glider's light frame and canvas shell provided little protection from gunfire, and their safe landing depended totally on the skill and luck of their pilots. As a result, many of the men, most of whom had never flown before, wanted to leave the glider units to which they had been forcibly assigned. Some men even preferred to join the paratroopers rather than become "glider riders." Despite the hazards inherent in this assignment, the glider men received no special pay like the paratroopers, nor were they allowed to wear the distinctive jump boots that had become the symbol of the paratroopers. Conditions for the glider men did not change until after the Normandy landings in July 1944.

Nevertheless, in spite of the drawbacks they faced, the glider men did not lose their sense of humor. Some of the glider men circulated their own homemade poster through their camps, which included photos of wrecked gliders and the following:

Join the Glider Troops!
No Flight Pay—No Jump Pay—
But Never a Dull Moment

The Glider Pilots

In 1942, the gliders were not ready for the newly created infantry regiments, and therefore there was a shortage of trained pilots. The army tried to rectify the problem by creating a large pool of glider pilots. Most of them were offered only the rank of staff sergeant, until November, when the rank of flight officer was authorized. Another disadvantage was that these pilots were not trained to operate with the infantry they carried once they landed behind enemy lines. Since they were considered a valuable commodity, they were expected to go back to the rear area, where they were to undertake various duties until they could be evacuated from the battlefield. Despite their skill and value, like the glider men, the pilots received no flight pay until 1944.

The first official glider pilot was S. Sgt. William T. Sampson, who earned his wings on June 28, 1942. Another glider pilot, Bill McFadden, remembers well his training sessions.

> Our classes seemed to never end: hand-to-hand combat, meteorology, navigation, chemical warfare, close-order drill, and physical training. After advanced training in the CG-4A at Lubbock, Texas, we were appointed flight officers.
>
> I had accumulated almost 200 hours of powered flight and had almost 300 glider flights, which included day and night precision landings. In dead-stick training, we took off in a light plane from a dirt field, would fly to a given altitude, turn off the ignition, and watch the propeller slow to a stop in front of our eyes. This indoctrinated us in what could be done without power.
>
> When you release the towrope on a glider, the sound dies away. You sit there in the quiet, under a Plexiglas canopy. At night, the stars are winking all around you. It's magical. I would sing all my favorite songs at the top of my lungs. What an assignment!

Another glider pilot, Charles V. Gauntt from Fort Worth, Texas, was drafted in November 1941 at the age of twenty-three. One of the first notices calling for volunteers for glider pilot training caught his eye in 1942. Enticed by the prospect of a promotion to staff sergeant within ninety days, he signed up and took the physical. Next, he went for his primary training to Fort

Morgan, Colorado, where he stayed until mid-August. He began flying on June 1, 1942. From Colorado, his class was sent to Twentynine Palms, California, the primary basic-training base at the time.

> They had a lot of Schweitzers, a soaring plane. It was a two-passenger plane, and you never got into it without an instructor. I stayed there until the middle of September 1942. At that time, we didn't have any CG-4A gliders, so in October 1942, they sent us to Stuttgart, Kentucky. I don't know when they opened, but when I arrived, the enlisted men were doing all kinds of manual work. We were all staff sergeants and we were under a Captain Slaughter. We had to do KP. We had this one staff sergeant who did not show up to do the pots and pans for KP. He said that NCOs do not do KP according to rules and regulations. He was told that if he didn't get over to that kitchen in five minutes, he wouldn't be an NCO.

When Gauntt graduated from Fort Sumner, New Mexico, as a flight officer, he was transferred to Bowman Field in Louisville, Kentucky, which happened to be the same base where he had done his infantry basic training. Then, between May and June 1943, Gauntt's group was sent to Fort Knox for additional infantry training, practice on the rifle range, and throwing live grenades. During the first week of July, Gauntt received orders to report to Pope Field, North Carolina, to join the 435th Troop Carrier Group.

Lambert Wilder, from Bogota, New Jersey, was already twenty-seven years old when he volunteered for military service in June 1942. Like Gauntt, he saw the call for glider pilots, and within seven days of reporting for active duty at Mitchell Field, Long Island, he became a staff sergeant. He underwent his primary training at Antigo, Wisconsin, where he trained on powered aircraft. The pilots practiced dead-stick landings, which consisted of cutting the engine and bringing the aircraft in for a landing. After graduating from Antigo, Wilder's group was sent to Mobile, Alabama, to train with the Schweitzers, the craft that Gauntt had used in his training. Like many fellow northerners, Wilder thought that summers in the South were "hotter than hell." The fact that they had left Wisconsin in the winter and had no summer uniforms made matters worse. According to Wilder, the entire glider-training program was riddled with problems.

> There were a lot of hang-ups in this program. I think I was in eight or ten bases before I graduated. After that, I went to Blockburne, Ohio, and we sat around there a while and didn't do anything until we were transferred to Smyrna, Tennessee. That turned out to be a B-24 outfit, and they didn't have any gliders. Some of us managed to get copilot time in a B-24, which I did not like. Next, we were shipped to Stuttgart, Arkansas, where we got our final advanced training in a CG-4. I think that was in September 1942. When we arrived at Stuttgart, it was a newly built base and not finished. The EM [enlisted men] were doing all kinds of manual work. We had a terrific rain that flooded the field, and they sent everybody home for two weeks. At Stuttgart, you had to fight for airspace with the ducks. The reason there were so many ducks there is that it was in rice country. Some people ran into ducks, but I don't recall any fatal accidents.

Wilder remained in Stuttgart until January 1, 1943, when it was decided that there were too many trainees at that location. About 120 men, including Wilder, were transferred to California. The week the group arrived at Bakersfield, the town was drenched in heavy rains that left it under six feet of water. About two or three weeks later, the first sergeant asked Wilder if he were ready to ship out. Wilder and about thirty of his comrades were sent to Fort Sumner, New Mexico. A week after that, ten of them transferred to Lubbock, Texas. Later, Wilder and his group found out that the men who had remained at Bakersfield had washed out and gone back to their old units. Wilder finally graduated at Fort Sumner, in the middle of April 1943.

Lambert Wilder's assignments closely paralleled Gauntt's. He too went on to Louisville for additional weapons training and classroom instruction at Bowman Field. Both men were surprised with a twenty-five-mile hike in the intolerable heat, and in both cases, their instructors followed them and their fellow pilots in training in jeeps for about half an hour on the march. Also like Gauntt, Wilder was assigned to the 435th Troop Carrier Group, stationed at Pope Field. The pilots in the group were sent to various parts of the United States to bring back their new gliders. Shortly after that, the group shipped out for England.

William Knickerbocker, a twenty-five-year-old Californian, was drafted in September 1941, becoming an infantryman at Camp Roberts. After Pearl Harbor, he was reassigned to the Signal Corps. Early in the summer of 1942, like the others, he too responded to a notice calling for volunteers for glider pilot training. The new assignment was more to his liking, because he had a private pilot's license and wanted out of the Signal Corps. He was sent to Plainview, Texas, for basic glider training, and then to Fort Sumner for primary glider training. After that, he trained in a CG-4A at Victorville, California. He did his primary glider training in a Cessna.

> We had a Taylor craft and a Piper Cub with the engine removed, and we flew them as gliders. We also had one Schweitzer. We took our primary glider training in that, and then on to Victorville. We were graduated there. I was lucky, because most glider pilots were left there for months before being transferred to an active outfit. I was sent to Louisville and assigned to the 315th Troop Carrier Group.

The first glider pilots from the class of 1942 completed their training and reported to their units in 1943. Some, like Flight Officer Knickerbocker, were sent overseas almost immediately to support the 82nd A/B Division; others were assigned to units still in the States. The pilots assigned to transport the troops of the 101st A/B Division had little time to train with the division before they too shipped out. Gliders and pilots were in short supply between 1942 and early 1943, and the glider regiments of the first two airborne divisions did not have the time to complete their training.

CHAPTER 7

Training and Equipping the Ground Troops

The Rangers

While the American 1st Ranger Battalion trained in Great Britain, a new program for Rangers was established in the United States. The training for this highly select group of men was as demanding as the one for the airborne troops, if not more so. The Rangers realized that they were expected to penetrate the enemy lines in difficult or almost impassable terrain, which required a great deal of endurance.

As William Darby's 1st Ranger Battalion took part in the invasion of Algeria, where it was attached to the 1st Infantry Division, a call went out for more volunteers back home. Of the men who were sent for Ranger training, only about 500 were selected to form the 2nd Ranger Battalion in April 1943.

James W. Eikner, the battalion's soon-to-be signal officer, had been rejected in the 1940 draft because of dental problems. Later, however, he took part in one of the Rangers' boldest and most celebrated exploits in World War II, the assault on Pointe du Hoc, Normandy. Eikner recalls when his draft number came up:

> I was one of the first people to be drafted. Some government official reached into the fishbowl and grabbed the numbers, and as luck would have it, he got my number on the second draw. I was living in Houston, Texas, at the time and working for the telephone company. Some of my fellow workers came in, and they were laughing. They had a copy of the newspaper, and they said good-bye. I asked, "What's the matter?" and they said to look here at the headline: "Houston Man First to Be Drafted," and there I was.
>
> I had signed up for the draft in my hometown in Mississippi and laughed that they would never find us in this little country courthouse, but they did. I was called up reasonably soon for my physical. The doctor examining me said I had an ill-fitting dental plate, and I told him it was a temporary plate and that my good plate was being repaired. He replied, "We only want good specimens." I said, "Hell, Doc, I don't want to bite them, I want to fight them!"[1] He replied that he was going to give me a 1-B classification, and he turned me down.

Disgruntled, James Eikner returned to work with the telephone company, but more than a year later, the situation changed.

Gen. Charles H. Gerhardt, commander of the 29th Infantry Division, swims a pond on his horse, September 23, 1942.
NATIONAL ARCHIVES

> Along came Pearl Harbor, my birthday. I was having a birthday dinner when the news came, so I said I had to go. I called the army, and they said they could not do a thing as long as the draft board had me, so I called the navy. The marine and navy recruiters both informed me that they could do nothing for me for the same reason. I talked to the people at the draft board several times.
>
> Finally I was called up for another examination, which was just a farce. They had a bunch of us strip in the old Herman Building in Houston, and it was cold as hell. We had to wait there forever, it seemed. The doctors came in and set up their little kits on apple crates. Nobody got completely through the line. The doctor looking at me

1. This seems to have been an often-used response during the war.

was interested in the instep of my foot. I informed him that they turned me down for my teeth. The doctor said, "You boys look like you are healthy, so that is it; put your clothes on." They gave us a 1-A classification. One boy there had a peg leg, and he wound up in San Antonio, where they finally rejected him. I was called up, and I went down to Dodd Field, the induction center in San Antonio [in March 1942].

I remember doing KP for 1,000 people, and it was rough. I had a medical problem, and the doctor said he could keep me out, while the telephone company also said that I was in an essential job, but I wanted to go. From the induction center, I went to Camp Barkeley in Abilene, Texas, to join the 90th Infantry Division, and in short order, I rose from private to buck sergeant in the headquarters company. I put in for the Signal Corps. On the basis of my IQ, they sent me to OCS. Time passed, and I decided I wanted to go to the infantry and not the Signal Corps after I graduated from Fort Benning in the fall of 1942. They sent me to Camp Forrest, Tennessee, to the newly activated 80th Division. Here I was, a trained infantry officer, but when they discovered that I had been at the telephone company, they made me the commo [communications] officer.

The first Ranger training school was set up by Colonel Saffarns. It was set up just up the street from my operations. We used to laugh at those boys with all the broken legs and arms from the training. After the school was over, old General Lear decided to organize a Ranger battalion, and they asked for volunteers. At the time, I was a first lieutenant communications officer in the 80th Infantry Division. When the call went out for volunteers, I made application . . . my chief interest was in infantry tactics, and I thought this would give me an opportunity to break away from communications. As to a selection process, this was just an interview by a staff officer and a review of my record. The 2nd Ranger Battalion began to organize on April 1, 1943, and I was one of the first members to join. Some lieutenants were handling all the inductees and making assignments. They made me an assistant S-3. When the commo officer came down with a bad hernia and had to go to the hospital, they stuck me back into commo. I stayed there all through the training in the States and into Europe.

We went through several commanding officers, and it did not seem any of them knew what to do with this type of unit. Finally we received James Rudder, who was just right for the job.

The standard training for the rangers at Camp Forrest was heavy on physical endurance, weapons expertise, tactics, both battalion and small units, motivation, to name a few. On a standard day, after reveille, we would take a mile run, eat breakfast, next about one hour of heavy calisthenics, and then into specific training: hand-to-hand combat, knife fighting, bayonet practice, handling explosives, training on all infantry weapons, running obstacle courses, some with live fire. We usually found time for a five-mile speed hike three days per week, a couple of nine-mile speed hikes twice per week, wind up with a twenty-five miler for Saturday morning, and get back to camp in time for lunch. One time, we pulled off a sixty-five miler, about half across-country on compass. My little communications section tied the commando world record of seven and a half miles per hour for sustained march—damned near killed the old man, but we made it.

We were not located in an area where we could have any real mountain training, and no one knew what type of mission we would be assigned. We did have some cliff climbing, and I remember the long hike out to a place where there was a sheer cliff that was undercut. We had several men wash out there—just refused to go. We also did a lot of stream crossing by constructing rope bridges or using our shelter halves to float on. In addition, we ran an obstacle course with live ammo, and the machine guns fired low enough over your head to hit you if you got up too high.

Everyone was expected to become expert in all types of infantry weapons. They made me the pistol instructor, because they said I should know about that because I was from Texas.

The 2nd Ranger Battalion was activated in April 1943, the first Ranger battalion to be formed on U.S. soil. It was followed by the 5th Ranger, created at Camp Forrest. In the meantime, their sister battalions, the 1st and 3rd Rangers, were already in action in North Africa. The Ranger School at Camp Forrest, Tennessee, set up in January 1943, was partially modeled after a marine combat training center in California. The school ran a two-week training course. Several NCOs from Darby's Rangers were assigned to train the men from other units. Initially the volunteers were sent back to their units after training, but General Lear, the commander of the second Army, decided before long that it was not practical to take the men away from their regular training duties.[2] As a result, a new Ranger battalion was created on April 1. Hundreds of volunteers came and went until a contingent with the required qualifications was selected. The battalion, housed in a tent city to toughen the men, went through a stringent training course. Lt. Col. William Saffarns, who organized the two-week training course and ran the school until he was needed elsewhere, was the first of a succession of officers assigned to command the newly formed 2nd Ranger Battalion. Maj. James

The 2nd Ranger Battalion

The 2nd Ranger Battalion included a Headquarters Company and six line companies: A, B, C, D, E, and F. There was no standard table of organization and equipment, since equipment and personnel were added or removed to fit the situation.

The Headquarters Company consisted of about ninety-five men, including the battalion commander and staff (S-1, S-2, S-3, S-4, and XO), a medical officer, a communications officer, a transportation officer, and the headquarters commandant. It had several sections: personnel, supply, intelligence and operations, communications, transportation, mess, medical detachment, cannon, and later, a special service section.

The line companies were each led by a company commander and two platoon leaders and numbered about sixty-two enlisted men, divided into two platoons, which were further divided into two rifle squads and a mortar section. Each company was equipped with a BAR in each rifle squad and 60-millimeter mortars in the mortar section. The rifle squads consisted of five to eight men and the mortar section of five men with a mortar.

2. Gen. Ben Lear was born in 1879, served in the Spanish American War and World War I, and was in his sixties when World War II began. From 1940 to 1943, he commanded the 2nd Army. From 1941 until 1943, he was involved mainly with defense of the United States and training units under the 2nd Army for overseas duty. He was retired because of mandatory age requirements in 1943 but recalled soon after. When Gen. Leslie McNair was killed in Normandy in July 1944, Lear replaced him as commander of the Army Ground Force that handled training and doctrine. After the war, he was again retired.

Rail movement at Fort Benning, 1943. NATIONAL ARCHIVES

Rudder, a former Texas schoolteacher and coach, took over at the end of June 1943, and stayed with the unit through the war until late 1944, when he was promoted to command a regiment.

In September 1943, as the 5th Rangers formed at Camp Forrest, the 2nd Ranger Battalion shipped out for Fort Pierce, Florida, for amphibious training at the naval Scouts and Raiders School, where it conducted exercises with rubber assault rafts. Late that year, the battalion departed for Fort Dix, New Jersey, and embarked for England in November 1943.

The Ground Pounders

As a rule, the men who volunteered for military service had a better chance of avoiding infantry duty than those who were drafted. Such was the case for twenty-two-year-old Floyd West of Portia, Arkansas, who enlisted on January 26, 1942, to beat the draft and get an assignment he liked. After signing up, he was sent to Camp Robinson near Little Rock, Arkansas, where he was sworn in the next day. Before long, he boarded a train bound for Camp Lee near Petersburg, Virginia, to join the Quartermaster Corps. In early March, after having trained for eight weeks, the last four in a workshop, he was ordered to prepare for shipping out for overseas duty.

> I was sent to Fort Slocum, New York, an island off the shore of New Rochelle. I was there a short while, and then transferred to Fort Hamilton in Brooklyn. We would fall out to be loaded on trucks, and we would wait and wait, and it would be canceled, and we would be assigned to volunteer duty over in New York City. This amounted to little jobs that didn't amount to much, but we got to see the city. We could have the day to spend any way we cared to. We could take a dime and five cents, and it would take us on the subway to downtown New York. We could do anything we liked

for free, as long as we were in uniform. We would have to spend the other nickel to get back to base. We had quite a good time in New York.

When the time came that we did fall out to go overseas, they began calling names starting with the A's and going down through the alphabet, as they needed men. They got down to VWXYZ, and they had all the men the ship had room to hold. My name being West, I was left behind. The rest went on. It wasn't but a few days until I was called, and I got on the trucks and we went down to the railway station. We were loaded on a train and were shipped to Boston, Massachusetts. At Boston, we were loaded onto a small ship.

West's trip began at the end of April 1942. Much later, he joined the 1st Division, which took part in extensive amphibious operations off the Virginia coast at the time he was still training early in 1942. The 1st "Big Red One" Division was constantly on the move that year. From Virginia, it went to Camp Blanding, Florida, in February; to Fort Benning, Georgia; to Indiantown Gap, Pennsylvania, at the end of June; and finally to New York in August. It was preparing to embark for overseas when West joined it.

In Southbridge, Massachusetts, Albert Mominee received a draft notice directing him to report for a physical examination. He had already tried to enlist in the navy before the outbreak of the war, but he had failed the physical because he was too short. The minimum height required by the navy was five feet, four inches. The army's physical qualifications, on the other hand, were much less exacting.

I passed quite easily; being a member of the YMCA and the gymnastics team was certainly a factor for me being in such good shape. I feared my height, which was five feet, one inch, might hurt my chances of passing, but now it was different because we were at war. The minimum was five feet, so I was accepted with open arms.

After spending a couple weeks at Fort Devens, Massachusetts, just long enough for me to get my clothing allowance and get my shots, I left by train for Camp Croft in South Carolina, where I received my basic training, which took about thirteen weeks. By the second week of June 1942, with basic training completed, I left Camp Croft for Indiantown Gap, Pennsylvania, to become a member of the 1st Infantry Division.

In the fall of 1942, Sgt. Herman Byram was ordered to leave his ROTC assignment at Ouachita College in Arkansas and report for OCS at Fort Benning. He graduated as a second lieutenant in class 192 on December 8 and was assigned to the 2nd Infantry Division at Camp McCoy, Wisconsin, where he was placed in the Division Headquarters Company. Here he remained until July 1943, when he took command of a platoon in the 9th Infantry.

Before the war, the 2nd "Indian Head" Division had been stationed in Texas, where it did most of its training.[3] It had also participated in exercises in the Louisiana maneuver area. The division moved to Camp McCoy, Wisconsin, in late 1942, and then to Iron River, Michigan, for a thirty-day ski maneuver in early 1943. Individual members of each of the division's regiments were sent to Michigan to train as ski instructors, lead-

3. The 2nd Division was a regular army formation, which was used before the war to experiment with the triangular type organization of three regiments. Other regular divisions like the 1st and the 3rd were employed in amphibious exercises before the war and the 4th was converted into a motorized division (and later changed back when it was found a poor use of transportation resources).

Elements of the 30th Infantry Division board a troop train early in the war. Note the bed-pan helmets still in use in early 1942.
NATIONAL ARCHIVES

ing most of the soldiers to conclude that they were bound for the upcoming Italian campaign. "I put in my required eight-hour skiing as well as I could," Lieutenant Byram recalls, "and finally they told me I had to go out again because doing it in the company area didn't count. We skied up and down a little hill there all day long. When we got to the bottom, I would be on my bottom! There were no trees there, except every time I started to ski, I would find some. The next morning, I was so sore I couldn't get out of bed; I had to roll out."

Finally, in October 1943, the 2nd Division moved east to Camp Shanks and embarked at New York for the sea voyage to the British Isles.

After the attack on Pearl Harbor, Sgt. Tom Cortright and his platoon were sent to guard a blanket factory in Lebanon, Tennessee, where they were quartered at the local fire station. A fortnight later, they were ordered back to Camp Forrest.

> Training was intensified, and recruiting for OCS and cadres for another division went out. The 33rd was purged of NCOs. I went to Fort Benning, graduated in August 1942 from OCS class 52, and was assigned to the 4th Motorized Division at Camp Gordon, Georgia. On reporting to the division, I was assigned to the 12th Infantry Regiment's AT Company. This company was commanded by an intense reserve officer whom the men alternately called "Wild Bill" or "The Whip." He was doing his job and was fair, and before long, I was a first lieutenant based on his recommendation.

Lieutenant Cortright arrived in time to witness the demotorization of the 4th "Ivy" Division. According to Walter Conrad of the 8th Infantry Regiment, "In 1942, we were given half-tracks and went into the Carolinas for training and testing the equipment. Upon returning from the Carolinas, the half-tracks were taken away from us, and we reverted to foot troops." The division returned from the Carolina maneuvers in August. In late 1942, as the armored divisions were reorganized in the aftermath of the North African campaign, it was decided to eliminate the motorized divisions. Each infantry division retained enough vehicles, however, to keep it relatively mobile compared with most European infantry divisions.[4] The 4th Division was redesignated as an infantry division early in 1943.

Harper Harvey Coleman of Shippensburg, Pennsylvania, joined the 4th Division in a roundabout way. He had tried to enlist in the Army Air Force during the summer of 1942. Even though he was twenty years old and worked at a furniture store as a salesman and truck deliveryman, his parents persuaded him not to enlist. About three months later, on October 2, he received his draft notice. He was inducted on October 16 and joined a group of other inductees on a chartered bus bound for the New Cumberland Army Induction Center, near Harrisburg. Coleman was one of those recruits that wound up doing their basic training with a newly formed division.

> On arrival at the center, we lined up for a count, and we were taken to a building for our new outfit. Starting at one end and going to the other, with all new clothing—one size fits all!—blanket, shoes, and all the things we would need. The last item being a box in which to pack everything—clothing, etc.—to send home, as we were not allowed to have civilian belongings.
>
> We were at the center for two or three days, in which there were many interviews, additional medical exams, and shots to be had, and then to the barbershop for the famous GI haircut. During our stay there, we were shown the proper way to make up the bunk. If a quarter did not bounce off the blanket, it was torn up, and you started over until it was right. In addition, while there, everyone was classified to an army occupation specialty. Almost everyone was classified infantry.
>
> After two or three days, we marched, with all equipment, to the rail yards down along the Susquehanna River, where we loaded in passenger cars. We did not know our destination. All window shades had to be kept down. After some time, we knew we were headed west, as we were going around the Horseshoe Curve at Altoona, Pennsylvania.
>
> We arrived at a camp, which we were told was Camp Atterbury, Indiana. This was a new camp and not yet completed. Most of the buildings were finished, but the streets consisted of mud or dust, depending on the weather. The barracks were two floors, forty men to a floor. This was the home of the 83rd Infantry Division, now being activated. I was assigned to Company M, 331st Regiment. Most of the cadre was cavalry soldiers who had lost their horses not long before and were not very happy about it. They were a close group and did not want any part of a bunch of new recruits. After we were settled in, life was somewhat routine. We had clothes altered to fit—almost! In

4. Some European armies, such as the British, Italian, Soviet, and German, used motorized divisions. In the German Army, the regular infantry divisions relied heavily on horses.

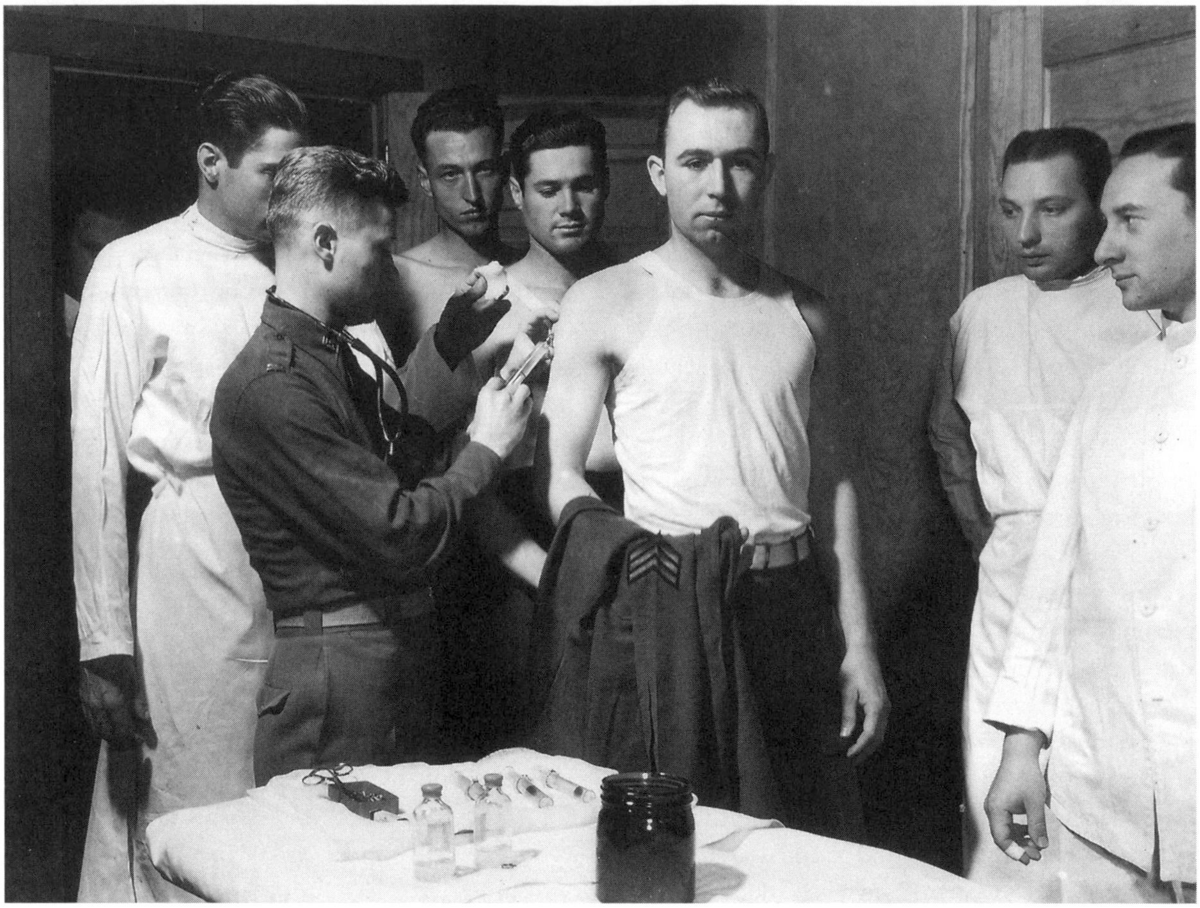

Troops receive injections at Fort Benning. NATIONAL ARCHIVES

addition, we were issued additional equipment, weapons, and other items.

The day's schedule was to rise at 5 in the morning, with about one hour to shower, shave, and make the bed. After this, there was a fall-out for roll call and instructions for the day. Following roll call, there was breakfast with never enough time. There was a noon break with a meal and mail call. In the evening, it would be retreat formation at 5 P.M., with evenings generally free and lights out at 10 P.M. The days were at first mostly made up of close-order drill, with and without weapons. Being in a heavy-weapons company, we did many days' training with the .30-caliber water-cooled machine gun. This was a six-man squad: a gunner, assistant gunner, and four ammo carriers. Everyone in the squad was required to know how to do everything from assembly and setup to firing. There were many hours of this, including cleaning, sometimes blindfolded. The gunner and assistant gunner were issued .45 automatic pistols, while the ammo carriers were issued carbines.

There were always Saturday morning inspections. This implied most of Friday night cleaning the barracks and equipments. Our sergeant's favorite saying was "House guys might never make good soldiers, but you sure as hell will make good barracks cleaners." We were made to clean the floor with toothbrushes until 1 or 2 in the morning. If we were lucky enough to pass the Saturday morning inspection, we generally had the rest of the day off. There were several theaters close by, also enlisted men's club, which generally had some kind of entertainment on weekends. Each company had its own dayroom that could be used for some activities.

After some weeks, we got into serious training. There was much physical training, long marches, with and without equipment. We had to learn how to assemble and disassemble all weapons blindfolded and to memorize the serial number of our weapons, our army serial number, and our general orders, as you could be, and were, stopped at any time and asked questions. Then there was guard duty and KP, which everyone had to do some of the time. Anyone doing KP was required to put a white towel on the bottom of his bunk so the duty sergeant would get him out in time in the morning (about 3 A.M.). There were obstacle courses of many designs—crawl in the mud, under wire with machine-gun fire over your head, also the usual up-and-down rope climb. There were many days on the range firing live ammunition and many days of going into the field with full equipment for training exercise, rain or shine or snow. The weather in Indiana can get very cold, with much snow, and there were many days like this. There were always foxholes to be dug every time we would stop for any length of time. In addition, being in a heavy-weapons company, there had to be a place for the machine guns, which required quite a large hole to be dug.

On one occasion, the division went by convoy to West Virginia (Parkersburg), where we stood guard along a section of railroad. There were two passenger trains that went by that night. We were told later that President Roosevelt was a passenger on one of them. In the morning, when everyone was picked up along the tracks, several of us were missed. We hitchhiked back to the base camp in Parkersburg, and I do not recall why they did not pick us up.

There were also some weekend passes to Indianapolis and one furlough home, February 22 to March 1, 1943. I took a steam train from Indianapolis to Harrisburg and hitchhiked to Shippensburg.

Coleman returned to Camp Atterbury for more training. Then he participated in the second Army's 1943 summer Tennessee maneuvers.

The division left Camp Atterbury by motor convoys during June 1943. We arrived in an area near Murfreesboro. The maneuver area was south of the Tennessee River, west of the area of Smithville, south near Manchester and west near Columbia. During this time, about six to eight weeks, we were living in the field. All equipment was carried, including machine-gun and blank ammunition. We lived in two-man tents or out in the open most of the time. Our food for the most part was K rations. Some meals were provided by our kitchen, if time and conditions permitted, and most often at night in the dark.

These maneuvers involved the red and blue units chasing each other all over this part of the state's backroads and hills—there seemed to be plenty of these. At the time, I did not know much about Tennessee. However, we had one person in our company who lived in the area of Smithville, and he kept us well informed. Any time we got close to his home, he would take off and come back with all the fried chicken he could carry. He also knew all the bootleggers in the area and kept the company well supplied with white lightning in pint jars. One of the best things to do was to get a white flag early on any day. This meant we

The 29th Infantry Division at Fort Benning. NATIONAL ARCHIVES

had most of the day to ourselves. On one occasion, after we received a white flag early in the morning, we took our jeep and went on a short sightseeing trip. We were near Kentucky and brought back some good watermelons.

At the completion of the maneuvers, half the division was given leave for seven to ten days in September. The other half moved to Fort Campbell, Kentucky, by foot. They walked most of the way, with some truck rides on and off. I was in that half that went on leave. After leave, I reported back to Fort Campbell, but I was not there very long. One of the highlights while there was a truck trip to Mammoth Cave. At this time, quite a few of the personnel of the 83rd Division were taken to other units. Most of us were sent to the 4th Infantry Division.

Coleman joined the 4th Division at Camp Gordon Johnson near Carabelle on the Gulf of Mexico. He had traveled with other soldiers by train from Kentucky to Tallahassee, Florida, where they were met by trucks and taken to the camp. He was then assigned to Company H, 2nd Battalion, 8th Infantry, and began amphibious training. The men jumped on and off Higgins boats in the Gulf of Mexico and took the landing craft back to the camp's beaches. They also had other forms of training, such as long hikes.

> One hike was for twenty-five miles in less than seven hours. Quite a few did not make this all the way, but I did. One of the incidents was in the Gulf of Mexico, off Dog Island. We had gone out one night, the day before Thanksgiving, and storms came up. The LCVPs were separated in the storm. The next day, the Coast Guard found our craft along with two others. We were headed toward Mexico, or so they told us. That was Thanksgiving Day 1943. They turned us around and took us back.
>
> After some time, in December, we left there and went to Fort Jackson, South

> Carolina. We were there only a few weeks, mostly to get new equipment and clothing. I did some guard duty and had a few times in town. Early in January 1944, we were sent to Camp Kilmer.

The 29th Division completed its guard duty and exercises on the Virginia coast in the winter months of early 1942. In March, this National Guard division reorganized as a triangular formation with three regiments. As a result, its fourth regiment, the 176th Infantry, was detached and sent to guard Washington, D.C. Gen. Leonard T. Gerow became the new divisional commander.[5]

The 29th "Blue & Gray" Division consisted of guardsmen from Pennsylvania, Maryland, and Virginia. The men settled at Camp A. P. Hill, where they underwent two additional months of training in the sweltering summer heat in this heavily wooded part of eastern Virginia. According to the hapless soldiers, it was the chigger capital of Virginia. Rows upon rows of eight-man pyramidal tents were planted in the clearings of the pine forest and swamps surrounding the camp.

In July, the division went to the Carolinas for maneuvers with the 4th and 36th Divisions. Walter Condon from Worcester, Massachusetts, who had joined the 29th Division in April 1942, was with the division at Camp A. P. Hill and in the Carolinas. For the young northerner, this stay in the South was a veritable eye-opener. The southern climate was quite oppressive for those used to milder summers. In addition, the sight of large numbers of African Americans and the notorious southern prison chain gangs toiling in the fields was quite shocking—even to John Slaughter, a Virginian. After weeks of misery in the searing heat and choking red dust, the division joined the 36th Division at Camp Blanding, Florida, which turned out to be a surprising improvement, according to Slaughter: "It was a beautiful setting: white-sand beach and crystal-clear Kingston Lake. Jacksonville was close by and the home of my sergeant, Jimmy L. Hamlin. He invited some of us for a night on the town. We had dinner at the Roosevelt Hotel, then went to a dance in the ballroom. I had never been to a place like that—crystal chandeliers, Oriental carpets, excellent food and drink. It couldn't last."

Several smaller elements of the 29th Division had already been scattered. Some troops from the engineer battalion were attached to another outfit and sent to the Pacific. Walter Condon was in the engineer battalion, most of whose men came from New England, Pennsylvania, and Ohio. It had a cadre of 29ers. Condon remained at Camp Blanding with much of the 121st Engineer Battalion until the 29th Division left that post. Meanwhile, the artillery battalions of the 29th boarded a train for Fort Sill for additional training. The division commander was ordered to prepare an infantry regiment to replace the demonstration unit at the Infantry School at Fort Benning. It was feared for a while that the division would be cannibalized to support other formations, but these concerns turned out to be unfounded.

After General Gerow notified his unit commanders on September 6, 1942, that the division was shipping out for overseas duty, a massive recall effort began. It was no simple task to retrieve the advance elements of the division artillery, which had already reached Fort Sill. Sound trucks cruised through the streets, ordering the troopers out on pass to hurry back to Camp Blanding, and shows in local theaters were interrupted so the loudspeaker could broadcast the call. It was time to say good-bye. Some of the soldiers had to part from families that had come

5. General Gerow was in George Marshall's War Plans Division in late 1941. He was called before Congress in the Pearl Harbor investigation, where he claimed the staff had failed. He was then given command of the 29th Division, and a year later, he took command of V Corps, which would conduct the landings at Omaha Beach.

Brig. Gen. Omar N. Bradley turns over command of Fort Benning and the Infantry School to Brig. Gen. Levin Allen. Allen would later become chief of staff for Bradley's 12th Army Group in France. NATIONAL ARCHIVES

to Florida to be with them, others from friends or sweethearts they had come to know in the area. As the troop trains pulled away from Camp Blanding, the soldiers of the 29th and their tearful wives and girlfriends on the station platform waved their final farewells.

The division arrived at Camp Kilmer, New Jersey, on September 20. It was the first major formation to use this camp in preparation for overseas duty. Encircled by a high fence topped with barbed wire, it was unlike any other camp John Slaughter had seen. But Slaughter had no intention of letting his last days on American soil go to waste.

> Kilmer was an East Coast embarkation post. Barbed wire enclosed the entire area, and military police patrolled from the outside. No one was allowed into the camp; those inside were not allowed out.
>
> Cpl. Richard W. Owensby of Roanoke had been on a war bond solicitation drive in Newark and said he really knew his way around town. He guaranteed me a good time if I went with him. We both knew the consequences if we were caught. Having dressed in our finest uniforms, we climbed over the fence that separated us from Owensby's description of "a night on the town." We hired a Checker Cab and were on our way to a nightspot in town. I've never forgotten that night of eating, drinking, and wandering around, lost. We decided we'd had enough, and it was getting very late. As we departed the cab, we could see Company D already in reveille formation. Knowing we would be reported absent and that Captain Schilling probably would skin us alive, we made up a tale of playing cards at Service Company. We tiptoed into the barracks, and First Sergeant Obenshain was waiting. With hands on hips, he asked us where in the hell we had been. In unison we answered, "Playing cards at Service Company." He then said, "You've just lost your ass!" The first sergeant took Owensby by the arm and jerked him roughly into the captain's office. In a few minutes, he and Schilling emerged, and I wanted to crawl under the table.
>
> I had never seen the captain so angry. He said, "Goddamn it, Slaughter, don't *you* lie to me! "He," said the captain, pointing to Owensby, "lied to me! I want to hear it from you. Just where have you two assholes been?" He told me that if I confessed, it might go easier. I knew my corporal stripes were gone. He had us dead to rights, and we both knew it. Confessing our sins and promising never to violate his trust again, we were sentenced on the spot to confinement to quarters until the captain could study the situation. Fortunately, the next day we were marching up the gangplank of the *Queen Mary* heading overseas.

In February 1942, the 1st Division went to Camp Blanding to join the 36th Division of the Texas National Guard. In the summer of 1942, the 36th Division took part in the IV Corps Carolina maneuvers with the 29th Division. At the time, PFC Bill Lewis had been in his company commander's bad graces, because he had been involved in a brawl in Orlando, Florida, and had sustained knife wounds before he managed to lay the man out. His injuries had required a stay in a private hospital in town. The upshot of the affair was that Capt. Sheldon Simpson, greatly put out, had kept him on his blacklist. Thus, at the earliest opportunity, the captain selected Bill Lewis and six other men—including Lewis's lifelong friend Ernest Lee, who was in another regiment—for "volunteer service." As the six men left their division for duty at Fort Ritchie, Maryland, little did they know that theirs was a plum assignment.

In 1943, the 36th "Texas" Division departed for North Africa to prepare for the invasion of Italy, while Lewis, Lee, and the other "volunteers" boarded a train at Greenville. After a nightlong ride, they got off at Fort Ritchie, where they joined 180 enlisted men from several divisions—including the 30th, 35th, and 36th—who had been sent to the Composite School Unit at the fort. This school trained mainly recruits from the East Coast of various ethnic backgrounds, such as Polish, German, and Italian, who later became known as the "Ritchie Boys." After they completed training, these soldiers were either integrated into other units or assigned to special intelligence teams. The draft boards had considered most of these immigrants, many of them Jews from German-speaking regions, as unreliable aliens only months before. After leaving Fort Ritchie, they were assigned to four-man interrogator of prisoner of war (IPW) teams, which each consisted of two NCOs and two officers and were attached to combat divisions. These IPW teams had jeeps and some specialized equipment. The Texans were sent to Fort Ritchie in 1943 to help the cadre impart to these immigrants basic military skills, including drill and courtesy. Life on the post was rather informal, however.

When Bill Lewis and his companions arrived, they were housed in pyramidal tents on concrete slabs. For Lewis, who had grown up in semiarid south Texas, the Blue Ridge Mountains towering over Fort Ritchie were the most beautiful sight he had ever beheld. To his surprise, the officers assigned to this special unit behaved in a very unmilitary manner. Eventually Lewis and his comrades moved into a new barracks in the mountains, where they were issued German uniforms and equipment. Between the end of July 1942 and February 1943, Bill Lewis, Ernest Lee, and the other "volunteers" were asked to demonstrate how a German field unit operated. Sporting enemy uniforms and small arms, antiaircraft guns, and field artillery, they rode German bicycles and motorcycles. Most of their large equipment was drawn by horses brought especially from Front Royal. Since these steeds had not been ridden in a long time, they had to be broken to the saddle once again. An old cavalry sergeant tried to convince the dubious troopers that they had nothing to fear from the half-broken, wild-eyed mounts, but he failed in this when one of the animals kicked him in the stomach. Once the horses were retrained, some ancient harness was unearthed for them, and the show was ready.

During the demonstrations, the entire group of more than 100 men took part in the act. Lewis and his comrades deployed their "German" unit in front of their audience and played out various scenarios. Sometimes, riding one of the team horses pulling a gun caisson, Lewis would gallop into an arena where bleachers were filled with officers from various units' S-2 and G-2 sections, showing them how the enemy operated. At other times, Lewis and his comrades unlimbered and limbered up the guns or came roaring onto the scene on motorcycles, kicking up a cloud of dust, followed by troops on bicycles.

A post exchange (PX) at Fort Benning. NATIONAL ARCHIVES

Except during rehearsals and demonstrations, Lewis and his comrades had little to do. Lee often exercised some of the sixty horses on the post. On one occasion, Lewis went to New York with another friend and came back several days late. Their commanding officer, who was very accommodating, was easily swayed into ignoring their escapade, the same way he treated infractions committed by others. Bill Lewis was also amazed at the lackadaisical attitude of the locals.

> Ernest Lee and I were in Gettysburg one time, and we pulled into a drive-in hamburger joint in full German uniform, jackboots, helmets, and things all over us. We went in and ordered a hamburger, and they brought it right out to us. We were waiting, sitting on our German motorcycle, with Ernest in the driver's seat and me in the sidecar. It was unbelievable that no one even asked, "What the hell you Germans doing here?"

The only mistake he and Ernest Lee made, Bill Lewis laments, was to request a transfer instead of sitting out the entire war at Fort Ritchie. Actually, he suspects the cadre wanted to get rid of some of the Texans, as they were encouraged to apply for transfers with promises of quick promotions. Bill Lewis was promoted from corporal to sergeant for agreeing to train about thirty of the "Ritchie Boys" and escort them to England. The men he trained became technical sergeants and master sergeants and went overseas to act as interpreters in IPW teams assigned to the 29th Infantry Division. Ernest Lee, G. T. Casner, Jack Hays, and J. Blanchard also volunteered to train this group and accompany it to England. (Except for Bill Lewis, all of these men became officers by the time the war ended.) En route, the group of sergeants was held up in Fort Hamilton, where they waited for a ship for several weeks. They took advantage of the opportunity to kick up their heels in New York with their charges, who showed them how to live it up. Soon, however, they were on their way to England.

Although the infantry was considered to be the "Queen of Battle" for much of the twentieth century, in World War II it needed, more than ever before, support from the artillery, the "King

Type 700 barracks, which were built at most military bases in the U.S. during the war. NATIONAL ARCHIVES

of Battle." Unfortunately, the U.S. artillery was not up to par on the eve of the war. The men who had joined the field artillery units before the war and until 1942 had to train on obsolete weapons. One of these young volunteers, Maynard E. Daggett of Waterville, Maine, enlisted on April 13, 1942. He was sent to Fort Devens, Maryland, where he joined long lines of men snaking through various stations. Here he received inoculations and a uniform, took intelligence tests, and was given physical exams. Within a short time, he was hustled onto a train bound for Fort Bragg, North Carolina. Daggett sent his civilian clothes home before he left Fort Devens, doubting he would need them in the near future.

Daggett underwent about seven weeks of basic training at Fort Bragg at the replacement training center, which he says was barely enough time to cover the basics. Nonetheless, his training was an improvement over the preparation artillerymen received before the war, when they reported to their assigned units and learned their skills on the job. At Fort Bragg, Daggett learned how to sight an artillery piece, load it, and set the elevation and deflection. He also learned how to handle a 105-millimeter artillery piece as well as small arms.

In the early summer, Daggett left for Fort Leonard Wood, Missouri, where he was assigned to the 978th Field Artillery Battalion, a Michigan National Guard outfit whose men mostly came from Detroit, Lansing, and Saginaw. Daggett was one of the many "fillers" assigned to bring the unit up to strength. The battalion artillery consisted of old French 155-millimeter GPF *(Grande Puissance Filloux)* guns. Like the old bedpan-style helmets, the guns were later replaced with the new, more effective 155-millimeter Long Toms.

> We trained on the old artillery pieces. I was assigned as a machine gunner and worked with the headquarters section of Battery A most of the time. Each gun crew had at least two men assigned to a machine gun. This was the advanced part of our training at Leonard Wood. I think there were ten or more men in the gun crew: ammo handlers, those that set the fuses, loading crew, one guy that fired the piece, and spare men as a backup.

The 155-Millimeter Field Artillery Battalion

The battery consisted of four artillery batteries with four guns each and a headquarters company, which included a fire control center, a survey section, and other battalion supporting services. There were only three officers in an artillery battery: the company commander and two officers who functioned as forward observers and assisted the commander in the battery area. The battery headquarters personnel included a first sergeant, mess sergeant, supply sergeant, and machine gunner. The machine gunner had no special assistant, but he was helped by one of the men not actively working on a gun crew. The machine gunner spent most of his time sending radio and telephone communications to the forward observer.

The advantage of the Long Tom over the old French GPF was that it was set up much more rapidly; otherwise there was little difference between the two guns, except the Long Tom had a range of 25,395 yards compared with the older weapon's 20,100 yards. On either side of the gun, two men with crowbars ratcheted the barrel forward, locked it, placed a large lug nut on its bottom to hold it forward, jacked up the front of the mount, and removed the back wheels in order to drop down and open the trails. It took about twenty minutes to setup a Long Tom, whereas the GPF took about twice that long.

During the firing operations of the 155-millimeter, fire control sent information about the mission of the battery and the type of shell to be fired. The gun had two types of powder charges: normal, which was used most of the time, and super. Two men, the loaders, carried the shell on a tray. Two more pushed it into the gun with a ramrod the same size as the shell. Two men took turns placing the powder charge in the breech. One of them stood ready, closed the breech, and screwed an adapter into the back of it that contained a special shell. Next, the gunner pulled a lanyard that released a flapper, which hit the firing pin behind the shell, igniting it. While the gunner, his ears plugged, stood at arm's length to pull the lanyard, the rest of the gun crew waited a safe distance away.

A fully tracked vehicle towed the Long Tom and carried the crew in addition to a driver and assistant driver who were not part of the gun crew. The vehicle also mounted a .50-caliber machine gun. An ammunition truck and trailer loaded with five to ten rounds followed the battery. The men of the gun crew carried the ammunition from the truck to the gunners. Everyone helped dig in and camouflage the gun. Each of the guns and the headquarters were assigned one machine gun that served as an antiaircraft and close-defense weapon.

At Fort Leonard Wood, several of the men in Daggett's battalion were trained to use TNT and other explosives. They also trained on obstacle courses and performed the long crawl while .30-caliber machine guns fired overhead. Although their training at Fort Leonard Wood was essentially the same as at Fort Bragg, it was more complete. Here Daggett first learned about gas on the battlefield.

> We went through gas chambers twice. They usually held meetings and passed out samples of what it smelled like. Just before the Tennessee maneuvers, we went out into an

open field with a little breeze. They set off hand grenades with mustard and phosgene in it, and we had to run through the smoke without gas masks. They used the real stuff. They said it was reduced in strength, but it would sure take your breath away if you tried to breathe it. Tear gas would make your eyes cry and hurt and burn your nose.

We had a lot of training on digging in 155-millimeter guns, foxholes, and machine-gun emplacements. An obstacle course was run everyday.

We went on to the Tennessee maneuvers, and I did think that was interesting. We were issued blank ammo and red or blue armbands. When you saw a red armband, you would yell, "Bang!" and he was supposed to be dead. They would set up the guns like in a real combat position.

After returning to Leonard Wood, we were sent off to the Desert Center in California for training. At that time, they had intentions of sending us to North Africa, so we stayed there over a month and a half.

Before it arrived in California, Daggett's battalion received its new 155-millimeter guns (M1A1) to replace the old 155-millimeter GPF model (M-1918M1). It spent the remainder of 1943 in the States.

The 35th "Santa Fe" Division, which included Dale Kearnes's 219th Field Artillery Battalion, prepared to move east in 1943. The division had been assigned to guard the California coast against a Japanese invasion the previous year, but it never materialized. During that time, this National Guard division changed from a square to a triangular organization. Its old French 75-millimeter guns of the 219th were replaced with 105-millimeter weapons.[6] The French guns of the other artillery battalions were also replaced with newer, American-made weapons. In early 1943, Dale Kearnes went to Camp Rucker, Alabama, with an advance party. The 35th Division soon followed.

That year, the 35th participated in the Tennessee maneuvers, and when the division engaged in the West Virginia maneuvers, it was snowing. During this time, Lt. Kenneth Jarvis, supply officer of the 1st Battalion, 137th Infantry, was sent to Camp Gordon, Georgia, to attend the Packaging and Crating School. "A captain and I were sent together," Jarvis recalls, "and then we went back to our outfits and instructed the supply officers and sergeants on how to prepare their equipment for overseas shipment." In addition to attending to his regular duties, Jarvis had to supervise the loading and unloading of his ship when the division departed the United States and arrived in Great Britain in the spring of 1944.

The Tank Men

When the armored divisions began expanding in 1942, recruits were urgently needed to fill the new divisions, independent armored battalions, and armored reconnaissance units. Although some men volunteered to serve in these mechanized units, the majority were assigned to them to fill vacant slots.

Robert T. Dove, one of the men who volunteered for military service in January 1942, went through basic training with a mechanized cavalry unit—Troop A, 6th Training Squadron Cavalry—at the Fort Riley, Kansas, Replacement Training Center. After basic, he was promoted to corporal

6. An infantry division (July 1943 table of organization and equipment) consisted of the divisional artillery of four battalions; three light battalions with three four-gun batteries of 105-millimeter howitzers; and one medium battalion with three four-gun batteries of 155-millimeter howitzers. The 155-millimeter Long Toms and other heavy weapons such as 8-inch guns were found in heavy artillery battalions attached to corps level or higher.

Completion of basic training at Camp Roberts, 1942. Left to right: Harrington, a Navajo nicknamed Chief, and Ray Hood.
PHOTO COURTESY OF RAY HOOD

and became a cadre instructor in Troop A, where he soon rose to the rank of sergeant. After two weeks of instruction, he also became the instructor for bayonet training and hand-to-hand combat. In the spring of 1943, he was sent to Cavalry OCS, where he underwent the same type of training he had given his own recruits when he had been an instructor. On July 1, 1943, eighty-six new cavalry lieutenants were commissioned, including Lieutenant Dove, who may be the only individual ever to have entered and completed OCS without passing a physical exam.

After enlisting in Los Angeles in January 1942, Dove failed his induction physical and those that followed, yet the doctors finally decided to drop his 4-F classification when they concluded that he was in better shape than most athletes were. Dove's lung capacity had been reduced by one-third after a bout of childhood pneumonia, and the operation that followed had caused his heart to shift slightly to the right, which mystified the doctors when they examined his X-rays. But the officers who sent him to OCS pulled some strings to make certain that he would never have to take a physical.

> We reported on Saturday morning, were given a made-up bunk, and were told to live out of our barracks bag. We were in a beautiful old barracks building at Fort Riley, Kansas. The post was "old cavalry," horses, stone, wooded, green, and historic. There were 120 of us, all corporals, and I was the only sergeant. We were given OCS patches and told where to sew them. We were told to remove all NCO stripes and to be ready for reveille in fatigues Monday morning. After lunch, I walked all over the

post. I remember very little except that the officers and senior NCOs had beautiful homes, and there was a hell of an obstacle course in a large draw east of the barracks. I changed into fatigues, studied, and ran the course for two hours. I tried each obstacle over and over again.

On that first Monday morning, I became a squad leader in the 1st Platoon, and I changed bunks and got a locker. I remember the opening pep talk because I've used variations over the years, and it was not just a pep talk. It included: "All of you are good soldiers or you wouldn't be here. All of you have the brains to learn the instruction material. All of you have the strength and agility to meet the physical requirements to be an officer. Over one-quarter of you will not become officers for two main reasons: The instructors determine you do not warrant a commission in the cavalry, or you do not want to become an officer. Each must do his own work. You will be dismissed if you cheat on a test or activity. There will be no sick call. You will never be late to a formation or a class. You will listen and you will do as you are told. If you leave tomorrow morning, you will be a better soldier for being here today. I am your senior tactical officer. I am Lieutenant Neville." If I missed anything in this speech, it couldn't be over two items!

Then we went out on the obstacle course. It was a Chinese fire drill! We were sent alphabetically at ten seconds apart. I was slightly slowed from time to time. I passed anyone if I did not take his right-of-way. I was the first D through. Many Bs and Cs were behind me. We were timed. After supper, I took my squad out on the obstacle course. About ten others joined us. I was the instructor for most. Two tac officers [tactical officers, who carry out tactical instruction during training] watched from a distance. I told my gang to ignore them. We were on time for study hour, but we were wet and a bit soiled. We were all clean, ready for Tuesday, shaved and dead at least fifteen minutes before lights-out.

Tuesday morning, I was told to lead off. I went for "show" not "go." Both show and speed on the monkey bars is every other rung underneath, grab the beam of the down ladder, and swing to the ground—running. Both show and speed on the suspension bridge, which is run full speed with knees bent. On the rope swing, you dive waist-high, both hands together, let your body drop fully, lift up to clear the far-side railroad ties, and drop off running before the end of the swing. Go over the wall on an angle; if you run to the wall straight, you hit the wall head-on, which stops forward movement. Use the corner turns of the zigzag trail out of the gully as stair steps. I hit the finish line with lots of wind to spare. Neville and another tac officer checked me in with questions. I said, "No, sir," to gymnast, circus, steel worker, etc. I said I studied the course on Saturday for two hours, Sunday for three hours, and Monday night for forty-five minutes.

On Wednesday, I went first and stopped at the rope swing. I was told to pretend I was cadre by the tac officer at the ropes. During a lull, the tac said, "Show or tell, don't help." I said, "Sir, both pushes were to ensure no accident or injury." Later, he said, "Do it your way—except kick ass."

The second Monday, we were told that we all met the obstacle course requirement. Many ran through the course each morning. The rest of us ran around the parade ground, which was over a mile.

One of my best memories of OCS involved swimming in the water survival phase.

I particularly liked our engineering training. The instructor was a full colonel, Corps of Engineers, and very old. He was a colonel in the [First] World War. Out of thirty or forty instructors, he and two others are the only ones I still recall by face. I got the only 100 percent he gave, though one other got a perfect test paper.

The customs-of-the-service instructor was outstanding. He said an officer commands best from a slight distance—that relaying distasteful or dangerous orders may not be done to a close friend. It *will* lessen your effectiveness if you send a close friend to his death. One quit the class, saying, "I am willing to take my chances on the battlefield, but I will not play God." He was a terrific person . . . and would not change his mind. Another good man quit when he was told a commission was a lifetime thing. He said, "I signed for the duration and months—and there it ends!"

The last inspection in ranks was a corker. We were told to be on our toes, as the failure quota wasn't met yet. We were at 27 percent, and the tacs were striving for 30 to 33 percent. We were slicked! All my squad passed but me. Lieutenant Neville found our barracks area perfect. He looked me over for at least two minutes. He then said, "Dove, we've a week to go, and you've never gotten a gig [a military demerit]." I said, "Sir." He then said, "Nobody goes through OCS without a gig—one gig. The underside of your belt tab is tarnished." I said, "Sir." Then he and the candidate platoon leader marched away. As he was turning the platoon back to the leader, the leader said, "Sir!!" Neville said, "Yes." It was an instant confrontation! The exchange: "Sir, you didn't look at the underside of Dove's belt tab." "So?" "You couldn't see the underside." "Did Dove complain?" "No." "What's your complaint?" "Sir, when I was made a corporal years ago, I was told to treat my men fairly and insist that they be treated fairly, sir." There was a long pause. Then Neville said, "Candidate Burton, yours is the school solution. Before you dismiss your platoon, tell them their area and themselves were perfection today." Burton said, "Sir." Neville walked away.

All hell broke loose when we got in the barracks. Our troop commander was Candidate Foote, the senior NCO of the original 120. He looked at my belt tab, and both sides were free of tarnish. "Chicken-shit bastard" was the kindest thing said. I quieted the crowd with "I'm proud of my gig; you bastards don't know a victory when you see one. Unless Foote or Burton says different, all of you shut up." The squawk box said, "Candidate Dove to the orderly room. Many times the person called was never seen again by other candidates.

When I got into the commandant's room, it was full of tac officers. A very glum bunch they were! After reporting, I heard, "At ease," and "Dove, are you pissed?" My answer was "No, sir, not in the least." There was a long pause. The conversation then was: "Sir." "Yes." "I wish to add to my answer." "Go ahead." "Sir, *sheeite no*!" The room exploded in laughter, and I grinned.

When I came into sight, the barracks windows were full of faces, followed by countless boxing victory signs. All candidates graduated ten or so days later.

In February 1942, Sgt. James Crutchfield left the 57th Field Artillery Battalion at Fort Ord to

Robert F. Mitchell handling a machine gun at Officer Candidate School at Fort Benning, October 1942. NATIONAL ARCHIVES

report at Fort Knox, Kentucky, where he entered the OCS program that produced the "ninety-day wonders." His OCS training was as rigorous as Robert Dove's, but possibly a little more vicious. According to Crutchfield, the staff there set a goal of at least 20 percent elimination. Candidates were allowed to fail only one exam and were brought before the board on the second failure. Crutchfield failed the map-reading test, even though he had become an expert at the skill at the survey school at Fort Sill. For him, as for many others, that was the "free one."

The candidates continued to go before the board until the night before graduation. Candidate Rosenblatt was called up the last night. He had already purchased the necessary insignia and uniform, assuming that he would graduate, only to be told by the board that he was overweight and was "canned." Rosenblatt, who had been a first sergeant before he entered OCS, would have made an excellent company officer, according to Crutchfield, who suspected that his removal was because he was Jewish, rather than any other factor.

Before graduating, each candidate had to rate the other thirty-four men in his training platoon. The candidates had to select five men with whom they would consider going into combat. Then they had to choose a second group, a third, and so on. If a man's name appeared too many times in the last-choice groups, he had to appear before the board.

At graduation, the candidates were asked if they wanted cavalry commissions. Crutchfield decided to pass on the opportunity and hold out for a position in the artillery. To his dismay, however, the speaker next announced that anyone who had not volunteered for cavalry would become an infantry officer. Crutchfield, like most of the other candidates, was eventually assigned to an armored unit.

The newly commissioned Second Lieutenant Crutchfield reported to the 6th Armored Division, which was forming at Fort Chaffee, Arkansas. The unit was in a state of flux as a constant stream of recruits swelled its numbers. Crutchfield's first command was a platoon in the cavalry reconnaissance battalion, but he soon became the battalion maintenance officer, a position he kept throughout the war.

In August 1942, the 6th Armored Division left the rolling, wooded hills surrounding Fort Chaffee in the Ozarks for Louisiana, where the unit had the maneuver area virtually to itself. In the sweltering heat of the Gulf Coast, Crutchfield and his men fondly remembered the more temperate climate of northwest Arkansas. The marsh and swamplands of Louisiana wreaked havoc among the division's mobile elements, and the men had to fight off hordes of pests. Every night, they had to take refuge behind their tents' mosquito netting to escape from swarming clouds of hungry insects.

As the maintenance officer, Crutchfield traveled with the battalion staff. He moved throughout the district, because the battalion's tanks and vehicles were scattered all over the maneuver area. In most cases, when a tracked vehicle tried to follow the same path as the one preceding it, it bogged down in the soft ground. The engineers had to cut down trees to build corduroy roads over small stretches of marsh and lay tread bridges over some of the streams. These bridges proved difficult for some vehicles to negotiate, however, especially the battalion's Harley-Davidson motorcycles. In one case, a soldier tried to ride his motorcycle over one of these bridges instead of walking it across and went over the side. He was picked up by a passing truck, and his Harley was recovered later. The battalion's 10-ton wrecker had to haul tanks out of the muck, but it was normally used only as a last result, when all other means, such as logs and winches, had failed to dislodge the mired vehicle.

Many areas in Louisiana, such as small towns and land tracts whose owner refused to grant access to the army, were marked as off-limits. Entering those zones could have serious repercussions and spark confrontations with irate, shotgun-wielding farmers. Although the soldiers were allowed to purchase alcohol during rest periods, they were not allowed to go into the towns to get it. One evening, when Lieutenant Crutchfield asked his driver to stop so he could check his location, he saw a civilian and asked him where he might purchase some alcohol. The man told him to wait there and he would be right back. Before long, the man returned with a fifth of liquor, for which he asked $1.75. Crutchfield took a swig and almost choked on the strong brew, which tasted as if it had been distilled in the moonshiner's bathtub. The next morning, Crutchfield came across an ordnance lieutenant who had been recovering vehicles. Since the poor lieutenant looked really beat, he offered him a swig of the moonshine. Watching the lieutenant down the concoction with relish, Crutchfield let him keep the entire bottle. In exchange, the grateful lieutenant asked Crutchfield the location of his broken-down vehicles and promised to recover them all.

7. Before the reorganization, the battalion included a headquarters troop and A, B, C, and D mechanized cavalry troops as well as a tank troop of Stuart light tanks. Each of the four troops included two 75-millimeter self-propelled guns. The reorganization removed the eight self-propelled guns from the mechanized cavalry troops and created a mechanized artillery troop of self-propelled guns.

After the 6th Armored Division completed its training in the Louisiana maneuver area, many of its troops concluded that that they might be headed for the Pacific. This rumor was quickly dispelled, however, when, soon after its return to Fort Chaffee and its reorganization, the division was shipped out to the desert maneuver area in California.[7] The trains on which the division traveled to California consisted of sleeper cars and boxcars, followed by flatcars carrying the battalion's tanks and vehicles. The troops were fed from one of the boxcars, where a kitchen had been set up for the long trip. The compartments of the sleeper cars each contained an upper bunk for one man and a lower bunk for two. Because the trains carrying the division had low priority, they frequently pulled over on sidings to allow other trains to pass. During some of these delays, the men got off the train to do calisthenics. When the 6th Armored Division finally reached Camp Young, California, in October 1942, it engaged in exercises at the Desert Training Center Maneuvers No. 1. This time, the men concluded that they were preparing for duty in North Africa. But by the time they finished in 1943, the Tunisian campaign had come to an end, and the North African theater of operations was closed.

The division's equipment was not yet ready for action, according to Lt. Rodney Mortensen of the 212th Armored Field Artillery Battalion.

> Our goddamn equipment wasn't any good. We didn't have volute springs on the half-tracks or anything. The volute spring allows a rock to get in the gears of the tracks so it doesn't tear up the idlers and drive wheels and so on. They had all kinds of technical representatives out there. We dreamed up the spring, and a whole bunch of us put it on, and soon the next tanks we got had these springs on them and they worked. I don't know who invented it.

The 6th Armored Division was the first armored unit to be deployed against fortifications in training, according to Lieutenant Mortensen, when it engaged a unit from the Presidio that set itself up in a fortified position. The desert training in California was truly a unique experience. Mortensen started out with eighteen half-tracks hauling ammunition for 105-millimeter guns of the M7 self-propelled guns and a jeep for his support section of the 212th Armored Field Artillery Battalion. After fifty miles through the desert terrain, all his half-tracks had broken down. "I lost one tank completely; it broke through the crust. They tried to pull it out. Then we lost two vehicles: the tank and the tank retriever. The last I saw of that, the ordnance came up and hooked on and issued us a new tank, and for all I know, they are still out there."

In the Catscombe Mountains, the terrain became the enemy for the vehicles. The greasewood native to the area punctured tires with annoying regularity, causing Lieutenant Crutchfield's maintenance section endless headaches. Occasionally one of the soldiers got slapped in the face with cactus and had to make the long trip to the medical facilities at San Diego. Mechanical problems did not let up. Some of the twenty-five motorcycle riders in Crutchfield's section got careless, leaving their Harley-Davidsons in the sand, which was too abrasive for them. The twenty-five diesel scout cars—the only ones the army owned—generally functioned well, but spare parts for them were virtually impossible to get. Thus Crutchfield heaved a great sigh of relief when he found out that the division would leave the motorcycles and diesel scout cars behind when he shipped out overseas.

During the desert maneuvers, the 6th Division tried out a variety of different techniques. One of the most common problems was that the soldiers often lost their way in the uniform terrain. "After maneuvers were over, we had to get in airplanes

Troop D, 91st Reconnaissance Squadron, 1st Cavalry Division, on maneuvers at Fort Bliss in July 1941. The 1st was one of two horse cavalry divisions in the U.S. Army when the U.S. entered the war. NATIONAL ARCHIVES

and look for people," said Crutchfield. Flying pennants from the vehicles' radio antennas proved to be very helpful. Most units were also equipped with signal flags during maneuvers.

> The idea was that everybody would take off at about 50 miles per hour in the half-tracks and spread out. Everybody was issued four flags: red, blue, white, and green. So when you came down in a single line, you would hold up a certain grouping of flags to create the formation, and somebody would always screw it up. About the time you got to some place where you couldn't get through, there would be large boulders, as big as a house, and somebody would give the wrong signal, and everybody would get jammed up. Sometimes you would reach a place where it was very dusty and you couldn't see anything, and they would get in line and you couldn't see where you were going, and by the time the order got to you it was too late. They didn't have many radios available.

By the end of the California maneuvers, the 6th Armored Division had acquired experience operating in jungle and desert conditions. It remained in California until early 1944, when it shipped out for Europe, where its troops would encounter neither desert nor jungle.

At the time the armored divisions formed up in 1941 and 1942, the first of many independent tank battalions became operational. One of these battalions was the 741st Tank Battalion, which had a unique future in store. It formed in March 1942 at Fort Meade, Maryland, with cadre from the 751st, which had been created the previous year. Training in Maryland was slow because of a lack of gasoline for the maneuvers. According to Crutchfield,

"There was not enough gas per tank per day even to warm up the engine. That could never stop the army from carrying out its training. The five-man crews played tank and ran about the field practicing tactics until their tongues hung out. We really looked silly. Gasoline wasn't all that was short; food was too. It didn't pay to be late for chow or to have an enormous appetite."

On January 12, 1942, eighteen-year-old Wardell Hopper enlisted in Chicago and reported to Fort Sheridan, outside the city, where he was given his physical. He had requested an assignment to the Air Corps, where he hoped to become an aerial gunner. After completing his physical, he was informed that at six feet, two inches, he was too tall to fit into a bomber turret, but his weight of 130 pounds would allow him to squeeze into a tank. Accordingly, he requested duty in the Tank Corps and was assigned to Fort Knox for ninety days of basic training at the replacement training center. At Fort Knox, it seemed to him that no one else wanted to be in the Tank Corps. "They used to threaten the tankers that if you goof up, you go into the infantry," he says.

> We did mostly infantry training and a little bit of tank training. They didn't have many tanks in those days. They had M-3 [Lee/Grant tanks] that we trained on.
>
> I went first to Fort Meade, Maryland, where I joined the 741st Tank Battalion in March 1942. We had a lot of Regular army men, cadre. We trained there, but I don't think we had too many tanks. We didn't have enough tanks, so we would take five guys with a broomstick for a gun and run out and play battle.

The 741st entrained for the desert training site in California, leaving its "soldier's paradise" at Fort Meade.

> On one of the stops for exercise, somewhere in Arizona, a rattlesnake sent the whole group into a swift retreat to the shelter of the train, which was something that in later months the German Army was unable to accomplish.
>
> As we debarked from the train at Indio, California, we stepped off into ankle-deep dust. It coated our clothes, filled our noses, and choked us. It was stinking hot. The town looked dead, almost deserted. We boarded trucks and headed out of town away from the dust.

The battalion settled at Camp Young, a tent camp located in a valley in the mountains where the climate was a little more tolerable, and stayed there for the remainder of 1942 and part of 1943. The tanks to be used for training were parked in long lines, but a good number were in need of repairs. Company B was allotted seventeen tanks, only two of which were in working order. These were used to help tow the other fifteen. Company B finally got all seventeen functioning, but on the first exercise, it lost so many of them to breakdowns that training had to be called off.

> The food at Camp Young was always covered with a layer of sand, and water was in short supply. Food consisted of canned goods classified as B, which usually consisted of sardines. None of this improved morale. One of the highlights of the stay was when the unit participated in the mak-

8. Released in May 1943, this was a fictional film about Rommel and the *Afrika Korps* with a secret plan to supply his army. The fictional secret was that at five sites on the road to Cairo, the Germans had secretly stored the supplies they would need for their troops to reach Cairo during the advance across Libya into Egypt in the summer of 1942.

The 206th Coastal Artillery (Anti-Aircraft) Regiment of the Alabama National Guard during maneuvers at Fort Bliss in July 1941.
NATIONAL ARCHIVES

ing of the Paramount film *Five Graves to Cairo,* about the campaign against Rommel in the desert.[8]

We trained there quite a while, and I guess they decided we weren't going to the desert in Africa, so they shipped us down to Camp Polk, Louisiana. We traveled there by train in January, I think. They were training us more for the South Pacific, because Camp Polk was swamplands. I don't remember how long we were there, but we did receive our Shermans.

Between 1940 and 1943, the towns of the Louisiana maneuver area were enlivened by the presence of the units taking part in maneuvers:

Leesville was a roaring one-horse country town, and during the day, it was dead. At night, the incoming soldier and the profiteering civilian brought it to life. Shooting galleries, popcorn stands, and a carnival sprang up. People milled about, walking in the muddy streets because the sidewalks could not accommodate them. Visiting wives and parents overflowed the rooming accommodations, and auto courts could get fabulous prices for their rooms. Liquor flowed freely, and the MPs had their hands full keeping order.

The tanks constantly became bogged down. The men were sure they would ship out after these exercises when they returned to Camp Polk, but once again, they were disappointed. In June 1943, the battalion moved to Camp Pickett, Virginia.

Here was another camp, just another camp. It was different only in that here we did our first amphibious training. There were dry land installations known as "mockups," designed to represent boats. Tall frameworks of boards with rope ladders stretched down represented the sides of ships. These could be made to rock back and forth and mimic the roll of the ocean. Up and down these ladders we played monkey, climbing with full field equipment.

From here we went to Camp Bradford, where we worked and lived with the navy. In our training here, we loaded and unloaded vehicles on LSTs and practiced climbing rope ladders up the sides of larger vessels. In boarding our first craft, the ramp wouldn't work, and we had to wade waist-deep to get in.

The men were told they would be going to the Solomon Islands; instead, they continued to practice landings and finally returned to Camp Pickett. In August 1943, they were sent to Camp Wellfleet on Cape Cod, where they did some antiaircraft training against targets pulled by naval aircraft. That concluded most of the battalion's training.

Obsolete M2 medium tank with 37-millimeter gun and machine guns used for bridging operations at Fort Benning.

CHAPTER 8

Preparing the Army for the Great Invasion

Special Amphibious Units

Three units that had participated in the North African campaign and the invasion of Sicily—the 1st Division, 2nd Armored Division, and 70th Tank Battalion, the oldest independent tank battalion in the army—became key elements in the Normandy campaign. The 1st "Big Red One" Division returned to Great Britain, from where it had staged the invasion of North Africa. The 82nd A/B Division participated in the Italian campaign for several weeks following the Sicilian campaign. Meanwhile, in the United States, units destined for the invasion of France continued to train before their departure in 1943.

In June 1942, shortly after the establishment of the Amphibious Training Command at Camp Edwards, Massachusetts, the Corps of Engineers created the 1st, 2nd, and 3rd Amphibian Brigades. Each of these units included an Engineer Shore Regiment and an Engineer Boat Regiment. The 2nd and 3rd Regiments, destined for the Pacific, also included an Engineer Amphibian unit, which was redesignated as an Engineer Special Brigade (ESB) in 1943.[1] The 1st ESB played a major role in the Normandy invasion. The 5th and 6th Engineer Special Brigades were formed from Engineer Combat Groups already in England—the 5th in November 1943 and the 6th in May 1944.

Lt. Sidney Berger joined the 1st ESB (then the 1st Amphibian Brigade) when it was organized at Camp Edwards. He had gone through a citizens' military training camp in 1938 at Fort Hoyle, Maryland, with the 6th Field Artillery, a horse-drawn outfit with 75-millimeter guns.[2] He also had ROTC schooling that included a training camp at Fort Belvoir, Virginia. When he graduated in May 1942, he received his commission, and within a month, he reported to Camp Edwards. Lieutenant Berger boarded a troop train in Massachusetts with the rest of the brigade, arrived in New York the next morning, and marched directly onto the waiting ships at Staten Island. The battalion headquarters sailed on the USS *Wakefield*. On August 5, the brigade sailed for Great Britain. It remained here until the end of November, when it went to North Africa and was redesignated as the 1st ESB.

A Stuart M3 light tank of the 1st Cavalry Division on desert maneuvers at Fort Bliss, July 1941. NATIONAL ARCHIVES

John P. Gallagher of Cleveland, Ohio, who was only eighteen when he was drafted in February 1943, shipped out to Oran after his thirteen weeks of basic training at Camp Wheeler, Georgia. At Oran, he joined the 1st ESB—a key unit for the upcoming invasions of Sicily and Salerno—as a replacement. The Corps of Engineers was short of trained replacements to meet all its needs, and soldiers like Gallagher were assigned to such specialized units as the 531st Engineer Shore Regiment of the brigade.[3] His few months of military service tested this young Ohioan's endurance. Though he had missed much of the sweltering heat of Georgia, he arrived in time for the arid heat of North Africa. He was quickly reconciled to his fate, however, once he realized that he would spend much of the remainder of his service at the beach. After he underwent several months of training with the unit in North Africa, he took part in the two invasions of 1943 with less than a year of military service.

1. These units remained in service even after the navy took control of all amphibious training in the United States and the army abandoned its amphibious training centers in the spring of 1943. They originally were organized to transport and support a reinforced division, but that role was reduced to mainly support. The 4th ESB was activated early in 1943 and sent to the Pacific.

2. By 1942, the field artillery battalions with 75-millimeter guns had traded them for 105-millimeter howitzers. The battalions with the old Model-1918 155-millimeter howitzers exchanged them for new 155-millimeter howitzers as they became available.

3. The 531st Engineer Shore Regiment was activated with the 1st Engineer Amphibious Brigade, which eventually became the 1st ESB, on June 15, 1942, and was the brigade's main unit. It landed in Northern Ireland in August 1942, and in November, it took part in the landings in Algeria.

Pvt. Otway Burns of Sarasota, Florida, enlisted in the army on August 22, 1940, at the age of sixteen, though he looked old enough to pass for eighteen. After undergoing his initial training at Fort Benning, he was assigned to a heavy pontoon company of the 87th Engineers.[4] This unit later became the cadre for the 531st Engineer Shore Regiment at Camp Edwards, where Burns, who served with Company A, was already an old hand and a member of the cadre by the ripe old age of eighteen. His job was to train the new recruits for their shore-to-shore mission. In August 1942, his brigade sailed for Scotland.

> We trained there with the Royal Marines near the Firth of Clyde at the towns of Troon and Ayre. While we were training, they took several companies, outfitted them in British uniforms, and sent us over to Northern Ireland. They were having trouble with the IRA. They sent Canadians too. The British troops had just come back from Dieppe and saw all the Americans dressed in British uniforms. I am sure all of the 1st Battalion went, but I don't know about the other two battalions. From there we went back to Scotland, and then to North Africa and landed in Arzou, near Oran.

Hyatt W. Moser of Greensboro, North Carolina, volunteered for the army on November 8, 1940, at age twenty. The recruiter at High Point gave him a bus ticket to Atlanta, where he joined the 62nd Signal Battalion and was trained within the unit by an old corporal named Lester P. Mendoza. In 1941, Moser's unit participated in the Louisiana maneuvers, providing communications for a corps-size unit. Moser, a radio operator, was placed in the telegraph section when his unit reached Fort McPherson for the maneuvers. At the time, he had not yet learned the Morse code and had to telephone the telegraph operator at division headquarters to send messages by telegraph. Unfortunately, the operator did not know the Morse code either, so they both tapped out the letters as they learned it and called each other to see if they had received the messages.

Moser's battalion next participated in the Carolina maneuvers, from where it went to Camp Blanding in November. Moser got his first leave on December 8, 1941, the day after Pearl Harbor. Within two weeks, his battalion was transferred to the Atlantic Fleet Amphibious Corps at Quantico, Virginia, where it engaged in communications training with the Marine Corps.

> I was assigned to the 71st Signal Company and was sent to a school run by marines for training personnel from the army, navy, and marines. We had the first amphibious training of army units [Moser is mistaken; this was not actually the first], and we went on practice invasions at Cove Point, Maryland. The 1st Division I think was one, and others came and made practice landings at Cove Point and the Chesapeake Bay. We ran that for some time. One of my jobs there was operating navy signal lights, which sent Morse code [which by this time he had mastered] by signal light. One of my jobs was to challenge all the ships entering the Chesapeake Bay, get their call signs, identify them, radio Washington, and tell them what ship it was.
>
> During this period of time, they decided to discontinue this Amphibious Corps and conceived the idea of the Amphibious Engineers, who were trained to do similar jobs.

4. There were various types of engineer units. A division had a combat engineer battalion, while at corps level and higher, other types existed, ranging from general service regiments to specialized heavy pontoon, water supply, topographic, and construction battalions that were not combat units. There were also the amphibian and aviation engineer units.

A select group of us from the 71st Signal Company was transferred to form two new units at Camp Edwards, Massachusetts: the 286th and 287th JASC. The 286th was to be in the 1st Engineer Special Brigade and the 287th in the 2nd Engineer Special Brigade. I was originally assigned to the 287th, but then to bring the 286th up to strength, I was assigned to them. All we did at Camp Edwards was draw new equipment, stencil it with our code, and get it ready to ship. We left there on August 5, 1942.

We were on the American passenger liner *Manhattan*.[5] We traveled independently, since it was a fast ship, and arrived in Northern Ireland on August 19, 1942.[6] We learned [at Camp Edwards] that the army's Amphibious Engineer Command was calling for volunteers that didn't require any training. They were looking for stevedores, boat operators, bulldozer operators, anything. They had an ad in a New England newspaper, which stated, "For adventure and a Fight, Join the Sea Taxis of the Army Engineers Amphibian Command." Consequently, when we left and got to Northern Ireland, we had people on our ship in civilian clothes that had no military training and not even a uniform. They were put on the ship and got uniforms in Ireland, half British and half American uniforms. I was assigned to give these men military training. Although they lacked the military training, they did an excellent job in what they were expected to do.

Some of us went to Scotland. I was with a group that had training with the British commandos. We made practice landings here with American and British units in the Hebrides Islands. All the boats were operated by British crews. We were next to one boat, and one coxswain was trying to talk to the other. He was saying, "Freddie, do you think we are going in the right direction?" and then they laughed. It was cold, foggy, and rainy, and they were setting off demolition and using live fire overhead.

From Glasgow, Scotland, we were loaded on ships. I was on an old ship the British had confiscated from the Spanish. On that ship were units of the 531st [Shore Regiment], 286th, 1st Division HQ with Terry Allen, and various British units. We were on that ship for thirty-two days. We sailed around and around until we got to the Mediterranean and joined the convoy for the invasion of North Africa. After the invasion, the 1st Brigade [1st ESB, to which the 286th JASC belonged] operated a basic training center in addition to running the port of Arzou near Oran and other places. We set up at Mestagna, Algeria, a basic training center where we trained units coming over from the States in practice landings. Then we organized and made the invasion of Sicily.

Emile Henry Sunier was an ROTC cadet at the University of Maryland when he decided to volunteer in October 1942 at the age of twenty-three. He reported for his basic infantry training at Fort McClellan, but once his instructors discovered he had some background in signal train-

5. Built in 1931 as a luxury liner for the North Atlantic, the *Manhattan* was taken over by the military in 1941 and renamed the *Wakefield*; it was operated by the U.S. Coast Guard as a troopship. The ship participated in amphibious training exercises at New River, North Carolina, in July 1941. In January 1942, it was damaged by Japanese bombs while evacuating civilians from Singapore. On September 3, while it traveled in a convoy returning to the United States after delivering Moser and others to Great Britain in August, fire broke out. It was abandoned and towed to Halifax, where it stayed until fires gutted it. Then it was towed to Boston and rebuilt as a troopship.

6. The trip was made in convoy. Convoy AT-18 included a dozen transports and a similar number of escorts. The *Wakefield* unloaded its troops in the River Clyde, not Northern Ireland. Moser was probably sent briefly to Northern Ireland with other elements of the brigade shortly after arriving.

A Stuart at Fort Bliss, July 1941. NATIONAL ARCHIVES

ing from ROTC, he was transferred to the Signal Corps Training Center that had been built in 1941 at Fort Crowder, Missouri. From there, he was transferred to the Pittsburg Replacement Center at Camp Stoneman Military Reservation in California. During his stay in California, Sunier came down with double pneumonia and missed being shipped to the Pacific. Instead, he was sent to Boston, where in February 1944 he boarded the *Empress of Australia,* which was bound for Liverpool. On the ship, he recalls, "the food was deplorable. There were maggots in the food, and if you had the guts to eat it, you were in trouble." He had to share his bunk with two other men in eight-hour shifts. According to Sunier, the ship was built to hold 4,500 troops but carried 6,000. Once he reached Liverpool, he headed for St. Austell, Cornwall, where the 286th JASC was stationed. The 286th and the 1st ESB had returned in early December 1943 from operations in Sicily and Italy.

The engineer special brigades absorbed other specialist units like the JASC and transportation companies. A unique type of battalion that was attached to these brigades was the specially created Naval Beach Battalion, which was primarily deployed in Europe. Like the ESB, the beach battalion's mission was to help establish a beachhead providing communications, medical, and boat repair personnel to maintain it logistically. The initial phases of their mission coincided with the landing of the last assault waves, whose responsibility was to secure the beach and penetrate inland.

Many young men who volunteered for service in 1942 tried to enlist in the navy or Army Air Corps, two branches of the service they considered not only more glamorous than the infantry, but also the most likely to strike first at the enemy—Japan, in the eyes of the American public during the early years of the war.

Frank D. Snyder, a seventeen-year-old from Florida, eagerly enlisted in the navy in December 1942, hoping to train in the medical field. After he was inducted, he was sent to Bainbridge, Maryland, for naval boot camp, where he trained with Company 100. Next, he attended the Hospital Corps School at the U.S. Naval Hospital at

Troops of the 206th Coastal Artillery (Anti-Aircraft) Regiment use a range finder to determine the elevation of "enemy" aircraft.
NATIONAL ARCHIVES

Bainbridge. After he finished his schooling as a pharmacist in August 1943, he was transferred to Camp Bradford near Norfolk, Virginia, where he joined the newly forming 6th Beach Battalion.

> The battalion, as organized, consisted of one-third each communications, medical, and demolitions men, and some miscellaneously assigned people. There were nine platoons, organized into companies, each with a platoon commander and an executive officer, both of whom were ensigns, and one doctor with each platoon who was an LTjg. Anywhere from seven to ten hospital corpsmen were assigned to each platoon. Approximately the same numbers of radio and signalmen in the communications section, and the remainder were made up primarily of seamen ratings of assignments of all kinds. I do not remember the name of our initial battalion commander. Our Company B commander was a Lieutenant Wood. At Camp Bradford, the battalion consisted of some 300 to 350 officers and enlisted men.

In October, Frank Snyder, by now a pharmacist mate, and his battalion boarded a troop train to his home state of Florida. He had no time to visit his family because the destination was Fort Pierce, where he underwent rigorous naval training in amphibious warfare. At the end of the year, Snyder took a train to Ledo Beach, Long Island, to await shipment overseas. Speculation about the eventual destination of the battalion was rife among the men. When the men were issued a complete set of arctic survival clothing and equipment, they concluded that the 6th Naval Beach Battalion was going to take part in the invasion of Norway.

The 44th Engineer Battalion

Like many other branches of the army, the Corps of Engineers was hard-pressed to find enough qualified recruits to serve in the numerous engineer battalions. Every combat division needed one of these specialized battalions. Unlike most service units, the engineer battalion also had a combat function. Corps- and army-level commands also required engineer combat and construction battalions. Even the invasion forces required the Engineer Special Brigades. Thus the Corps of Engineers was required to create many new battalions to meet the demand.

Among the newly created units was the 44th Engineer Battalion, which was formed in April 1943 from the 1st Battalion of the 44th Engineer Combat Regiment, itself created in August 1942. The 44th Regiment was broken up to form other units. The 44th Engineer Regiment was at Camp McCoy at the time the 2nd Division underwent its cold-weather training. Although the 2nd Division was well equipped for the task, the 44th Regiment had no special winter gear, and its men had to survive as best they could in temperatures ranging from 0 to minus 20 degrees F.

> To fire on the firing range was difficult enough under normal conditions, but when it reached the point where someone had to hold shelter halves to keep the wind off the men trying to fire their weapons, it certainly created a problem. Another problem in firing in such cold weather was the possibility of your hands sticking to the metal part of your weapon. The weapon had to be cleaned of all oil; any oil or grease left on the working parts of the weapon would freeze and cause the weapon to misfire, which could be very dangerous. No one wanted to lay flat on his stomach or sit on the frozen ground in the snow and fire his weapon; no one even wanted to fire from the standing position when the wind made it difficult to even stand.

The situation was exacerbated by the fact that most of the new men, who came from the Southeast and Southwest, wore summer uniforms. In one platoon, no one spoke English, only Spanish, but with the help of a Spanish-speaking officer, it became an efficient unit. Despite the fierce cold, the men of the 44th carried on with their training, which included, among other things, the art of building bridges of various types.

Eventually the 44th Regiment was dissolved at Camp McCoy, and the 44th Combat Engineer Battalion was created. Capt. Andrew P. Rollins Jr. became the first commander of the 44th Engineer. He had graduated from ROTC at Texas A&M in 1939, and he led the battalion until November 1943, finally ending up in the Pacific theater.

> The 2nd Infantry Division from Texas had been moved into Camp McCoy for special winter training. They were issued special winter gear, special clothing, skis, snowshoes, and everything. We laughed at them because they spent less time outside than the 44th Engineers did, and the 44th had no special gear. We learned to meet our troops at the railhead, put hay in the bottom of the dump truck to cover the metal bottom. The hay would help keep their feet warm. We would bring them straight to the mess hall for coffee or cocoa and something to eat.
>
> We learned one thing or two, such as building bridges. When we were teaching how to build floating bridges, we would push the boats out on the ice. The ice was too thick to break, so we would build a floating bridge with the boats sitting on top of the ice.

In April 1943, the 44th boarded a train for the Tennessee maneuver area, where it went through all phases of training related to the operations of a combat engineer battalion. In July, the unit returned to Camp McCoy, where it trained until August. Next, the 44th took to the fields of

A tank destroyer unit consisting of half-tracks mounting 75-millimeter guns lined up at Fort Hood, February 1944. NATIONAL ARCHIVES

North Dakota in the company of other units, a force of up to 3,000 men, to harvest crops until September. (In 1944, POWs replaced the army troops in the fields.) Later that month, the 44th returned to the Tennessee maneuver area to maintain the roads and bridges during the exercises.

Before he joined the 44th, PFC Romauld D. Ellegood, who was inducted into the army in April 1942, underwent training typical for engineer personnel. During his eight weeks of basic training at Fort Leonard Wood, Missouri, he participated in the construction of his first pontoon bridge. The companies competed with each other to finish their bridges across the Big Piney River. The first to complete the task was to receive a prize. In August 1942, Ellegood took part in the Tennessee maneuvers.

> While we were playing warfare in 1942, Company B wore blue armbands and the other side wore the red armbands. Some of us were guarding different bridges. Sergeant Wilkins and I were together guarding the bridge around Gallatin, Tennessee. If we didn't do a good job, they would bomb it all, dropping a sack of flour on it, and we would lose some points.
>
> We built a pontoon bridge across the Cumberland River at night. Every vehicle had to drive with their blackout lights on across the bridge. The tanks also drove with blackout lights on. There was a first lieutenant with a small flashlight directing or leading these tanks across the bridge. I think he wasn't in the center of the bridge with his light. The first tank made it to the middle of the bridge, went off in the river, and capsized. The second tank was so close to the first tank it couldn't stop and also went off into the river. The third tank managed to back off without going in the river. There were three men in each tank, so that made six men that drowned in this accident. After this, we were on maneuvers for two more months. We were assigned, and we began to load our half-track and other

> equipment on flatcars. We had to fasten and nail down all heavy equipment with straps. We arrived at Camp McCoy, Wisconsin, in the late fall. We had several recruits or new men join us there. These men had to take their basic training there.

When the 44th left for the Tennessee maneuvers in 1943, Ellegood's Company B went to Fort Knox, where it built a camp on a hill overlooking the Ohio River, about ten miles from the main post, and began special training.

> I helped to lay antipersonnel mines, sometimes called knee mines. Another one of our main training missions was to build what some called a "snake." It was steel pipes made in two sections and made lengthwise, top and bottom, so you could put TNT inside one half of the pipe and buckle the top of the upper side with bolts. Both of these pipes lengthwise had two inches or more straight edge with holes for bolts to hold them together. I don't remember how many pounds of TNT would be put in each length of pipe. It would be enough pipes to cover 500, 600 feet or more. They would take a tank and hook onto one end of this long section of pipe and push it forward: it would work back and forth like a snake. It would go in between military obstacles and strong outposts like those that would be found in fixed positions in France and Germany. The men in tanks could trigger this large explosive from their tanks. When they were shooting one of these explosives from the tank, it shook windows out of the train passing on the tracks, which was between our camp and the Ohio River.

Training in the United States, Late 1942–43

As the major units of the U.S. Army moved into action overseas in 1942, the training structure had to adapt, and the men were not necessarily fully prepared for their assignments or the conditions they would encounter. Many units, like the 6th Armored Division, trained for conditions they would never encounter on the battlefield.

John A. Kirchner, a lieutenant in the Medical Corps, went on active duty in April 1942 and joined the newly forming 79th Division at Camp Pickett, Virginia, in the summer of 1942. He was assigned to Company A of the 304th Medical Battalion, which usually served with the 314th Infantry Regiment of the division.

> I was originally in Company A of the 304th and started out in Camp Pickett. From Camp Pickett, we were moved to Camp Blanding, Florida, where we had what I suppose was jungle training. From there we were sent to Camp Forrest, Tennessee, for maneuvers in the woods and the mud [in September 1942 with the 2nd Army no. 1 Tennessee maneuvers]. From there we were sent to Camp Laguna, Arizona, about thirty miles northeast of Yuma, in August 1943 for desert maneuvers until December 1943. From there we were sent to Camp Phillips, Kansas, before Christmas in December.[7]

Although much of this training turned out to be of little practical value to units like Kirchner's, it did condition the troops physically.

John F. Troy of Gary, Indiana, also underwent unusual training procedures in 1943. After graduating from high school in the summer of 1942, he tried to join the marines but was rejected because of a weak right eye. Ironically, he received a draft

7. Camp Phillips was built in the summer of 1942 and in use until late 1944. Four divisions, including the 79th, trained here, along with several noncombat units.

notice several months later and was inducted at Fort Benjamin Harrison in February or March 1943, after it was determined that he was fit for service in the infantry. He was then sent to Camp Swift, Texas, for basic training with the newly formed 97th Division.

> Since I was in a rifle company, I received the standard infantry training: M-1 rifle, .03 grenade launcher, bazooka, BAR, but *no* infantry tank tactics. This, later, we had to learn the hard way!
>
> In August, they started to break us up piecemeal. A shipping notice would be posted; if your name was on it, you were sent by train either east or west—west to the Pacific or east to the ETO. They gave us a seven-day furlough in August before we left. I don't remember anybody going AWOL at that point. I left in late August, headed east, but the train dropped us off in Tennessee at Camp Forrest, where I joined the 8th Division. I was put in Company E, 13th Infantry, and stayed there. Later our platoon took part in division maneuvers and served as an enemy raiding party at night.

The 8th Division had only recently returned from training in the desert maneuver area in California when Troy joined it. In November, it moved east to its port of embarkation.

In 1943, Albert Littke of Niagara Falls, New York, received a "Greetings" notice informing him that he had been drafted. Only a year earlier, when he was eighteen years old, he had opted for U.S. citizenship while his family returned to its native Canada. At the time, he worked on the production of P-39s at the Bell Aircraft plant.

> On March 3, I received notice to report and was inducted into the armed services. I reported to Buffalo, New York, where I took my physical and was sworn in. I was bused to Fort Niagara for approximately three or four days, where I was given clothing, shots, and an aptitude test. From there I was bused back to Niagara Falls, New York, where I was put on a troop train—destination unknown. Halfway across the States, we were told that we would be joining an engineer outfit. Nobody knew what their duty would be, and somebody mentioned that we had to dig foxholes for the infantry.
>
> Upon arrival at Bedford, Oregon, we were then bused to Camp White, where, in an open field with barracks all around, our battalion commander introduced himself and welcomed us to the 299th Combat Engineers. I was assigned to Company A, 3rd Platoon, 3rd Squad. Basic training

Divisional Medical Battalion

The Medical Battalion consisted of three collecting companies, A, B, and C, which included five officers—three medical doctors (MDs) and two medical administrative officers (MACs)—and ninety-six enlisted men. The MACs took care of supporting activities for the unit, such as the motor pool, supplies, and kitchen.

A collecting company provided service for three battalion aid stations of an infantry regiment. It supplied an ambulance and a ¾-ton weapons carrier or even a jeep to take casualties from the aid stations to the company's location, where they could receive medical attention beyond first aid. The collecting company's aid station maintained a supply of splints, bandages, plasma, morphine, and other supplies, but it was unable to perform any definitive surgery. Its primary purpose was to stabilize the casualties for an ambulance ride to a clearing station.

Troops demonstrate attacking a simulated Japanese tank with "sticky" grenades at Fort Hood, February 1944. NATIONAL ARCHIVES

included marksmanship, forced marches, building bridges, etc. After that, we were trucked to Lapine, in the central part of Oregon, where we installed communication lines—telephone poles.

I was assigned, with the rest of the platoon, to go and cut down trees, trim them, remove the bark, and help transport them out to the middle of the desert. From there we went on maneuvers through the months of September and October in the northern part of Oregon and the tip of Washington. There we had about six to eight problems in which we learned how to put up the Bailey bridges again, roadblocks, and line of defense.[8] During that time, they had the air force flying over and dropping five-pound flour bags, simulating them as bombs.

From there we proceeded by trucks to Fort Lewis, Washington, where I was made PFC and given my first furlough home, which consisted of eleven days, plus three days grace. I spent approximately six days home; the rest was traveling time.

Upon returning to Fort Lewis, that evening I was put through a night infiltration course and a forced march, getting back to the barracks at approximately two o'clock in the morning. The following day, we were told to be ready to move out. We were put on trucks, transported to the train station, and put on a troop train. Another GI and I were to board the caboose. At every stop, we were supposed to get out and guard our vehicles that were on the flatcars.

After traveling for about six days and seven nights, we arrived at Fort Pierce, Florida, which was a U.S. Navy base. Here we were put through intensive amphibious training and underwater demolition, as well as hand-to-hand combat, with a few

8. The British developed the prefabricated Bailey bridge early in the war, and it was adopted by the U.S. Army. A series of panels were put together by the engineers, and then the completed bridge was pushed over the gap it was to span. The sections were light enough that no heavy equipment was needed.

Rangers as teachers. We stayed there approximately three months. Around March 1, we departed for Camp Pickett, Virginia, where we took a night map-reading course with a compass, threw live grenades, and had a few lessons on different things such as identification of planes and the uniforms of German soldiers.

Private Littke was trained in the 299th Combat Engineer Battalion, formed on March 1, 1943, at Camp White just days before he arrived. He remained with this unit for the duration of the war. This battalion received special training because it was slated to participate in the assault wave during the invasion of France. It was the only unit to land companies on both Omaha and Utah Beaches.

During the first part of 1944, preparations for the invasion picked up their pace. The 82nd A/B Division, a veteran combat unit that had undergone its baptism of fire in 1943 during operations in Sicily and at Salerno, did not let up on its training. Its sister division, the 101st, which had barely finished its training and would not see action until mid-1944, and other airborne units such as the 508th PIR, which was attached to the 82nd Airborne Division in 1944, also continued to prepare. Maj. David Thomas, who had been with the 505th PIR in the spring of 1943, did not go with that unit to North Africa, where it prepared for the drop into Sicily that summer.

I was with the 505th Parachute Infantry Regiment until the winter of 1942–43, and I broke my leg on a tree landing on a parachute jump and wound up in the hospital. This was at the Alabama Training Area at Fort Benning. When I got out of the hospital, the 505th was shipping out for Africa, and I wound up with the 508th, which was further down the line in the training schedule.

Regimental show put on by the 12th Training Regiment at Camp Robinson, November 1942. NATIONAL ARCHIVES

Night jumps are a real mess. We had one on a dark night on Tennessee maneuvers. If you have ever been in Tennessee, you will notice there are a lot of big stones lying around here and there. On those Tennessee maneuvers, we jumped the regiment on this problem. One battalion was ten miles away from the objective, and the other battalions that were near the objective could not see anything. It was totally dark, and we put 1,200 out of a 2,000-man regiment in the hospital. As a matter of fact, we had scout dogs out there locating the wounded.

According to David Thomas, however, the parachutists who died during that jump usually had no one to blame but themselves.

When you parachute jump, you have a set manner of attaching your static line to the anchor cable in the aircraft. You have to snap your static line onto the anchor cable so your static line comes up over the outside of your left arm and shoulder. I have never seen anybody die parachute jumping that did not have a lot of ecchymoses and

An inspection at the Second Army's Tennessee Maneuvers, May 1943. NATIONAL ARCHIVES

> bruises under their left armpit. What they did was let their static line get under their armpit and they cleared the aircraft. When you clear the aircraft, you hug your reserve chute, tuck in your head, and wait for the opening shock. What happens is the static line comes under the guy's armpit, the canopy comes under his armpit, he is holding on to the canopy, the break line breaks, he has his canopy held under his armpit, and he just spins, crashes, and burns.

During the winter of 1942–43, Pvt. Ray Hood attended the Communications School at Fort Benning after he completed airborne training. He learned Morse code and was able to send and receive fifteen words a minute. He also received training in splicing, switchboard operation, and radio and telephone voice procedure. While at Fort Benning, he had time to become acquainted with Columbus, Georgia, and Phenix City, Alabama, which were near the fort.

> They were absolutely full of soldiers. Phenix City consisted of bars, bootleggers (on Sunday), cathouses, and gambling joints. Any ex-paratrooper from that era will remember a place in Phenix City called Beechie Howard's. It was a real dive, ill lit and smoky, watered down and overpriced drinks. There was a very well-known hooker called "Parachute Blondie," who auctioned herself to the highest bidder quite regularly. She would climb up on the bar, exhibit the merchandise, and graphically describe the available action. Literally thousands of men must remember her. In 1942, she was still very attractive but becoming a bit shopworn. Beechie Howard's was a paratrooper hangout. Brawls were nightly affairs.

After completing his communications training, Ray Hood was sent to Fort Bragg to join the 502nd PIR. He also made a training excursion to the Tennessee maneuver area in June 1943. Next, his unit traveled by train from Fort Bragg to Evansville, Indiana. His battalion set up pup tents near a lake fifteen miles from Evansville, in the vicinity of the small village of McKutcheonville. Life in the regiment was enlivened by a young lieutenant named Carp, who was "a one-man USO show," according to Hood. Although he was very brave, Carp was a little immature and fell into one misadventure after another, to the delight of the troops.

> Lieutenant Carp distinguished himself there by driving into the lake while carrying as a passenger a spit-shined major in class A uniform from division headquarters. When the jeep came to a halt, both men were waist-

A vehicle with a 37-millimeter gun on its rear and a .50-caliber machine gun on its front during the Second Army's Tennessee maneuvers, June 1943. NATIONAL ARCHIVES

deep in water. The major's dignity was a shambles, and he had a very colorful vocabulary—lots of witnesses, lots of laughter, but not much surprise. This was one of the first of "Carp's Capers."

During the maneuvers, Hood's unit made two daylight jumps and later spent several days "playing blue army-red army." Nothing of special interest occurred, and the weather was perfect, so the troops could relax and enjoy swimming in the lake.

The village had one store, a combination service station-grocery, and we really mobbed the place. It was located at a crossroads among a scatter of houses, and our tent city was only about 300 yards away. Everything went: lunch meat, cheese, peanut butter, candy, milk, soft drinks, canned goods—the whole nine yards.

The very nice elderly couple who ran the place simply couldn't keep their shelves stocked—we bought everything as soon as it appeared. Our cooks, all nonjumpers, had the battalion field kitchen set up, but the food was lousy. Even had it been acceptable, we would still have stormed that small store: Different is better.

I was in the Battalion Communications Platoon, and we had a switchboard in operation, connected to regimental headquarters, division headquarters—and, we discovered, Ma Bell, though the term was not in use at the time.

There were twenty-eight of us. We each called parents, girlfriends, wives, casual acquaintances—literally hundreds of phone

377th Parachute Field Artillery Battalion, 101st Airborne Division

The 377th battalion included a headquarters battery; three gun batteries, A, B, and C, each of which had four 75-millimeter pack howitzers (six after Normandy); and a service battery denominated Battery D. Each battery consisted of 120 to 130 men, and each of its four gun sections numbered 10 men. Each firing battery also included a wire section, an instrument section, and truck drivers.

The 10-man gun section included a gunner corporal, a number one man who opened the breach and fired the gun, a number two man who loaded the gun, and numbers three and four men who delivered the round and set the fuse and charge. The remaining men shifted the trail, carried ammunition, and performed other miscellaneous duties. Machine gunners were assigned to the guns from the machine-gun section.

calls at government expense. We were a very popular group when the other men in the outfit learned of long-distance availability.

Life in the field on maneuvers was not without funny mishaps. "Bud" Houser, who also took part in the Tennessee maneuvers with the 502nd PIR, remembers one particular incident when the men bedded down for the night.

We came into these two fields. One field was used for the headquarters and the officers, while the troops were on the larger field. We could hear the talking that night that they were getting bit. The next morning, that field was a bed of red color; they were just filled with chiggers. You talk about people with chigger bites!

When going up and down some of those steep hills in Tennessee, the machine gunner got tired of carrying that machine gun because it was quite heavy. So word went to pass it around. It went down one line and came back up the other. The first lieutenant walked ahead of me. After I got through carrying it, I told him it was his turn, and he said he had already carried that thing. He forgot that he was in the other line when it came that way, but we convinced him that he hadn't carried it, so he did.

The 377th Field Artillery, which usually backed up the 502nd PIR, participated in the Tennessee maneuvers.[9] William Gammon was replaced as a machine gunner in Battery B and put in charge of the Commo Section. The Tennessee maneuvers were not as memorable for him as the South Carolina maneuvers had been a month earlier, however.

We made a jump in South Carolina, and it was very low, maybe just under 400 feet, and we established communications. I was in the Commo Section then. A boy in the 326th Engineers unbuckled the straps on his chute because it was a long ride and hot. They gave the order to jump, but he never buckled up the straps, and when he jumped, the chute opened and he kept on going. He was in another plane, and the jumpmaster was supposed to check them before the jump.

---

9. An airborne division's divisional artillery consisted of three battalions of 75-millimeter pack howitzers—two with twelve guns each and one of sixteen guns, the latter parachute-dropped.

Parachute Battalion

A parachute battalion included a headquarters company and three rifle companies. The headquarters company included a commo platoon, a machine-gun platoon with six .30-caliber air-cooled machine guns, and a mortar platoon with four 81-millimeter mortars. For inspections, there was also a headquarters section.

Each of the three rifle companies consisted of a headquarters section and three rifle platoons. Each platoon, according to the 1942 table of organization and equipment, comprised two twelve-man rifle squads and a six-man mortar squad. Later, in 1944, a third rifle squad was added. For Normandy, the table of organization and equipment was not followed, and some rifle platoons consisted of three squads of twelve men that included a squad leader, an assistant squad leader, a three-man machine-gun team, and seven riflemen. The mortar squad of six men with a single 60-millimeter mortar was part of the parachute rifle platoon. The armament of the squad included one light .30-caliber machine gun and M-1 rifles (carbines for the machine-gun team).

A 60-millimeter mortar for airborne troops in a parapack.
NATIONAL ARCHIVES

In Tennessee, it went well. We assembled the guns and fired the battery about six minutes after the first man jumped.

Robert Flory was with the 506th PIR during the June maneuvers in Tennessee and the earlier exercise in South Carolina.

On the exercise in South Carolina, we were supposed to jump in Camden. We flew gliders down there that time. That was the first time we had done that [had C-47s loaded with paratroopers towing gliders]. We had flown through a rainstorm, but they decided it was too dangerous to jump through the clouds, and we flew back to Camp Mackall. That was the first time I ever landed in an airplane. They released the gliders first before we returned. We were towing Colonel Allen's battalion, and we were to drop the gliders, come around, and jump the other side of Camden. When the weather cleared, we left Camp MacKall and made our jump.

As I recall, the 506th was sent to Camp Breckenridge, Kentucky, and we were to take off from Sturgis Field and jump outside of Lebanon, Tennessee. The first jump was scary, because we jumped at a low altitude; I would say under 500 feet. I know because when my chute opened, I swung once, and bang, I hit the ground. We were

A 37-millimeter antitank gun during maneuvers of the 1st Cavalry Division at Fort Bliss. NATIONAL ARCHIVES

in the maneuvers for ten days and two weeks. We were supplied by air. They dropped these big plastic bags of water, which burst on hitting.

We jumped with a canteen of water, and we were told anyone getting more water would be court-martialed. Being a smart aleck that I was, I drank my water right away because it was hot. We were in a farmyard, so I went in a barn, found a couple of cows, and milked them to fill my canteen. The lieutenant walked in, caught me, and said I was subject to court-martial, and I replied that it wasn't water. He told me to let him have some of that, and he drank it too.

Later on, we were captured by the other army, and that phase of the maneuver was over. We were released in Bowling Green, Kentucky, and told to rejoin our outfit.

The second jump, not too far from the original, I don't remember much about, except that a buddy and I got hungry, so we stole some chickens and cooked them. I remember the farmers were upset, because one of them caught me and asked when we were going to get those balloons off his cornfield!

FO John Schumacher, who graduated as a glider pilot in February 1943, shifted from assignment to assignment around the country before he landed at Camp Campbell, Kentucky, to take part in the Tennessee maneuvers. The CG-4A gliders that participated in this operation had wheels that could be dropped off to allow the craft to land on the skid, which had been modified for the purpose. This was the only time in his career as a glider pilot that Schumacher jettisoned his gear and landed on his skids in an open field. Many of the gliders skidded across the landing zone, crashed to a stop, and ended up in a heap of wreckage. Soon after this exercise, all CG-4As were outfitted only with fixed wheels to allow better landing control.

After the Tennessee maneuvers, Flory returned to Fort Bragg with the 506th PIR.

> We were informed we were going overseas. We were issued dust masks and sunglasses, I guess to give the Germans the idea we were going to North Africa.
>
> Before we went overseas, they came through each regiment and picked out certain men for assignment X. They were replacements for 82nd people injured or killed. The first sergeant in our company selected all the screwups and sent them out, including one platoon sergeant.

During the company formations within the 502nd PIR that took place after the regiment's return to Fort Bragg, the commanding officer announced that the soldiers would have to remove or cover at their own expense all tattoos with military unit designations. PFC Ray Hood, who had not succumbed to the tattoo fashion, wryly watched his disgruntled comrades scurry to obey their commander's order.

> One man, known as "Drinkin' George" for excellent reasons, had on his left shoulder an open parachute that was five or six inches in height. Beneath the chute were the words "Co C, 501st Parachute Battalion." The tattooist attempted to change the parachute into an eagle with folded wings. Since our division insignia showed an eagle's head, this correction was considered unsatisfactory, and additional work gave him a nice eight-inch scab, which finally fell off to reveal a tattoo that resembled nothing on this earth. He's lucky his arm didn't fall off.

As it turned out, this order was an exercise in futility, because every time the paratroopers jumped in Europe, they wore their division patches on their uniform sleeves.

The 31st Infantry Division's mobile library at the Third Army's Louisiana maneuvers, August 1943. NATIONAL ARCHIVES

While the 82nd Airborne Division was engaged in combat in the Mediterranean and the 101st honed its skills, a flood of volunteers manned additional newly forming units. Among the volunteers was James "Jas" David Purifoy of Texarkana, Arkansas, who was drafted at age nineteen and inducted on April 1, 1943. At Camp Robinson, Arkansas, he was issued his uniforms, given some basic military instruction, and put on a train destined for Camp Roberts. By then the camp was a sprawling post with more than 30,000 men. Although this was Purifoy's first time away from home and he was homesick, he enjoyed the mild California climate. In the tenth week of his training, a small contingent from Fort Benning came to recruit volunteers for the paratroopers, and Purifoy jumped at the chance to join them.

> They sent us on a regular train to Fort Benning in July, without leave. It took seven days to get there. We were tired, dirty, and nasty and looked like a bunch of bums when we arrived with only one change of clothes.
>
> They assigned me to class 89. The first week was all running and calisthenics, the

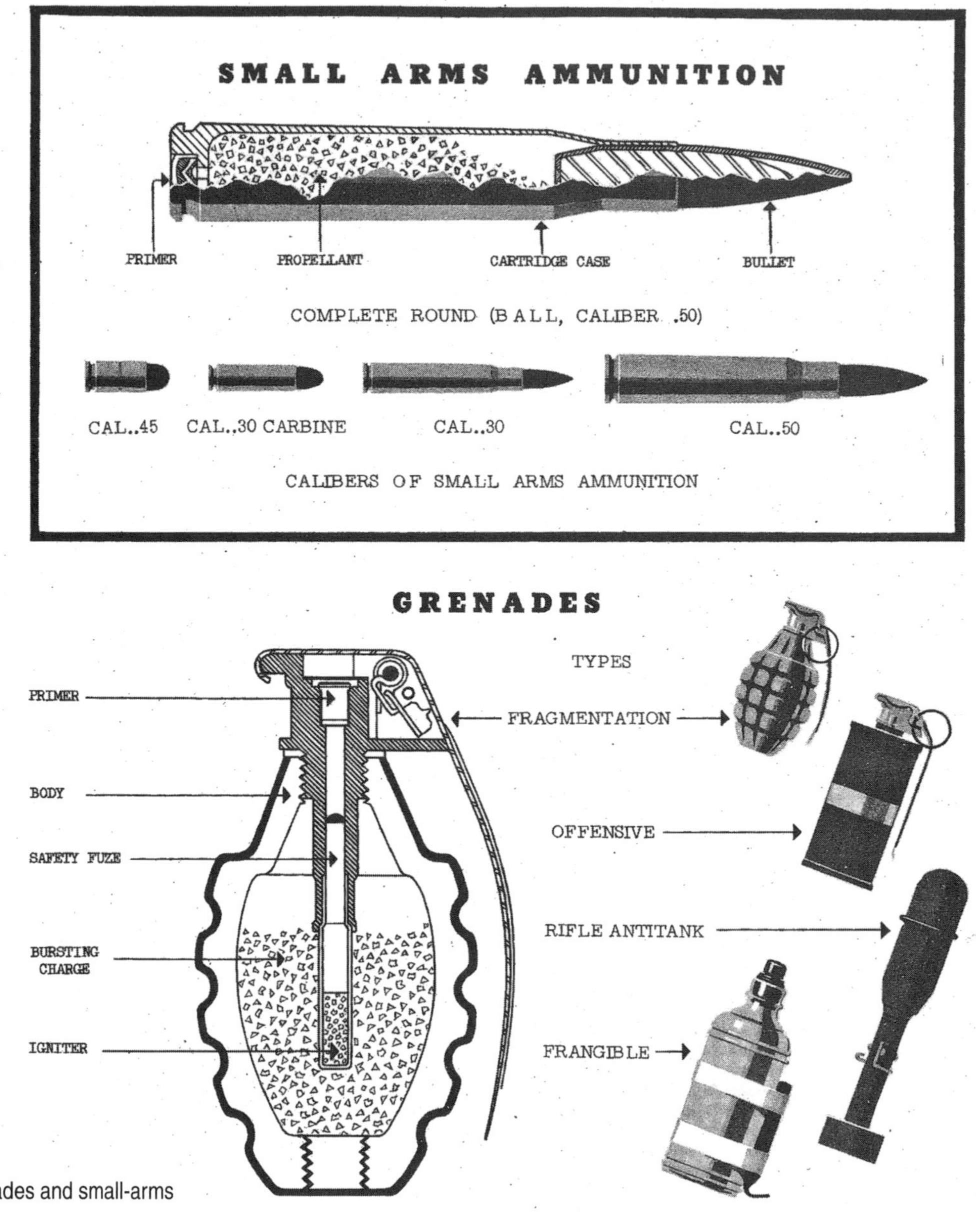

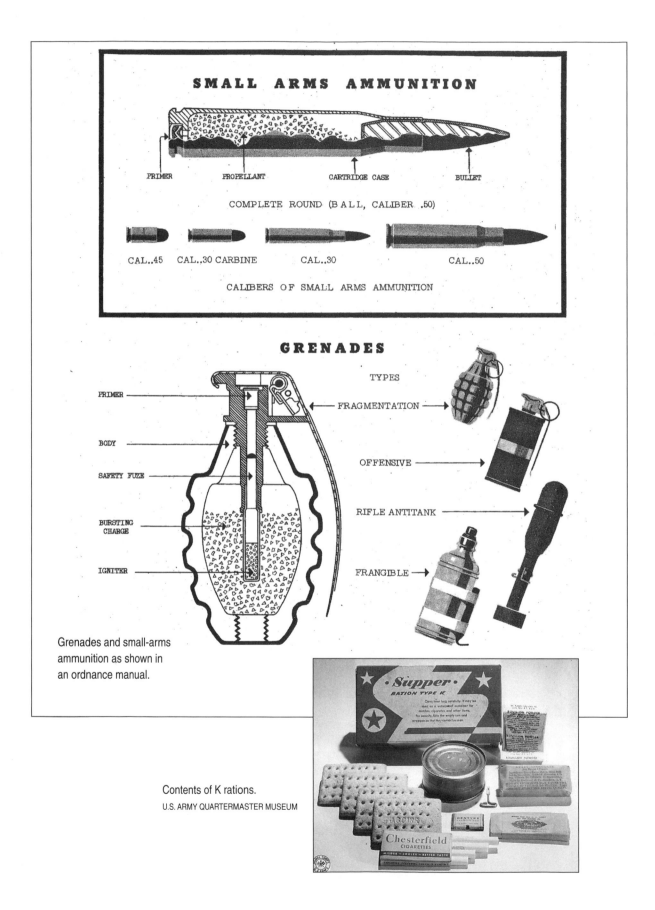

Grenades and small-arms ammunition as shown in an ordnance manual.

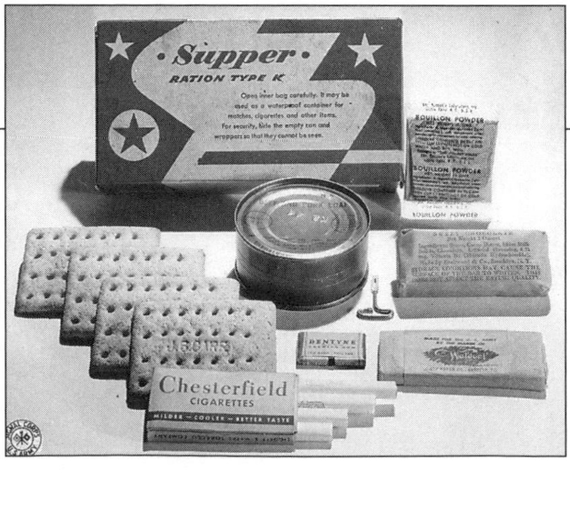

Contents of K rations.

U.S. ARMY QUARTERMASTER MUSEUM

> second week running and packing parachutes, the third week jumping from the tower. I thought the sudden stop was pretty thrilling. I was nervous on the first jump. Once you got out the door and your parachute opened, you felt good, but you hit the ground awful hard. The other four jumps, I started dreading it when I got close to the ground.

Purifoy finished jump school at the end of August 1943. He joined the 542nd PIR, forming at Fort Benning and later was sent to North Carolina to join the 13th A/B Division.

During their practice jumps, these paratroopers carried their M-1s in a single piece strapped around their shoulders. Until the time of the Normandy drop, however, many paratroopers still carried the rifles broken down into their three major components. The largest training exercise in which Purifoy participated took place in the fall of 1943 in North Carolina. "The first was at night with full equipment," he recalls, "and that was my first time jumping with full equipment. It worked out well." In December, his battalion was broken up, and the troops were sent overseas as replacements. He caught up with the 101st A/B Division in England to fill out its ranks.

From 1942 through 1943, even into 1944, troop trains rumbled through the country virtually every day. As the training bases rapidly grew in size, soldiers and airmen crisscrossed the country moving to their assigned units. In addition, whole battalions, regiments, divisions, and air units were often shuffled from one post to another. A constant flow of men and units passed through the basic and specialized training centers. In addition to the troops, the trains ferried everything from bullets and beans to tanks and other heavy equipment from factories to military posts and embarkation ports on the both coasts. Despite the added activity, the railroads successfully managed to handle the needs of the civilian population. Most troop trains were given low priority and shunted onto sidings.[10]

As soon as the units completed their training, they moved to their ports of embarkation. The units earmarked for the invasion of Northern France began landing in Great Britain between 1942 and mid-1944. Most were green formations that needed additional training. On the other hand, the forces destined to invade Southern France had already undergone their baptism of fire fighting the Germans in Tunisia, Sicily, and the Italian mainland in 1943.[11] Some of the units in the Mediterranean theater were eventually withdrawn and sent to England to provide a veteran force to spearhead the Normandy invasion. The forces that formed up in Great Britain between late 1943 and 1944 were better equipped and prepared than units the Allies had mustered for a possible cross-Channel invasion in 1942 or 1943.

10. At this time, moving cross-country by road was not a practical option. President Eisenhower created the interstate highway system in the 1950s, based on the German *Autobahn,* in order to improve logistics for future military needs.

11. Those assigned to take part in the invasion of South France for the most part were pulled from the battlefront only in the summer of 1944 and given less preparation time than those that went into Normandy.

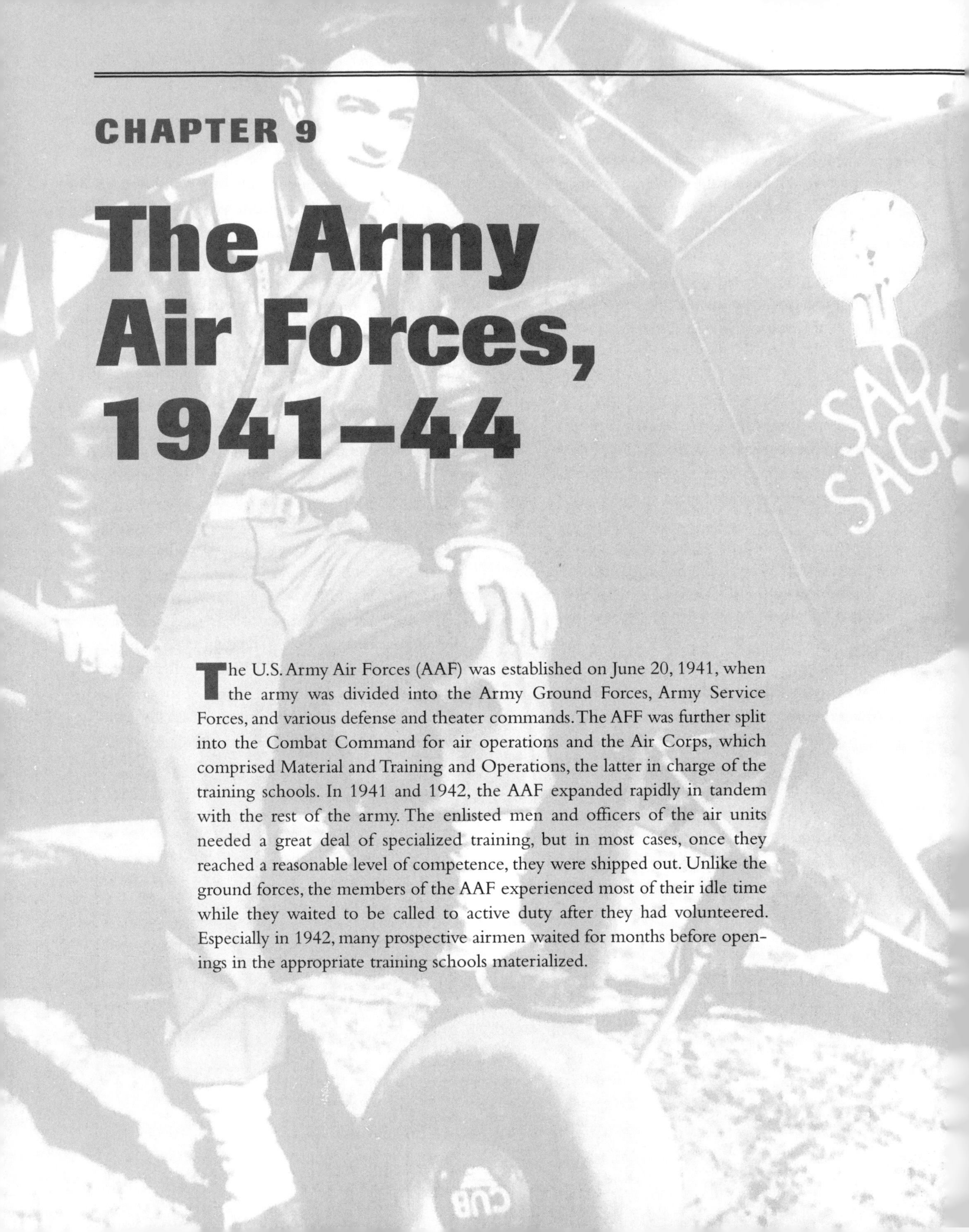

CHAPTER 9

The Army Air Forces, 1941–44

The U.S. Army Air Forces (AAF) was established on June 20, 1941, when the army was divided into the Army Ground Forces, Army Service Forces, and various defense and theater commands. The AFF was further split into the Combat Command for air operations and the Air Corps, which comprised Material and Training and Operations, the latter in charge of the training schools. In 1941 and 1942, the AAF expanded rapidly in tandem with the rest of the army. The enlisted men and officers of the air units needed a great deal of specialized training, but in most cases, once they reached a reasonable level of competence, they were shipped out. Unlike the ground forces, the members of the AAF experienced most of their idle time while they waited to be called to active duty after they had volunteered. Especially in 1942, many prospective airmen waited for months before openings in the appropriate training schools materialized.

At the time of the attack on Pearl Harbor, the AAF numbered more than 350,000 men; a year later, it had almost five times as many. The AAF Officer Candidate School was located at Miami Beach, Florida; however, most of its officers were graduates of the Aviation Cadet Recruiting Program. Early in the war, there was a brief shortage of trained technicians, especially aviation mechanics. But thanks to a massive expansion of the training command, more than sixty civilian mechanic schools were leased, and the number of military schools increased from three to thirty-three during 1942. As a result, the shortage of trained technicians rapidly dwindled.

On March 2, 1942, the structure of the AAF included four air forces in the continental United States, several combat air forces overseas, and the following specialized commands:

1. Flying Training and Technical Training Commands, which were united in 1943 into the Training Command, with HQ in Fort Worth, Texas
   a. Three Flight Training Commands, made of one to four wings
      - Eastern Flying Training Command, with HQ at Maxwell Air Base, Alabama
      - Central Flying Training Command, with HQ at Randolph Air Base, Texas
      - Western Flying Training Command, HQ in Santa Ana, California
   b. Three Technical Training Commands
      - Eastern Technical Training Command, with HQ in Greensboro, North Carolina
      - Central Technical Training Command, with HQ in St. Louis
      - Western Technical Training Command, with HQ in Denver
2. Material Command, responsible for development, testing, inspection, and procurement, with HQ at Wright Field, Ohio
3. Air Service Command, which handled repair, rebuilding, and preparations for overseas shipment of aircraft, with HQ at Patterson Field, Ohio
4. Air Transport Command, which replaced the Ferrying Command on July 1, 1942, and was responsible for all transportation, with HQ in Washington, D.C. Within the United States, the Women's Air Force Service Pilots (WASPs) performed most of the ferrying functions and were assigned to tow targets.
5. Troop Carrier Command, which was created in 1942 and worked closely with the army airborne forces and provided the troop transports and gliders with pilots, as well as controlling their training and deployment, with HQ Indianapolis

The ground crews, especially the mechanics, were the unsung heroes of the AAF. Although their job lacked glamour, they were indispensable for the smooth functioning of the air unit. William J. Hart from Arkansas, one of the thousands of men providing these vital services, had enlisted in the Army Air Corps as early as in August 1940. He was assigned to the 3rd Transport Air Squadron at Duncan Field in San Antonio. He trained as a mechanic at Chanute Field, Illinois. Shortly before the outbreak of the war, he attended a school in Georgia, where he and his fellow apprentices practiced on three B-18 bombers.

> The outfit I joined in Georgia split and went to Louisiana before the war. Here again, we had an old B-18. When the war started, we didn't go overseas, but to Camp Douglas, Wisconsin. At that time, we received the aircraft from the airlines, which also flew DC-3s, and we took those birds to train our pilots and mechanics. It was fun because the civilian aircraft weren't all equipped the same way, and the accessories on the engines weren't all the same and

The 84th Squadron

In England, the 84th Squadron consisted of the following:

1. Maintenance Section
   - Maintenance officer
   - Assistant maintenance officer
   - Crew chief for each aircraft, about forty to fifty men
2. Pilot Section
   - Power pilots, twenty to twenty-five, including spares
   - Glider pilots, twenty to twenty-five men
3. Administrative Section
   - CO, a major
   - XO, a captain
   - Adjutant, a lieutenant
   - Administration officer
   - Supply officer
   - Technical supply officer for aircraft parts
   - Communications officer
   - Intelligence officer
   - Legal officer, who was also a glider pilot

> were also mounted differently. You had to have a separate supply catalog for each.
>
> We moved to Sedalia, Missouri, and from there we came down to open the air base at Austin. At Bergstrom, in Austin, I passed the warrant officer test. When I made warrant, I went to California to visit the Douglas plant. Before the war, it was the policy to send the crew chief to the Long Beach plant to see his bird and follow it through so he knew everything about it. I spent about a month there. When I returned, I was sent to Fort Wayne, Indiana, to join my new outfit, the 84th Squadron of the 437th Group, as the assistant maintenance officer.

Not all ground support personnel were part of fighter and bomber squadrons. Other special service units, such as service squadrons, were formed to maintain everything from airfields to equipment supply. In 1942, Lt. Robert Hahlen, who had suffered from a collapsed lung and no longer qualified to fly B-26s, was assigned to the newly organized 312th Air Base Group, which included a headquarters squadron and two service and supply squadrons.

> There were a few cadre troops and so forth, but most were new recruits they shipped in. They made some mistakes, of course, but we survived it. Eventually we were transferred to Columbia, South Carolina. I don't remember exactly when we moved, but it was real cold in Columbia. When we got there, our group was filled up. We had a lot of troops. We sent people to service and technical schools to get them qualified.
>
> A service group comprised a headquarters squadron and two service squadrons. The service squadrons were developed to provide third-echelon service and supply for any combat group they were servicing. We were supposed to service two combat groups.
>
> In Columbia, I was put in command of the headquarters squadron and later the 331st Service Squadron. We lived in tents because it was a brand new base. They had a quartermaster building and a few wooden structures. I don't recall how long we were there before we transferred to a field outside of Savannah, Georgia. From there we trained and sent people out to tech schools.
>
> We transferred to Lakeland, Florida, right after Christmas 1942. They were training

B-26s out there; it was a cadre group. At Columbia, they had B-25s. At Savannah, there were A-36s and P-51s. We didn't do much work with the combat groups then.

At Lakeland, we were almost a complete unit. People came back from North Africa while we were getting ready to go overseas. We presumed we were going to North Africa. We packed our stuff and carried our own toolboxes. Finally, in about April 1943, we were taken to Camp Shanks, New York.

Many of the men who volunteered for the Air Corps wanted to become pilots, but they did not meet the standards required to qualify. In addition, many of those who passed the initial tests failed to meet the requirements for piloting and had to content themselves with other positions, such as bombardiers or navigators. In some cases, however, draftees like William M. Thompson wound up in the cadet program and carved a career in the military.

I was about the third one in my hometown in Missouri to be drafted into service. I was drafted in March 1941 and sent to the infantry. After Pearl Harbor came along, I tried to get assigned to the Air Corps for pilot training. I decided if there was a war, I wanted to go as a pilot. In 1942, I was accepted into the pilot training program after almost a year as an aid man in the infantry. As a cadet, I went to Lackland (San Antonio) for my preflight training. From San Antonio, I went to Vernon, Texas, for primary training in a PT-19; then to Waco, Texas, for training in a BT-13; then to Victoria, Texas, for training in an AT-6, and I graduated there.

It was not determined what I would fly until I graduated and got my assignment. When I went down to Matagorda Island for gunnery as part of our advanced training, I assumed I was going to be a fighter pilot, but when I got my orders on graduation, it read "Austin, Texas, Troop Carrier." Back in 1943, we didn't even know what a troop carrier was. We proceeded to Austin and checked in. The first thing I did was look for the fighters, because in my mind I thought I was going to be a fighter escort for these troop carriers. I rudely found out when I saw these big twin- engine DC-3s that that was what I was going to be flying. I graduated on April 22, 1943. I was processed to Austin, and I checked in in May 1943. I checked out in a C-47, went to Sedalia Air Base in Missouri, and was assigned to the 437th Group. I was one of the first assigned as cadre to the group. We trained from June to about September 1943; moved the whole group, when fully

Cadet Pilot Training

Cadets were commissioned after successfully completing the following training:

- Pre-Flight School: ten weeks, including course work, code, map reading, physical and military training
- Primary Flying School: ten weeks, including seventy hours flying plus course work
- Basic Flying School: ten weeks, including seventy hours flying in basic trainer plus ground school. Pilots were selected for single- or multiengine training after this school.
- Advanced Flying Training: ten weeks, including seventy hours flying, AT-6 for single-engine pilots, AT-9, AT-10, AT-17, or AT-24 for twin-engine pilots.

Cadet Bombardier and Navigator Training

- Pre-Flight School: ten weeks, same school as for pilots
- Gunnery School: six weeks, for both navigator and bombardier, training mainly with flexible mounts including maintenance
- Bombardier School: twenty weeks, with 120 hours in AT-11 trainer for practice bombing, plus ground school, including navigation, bombing, code, recognition, and meteorology
- Navigator School: twenty weeks, with 104 hours flying on navigation problems, plus ground school, including pilotage, instruments, dead reckoning, radio, celestial navigation, meteorology, and code
- Bombardier-Navigator School: twelve weeks, bombardier training for navigators who were to be assigned to medium bombers

manned, to Pope Field, North Carolina; and trained there with the 101st Airborne Division until about December 1943, and then prepared for overseas.

Frank Gallagher joined the navy in February 1941 to become a pilot. He signed up for the Naval Air Corps in his hometown of Des Moines, and he was sent to Fairfax in Kansas City, Kansas, for his primary flight training. In June, he reported at Jacksonville for his basic training or "boot camp," according to the navy. From there he traveled to Corpus Christi, Texas, for further flight instruction. "I had ninety hours of log time," he recalls, "but I had a little difficulty in slipping into a 100-foot circle (to represent a carrier deck) and picking up the instructor and returning. When I landed on the King Ranch [in south Texas], it was rough: My tail wheel came loose, I ended up in the flight pattern of another cadet, and he collided with me. I had to meet a board, and we were both washed out."

Disconsolate, Gallagher returned to Des Moines in August and waited for his discharge, which he received in November. Within a month, the United States entered the war. Still burning with patriotic fervor and a passion to fly, Gallagher reported at Fort Crook, Nebraska, and enlisted in the AAF for flight training. Thirty days later, he reported at Santa Ana, California, and from there he went to Visalia for primary flight training, but bad luck seemed to dog his steps. "I soloed there and, getting excited, I took a plane, went up for a solo, ran out of gas, spun in from 400 feet, and that was the end of my flying. They asked me if I wanted to continue flying, and I said yes, so they assigned me to the Bombardier School at Roswell, New Mexico."

Gallagher attended the bombardier course between August and October 1942. He learned how to operate the Norden bombsight, which he never used again after he graduated, since he was assigned to B-26s, which used a system with crosshairs and manual release. He also learned how to load and arm the bombs and handle navigation. After he received his commission from the school, he reported to a B-26 training unit at Barksdale Field in Louisiana. In February 1943, he went to West Palm Beach, Florida, where he boarded a C-47 bound for England, which flew unescorted and alone and was full of civilian engineers. The route took Lieutenant Gallagher to Port-au-Prince, Haiti, for an overnight stop, then to Natal, Brazil, across the Atlantic to the Azores, and finally to Marrakech in Morocco. Since replacements did not have priority, the journey went at a leisurely pace as the aircraft was held over at Marrakech for thirty days. In the meantime, virtually every day, B-26s from West Palm Beach landed and took off for England. Frustrated, Lieutenant Gallagher decided to leave the group waiting for the next C-47 to depart Morocco and hitch a ride on one of the flights bound for England. In March 1943, he landed at Braintree, where he reported to the 450th Squadron, 322nd Bombardment Group.

Graydon K. Eubank, a nineteen-year-old student at Texas A&M who had already obtained a civilian pilot's license in 1941, was toying with the idea of enlisting in the army when the Japanese attacked Pearl Harbor. He enlisted on January 23, 1942, and was soon on his way to San Antonio for preflight training. Next, he underwent his primary training at Uvalde, Texas. In his class, there were a number of "flying sergeants," who, if they graduated, would become flight officers in 1943. Although no distinction was made between the cadets and the sergeants during training, the NCOs stayed in separate barracks. In Uvalde, Eubank flew in a two-seater Fairchild PT-19 with standard blue fuselage and bright yellow wings. During the next phase, he flew the North American BT-9 Yale trainer at Randolph Field in San Antonio. After he received his commission, Eubank was assigned to a B-26 unit at MacDill Field, Florida, with about six other classmates of the class of sixty. The rest were mainly assigned to B-17s.

> Later in September, I was flying in the short-wing Martin B-26, known in those days as the "Prostitute" and the "Widow Maker" because it was a short-wing airplane with no means of support. Later on, we went to a longer wing; they added four feet to each side, making it easier to fly. We had lost many, many people in training. The old saying was "One a day in Tampa Bay," primarily because it was a very hot aircraft. It would come into the final approach at 150 miles per hour and had electric props that were not too good and would go out of control.

Training Aircraft

- Beech AT-7 Navigator: twin-engine aircraft with a crew of two plus three student navigators
- Beech AT-10 Wichita: twin-engine wooden aircraft used to train multiengine pilots
- Beech AT-11 Kansan: twin-engine training aircraft for bombardiers and gunners, with a crew of 3 to 4; included flexible guns, bomb rack, and clear nose
- Boeing AT-15 Crewmaker
- Cessna AT-17 Bobcat: twin-engine five-seater
- Fairchild AT-21 Gunner: twin-engine five-seater with .30-caliber turret guns and nose gun; carried two gunners and a relief gunner
- Fairchild PT-19, PT-23, and PT-26 Cornell: single-engine two-seater with open cockpit
- North American AT-6 Texan: single-engine advanced trainer
- North American AT-16 Harvard
- North American BT-9 and BT-14 Yale
- Ryan PT-21 and PT-22 Recruit
- Stearman PT-13, PT-17, PT-18, and PT-27 Caydet (also known to cadets as the "Yellow Peril"): single-engine two-seater with open cockpit (PT-27 had closed cockpit)
- Vultee AT-19 Reliant: single-engine five-seater
- Vultee BT-13 and BT-15 Valiant (also known to cadets as the "Vibrator" or "Bamboo Bomber")

The Martin Marauder B-26 Medium Bomber

The B-26 A model with short wings reached speeds of 315 miles per hour and carried up to 3,000 pounds of bombs at a ceiling of 25,000 feet. The B model had a speed of 282 miles per hour and included four additional machine guns fixed in the fuselage. The aircraft was also armed with a .50-caliber machine gun in the nose operated by the navigator-bombardier, a top turret with two .50-caliber guns manned by the engineer, two .50-caliber tail guns operated by the tail gunner, and two waist guns used by the radio operator. This twin-engine bomber required a high landing and takeoff speed and more effort and skill to land and take off than most aircraft. John B. Walters described it in his article "The B-26 Martin Marauder":

> Because the aircraft was, for its time, so revolutionary in design, it was difficult to learn to fly. It had two huge 2,000 horsepower engines attached to very short 65 foot long wings. . . . Its huge propellers were the first four-bladed props used on bombers and they often time "ran away" on take off. To achieve the 110-115 mph required for takeoff usually meant using all of the runway if any sizable load was on board. Landings were accomplished with 150 mph on the approach, rounding out with touch-down at around 115 mph . . . those characteristics made the B-26 a "hot" bomber. . . .
>
> Though takeoffs and landings were combinations of excitement, madness and sheer terror, all of us who flew the Marauder learned to respect and love her. (*Military* magazine)

Eubank's unit moved to Lakeland, Florida, where it stayed between September and December 1942. The men were quartered in tents on concrete slabs.

Lieutenant Eubank's unit moved to West Palm Beach in May 1943 before it went to England. His crew consisted of Lt. Elwood Lunkenheimer, the copilot; Lt. Tom Bowdre, the navigator-bombardier; Sergeant Walker, the crew chief; and a radio operator.

> We left Puerto Rico and went on to British Guiana. We were flying at several-minute intervals between planes, from there to Belem and then to Natal. We were flying in loose formation to Ascension Island. That was one long flight, and if you missed it, you had to ditch. We had one of our best navigators in the lead ship. The German submarines would beacon us; they would put out false signals to try to lead us off course. I think we spotted one German submarine on the trip over. We carried two huge collapsible tanks in the bomb bay. I saw the island and I was happy. We stayed there a couple of days. Then we went on to Roberts Field at Monrovia, Liberia, and stayed there a couple of days. We went up to the Firestone rubber plantation with a little time off. From there, we flew to Dakar; then we went over the Sahara Desert to a place called Tendu, where we refueled and waited for the weather to change. It was nothing but a strip. From there we flew to Marrakech, and there we had some engine trouble. It took four or five days to get that fixed. From there we went to Port Lyautey on the coast, and then non-stop out over the ocean into England. On landing, we put our gear down. We had three green lights, and the left main gear light was not on. We had no fuel to go anywhere else, so we came down on the right main gear

> and hit hard on it, which caused the other gear to snap into place. I remember this well because the copilot pulled out a bottle of scotch whiskey, and I had never had scotch whiskey in my life.

Robert Raoul Walsh, son of the famous film director Raoul Walsh, enlisted on January 12, 1942, at Los Angeles. Interestingly, he later served in the 8th Air Force, which became known as the "Hollywood Air Force" because of the movie stars, such as Jimmy Stewart, who were associated with it.

Sergeant Walsh had completed gunnery school at Albuquerque, New Mexico, and was on a B-17, ready to cross the Atlantic as a tail gunner, when his application for cadet training was approved. He suspected that his father might have had a hand in his acceptance. First he trained at Santa Ana, California, and then at Kirtland Field, New Mexico, as a bombardier and learned to operate the Norden bombsight.

> You were in control of the aircraft on the bomb run as far as making it go left or right, but you could not make it go up or down. You would put crosshairs on target with trail set in there and the height, which determined how far ahead to drop the bombs. The crosswinds too—we had to compensate for that. We had about 100 hours of training on a twin-engine Beech AT-11 Kansan from which we dropped little blue practice bombs, which had some type of powder in them so we could see them when they burst.

In November 1943, his training completed, Walsh went to Fort Dix, New Jersey, where he boarded the *Queen Elizabeth* with 20,000 other airmen. The liner crossed the Atlantic in five days and docked in Scotland. From there Walsh headed south to report for duty with the 379th Bombardment Group at Kimbolton.

Chester L. Pietrzak, a volunteer for the AAF, enlisted in his hometown of Erie, Pennsylvania, in June 1942. He also went through preflight training at Santa Ana before he attended Bombardier School at Victorville, California. During his gunnery training, he had to learn to take apart the .50-caliber machine guns and reassemble them blindfolded. He also had to do a good deal of skeet shooting and fire at tow targets during a whole week in the skies off Galveston, Texas, over the Gulf of Mexico.

At Bombardier School, instructors explained the operation of the Norden bombsight, but to keep the instrument secret, there were no user manuals. The bombsight allegedly was an early form of computer with a telescope that aimed ahead of the aircraft. With the proper adjustments on the target, the bombs were released automatically, while the sight carried its own gyroscopes to keep it on target. Pietrzak began his training by maneuvering an instrument mounted on wheels around a hangar floor to "bomb" a small moving target. During the next phase, Pietrzak flew in a twin-engine AT-11 over the Mojave Desert. The plane carried a pilot and two bombardier cadets. As the pilot maneuvered the plane, the cadets took turns lining up targets and dropping 100-pound bombs containing sand and a small incendiary device that gave off a puff of smoke as it hit the ground. While one cadet operated the Norden bombsight, the other took pictures through the rear floor opening. After they returned to base at Victorville, the photos were processed and evaluated to determine the student's bombing score. If the score was to low, the cadet washed out.

After he was commissioned in September 1943, Lieutenant Pietrzak transferred north to Spokane, to a B-17 base where he met his pilot, Frank Prendergast. In due course, they acquired a navigator, copilot, and engineer. Poor weather slowed their training, but eventually the crew transferred to Admore, Oklahoma, where it was joined by the rest of its members, fresh from their training schools. The entire crew trained as a unit for three more months before it departed for England in February 1944.

For William E. Denham, the road to cadet school was more convoluted. He enlisted in April 1941 at the age of twenty-four and was assigned to a special air corps unit, the School Reception Squadron, which moved around the country processing inductees. As a private, Denham served as a clerk. When his unit reached Scott Field, Illinois, he was ordered to attend Clerical School at Fort Logan, Colorado—to his great amusement, because he had never been good at typing, even in his typing days. He rejoined the squadron at Keyster Field, Mississippi, where he received the news that he had been accepted for cadet training. He reported for Pre-Flight School in San Antonio, only to find out that the school was full. In July 1942, Denham and 600 other cadets were sent to Santa Ana, California, where there were openings for them.

From California, Cadet Denham went on to Glendale, Arizona, where he flew the Stearman PT-17 biplane in Primary Flight School. Next, he went to Tucson for Basic Flying School, where he qualified in the BT-13 twin-engine aircraft, and his instructors decided that he would fly multiengine aircraft. After that, he completed Advanced Flying School at Marfa, Texas, where he flew the AT-17 and received his commission in May 1943. Before he could complete his training that summer, he was sent to Moses Lake, Washington, for transition training on the B-17. On his maiden flight in a B-17 Denham, a lieutenant by now, he was accompanied by an instructor pilot. After ten hours of flying, he flew his first solo mission on a B-17.

To his chagrin, Denham soon found out that his status as pilot was by no means assured. The positions of pilot and copilot were determined by the number of flying hours; the man with fewer hours became the copilot, and many of the newly arriving pilots at Moses Lake had already been through a special B-17 training course that was part of Transition Flying Training. Since he was one of the few pilots not to have this training, he endeavored to get the extra flying hours before aircraft assignments were issued. When the time came, he made it to pilot status and got to pick a crew for his plane. Then Denham and his crew flew to various bases between Washington and Texas for training operations, during which they practiced high-altitude gunnery and bombing, among other things. "We had a target at Moses Lake," he says. "Moses Lake consisted of an X with streetlights going in two directions, and a short distance away was the target. It had about the same identification, and I believe someone did drop a little 6-pound charge of black powder in the town a time or two by mistake."

Once Denham and his crew completed their training, they joined the 452nd Bombardment Group (BG) at Pyote, Texas. By the time they got there, almost two-thirds of the air crews had been there for more than a month. Denham and his crew were assigned a new B-17 and flew to Minnesota. In December 1943, they flew to Presque Isle, Maine, to stage for their departure to Great Britain. Their next stop was Newfoundland, where they remained for almost two weeks before the 452nd BG began flying its aircraft individually across the Atlantic.

> Some went the southern route, and others the northern route. We carried the customary full load. It was around Christmastime when we took off, but engine trouble caused us to come right back. A few days later, we tried again. I got in the middle of the North Atlantic flying in and out of clouds in icing conditions, going up and down to melt that ice and find a warm place. Right about in

the middle, I looked up, and there was a B-24 just passing over, about 1,000 feet above me. He was going in a southerly direction, and I was going easterly. We finally got across and landed in Nutts Corner, Northern Ireland, and a few days later, we flew on to our group in England.[1]

Douglas G. McArthur received his draft notice in the spring of 1942 and reported for induction into the army at Fort Lewis, Washington, in March. After basic training at Sheppard Field, Texas, he attended a Radio Maintenance and Operation School at Scott Field, Illinois. Next, he moved to Boca Raton, Florida, for radar training. After he had undergone all this specialized training, McArthur was admitted to the pilot training program. He passed the physical at Nashville in November and reported first at Maxwell Field in Montgomery, Alabama, for Pre-Flight Training. His training went as follows:

December 19, 1942: Pre-Flight Training at Maxwell Field. All ground school with lots of physical training including obstacle courses and eight-mile runs every week, as well as hazing. Subjects included math, maps and charts, communications, code, physics, chemical warfare, and army, air, and naval forces.

February 28, 1943: Primary Flight Training at Bennettsville, South Carolina. Soloed in a PT-17 Stearman on March 12; about 35 percent washed out.

May 1, 1943: Basic Flight Training at Shaw Field near Sumter, South Carolina. Flew BT-13 and BT-15 Vultee "Vibrators." First night flying and instrument flying; about 15 percent washed out.

July 2, 1943: Advanced Flight Training at Moody Field near Valdosta, Georgia. Flew mostly AT-10 twin-engine Beech and some AT-6 single-engine time; about 5 percent washed out.

On August 27, 1943, Douglas McArthur received his wings and commission and moved on to Transition Training at Hendricks Field in Sebring, Florida, where, on September 11, he began to learn how to fly a B-17. He finished this phase of his training on November 8. On November 18, Lieutenant McArthur reported to the 18th Replacement Air Wing at Salt Lake City, where he picked up a crew and engaged in more training. He had to replace his top turret gunner and a waist gunner because one went haywire at high altitude and the other could not get along with the rest of the crew. On January 1, 1944, McArthur and his crew arrived by troop train at Dyersburg, Tennessee, where they received their vaccinations—all eight of them. The training at Dyersburg concentrated on formation flying—McArthur's first experience at it—as well as instrument flying on a trainer, simulated bombing, and other skills. During this last phase of its training, the crew bonded into a close-knit unit.

AAF Personnel Training

Many different schools were available for AAF personnel, including about two dozen types of ground support units, and OCS courses provided leaders for these support and service units. Many of the enlisted men were trained to take their place in aircrews and had to learn many other skills in addition to gunnery training. Each combat aircraft had a flight engineer and one or two assistants. The transport aircraft also carried a

1. Located near Belfast, Nutts Corner was an RAF Coastal Command base that also served as a center for aircraft being ferried over from the United States during the war.

Lt. William Boucher at Camp McCoy with his observation aircraft *Sad Sack*. PHOTO COURTESY OF WILLIAM BOUCHER

crew chief. These men, who performed tasks in preparation for takeoff before the pilots showed up, had to be trained in the proper operation and function of their aircraft. The crew usually included a radioman, who also needed special training. The training of the enlisted members of the aircrew took as long as that of the officer personnel in most cases.

Bonnie Skloss, from a small, dusty Texas town, was drafted and entered military service in July 1942. After he completed the examination, he was sent to Wichita Falls, Texas, for basic training in the AAF instead of the infantry. At Sheppard Field, northwest of Fort Worth, he began training as a flight engineer. Part of this training included a trip to a facility in Boise, Idaho, where B-17s were maintained and rebuilt.[2] Like so many other potential flight engineers, he followed the construction process for a B-17 so that by the time his stay in Boise came to an end, he knew the aircraft inside out. One of the more challenging tasks for him was memorizing all the color-coded wires that ran through the fuselage.

The next phase of Skloss's training was gunnery school in Las Vegas, where he practiced firing at targets from the open cockpit of a two-

2. The B-17s were built only on the West Coast, although Skloss says he watched them being built at Boise. He was apparently sent to the depot there where older aircraft were refurbished and probably rebuilt, possibly for training purposes.

seater plane. "The target towing aircraft was flown by lady pilots, and we were flown by young cadets learning how to fly," he recalls. He also learned how to assemble and disassemble a .50-caliber machine gun blindfolded.

Skloss traveled from one assignment to another by train. When he finally finished his training, he stayed in Salt Lake City for a month awaiting orders. Eventually he was ordered to report at Gowen Field, Idaho, where he joined a B-17 crew. Shortly after his arrival, the 388th BG began to form, and Skloss's aircrew began training. In Boise, the crew was assigned a brand new B-17 on which it trained and flew to England. By this time, Skloss had attained the rank of staff sergeant. "We flew almost every day, weather permitting. We were trained to fly at night and in formation." Formation flying intensified when his outfit moved to Wendover Field, Utah. "We would be taking off and going into formation, and fly a couple hours and come back."

In June 1943, the 388th BG began a cross-country flight from Idaho to the East Coast in preparation for departure. While the ground crews traveled by troop train to their port of embarkation, the aircrews flew across the country, stopping along the way in Kansas and New York. Sergeant Skloss's aircraft took off from Gander Bay, Newfoundland, at 8 A.M. on the Fourth of July.

> We saw nothing but water. We arrived in Reykjavik, Iceland. It was right about sundown, and the sun never did go down. We walked around till midnight, and the sun still did not go down. The island was a green volcanic rock. All your sidewalks were made of real fine crushed rocks. Inside the barracks, each door had a black board to cover up the windows so you could sleep. That was the fifth of July.
>
> We left Reykjavik on the sixth of July. As we began to take off, our number 3 engine caught on fire. The navigator jumped out and put out the fire. We taxied back to park it and check it out. We found that somebody had stuck a bunch of oily rags into that engine. It took about an hour or so before we took off.
>
> After leaving Iceland, we got lost because we hit a storm and had to climb up to 37,000 feet to get above it. For some reason, we didn't hit land. We were about 350 miles north of our designated landing spot. I think that little town we saw was Prestwick (south of Glasgow), Scotland. We were running out of fuel, and it was an hour or so before sundown when we saw a little bitty airstrip, so we just set our B-17 down on it.
>
> I think there was a little single-engine aircraft there. It was an asphalt strip, which made our landing easier. A truck came by and went back. We waited about thirty

Training and Assignment of a Flight Engineer

T. Sgt. Javis J. Roberts, who was drafted in December 1942 and assigned to the 388th Bombardment Group, went through the following training program to become a flight engineer for combat:

- Basic training at Sheppard Field, Wichita Falls, Texas
- Gunnery School in Las Vegas
- Aircraft Engineering School in Amarillo, Texas
- 1st Phase Combat Training at Rattlesnake Bomber Base, Pyote, Texas
- 2nd and 3rd Phases Combat Training in Dyersburg, Tennessee
- Departed for England in February 1944 with training completed

> minutes, and they returned with enough gas to make another 200 or so mile trip to Knettishall, England.

The first aircraft of the 388th BG had landed in England in May. Skloss's plane was one of the last of its unit to arrive.

On December 2, 1942, William F. French, another teenager, volunteered for the army. After he was inducted in San Francisco, he reported first to Fort Ord in his home state of California. After he requested an assignment to the Air Corps, he was sent to St. Petersburg, Florida, to complete his basic training, which consisted of a lot of calisthenics, marching, and military operations. From there he went to Scott Field, Illinois, to train as a radio operator from January to July 1943. He learned Morse code, how to send and receive messages, and how to repair radios.

After he graduated from radio school, he was assigned to the 452nd Bombardment Group at Moses Lake, Washington. The 452nd moved to different sites during the fall of 1943, finally ending up at the Rattlesnake Bomber Base, in a barren desolate area of west Texas near the town of Pyote.[3] From there it traveled to Europe in stages.

> We had new [B-17] aircraft and had to calibrate all the instruments and practice formation flying. From there we went to Grand Island, Nebraska, and on to Presque Isle, Maine, and Goose Bay, Newfoundland. It was early January 1944 when we departed and flew on to Nutts Corner, Northern Ireland.
>
> I think we carried fifty rounds of ammunition per gun when we went over, some K rations, as well as personal gear. The flight over was scary. Most of it was at night, and it was winter. Sometimes they warned us there might be German planes on the route. Sometime during the night, one of us looked up and saw a star, and everybody thought it was blue and the exhaust of a plane. We watched that thing all night long.

French's plane flew from Nutts Corner to Deopham Green, England, to join the rest of the unit.[4]

Alvin J. Anderson, born and raised on a farm in Indiana, graduated from high school in Buffalo, Indiana, in April 1942, when the United States became more heavily engaged in the war. He worked on the family farm throughout the summer, but when winter came, he and one of his neighbors decided to join up before they were drafted. They both went to Lafayette, Indiana, where Anderson signed up for the Army Air Corps and his friend for the Naval Air Corps. The very next day, December 14, Anderson left for Fort Benjamin Harrison in Indianapolis. On the following afternoon, he stood with several hundred men, right hands raised, during the reading of the oath that made them members of the U.S. armed forces.

After a few days, Anderson and his new comrades boarded a train for Miami Beach, Florida, to begin basic training on the sun-drenched beaches.[5] Several exams determined the qualifications of the would-be airmen. After only two and a half days of basic training, Anderson was ordered to report to the less exotic coastal town of Fort Myers, Florida, for gunnery training.

> While at Fort Myers, we practiced with shotguns, firing at skeet and so forth to get

3. During construction on the base, which began in September 1942, an unusually large number of rattlesnake dens were uncovered, hence the name.

4. The airfield was built from 1942 to 1943 in the county of Norfolk in East Anglia, a region of lowlands. It became a USAAF base for the 452nd BG in February 1944.

5. Miami Beach is located on barrier islands, and its desirable location later turned it into a major tourist area. To the west, across the bay, stands Miami, and farther west begin the Everglades.

used to leading your targets, as you would have to do in the air. We were also qualified with the .30-caliber carbine, the .45-caliber handgun, the submachine gun, and the .30-caliber air-cooled machine gun. We also got to go up in the air to practice shooting from an airplane at a target towed by another plane. We were put on an AT-6, which was an advanced trainer for the time, for our aerial gunnery practice.

The projectiles of our bullets were covered with grease paint of different colors so whenever you hit the sleeve target, they could tell what gunner had hit it. This was the second or third time I had even been up in an airplane. When we were done firing at the targets, those pilots dogfought all the way back to the landing field. I was not only scared, but three-quarters sick and shook up visibly. One of the boys with us went over to the officer in charge and told him he better send me back up or I would never fly again. The second trip up, I drew a captain who to me looked like an old man, but he gave me a nice easy ride. From then on, I had no trouble with flights, rough or easy. After some three months there—a twelve-week course, I believe—I graduated in the upper 10 percent of the class. That meant that the colonel pinned your wings on. So we had the coveted silver wings of an air crewman, and I also had sergeant stripes.

Because he had a high score in mechanical aptitude, Sergeant Anderson was ordered to report to an aircraft mechanics school at Goldsboro, North Carolina. Early in the spring, he boarded a train at Fort Myers, leaving Florida before the hot, muggy summer weather set in. In early April, he reached Goldsboro, where "various phases of work on the planes, from the engines down, were studied. A week was spent out in the field in tents and under simulated combat conditions. In fact, while we were out there, we had a severe lightning storm, and two men were killed. One of them was from Indiana."

After he completed his training, Anderson waited for thirty days in the company of two other men for his next assignment.

We were shipped to Pyote, Texas, which was the Rattlesnake Bomber Base and the home of the B-17. To us at that time, the B-17 was the best airship in the air. Not only that, it was practically the biggest airplane the U.S. had. I was with my first crew only a short time because I got tonsillitis, and after the doctors discussed it for some time, they gave me some sulfa to take for it. This was the first time sulfa was used for tonsillitis that they knew of, and for taking sulfa, I was consequently grounded. The crew I was on went on, and I was placed with another crew.

The second crew I was put on was led by the pilot W. W. Smith, so we were known as "Smithy's crew." The copilot was Ralph Bracato; in the nose were the navigator, Lt. Frederick Ford, and the bombardier, Lt. Raymond Conner. The men in the back included me in the top turret; Sgt. Orville Greenmager in the radio room; the waist gunners, Sgt. Junior Leady and Sgt. Ernest Falbo; and the tail gunner, Sgt. Joe Prevost, who was called "Red."

While at the Rattlesnake Bomber Base, we started getting used to our crews and flew daylight-simulated missions, dropped practice bombs, and had air-to-air gunnery, again shooting at a towed target. We had some air-to-ground gunnery also. We had lots of hours in the classroom. The engineers had to get familiar with the mechanical parts of the B-17. There were two assistants to me. The pilot and copilots had their schools to attend, as did the navigators. "Red" Prevost, the tail gunner, was also the armorer, and it was his job to learn all he could about the machine guns and so forth to make them work in case the gunner could not fix them. Most of us on the guns were proficient enough to fix our own guns due to any kind of malfunction.

We also got to go on cross-country flights; the pilots practiced formation flying. There were two or three of us who got some stick time on the plane. We were told, in case the pilot and copilot were injured or killed, some other crewmember had to be proficient to keep it in the air, and if you got back to base, if nothing else, you could belly-land it.

That training lasted through August and September 1943. Then we were sent to Dyersburg, Tennessee, for our advanced training, which was practically the same thing. It was more detailed, with more night flights. On the gunnery, we had air-to-ground and air-to-air practice.

We were on a mock bombing run to Chicago, Illinois, one day when the pilot said to me, "Andy, you live up here, don't you?" I said, "Yes, I do." He told me, "Go down to the navigator and pick out the route to your place." We picked out Monticello and headed up the Tippecanoe River to Buffalo, where I had graduated from school. Before we got to Buffalo, the copilot slid out of his seat, and I slid in. As we went passed the Buffalo school, we were quite low. I could see the boys and girls in the window, and we waved as we went past. The overcast was under 1,000 feet that day, so we went out to my home. The first pass, we went over the house, and my mother and youngest brother were standing on the porch. Smithy said, "Your mother wears glasses." I said, "Yes, she always has, as I can remember." Well, we made three passes; by putting those Wright Cyclones that had 1,200 horses per engine in low pitch and high revolutions per minute, they would shake the house almost off its foundation. Mom said she laughed awhile and swore awhile. On the way back, we were so low the boys in the nose got in an argument whether we went over the high line transmission wires that ran through the farm or under them. The third guy said, "You are both crazy! We went between the wires!" We were low, but not quite that low.

After going through Dyersburg, we went through the overcast that covered the area and couldn't find the base. The gas gauges were getting mighty low. The pilot got on the intercom and asked the crewmembers whether they wanted to bail out or ride the plane down into the cornfield. The consensus of opinion was nobody was going to jump. He got underneath the overcast, and the navigator saw a water tower on a small town, which indicated we weren't very far from Vincennes. Vincennes had an airstrip long enough for a B-17. The pilot radioed for clearance, and they told him to keep his wheels off the runway because they had a plane taking off. He said, "You can go to hell too!" and as he set down on the end of the runway, the other plane was just taking off. The number four engine on our plane quit; it was out of fuel. We got more fuel there and a sack of sandwiches and headed for Dyersburg, making it this time.

The men on Anderson's crew were all young, and the pilots were no older than twenty-three, and they took a lot of risks.

One night, while we were out on a night flight, I was back in the radio room practicing breathing oxygen, the pilot was down in the nose of the plane, and the armorer was messing around with a flare gun. The flare pistol had a port in the nose of the plane where you fastened it in and fired it. They had done that, but for some reason, the pistol had misfired. They drew it back inside the plane, and consequently it went off. It was a terrible sight and feeling at night to see a red flash in the nose of the plane, while you are back in the radio room. About that time, one of my assistants, who was flying copilot, left the copilot seat and came back through the bomb bay to get his parachute. One of the waist gunners, Ernest Falbo, who had his chute harness on upside down, said, "Help me, boys! Help me!" We straightened his chute out and put in on right. The pilot came back and said, "Don't jump, boys; we got everything under control!" By that time, we got to looking around and found the main escape hatch had been jettisoned, and nobody would admit he had done it. When we got back to the base, the pilot said he would take care of it. Of course, it was my job, and my assistants were supposed to help me service the plane. Well, they took off and I was by myself, and the ground crew was very inquisitive. I really didn't know what to say, so I kept my mouth shut. Pretty soon the pilot came back; he was going to help work all night to get that plane ready to fly. Afterwards, we found out that his parachute had been on fire; he had kicked it out the front escape hatch, which had broken the oxygen lines—whatever kept that plane from blowing up, I will never know.

Another day, on a practice mission down to the Gulf of Mexico, I happened to look out and check on the engines on the left side. Number two had smoke pouring out of it. Now, that is an experience that will give you an awful feeling. We shut the engine down and feathered the props. You have an emergency button on the dash, you push it, and duc to oil prcssure, it will turn the props to an angle where they will not windmill with the engine shut off. We landed in Mobile, Alabama, and they telephoned back to Dyersburg to send a plane to pick us up. They sent two planes, but one of them never got off the runway, and the other one lost an engine before it got down there—it blew a cylinder, the same as ours did. Before midnight, they got another plane down there to take two crews back to Dyersburg. The planes that we were flying in the States and training on had a lot of hours on them.

One of the jobs of the engineer, the pilot, and copilot was to inspect visually the plane before you got in it. You checked it from one end to the other. Then you started up the engines. The pilot and copilot had a checklist. I know they revved the engine up. It had two magnetos. You would check the magnetos, and if you had over 150 revolutions per minute drop from one to the other, you didn't have to fly the plane. This happened to us one night. We were running the engines up, ready to take off, but we had over 250 revolutions per minute drop, so the pilot shut it down and radioed the tower. We refused to fly. Well, here comes the engineering officer, the ground crew chief, the line officer, and all of them. They wanted to know why we wouldn't fly, and after the explanation, they still asked the pilot to take off. He said his engineer said no, and consequently they gave us another plane.

I happened to be the only one close enough to get home before we went overseas. The pilot covered for me a day early and a day late, and I hitchhiked home. To get back, my dad, my brother Chuck, and two neighbors, Esper Hutton and Bill Brooks, went back with us. We had quite an enjoyable time down there. Mom had baked some things and canned fried chicken and so forth and sent it with us. Two of our crewmen were married, Lieutenants Smith and Conner, and their wives came up and visited. We met when I returned with my family and friends, and somebody mentioned we ought to take Dad and the boys out for a ride that night. We were going to take them out for a ride in the B-17! It is a good thing it didn't happen, for if we had been caught, I am afraid the Air Force would have frowned on that. Thankfully, the base had fogged in. Dad and the others had to leave the next day, and it was back to the regular routine of schoolwork and flying. Our training was over at the last of December.

On December 24, 1943, they put us on a train for Kearney, Nebraska, where we picked up a new plane to go overseas. We did a lot of poker playing that night on the train. The train pulled off to a siding for a passenger train to pass. We were supposed to be on the siding for ten to fifteen minutes, but you know servicemen—they took off! After they got everybody rounded up some way or another, a few bottles were brought back on the train, and we had a Christmas Eve celebration.

When the train finally reached Kearney, Anderson's crew picked up its aircraft. The men were told not to write home or tell anyone what route they were taking overseas. Anderson's group followed the northern route through Goose Bay, Labrador.

We got into Goose Bay, where it was colder than the dickens. It was January—a lot of snow and ice. The night we were to take off for overseas, we had to put cowls around the engines and start heaters up for about two hours before we could get them to turn over. I don't know what the temperature was, but it was quite cold. When we were on the way, taking off, the pilot's last transmission to clear the tower received the reply "May God be with you boys tonight!" I think at that time we realized we were on our way.

Several planes were going, but each was on its own. During that flight over, we carried an extra fuel tank in the bomb bay, because we didn't have enough fuel to reach Ireland. Due to the storm front that came through, we had to climb to a higher altitude. I was back in the radio room trying to catch a little sleep. An assistant was taking over for me. The next thing I remember is that one of them woke me up and said, "Andy, where is your parachute?" I said it was up in the nose. He said, "If I were you, I would check the gauges up there." Whenever you are awakened out of sleep and somebody asks you where your parachute is, that sort of gives you a shock in a hurry. So I went up to the cockpit area and checked the gauges on the fuel. All four of them were reading on almost zero. I looked at Smithy and asked him where we were. It was overcast and you couldn't see anything. He said he didn't know if we were over land or sea. At about that time, a B-17 came up out of the overcast. There was a hole through there, and we could see a runway underneath it. That is one time I am sure we didn't follow the regular procedure; we didn't fly any better. We went down through the hole, found the airstrip, and landed. I will tell you that there were ten fellows very glad to be on the ground.

One of the other planes that came over the same time we did, and behind us just a little bit, wasn't quite so fortunate. He got down underneath the overcast to see if he could see where he was. He hit a brick building that took off five feet of the end of his wing. He got his plane back up to over 1,000 feet and had his crew bail out. He and the copilot set the plane on automatic pilot and set it out over the ocean. Somehow the pilot's parachute opened in the plane and he had no way to jump, so they brought that plane back in. Normally we landed at close to 110 to 115 miles per hour, but he had to keep that plane up over 150 miles per hour to keep it from stalling out. Well, he got it on the ground anyway and saved the plane. You have to give the man credit, because we really didn't have a lot of flying, and he did a wonderful job.

Anderson's aircraft successfully made it to Nutts Corner, Northern Ireland. Although he felt he had had enough excitement to last a lifetime, he now had to prepare for an even greater adventure.

A large number of B-24 squadrons flew over to the European theater in addition to the B-17s, but the Flying Fortress captured the limelight. The B-24 carried a heavier bomb load and had a greater range, but it usually flew at lower levels, drawing most of the enemy's flak, and was less maneuverable than the B-17.

One of the men who flew a B-24 was David C. Burton, who had enlisted in March or April 1942 at the Presidio of Monterey after leaving the University of California. He began his training as an aviation cadet in June 1942 and graduated as a pilot in April 1943. His training followed the same pattern as the B-17 pilots', but he drew an assignment to fly a B-24. He trained in the B-24 at Clovis Field.

The first time I climbed into the cockpit of a B-24, I sat in the pilot's seat and looked at all the instruments, dials, levers, and switches. It was an exhilarating experience but almost overwhelming to a twenty-one-year-old with shiny new pilot's wings. I looked out the windows at four huge engines with props higher than a house and the ground twelve feet below the pilot's window. This was a great transition from the little twin-engine Cessna AT-17s and Curtis AT-9s I had flown at Roswell, New Mexico, during my Advanced Cadet Pilot Training.

The B-24 was a pilot's plane. It had to be flown with positive action of the control wheel and rudder pedals, and surprisingly, it would respond very well to aerobatic maneuvers that were not expected from four-engine heavy bombers.

At Biggs Field, my crew decided to test the limits of the B-24D we were assigned. Many times, after finishing our routine training in gunnery and bombing, we would fly the B-24D to its maximum altitude of about 32,500 feet. As it mushed along, we would cut all four engines, push forward on the control wheel, and hold it in a vertical dive until the airspeed needle passed the red line. At other times, we might drop full flaps as we nosed over. It felt like we were suspended in midair with zero gravity. At night, we would seek out thunderheads and stay in the center of the storm, bouncing up and down with the vertical wind shears.

A "vertical reverse" was one maneuver my gunner especially liked. It was when I would make a left turn in a near vertical bank, pull the control wheel to my lap, and kick full right rudder. The plane would shudder in a high-speed stall and do a half

Glacier located behind this
morraine
Airfield outlined in white.
The aircraft landed on this
side adjacent the fjord and rolled uphill
to the other side. They took off from that
higher side and went downhill toward the fjord.

Bluie West 1, Greenland. RAY MERRIAM

snap roll to the right, while the men in the back of the plane would hang on.

Other times we would "hit the deck" and fly five to ten feet off rural highways to see if we could chase cars off the road or spin farmers' windmills. One day we met a regiment of army soldiers on the road, and they scattered like chickens in a farmyard. That caper nearly cost me my wings and my commission.

Lieutenant Burton and the crew he picked out made it together through fifty missions. The crewmembers were copilot Lt. Milton Shuman, navigator Lt. Hugh Banta, bombardier Lt. Dan Delaney, engineer Sgt. Ed Steiner, assistant engineer Sgt. Al Kurzonkowski, nose gunner Sgt. Harold Furney, waist gunner Sgt. John Knoll, tail gunner Bob Mellinger, and radio operator Sgt. Herb Graham. They joined the 376th Bombardment Group of the 15th Air Force operation in the Mediterranean.

Fighter Pilots

A large number of fighter pilots had to be trained to provide protection for the medium and heavy bombers that flew over to Europe and to take part in ground support operations. During flight training, the instructors determined who was more suited to handle multiengine aircraft and who would make a better fighter pilot.

Robert S. Johnson, who volunteered for the AAF before America entered the war, was selected to be a fighter pilot. He had left college to enlist as an aviation cadet in Oklahoma City on November 11, 1941. Having acquired some flying experience as a teenager, he went through flight training and graduated in July 1942. In January 1943, he departed for England, where he

The Ilfrey and Bennett Odyssey

Lt. John Bennett flew his aircraft on the first bombing raid of the 97th Bombardment Group on August 17, 1942, against Rouen. A few weeks later, on September 1, Lieutenant Ilfrey took part in the first sweep of Northern France by a fighter unit of the 8th Air Force. The odds against them grew with additional missions they flew. On October 21, the 1st Bombardment Wing sent ninety B-17s and B-24s on their first mission. They were to bomb the submarine pens at Lorient, but cloud cover prevented most of the aircraft from finding their target, and three B-17s—all from the 97th Bombardment Group—were lost. Bennett's was one of the planes that were hit.

> The entire rear element was shot out of the sky—I including my aircraft. Jackson (the navigator) and I were the only survivors from our aircraft and neither of us knows how we got out of the aircraft. The aircraft was torn apart somehow. I speculate that when we snapped, violently, the 2,000-pound bombs may have torn through the nose of the aircraft and thrown us out. I have no other thought. All I know is that after being thrown forward violently I found myself falling with a piece of wreckage—with my right foot lodged firmly in it. I was able to force myself loose and pull the ripcord.

Bennett spent the remainder of the war in Stalag Luft III. This was the last mission the 97th staged over France before it moved south for the North African invasion. Jack Ilfrey departed for Gibraltar in his P-38 on November 15. After he lost his belly tank, he overestimated his capability to reach his destination and was forced to land at Lisbon, where officials at the airport told him that he was to be interned. Luckily he was able to talk himself out of the situation, and he even persuaded the Portuguese officials to refuel his aircraft and let him continue his journey. General Eisenhower, who wanted to avoid any diplomatic problems, threatened to send Ilfrey back to Portugal for internment, and only Gen. Jimmy Doolittle's intervention saved him from this fate.

After he completed seventy-two missions with the 12th Air Force and became an ace, Capt. Jack Ilfrey returned to the United States in 1943. He became an instructor for P-38 and P-47 pilots, preparing them for combat. In April 1944, he returned to join the 20th Fighter Group of the 8th Air Force at Kings Cliff, England.

flew the P-47 Thunderbolt and became one of America's first aces as a member of one of the most famous fighter groups, the 56th.[6]

Jack J. Ilfrey signed up in Houston as an aviation cadet in March 1941. He had already learned how to fly in the Civilian Pilot Training Program in 1939 and 1940 while he attended the University of Houston. He began flight training in April 1941 and graduated on December 12 at Luke Field, Arizona. As a member of the 94th Pursuit Squadron, 1st Pursuit Group, he patrolled the California coast in P-38 D and E models

6. See the book *Thunderbolt,* coauthored by Johnson, for more details on his wartime experiences.

American Fighter Aircraft

Aircraft	Speed (max.)	Ceiling (feet)	Range (miles)	Weapons	European service
Lightning P-38 F	347 mph	39,000	1,425	1 x 20-mm Hispano cannon, 4 x .50-cal. MG in nose. 2,000 lbs bombs	1942
Lightning P-38 J	414 mph	44,000	2,260	1 x 20-mm Hispano cannon, 4 x .50-cal. MG in nose. 2 x 500-lb. bombs or 10 x 5" rockets	1943
Thunderbolt P-47 B	429 mph	42,000	1,100	8 x .50-cal. MG in wings	1943
Thunderbolt P-47 D	433 mph	42,000	1,000	6 to 8 x .50-cal. MG and racks for up to 2,500 lbs. of bombs or 10 x 5" rockets	1943
Mustang P-51 B & C	440 mph	42,000	2,200	4 x .50-cal. MG in wings and racks for 2 x 1,000-lb. bombs	1943
Mustang P-51 D	437 mph	41,900	2,300	6 x .50-cal. MG in wings and racks for 2 x 1,000-lb. bombs or 6 x 5" rockets	1944

Note: The combat range of the aircraft above was approximately half the range given.

after the attack on Pearl Harbor. In the spring of 1942, his fighter group received the newer P-38 F and departed for Dow Field, Maine, to escort the 97th Bombardment Group over the Atlantic in the first mass crossing of aircraft for the buildup in England.[7]

The 94th Fighter Squadron, with four P-38s and a B-17, departed the United States on July 4, 1942. Their flight took them from Presque Isle, Maine, to Goose Bay, Labrador where they refueled. On July 6, they took off for Bluie West 1 (BW1), Greenland, a base that later served as an emergency stop for bombers.[8] They approached BW1 by flying up a fjord about fifty miles at low altitude, with mountains rising 1,000 feet on either side. The pilots had to be careful not to fly up a similar L-shaped fjord about ten miles to the north. Once they neared the end of the fjord, they made a sharp turn into a valley where the air base was. It was a difficult approach, with little opportunity for a second chance. After several days' layover, the squadron departed for Reykjavik, Iceland, on July 15. According to Lieutenant Ilfrey, "It was on that day that six of the 94th's P-38s and two B-17 Es, low on fuel, went down on Greenland's Icecap." The crews were rescued, but the planes were abandoned and swallowed up in the ice. What remained of the 94th flew on to Great Britain, landing at Kirton in Lindsey, England, on July 26. Ilfrey and his comrades were stationed with the famous Polish 303rd Kosciuszko Squadron, which "taught them many tricks of the trade." The pilots that successfully completed the trip received the first Air Medals awarded by the 8th Air Force.

John Bennett, one of the B-17 pilots crossing the Atlantic on that trip, reminisced years later in Ilfrey's book:

7. See Ilfrey's book *Happy Jack's Go-Buggy* for more details on his wartime experiences.
8. Bluie West I was constructed by a battalion of the 21st Aviation Engineer Regiment between July 1941 and the end of the year and went into operation at the beginning of 1942. It was located on the southwestern coast of Greenland, at the village of Narsarsuaq. Made of pierced steel planking, the airfield was also used by Catalina PBYs for antisubmarine patrols. Bluie West 8 was much farther north on the west coast.

You [Jack Ilfrey], Cy Widen, Harmon, and Pringle (flying P-38s) were on my wings. We had been instructed not to fly above 14,000 feet, but the weather front went above 14. We climbed up to about 18,000 and suddenly, when we were not expecting it, we hit the cloud. We did a 180° turn and talked about what to do next. Harmon was not tucked in tight enough when we hit the cloud so he just kept doing on his own (toward BW-1). The second B-17 and four P-38s turned around and returned to Goose Bay. Someone among you remaining three P-38 guys indicated by radio that you might not have sufficient fuel to return to Goose. So "Ole" John Bennett (with his 450 flying hours) said, "OK, tuck in tight! We are going through the weather." We did. . . . You will recall that we collected some ice and I was very concerned about your visibility and your ability to fly formation safely. You guys did it beautifully. You were in so tight that my crew said they could practically read the instruments in your cockpit.

I remember the horror with which I contemplated a possible letdown in BW-1 (Bluie West 1). I knew that I could do it, but I worried about doing it in tight formation. My radioman was able to get the weather from BW-1 and I was overjoyed to find that the weather there was good.

The airport strip was situated at the head of a long fjord. We made our CAVU let down in the fjord, then flew up the fjord, turned right, and there it was. At that point, we pulled back on the throttles and landed because there was no place else to go. You guys might have been able to make a 180° turn and get out of there, but I doubt that we could. Harmon was there just ahead of us and in good shape.

The Training of a Bomber Crew

The following is the account of six members of a ten-man B-24 bomber crew that trained in 1943, went overseas, and fought as a unit. Only the nose gunner, whose account is not included, did not remain with this crew, because it converted from B-24s to B-17s, which carried one less man.

James C. Williams of Medford, Oregon, was the pilot. He signed up for what he called "Aviation Cadets" in November 1942, but he had to wait for several months due to a long waiting list. He finally reported for duty in June 1943.

> The physical was very minor; you lined up and they took you through real fast. It was nothing in depth. I think in Santa Ana, they gave us the big physical. I had some teeth that overlapped; if you had too much overlap, they would not accept you as a pilot. If you were warm, you were in.
>
> I went through preflight in Santa Ana for twelve weeks, then to primary flight school in Santa Maria, California, where we flew Stearman aircraft for about eight weeks. Then we went on to Chico, California, where we flew Vultee Vibrators for about twelve weeks; then to Stockton, California, where we flew Beechcraft AT-17s for another twelve weeks; and then we graduated in late December 1943. At that point, it was determined that the group from Stockton would become first pilots, so they were sent to Albuquerque, New Mexico, for B-24 training. We took B-24 training until midspring, and then we were sent to Fresno, California, where we were to be assigned a crew.

William Laahs from Klamath Falls, Oregon, also signed up for the Aviation Cadets program, but earlier in July 1942.

There were slots programmed in advance, as to which class into which you were going to fit. We went in for a physical and mental test in July 1942. They accepted us in about a three-day period and told us to wait to receive orders.

I reported to Santa Ana in January 1943 for preflight. They had a screening process to decide who was going to go to Pilot, Bombardier, and Navigation School. They told me I tested best for navigator, but I said I wanted to be a pilot, so I reported twelve weeks later to Gary Field in Blight, California, for flight training. I had seven hours' pilot training in a Fairchild PT-21, I believe. I was washed out for lack of progress, because I guess I didn't learn fast enough.

I was sent back to Santa Ana, and this time I went to Navigation School, and then to Indian Springs and Las Vegas, Nevada, for gunnery training. We had a turret mounted on the back of a pickup so you could swivel it as they went around in a circle. We also went around and shot at skeet while driving in a circle. We also trained on an AT-6 during this six-week period of training, although we never trained with a turret in the air.

Next, I was sent to Mayfair, California, for Advanced Navigation School. I spent twelve weeks in Navigation School. They had both a pilot and navigator school at Mayfield, and while I was there, they moved the whole Navigation School to Ellington Field (near Houston) in Texas, so we went there on a troop train in December 1943. At this time, we were flying AT-18 (Hudson) for advanced navigation, both with maps and with what we called pilotage—looking out the window and seeing where you were. We did that mostly over Texas and Louisiana. I graduated on February 5, 1944, and had about three weeks of vacation before I was sent to the 4th Air Force Replacement Depot at Hamerfield, Fresno, California, where I met the rest of the crew.

At age twenty-five, Douglas Morilon of Portland, Oregon, was several years older than his comrades. He signed up for the cadets on September 19, 1942. After the physical, he was told that he was too short to be a pilot but could be either a bombardier or navigator. He too had to wait for a period of six months before reporting.

I went to aerial gunnery before Bombardier School, because the bombardier was also the armorer and had the responsibility for the armament of the plane. I took the basic gunnery at Kingman, Arizona. We did our air-to-air in an AT-18, which carried four or five men. On my first mission up, I shot the cable on the tow plane in two, so I was popular.

I was then sent to Kingman, Arizona, where we had six weeks of basic training and studied code, mathematics, meteorology, and so forth—an intensive course. We also had navigation training, which consisted of dead reckoning and pilotage. The bombardier's duty consisted of dropping practice bombs of 100 pounds—that was 94 pounds of sand and 6 pounds of powder—so they would know where the bombs hit. We had to graduate with a CE [circle of error] of, I think, about 200 feet. We dropped about 100 bombs. We used the Norden bombsight continually. We had to know it well, and the charts and graphs that went with it had to be understood. I graduated on February 5, 1944.

While the officers of the crew were training, most of the enlisted men had not yet been called

American Aircraft Production

Types	1940	1941	1942	1943	1944
Bombers	623	4,115	12,627	29,355	35,003
Fighters	1,162	4,416	10,769	23,988	38,873
Recon	63	727	1,468	734	259
Transports	164	532	1,984	7,012	9,834

Bomber types	B-17	B-24	B-25, B-26, A-26, A-20
July 1940–August 1945	12,677	18,188	24,848

Fighter types	P-38	P-39	P-40	P-47	P-51
July 1940–August 1945	9,535	9,585	13,700	15,579	14,490

Transport types	C-46	C-47	C-54
July 1940–August 1945	3,144	10,245	1,089

up. Ralph D. Rickel of Elyria, Ohio, was nineteen when he was drafted in August 1943.

I went to Cleveland for induction. At the induction center, they gave us our physical. They told us to take off our clothes, and line up and spread your cheeks. It was the standard physical. They put their finger up your hind end, and then they'd tell you to open your mouth. I said, "No, my throat is OK!" because I thought they were going to use the same finger. They sent you into a little cubbyhole. There is one guy sitting there with a white coat on; you're standing there with no clothes on in front of him, and he asks, "Do you like boys? Girls?" Later, they told me that all you had to tell him was you like boys, and they wouldn't take you in the service.

Then they sent me to Fort Hays, Columbus, Ohio. There was some corporal there that I thought was a general. He told us what we were supposed to do and when to do it. We all lined up there, and he came out and said, "Hey, the first sergeant's mother just passed away, and I think it would be good for you guys to chip in a little money for flowers and everything." Well, we all chipped in a buck apiece. The next day, I was standing there watching, and another group came in and he did the same thing. We were there three or four days, and that woman died every day!

The next thing you know, I was on a slow train to Amarillo, Texas, for basic training, and then to Laredo for gunnery. The first thing they gave you was nomenclature, and then later, field-stripping it blindfolded.

We trained in the AT-6, and I thought, "What am I doing in this? I'd rather be on the ground, because I don't like flying!"

James William Henkel of Galveston, Texas, was inducted in May 1943 at Dodd Field in San Antonio. He reported to Miami, Florida, for

The B-24 Ball Turret

The lower turret of the B-24, which was hydraulically operated, had to be raised into the fuselage of the plane for takeoff and landing. After the gunner climbed into it, the waist gunners lowered it. The gunner could also climb into it once it was lowered. If the turret was not in the correct position, guns down and forward, it became jammed in the lowered position, preventing the gunner from exiting. According to Ralph Rickel, "If it jammed down, it would stay there with the guy in it, and if the landing gear collapsed, he was going to be scraped off the runway." The turret had an emergency exit, but it required the gunner to use his parachute. Unfortunately, many of the gunners did not fit into the ball turret with their parachutes.

his basic training and transferred to Gulfport, Mississippi, where he tried to join the Aviation Cadets.

> They put a bunch of numbers in front of you with different colors, and they said I was color-blind. Then they informed me I was going to gunnery school, and they sent me to Laredo, Texas. I was a PFC when I reached Laredo, and they promised me I would come out a staff sergeant.
>
> It took a month for gunnery school, and I really thought I was moving quickly with my promotion to staff sergeant. We shot skeet for many hours every day with shotguns, until your arm turned black and blue. I got pretty good: I could hit forty-eight out of fifty. We shot from raised towers, off the back end of jeeps, in just about every form and fashion you could think of before we got the .50-caliber machine gun. Then we got up in this AT-6 and shot at socks (tow targets). The pilot in the AT-6 enjoyed scaring you. He could go up and drop down, and he would flop around.
>
> In Gunnery School, they had us sit by a large screen where you would identify every aircraft, and you had to identify all these airplanes fast. They also had a turret where you sighted, and you had to track them and identify them before you shot them.

James C. Ross of Mansfield, Ohio, was drafted in August 1943 and went through the same routine as the others in gunnery training.

Second Lt. James Williams collected part of his crew at Fresno. The pilots there were allowed to pick their own copilots, navigators, and bombardiers. According to Williams, they usually made the selection while "walking up the avenue of the base."

> In my case, I kept saying, "Oregon! Oregon!" and anybody that was from Oregon would normally come by and we got together. So my officer crew was all from Oregon. The enlisted people for gunnery, the engineer, assistant engineer, and radio operator were assigned, so we had a crew of four from Oregon, two from Ohio, two from Texas, and two from Alabama. Then we were sent to March Field, Riverside, California, for training on a B-24. We trained with the whole crew.

At March Field, Lieutenant Laahs, the navigator, was cross-trained as a bombardier on a bombsight mounted on a little stand about ten feet off the ground. Sergeant Henkel ran into a problem:

> Our plane came in on two landing wheels and did several spins on the runway, so the FBI began to investigate for possible sabo-

tage. They took me out of the airplane and acted like I should know how to fly it. They took me up into the cockpit and asked me what each gauge was, and I didn't know. It scared me to death, so I told Jim Williams, the pilot, to have another engineer gunner aboard, and I would be a gunner.

Jim Williams had another perspective on the incident:

> This was one of our earlier landings at March Field, when our gear collapsed and we ended up ruining a pretty good aircraft on the ground. The reason Jim Henkel got in a little trouble is because it was the engineer's responsibility to go back to the waist window and look to make sure that the knuckles on the landing gear protruded, which meant the gear was down and locked. In his case, maybe he did or didn't do this, and the gear collapsed. That is why the FBI took after him.

Jim Henkel was not the only one to be dissatisfied with his original assignment. Ralph Rickel, the ball turret gunner, did not like his either. Although the turret was lowered only when the B-24 was airborne, it was possible for the gunner to become trapped in it if a problem occurred when it was cranked back up. "I had a yellow stripe down my back about a foot wide. When we got assigned as gunners on the aircraft and they told me I was ball turret gunner, I had a scared fit. When I found out Henkel was available, I said, 'Hey Henk, why don't you take that ball?' and he said he would love it. I became the waist gunner, where all the toilet paper was."

By early summer of 1944, Lieutenant Williams's bomber crew was ready to ship out from the East Coast as a replacement bomber crew.

Between 1940 and the end of 1944, the U.S. defense industries far outstripped those of their opponents in the production of aircraft and training of men qualified to fly them. The tables on page 173 are summarized from *The Army Air Forces in World War II,* a history by Wesley Craven and James Cates.

Between the summer of 1939 and 1945, the AAF trained 193,440 pilots; 124,000 cadets failed to complete the training. These results were achieved through rapid expansion. When the war began in 1941, there were few bases where pilots could be trained, and civilian schools had to take up the slack. During 1942, a surplus of volunteers made it necessary to establish a waiting list for cadets. In 1943, between 50,000 and 60,000 pilots were trained, but there was a shortage of volunteers for the positions of navigators and bombardiers. To help solve this problem, the AAF resorted to various forms of propaganda to glamorize these positions.

Schools and practice ranges had to be established for bombardiers and gunners in 1941. Despite the rapid expansion, the AAF was able to produce relatively well-trained men for these positions. During most of 1942, the personnel in the European and Pacific theaters was mainly able to hold the status quo or maintain an American presence in those areas until the properly trained crews came in sufficient numbers in 1943 to decisively tip the scales.

CHAPTER 10

The Naval Arm, 1942–43

Even though the importance of its operations in the Atlantic is often overlooked, the navy played an important role in the Allies' success in the European theater of war. During the critical buildup in the British Isles, the army and its air units depended on the navy to secure their lines of communication. The Coast Guard patrolled Greenland and even prevented the Germans from setting up weather stations in the area. The navy also escorted ships across the Atlantic and guided aircraft. This increased activity, and the operations in the Pacific required a great deal of manpower. Thus expansion progressed as rapidly in the U.S. Navy as in the U.S. Army and Army Air Forces.

Operation Torch, in North Africa, required the participation of major surface ships from the British and American fleets. The next summer, the invasion of Sicily also involved naval forces not only to transport and support the invading troops, but also to neutralize thc Italian fleet. The follow-up invasion of the Italian peninsula in September necessitated another massive naval effort. Although the Royal Navy dominated in all these endeavors, the U.S. Navy and Coast Guard supplied personnel to man the landing craft transporting the assault forces.

The buildup for the great invasion in Normandy in 1944 and, later, Southern France once again depended on a large naval force that also supported ground operations after the attack. At the same time, the navy had to maintain the security of the sea-lanes between England and the States. After 1942, fewer fleet units were deployed in the Atlantic than in the Pacific, but the landing operations they made possible dwarfed in scope those of the Pacific.

Although the American navy was able to deploy only battleships on the verge of obsolescence in the European theater, the Allies quickly neutralized the Italian fleet. The German surface fleet, on the other hand, was a minimal threat after 1943, so the older ships were perfect for supporting amphibious operations.

The Ships of the Atlantic Fleet

Many of the more modern warships that participated in operations in the Atlantic and Mediterranean served there for only a short period before they went on to the Pacific. Some, however, like the three oldest battleships, remained there during most of the period between 1942 and 1944. The *Arkansas,* the most ancient of the American battleships completed in 1911, mounted twelve 12-inch guns, four of which were mounted in two turrets behind the stacks, near the center of the ship, and could be fired only broadside. But this was sufficient for shore bombardment missions. Its maximum speed of 20.5 knots was too slow to challenge other warships of the time. The 12-inch guns had a range of 23,500 yards. Eight 3-inch antiaircraft guns added between 1940 and 1941 provided extra protection.

Two other elder "battle wagons" serving in the Atlantic Fleet were the *New York* and *Texas,* completed in 1914 and only slightly newer than the *Arkansas.* They carried ten 14-inch guns and had one less turret than the *Arkansas,* but one of their turrets was located near the center of the ship, behind the stack. Between 1940 and 1941, the elevation of the 14-inch guns was increased to 30 degrees, which extended the maximum range of these guns from 23,000 to 34,300 yards. These ships also had eight 3-inch antiaircraft guns and numerous smaller antiaircraft weapons.

The battleships *Arkansas* and *Texas* played a prominent role in the invasions of France, whereas the more "modern" *Nevada,* a newer ship completed in 1916, made an appearance only for the Normandy campaign. New ships with 16-inch guns such as the *Massachusetts,* which took part in the North African campaign, did not play any role in the French campaign. The older battleships, although slow, were fast enough for escorting convoys in the Atlantic, but they were not used in the Mediterranean landings of 1943. Later, in 1944, they were sent to the Pacific to participate in landings in places such as Iwo Jima, where their heavy guns were still valuable for shore bombardment.

Except during the North African campaign, no American fleet aircraft carriers took part in the European theater, but several escort carriers participated in some invasions along the Mediterranean and performed convoy duty in the Atlantic. The four escort carriers of *Sangamon* class, converted oilers, carried up to thirty-six aircraft and had a speed of 18 knots. They served in the Atlantic in 1942 but were gone by the end of 1943. Some escort carriers of the *Bogue* and *Casablanca* classes, which carried about twenty aircraft and had a speed of 17 to 18 knots, were present throughout 1943 and 1944.

Several types of cruisers, destroyers, and smaller destroyer escorts served in the Atlantic as well, but compared with those used in the area of operations in the Pacific, their number was small throughout the war. The *Augusta,* a heavy cruiser built in 1931, served as the flagship in the North African and Normandy landings. It was the oldest American heavy cruiser and one of only about half a dozen that served in the Atlantic in

American Warships in the ETO, 1943–44

Ship	Built	Main Weapons	Speed	Aircraft	Crew
Aircraft carriers					
Ranger	1934	8 x 5"	29 knots	36	2,300
Bogue class[a]	1942		17 knots	20–28	890
Battleships					
Arkansas	1912	16 x 12"	20 knots	3	1,330
New York class[b]	1914	10 x 14"	21 knots	3	1,031
Nevada	1916	10 x 14"	20 knots	3	1,300
Heavy cruisers					
Augusta	1931	9 x 8"	33 knots	4	900
New Orleans class[c]	1934	9 x 8"	33 knots	8	919
Light cruisers					
Brooklyn	1938	15 x 6"	33 knots	8	900
Destroyers					
Bristol class[d]	1943	4 x 5"	37 knots		250
Sumner class[e]	1944	6 x 5"	35 knots		350

[a] Similar to *Casablanca* class of 1943
[b] *Texas* and *New York*
[c] *Tuscaloosa* and *Quincy*
[d] *Frankford* and *Satterley*
[e] *Meredith* and *Laffey*
Note: The *Sumner* and *Bristol* classes dated from about a year earlier than indicated on the chart; the date of the ships named in the footnotes is given.
Source: Rimington, 1944; Fahey, 1945.

1944. This ship mounted nine 8-inch guns with a range of about 30,000 yards, like those of the slightly newer *Tuscaloosa*.

There were numerous small ships as well, including tugs and landing craft. The U.S. Coast Guard also contributed the LCI Flotilla Number 4, with twenty-four LCI(L)s, and participated in the invasions of Sicily, Salerno, and Normandy before being shifted into the Pacific. The same fate awaited many of the navy LSTs, LCIs, and smaller landing craft after the invasion of Southern France.

The Men of the Fleet

Throughout the war, the U.S. Navy, Merchant Marine, and Coast Guard strove to maintain lines of supply for the rest of the armed forces. Although the navy suffered a heavy blow at Pearl Harbor, it was not crippled, because it lost only a small number of experienced sailors. In addition, it received a flood of volunteers to fill the slots on the numerous ships of all sizes and types built in the early years of the war. Most navy inductees reported to a boot camp for basic training, attended some type of service school, and went on to serve on a naval base or ship. In some cases, they were trained onboard ship.

James J. Bennett, who enlisted in the navy in July 1942, was sent to Great Lakes, Illinois, for boot camp. Several weeks later, he attended a radio school at Miami University in Oxford, Ohio. Once he completed that course, he went to Norton Heights, Connecticut, for instruction at a signalman school. Next, after attaining the rank of radioman third class, he reported to the U.S. Naval Armed Guard Center at Brooklyn, New York.

Naval Training Camps

Like the army, the navy set up camps for the recruits' basic training, which the navy and marines referred to as boot camp. The U.S. Naval Training Station at Newport, Rhode Island, one of five such facilities, trained recruits for the fleet between 1939 and February 1944. Training, which was not standardized until late 1943, included swimming, and 91.4 percent of the recruits became qualified swimmers. After the United States entered the war, Service Schools were established at the facility. Beginning in December 1943, the facilities of the Training Station were gradually taken over by the Large Ship Pre-Commissioning Center. In 1942, a single class of 1,600 officers attended only a Reserve Officers Indoctrination School to meet the immediate demands of the war. No further classes were held at Newport.

Four training stations had been charged with processing recruits for fleet duty since 1883 by the Bureau of Navigation. When the war began, 1,023 recruits went into training under the supervision and instruction of a ship's company of 234 men.

In 1939, the quota for raw recruits for Newport was set at 200 to 300 a month, with a training period of twelve weeks. After September 1939, the new instructions reduced the training period to eight weeks and raised the quota of recruits to 731 for September and 1,000 for October and succeeding months. The eight-week program began with a physical examination, and the men were issued a complete outfit. Goals of the program were to keep recruits in good health, accustom them to naval routine, and instruct them in the following: basics of the Infantry Manual, government insurance, ordnance safety and firing a rifle, rudimentary skills in seamanship, swimming, use of a gas mask, how to stand watch, and mess duty. Also included were information on and selection for trade school.

Quarters were available for 2,100 men, which stretched the base to the limit in 1939, until Quonset huts were set up later. Early in 1940, the quota of recruits was reduced to 600 a month, which eased the situation. By the end of the year, the number of recruits rose to 3,845, but it dropped by half the following year. After the attack on Pearl Harbor, the number of recruits rose above 3,000 again, resulting in a reduction of the training period to four weeks after mid-December 1941. In April 1942, the basic training was increased to five weeks. In September, it was reduced to four, only to be raised to eight weeks in early November and twelve by the end of the month. As 1943 wore on, the training period was reduced once more. These constant changes reflected the navy's needs, but it did little to ensure consistency in the quality of seamen it produced.

When the Service Schools were founded, a two-brigade training organization was created. The Service Schools, which were to accommodate four classes of 1,000 men at one time, required the construction of buildings and barracks. Classes began each month and lasted sixteen weeks. There were schools for electricians' mates, fire control men, gunners' mates, torpedo men, radiomen, quartermasters, signalmen, yeomen, storekeepers, and stenographers.

Among the training aids in use was the Mark 1 Trainer (Polaroid) for machine-gun practice, which simulated very realistically fast-moving targets and allowed the students

continued

Naval Training Camps *continued*

to develop the proper technique for leading the target.

The length of courses varied; gunners' mates attended thirteen weeks, but radiomen as many as twenty weeks. The Radiomen, Quartermaster, and Electricians' Mate Schools were transferred to other sites after May 1944, the Stenography School after December. Most of the other schools were simply closed after August 1944. The Service School graduates qualified for the rank of petty officer, third class, and their graduation rate was just over 90 percent.

The mission of the Large Ship Pre-Commissioning Training Center, established at the end of 1943, was to impart the skills necessary for service on the type of ship to which the men were going to be assigned, from battleships and carriers to smaller fleet units. More than 40,000 men, both officers and enlisted, passed through this center between the time it opened and the end of May 1944. Few of the new ships were destined for the European theater.

Bennett's story is similar to those of many others who served in the Naval Armed Guard. Between 1943 and 1945, he crossed the Atlantic several times and even sailed into the Mediterranean. Between February and September 1943, he crossed the Atlantic and sailed into the North African war zone on the cargo vessel SS *Richard J. Gatling*. Between November 1943 and March 1944, he served on another cargo ship, the SS *Charles W. Eliot*. By the time the war ended, he had served on six other ships. According to Bennett, "The size of the Armed Guard gun crews was determined by the weaponry aboard that particular ship. It was usually some combination of the older .50-caliber machine guns and 4-inch .50-caliber surface guns, and the newer 20-millimeter and 40-millimeter, 3-inch .50 and 5-inch .38 dual-purpose guns."

Bennett says the cargo ships on which he served carried all types of war supplies, from chewing gum to aircraft. The escorts—battleships, destroyers, and other types—fought the battle of the Atlantic to protect the cargo ships, troopships, and tankers from falling prey to the U-boats and surface raiders.

For Carl J. Hummel, the navy was a family tradition. His father had served in that branch in 1910, and his brother was already serving as a frogman. Hummel and his brother decided to join the navy in 1942, while another brother joined the army.

> My brother and I often talked about being in the navy, so I mentioned to my parents that I wanted to enlist for the duration of the war. Naturally, they did not want me to do this, but I explained that I wanted the navy, and if I waited, sooner or later, I would be drafted into a branch of the service that I did not want. So I went to the post office where the navy recruiting office was and signed up. My brother signed up about six weeks later.
>
> They gave us our physicals and told us we had two weeks to wait until we were called to go to a training camp. Two weeks later, they called us in, lined about fifteen of us up on the post office steps, took our picture, and said, "Good-bye and good luck!"
>
> We went by train to Newport, Rhode Island, and we were put into Company 525,

a company of about 150 men. There they outfitted us, made us look like a bunch of bald-headed guys, and taught us to say, "Sir!" in a big hurry.

Boot camp was rough, as they had to make a man out of you in a hurry. Normally boot camp took four months to complete, but since the war was on, they pushed you through in six weeks. Our "igloos," curved galvanized buildings that we slept in, were out on Cottendon Point. Out of the six weeks that I was there, I believe it rained four weeks nonstop. We had one great big mud hole to train in. Guess what our white lace-up leggings looked like?

I met my best buddy the first day in camp. He was from Thomaston, Maine. His bunk was beside mine. He introduced himself as Eddie Harrington. I told him I was Carl Hummel, and I looked at my dog tag and said, "650 93 03." We both got a kick out of that. Eddie and I stayed together all through boot and Radio School. We went aboard the *Augusta* together, and we both got discharged together.

During our training, we were given an aptitude test to find out what we wanted to be and if we were qualified to do what we wanted. Eddie and I both put down that we wanted to be aviation radiomen, radio technicians, or in communications.

We were assigned to RCA Radio School on 52nd Street in New York City. It was the end of September 1942, and we were told that the radio course was about four months. That is, if we made it to the end.

School was very much like school at home. Reported at 8 A.M. to first class and changed classes throughout the day. First class of code, then typing class, then theory, etc., until 4 P.M., after which our time was our own to do as we pleased.

This school was tough, and we were losing about fifteen or twenty men a week that could not hack it. Out of a class of about 150, only 48 graduated.

Here we were in New York in the years of the big band era, and every theater had at that time a Fox Movietone News, a short movie, and then the band would come onstage. Big band was the thing in those days. My buddy and I talked it over and decided that we would study three nights a week and go out the other two. We would go to the USO and bum tickets to a theater or to Madison Square Garden to watch fights and basketball. Guess we must have seen every big band there was in those days, and there were many of them.

I passed thanks to a couple of other good buddies, Vince Femia and Bill Driscoll, a couple of guys from the Philadelphia area that took me under their wing and helped me pass the course, because I was not the smartest one in the class.

About January 15, 1943, I was assigned to the cruiser *Augusta*. It was in the Todd shipyard in New York, and they were working it over. My buddy Eddie and three others reported to Chief Jim "Wag" Wagner in the radio shack. All five of us reported on as third-class petty officers.

As I understand it, the *Augusta* just came from China, as she was a flagship over there.[1] The original crew all had long beards, and they looked like the baseball players on the House of David team.

The *Augusta* was painted white, had red poured decks and cork-lined bulkheads. It was a beautiful ship. They were removing

1. Actually, the *Augusta* was back from the North African invasion of November 1942.

the cork and decks and painting the ship dark gray, getting her ready for battle.

The first year or so, the *Augusta* was in charge of a task force that patrolled the North Atlantic looking for trouble that we sometimes found. We were eight destroyers, four battleships, six cruisers, and one aircraft carrier. I do remember cruisers *Quincy* and *Tuscaloosa;* the aircraft carrier *Ranger;* battleships *Nevada, Arkansas,* and *Texas;* as well as the destroyers *Endicott, Fitch, Corry,* and *Hobson.*

We crossed the Atlantic from Iceland to the Orkney Islands, back to Nova Scotia, and then over to Scapa Flow in the Orkneys. All these ships stayed together all the time that I served on the *Augusta.* At one time we were 800 miles from the North Pole as we crossed the Arctic Circle in October 1943 and awarded a certificate signed by Commander Phares.

After about one year of cookie tossing—and I tossed them often—we went south to Gitmo Bay, San Juan, and Trinidad, and that area we did a lot of training.[2] How long we stayed in that area, I do not remember.

We did a lot of patrolling from Norfolk to Italy, Algeria, and that area. Then we spent some time around the British Isles, Scotland, and Ireland.

John L. Evans, another member of the *Augusta* crew, had entered the navy in 1941 as an ensign. He served at U.S. Navy, Headquarters 8th Naval District, in New Orleans from December 1941 until the end of 1942. Next, he attended the Navy Supply School at Harvard University in Massachusetts between January and May 1943. After he graduated, he was assigned to the *Augusta.* While he served on the vessel, he took part in convoy duty in the Atlantic and the Murmansk run to Russia.

Marine Lt. William H. McDaniel, a Californian who served on the *Augusta* in 1944, was one of a handful of marines who took part in the landings during the invasions of France, leading a landing party in South France.

I first enlisted in the Marine Corps on April 22, 1937, at Kansas City, Missouri. After basic training at the Recruit Depot at San Diego, I transferred to the marine detachment aboard the USS *Maryland.* I served aboard her for three and a half years as a seagoing marine, so sea duty was not new to me. I finished my enlistment at the Marine Corps Base in San Diego, and I was discharged on April 21, 1941, with the rank of sergeant. I reenlisted on December 14, 1941, at San Diego, and I was assigned to Company C, 2nd Pioneer Battalion, as acting first sergeant. As a result of my request and my two and a half years of college, in September 1942 I was transferred to the Officer Candidate School at Quantico and was commissioned on December 2, 1942.

After graduating from the sixteenth reserve officers' class, he received the rank of second lieutenant and reported to the marine barracks at Norfolk Navy Yard on temporary duty, awaiting assignment to a ship. In early July, he was ordered to report to First District Headquarters in New York for transfer to the heavy cruiser *Augusta.* He flew on a naval aircraft from Floyd Bennet Field on Long Island to Argentia, Newfoundland. Here he joined the *Augusta*'s marine detachment, which included two officers and forty enlisted men who manned antiaircraft guns. Within a few days, his ship escorted a convoy to Grenoch, Scot-

2. Gitmo Bay is a nickname for the U.S. Naval Base at Guantanamo, which was leased from Cuba after the Spanish American War and Cuban independence in 1898.

land, and returned to Halifax to pick up another convoy during the last great U-boat campaign in the North Atlantic.

Later in the spring, the *Augusta* sailed into Scapa Flow, the main British naval base situated in the Orkney Islands of Scotland, and served in the Arctic with the British fleet for the remainder of the year. The heavy cruiser *Tuscaloosa* and aircraft carrier *Ranger* also operated with the *Augusta* at the time. In December 1943, the Augusta sailed for Boston and then to Portland, Maine, where she stayed for about a month. In March, she set sail in convoy for Plymouth, England, to prepare for the invasion.

A fair number of sailors, such as Seaman 1/C Clarence Douglas of Lexington, Tennessee, served on the smaller ships of the fleet. Douglas, who joined the navy in October 1943 at age eighteen, went through boot camp at Great Lakes, Illinois. Next, he trained for two more months at Norfolk, Virginia, after which he was assigned to the destroyer *Meredith,* named after a ship that had been sunk in the Pacific in October 1942.[3] Seaman Douglas joined its crew at Boston and went on a shakedown cruise to Bermuda before heading for Europe.

The destroyers were called "tin cans" because for the crews, they did not represent much more than that, compared with the larger warships. If Hummel often became seasick on a heavy cruiser, it is not difficult to imagine what it was like on a destroyer in heavy seas. Douglas experienced many rough rides across the Atlantic. Only a sea journey on a flat-bottomed landing craft could be worse.

While a large number of sailors sailed on warships, many others served on the more humble and less protected landing ships. Their role was as vital as that of the sailors on the fighting ships, however, because they provided support for the fleet as well as the troops that conducted the ground campaign against the Axis. Among these men was Ens. Walter G. Treanor of New York City, a student at Principia College in Elsah, Illinois, who entered the Navy V-7 Officer Candidate Program in July 1942.[4] After receiving his bachelor's degree in 1943 by cramming two academic years into one, he entered Midshipman School at Northwestern University in Chicago on September 22, 1943.

Men aboard U.S. Coast Guard cutter *Spencer* watch a depth charge explode during the hunt for a U-boat in the Atlantic, April 1943. NATIONAL ARCHIVES

> Midshipman School was designed to fashion naval officers out of civilians in a very short time. The curriculum consisted of four main courses. First, of course, was physical fitness. We had to engage in hand-to-hand combat,

3. This would not be the last destroyer to bear the name of *Meredith* during the war. Another new *Meredith,* DD-726, was launched in December 1944 and commissioned in March 1945.

4. The Navy V programs included the V-1 program, a preinduction curriculum at universities, which allowed the student to enter an advanced program after two years; the V-5 program, for aviation cadets; and the V-7 program, for midshipman training to become ensigns. If the men in the V-1 program did not qualify for the V-5 or V-7 program after their two years in college, they went on active duty as apprentice seamen.

rope climbing, the obstacle course, and gymnastics, in addition to some recreation-type sport. The three academic courses were ordnance, seamanship, and navigation.

One time, going aboard a ship in the Illinois River, we committed the horrendous crime of failing to salute the quarterdeck as we came up the gangway and requested permission of the officer of the deck to come aboard. Another midshipman and I were very quickly well educated into the niceties of naval etiquette and requirements for boarding and leaving ships. The first time we were let out on holiday leave on the streets of Chicago, we were saluting everything in sight. I actually did salute the doorman at the hotel!

About three weeks prior to the completion of our program, I received orders to the ship to which I was assigned. I was the first member of the class to receive such orders. During class, one of the instructors said that one of the midshipmen present had received orders, and if he would get up and identify himself and tell us the type of ship, the watertight integrity would be discussed that day. The watertight integrity was the efforts that had to be taken after a ship had been hit to keep it afloat and presumably flooded in some area. I identified myself and told the instructor I had been ordered to an LST. The instructor looked at me in an almost stricken way and said very sympathetically, "I am sorry, sailor; there is no watertight integrity aboard an LST." The group all laughed, and I laughed too, although a bit nervously. This turned out not to be true, but LSTs were not well known to the instructors at the time. They proved very seaworthy and hard to sink.

Treanor received his commission after ninety days.

I was immediately ordered to report to LST 58 at the Algiers Naval Station, Louisiana. The ship had just been built by the facility on the Upper Mississippi River, and it was manned by a very green and inexperienced complement of officers and enlisted personnel. After spending several weeks in a New Orleans shipyard for numerous alterations, including the installation of newly developed radar equipment and additional 40-millimeter AA guns, we embarked on maneuvers in the Gulf of Mexico. These included landing operations and learning to fight shipboard fires over a period of several weeks. Ship-handling experience and movement in convoy and undergoing various intricate maneuvers in convoy. I, the youngest and least experienced officer, was during these maneuvers designated to serve as one of only three underway officers of the deck.

We sailed on to Halifax, Nova Scotia, after having made some stops in the ports of New York and Boston, where we picked up passengers for the journey to England. The passengers consisted of 10 to 12 army officers of various specialties. On the main deck, we carried an LCT, which was not designed for ocean travel but could navigate, as it did, a channel crossing. This craft was manned by an ensign and 12 enlisted men.

Our normal complement consisted of 10 to 11 officers and approximately 110 enlisted men; however, we had six LCVP (landing craft, vehicle personnel) assault craft, and therefore we carried two additional ensigns serving as small-boat officers along with three-man crews for each of these assault craft.

Tom Clark, a junior at Southern Illinois University and another New Yorker, enlisted in the navy right after the attack on Pearl Harbor in January 1942.

A group of us went up to St. Louis and took some examinations. I took exams for V-7, which was navy midshipman, and for V-5, navy flight training. I never heard from navy flight, but I did hear from V-7, and I was accepted. I continued in school and had to take certain courses in math. I went on active duty on April 28 and went to boot camp at Great Lakes. I went through midshipman school up in Chicago; it was conducted by Northwestern University; from there, down to Damn Neck, Virginia, and the Virginia area for training of all the amphibs. I went through gunnery training down at Damn Neck, Virginia, and then back to Great Lakes for more gunnery training. Then I was a plank owner on the ship; a group of seven officers and enlisted cadre was assembled. We trained together on the Great Lakes and somewhat in Virginia at the amphibious base there. We reassembled at Chicago.

Lt. James Swarts, Lieutenant Murdoch, Lieutenant Smith, Ens. Jerry Brown, Ted Beattie, Lieutenant Scotty Gil, and I were assembled at Great Lakes Naval Station, assigned a crew, sent by sealed train to Jeffersonville, Indiana, where we saw the 507 launched on November 16, 1943—keel laid down on September 8—and departed January 1, 1944, for New Orleans.[5] We arrived in New Orleans on January 8. We went for a shakedown and various maneuvers and such in the Gulf of Mexico.

We loaded LCT 663 on the main deck on March 7, 1944. We sailed up the East Coast and picked up extra men and medical officers at New York while the 507 was in the Brooklyn Navy Yard. By March 14, we were at sea after forming up in an eighty-ship convoy at Boston. En route, we lost power to our rudder and lost our convoy in the Atlantic. We regained the convoy by skimming at flank speed.

I am compelled to say that it was hellish on an LST when the sea got up and her screws pitched partially out of the water. One feared she would break in two, since she had no keel. When the screws came out of the water, the whole ship would vibrate seemingly to buckle amidships. However, the LST cannot be put down; it was a remarkable vessel, and it did well.

We got to England at the end of February or the early part of March. A year to the day after I went on active duty, as luck would have it, we were torpedoed (April 28, 1944).[6] That is just one of the quirks of the thing.

Donald Irwin of Iowa also entered the V-7 program in 1942 and went to the Midshipman School at Columbia University in New York. After he was commissioned, he was sent for additional training first to Solomons Island, Maryland; then to Little Creek, Virginia; and finally to Camp Bradford, Virginia. By the time Ensign Irwin reported to New Orleans, Ensign Treanor was already on his way across the Atlantic.

I received orders to report to LST 291 New Orleans, and here I took charge of my brand new LCT, LCT 614, which had been built in New Orleans, with all new gear aboard. The LCT was lifted by a giant crane to the main deck of the LST and securely fastened by heavy chains and wire cables to the deck of the LST so it would withstand

5. LST 507 was accepted by the U.S. Navy on December 31, 1943, and placed in reduced commission. It departed Jeffersonville on January 1, 1944; arrived in New Orleans on January 8, 1944; and was placed in full commission on January 10, 1944.

6. LST 507 was one of the vessels sunk by German E-boats during Exercise Tiger (details in a later chapter).

the rough seas that would be encountered in the Atlantic Ocean.

I traveled on LST 291 down the Mississippi to the Gulf, then along the East Coast, with stops in New York Harbor, Boston Harbor, and Halifax, Nova Scotia.

From Halifax, we joined a sixty-five-ship convoy across the Atlantic, with only a stop at the Azores for refueling before arriving at Londonderry, Ireland, approximately fourteen days later. En route, we encountered very rough seas, with one storm so severe, it scattered the sixty-five-ship convoy so much that only three or four ships were in view when the storm ended. Word was that the German subs sank one of the ships, but we got back into formation again and proceeded on our way. The only other unusual happening I can recall was that an iceberg floated through the middle of our convoy during the night. This was cause for some emergency-type maneuvers, but no ships were hit.

The navy also played an important role in maintaining medical services for the invasion forces. The navy provided medics for marines, and the beach battalions assisted the army with landing operations. Some LSTs were reserved for service as hospital ships after their cargo was unloaded. Medical personnel constituted almost one-third of the special naval beach battalions.

Eugene Eckstam of Madison, Wisconsin, who entered the U.S. Naval Reserve (USNR) program in January 1942, became a seagoing medical officer in the navy. When he completed his medical degree in March 1943, he received a commission as an ensign in the Naval Hospital Corps.

We were issued a copy of naval regulations and the manual of the Medical Department of the Navy. We had to read those publications and had to turn in answers, on which we were graded. After completion of internship at St. Luke's Hospital in Duluth, Minnesota, for nine months in 1943, I was assigned to the Great Lakes Training Station in Illinois in January 1944 as a lieutenant, junior grade, in the Medical Corps, USNR. At Great Lakes, I was on the examination line for new recruits, and we examined about 1,600 of them a day.

After that week, I was transferred to Ledo Beach on Long Island for amphibious warfare training. We saw many films, and there were models of LSTs. We were taught marching techniques as well. It was quite hilarious watching some new doctors teaching hospital corpsmen, who had been in the service longer than we had, military discipline.

At Ledo Beach, doctors and corpsmen were paired up in units of size and periodically assigned to ships for departure to Europe. Early in March 1944, two doctors (including myself) and forty corpsmen boarded the LST 507 in the harbor at Brooklyn, New York. We stopped at Boston and Halifax and joined an eighty-ship convoy to cross the Atlantic. Halfway across, our rudder mechanism went out of order, and as things would have it, there were two left-control springs in the reserve repair box, but no right-control springs, which we needed. We fixed it with rubber bands and made the journey uneventfully. I suppose the rubber band is still there!

LST 507, carrying Dr. Eckstam and Tom Clark, arrived at Roysth, Scotland, where it delivered LCT 663. From there it proceeded to Bristol, but then it had to move on to Falmouth, England, because of damage caused when, Dr. Eckstam says, "a drunken British pilot took us over one of those metal buoys at the entrance to a harbor." Possibly these mishaps were bad omens for LST 509, presaging worse to come.

Early in the war, the navy created special naval beach battalions to support amphibious operations. These units included a large signal section, a medical section, and a boat section for beach control. The battalion was expected to act as a liaison between the navy and army troops on a beachhead. Some veterans of these units opine that they replaced specialized marine units, which were committed to the Pacific.[7]

The 3rd Naval Beach Battalion had trained with the 1119th Army Engineer Combat Group at the Naval Amphibious Center at Fort Pierce, Florida, and Camp Pickett, Virginia. In October 1943, it was split up to create the 6th and 7th Naval Beach Battalions. After several additional weeks of training in 1943, the 6th Naval Beach Battalion, under the command of Lt. Cmdr. E. C. Carusi, set sail for England from New York in January 1944. After it disembarked in England, it moved to its base at Salcombe, Devon, on January 20 and continued its training.

The men, ships, and aircraft of the Coast Guard not only patrolled the beaches and coastal waters of America and protected the seaports, but also provided transports, destroyer escorts, and landing craft of various types.[8] When LCI Flotilla 4 was created in January 1944, it numbered twenty-four of seventy-six LCIs built by the Consolidated Steel Corporation's Shipbuilding Division at Orange, Texas. Eventually it took part in the Mediterranean campaign. Although the Coast Guard manned a number LSTs and other landing craft, this was the only flotilla fully manned and controlled by coast guardsmen.

Dockyard workers finished the twenty-four LCIs allotted to the Coast Guard during the last weeks of 1942 and beginning of 1943. The completed ships assembled in Galveston, Texas, under the command of Capt. Myles Imlay, USCG, early in 1943. The flotilla consisted of two groups: Group 7 under Commander Bresnan and Group 8 under Commander Unger. On February 20, 1943, the LCIs cast off from Galveston on the first leg of their voyage to North Africa. En route to Key West, Florida, these small flat-bottomed ships ran into rough weather. Their largely untrained crews, who had yet to find their sea legs, literally turned green and found a new use for the buckets by their bunks as the rail riders were busy depositing their meals in the sea. By the time they reached Key West on March 5, 1943, the coast guardsmen had developed their sea legs, but they concluded that LCI stood for "lousy civilian idea."

On March 11, the flotilla pulled into Norfolk, Virginia, and loaded with provisions in preparation for their ocean crossing, while the crewmen experienced their first beach landing at Virginia Beach. The ships then proceeded to a degaussing station, where their magnetic field was neutralized to protect them from magnetic mines. Finally, on April 1, the flotilla sailed with a convoy to Bermuda, where it arrived on April 5. After the crews enjoyed several days of liberty, the flotilla set sail on April 12 for Port Lyautey, French Morocco, where it arrived on April 31, entering the European-Mediterranean theater of war.

The Coast Guard had limited facilities, and its inductees went through basic training in boot camps at Port Townsend, Washington; New Orleans; or the Coast Guard yard at Curtis Bay, Maryland. Two additional bases were opened early in the war, but because of a lack of time and an excess of volunteers, basic training was reduced to about one month. The majority of the men in the LCI flotilla entered the service in 1941 or 1942. Recruits who entered the Coast Guard later came to join them in Europe.

7. Some beach battalions did serve in the Pacific, since they fulfilled a function the marines could not in addition to providing medical services.

8. The destroyer escort (DE) was smaller and more lightly armed than the faster fleet destroyer (DD) but had sufficient antiaircraft armament to defend itself. The DEs served as convoy escorts and in antisubmarine operations.

Yeoman 2/C George Gray from McFall, Missouri, was typical of most members of the flotilla crew. He enlisted in 1942, and after he went through a six-week boot camp at Algiers, New Orleans, he joined Flotilla 4 at Galveston on February 23, 1943, with an assignment as a personnel yeoman. He was stationed on the flagship of the unit LCI 87. Whenever the flotilla put into port for a period of more than two days, the whole crew moved the office equipment ashore, where all the personnel administrative work for the flotilla, such as transfers, medical records, promotions, and reports, was performed.

Allen Aylward of Beverly, Massachusetts, joined the flotilla by a more indirect route. After he enlisted in 1942, he attended one of the new training bases near Brooklyn, New York, for his boot camp and a Radio School at Atlantic City for his advanced training. Having attained the rank of radioman third class, Aylward served at a Coast Guard radio station on Long Island, New York. Later he was assigned to the Liberty ship *Stephen Austin*. Finally, in 1944, he reported for duty with the flotilla as a radioman on LCI 326.

The Civilian War Industries

The most noticeable of the war industries were the shipyards where thousands of workers built all types of ships for the war. Large factories, many in the automotive industry, produced a wide variety of vehicles for the war, from jeeps to tanks and artillery. Thousands of smaller sites manufactured everything the American war machine might need, from uniforms and equipment to bullets and bombs.

Although the capital ships drew most attention, many shipyards worked around the clock to turn out the landing craft vital for the amphibious operations that would place American troops on European shores and in the Pacific.

The LSTs, the largest of the landing craft, required the most work and space. To meet the demand, numerous shipyards along the Mississippi River and its tributaries produced LSTs and other landing craft. Farther up the Ohio River from Jeffersonville were the Dravo Shipyards on Neville Island, on the outskirts of Pittsburgh. Even this far up the river, LSTs were laid down. Harvey Kaufmann describes the operations:

> The Dravo works consisted of two large yards, each capable of constructing at least two LSTs at once, and in 1942, work in the yards continued night and day, seven days a week. Like the troops preparing for the war or already shipped out, the workers had a sense of duty leavened by their own brand of humor.
>
> Once, while one of the workers was busy at his assigned task on the bow of the ship, his coworkers welded a piece of chain wrapped around his ankle to the ship. Everyone one in the yard had a good laugh except the victim until the chain was removed.
>
> Equipment needed for daily operation of the vessels was not always available at the shipyards. For example, the navy had to buy presses for the crew's laundry from civilian tailor or cleaning shops.

Some of the small but just as vital items, such as shells for the guns, were also produced at a frantic pace.

> The workers here were not paid by the hour, but instead by what they produced. The production of shells was not easy or safe. For example, at a plant in Pittsburgh, to produce the [90-millimeter] shell required an eleven-man crew. The men alternated in their workstations. They had to place a 10-foot prong into a huge circular oven and pull out a red-hot billet—a solid piece of steel that was to become the shell—and carry it over to a large piece of machinery

known as a reamer. This reamer stamped out a shell by penetrating the red-hot billet and hollowing it out. Next, another man, known as a scaler, removed the excess material from the billet. Finally, the completed shell was placed in a large steel crate that held 75 to 100 rounds, which was picked up and stacked in a pile with a forklift. The workers had to provide their own gloves—difficult to obtain at the time—for this hard work. Many a man passed out from the heat of the furnaces, and serious accidents also occurred. One man, while working at the reamer, was hit in the chest by the red-hot billet when it popped out of position as the reamer came down to hollow it out. Although the man was rushed to the hospital, his coworkers never saw him again.

Working in civilian industries producing war materiel from uniforms to tanks could be as dangerous as combat, since speed was important and long work hours were needed. Some workers left messages of thanks for the men in the armed forces in some of the items produced. These were later found by crew members, some of whom struck up a correspondence with them. Although skilled workers had to be protected from the draft after 1942 and also were discouraged from enlisting, women contributed heavily to the workforce.

During most of the war, Mary Stokes worked for the Olin Corporation in East Alton, Illinois, in America's heartland. That company owned several factories and produced and distributed ammunition around the world, and had been known for their variety of shotgun shells and taking over the Winchester company early in the 1930s. Her father, Emil Hanson, who had risen from private to first lieutenant, had retired from the army after thirty years of service. He had volunteered for active military service during the war but was told he was too old, so he took a job as a guard at the site and may have helped her secure a position there.[9] Mary Stokes did not have one of the more publicized positions, like that of a "Rosie the Riveter," but instead had more of a desk job in an office. She gave up that position when there was an opening in the factory for an inspector on the floor to check the ammunition being produced. When she found the quality of the bullets not up to standards, she sent them back. This soon made her very unpopular with many of the workers, who seemed not to be as concerned about sending out substandard munitions. She felt strongly about this as her patriotic duty and not a $14-a-week job, since she had been an "army brat." During the war, all the ammunition plants of the Olin Corporation had produced a combined total of over 15 billion rounds for M-1 rifles and carbines, employing 62,000 men and women.

Although the government imposed rationing on the civilian population, once the war industries got in gear, the troops lacked little. Even though some materials were in short supply at one time or another, no other nation came even close to matching the U.S. output. Nonetheless, the United States still was not ready to begin its great offensive operations against the Axis before 1943, because it took time not only to train and ship the troops overseas, but also to produce the munitions and equipment necessary to win the war. Many Americans sanguinely believed that victory would come in 1943, but despite the massive U.S. war effort, more time was needed to launch the great invasion that would eventually bring an end to the war.

9. Harrison died in May 1943.

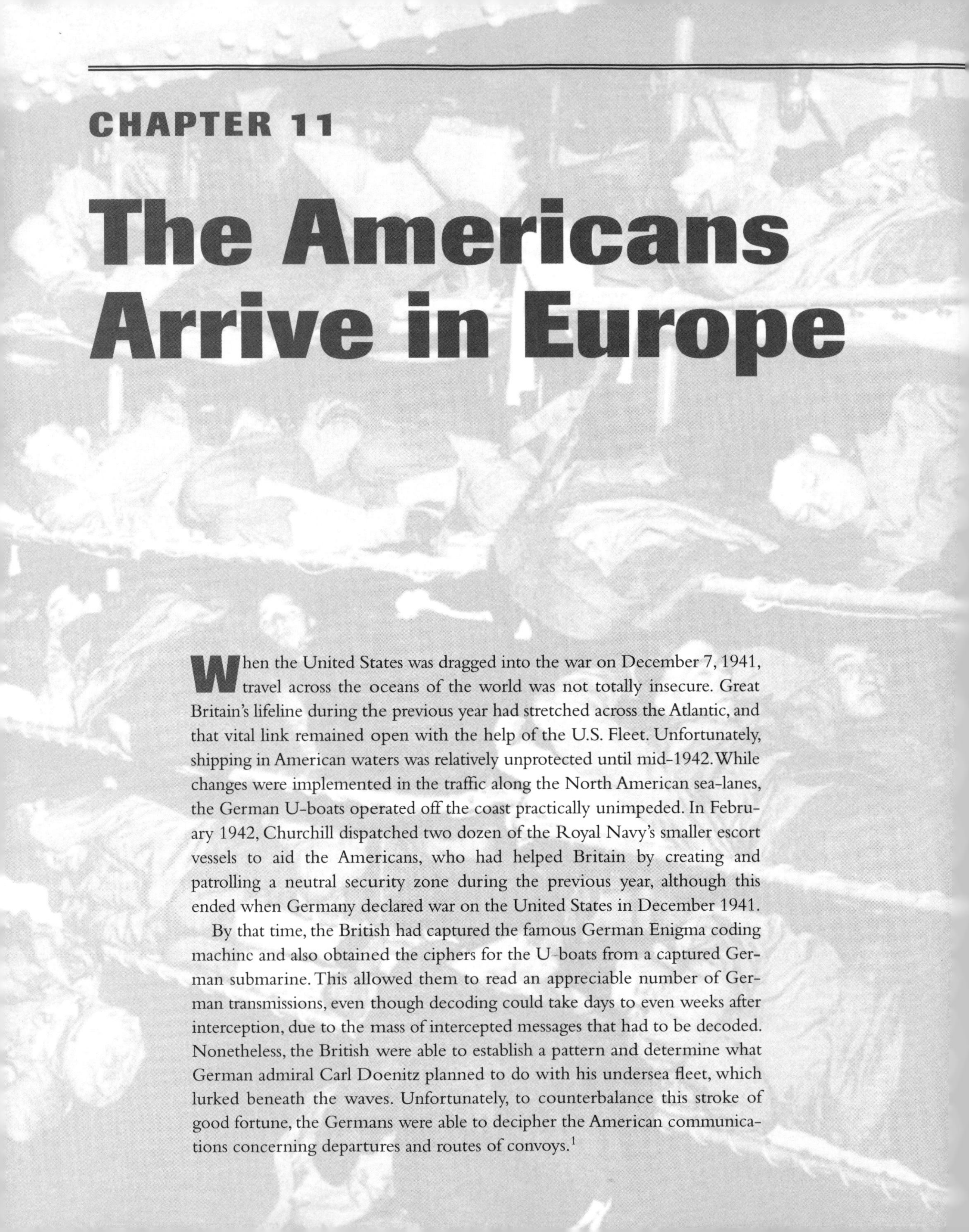

CHAPTER 11

The Americans Arrive in Europe

When the United States was dragged into the war on December 7, 1941, travel across the oceans of the world was not totally insecure. Great Britain's lifeline during the previous year had stretched across the Atlantic, and that vital link remained open with the help of the U.S. Fleet. Unfortunately, shipping in American waters was relatively unprotected until mid-1942. While changes were implemented in the traffic along the North American sea-lanes, the German U-boats operated off the coast practically unimpeded. In February 1942, Churchill dispatched two dozen of the Royal Navy's smaller escort vessels to aid the Americans, who had helped Britain by creating and patrolling a neutral security zone during the previous year, although this ended when Germany declared war on the United States in December 1941.

By that time, the British had captured the famous German Enigma coding machine and also obtained the ciphers for the U-boats from a captured German submarine. This allowed them to read an appreciable number of German transmissions, even though decoding could take days to even weeks after interception, due to the mass of intercepted messages that had to be decoded. Nonetheless, the British were able to establish a pattern and determine what German admiral Carl Doenitz planned to do with his undersea fleet, which lurked beneath the waves. Unfortunately, to counterbalance this stroke of good fortune, the Germans were able to decipher the American communications concerning departures and routes of convoys.[1]

For the Axis and Allied forces alike, radar became a key element in the struggle for control of the seas, even though it was still riddled with problems in 1942. War correspondent Walter Cronkite witnessed firsthand a radar glitch as he traveled along the American coast early in the war. His convoy sailed into a fog bank, and its commander considered dispersing the ships to avoid collisions, but the radar operator convinced him that the vessels could rely on their radar to steer clear from each other. Thus the ships continued on their way, relying on radar to maintain the proper alignment and distance. When the fog began to lift, everyone standing along the side of the ship was taken aback to see the other ship off the port side only a few yards away. It was clear that there were kinks to work out of the newfangled contraption and that its operators needed more experience using it.

While the battle of the Atlantic raged throughout the spring and summer of 1942, the Allied planners argued over the feasibility of a cross-Channel invasion. The 1st Armored and 5th Infantry Divisions crossed the dangerous waters of the North Atlantic in the spring of 1942, followed, at the end of the summer, by the 1st Infantry Division, which sped across in the fast liner *Queen Mary.* During the summer, to keep their Soviet ally in the war, the Allies sent convoys to Murmansk in the Arctic, where units of the German surface fleet, including the battleship *Tirpitz* and U-boats, posed a serious threat.[2] The Allied fleet was stretched trying to patrol the Arctic and Atlantic, back the 8th British Army in North Africa, maintain Malta, and later in the year, support the invasion of French North Africa. In early 1942, transporting troops to the British Isles through U-boat-infested waters presented a great risk. The Allies did not take control of the situation in the Atlantic until the latter part of the year, when the employment of the new destroyer escorts and small escort aircraft carriers helped turn the tide.

Only one other American division, the 29th, crossed the Atlantic to Great Britain in 1942. The first half of 1943 saw the situation in the North Atlantic again getting out of hand. After several battles with the U-boat wolf packs, the Allies improved their weapon systems, forcing Doenitz to pull his undersea raiders back at the beginning of June 1943.[3] Several weeks later, the convoys began transporting the divisions needed for an invasion.

While convoys gathered on the East Coast of North America to cross the Atlantic, a stream of aircraft flew above them toward the same destination. The air journey could be as hazardous as the ocean voyage. Though it was uncommon to lose a ship to the elements, losing them to the enemy was routine. On the other hand, more aircraft were lost to the elements than to interception by enemy aircraft. Bad navigation, engine problems, or plain bad luck could spell disaster for a flight crew.

In the early years of the war, the aircraft usually stayed far to the north. The trip across the Atlantic began in New England, stopped over in Newfoundland and Iceland, and proceeded to the British Isles. Pilots occasionally made emergency landings in Greenland, at bases such as Bluie West

1. German intelligence reports included newspaper clippings on troop movements and any other information they could garner from agents, but the accuracy of this information was not nearly as reliable as data culled from message decoding.

2. The sister ship of the battleship *Bismarck* when it broke out into the Atlantic, the *Tirpitz* was hunted down by the Royal Navy and sunk in 1941. The *Tirpitz* was based in Norway, and a sortie by the vessel in July 1942 led to the dispersal and destruction of Murmansk-bound convoy PQ 17. British midget submarines damaged the *Tirpitz* in September 1943, and several bombing missions targeted the warship in 1944. The RAF finally brought about the ship's demise using 5-ton Tallboy "Earthquake" bombs in November 1944.

3. The Germans built huge submarine pens on the French Atlantic coast to provide secure bases for their U-boats. These included the pens at Brest, St. Lorient, St. Nazaire, La Rochelle, and Bordeaux. Although targeted by the 8th Air Force many times, they proved immune to the heaviest Allied bombs until late 1944. Similar pens also existed in Norway at Trondheim.

Troop ships were crowded and uncomfortable.

1 or 8. The planes usually flew individually, although the first major air crossings were made by groups flying in formation.

After the occupation of French North Africa, the southern route came into use. Aircraft departed from Florida, with possible stops in the West Indies en route to Brazil, from whence they continued to West Africa and Morocco if their destination was England. Some aircraft flew on to join with the 12th and 15th Air Forces in the Mediterranean.

The 29th Division's Deployment Overseas

The 1st Infantry Division, which did not ship out until August 1942, made the journey on the converted British luxury liner *Queen Mary.* During its short stay at Tidworth Barracks in England, it engaged in some training. In October 1942, it embarked for the invasion of North Africa with the 1st "Old Ironsides" Armored Division, which had arrived in May.[5] They were joined by elements of the 34th "Red Bull" Division that had been stationed in Northern Ireland since January 1942. The remainder of the 34th Division left for North Africa in January 1943. The 5th "Red Diamond" Division, garrisoned in Iceland since May 1942, stayed behind, but it was in no position to train for amphibious operations.

The departure of all these divisions for North Africa meant that no American divisions remained in Great Britain to continue preparations for the cross-Channel assault. When the 29th Division, a National Guard outfit like the 34th, came off the summer maneuvers in the Carolinas, the Washington planners decided that it was ready for overseas deployment.

The 29th Division traveled by train from Camp Blanding, Florida, to Camp Kilmer, New Jersey, where it arrived on September 20, 1942. About a week later, the two huge liners *Queen Mary* and *Queen Elizabeth,* their transportation for their Atlantic crossing, arrived at the port of New York. Each ship, with a capacity for over 10,000 men, was more than sufficient to carry the entire division. They could reach speeds of 30 knots, which was twice as fast as any U-boat. On previous journeys in September and October, they had transported ground elements of the 8th Air Force units. There would be no convoy, just a mad dash. The only escort would be provided by several British warships that would meet them off the coast of Ireland.

The 29th was the first American division to depart from New York under the cloak of secrecy as described by Joseph Balkoski in *Beyond the Beachhead.* Orders for the division's movement never included its number. Troops detrained and moved as inconspicuously as possible through the night to the ferries that carried them to great liners. The *Queen Mary* slipped out of New York on the morning of September 27, and the *Queen Elizabeth* followed her on October 5. Both ships

5. General Patton had nicknamed his 2nd Armored Division "Hell on Wheels" in 1941. Gen. Bruce Magruder, who commanded the 1st Armored Division until March 1942, need a name to match him. A competition failed to produce anything he liked until he noticed "Old Ironsides" on a painting of the USS *Constitution*.

The Battle of the Atlantic

German U-boats went on a rampage during the first half of 1942, especially along the American Eastern Seaboard and in the Caribbean. They sank 465 ships, losing only 21 of their submarines. As the Allies gradually expanded air cover over the North Atlantic, German losses began to rise. During the last half of the year, the U-boats sank 550 ships, but their losses had increased to 66.

Allied bombing of German submarine pens and shipyards was fruitless, and U-boat production continued unabated. It was not until the Allies developed new, more effective radar and other electronic devices that they were able to turn the tide.

In the meantime, the development of prefabricated, mass-produced merchant ships, which took six months to build, counterbalanced the heavy losses incurred by Allied shipping. The first of these vessels, known as Liberty ships, was launched in September 1941. Before the end of 1942, shipyards working around the clock produced one a month, so that before the war ended, more than 2,700 plied the oceans. These Liberty ships, used as troop transports, were slow and lacked basic amenities, but they quickly filled the gaps produced by the losses.

In 1943, the U-boats launched a new campaign in the North Atlantic, wreaking havoc on the convoys. On more than one occasion, violent weather saved a convoy from U-boat depredations. At other times, however, storms separated the ships from their convoys, allowing them to fall prey to the lurking danger. In the first half of 1943, 320 Allied ships went down in the Atlantic, while U-boat losses were relatively light. The Germans lost just 40 submarines during the winter months, but between April and June, the gray wolves sank only 120 ships as 73 U-boats never surfaced again.

When Allied aircraft from land bases on both sides of the Atlantic and from escort carriers began to maintain an almost constant patrol over the sea-lanes, the U-boats were forced to spend most of their time underwater at reduced speeds.[4] The endless vigil of the escorts made it impossible for the U-boats to continue their depredations with immunity. In addition, once they located the enemy submarines, they mercilessly depth-charged them. By August 1942, 105 of the 344 submarines that had gone to sea never returned to their bases. The increased efficiency of Allied antisubmarine measures in 1943 also had a negative impact on the German submariners' morale once they realized that the odds were against them. During their arduous trips across the Atlantic, the Allied soldiers could feel a measure of reassurance knowing that if anything happened to their ships, their chances of being rescued were good. The German submariners, on the other hand, could not count on being rescued at sea. On a U-boat destroyed underwater, its crew of about fifty men had no chance of escape, even on one destroyed on the surface, the chance of rescue remained slim.

The month of May 1943 was disastrous for U-boats in the Atlantic, as many of them slipped beneath the waves, never to be seen again. Doenitz called off his campaign in the

continued

4. Submerged submarines reached just a fraction of their surface speed because they had to run on batteries, which could be recharged only on the surface. In addition, the air supply soon became exhausted while underwater for long periods. These drawbacks did not disappear until the snorkel was developed late in the war. One other problem was that most submarines could submerge only about 200 to 350 feet, and in clear water, they could be spotted by patrol aircraft and blimps that carried depth charges.

The Battle of the Atlantic *continued*

North Atlantic. In September, the U-boats made a brief comeback when they attacked one convoy, but it was a flash in the pan. Despite improved antiaircraft armament, the U-boats were not able to withstand air attacks. During the last half of 1944, Doenitz's underwater fleet accounted for another 115 Allied ships sunk in the Atlantic but lost 124 U-boats. This was a loss ratio of more than 1:1, not a satisfactory exchange for the Germans.

In early 1944, a new generation of U-boats made its debut. Equipped with a snorkel and other innovations, it was more effective. These changes had come too late, however, and the new submarines were not produced in large enough numbers to save Germany. During the first three months of 1944, the Germans sank 45 Allied ships in the Atlantic while losing 60 U-boats. The same U-boat fleet was expected to break up the Allied invasion fleet that year.

American and Foreign Troop Transports

The American troops quickly found that the worst way to travel to Europe was on a foreign ship. The Americans were not accustomed to the cuisine served on British ships. In addition, the British merchant marine sailors, who had already been at war for well over two years, seemed to have an "attitude" toward their better-paid and more privileged American passengers.

According to most GIs, the American ships were clean and the food onboard was palatable, whereas the foreign-flagged vessels were usually dirty, and the food did nothing to help stomachs already unsettled by the rough seas and zigzagging course of the vessel. A few GIs tried to survive the trip on nothing but candy bars.

The quality of the trans-Atlantic trip varied greatly from unit to unit. The troops usually had little time on deck, and the air was stuffy belowdecks. When the seas got rough, enormous waves smashed against the ship, and many a soldier succumbed to seasickness. When the sea was serene, an eerie sense of calm pervaded the ship. All the while, the ever-present fear of U-boats kept everybody on edge as the ship zigzagged across the ocean in an effort to evade the enemy. Under these circumstances, the cleanliness of the ship and quality of the food greatly affected the condition and morale of the men by the time they disembarked in the British Isles.

successful negotiated the U-boat-infested waters, but the *Queen Mary,* which was in the lead, was involved in a tragic accident when it sliced through the British cruiser *Curacao.* The majority of the men of the 29th never knew what happened.

The *Queen Mary* sailed up the Firth of Clyde to the port of Greenock, Scotland, on October 3, followed by the *Queen Elizabeth* on October 11. They were the first of many ships carrying American soldiers to arrive at Greenock over the next eighteen months.

Fast Liners and Troop Movements

The British discovered early in the war that their large oceangoing luxury liners could carry up to a full division of army troops if the interior fixtures were removed to make room for the men. Their high speeds allowed these liners to cruise twice as fast as the German submarines at surface velocity.

When the Americans entered the war, they needed to get a large number of troops across the Atlantic as speedily as possible. Although it might seem that a large convoy would be the safest method, statistics proved that it was not so. Convoys were slow, taking from ten to fifteen days to make the crossing, and even though the escorts were able to ward off the German wolf packs, in 1942 and 1943, the odds were that most convoys would lose at least a ship or two. Since those ships carried several hundred men, their loss was a tremendous setback for the Allies, especially from the standpoint of morale. For example, when the *Dorchester,* one of the few troopships sunk by a U-boat, went down off the coast of Greenland in February 1943; about 600 of the 900 men aboard were lost. On this ship, four chaplains gave their life preservers to other men and remained behind.

Transporting elements of more than fifty air groups, almost twenty army divisions, and their supporting units to Great Britain in ships that carried an average of 500 men probably would have required more than 700 shiploads between 1942 and the early summer of 1944. Chances were good that the U-boats might have successfully sunk at least ten to thirty of the ships, which would have meant the loss of at least 5,000 troops.

Although the decision to use the *Queen Elizabeth* and *Queen Mary*—each carrying up to 15,000 men—was not without risk, the odds were in favor of the Allies. If one of these 80,000-ton ships were hit by a torpedo, the chance of its going down quickly with all aboard was unlikely. Even the *Titanic* had remained afloat for a while after it hit an iceberg in 1912. Most ships of this tonnage were provided with watertight compartments that would allow them to stay afloat for a considerable amount of time. In addition, these liners carried little in the way of munitions and had a better chance of staying afloat than the large warships, which were usually able to sustain a number of torpedo hits as long as they did not detonate a magazine. If a liner were hit and disabled, several factors would come into play. Would the rescue ships or U-boat wolf pack get to the scene first? Did the U-boats carry enough ammunition to kill all the survivors? Would the Germans actually massacre thousands of men in lifeboats and rafts? Another problem was the scarcity of lifeboats on the liners. There were probably not enough to accommodate even half of the passengers. If a ship were sunk during the winter months, what would happen to the men? Fortunately for the Allies, these questions never required answers, since none of the fast liners were sunk.

In 1942 and 1943, the *Queen Elizabeth* and *Queen Mary* alone transported the ground echelons of more than fifty bomber and fighter groups of the 8th Air Force, as well as the crews of some of the squadrons. The *Queen Mary* carried the ground echelons of eight bomber groups in a single trip. In 1942, the *Queens* also carried the 1st Division and two months later its replacement, the 29th Division, to England. Many of the army divi-

continued

Fast Liners and Troop Movements *continued*

sions, even if not sent on one of the great liners alone, still traveled crammed into large transports. Thus instead of the need for an estimated 700 shiploads of troops to transport more than twenty divisions, it took closer to 50. This reduced the chances that one of the ships loaded with troops, either transports in convoy or fast liners traveling independently would be hit, and may have been the overriding factor in taking the risk.

Liners Converted for Troop Duty

Ship	Built	Displacement	Speed	Passengers (troops)
Queen Elizabeth (U.K.)	1940	83,673 tons	28 knots	2,240 (11,027[a])
Queen Mary (U.K.)	1936	81,235 tons	28 knots	2,139 (10,595[a])
Normandie[b] (France)	1935	82,792 tons	30 knots	2,000 (?)
Ile de France[c] (France)	1926	43,450 tons	22 knots	1,300 (9,706)
Aquitaine (U.K.)	1914	44,786 tons	25 knots	1,000 (7,725)
Mauritania (U.K.)	1939	35,739 tons	23 knots	1,100 (7,124)
West Point[d] (U.S.)	1939	35,400 tons	25 knots	1,200 (7,600)
Wakefield[e] (U.S.)	1931	33,600 tons	22 knots	1,000 (6,000)

[a] Normal troop load, maximum about 15,000
[b] The United States took over the ship and attempted to convert it, but it was damaged in a fire
[c] Taken over by the British in 1940
[d] Formerly the liner *America*
[e] Formerly the liner *Manhattan*

The next table lists all major movements of army divisions and 8th Air Force units from the United States to the United Kingdom between January 1942 and May 1944.

Major Cross-Atlantic Troop Movements, January 1942–May 1944

Date	Ship or convoy	Units
Jan 16–25, 1942	Convoy	34th Division (part of division) (to Northern Ireland)
Feb 19–Mar 2	Convoy	34th Division (part of division)
Apr 30–May 5	Convoy	34th Division[a] (remaining units)
May 11–16	*Queen Mary*	1st Armored Division (part of division)
May 25–Jun 10	Convoy	1st Armored Division[a] (remaining units)
June 3–10	*Queen Elizabeth*	1st & 31st Fighter Gp, 97th Bomb Gp
July 16–Aug 16	*West Point* (in convoy)	14th Fighter Gp, 92nd Bomb Gp
Aug 5–11	*Queen Mary*	1st Division[a]
Aug 9–18	Uruguay (in convoy)	301st Bomb Gp
Aug 30–Sept 5	*Queen Elizabeth*	67th Recon Gp, 93rd & 306th Bomb Gp

[a] Divisions sent to take part in the North African and Mediterranean campaign

Fast Liners and Troop Movements *continued*

Major Cross-Atlantic Troop Movements, January 1942–May 1944

Date	Ship or convoy	Units
Sept 3–11	*Queen Mary*	44th, 47th, 91st, 303rd, 305th, 310th, 319th, & 320th Bomb Gp
Sept 28–Oct 8	*Queen Mary* and *Elizabeth*	29th Division
Nov 24–30	*Queen Elizabeth*	315th Troop Carrier, 78th Fighter Gp, & 322nd Bomb Gp
Jan 1–11, 1943	*Queen Mary*	56th Fighter Gp
April 12	Convoy	351st Bomb Gp
May 5–11	*Queen Elizabeth*	94th, 95th, 96th, & 323rd Bomb Gp
May 10–18	*Argentina* (in convoy)	379th Bomb Gp
May 27–Jun 3	*Queen Elizabeth*	100th, 381st, 384th, & 386th Bomb Gp
June 1–6	*Queen Mary*	353rd Fighter Gp
June 23–July 1	*Queen Mary*	38th & 387th Bomb Gp
July 1–6	*Queen Elizabeth*	352nd & 355th Fighter Grp, 388th Bomb Gp
July 17–27	*James Parker* (in convoy)	390th Bomb Gp
July ?	Convoy	392nd Bomb Gp
Aug 5 (arrives)	Convoy	5th Division (from Iceland to Northern Ireland)
Aug 20–25	*Queen Elizabeth*	20th & 356th Fighter Gp
Sept 6–14	*Orion* (in convoy)	55th Fighter Gp
Sept 11 (arrives)	Convoy	101st A/B Division
Sept 18 (arrives)	Convoy	3rd Armored Division
Oct 18 (arrives)	Convoy	2nd & 28th Divisions
Oct 8–20	*Monterey* (in convoy)	358th Fighter Gp (359th Fighter Gp on 3 ships)
Oct 27–Nov 2	*Queen Mary*	401st, 445th & 446th Bomb Gp
Nov 11 (arrives)	Convoy	1st Division (from Mediterranean theater)
Nov 23 (arrives)	Convoy	2nd Armored Division (from Mediterranean theater)
Nov 23–29	*Queen Elizabeth*	357th & 361st Fighter Gp, 447th & 448th Bomb Gp
Nov 25 (arrives)	Convoy	9th Division (from Mediterranean theater)
Dec 9 (arrives)	Convoy	82nd A/B Division (to Northern Ireland) & 1st ESB (from Mediterranean theater)
Dec 16 (arrives)	Convoy	1116th Engineer Combat Gp (redesignated 6th ESB)
Dec 5–18	Convoy	8th Division (to Northern Ireland)
Dec 23–29	*Queen Mary*	5th ESB
Jan 26, 1944	Convoy	4th Division
Feb 23 (arrives)	Convoy	30th Division
Feb 24 (arrives)	Convoy	5th Armored Division
Apr 4 (arrives)	Convoy	90th Division
Apr 16 (arrives)	Convoy	79th & 83rd Divisions
May 26(arrives)	Convoy	35th Division

While the troops were at Camp Kilmer waiting to embark, many were not happy. Despite the attempt at secrecy, families, wives, and girlfriends were waiting near the camp, so during the next week, each soldier received a twenty-four-hour pass. Apparently the one pass was not enough for John R. "Bob" Slaughter of Company D, 116th Infantry, who was chewed out for a little escapade that involved sneaking off the post and going into town the day before he boarded the *Queen Mary* in New York Harbor. His regiment was taken by train to Hoboken on September 26 to board ferries to take them across the Hudson, where their ship awaited.

> [Before departing Kilmer,] photographs were taken and identification cards issued that would be carried until our separation from the army. Immunization shots for every disease known to man were given in both arms and where the sun doesn't shine. New weapons, equipment, and clothing were handed out.
>
> [After crossing the Hudson and leaving the ferry,] loaded down with two barracks bags filled to the brim and weapons slung over our shoulders, we marched two miles, double file, to dockside and the awaiting ship. A miserable downpour and the ever-shifting load caused some of the men to say that this hike was one of worst they ever took.
>
> An unforgettable incident occurred concerning the two barracks bags. One bag was the A bag and the other the B bag. One bag was to stay with the soldier aboard ship, the other stored in the hold. Typical army instructions were issued on what went into the bag that was stored—items not needed on the journey. No sooner had the bags been packed as per instructions than a new order came to take item so-and-so from the A bag and put it in the B bag. This went on and on. Soon we had dumped the contents of both bags in a pile, starting over.

Finally the men of the 116th marched alongside the huge liner on the quay. As his last name was yelled out, each man called back his first name and middle initial and marched up the gangplank onto the largest and once the most fashionable ships afloat. Luxury, however, was no longer evident. The *Queen Mary*'s colorful exterior had been toned down to a dull gray to reduce the ship's visibility. The spacious cabins that had once accommodated families of two to four had been stripped of all furniture and luxury appointments and were now hung with hammocks for 20 men each. The liner was crammed to the rafters with up to 15,000 men. Instead of gourmet meals, the cooks now served a revolting mess that passed for food. For many of the soldiers, this was not only their first trip overseas, but the only trip they would ever take on a "luxury" ocean liner. The trip was memorable for Bob Slaughter.

> The weather was almost perfect, and the trip could have been enjoyable if the food had been edible and conditions in the sleeping quarters had not been so crowded. We slept in shifts. Sailing in the warm waters of the Gulf Stream enticed many of us to sunbathe on topside. A school of playful porpoises followed us, and some misguided flying fish landed on deck. A whale was sighted one day off the starboard side, spewing water and rolling in the glass-smooth waters.

It was not until they were approaching Scotland that problems arose when the escorting cruiser HMS *Curacao* cut in front of the *Queen Mary.*

> There was a distinct bump that caused many of us to run to the rail just in time to

> see the bow, nose up, scraping our port side. It was shocking to see a frightened sailor giving semaphore signals from the crow's nest. I couldn't imagine who he was signaling to. There was very little we could do except throw life preservers to the stricken ship.

Although most of the men of the 29th were belowdecks and did not witness the event, they wondered about the scraping noise on the hull. The cruiser *Curacao* had come out to escort the liner but then cut in front of it. The *Queen Mary* could not avoid slicing the warship in half, and about three-quarters of her 400 sailors went down with the ship. The British captain ordered the men of the 29th Division to keep quiet about the event, which could have been detrimental to morale and the war effort.

As the *Queen Mary* slowed in British home waters, new measures for the ship's protection went into operation.

> Orders came for all Browning automatic rifle men to assemble on deck. Curtis Moore was stationed on one of the upper decks, with his loaded BAR guarding against possible attack by *Luftwaffe* or U-boat during this vulnerable time. While on guard, Moore remembers forty-four years later, the ship listed so far that it came dangerously close to capsizing. We stared in amazement at the gaping hole in the bow of the ship as we exited.

As the 116th disembarked at Greenock, Scotland, they were greeted by a British army band and Red Cross girls serving coffee and doughnuts. This warm welcome, in such contrast with their furtive departure from New York, warmed the men's hearts. It could not, however, erase the heartrending sight of the sailors of the HMS *Curacao* floating abandoned in the ocean from the minds of the soldiers who had witnessed the whole incident. Later that afternoon, the men of the 29th Division boarded a southbound British passenger train.

> We sped under blackout conditions through the afternoon and the night. High-stake poker games occupied some; others of us just sat in silence. The high-speed little train shook the passengers from side to side, and the eerie whistle shrilled its cry through the dark night.
>
> British troop-carrying "lorries" were waiting at the train station at Andover to transport the tired soldiers to their new abode at Tidworth Barracks. This old cavalry base, situated between Salisbury and Andover, became home for a few months to the men of the 29th.

As the first units of the 29th Division arrived at Tidworth, the last units of the 1st Division headed for ports of embarkation for the invasion of North Africa. The 115th, which arrived shortly after the 116th, stayed at Oxford until room was available at Tidworth. Although no one realized it at the time, the 29th Division would be the only American division left in England for many months.

On October 5, 1942, the *Queen Elizabeth* sailed from New York with the remainder of the division onboard. One of its passengers was Lt. Carl A. Hobbs of the 175th, who had been assigned to the division on September 5. He was a little older than most of the other lieutenants, since he had volunteered for military service in February at the ripe old age of twenty-seven. After three months of basic training, he had been sent to the Officer Candidate School at Fort Benning. His first and only assignment had come through after he graduated. He had reported to the 29th Division at Camp Blanding, Florida, where he was appointed a platoon leader. Despite

The *Bayfield*. PHOTO COURTESY OF ED FABIAN

a shortage of officers, there were many good sergeants in the line companies at the time. For some unknown reason, probably his age, Hobbs was replaced as a platoon leader and assigned as the battalion intelligence officer (S-2). His experience in crossing the Atlantic was very different from the enlisted men's because, as an officer, he was accorded a few privileges.

> I was assigned to a detail on battalion staff with ten men and a Major Gill for security on the *Queen Elizabeth*. We toured that big ship for two days. We had some 15,000 men, I would guess, on that ship. The men had to share bunks. We had three men assigned to a bunk. The British had food for the infantry soldiers that was inferior, although the food for their officers was superior. I was a second lieutenant and I was assigned to a table. I had a steward and a printed menu for every meal. It was quite exciting to see the whole ship. The *Queen Elizabeth* and *Queen Mary* traveled alone and changed direction about every five to seven minutes. It was fast enough and changed course often enough that a submarine couldn't track it.
>
> We traveled by ourselves, and I never saw any ship in crossing the Atlantic, but I wasn't on the outside that much.
>
> We had guards on all the water points because we rationed water. When we showered, it had to be salt water. We had huge swimming pools converted into showers, a series of showers. The salt water was pretty sticky when you got through. In addition to water points, we had to make sure all portholes were covered so that when we traveled at night, it was completely dark. We had some boat drills, but we had so many people on the ship that we could not possibly put them in lifeboats.
>
> It was a fast, smooth, exciting five-day trip across the ocean. We landed in Scotland, and from there, we boarded a train and ended up in North Tidworth at an army barracks.

A member of the division's 121st Engineer Battalion, Walter Condon, who also sailed on the

Queen Elizabeth, had a different perspective of the trip.

> The British sailors on the ship were selling us British pounds at $5 each. When we got to England, they were worth $4.07 each at the official U.S. rate. They were also selling us food. There were two meals a day on the ship. There were long, long lines. You might be an hour or two in line getting ready to eat and might get two hard-boiled eggs, a slice of bread, and a cup of tea. The meals were not too great. We made the trip in several days, zigzagging every three minutes and going fast.
>
> On the *Queen Elizabeth,* I was assigned to one of the 5-inch guns on the deck and was part of the crew, although the chance of being torpedoed was very slim at high speed.
>
> We went up the river as far as we could and arrived at Greenock in Scotland. We unloaded at night onto barges. There were Red Cross ladies there serving coffee, tea, and doughnuts as we got on the train and traveled to Tidworth Barracks.

Lt. John A. McAllister, a New Yorker, volunteered at age twenty for military service in January 1941 and was later sent to OCS at Fort Sill. He commanded an antitank platoon of eight 37-millimeter guns in the 29th Division when he sailed on the *Queen Elizabeth.* (This antitank unit was eliminated in 1943, and after several other assignments, McAllister was put in a 155-millimeter gun battery.) When he arrived in England, he was sent on temporary duty to Liverpool to help in loading for the North African invasion. His men handled mainly large items, such as oil drums. In November, the 29th Division settled in southern England, where it began to train. No other divisional formations sailed to Great Britain until the end of the summer of 1943 because of the risks involved in crossing the Atlantic.

Most to the soldiers who boarded their transport ships prior to the summer of 1943 were blissfully unaware of the dangers lurking in the ocean. That was the case for Ernest Lee and William Lewis, who had transferred from their 36th Texas National Guard Division to a demonstration unit at Fort Ritchie and volunteered for another reassignment. After waiting a long time for a ship to take them from New York to England, they finally got berths on a vessel that joined a large convoy. It was February 1943, one of the deadliest months for Allied convoys because the frightful weather compounded the danger from the wolf packs running rampant in the Atlantic. Neither of the two friends remembers exactly how long the journey lasted, though Lewis is sure it took at least nineteen days, while Lee asserts that they spent no less than twenty-nine days at sea. During the crossing, they both regretted having given up safe, cushy jobs for this nightmarish journey.

> We were in a convoy that seemed to be 100 ships. We went through Newfoundland, Greenland, and Iceland. We were in storms and ice; it was winter. You talk about snow, storms, and confusion in the night. The convoy would split and would be in ice all night. Whistles and foghorns blowing, trying to gather them all back up in the morning. We were escorted by little Canadian corvettes.
>
> One time at sea, a large group of American ships with a couple of cruisers passed by us. We were in the flagship. It was an old ship, the HMS *Esperance Bay.* It had been down at Tobruk in the Mediterranean. Its sister ship, the *Empress Bay,* had been sunk.
>
> It was cold, and we slept in hammocks that were jammed together. It had one heated mess deck. They had things like fish for breakfast. We never had eaten fish for breakfast before. They would give you some old tea with milk or cream in it and a fish.

We would say, "What is this?" and they replied, "Breakfast."

We could see ships burning. They attacked the convoys ahead of us, and you could see the fires way out there at night in the North Atlantic. They had us on the 6-inch guns. We would not have known how to pull the trigger on them! We kept the ice chipped off. We received big parkas to wear when on duty. We would be chipping ice all night long. They told us to keep a lookout. If you keep staring into the dark, you will see submarines sure as hell.

We cut loose from the convoy and started running. When we got within range of the RAF and *Luftwaffe,* we cut loose and ran for it. Zigged and zagged. Finally, we landed at Liverpool, and they took us down to Tidworth on the Salisbury Plain, where the 29th was.

Sergeant Lewis was assigned to an antitank platoon of the 116th Infantry, and his friend, Sergeant Lee, was placed in an Intelligence and Recon (I&R) Platoon of the 175th Infantry.

The 29th Division settled in at Tidworth Barracks to prepare for the cross-Channel invasion. Except for the men of the AAF, the service units, and a few smaller formations such as engineer battalions, the 29th Division was the only major American unit in England at the time. Meanwhile, the 5th Division continued its lonely vigil in Iceland. It would be almost another year before the next American combat division arrived in England. As winter set in and the daylight hours dwindled to fewer than eight, the "Twenty Niners," as they were called, discovered the meaning of long nights. The following summer, when the situation reversed, they learned the meaning of long days. The cool, wet English climate exacerbated the feeling of homesickness, especially for the men from the South. English customs and food exacerbated the alienation the men felt. Tea break seemed a bit strange to most men of the "Blue and Gray" Division, and the warm beer failed to satisfy their taste buds. Adjusting to the blackout conditions was also a challenge for many of the servicemen, especially on moonless nights.

The sleeping quarters were too spartan for Bob Slaughter and his comrades. The double-decker bunks with straw filled-mattresses did little to ensure a good night's sleep. The two GI blankets each man had been issued were insufficient to ward off the chill that pervaded the unheated barracks. The men in Slaughter's barracks slept in their uniforms and thus were already dressed when they woke up at 5:30 A.M.

Several British divisions still remained in Great Britain, along with the badly bruised 2nd Canadian Division, recovering from its painful experiences at Dieppe, and numerous formations of foreign armies in exile, but Americans now formed the majority of the foreign forces. The Twenty Niners, under the command of the demanding General Gerow, trained intensively during the remainder of 1942 and went weeks without a pass. Gerow turned the twenty-five-mile march into a routine exercise to keep them physically fit.

On December 20, a special volunteer unit, the 29th Provisional Ranger Battalion with a small cadre from Darby's 1st Rangers, formed and underwent Ranger training before it was attached to the British No. 4 Commando. A few of the men took part in three small raids on the Norwegian coast before they returned to the division early in 1943. In July, the 29th Ranger Battalion participated with British commandos in a raid against a small German radar station on Île d'Ouessant, off the west coast of Brittany. The raid was successful, except that the attackers were unable to take any prisoners. They left behind a helmet and cartridge belt to identify themselves to the Germans. After the unit was disbanded in October 1943, the men returned to their original regiments.

The Engineers in Great Britain: Preparing the Way

The 107th Combat Engineer Battalion was one of the first American combat units to arrive in the United Kingdom after December 7, 1941. It departed New York on the *George F. Elliot* on February 18, 1942, escorted by the battleship *New York* and cruiser *Philadelphia*. While the 107th was crossing the Atlantic, its parent division, the 32nd, was dispatched to the Pacific. After the 107th disembarked at Belfast on March 3, 1942, it was reassigned to the V Corps. This Michigan National Guard unit combined with the 112th Engineer Combat Battalion from the Ohio National Guard to create the 112th Engineer Combat Regiment, the 107th forming the 2nd Battalion, and the 112th the 1st Battalion. The regiment transferred from Ulster to Devized, England, where the unit gained expertise in the use of Bailey bridges. The regiment's Company F sailed for North Africa in December 1942 and hence to Italy. In August 1943, the regiment's 2nd Battalion became the 254th Engineer Combat Battalion, which consisted of a headquarters company and three engineer companies with a total of 664 men. The 1st Battalion, with the regimental headquarters, became the 1121st Engineer (Construction) Group Headquarters and prepared for the Normandy invasion in the months that followed.

The 254th took part in the construction of assault-training centers at Barnstable and Slapton Sands. It built bunkers, laid wire entanglements, and set up the special demolition courses at these sites built to train the designated assault divisions. After completion of the training center, the 254th continued to maintain it. One of the battalion's companies had the difficult task of removing 6,000 British mines from the beaches of Thurlestone, a few miles northwest of Salcombe, suffering several casualties in the process. The British had emplaced these mines in 1940, when the threat of a German invasion existed after the fall of France.

Meanwhile, at Camp White in Oregon, the 299th Combat Engineer Battalion, under the command of Lt. Col. Milton A. Jewitt, came into existence on March 3, 1943. The men underwent basic training at Camp White before boarding a train at Fort Lewis, Washington, in December for a six-day trip to Fort Pierce, Florida. Over the next three months, they practiced underwater demolitions at the U.S. Naval Amphibian Training Base. Then they went on to Camp Pickett, Virginia, for advanced infantry training. In April, the unit set sail from New York on the SS *Exchequer*, escorted by a battleship and some destroyers, arriving in England in mid-April 1944. There it continued training in underwater demolitions in preparation for the invasion. During the few weeks the 299th was stationed in England, the men had a few practice sessions disembarking from large ships onto LCMs. The 299th was the only engineer unit to land companies with the first waves on both Utah and Omaha Beaches.

The 29th Division borrowed 75-millimeter guns from the British for firing practice until its own division artillery arrived. Early in 1943, the men were introduced to the bazooka. The weapon had become available to combat units in the fall of 1942 and proved to be the first successful shoulder-mounted antitank weapon of World War II. The American soldiers who first saw this rocket launcher called it a bazooka because it reminded them of the instrument played by musician Bob Burns.

During the month of May 1943, the 175th Infantry Regiment, 29th Division, took part in *Exercise Columbus,* in which a British armored division played the aggressor, and the 29th the German defender. The 29th Rangers launched a raid, capturing the British headquarters. In the spring, the division moved into the southwest corner of England, Cornwall, and Devon to relieve the British 55th Division from coastal defense duty. Training took place in the wet and barren terrain of Dartmoor and Bodmin Moors. The troopers concluded that southern wetlands of Virginia had been more welcoming, because they had provided more cover and had not been as bitterly cold.

In July 1943, Maj. Gen. Charles H. Gerhardt replaced General Gerow, who took command of the V Corps. The troopers had hoped that the change in command would lighten their grueling training routine but were soon disabused of that notion. Gerhardt first grilled the division officers, making sure they knew what he wanted, even if that meant humiliating them. His officers were to master all the skills required of the common soldiers and set an example for their subordinates. To that end, he rode them as hard as everybody else in the division. General Gerhardt's trademark demand was to have every man buckle his helmet chinstrap, and woe betide the soldier who failed to do so. From the moment he took over the reins, the 29th became the sharpest and neatest-looking American unit in England, because he tolerated nothing less. Even the equipment and vehicles had to be kept spick-and-span. Despite his unbending perfectionism, General Gerhardt managed to raise the morale of his men to a new high.

That same month, the 29th Division was ordered to prepare for amphibious training. It received landing craft from the British and used a small section of coast to practice. The Twenty Niners were the first to train at the new Assault Training Center established by the U.S. Army Engineers at Woolacombe Beach on the northwestern coast of Devon.

Individual Accounts of Training

According to Lt. John McAllister, General Gerow transferred a large number of men out of the 29th Division because they failed to complete the long twenty-five-mile marches loaded with full field equipment. The Twenty Niners did so much marching that the locals took to calling them "foot cavalry." In 1943, after his antitank platoon was eliminated, McAllister was assigned various other functions in the battalion.

Bob Slaughter of the 116th Infantry, 29th Division, had to make many adjustments to adapt to life in wartime England. The sweets were not really sweet, and the soft drinks were semisweet and warm. Coca-Cola was sold in clear bottles instead of the customary green and was considerably watered down. The short winter days added to Slaughter's feelings of gloom. He shivered in the biting wind and constant drizzle, and his teeth never seemed to stop chattering. There were few breaks during his training, and the highlight of his day was mail call, when boxes of homemade goodies were delivered to the men and shared all around. As part of the exchange program with the British, which enlightened many of the American troops to the hardships their counterparts had been going through, Slaughter spent a week aboard a Royal minesweeper in the Channel.

First Lady Eleanor Roosevelt's visit was a major event for the 29th Division. During the weeks preceding her arrival, the men toiled so hard to spruce up their camp that by the time she arrived, they were ready to drop from sheer exhaustion. On that fateful day, the soldiers trooped into the church, where she delivered a speech. One of the privates stood up and said,

"Mrs. Roosevelt, ma'am, wouldn't it be better for the taxpayer and for *our* morale to send one of us home rather than sending you over here?" The rest of the assembly gasped in shock at his cheek, even though many of the troops tacitly sympathized with his sentiments.

In December 1942, Bob Slaughter joined the 29th Provisional Ranger Battalion in response to a call for volunteers.

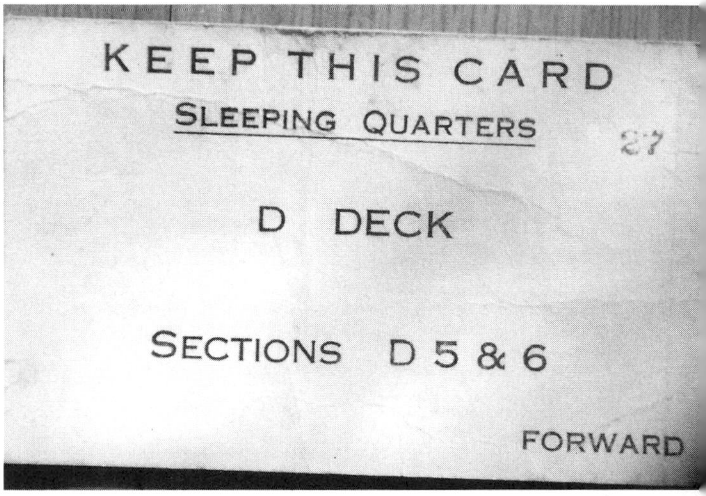

Berth ticket for transport. COURTESY OF CHARLES SCHEFFEL

> I didn't want to spend the war guarding the shores of Great Britain, so I volunteered. Approximately 500 zealots and I were selected after passing rigid physical and mental examinations. The candidates were sent north to the Commando Depot at Achnacarry House, Spean Bridge, Scotland, which was situated near the shores of beautiful Loch Lochy.
>
> This area was the Highlands—desolate, craggy hillsides, blue lochs between the low mountains, green heather growing on the waterlogged moors. Herds of wild deer roamed in relative peace on this wilderness expanse. It rained often, and the wind was constant. One would have to agree that the scenery was beautiful to the eye but unpleasant to the skin.
>
> Basic commando training was given under the tutelage of battle-hardened instructors from Lord Lovatt's No. 4 Commando. These officers and noncommissioned officers were from the old school, ruthlessly harsh and strict disciplinarians. Within a short time, half the candidates threw in the towel and returned to their outfits. Those that finished the course were dubbed 29th Provisional Rangers.
>
> Grueling speed marches, reportedly the toughest obstacle course in the world, mountain and cliff climbing, unarmed combat, boat drills, log PT [physical training] and finding one's way on the desolate Scottish moors with nothing but a compass and a map caused some of us to wonder if we had made a mistake.
>
> The obstacle course's path was five miles long and over hilly terrain. It had the usual obstacles: walls to climb, log and rope bridges traversing steep ravines, rope swings over water hazards. Umpires were stationed along the route. Their job was to determine if contestants performed correctly. Lifesize targets appeared, and the candidate had to decide quickly whether to shoot or bayonet it. A wrong decision or a missed target might declare him a casualty, and then he must be carried by his squad members over the rest of the course. When the last man of the squad finished the course, the time was taken, and if it wasn't within the prescribed time, the squad had to run the "Black Mile," which was running the course on Sunday.
>
> Our instructor, Captain Hoar, a veteran of the Dieppe Raid, carried a swagger stick, a foot-long leather-wrapped stick. I had never seen one, and I wondered what it was used for. On one of the first speed marches, one of the men dropped out along the road. That stick went into action around the shoulders of this "yellow-bellied coward that wasn't fit to breathe fresh air!" He also

> was observed rib-kicking a slackard who couldn't take one of the rigorous exercises and was soon sent packing back to his original outfit in disgrace.
>
> The time for short hikes was seven-miles an hour, longer ones five miles an hour. We traveled light—rifle or carbine, cartridge belt, and light pack.
>
> Near the conclusion of these debilitating hikes, just before rounding the curve and up the last hill to camp, Captain Hoar would yell, "Straighten up, mates! Get in step!" Camp was still a mile away, and the wail of bagpipes could be heard in the distance. The kilted pipers, standing at the entrance of the camp, greeted us with one of the traditional Highland tunes. This did wonders for morale and pride.
>
> After completion of the rugged training, our reward was a pair of paratrooper boots and a 29th Ranger patch sewn on an Eisenhower jacket. The patch was rainbow shaped with a red background and blue lettering, "29th Ranger," bordered with blue piping.

On his first eight-day pass to London in a Red Cross facility, Slaughter ran into an American paratrooper, who ordered him to take off the paratroop boots. The six-foot, five-inch Slaughter stared down his nose at the five-foot, 8-inch upstart and dared him to take them off himself. Before the incident could deteriorate into an out-and-out brawl, however, the paratrooper's buddies dragged him away.

On one of the battalion's speed marches, Slaughter's feet blistered and bled. That evening on the moors, unable to get his tent pegs into the ground, he slept on his shelter half wrapped in a blanket. Despite the pain and misery, he survived the exercise and avoided being transferred.

Any new or modified rations were usually tested on the 29th Rangers. One company received C rations, another K rations, and two got the new ten-in-one and the chocolate D bar. The K rations proved to be the most practical in combat.

Finally the battalion went to prepare for a commando mission at Dover, where it came under the fire of heavy German coastal guns across the channel and observed German bombers on their way to London. One evening, Slaughter watched a damaged Lancaster, returning from a bombing raid and flying at low level, snag a barrage balloon and crash in an empty lot. In October 1943, before the battalion could carry out a raid, the division ordered it to be disbanded, and the men returned to their former units. Large-scale commando raids no longer took place on the Channel coast after 1942, and even small actions were beginning to decline after late 1943.

Lt. Carl Hobbs, S-2 for the 1st Battalion, 175th Infantry, felt he was more a patrol leader than a gatherer of intelligence. His section included sixteen well-trained riflemen and experts at map reading and navigating with a compass. They had been well trained in patrolling.

> I had two men who spoke French, they were French-Canadians, and one young boy, about nineteen, who was a German and spoke the language fluently, although his parents had lived in the U.S. a long time. He was born in the U.S.
>
> Our job was gathering information through patrolling more than interviewing prisoners. Some of the men had been in the National Guard unit some time, and others were draftees. We had a sergeant and two corporals, but the sergeant didn't arrive until we were overseas. About half the men were in the National Guard, and many from the Baltimore area.
>
> We would have two or three men go out with a company patrol. On occasion, we would have a patrol strictly from our unit.

We were with the frontline companies in combat, gathering as much information as we could during active combat to try to be able to give an answer to the battalion command as to what the conditions were.

The intelligence section would help determine some of the routes of travel during planning. When we were in training in England, it was the responsibility of this section to plan some of the routes to and from training. Training, for example, in the Dartmoor, you could get lost pretty easily; it was forty miles wide and forty miles long. There wasn't anything special about this group other than they were a notch or two above the average privates.

In North Tidworth, we had an officer from Scotland on the exchange program. Periodically, we had British soldiers and officers billeting with us, observing our training. We had a Canadian officer or two. I attended a British military intelligence school for three weeks at Cambridge University. I was the only American, and there were two Canadians. They also had soldiers attending our military institute in one of their English towns. I was in the British school in the fall of 1943.

We went on a week's assignment with the British navy. We boarded a British destroyer that convoyed ships up and down the English Channel. On a couple of occasions, we escorted minelaying details over to the French coast. There was quite a bit of exchange. On this ship, my intelligence unit, about twelve men then, were free to do what they wanted to. I helped plot the course and on occasion man the helm and steer the destroyer. It was all public relations, for the most part.

The whole division was scattered up and down the British coast for literally hundreds of miles. Most of the training was in small-unit training. The battalion did its own training. We lived about twelve miles from Plymouth in the Dartmoor for several months. We broke up into twenty-five man units and lived out in the Dartmoor. We did not know where we would get our next meal. You would get a radio message that you would have to go to a point on a map. You might have to go twenty miles, and you had to make sure you were right or you would not get anything to eat. We did a lot of that. You went out on Monday morning and came in on Friday afternoon. A lot of that time, you were wet all the time. We lived in pup tents and we rated one another in a planned way. It was good training, hard training. We didn't begin amphibious training until about six months before the invasion. At the final stages of that training, we would get on a larger craft like an LST. We even spent the night on one and landed the next morning in the dark.

They spent a lot of money and had a lot of high-ranking officers, including British, observing the hedgerow problem. The first attempt to knock the hedgerows down, they fastened two iron attachments to a tank and a cylinder about eight inches in diameter and twenty-four inches long. A tank would hit the hedgerow and back off, and a soldier would run in with dynamite, stick it in the holes, and explode the hedge. Later, they welded V-shaped bars on the tanks. We practiced with the tanks with the round cylinders in England; the other thing was devised when we were in combat. They didn't practice extensively, because we were on somebody's farm and they had to pay for whatever damage they did. Once this technique was perfected, we didn't damage the hedgerow. We had a tank and a platoon of soldiers, and we would practice how to move with the tank, attack the hedgerow, and move forward. The tanks were attached to the regiment.

There were lots of areas in England that were open. France was an older country with hedgerows that were older, and over the years, trees and shrubs made these hedgerows difficult to go through, although you could go over them, which was dangerous.

As battalion S-2 in training, we had maps of France, not of any particular area, and we had maps with hedgerows on them. We knew of the hedgerows. Also in training, we would take two twenty-five-mile hikes a week. We also practiced with our weapons on the firing range.

I was training a group of men who had come into our battalion who were cooks, truck drivers, etc. We had them in an exercise. I got into a position where I sent out the scouts and maneuvered my company around. I thought I did a great job, but at the critique, the regimental commander said, "Who was the company commander? Who went down this draw over here?" I stood up, and he said, "Lieutenant, you killed your whole damn company! Sit down!" Of course, that was a training exercise; it was really something you would sit down at night and break out into a cold sweat over.

S. Sgt. William Lewis, AT Platoon, HQ Company, 1st Battalion, 116th Infantry, enjoyed the twenty-five-mile hikes over the lovely English countryside until his unit went into the moors.

We used to have to swim across a low-water area that was supposed to represent a swamp somewhere that I never did see on the beach. That was part of the training. Before that, we did not have any landing craft, so we would go into the moor, and they would scratch out a hole in the shape of the inside of a landing craft; then we got in, and on a given signal, we would charge out and disperse. We had a National Guard major as the battalion commander, who in civilian life was an official of the telephone company. He was a political appointee, and they disposed of him before the fighting started. Anyway, we used to call that part of the moor his beach.

We trained in the Dartmoor and crossed it where no troops had ever crossed it before.

I took over the squad, although I never went to any special school like the others in it. We sat in groups and talked about antitank guns. Twice we had practice firing at the range. We fired against paper targets. The 57-millimeter AT shoots like a rifle; you just aim it because it has a flat trajectory. It fired two types of ammunition. With the armor-piercing with baker light on the outside of it, when a 57-millimeter hit the target, the baker light sheared, and the projectile, which was not much bigger than a pencil, would penetrate and bounce around inside the tank. We also had canister, like the artillery, which was like BBs for antipersonnel work. We would fire those rounds also, but not many during practice. There were ten men on the antitank gun. We had a gunner sight the gun, usually me, plus a sight setter, a range finder, and ammo bearers. We always had to dig the gun in, because if you fired that son of a gun, it would run a mile backwards. You would have to get it dug also to keep from being exposed. Three or four men could load and fire the gun. The range finder wasn't always just right on the money. We pulled it with half-tracks in France, but in training, we used a ¾-ton weapons carrier. When we got over there, we had a half-track with a mounted .50-caliber gun. In

England, a couple of times we practiced with a DUKW, but we didn't have anything like the load we had on the beach.

As part of the exchange program, we had a Scotsman come over wearing those kilts and everything. He stayed with the division for two weeks. The day he came, I went and joined their glider unit for two weeks. Every day, we would go out and take off in these gliders pulled by Lancaster bombers. God, it took forever to get you airborne! They would get you up there and release them. All you would hear was the wind whistling through all the cracks. You had some twenty-year-old boy driving it, and every landing was damn near a crash landing, but that is the way we got back every time. I did that for two weeks; we didn't fly every day, but close to it. I learned that they took off at 10 A.M. and 4 P.M. for tea, and they did a lot of things that were different. I do not remember ever eating a good, solid meal. They ate potatoes and goat or sheep.

During the first few days we had off, the hostility of the people when we came into Devonshire was like at Ivybridge. They really didn't cater to us too much, but before we left, the economy boomed and everything got much better. They truly came to the streets and cried when we left, so they did like us. At Tidworth, there was nothing to drink. They did have one bottle of scotch at night in the pub, a bottle of gin, maybe some wine, and that old bitter beer that would give you heartburn. When we got to Ivybridge, they hadn't any soldiers before, and the bars were full. So we went down there and whipped all the Englishmen, then whipped each other, and the people thought we were all maniacs. At that time, I was delivering the mail. I would go to Plymouth every day—ten miles—get the mail, bring it back to the local post office, and check it in. I will never forget that first morning I went to get the mail after we had a night on the town. The people pulled back the drapes, and you could see just half their faces looking, saying, "Goddamn! There is one of them!"

General Gerhardt's high standards left an indelible mark on Bill Lewis's friend, 1st Sgt. Ernest Lee, I&R Platoon, HQ Company, 175th Infantry.

General Gerhardt was very sticky about the equipment of the division. Of course, it rained quite a bit in southern England, where we were stationed most of the time, near Land's End, which encompassed the Devonshire area and the Bodmin Moors. We would be out training all week long, and every time we came back to our billets, we had to make sure the jeeps were clean, the weapons were clean, and our equipment was clean. The general would not tolerate any equipment not being kept up to first-class condition, just as if it were issued to you that day.

Army Air Force

Although no other division-size American formations went to Great Britain for many months, smaller units and replacements continued to flow in. Ground echelons for the Air Corps constantly crossed by the Atlantic sea route, while most multiengine aircraft flew overhead.

Lt. Robert Hahlen left Camp Shanks on May 7, 1943, with the 312th Service Group to board the *Queen Mary* in New York. At this time, the trans-Atlantic crossing was particularly hazardous, because the U-boat wolf packs were striving to establish German dominance of the sea routes. The men of the 312th were led to believe that

The transport *Wakefield* unloading troops in England.

they were heading to North Africa to join a B-17 unit, an assignment that puzzled them because they had never seen, much less worked on, this type of aircraft before. After seven days, however, the *Queen Mary* anchored at Greenock in the Firth of Clyde, Scotland. "They put us on a train there and shipped us out to a little place in the Midlands called Tigershaw," Hahlen recalls, apparently referring to Eccleshall. "By that time, I had been working a seven-day week and ended up in a field hospital there for a week with a bad cold. We were matched up with the 94th Bomb Group, a B-17 group."

The aircraft of the 94th Bomb Group flew over in April, and its ground echelon arrived two days ahead of the 312th Service Group aboard the *Queen Elizabeth*. The 312th moved from the Midlands to Bury St. Edmunds for the remainder of the war. The unit was not part of the 8th Air Force, but rather the Service Command.

In May and June, 1943, the B-17s of the 8th Air Force flew over the Atlantic. They were joined on July 7 by the ground echelon, arriving from Sioux City, South Dakota, via New York, where the troops had boarded the *Queen Elizabeth* on July 1.

The buildup for the planned invasion of France began during the summer of 1943. The 5th Division transferred its units from Iceland to Northern Ireland in August. The 101st Airborne and 3rd Armored Divisions crossed the Atlantic in September. Additional units of the 8th Air Force continued to arrive throughout the summer. Fortunately, by that time, the U-boats no longer dominated the Atlantic.

Having completed their training, the men of the 101st A/B were ready and anxious to go. They left Fort Bragg for New York in August 1943. One year earlier, on August 19, 1942, the new commander of the division, recognized as the "Father of the Airborne," had issued this prophetic message: "The 101st Airborne Division, which was activated on August 16, 1942, at Camp Claiborne, Louisiana, has no history, but it has a rendezvous with destiny." The troops of the division were anxious to live up to this prediction.

By the end of August, twenty troop trains delivered the two glider regiments, the parachute regiment, and the remaining smaller units of the 101st A/B to Camp Shanks, where the units made final preembarkation preparations: inoculations, inspection, and packing. During the first days of September, the troopers boarded the two British ships assigned to transport them. The SS *Samaria* took on the 506th Parachute Infantry Regiment, 327th Glider Infantry Regiment, 81st Airborne AAA Battalion, 321st Glider Field Artillery Battalion, and 326th Airborne Medical Company. The SS *Strathnaver,* a 22,000-ton British liner built in 1931 and converted to use as a troopship in 1940, carried the 401st Glider Infantry Regiment, 502nd Parachute Infantry Regiment, 377th Parachute Field Artillery Battalion, 907th Glider Field Artillery Battalion, 101st Airborne Signal Company, 326th Airborne Engineer Battalion, 426th Airborne Quartermaster Company, a detachment of WACs, and members of the Canadian Air Force. Although the SS *Strathnaver* had been converted to carry 4,300 men, on this trip it transported 5,800. Because of the overcrowding, conditions on both ships were uncomfortable. The troops complained about the filth and unpalatable food. Fortunately for its passengers, the *Samaria* reached England without incident, according to one of her passengers, Capt. X. B. Cox Jr., with the 81st A/B AAA Battalion.

> On September 5, 1943, we sailed from Pier 90, North River, New York, aboard the HMS *Samaria* for England. The battalion was designated as the work unit for the ship, so we manned the antiaircraft guns and did watch duty for submarines and all other fatigue duties required aboard the ship. Colonel Scoggins, our battalion commander, was commander of all troops on board.

The 388th Bombardment Group

The 388th Bombardment Group was activated on December 24, 1942, at Gowen Field, Idaho, and formed in February 1943 at Wendover Field, Utah. The group consisted of the 560th, 561st, 652nd, and 653rd Squadrons of B-17F and B-17G models.

In England, the group was stationed at Knettishall, from whence it flew its first mission on July 17, 1943. A year later, the group was assigned to the unsuccessful Aphrodite Project, which involved explosive-filled old B-17s used as guided missiles.

> The trip was uneventful, except for a near ship collision and the stress of an overcrowded ship with British rations and a two-meal-a-day schedule. We landed at Mersey Dock, Liverpool, England, on September 15 and traveled by train to Basildon Park, Berkshire, near Reading, England. Basildon was a 600-acre estate with a ninety-one-room manor house, all of which was enclosed within a stone wall. This was to be our home along with the 326th Airborne Engineer Battalion, which was about our size, with 550 men and officers in each battalion.

According to Cpl. Harold S. Martino and PFC Ray Hood, the passengers of the *Strathnaver* were not as fortunate. Drafted on March 19, 1942, at age 19, Harold Martino was "volunteered" into the 401st Glider Infantry Regiment. He prepared to leave for Europe at the end of August 1943. Martino recorded his experiences in a diary at the time:

> Well it's here at last, your brother has finally been selected as a member of a new A.E.F.

[the American Expeditionary Force, a term used during World War I]. There was a lot of confusion before we left our P.O.E. [port of embarkation] camp. Old and unserviceable clothing and equipment were taken in and new ones were issued. Then there were talks about life insurance and allotments, mail censorship, physicals, etc. all of this was called "being processed" [at Camp Shanks].

Finally, our A and B barracks bags were packed and set out in the company street, awaiting our orders to move to the train. Full field packs were made with another compact roll, which fit over the pack in a horseshoe shape. Fully equipped and ready to move out, we looked like some beast of burden.

Early in the morning of the 5th, our orders came to move out to the train. A light drizzling rain made the soldiers around you take on an almost ghostly appearance in the early morning air. There was no confusion, no fuss; a few quiet orders were barked and immediately the sound of marching feet filled the early morning air.

It was quite a long march to the train and the load was heavy. As far as I could see, helmeted heads glistening from the light drizzle gave off an eerie appearance. Lights from nearby ordnance buildings cast long, thin shadows of soldiers marching by. It was quiet save for the sound of marching feet. I've wondered since if every man was thinking of the same things I was. It was a strange feeling that cannot be described; it must be lived.

Soon, the coaches waiting on the siding with drawn shades came into view. Our A bags were lined up in order on the platform beside the train. By this time, the drizzle had stopped and so had our marching column. Cigarettes were being lit throughout the entire column giving the appearance of a thousand fireflies dancing through the ranks. Slightly muffled sounds of conversation, could be heard and now and then a laugh. Nervously, I lit a cigarette and a small group congregated and engaged in a meaningless conversation, more to act nonchalant than anything else. I must admit I had a peculiar feeling in the pit of my stomach. "Cigarettes out" was the next order given by an officer who was checking each soldier as he filed past and picked up his barracks bag. . . .

Once we were loaded on the train, the car commander, an officer, called a roll and checked to see that each man was in his assigned seat. As soon as he made sure all his men were there, the car became crowded and clouded with cigarette smoke pouring from nervous smokers. This was it! Funny what can run through your mind in such a short time! Thoughts of my training days in Louisiana and North Carolina were racing through my brain mingled in with thoughts of home and what Mother was doing at the exact moment, wondering if she knew her son was at last on his way. To banish these thoughts, I struck out with a song and everyone honed in at once as if they were thinking the same thoughts and just waiting for someone to break the ice.

When the train pulled into the 42nd Street Ferry, most of the men were asleep. Drowsily, they dragged their weary bodies and heavy bags off the train onto the platform; and after the usual waiting around, we marched off towards the ferry. We poured into the ferry and, as large as it was, we loaded it completely.

Making sure to get a good position on the boat to get a good view of the New York skyline, I stood by my barracks bag with rifle in hand staring at "sleeping New York" asleep in its war time dim out. The motors churned and we slowly moved out into the bay.

There it was, my first view of the famous New York skyline, and wondering if those thousands of people knew that a cargo of men were puffing out to board a steamer with hearts full of anxiety and fear.

Off to the left of the ferry appeared the once luxury liner *"Normandie,"* still on her side, and men still working on the stripped decks so that some day she may once again sail in all her splendor.[6] At the sight of the *"Normandie,"* quiet murmurs arose from the mass of men discussing the sight. New York natives explaining to men of farther away states the interesting sights New York has to offer. West Virginians and Kentuckians, who probably have never seen such a sight before, were thrilled and stood gazing with open mouths.

Presently, the ferry pulled into the dock and the men started to file off, carrying their heavy bags on one shoulder and trying to balance a rifle loosely slung on the other. Once off the ferry, men lined up in four columns waiting for their last names to be called to which they would answer in a loud, clear voice their first name and middle initial.

Men sitting on their bags in a dimly lighted pier with large white numerals printed on their steel helmets and a huge horseshoe-shaped pack looked more like mechanical robots than human beings. Red Cross workers had more than their hands full doing their best trying to give as many soldiers as they could, "Coffee and Donuts" before they boarded the ship. After gulping down a donut, stuffing two or three in my pockets, and downing a hot cup of coffee, I found it was none too soon for already my file began to move, filing past an officer with a stack of papers checking off the names of each individual soldier. Barracks bag on one shoulder, rifle on the other, I filed past. "Martino!" the officer struck a pink card in my hand and I staggered up the gangplank, leaving good solid ground behind for a long time. I was finally leaving U.S. soil. How long would it be before I once again planted my feet on the same soil? Or would I ever? Surely, these thoughts were shared by many more men. Once on the boat, I ran into two more assistants. One gave me a life jacket, which to this day I don't know how I managed to stack on my already overloaded body. The other looked at my pink ticket, gave me a slight shove, and said, "Two flights up and to the left!" After struggling up the two flights, I found myself staring at a mass of men and equipment sprawled out on the open deck, asleep, for it was now rather late, or, should I say, early in the morning—5:00 A.M. "Find a space, soldier, and get some sleep!" was all I heard after an officer gave me a nudge in the direction of the sprawled-out mass of humanity and equipment. After finding a space large enough for my tired body, I literally tore off my heavy pack, threw my rifle down, and in a few seconds was in a deep slumber.

About 9:00 A.M., we were aroused from a not too comfortable but restful sleep and some semblance of routine was made where a few companies were assigned deck space for sleeping quarters and a few in regular sleeping quarters below deck in hammocks. Fortunately, I was with the first group on deck thereby being able to watch from the railing as the boat [the *Strathnaver*] was being tugged out to the open sea.

6. A fire had gutted the liner early in 1942, when it was being converted into a troopship. The ship never sailed again.

The skyline was quite different in daylight and was the main interest of all leaning against the rail. Here again, the New York natives were proudly pointing out interesting and famous buildings. . . .

The Staten Island ferry passed close by, carrying holiday picnickers for it was the day before Labor Day.

As the huge ship was slowly slipping out to sea with its human cargo leaning over deck railings and out of portholes frantically waving at every passer by, I knew every soldier aboard felt as I did. . . . Then came what everybody was waiting for. There she stood as majestically as ever, the symbol of freedom and liberty. That's why we were on this boat, to fight and preserve what that symbol stands for. As the "Statue of Liberty" slowly faded off into the horizon with the New York skyline silhouetted in the background, we were ordered to take our last look and then clear all decks and fasten portholes.

Our eventful journey had now begun, destination unknown, but, as always, rumors had us all over the European continent before we had even left port.

Over the ship's loud speakers came the message that the troops were now allowed the freedom of the deck, without awaiting further orders, I was one of the first to rush on deck to see where we were. Water is all that I could see, a huge vast world of water rolling in small, calm like white capped waves. This brought about a lonely feeling with the grim realization of what is yet to come.

Suddenly, as if from nowhere, appeared a ship on the horizon, then another, and another. Cruisers and destroyers were all around us, a blimp soared overhead; the convoy was being formed! Look out Hitler and Tojo! Here comes a new batch of headaches. This was a sight I shall never forget. With such a wall of security built around us, you wonder how a sub could possibly penetrate it, but they can—and—they have.

What fascinated me most was the crew, half of which were Indian Hindu in their native attire, which consisted of bright red turbans and chain necklaces. Naturally, since these were the first foreign natives we have seen, we were more than amused at their actions and seemingly endless chatter when they were working. The presence of these natives more than ever made me realize that each day I was getting farther away from home.

Nightfall on the Atlantic is more breathtaking than beautiful. As the sun sank into the horizon, so did my heart. It had the appearance of a ball of fire that sent out arms of flame that lit up the sky when it struck the ocean. Watching the sunset from the deck of a troop transport is far from romantic, but it did send romantic thoughts of home running through my brain.

After our second meal, which incidentally was the last one of the day since we had only two meals a day, we were issued hammocks and two blankets. Our bedroom was the mess hall, we simply stretched our hammocks on bars provided for the purpose on the ceiling, and then, if you were lucky, you would crawl into it without tipping it, gently but firmly planting your body on the table below or the mess hall floor. But after a few nights' practice, you became quite expert at the art of "Hammock Dreaming," and find that it isn't bad at all. After successfully crawling into my hammock, I lay there quite awake and just let my thoughts drift off. . . . Underneath the hammocks, on the tables, small groups of soldiers were huddled around one of the wall lights, indulging in the army's most popular pastime, "Blackjack" and "Poker."

Morning found me quite rested despite the fact that I fought my hammock most of the night and also with huge appetite. By this time, the sea was beginning to get quite rough and with some difficulty in maneuvering around, I finally made my way to the washroom. After waiting for quite some time, I did a very poor job getting rid of the grime with salt water. Breakfast, or whatever the first meal may be called, was served at 10:00 A.M. It was really something to remember, as was the other meal as disappointing as the first. To stave off the pangs of hunger between the long intervals of feeding, the ship's P.X. came to the rescue. They sold practically everything that a soldier could use during the voyage.

The first day aboard was spent looking over the ship from stem to stern. . . . The ship's swimming pool was used as a storage bin and the sergeants' mess was a Chapel. The officer's mess was probably the only part of the ship that wasn't stripped of its peacetime fancy frills. It was there our regimental orchestra and a few local talents put on some darn good shows when the officers weren't messing. Their last show was a command performance before the ship's Captain, the Division Commander, and all the Brass on board.

Ray Hood's memories of the *Strathnaver,* more than forty years later, are less charitable than Martino's diary reflections.

The ship's captain and the other officers were British, deckhands French Moroccan. We were fed twice each day. Breakfast consisted of one hard-boiled egg per man, one slice of grease-drenched toast, porridge, and marmalade. These items were all dumped in layers into one steel bucket, each bucket holding enough for ten to twenty men. Today, greasy bread on marmalade on porridge on hard-boiled eggs. Tomorrow, the order in which they appeared might vary, with cockroaches included at the chef's pleasure. Another bucket contained tea. No milk, no sugar, no salt, no pepper. Ever. The last meal of the day almost always included boiled potatoes, boiled fish or mutton, boiled brussels sprouts. We were insulted, and the complaints were loud and profane. Our comments to our own cooks included remarks like "Now you're getting a dose of your own medicine!"

The overcrowding was such that we took turns sleeping on the open deck—either one night in three or every other night, I have forgotten which. At any rate, there were plenty of very heavy woolen blankets, and the fresh air on deck was a damn sight more pleasant than those airless compartments.

Belowdecks, we slept in old-fashioned navy hammocks, which, if strung too tight, had a decided tendency to slam-dunk the occupant. String 'em too loosely, and the upper body and legs formed the letter V. They were roundly cursed by one and all.

Hood also bemoans "the lack of fresh water and soap" and says that "all this with the food caused profanity to became an art form." Romance and the resultant gossip helped while away the time for the idle soldiers.

The WAC detachment caused problems. The two sexes were only allowed to mingle aboard ship during church services (held twice daily). Not at all surprisingly, church services were exceptionally well attended. Romances bloomed, with much passing of notes tied to strings and lowered down the side of the ship to waiting female hands.

One officer was caught with his trousers at half-mast by a junior officer who was acting as officer of the day. It seems that he was discovered in a lifeboat with a rather muscular member of the WAC detachment, which sailed with us. The WAC in the lifeboat was large enough to play for Green Bay, and far too formidable in appearance to excite a hell of a lot of sexual interest in the average human male—an orangutan, maybe, not me. The officer of the day reported it to the ship's captain, who was not at all interested.

As the journey dragged on, Harold Martino noticed that the atmosphere changed dramatically.

Every day at a specified time, the general alarm would be sounded, and we would run to a previously assigned "abandon ship" station, clad in our life jackets, which made us look like something out of a "Flash Gordon" comic strip. This boat drill was carried on every day.

As the days went by, the sea got rougher; huge waves would send the ship rocking and rolling until you thought that seasickness was a prelude to death. Luckily, I only got slightly seasick, which was quickly remedied by some PX rations, cakes, candy, pop, etc.

One morning, I noticed the ship's engines had stopped. After making my way to the deck, edging through groups, soldiers were already boasting of how they had overheard the major tell the captain (and presto! a new rumor was born). I noticed our ship was no longer in the convoy and we were just standing still, riding the crest of the waves. What had happened? Had we encountered something during the night? Why did we drop out of the well-protected convoy and dare to brave the subinfested waters alone? Half-confirmed rumors had it that we had developed engine trouble and were to turn back and go to a nearby port for repairs.

Two days later, we pulled into the historic harbor of St. John's Newfoundland, to have the engines repaired. Dropping anchor in the middle of the harbor, we found ourselves alongside a U.S. Merchant Marine vessel. The sailors were glad to see someone from the U.S., and we were equally happy to see an American vessel, which resulted in a very pleasant conversation between ships.

The *Strathnaver* docked at St. John's on September 11. According to Ray Hood, the ship had been forced to leave the convoy after three days at sea as a result of engine trouble. Lt. Col. William P. Machemehl, who had been in the reserves, was ordered back to active duty on July 10, 1941, at the age of thirty and was serving as the Division Finance Officer. "The turbines started taking water," he recalls, "so the convoy commander ordered the ship to leave the convoy and head for the nearest port, accompanied by a Canadian corvette."

For Harold Martino, the stopover in Newfoundland was quite a welcome respite from the tedium of the sea voyage.

Upon awakening the following morning, we found that our ship had moved in close to the dock and already a crew was working on the engines.

I went up to B deck to see more of this old city. I had seen it before in a movie travel log but now I was seeing it with my own eyes. Before me, built on rocky cliffs, were quaint old villages scattered over the entire hillside. Well-camouflaged gun positions, few of which could easily be spotted, were well spaced and very well concealed. This was a well-fortified harbor. . . .

Directly in front of the ship on the hillside, was a group of native girls who put on

Yanks at Home in the ETO
"SO THAT'S ENGLAND! . . . I DON'T LIKE IT!"
—Pvt. Tom Flannery

Cartoon from the April 30, 1944, issue of *Yank*.

quite an entertainment for the boys on the ship with their burlesque antics. This was an every day occurrence, which, of course, was very popular with us, consequently the hill was christened "Burlesque Hill". . . yes, I must confess I was among the anxious audience waving, whistling, and applauding.

Since repairs to the ship were slow, it was arranged on September 14, 1943, for some of the troops to go into Fort Pepperrell while others went on an eight-and-a-half-mile hike into the countryside. Martino was in the group that went on the hike.

Our first hike was not bad at all, as a matter-of fact it was quite enjoyable. We had to march through town to get to the open country . . . the entire population was on the sidewalks to look us over. The younger females were the receivers of whistles and catcalls, which is a good ole American custom and very popular with the Yankee Soldiers. Not much could be said about the women, no comparison at all to our own American girls. But since it had been quite some time since we had seen a woman each day they seemed to improve in looks.

Small native youngsters would follow along our marching column begging pennies. You could hear that same cry all along the line, "Copper, Yankee! Copper!"

The country we were marching through, although very hilly and rocky, was very beautiful. Although fishing was the chief industry, the vast grazing lands and farms indicated that farming and dairy products ran a close second.

Returning to the ship none too weary from our sightseeing tour with the exception of additional perspiration, which clung to our already dirty fatigues, we found that we were to be allowed to go to an American outpost camp, a half a company at a time. Of course, we were all jubilant for that meant good American chow, best of all, a bath and clean clothes.

Expecting to see the usual drab G.I. buildings that make up an Army Camp, I was surprised to see a small city of gleaming white buildings. It was almost unbelievable. . . . I was even more surprised to find the interior to be so constructed and arranged that I felt as if I were in a college dormitory rather than an Army barracks. After being assigned a bunk with a mattress I hurriedly took off my equipment and clothes and, with a towel around my mid-section and soap in hand and childish glint in my eye, I made tracks to the shower room like a child running to a Xmas Tree for this, my first bath in two weeks. . . . After a shower, a shave, and fresh, clean clothes, another surprise was in store for me, the mess hall and what we had all been dreaming of, good ole "American" steak and French fried potatoes. . . .

There wasn't a more contented soldier than I when I left the mess hall and laid my well-bathed and well-fed body on my cot and drifted off into a happy and peaceful slumber for two hours or more.

The time between my nap and supper was spent in doing my personal laundry, underwear, socks, and fatigues. Oh yes, I have become very well adept in the art of laundering.

The evening was spent in absorbing a few beers that tasted like rust water out of a three-month old rain barrel, but they called it beer so I used my imagination and shouted SCHLITZ before each drink. . . . A G.I. dance was also on the bill so who was I to miss anything, especially a dance with real live girls. Eleven O'clock found me in bed with a day well spent. . . .

The following morning, we marched back to the ship to allow another group to enjoy the luxury of what I had just experienced.

When the *Strathnaver* finally pulled away from the dock on September 26, the vessel struck a rock in the harbor and was forced to return to have its hull inspected by divers. The next day, the ship ventured out again but started taking on water.

Men were still discussing their various adventures in the Army Camp we had just visited when, suddenly, the ship's engines once more stopped. The tugboats had just broken away from our huge boat when they returned to once more tug the soldier-laden vessel back into the harbor. The ship's engines again failed under the terrific strain of the heavily loaded ship. Again, we found ourselves in the harbor in exactly the same place we had left. How long we would remain this time, no one even dared to guess. This provided additional material for our rumor manufacturers. Talk of sabotage was all over the ship for the city of Newfoundland was known to be pro-Nazi and in sympathy with the Axis in spite of the American and Canadian outpost there.

The same routine prevailed as before, daily hikes and visits to the camp for additional meals and showers that were always welcomed.

Ray Hood is less philosophical than Martino. "We remained aboard the *Strathnaver,* aside from a couple of overnight visits to Fort Pepperrell and a few hikes into the Newfoundland hills, until October 3," he grouses. He was among the group of soldiers who did not get off the ship until the arrival of the SS *John Ericsson,* an American troopship returning from Europe.[7]

The *John Ericsson* picked up the stranded troopers of the 101st Airborne Division and sailed out on October 4. A whole month had elapsed since the *Strathnaver* had left New York. Martino noted the arrival in his diary:

> When the last of the equipment was unloaded, the ship (the *Strathnaver*) slowly pulled into the middle of the harbor as we, who by this time were sprawled over our barracks bags, watched her. The docks and warehouse was now assuming the appearance of a haven for shipwrecked soldiers. Men were sprawled on bags trying to make themselves comfortable for the long wait. They knew what was in store for them. Many by this time were already asleep, others were congregated in small groups indulging in the Army's pastime, "Gambling," and, as always, the inevitable rumormongers were on the job having us on every ship from the *Normandie* to a rowboat. . . . The wait wasn't as long as we had expected for late that afternoon I was awakened by a rousing cheer and everybody pointing to the harbor's entrance. The first thing that caught my eye was the good old American flag flying from the mast and I too joined in with a throaty cheer. . . . The faithful old tugs were chugging out to meet her as she was drawing closer to the docks.
>
> Already the officers were barking out orders as men were forming in columns beside their respective barracks bags preparing to board our new ship. By this time, the liner was broadside to the dock. The ship's crew was busy throwing huge ropes outside while the land crew was making fast the ropes to the pier. The merchant marines and gun crews were waving from the rails and shouting out their home states, hoping to find someone from their hometowns. . . .
>
> Again, we went up the gangplank with our huge load as we did in New York. . . . Once aboard ship, we again began to explore this ship as we had the other and found it to be a much better ship. . . . A onetime luxury liner converted into a transport carrier. Our quarters this time were much better; we were assigned to the promenade deck in the ballroom. . . .
>
> The ship lifted anchor and silently sailed from the harbor late that night. We were all aware of the fact that this part of the trip would be the most perilous of the voyage, for we were to sail alone without convoy protection to Halifax to take on supplies and continue our journey.
>
> The food aboard that ship was so much better that all men aboard felt so much better both mentally and physically. Early the next morning, we were awakened by a series of dull thuds that vibrated the entire ship. Instructions blared over the loud speaker for every one to remain in their quarters until otherwise instructed. Everyone sat upright in his bunks, life jackets securely fastened, talking of how cold it would be in the cold icy Atlantic. Blam! Another ash can went [off], and then we were put at ease by the news that all danger had passed. Later we learned that we were dropping depth charges on a lurking sub, the results were never known.

7. Former the *Kungsholm,* the ship was taken over in 1942 by the government and converted into a troopship.

> Late the following night, we sailed into the harbor (Halifax) where supplies were to be taken on. . . . Daylight found us all leaning over the rails, trying to see all we could of the city spread out before our eyes, but only the skyline could be seen for we were far out in the harbor. Ships were forming inside and out of the harbor for the convoy that was to escort us to England. The following morning found us once again rolling over the bounding main with the protection of a huge convoy sailing for Merry Ole England.
>
> Now that our destination was known, the trend of conversation amongst the men was somewhat different. Small booklets on British traditions and customs were distributed. . . .
>
> That night, I was on guard. My post took me completely around the top deck. It was a cold, lonely, bright night and the sea was calm. On either side of the front and rear, ships of the convoy could be seen silently bobbing up and down. That night is one that won't be easily forgotten. It was a beautiful night with a large, orange moon lighting up practically every ship in the convoy. Off in the distant horizon, the faint "rat-tat-tat" of antiaircraft guns could be heard as they shot off a few rounds testing their guns.
>
> Early next morning, just as I was being relieved, the rumble of a muffled depth charge explosion brought me running to the ship's side to see where the charges came from. One of the ships was dropping practice charges.
>
> The days went by with usual routine: boat drills, lining up for chow, and an occasional shuffle board game on deck if you were lucky. There was always a boxing match on the open deck after supper until black out time when everyone had to return to his quarters. Then the rest of the evening was spent by playing cards, cleaning rifles, or singing. A few of the boys were still making rings from the foreign coins they had acquired during the voyage. . . .
>
> A few days later, as I was returning from mass, I noticed a small group gathered along the rail pointing off into the horizon. Then I saw it. Through the fog, I could barely see land, rolling hills rising up into the fog and off to the left a lighthouse blinking signals to the ship. It was then I noticed our ship was alone. We had broken off from the convoy. This was the coastline of Ireland. . . .
>
> I arrived in my company quarters just in time to hear the order given for all men to get their equipment together and be prepared to disembark. That's all I needed to hear, I was overjoyed at the idea of getting off this boat and once more placing my own two feet on good solid earth.

More than forty days after leaving New York, the last half of the 101st A/B Division finally made it to England after one of the longest Atlantic crossings of the war. The men on the *Samaria* had disembarked a whole month earlier at Liverpool and settled into their new quarters in Berkshire and Wiltshire. The troops got off the Ericsson on October 18 and proceeded to their camps, located in the same general area as the rest of the regiment, about midway between London and Bristol.

In his diary, Harold Martino also gave a detailed account of the arrival of the 401st Glider Infantry in England.

> Early the following morning, the disembarkation orders were given and we were all marched on deck and lined up in two columns. Dawn was just breaking and through the semi-dense fog lay the city of Liverpool. I could barely see the buildings,

and the warehouses on the docks, but I just stood there and stared, before me lay a world-renowned city in England and I was about to land there, for the duration. . . . Then suddenly I wasn't standing on deck, trying to see a harbor city through the fog. I was home working in a grocery store, laughing, eating a real home cooked meal with my family, dancing with my girl friend in a night club, drinking, racing over the countryside in a fine automobile. I was awakened from these dreams with a start when I heard my name shouted by an officer checking the men according to passenger list order. With a meek "Here sir!" I threw my barracks bag over my shoulder and started down the gangplank into a war torn country. The load wasn't as heavy as it was when we boarded the ship in New York for this time we left on board one of our bags, which was to be shipped to us later. As I walked quickly to keep up with the men in front of me, I was all eyes looking over the bomb-scarred buildings along the harbor front. . . . Then before me was the strangest sight I have ever seen in all my life, an English train. It looked more like a toy than the real thing. So strange was this sight that it brought roars of laughter from the men. As we moved alongside the train, we dropped our barracks bags in a baggage car and moved along to the passenger coaches. These were constructed exactly like I've seen in the movies, divided into compartments with an entrance to each compartment facing the station side. Once inside these compartments, we found they seated six very comfortably.

We were told we would be riding for five hours so we took off our equipment, placed it in the baggage racks above our heads, and all of us who could stuck our heads out the windows to see what we could of the city.

American Red Cross girls were busy preparing coffee and donuts on the station platform and naturally, they were the recipients of whistles and cheers from the soldiers. An attractive redhead was yelling, "Pittsburgh! Pittsburgh!" That was awfully close to home so I yelled and frantically waved for her to come down to my window. As she came, the train whistle let out a terrifying "Peep," a warning that the train was ready to move out. . . .

As we passed through the outer freight yards women workers in soiled overalls stood along the tracks waving at us and giving us the "V" for victory sign.

As the train was gradually gaining momentum, passing through the yards and heading for the open country, we all marveled at the speed and comfort of this toy-like train.

The fog had now lifted to a drizzling mist as we sped over the English countryside. The country was level and very little vegetation other than a few wooded areas. The thing that seemed peculiar was the fact that all the buildings, farmhouses, barns, etc. were constructed of brick or stone. I have yet to see a wooden building in England.

Hours flew by as we sped along in our trip to our base camp—where, we did not know. Darkness started to fall and in the dim twilight a formation of bombers were flying low, heading from the west out of the setting sun. They were strange planes, English bombers probably, heading out for a mission. As they came closer, we tried to identify them, but it didn't take long for us to realize that none of us knew a thing about English planes. . . .

A conductor popped his head in the compartment and said "Draw the shades please, black out you know." Shades drawn, there was nothing to do to pass time now

A life boat drill en route to Ireland, January 1942.
NATIONAL ARCHIVES

except the old Army sport of cards. . . . The company commander saved me from financial disaster in that game when he opened the compartment door to inform us to get our mess cups ready, for in a few minutes we were stopping for tea. Soon the train came to what we thought a very easy stop and we piled out into the cold foggy black night and mess cups in hand we lined up for our first taste of English Tea. Back in the compartment, we had a good laugh making fun of the tea. . . .

Our journey continued and so did the card game. Again, the train stopped and the same conductor came through and in a very calm manner said, "Turn out the lights please, there's an air raid in progress." Our first day in England in a troop train and in the midst of an air raid! You can well imagine how I felt or for that matter how we all felt. We were straining our ears for the roar of enemy bombers and the explosion of bombs. I don't know whether I was disappointed or relieved when I didn't hear either. We were held up for about an hour and then our journey resumed, lights were on and so was the game, but I assure you our minds weren't on the game so we decided to call it quits and get some sleep for our trip now was to be much longer than we had anticipated.

A few hours later, we were awakened by an order to get our equipment on and be ready to leave in 15 minutes. We were a sleepy, half-awake bunch of soldiers when we got off the train in Reading Station, trying to see where we were through the English fog, when the officer in charge barked out an order to fall in and went through the process of checking men, which by this time we had experienced so many times.

After making sure each man was accounted for, our column began moving forward off the station platform into the backed out city. Silence reigned throughout the column, save for the sound of marching feet and rustling equipment.

It was a strange and very different sight, this city, much different from our American cities. Early morning workers were either walking to work or bicycling and paying no attention to this huge marching column of men, as if it were a part of the daily routine. . . . Double-decker buses were moving noiselessly about with practically no headlights at all except for a small one about the size of a flashlight. This was all the traffic there was. . . .

The fog was now lifting a little, revealing the glistening helmets of the marching men. We had now passed through the business district of the town and were approaching the residential sector. The houses were all of brick or stone and built close together. Air raid shelters were built just off the sidewalk directly in front of the houses and conveniently marked with a red reflector and a huge numeral painted in white so that they can be easily found in the dark, I assumed.

I was now wondering just where we were going for we had now been marching for about 30 minutes through a city about as large as my hometown. Presently, the marching column turned left and passed through a huge iron gate. We were halted and I found myself staring at a group of two-story red brick buildings in an enclosure of a ten-foot iron fence. This was to be our English home, and, I must say, it was much more than I expected. Soon, the early morning air was filled with murmuring voices—all of the men talking about the setup and what they had expected.

The mass of men were divided off into their own respective companies, and each company filed off into a separate building. Wearily, I picked up my rifle and pack, followed my company into a red building, and found myself staring into a huge drab room with double-decker bunks lining each side of the wall. So this was it! Our home for how long we did not know, but for the time being it didn't matter. I was tired and I didn't need anyone to tell me where my bunk was. I picked out the nearest one, threw my equipment in a pile, spread a couple blankets over the straw mattress, and in no time at all was in a deep slumber.

The Mass Movement of Divisions, Fall 1943–Spring 1944

In October, after the 101st "Screaming Eagles" Airborne Division settled into its new quarters in England, the Americans had a three-division force for the buildup. The 3rd "Spearhead" Armored Division had arrived before the *John Ericsson* delivered the last half of the 101st A/B. The 29th "Blue and Gray" Division, which had trained in England for about a year for the planned invasion, was joined by the 2nd "Indianhead" Infantry Division, which landed in Northern Ireland at the same time as the *John Ericsson* docked in Liverpool.

The 2nd Division moved from Camp McCoy, Wisconsin, where it trained for arctic warfare, to Camp Shanks in October and departed from New York on October 8. It is probable that its convoy picked up the *John Ericsson* at Halifax.

The trans-Atlantic crossing was as memorable for Lt. Herman Byram, 9th Infantry, 2nd Division, as it had been for Martino and Hood, but for different reasons.

The ship was loaded by battalions, and there were about 1,500 people on the ship I was on, the *Susan B. Anthony*.[8] It was a troopship. The trip across was rough. I got up on deck one time and counted 100 ships. We had air protection; planes flew over. The sea got rough.

We had to have an officer in each compartment as a watch for the enlisted men. They would assign you to a compartment, and when you got three decks down on that ship, it was smelly; it was hell. It was a problem not to get seasick. Many times, I would begin to feel nauseous, and I would sneak up on top for some fresh air and then go back to my post. I never got seasick or missed a meal. If you quit eating, you would get seasick.

That ship got so rough that it would lay over, and it would feel like you were on the side, and then it would move back over to the other side slowly. That worried you too, whether it would come back or not. We almost had an accident. All of a sudden, every ship horn was blowing. The water

8. This was the former cargo liner *Santa Clara* of Grace Lines, built in 1929. Taken over by the navy in 1942, it was renamed and designated AP-72.

was so rough. One of our ships, a troopship, moved in front of us, and we almost collided.

Just a few days of rough weather, it was really rough. Then we got into Ireland, and the regiment was bivouacked out in towns around Armagh.

The trans-Atlantic trip on a converted cargo ship was no picnic either, according to PFC A. J. Hester, who had been with the 12th Field Artillery Battalion, 2nd Division, since joining up in 1940. He was on a ship he believed carried far more men than it was designed to do.

We moved at night to board the *Sea Tiger,* which was a converted Liberty ship.[9] They took the whole Service Battery and other units. The accommodations? Ha! Ha! We had pretty good food, but out of 5,000 men, I imagine 4,500 had dysentery or were seasick.[10] You had to go down into the hold to eat, and it was all steam-cooked food. The tables were covered with stainless steel, the ship was rocking and pitching, your mess kit might slide down in front of some guy, and he would vomit in it, and it would come right back to you. The only thing a lot of them ate was fruit and these little lemon sour balls. I didn't eat anything but fruit and those sour balls.

You took turns up on deck. One time we were in a storm—I would say it lasted for three days and nights—and you had to tie yourself into the bunk to stay in it. The bunks were in tiers, and we had to alternate eating and sleeping. When you came up on deck, the waves were coming over the deck of that ship so high you would see the flying fish go over the deck. During that storm, you didn't get up on deck. In times of calm, there was always some unit on deck for fresh air; they just alternated. The storm was a good thing, as it were, because by the time we left New York, a pack of German submarines must have been on our tail. The destroyers were running complete circles twenty-four hours a day around us. We were back on the left side of the convoy. The battleships and the destroyers were patrolling. Before we got to Belfast, the convoy split up, and part went to Ireland and part to England.

Although Hester thought his convoy was larger than it actually was, he did not overestimate the threat from the U-boats. In general, the soldiers on the transport ships were never informed about the size of their convoys, and unless they actually saw burning ships, they remained in blissful ignorance of the dangers lurking in the ocean. Many of them had never seen the ocean before and did not know the difference between a battleship and a cruiser. Although a substantial number of soldiers claimed to have seen the battleship *Texas* with their convoys or at Normandy, it is unlikely that they would have known the difference between the *Texas* and the *Arkansas,* much less its sister ship, the *New York.*

Lt. Luther R. Underwood had been with the 8th Infantry, 4th "Ivy" Division, since 1936. His regiment, stationed not far his home in Macon, Georgia, had gone through extensive maneuvers early in the war. Underwood, who had been

9. Hester possibly has confused the name of the ship with one he returned on or simply incorrectly remembers the name. The *Sea Tiger* was not a Liberty ship, but a converted C-3 cargo ship, and was not built until 1944. A converted Liberty ship would not hold more than about 500 troops, so it is more likely that he was on a converted cargo ship. The field artillery battalions of the division were usually paired with the regiment they supported; however, the 15th Field Artillery was not on the *Susan Anthony,* but instead, the modified C-3 ship the SS *Hawaiian Shipper* probably could have carried all the division artillery units, with a troop capacity of about 1,500 men.

10. This number must be exaggerated, since the 2nd Division was spread among five ships: *Ann Arundel, Edmund Alexander, Thomas Barry, Susan Anthony,* and *Hawaiian Shipper,* with a combined capacity for about 15,000 men.

assigned to personnel, rose to the rank of master sergeant and warrant officer. In January 1943, he reported to Finance OCS at Duke University. The courses were mainly for finance and infantry officers, but since he already had experience in military finance and infantry training, he became a "sixty-day wonder" instead of the typical "ninety-day wonder." In August, his assignment to Fort Barrancas, within sight of the white beaches and blue waters of the Florida Panhandle, came to an end.

> On August 27, 1943, I left Fort Barrancas, Florida, en route to Shenango Personnel Replacement Center, Pennsylvania. I did not leave there until October 10 or 11 and went to Camp Shanks, Orangeburg, New York. We were there a few days and boarded the ship the *Capetown Castle* on the eighteenth. We left New York on October 21, when I saw the Statue of Liberty for the first time. We were part of a convoy of about thirty ships, including the battleship *Texas* and two aircraft carriers. We had about 6,000 troops onboard, and 2,000 alternated sleeping on the deck at night. We had a nice crossing without any rough weather or enemy attacks. We docked at Liverpool on November 1 and left the next day by train for Litchfield, near Birmingham. We were placed in the 10th Personnel Replacement Depot.

The 28th "Keystone" Division, a Pennsylvania National Guard outfit, and the 2nd Division left for England at about the same time as Lieutenant Underwood.[11] Their troopships may have been in the same convoy as Underwood's.

Smaller army units of various types were shipped to the British Isles at the same time as the army divisions. They were usually battalion size and included antiaircraft and tank battalions, quartermaster units, and so on. Two of these specialized units were the 430th Anti-Aircraft Artillery Automatic Weapons (AAA AW) Battalion, which departed from Boston, and the 741st Tank Battalion, which embarked at New York. Both units sailed in the convoy that carried Lieutenant Underwood's division. The 430th had begun its journey at Camp Davis in Wilmington, North Carolina, where the Anti-Aircraft Artillery School was located, and had gone to Camp Miles Standish to await its departure.

Pvt. Edward A. Trennert from Chicago was drafted in 1943, and on March 2, after passing his physical, he was sent to the induction center at Fort Sheridan, Illinois. After three days of instruction, a uniform issue, and immunizations, he was on a train to Wilmington, North Carolina. He went through basic training and antiaircraft instruction at Camp Davis. Trennert and his fellow recruits practiced firing at aircraft-towed targets among the ruins of old Fort Fisher and on the nearby beach, where they trained with the Swedish 40-millimeter Bofors antiaircraft gun.[12] After the basics, Trennert was assigned to the 430th AAA AW Battalion (Mobile). The unit's continued training at Fort Fisher included everything from target practice to obstacle courses. There was only one furlough in July.

> We left Camp Davis, went by train along the East Coast, and ended up in a very nice camp called Fort Devens, Massachusetts. We were there for a couple of weeks. It was really nice, things you don't see down south. We were sent to Camp Miles Standish, which was the staging area for going overseas. Finally we boarded the SS *Shawnee.* It was a cruise ship, which was

11. Because of the shape of their red-colored keystone, the Germans called the 28th the "Bloody Bucket" Division after engaging it in the Huertegen and Ardennes late in 1944.
12. Fort Fisher was an earthen fort built by the Confederates during the Civil War at the mouth of the Cape Fear River to protect Wilmington.

used for island cruises in the Mediterranean or Caribbean. It was a nice ship. There were at least four of us in a small cabin. We boarded one afternoon, and when we woke up the next morning, we were out at sea off of Nova Scotia or somewhere out there. You could see a lot of other ships, and we were forming in a large convoy to cross the North Atlantic. It didn't take long to form up, and it took us eleven days to cross.

I remember a few incidents on that trip. The battleship *Texas* was the leader of the convoy, and the escorts protected us. We were on one of the add-ons on the last column. That was not an enviable position because of the wolf packs. Another thing I thought quite precarious was that there was a Liberty ship carrying ammunition, which would have been big trouble if hit. In the evening, you couldn't light a cigarette. Looking over the side of the ship, I could see all the phosphorescence in the water. It was pitch-black, and my buddy from Detroit always helped to harmonize and sing old songs to pass the time.

The convoy would always proceed on a zigzag course, and every twenty minutes, we would change course. The weather was not too bad, and I don't recall any big problems of any kind. We did receive a little booklet about customs and the people of England a few days out, so we knew our destination. We entered the Irish Sea, and there were a lot of mines laid by the Germans floating in the water. It was the duty of our sailors to shoot those mines, and they exploded when hit. They created a lane for the ships, and we went through single file. We landed in Cardiff, Wales. We disembarked and we couldn't see anything. We went on a train and proceeded to the Liverpool area and a town called Huitton.

The 430th AAA AW Battalion Mobile

The 430th was an antiaircraft artillery automatic weapons unit that consisted of a headquarters battery and four antiaircraft gun batteries identified as A through D. Each battery consisted of a headquarters section and two platoons totaling eight 40-millimeter guns towed by 2½-ton trucks, which also carried the sixteen-man crew. Each platoon had four 40-millimeter guns and two half-tracks mounting quad .50-caliber machine guns. Each 40-millimeter gun crew had a .50-caliber water-cooled machine gun mounted on a tripod in a manner that allowed it to protect the rear of the gun crew when it was deployed.

Edward Trennert was a member of the 1st Platoon of Battery C. His duty as an azimuth tracker for the 40-millimeter gun placed him on a seat on the right-hand side of the gun-turning handle. When an enemy aircraft was sighted, he was to give the lead on the plane. Opposite sat the elevation man, who moved the gun up and down. Once they were on target, the gunner gave the command to fire. A loader on the platform fed shells from a case of four into the gun, and then pressed the pedal to fire them.

In the ETO, the battalion always carried armor-piercing shells, because its secondary mission was to operate as an antitank unit. When the American army was crossing the Roer and Elbe Rivers in Germany, the battalion was ordered to fire at enemy troops on the opposite banks. At one point in Germany, the men of the battalion were unable to disable three Tiger tanks and had to call on a P-47 squadron to knock them out. The battalion's main role in Germany was to protect bridges over the Rhine and Elbe Rivers.

Pvt. Fred W. Bewersdorf, who had volunteered in 1943 at age twenty-three, was also sailing with the 430th AAA AW Battalion in October 1943. Before shipping out, he had been assigned to Camp Grant, Illinois, where he did little training but participated in athletics to entertain the troops. He and his small group were assigned to the 430th in North Carolina and were detached most of the time to engage in sports. His first sergeant even picked him up at a game park and drove him to the rifle range, still in his baseball uniform, to make sure he qualified so he could ship out with the battalion.

The 741st Tank Battalion, which had recently returned from the Cape Cod area, traveled in the same convoy as the 430th. It boarded the converted luxury liner *Capetown Castle* with Lieutenant Underwood and elements of his division. One of the 741st's companies had deck gun duty, which meant that each of its men got individual bunks and the best accommodations for any enlisted men on the ship. The battalion boarded on October 19 and sailed on October 21. According to the unit history, the *Capetown Castle* was part of a convoy escorted by the *Texas* and several destroyers. Cpl. Wardell Hopper recalls:

> They had ripped out all the pleasure stuff from this onetime ocean liner. The men were sleeping in the swimming pool, the bars, and everywhere else on the ship. I do not think our tanks were on the ship, but I do not know what it carried. We took our personal weapons with us. We had M-1 rifles but no pistols. We were in good quarters because of our gun duty. I do not recall bad weather and I did not get seasick. There was nothing outstanding about the trip; it was just long.

Corporal Hopper forgot the bone-chilling nights the gun crews spent on watch. But considering the events he lived through on June 6, 1944, and after, it is not surprising that the cold weather and unpalatable food prepared by the English crew slipped from his mind. The *Capetown Castle* finally docked at Liverpool, where the 741st officially unloaded on November 2. The next month, the 741st battalion moved from one part of England to another. On D-Day, its 33-ton tanks were unloaded into the sea.

Another unit that sailed with this large convoy was the 1119th Engineer Combat Group, which later converted into the 5th Engineer Special Brigade. This unit had undergone some amphibious training not long before its departure and had practiced with the new DUKW vehicles, floating 2½-ton trucks.

Pvt. Herbert Campbell, a draftee from a small town near Cincinnati who had reported for duty in March 1943, had undergone his basic training in California. That summer, he crossed the country to take part in amphibious training at Little Creek, Virginia, where he was introduced to the DUKW. After eight months in service, he was deemed ready to ship out.

> We were shipped to an embarkation point up in New York, where we got all of our shots, had our general health checked, and got ready for overseas duty.
>
> We boarded a Liberty ship to sail overseas. While we were going up the gangplank, the Red Cross was there with coffee and doughnuts, giving all the troops a little treat. We were eleven days going over, and I was seasick for ten of the eleven days. Even the seasickness pills that the army provided did not help me. Even some of the sailors were sick, so I did not feel too bad when they got sick.
>
> We arrived in Glasgow, Scotland, November 1, 1943, and from there, went to England for more amphibious training.

CHAPTER 12

North Africa to Sicily, 1943

The conquest of Tunisia was the final phase of the North African campaign. The British spearheaded a drive that was stopped after they reached the Tunisian border in November 1942. An American paratroop battalion finally made a successful drop, taking an airfield near Tebessa.[1] During the first weeks after they stormed ashore in Morocco and Algeria, the Allies experienced tough logistical problems. Their supply line extended all the way to America and Great Britain. Once they unloaded their supplies in North African ports strung out from Casablanca to Algiers, the Allies had to rely on a rickety French rail line and a couple of east-west roads along the northern coastal areas where the Mediterranean and mountains tempered the climate. Beyond the mountains lay the Sahara, with vast expanses unsuited to modern mechanized warfare. Similar conditions prevailed in Libya and Egypt south of the inhabitable coastal strip to which were limited the "desert campaigns" of 1940 to 1942.

The inadequate transportation system and the problem of landing and maintaining the army's vehicles seriously hampered the Allies' progress. To compound the problem, the army lacked advance airfields to support the ground forces. In December, the British forces, elements of the U.S. 1st Armored Division, and some infantry moved forward, but they were beaten back several miles from Tunis in a tank battle.[2] A second advance in late December also failed.[3] The Germans managed to rush enough troops into Tunisia to force the French at Tunis and Bizerte, which were not properly equipped, to pull back.

As the Allies regrouped, winter arrived in the coastal regions, turning roads into rivers and even flooding some airfields. The small Allied force that had advanced into Tunisia had to be built up, so it took up positions along the Dorsal Mountains, where it tried to defend the few passes. By February, Hitler had dispatched 100,000 Axis troops to Tunisia, including three German and two Italian divisions, which had been there since November.[4] He opted to reinforce his shrinking foothold in Africa after the defeat of his 6th Army at Stalingrad and the desperate situation it left on the Eastern Front.

In February, the American forces suffered heavy losses at the battle of the Kasserine Pass when Rommel, convinced that their lack of combat experience made them easy prey, decided to strike. On February 4, before the battle, General Eisenhower, commander of the Allied Forces in Northwest Africa, wrote to General Marshall, chief of staff, that his divisions in Morocco and Algeria were "almost completely immobile" because he had "stripped them ruthlessly" to support the operations in Tunisia. As the battle began, the 1st and 34th Divisions moved forward to bolster the deteriorating French position. On February 15, Eisenhower reported the loss of half a tank battalion of the Combat Command A (CCA) of the 1st Armored Division. A few days later, as the battle reached its climax, he noted that the 1st Armored had been held back and its forward detachments had been expended in piecemeal actions, which led in part to the loss of 112 medium tanks, about 80 half-tracks, and 20 self-propelled guns.

Gen. Orlando Ward, the division commander, complained that Gen. Lloyd Fredendall, the II Corps commander, had ordered him to place his infantry on hills up to fifteen miles apart, leaving his tank force on the plain beyond their support, which contributed to the heavy losses.[5] The high-silhouetted American M3 tanks proved inferior to the German medium and heavy tanks.[6] Fredendall had set up his command post in an underground headquarters he had built near the big supply dump at Tebessa, many miles behind the front, making it difficult for him to control his II Corps. A counterattack by Ward's division on February 15 failed, and Eisenhower ordered a withdrawal to the

1. The 509th Parachute Battalion successful dropped and took the airfields, only to be greeted by a French commander who showed the officer in charge that the paratroopers had dropped into a zone surrounded by his regiment, and that they would have taken severe losses if he had not been waiting to join the Allies with his unit. Later, a German air-landing attempt to take the airfield was repulsed.
2. Without advance bases, the Allied aircraft were unable to establish air superiority in Tunisia for many weeks. In addition, aircraft like the P-40 were inferior to the German fighters.
3. Maintaining lines of communication and providing security in 1942 tied down many American units, limiting their offensive capabilities. For four months, the 39th Infantry and French troops had to maintain security in the rear area.
4. The British 8th Army won the battle of El Alamein on November 5, 1942, and chased Rommel's Axis forces back into Tunisia by late January 1943.
5. As commander of the I Armored Corps in 1942, Patton helped create the Desert Training Center (the California-Arizona Maneuver Area) in southern California and Arizona. Neither the 1st nor 2nd Armored Division trained there, however. The armored divisions that did were not sent to North Africa.
6. The sponson-mounted 75-millimeter gun of the M-3 tank had a limited field of fire, unlike the turret-mounted guns of the German tanks. The M-3 had a height of 10.2 feet while the German Panzer IV was 8.8 feet high and the more heavily armored Panzer VI Tiger was just under 10 feet high. The Sherman M-4 was 9 feet high.

U.S. Army Chief of Staff George C. Marshall (right) with Dwight D. Eisenhower, the commander of the North African theater of operations, confer over victory in Tunisia, 1943. NATIONAL ARCHIVES

west of Kasserine to prevent a disaster. On February 20, the Germans took the key pass, putting out of action 100 medium American tanks.

After a "violent tank battle" on February 14, Rommel had concluded that the Americans were inexperienced. "Steadily battered down by my tankmen . . . ," he observed, "the bulk of the American force [was] destroyed and the remainder fled to the west." He wanted to pursue the American forces but was unable to advance his 21st Panzer Division until the night of February 16. "The delay," he wrote, "enabled the Americans to organize some sort of a defense and they now fought back skillfully and bitterly," but "enemy resistance was overcome by evening." Rommel also received reports that "Allied depots were already burning even in Tebessa" as his forces advanced to the airfield at Thelepte. "The Americans seemed to be pulling back to Tebessa. Their command appeared to be getting jittery and they were showing the lack of decision typical of men commanding for the first time in a difficult situation. I wanted to push forward with all our strength to Tebessa . . . and strike on deep into the Allied rear."

He blamed General von Arnim, commander of the 5th Panzer Army, for preventing him from carrying out his plan. Arnim, almost as ineffective as Fredendall, saved the day for the Allied forces, although the U.S. Army took one of its worst beatings of the war. Soon the Americans retook Kasserine Pass, driving the Germans back.

By March and April, except for the 2nd "Hell on Wheels" Armored and 3rd "Rock of the Marne" Infantry Divisions, waiting for their first real battle with Axis forces, most of the American divisions in North Africa moved into Tunisia.[7] Eisenhower relieved some of his officers, including General Fredendall, who was replaced by George Patton. After a quick inspection, Patton concluded that the American soldiers were slovenly and imposed fines on them for not wearing ties or leggings and not shaving. Even Lt. Charles Scheffel later had to talk his way out of a fine for not being shaved after coming out of combat in Tunisia. Before long, Patton whipped the divisions into shape and pushed the II Corps forward. At this point, his greatest enemy was Mother Nature, as mud from spring rains and hailstorms delayed his columns. On April 15, Patton's deputy, Omar Bradley, took over in North Africa. Patton was sent back to Morocco to plan for the invasion of Sicily, during which he would command the 7th Army. By this time, the Allies had reestablished their position along the Dorsal Mountains where they had been before the German offensive in February.

7. The 3rd Division took part in further amphibious exercises at Arzew in late March, maintained the lines of communications, and guarded the Spanish Moroccan border before that. Both the 2nd Armored and 3rd Infantry Divisions did not have to wait long before being engaged in major combat operations.

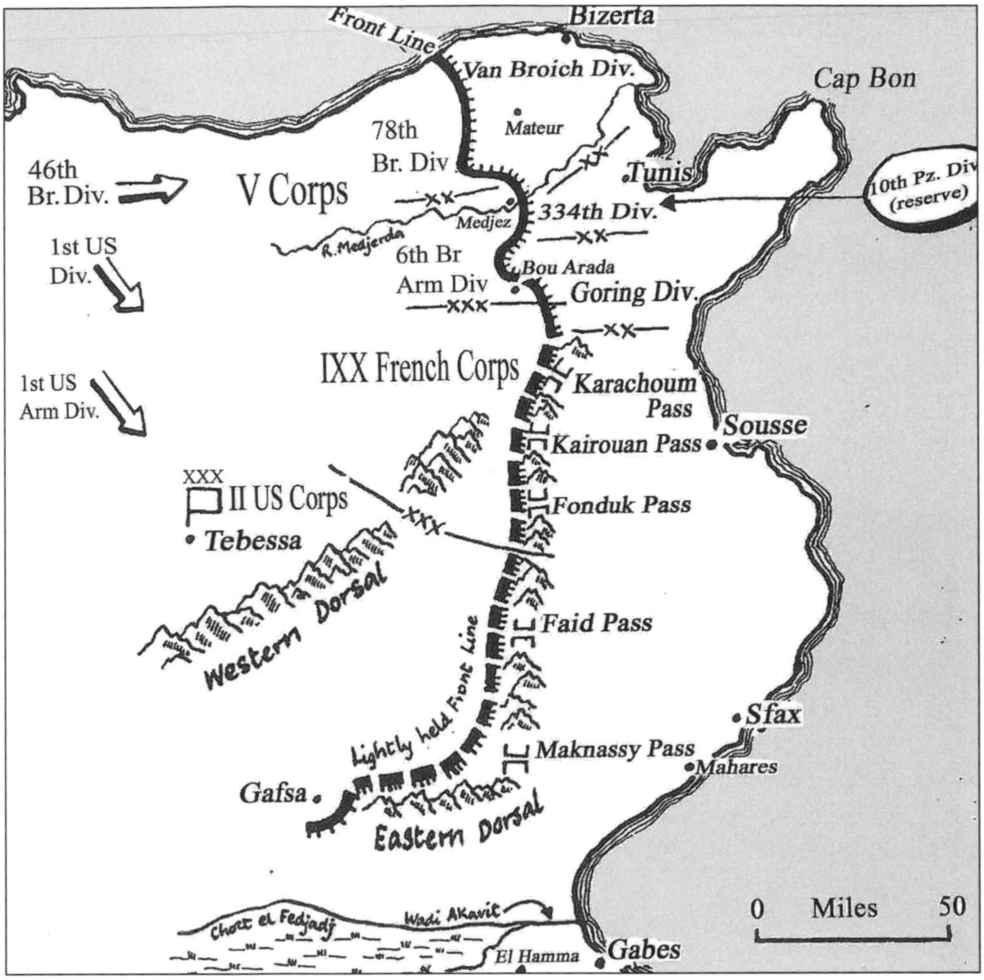

Tunisia

During the spring, the Allies, having acquired additional forward airfields and new aircraft, finally controlled the airspace over Tunisia and cut the Axis logistical lifeline to Italy across the Mediterranean. The navy had not been able to concentrate in order to cut the Axis supply lines, however. On January 4, 1943, Eisenhower told the Joint Chiefs of Staff that the air situation was "critical because of lack of suitable landing fields" and light antiaircraft weapons to protect landing field in Tunisia. That situation changed during the month of March. But the American tanks were still no match for the new German Tigers or even the Panzer IVs. Luckily, in March 1943, the Royal Navy, reinforced by the American Fleet, was more effective against the Germans and Italians than were the Allied armored units.

The final offensive, which began late in April, involved Bradley's II Corps, which formed the northern wing of the British 1st Army, and three French divisions, one of which, the Corps Franc d'Afrique, was attached to the II Corps. The II Corps also included the 1st Armored Division and 1st, 9th, and 34th Infantry Divisions.

In May 1943, while the 1st Armored Division broke out toward Ferryville, the 9th Division undertook a holding action to the north. Then its regiments moved forward with the 60th Infantry, launching a holding attack against Hills 168 and 207. In the meantime, the 47th Infantry advanced to the north. On May 6, the attack on Hill 168 began at 1 P.M. and lasted three hours. The resistance was more stubborn and lasted longer on Hill 207. On May 7, the advance continued, and the enemy was in full retreat.

The Tunisian campaign was tough on the American soldiers who underwent their baptism of fire. When they moved back to port areas, many of the soldiers hoped to be sent home, since casualties were heavy. The 1st Division alone suffered about 30 percent casualties, and the casualty total for the American army was estimated at about 16,000 men.

The Veterans of North Africa

Sgt. Glenn Edward Gibson, now an old-timer, had joined the army at age twenty in December 1936. In 1942, he was a senior NCO in the 70th Tank Battalion. When the 67th Infantry (Tank) Battalion was redesignated as the 70th Tank Battalion in mid-1941, Gibson was in Company A. His battalion was equipped with light tanks through 1943.

> We departed New York Harbor September 12, 1942, and moved to Halifax, Nova Scotia, where we laid over for three or four days to allow for the convoy to form before crossing the North Atlantic, which was rough as hell. We landed in Glasgow, Scotland, and laid over there for a few days to allow for another convoy to form. Part of the 70th Tank Battalion laid over in Ireland. We did not know we were to be one of the units to make the assault in North Africa.
>
> Since the 70th Tank Battalion was the first unit of its kind trained for amphibious warfare, and the only one ready for such operations in November 1942, its companies were assigned to various infantry regiments involved in the landings. Then in 1943, the battalion moved into Tunisia, where it supported the underequipped French troops.
>
> My company landed on D-Day, November 8,1942, at Algiers. We stayed in Algiers for a couple of weeks and then A Company of the 70th, of which I am an original member, was sent to Tunisia, where we fought with the Free French until the war ended in North Africa. After a victory parade in Tunis, we moved back to rejoin the remainder of the battalion. We then moved to Algiers to prepare for Sicily.

Sgt. Gino Mercuriali, with the 1st Ranger Battalion, found that after securing Arzew, the men spent much time in training, especially for nighttime operations. In December, they trained on the LSI *Queen Emma* for a raid on the island of Galita, an Italian-held island off the Tunisia coast with an important radar installation, where the Italians had also set up beach defenses, but that mission was canceled in late December 1942. In February 1943, the battalion went into Tunisia. At one point, Company D was scheduled for a raid on a tank bivouac, but it was canceled because the Germans moved out before nightfall.

> Most of our duties during this campaign consisted of scouting patrols deep into enemy territory—sometimes hazardous. One of our company's missions involved climbing a mountainside by scaling it via goat tracks. Once established on the downside crest, we were attacked by a crack German force. Sergeant Yurko and Corporal Rote were on outpost and held the Germans at bay until they had run out of ammunition. Meanwhile, the rest of the company was on higher ground, but not in a good position for firing. Still, the German fire was reaching our area, as we discovered when Gunner Wilson started complaining about bees buzzing him. They were bullets ricocheting

The 1941 Maneuvers and the Tunisian Campaign

All the divisions that took part in one or more exercises of the 1941 maneuvers in Tennessee, Louisiana, and the Carolinas, except the 3rd, also took part in the North African campaign. Many of the generals and colonels, including Mark Clark, Dwight Eisenhower, Lloyd Fredendall, George Patton, and Orlando Ward, were also involved.

Gen. Lesley McNair, who was in charge of the Army Ground Forces when the Army GHQ was dissolved, played a key role in the 1941 maneuvers. He helped develop a new handbook for umpires, because he wanted these war exercises to be more realistic. In the 1930s, since he had a keen interest in the development of antitank units, he tried to incorporate them in the war games. The rules he tried to impose were so distorted, however, that the antitank guns ended up having a higher kill rate than tanks. Umpires were told that the already obsolete 37-millimeter antitank gun could take out a light tank at 1,000 yards and a medium one at 500, when in reality these "pop" guns could not penetrate the light tanks' armor at more than 100 yards. Even the .50-caliber machine gun was allowed to take out a light tank at 1,000 yards in these games.

Since McNair wanted the antitank guns to move swiftly and serve in an offensive role, he was instrumental in the creation of tank destroyer units and a Tank Destroyer School. Unfortunately, the antitank guns and the mechanized elements were not as effective as he had hoped, and the Tunisian battlefields became littered with them. Maj. Allerton Cushman, an observer from the Tank Destroyer Center, pointed out in a report that the tank destroyers with 75-millimeter guns were used as supporting artillery, placed up to 1,000 yards behind the tanks, and used high explosives to take out enemy antitank guns. He also expressed doubt that the 57-millimeter antitank gun would be more effective than the 37-millimeter, because it was too large for the infantry to deploy. He conceded, however, that the recon companies needed a towed 57-millimeter antitank gun, because he had observed the 37-millimeter weapons engage a Panzer IV, hitting it five times at 1,000 yards without inflicting any damage.

Gen. Orlando Ward, commander of the armored brigade of the 1st Armored Division at the time, realized why his tanks had problems dealing with antitank units during the maneuvers and recommended to General Marshall the formations of teams consisting of infantry, artillery, and tanks, although plans for this were already underway before he suggested it. At the time of Rommel's February offensive, Fredendall had ordered General Ward to separate his infantry from his tanks, leaving the armor alone on the plains to be overwhelmed by the Germans.

The 1941 maneuvers revealed that the infantry commanders tended to deploy their troops improperly and failed to maintain good lines of communications. There was time to improve these problems before Operation Torch took place. The war games also showed that close air support was another problem. Requests had to be sent to the corps headquarters before permission was granted to request air support. Little was done to resolve this problem in time for the North African campaign. According to Major Cushman, communications were unreliable because of problems with the SCR-508, which was effective only at short ranges.

continued

The 1941 Maneuvers and the Tunisian Campaign *continued*

Among the few positive results of these maneuvers was the use of small Piper Cub aircraft equipped with radios for artillery spotting and liaison. The army decided that every division should have about half a dozen of these aircraft, which proved to be quite effective in the campaigns of 1943 and 1944. Pierced steel planking (PSP), which was used by aviation engineers during the Carolina maneuvers to lay out a 3,000-foot airfield on open ground, later speeded up the construction of airfields in most theaters of war. In fact, one of the first airstrips made of PSP was already being laid out at Bluie West 1 in southern Greenland at the time of the 1941 maneuvers in the United States.

> off the rocks, and Wilson was never allowed to forget it. Also about this time, the rest of the company started down the mountainside, and we could see them moving out. That left me with about one squad of men and no lieutenant or radioman. We couldn't very well leave while Yurko and Rote were under fire, but after they ran out of ammo, I called them back to our position. We then relocated and returned German fire while they advanced in an upright position—up a slope on that side of the mountain well within rifle range. We were probably about eight to ten men, and our fire, along with that of Larry Troxel and his old Springfield rifle grenade launcher, really did the job of driving them back. Then returning to our unit, we found we had been reported as missing.

As the Tunisian campaign came to an end, two new Ranger battalions, the 3rd and 4th, were formed using members from the 1st as cadre and filling all three battalions with new recruits. Mercuriali remained with Company D, and three new officers, two second lieutenants and a captain, arrived. The new commander, Capt. Ralph A. Colby, a West Pointer, called together his two lieutenants and Sergeant Mercuriali. He introduced himself and said, "Sergeant Mercuriali, you will run this company, and that includes the officers too." Mercuriali sensed this would be trouble, as the two lieutenants appeared mortified at this announcement.

According to Verl Pendleton, 7th Infantry, 3rd Division, after landing and occupying Morocco, the division remained in training and patrolled the border with Spanish Morocco. In 1943, Lucian Truscott, who took over the command of the 3rd Division, had his men make long marches to keep in form. Only the 15th Infantry went to Tunisia, but the fighting was over by the time it moved into line. Pendleton recalls some of his experiences in Tunisia.

> We mostly continued training. I was on detached service to the motor pool, because the army forgot to put master cylinders in the jeeps, and they got water in the brake lines during the landing. This also gave me access to a jeep when I wanted one.
>
> Once, my friends Deacon Thompson and Pete Alkire and I made a wrong turn in an Arab village and wound up in a dead-end alley. The Arabs surrounded us and made threatening noises. I fired a few rounds above their heads, and we got out of there. The next day, the town was posted "OFF LIMITS."
>
> When we got to Tunisia, we did policing work, gathering up guns, cars, and ammuni-

tion. We found an old car and didn't turn it in so we could use it. Deacon was smoking in the back and set it on fire.

The motor pool guys drank from two to five gallons of wine every night. I don't like wine to this day.

From age eighteen to twenty-two, PFC Joseph Foye of Iowa had sold magazines door-to-door in thirty-two states. After the attack on Pearl Harbor, he decided to join the army and enlisted on July 2, 1942. He went through thirteen weeks of basic training before he was sent to the 60th Infantry Regiment, 9th Infantry Division, in time for the Tunisian campaign.

German commander Erwin Rommel with the 15th Panzer Division in North Africa, 1941. NATIONAL ARCHIVES

I was a replacement for the 9th Division in February 1943. A truck load of us headed for MacNasy. They asked for volunteers for night patrol in the wadis. Having an army jeep and command car license, I was chosen.

After the battles were over in that area, I was sent to C Company [1st Battalion, 60th Infantry] in late March. In the Sedjenane valley, we were committed to fight to Bizerte and finish off the war in Africa. In April, I was knocked unconscious by a German 88 that landed ten feet from my foxhole. The next day, we fought for the next piece of high ground. We spent three days there being pinned down.

We could not keep lieutenants. They were always getting wounded or killed, and we did not have one then. The artillery was really coming in, and all of a sudden, a big fellow fell in my rock foxhole. Well, he had second lieutenant bars on, and we introduced ourselves. He said his name was Arnold Herfkins. I told him I knew some Herfkins in Hartington, Nebraska, that owned the grain elevator. He said that was his father's. Then he said he used to watch me pitch baseball in Hartington. To me, this was a real coincidence. To make a long story short, we fought to our last attack in Africa.

Our BAR gunner and myself got the command to cover the open ground to Hill 168. As we did, we got separated. He waited for the rest of the company. I will never forget going up that hill with our artillery going over my head and being shot at. My M-1 got so hot it jammed. Then a German hand grenade came at me but landed short. I threw two of ours, and that was when I started to get prisoners. I took two prisoners, and I made them go up the hill. When I got to the top, five more gave up. I was the first up Hill 168.[8] When I got to the ridge, I had seven prisoners, so I took them down to the captain at the command post. Then I went back up to join in with the rest of the company. When I arrived, my sergeant said, "Your friend Lieutenant Herfkins has been

8. This action was important in conjunction with the fall of another nearby hill for the advance of the division, but it was not as well known as the more critical operation involving the 34th Division, whick took Hill 609, several miles to the south.

Valenti in the North African desert, January 1943.
PHOTO COURTESY OF I. VALENTI

hit." So I went to where he was. I did not recognize him. Being a 240-pound man, and being shot, he did not look like himself, so I unbuttoned his shirt to look at his dog tags. It was him and a bullet in his chest, and of course he was dead. I did visit his parents when I got home.

Things like this change one's way of thinking throughout life, and this was just one skirmish of many. I am glad to have gotten home in one piece, except my left ear has been ringing since 1943.

Private Foye and his platoon slept that night, and soon the campaign came to an end. Foye received a Bronze Star for his action at Hill 168. Lieutenants remained in short supply as he soldiered on through the campaign in Sicily.

Herbert U. Stern, a Jewish refugee from Germany who arrived in the United States in 1936 at age sixteen, lived with relatives in Ohio, where he completed high school and entered college. He was drafted during his senior year, in mid-1941, and received his diploma while he was in basic training in Virginia. Shortly afterward, he was called back to Ohio to receive his citizenship papers. Unlike other many Jewish refugees, he was not sent to Camp Ritchie for intelligence training. Instead, he took part in the division's amphibious training exercises. During the operations in North Africa, he was assigned to the division G-2 (intelligence) as an interrogator. He took part in the landings in North Africa, where he and his comrades learned how to gather intelligence, honing their skills as they moved into Sicily and developing methods of interrogating Germans that he prefers not to describe.

Aaron David Lubin, 84th Field Artillery Battalion, 9th Division, was a late arrival in North Africa. He was drafted in 1942 at age twenty-four and was inducted at Fort Dix. He was supposed to go to Camp Monmouth for Signal Corps training, but he was reassigned to the Field Artillery Replacement Center at Fort Bragg, because, he says, it took time for the army to find a pair of shoes large enough to fit his big feet. He trained on 105-millimeter howitzers and antitank guns. His prowess with an antitank gun surprised even Lubin. The target consisted of a pipe frame covered with a sheet. With his first shot, he collapsed the entire frame, gaining the admiration of everyone around him. He turned out to be a terrible shot with a rifle, however. During his training period, this New Yorker did not get far from home, because his unit had staged at Fort Dix, arrived by train at Staten Island, and boarded a troopship that did not sail far before it broke down in the Atlantic. "During the night," he recalls, "we were awakened and brought up on deck with our life belts on, and we stayed there for most of the day. We were fed sandwiches on deck. Finally a blimp came overhead, and then a ship arrived to tow us back to port."

Lubin was happy to spend Christmas and New Year's Day at home while his division was already in Africa. He finally disembarked at Casablanca on January 25, after a trip of about eleven days. His unit was employed in the rear area, but during the battle at Kasserine in February 1943, he was in a convoy that traveled more than 700 miles in four days to reach the Thala Pass and join a mixture of British and American troops.[9]

> On the way in, we passed long trains of ambulances going in the opposite direction with British and American wounded. Some were screaming "Shake 'em up!" "Beat 'em up!" or "Stop them!" We were green as only first-time combat soldiers can be. We went into position. During the night of February 21, the Thala Pass was ahead of us, and we were in a valley shaped like a bowl. On February 22, we were dive-bombed, and I remember watching the bombs that seemed to head straight at us. Then they drifted beyond us and fell well to our rear. We saw a British plane shot down by a German.
>
> Since they had learned at Kasserine Pass that our 37s were useless, they moved the 105 howitzers of our C Battery directly to the top of the hill opposite us to fire directly at Rommel's Panzers.[10] This was the height of unorthodox tactics. Mortar shells seem to fall all around them. It was a miracle that anyone survived, but they stopped the panzers, and Rommel withdrew. For this we received a unit citation. We had done nothing but present a target and had no function. C Battery's first sergeant told me later that they had practiced direct fire even though the 105s were not well suited to this tactic.[11]

During the next few weeks, the Allied lines moved forward, and by mid-March, the 1st Armored and 1st Infantry Divisions were marching on El Guettar, and the 9th and 34th Divisions advanced in support.

> El Guettar was a major battle, and our useless pop guns [37-millimeter antitank guns] were in position alongside the main road. Our kitchens were set up in a wadi, across an open field. Around noon, we were attacked by Ju-88s with no sign of our air force. It got so that fellows wouldn't get out of their holes to get their food. I would take a group of mess kits and start across the field. One day, as I was heading back loaded with filled mess kits, the guys in my crew were pointing behind me. I looked over my shoulder and saw a plane heading toward me. I took off, trying to outrun it, and dove in a foxhole, spilling everything. Then the plane flashed over me, and it had a big star on it—ours. I changed my eating habits.
>
> Shortly thereafter, we were in our holes at lunchtime, eating C rations, when the Ju-88s came over. All of a sudden, they were attacked by American fighters and were crashing and burning all over the place. I yelled out, "The food is terrible, but the floor show is great!"
>
> One other event took place at El Guettar. A general's staff car came down the road, followed by two truckloads of what we thought must be war correspondents. A single shell struck alongside the road. Patton's car made a U-turn along with the two trucks and got out of there. I guess George wasn't ready to shed his own "blood and guts" that day.

---

9. Rommel wanted to attack westward toward Tebessa and its supply dumps, but Arnim ordered the 10th Panzer Division to move northward from Kasserine to Le Kef via Thala.

10. Each artillery battalion of the division artillery included six 37-millimeter antitank guns in the 1942 TO&E, which was part of the HQ Battery. The division traveled 777 miles across North Africa.

11. The artillery of the 9th Division (34th, 60th and 84th Field Artillery Battalions) joined a company of the British 2nd Hampshires at the pass. The British troops, supported by American artillery, repelled an attack of a battle group from the 10th Panzer Division during the morning of February 22.

> We were in the Sedjamene Valley, and they were talking of moving our 37s up to fire directly into German foxholes, but it never happened.
>
> After the fighting ended in Africa, one of the greatest thrills was seeing what seemed to be miles of prison stockades with thousands of prisoners. This was the first sign that we were on our way.

The campaign in North Africa proved to be decisive for the American armed forces during World War II. If Hitler had not sent General von Arnim's 5th Panzer Army to Tunisia with some of his best weapons, like the new heavy Tiger tanks, and allowed Rommel to launch a major attack with the remnants of the Afrika Korps, the Americans would not have suffered their first major defeat. This defeat, as well as earlier setbacks in Tunisia, revealed many weaknesses in the American army, including ineffectual commanders, outmoded tactics, obsolete weapons, and logistical problems.

By the summer of 1943, the standard TO&E for infantry and armored divisions was changed, and some commanders were replaced. It took longer, however, to replace inferior weapons, such as the 37-millimeter antitank guns with 57-millimeter antitank guns, and to receive sufficient M4 Sherman tanks to replace the M3 Grants. With the fall of Tunisia, the capture of more than 275,000 prisoners almost overwhelmed the conquerors, who realized they would need to make better preparations for POWs in future operations.[12] If these problems had not been exposed, the outcome of the operations in Sicily and Italy might have been different.

Preparations for the Invasion of Sicily

Operation Husky, the invasion of Sicily, was agreed upon when Roosevelt and Churchill held a conference at Casablanca in January 1943. The next month, the planning for this joint operation was under way, but this time the British would have their own beaches to avoid problems like those that developed in Africa. The Americans would still have to depend in part on British-manned vessels, however, The length of the invasion coast was reduced to about seventy miles. British air bases on Malta and the bases captured in Tunisia would provide air support to the Allied forces. New types of landing craft from America, including the LST, LSI, LCT, and LCVP, became the key vessels in all future landings, replacing the old Higgins boat and LCP.[13] For the North African landings, which had been operated on a shoestring, the Allies had attempted to get a large force ashore by whatever means possible. The invasion of Sicily, on the other hand, turned out to be a demonstration of the proper techniques for an assault landing. Operation Husky most resembled Operation Overlord, because it would be launched against a defended coastline. For the first time, it would use all elements, and it would involve airborne forces in close conjunction to establish a bridgehead from which the invasion force was to break out.[14]

Since the campaign in Tunisia still had many weeks to go before its conclusion, the 3rd

---

12. The Axis forces suffered 200,000 battle casualties while the Allies had 70,000, including American losses of 2,715 killed, 6,528 missing in action, and about 9,000 wounded.

13. LCTs had participated in the Dieppe raid of August 1942, but American forces did not use them in Operation Torch.

14. Neither at Salerno nor at Anzio, which followed Sicily, would a major airborne force be dropped behind enemy lines. Close air support was important in all these operations, but coordination was lacking for Husky, and ground support was not given. This operation served as a blueprint for Overlord. Eisenhower later returned to London with this experience under his belt when he took over the Allied forces preparing for Overlord. His troops had less time to prepare and train for the landings in Salerno.

Infantry and 2nd Armored Divisions began training during March 1943 for the next invasion.[15] General Truscott took over the 3rd Division in March and began new training procedures. After being battered by bad weather on their trip from the United States via Bermuda, six LSTs and one LCI flotilla arrived at Arzew, on the western side of the Gulf of Arzew, about fifteen miles northwest of Oran, late in March. Another convoy with thirty LCIs and twenty-one LSTs carrying LCTs left Bermuda on March 27 and arrived in April. The fifth and last convoy with landing craft arrived at the end of May.

The Amphibious Training Center was finally able to carry out practice landings, but the sites at Arzew did not have steep enough gradients for the LSTs and LCIs to unload on the beach, and sandbars presented further limitations. During this training, Truscott required the troops of his division to practice speed marching at the training center, demanding a rate of five miles per hour, or four miles per hour for distances over five miles.

The training included the laying and removal of foreign and Allied mines, familiarization with the various types of booby traps found in Tunisia, and practice with antitank and antiaircraft weapons in the reduction of enemy bunkers. The two weeks at Arzew concluded with a landing exercise for each regiment in the vicinity of Pont du Cheliff, on the eastern side of the Gulf of Arzew, about twenty miles directly east of Arzew, in a region of rough terrain that resembled the area of the intended landing in Sicily. Other elements of the training included combined infantry-artillery problems, during which the foot soldiers advanced within 100 yards of artillery concentrations. For realism, gunners fired live machine-gun and mortar rounds overhead. During the training, each regiment had to go through a two-week course at the Mountain Warfare Training Center, established in the Pont du Cheliff area, where the troops practiced map-reading skills, climbed hills, and set up defensive positions. They also took part in offensive operations that included scouting, patrolling, and night raids. Experiments with local pack animals were unsatisfactory, because the Arab burros had not received proper care. Only the 15th Infantry completed this part of the training; the 7th, on the other hand, was just beginning to train when the division was ordered into Tunisia. The 15th Infantry departed first to relieve the 1st Division, but by the time it reached the outskirts of Bizerte on May 12, the campaign was over.

On May 15, the 3rd Division returned to Algeria and concentrated at Jemmapes, where the assault battalions practiced assaulting beach fortifications and maneuvering.[16] According to a British observer, the area was located in a cork forest with heavy undergrowth rather suitable for jungle warfare. Despite the terrain, the troops underwent intensive training. General Truscott selected one battalion from each regiment for specialized training, which included antipillbox teams consisting of two bazooka men, two antitank grenadiers, two BAR men, and two riflemen with explosives led by two NCOs. The other infantry battalions were trained to follow these assault battalions and seize key terrain several miles inland. A single battalion was selected for training in street fighting, and all its training was conducted at night.

Meanwhile, between May 16 and June 19, the 2nd Armored Division was involved in intensive

15. Since the landings in November, these two divisions served mainly as occupation forces and patrolled the border with Spanish Morocco to prevent the Spanish forces from expanding the frontiers of their colony. A couple of companies of the 2nd Armored Division were sent into Tunisia and January with their Sherman tanks, but had to be brought back. These two divisions sent many replacements to replenish the 1st Armored Division during the campaign.

16. Eisenhower did not make the decision to use the 3rd Division for Husky until May 11 when he cabled Marshall informing him that he needed it because of its amphibious training. He also informed him that the 1st Division would be sent for amphibious training.

training and amphibious exercises, which included waterproofing vehicles at Arzew. The division, which came from Morocco, had been on the move since April 22, because the single railroad and the overcrowded roads were inadequate for a quick advance. En route, some of its units were delayed by flash flooding for two days near Meknes, Morocco. A full-scale rehearsal landing took place from June 17 to 19, but there weren't enough ships for the operation, and only 50 percent of the assault units and 75 percent of the armor were able to take part.

At Mostaganem, about five miles to the south of Arzew, the 7th Army headquarters worked out the details of the operation. Truscott's 3rd Division was reinforced and became the Joss Force under Admiral Connolly. The army-navy team worked well together, but the AAF refused to take an active part in the planning and turned down requests for information concerning air support operations for the invasion. Finally in June, less than a month before the invasion, the AAF sent a senior officer to the 7th Army headquarters to assist in drawing up a new list of targets. When the invasion fleet sailed, the Allied forces still did not have a satisfactory method of obtaining direct air support. As a result, many of the problems encountered in the 1941 maneuvers resurfaced. As a matter of fact, the task forces sailing for Sicily did not even know what type of fighter cover, if any, to expect.

The Allied staff planners also had to decide how to employ the new LSTs. No one even knew how many men the LSTs and LCTs could carry. After careful consideration, they found that the LST could accommodate 500 men instead of the official number of 250. Only limited exercises were done to see how much equipment could be loaded on these vessels. Since they had not been able to beach LCIs at a depth practical for infantry to wade ashore in North Africa, they had to consider using smaller boats to disembark the troops.

Exercise Copybook, the 3rd Division's full-scale rehearsal, took place from June 22 to 26. This time the AAF participated, along with other elements of Joss Force, including the 3rd Ranger Battalion. Most of the vehicles involved did not disembark from the landing craft, because there was not enough waterproofing material to cover the rehearsal as well as Operation Husky. Thanks to this exercise, many problems were corrected, including communication and waterproofing problems.

The 1st Infantry Division, which was also slated for Operation Husky, was pulled out of the line on May 7 and trucked back to Algeria. Its infantry battalions, which had been heavily engaged in Tunisia, had to take on many replacements. The battle-worn troops looted shops between Tunisia and Oran, causing riots to break out in Oran. A major morale problem developed among the men. It culminated when the soldiers back from the front saw the service troops in the rear areas wearing summer khakis, while they sweltered in the North African heat in heavy woolen uniforms. When order was finally restored, the troops of the 1st Infantry Division were ordered to undergo weeks of training similar to that of the other divisions earmarked to land in Sicily. The 1st Division formed Dime Force for Husky. The 9th Division was sent to the fringe of the Sahara, where it stayed out of trouble.

The 45th Infantry Division, a National Guard unit from the southwestern states, departed from Hampton Roads, Virginia, on June 3, 1943, and arrived in Africa on June 22. Its troops had undergone amphibious training in the Chesapeake before they left, but after disembarking, they moved to Arzew for additional exercises before the upcoming invasion. These were designated as Cent Force landings.

The 82nd A/B Division arrived by sea from the States at Casablanca on May 10 and then moved by train to Oujda near the Algerian border, where it began training. Early in July, the

An M3 tank crew at Souk el Arba, Tunisia, November 1942. NATIONAL ARCHIVES

division assembled at the airfields near Kairounan, Tunisia. Colonel Gavin's 505th PIR was to drop into Sicily after midnight while the moon was still up, and the division's 504th PIR was to be ready to follow on another night after the landings.

Even though several months went into its planning, Operation Husky, like Operation Torch, may be considered a rush job, because some of the divisions were selected only a month or two before the action started. The same may be said of Avalanche, the invasion of the Italian mainland, which followed shortly after the fall of Sicily. Husky was the largest amphibious operation undertaken until the invasion of Normandy. The invasion fleet consisted of more than 2,500 ships and landing craft, landing three American and three British divisions on a hostile shore. Eisenhower later observed that the pieces of equipment that were the keys to Allied success in Africa and all the succeeding campaigns were not even war machines, but the bulldozer, jeep, 2½-ton truck, and C-47.

One of the preliminarily actions before the invasion was to clear the Axis forces from the island fortresses of Pantelleria, located between Cap Bon in Tunisia and Sicily, and Lampedusa, which lay between Sousse, Tunisia, and Malta. Pantelleria had underground hangars that could support several hundred aircraft. Aerial and naval bombardment lasted from May 9 to June 10, bringing about the quick surrender of the Italian garrison to a British landing force on June 11. Lampedusa's defenders surrendered after a round-the-clock air bombardment. More than 11,000 Italians surrendered at Pantelleria, and another 4,600 at Lampedusa.

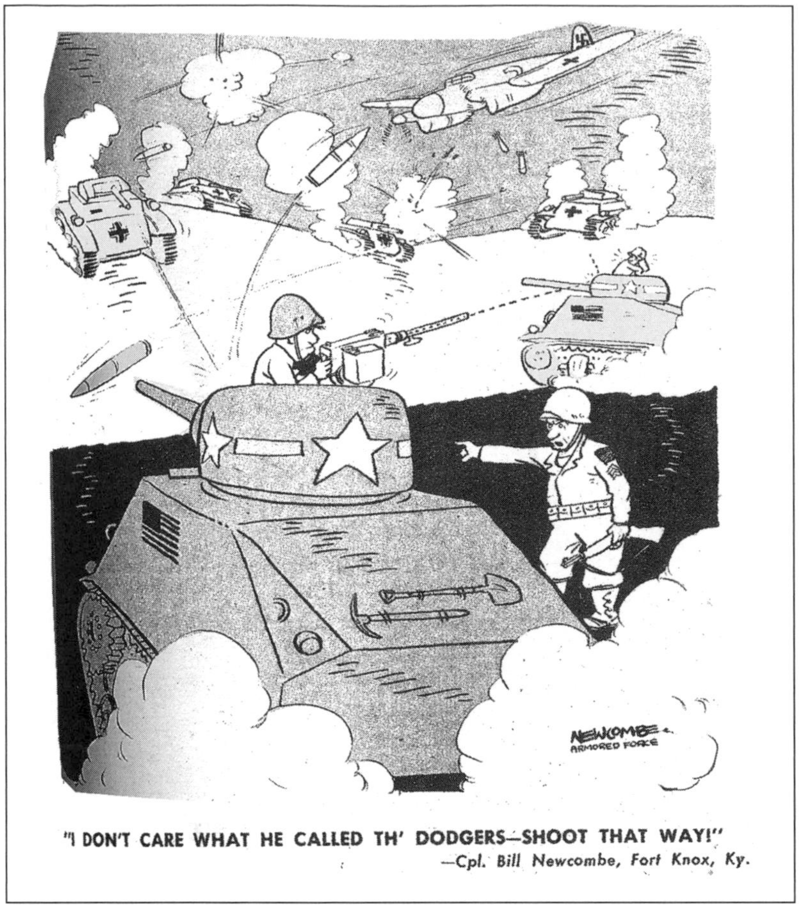

NEWCOMBE
ARMORED FORCE
"I DON'T CARE WHAT HE CALLED TH' DODGERS—SHOOT THAT WAY!"
—Cpl. Bill Newcombe, Fort Knox, Ky.

Cartoon from the June 25, 1943, issue of *Yank*.

To the enemy, it may have seemed that the last major obstruction to the Allied sea-lanes along the North African coast had been cleared, but in actuality, the fall of these two islands opened the invasion route to Sicily.

Railroad Men Go to War

Sgt. Keith Wilson of Roanoke, Indiana, was drafted in March 1942 at age thirty-two. He had worked as a brakeman on the Erie Railroad in Huntington, Indiana. After his induction at Fort Benjamin Harrison, he was sent to Camp Livingston, Los Angeles, for infantry training. Only months earlier, the military railway system was being activated at the end of 1941, and during the months that followed, records were checked for recruits with experience on the nation's railroads. On March 14, 1942, the 727th Railway Operating Battalion (ROB) was the first such unit activated. The battalion was at Camp Shelby, and men were needed to fill its companies.

The ROBs included a headquarters company and three operating companies. Company A handled maintenance and engineering work. Company B's men operated the facilities used by the trains, including manning switches and roundhouses. Company C comprised the train crews, usually about fifty of them. An army engineer battalion created a rail line at Camp Shelby for training, and the Southern Railroad sponsored this unit, just as other railroad companies did with other ROBs in other part parts of the country.

Soon Wilson was transferred into the 727th ROB. "We operated between New Orleans and Meridian, Mississippi," he recalls. "Some of our fellas came from the combat engineers at Fort Leonard Wood and other branches. We trained from May until November 1942 on the Southern Railroad, running their trains, and doubled with civilian crews."

William Fred Buffington of Kansas City, Missouri, was drafted in June 1941. He had worked on the St. Louis–San Francisco Railway. Not long after basic training, he was assigned to the newly forming 727th ROB. Before the end of the year, both he and Wilson were shipped to Fort Dix. "We boarded the *Dorothy Dix* on December 11, 1942, for North Africa. We were on the water for fourteen days and landed in North Africa the day after Christmas at an Arab town called Mers el Kebir, Algeria, and then went into Oran. We were there for three weeks and used as stevedores because they didn't know what to do with a railroad unit."

By early 1943, three ROBs and a shop battalion were operating in North Africa. The first ROB had arrived from England shortly after the landings in November 1942. The French rail system in North Africa was small and not adequate for the needs of a modern army. New equipment arrived from the United States, but the capacity remained limited. Trains carrying ammunition and other supplies chugged toward the front in Tunisia throughout the campaign. MPs joined the munitions trains to prevent looting. In Tunisia, the Germans created many problems by destroying bridges and facilities and trying to sabotage operations behind the lines. The railroad men could do little to counter this, and during the night, when the trains traveled without lights through the darkness, they never knew if a bridge or piece of track had been sabotaged until it was too late.

After the 727th ROB finally got organized and received equipment, Wilson recalls,

"Finally, we moved up. We rode with the French to Constantine and ran a narrow-gauge railroad for 122 miles from Oulid Ramon to Tebessa, Tunisia. We were there from January through possibly July. We had five-man teams—conductor, engineer, flagman, fireman, and hand brakeman—three in front and two in the rear. The conductor was in charge and rode where he wanted and was needed." But it took more than five GIs to operate these French trains. "In North Africa, we had an Arab brakeman for every seven cars and our regular train crew. We used one whistle from the engine for brakes and two to release. We needed the extra men because there were no air brakes, only hand brakes. They would cut the lining for shoes."

Lawrence R. Langley of Wartburg, Tennessee, enlisted at Fort Oglethorpe, Georgia, in March 1942 at age twenty-eight. A civilian railroad man, he was assigned to the 727th ROB. He found that not all operations in North Africa were well behind friendly lines. His commanding officer, Lt. Col. Fred Oakie, was attempting to recover equipment and supplies at Gafsa when the Germans launched their February attack.

> We were behind the lines for three days in Africa near the Kasserine Pass. We had been sent to Gafsa to get the trains when Rommel made his advance. When we brought them up to near Kasserine, we couldn't get across, so we backed the trains into a tunnel and took the side bars off [the wheels] and got in a truck with our colonel and drove across the desert and got to Tebessa. They gave us up as captured or missing, and we showed up the third day with five crews and our CO—he got a Legion of Merit for that.

The trains were concealed in a mine tunnel near Moulares just as German tanks arrived. According to Langley, the crews escaped across the desert, reaching Tebessa on February 16, but they had more than one truck.

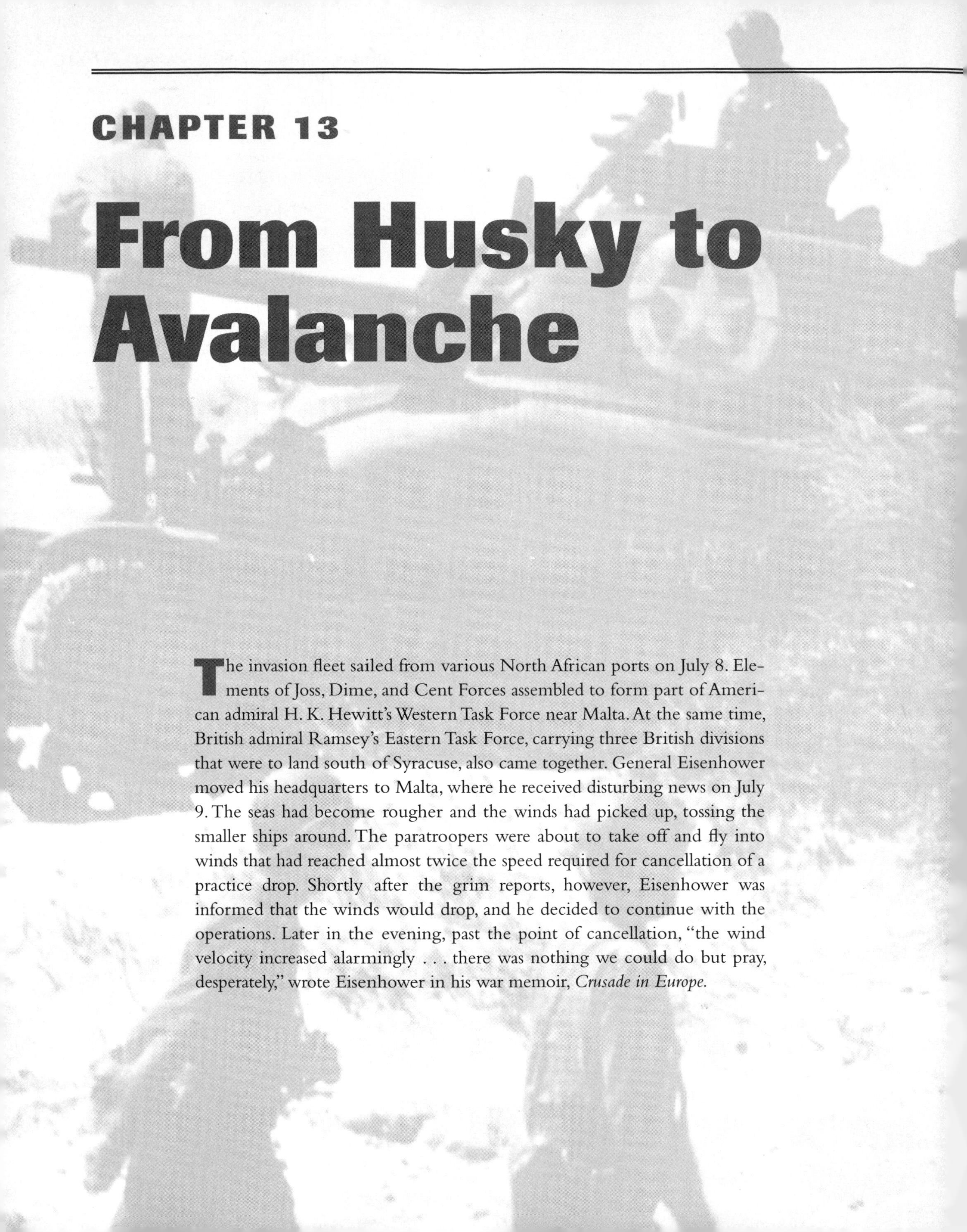

CHAPTER 13

From Husky to Avalanche

The invasion fleet sailed from various North African ports on July 8. Elements of Joss, Dime, and Cent Forces assembled to form part of American admiral H. K. Hewitt's Western Task Force near Malta. At the same time, British admiral Ramsey's Eastern Task Force, carrying three British divisions that were to land south of Syracuse, also came together. General Eisenhower moved his headquarters to Malta, where he received disturbing news on July 9. The seas had become rougher and the winds had picked up, tossing the smaller ships around. The paratroopers were about to take off and fly into winds that had reached almost twice the speed required for cancellation of a practice drop. Shortly after the grim reports, however, Eisenhower was informed that the winds would drop, and he decided to continue with the operations. Later in the evening, past the point of cancellation, "the wind velocity increased alarmingly . . . there was nothing we could do but pray, desperately," wrote Eisenhower in his war memoir, *Crusade in Europe*.

To his disgust, Col. James Gavin, who led his 505th PIR into Sicily, discovered that the preinvasion bombings had left no fires burning to mark the way for his regiment in the moonlit night. Instead, a pall of smoke hung over the region, making it impossible for the pilots to find the drop zone. As a result, Gavin's paratroopers failed to find their drop zone, and they were scattered throughout southeast Sicily, spreading confusion among the Italian commanders. This helped the Allies, because it prevented the enemy from rushing to the invasion beaches.

Late on the evening of July 11, D+2, two days after the landings, aircraft carrying the 504th PIR, flew over the invasion fleet on the heels of an enemy air attack on the Gela area and the fleet. The American antiaircraft gunners, who did not know about the airborne mission that evening and were still jumpy from the air raid, let loose on the troop carriers, destroying or badly damaging about one-third of the 144 C-47s. Twenty-three planes either crashed into the sea or made forced landings, and six went down before their loads of paratroopers could get out. Only about a quarter of the 2,000 paratroopers on the mission assembled that night, although others showed up later. The failure of the paratroop drop and the number of casualties inflicted by friendly fire led Eisenhower to conclude that airborne operations were impractical and recommend to Marshall that he break up the airborne divisions. Two months later, Eisenhower used the 82nd A/B to reinforce the Salerno bridgehead. The airborne troops proved him wrong in Normandy, however, when they became one of the keys to Allied success.

The amphibious landings in Sicily were to begin about two hours before dawn. On the right, when the 1st and 45th Infantry Divisions of the II Corps landed, the surf was up, causing the troops to scatter somewhat. The 1st and 4th Rangers went ashore first, seizing Gela, situated on a plateau about 150 feet above the sea, by 8 A.M. To the east, on the other side of the mouth of the Gela River, the 16th and 26th Regiments of the 1st Division stormed four beaches at 2:45 *a.m.* Only half of the LCIs, which they arrived in the fourth wave, were able to reach the beach. The remaining LCIs were prevented from coming ashore by sandbars, and the troops they carried transferred to rubber boats or waited for LCVPs. On the beach, the DUKWs, which were used in combat landings for the first time, ran into mines, which also caused problems for other vehicles. After dawn, as the LSTs began to disgorge the tanks, they were met by the *Luftwaffe.* The lone pier was damaged, and the LSTs needed pontoon causeways to reach the beaches, but only three were available. Prefabricated beach matting that would allow vehicles to cross the sandy beaches was delivered by sled-towing LCTs. Dime Force moved off the beaches with few problems until an air observer spotted approaching German and Italian armored units. These enemy formations were broken up by naval gunfire, however, which intervened on July 10 through 12.

Cent Force, the 45th Division, landed on the beaches of Scoglitti, on the right flank of the American invasion beaches. The 157th Infantry landed about two miles south of the town, and the 179th Infantry went in about four miles north, heavily hampered by the pounding surf. Although unloading was delayed because the beaches were not being cleared fast enough, the enemy was forced back with the help of naval gunfire. Thus Cent Force continued to move inland.

The mission of Joss Force, the reinforced 3rd Division, was to secure the left flank of the invasion front by taking the port of Licata and moving inland. The capture of Licata was vital in securing the Allies' left flank, so Patton, the army commander, sailed with Joss Force. The landing beaches were more than ten miles distant from Cent Force at Gela. To the west of Licata, a small port at the mouth of the Salso River, was Monte Sole, which stretched for about three miles along the cliffs overlooking the sea. An Italian fort and

A tank crew checks its tank after landing on Sicily, July 10, 1943. NATIONAL ARCHIVES

artillery battery on this hill commanded the beaches in the area. The 3rd Ranger Battalion was to land at Green Beach in coves on the west of Monte Sole, and was to be reinforced with a battalion of the 15th Infantry. This force's mission was first to neutralize the Italian positions on Monte Sole, and next to advance on Licata and the airfield to the northwest of it.

To the northwest of Monte Sole was a long expanse of narrow beach backed by cliffs of moderate height, which was designated Red Beach. The 7th Infantry was to launch its assault there and secure the beach exits leading onto the Licata plain, only one of which was large enough for vehicles. Beyond the beach, defended by bunkers, wire obstacles, and mines, was an open plain bounded by a semicircle of hills or mountains. After eliminating the resistance, the 7th Infantry was to move over the plain and secure the exit of the coastal road that led to the west.

There were broader beaches near the coastal road that ran between Licata and Gela east of the Salso River, but beyond the road, the terrain was hilly and mountainous. The beaches were almost ideal for this type of operation, but they were defended. The 15th Infantry was to land at Yellow Beach and advance toward Licata. To its right, the 30th Infantry would land at Blue Beach and secure the heights beyond and the coastal road running to the east.

The ships of Joss Force assembled off the coast early in the morning after the moon went down. Shortly after 1 A.M., most of the LSTs began lowering the six LCVPs they carried and the boats began to assemble. At about 2 A.M., in the distance near Gela, Italian antiaircraft guns shat-

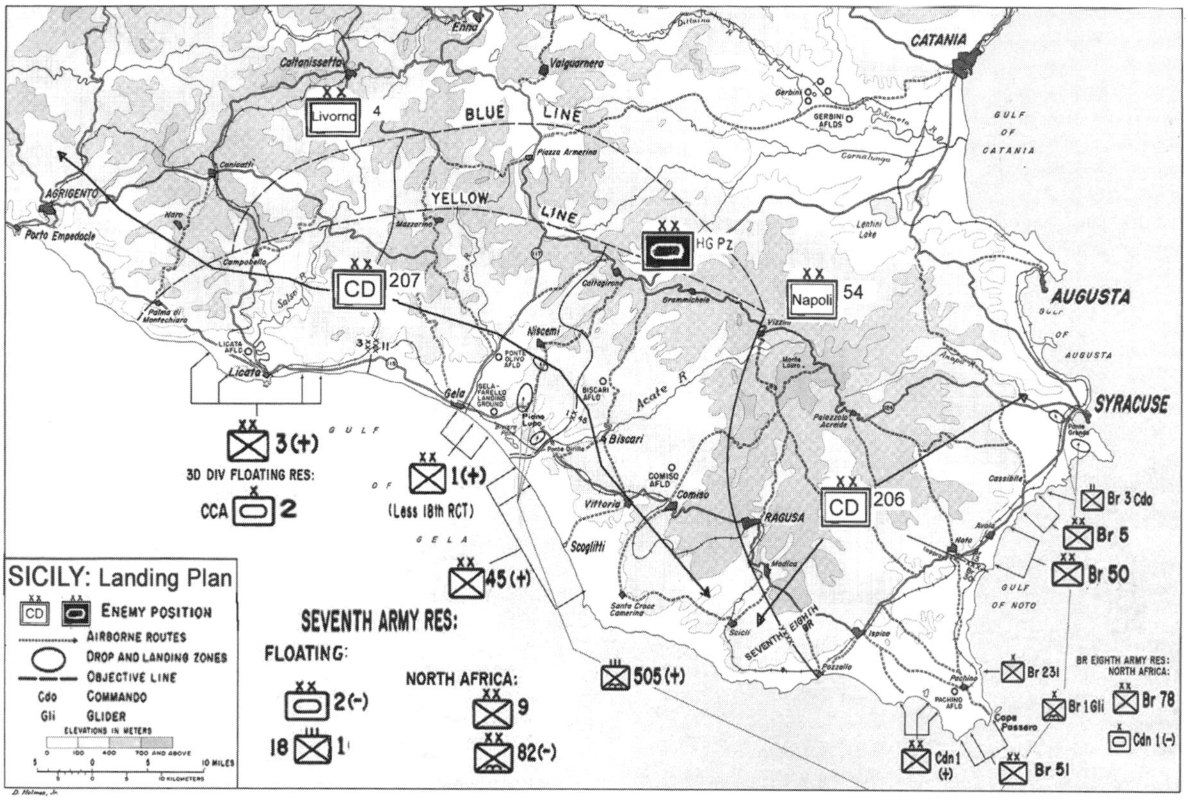

tered the silence as they fired on the C-47s dropping paratroopers. Later, parachute flares exploded over Cent Force, but silence continued to reign in the darkness enveloping the Joss Force assembly area. When Italian searchlights lit up the flagship *Biscayne* for almost twenty minutes, everyone held his breath, but nothing happened. Apparently the ship was beyond the range of the Italian weapons. The force leaders knew, however, that the defenders had been alerted. At 3:00 A.M., the LCTs, which had plowed their way through rough water since July 9, moved into position with their sodden occupants. Before the landings began, two cruisers unleashed their guns on the Agrigento area to divert the enemy's attention from the landing forces. After the first waves of Joss Force reached the shore, the naval guns ceased to fire in its support.

The battalions leading the first waves on all of the beaches came ashore in LCVPs and began landing at 4:35 A.M. Ten minutes later, they were followed by the second wave, as planned. The Rangers had landed earlier, at 3 A.M., followed by the 2nd Battalion and 15th Infantry. When Patton was informed at about 4:40 A.M. that the first battalions were ashore, however, there was no news from the Rangers at Green Beach. They had come under machine-gun fire after moving through a dense wire barrier but quickly had overrun the enemy position. An LST rigged to launch small Cub aircraft used to spot for the division artillery launched two aircraft to search for the Rangers. The pilots spotted them climbing toward Monte Sole on their way to eliminate the Italian fortified position located there.

On Red Beach, the first troops did not encounter any resistance until they reached the cliffs, at which point they came under machine-gun and light-artillery fire. Undaunted, they quickly moved up the gullies to the top of the cliffs and cleared the area under cover of a smoke barrage. Naval gunfire silenced the enemy batteries. The next two battalions and a tank company from Combat Command A, 2nd Armored Division, landed at Red Beach in LCTs. At Yellow Beach, the assault troops were met by machine-gun fire when they landed, but they quickly overcame the resistance and moved forward, clearing the beach defenses. The situation at Blue Beach was similar, but as at Red Beach, bunkers and a strongpoint east of the beach had to be silenced with the help of naval gunfire and Truscott's antipillbox squads.

The next two battalions disembarked from LCIs. On their heels came a tank company in LCTs.[1] Although the LCIs came under enemy fire, they managed to get their troops ashore. Enemy aircraft showed up early during the landings but inflicted little damage on the Allied troops. Italian artillery batteries posed some difficulties, but shore fire control teams helped direct naval gunfire several hours after the initial landings began. Before that, spotter aircraft from the cruisers and the Cub aircraft identified targets for the ships. Once the field artillery battalions reached the shore that morning, they went into action. Licata surrendered before noon, and its port facilities were put back in order so that by dark, the LSTs were able to unload their cargoes in the port rather than the beaches.

At the close of the first day, the hills surrounding the area were occupied by the 3rd Division, and the beachhead was two to three miles deep. The Allied forces took more than 2,000 prisoners, having sustained little over 100 casualties. By midday, the division had reached Phase Line Yellow, a position that put the enemy artillery beyond the range of the ports of Licata and Gela.

In the landings at Licata, the American forces had used LCVPs, LCIs, LSTs, and DUKWs for the first time in combat operations and found that they operated rather effectively. The DUKWs proved invaluable and exceeded all expectations in building up the stores on the beachhead. Naval fire support guided by spotter aircraft and shore fire-control parties proved to be extremely effective as well. Only the AAF failed to play a role in supporting the ground troops; aside from engaging the enemy air forces, the AAF craft were notable for their absence. Although the operation went better than expected, its commander was prepared for failure on two of the three main landing beaches. In that event, he intended to commit all his available forces and materiel to the successful landing.

The landing at Licata went so well that it served as a blueprint for the operation in Normandy. The only problem was that the Licata landings made it look easy.

By July 11, the key ports of Licata and Syracuse were controlled by the Allies. The Joss Force had taken Licata, and the British took Syracuse. The landings in Sicily had gone almost exactly as planned, and the Italian defenders had been easily overcome. Things were not going as well for Cent and Dime Forces, however, which faced counterattacks from Italian and German armor.

The American troops reached the Phase Lines Yellow on July 15 and Blue shortly after they secured the entire 7th Army bridgehead and drove back the German Hermann Goering Panzer Division and Italian mobile reserves. The German divisions, reinforced by the 1st Parachute and 29th Panzer Grenadier Divisions, began to retreat toward the Etna Line to defend the northeast end of Sicily. Patton was ordered to hold the Blue Line and secure the flank of the British 8th Army as it advanced toward Messina to cut off an Axis retreat to the mainland across the straits. When it dawned on him that the British did not trust the American army to be able to handle the Germans, Patton was livid. He sought permission to launch a recon mission toward the west end of the island and dispatched the 82nd A/B, 3rd Infantry, and 2nd

1. Each regiment had a company of seventeen Sherman medium tanks in support from CCA. The remainder of CCA was in the floating reserve.

Armored Divisions toward Palermo. By July 23, he had taken the city and captured a large number of Italian prisoners, and the German 15th Panzer Grenadier Division had moved east.

In the meantime, the British were bogged down and had not yet reached the German Etna Line. At this point, Patton was allowed to move the II Corps northward to take up a position on the British left flank and advance on the northern section of the Etna Line. At the end of July, the 1st Infantry Division engaged the enemy in a bloody six-day battle for the town of Troian on the Etna Line. Between August 7 and 16, the 3rd and 45th Divisions launched battalion-size amphibious operations to outflank the Germans on the north coast. By August 17, the Germans had withdrawn their forces from the island, but the American advance was delayed by obstacles. That same morning, the 7th Infantry, 3rd Division, entered Messina, hours ahead of the British.

By the end of the campaign, 29,000 Axis soldiers were killed and 140,000 captured. The Americans suffered about 9,000 casualties, including a little over 2,300 killed in action. The British had more than 12,000 casualties, including over 2,700 dead. The American 7th Army numbered 200,000 plus men on the island. The enemy evacuated more than 100,000 soldiers and 10,000 vehicles, including all the German divisions. Unexpectedly, Mussolini was removed from power and arrested during the campaign. Secret negotiations were soon underway for the surrender of Italy.

Operation Avalanche

The invasion of the Italian mainland began barely three weeks later with another major amphibious invasion, Operation Avalanche, which was launched in the Gulf of Salerno on September 9. Planning for this operation had begun after July 26. It was a smaller operation than Husky, if the British landings on the toe of Italy and at Taranto are excluded. Two British divisions, one American division, and other specialized units conducted the initial landings, with several other division, both British and American, in reserve.

The two British divisions departed from Bizerte and Tripoli, the untested 36th "Texas" Division from Oran, and the 45th Division, which served as a floating reserve, from Palermo. Both the 36th and 45th Divisions were National Guard units. The British beaches were north of the Sele River, and the 36th Division was to the south, near the ruins of ancient Paestum. The plain of Salerno, between the coast and mountains, formed a crescent about ten miles deep at its widest point along the Sele River. American Rangers and British commandos landed on the left flank near the base of the Sorrento Peninsula east of Amalfi. To the north, beyond that peninsula, lay the prize: Naples. Mark Clark's new 5th Army commanded all the British and American units in this operation, which included a British armored division, the 82nd A/B, 3rd, and 34th Divisions in reserve.

The "T-Patchers" of the 36th Division underwent amphibious training at Arzew, with the 34th Division acting as the enemy, while the Sicilian campaign was nearing its end. Because of limited shipping, the only immediate reinforcement for the 36th Division would be one regiment of the 45th, which trained a little in Sicily shortly before Operation Avalanche. The rest of the invasion fleet sailed from Oran on September 5, two days after the British 8th Army landed in Calabria, on the toe of the Italian Peninsula. The Italian Army surrendered on September 8, but the German 16th Panzer Division in the Salerno area continued to fight, covering the beaches where no significant coastal defenses existed.[2]

At 3:30 A.M., four battalions from the 36th Division began landing on four adjacent beaches,

2. Before the armistice, the Italian 222nd Coastal Division helped the Germans lay down minefields and set up strongpoints that included 75- and 88-millimeter guns.

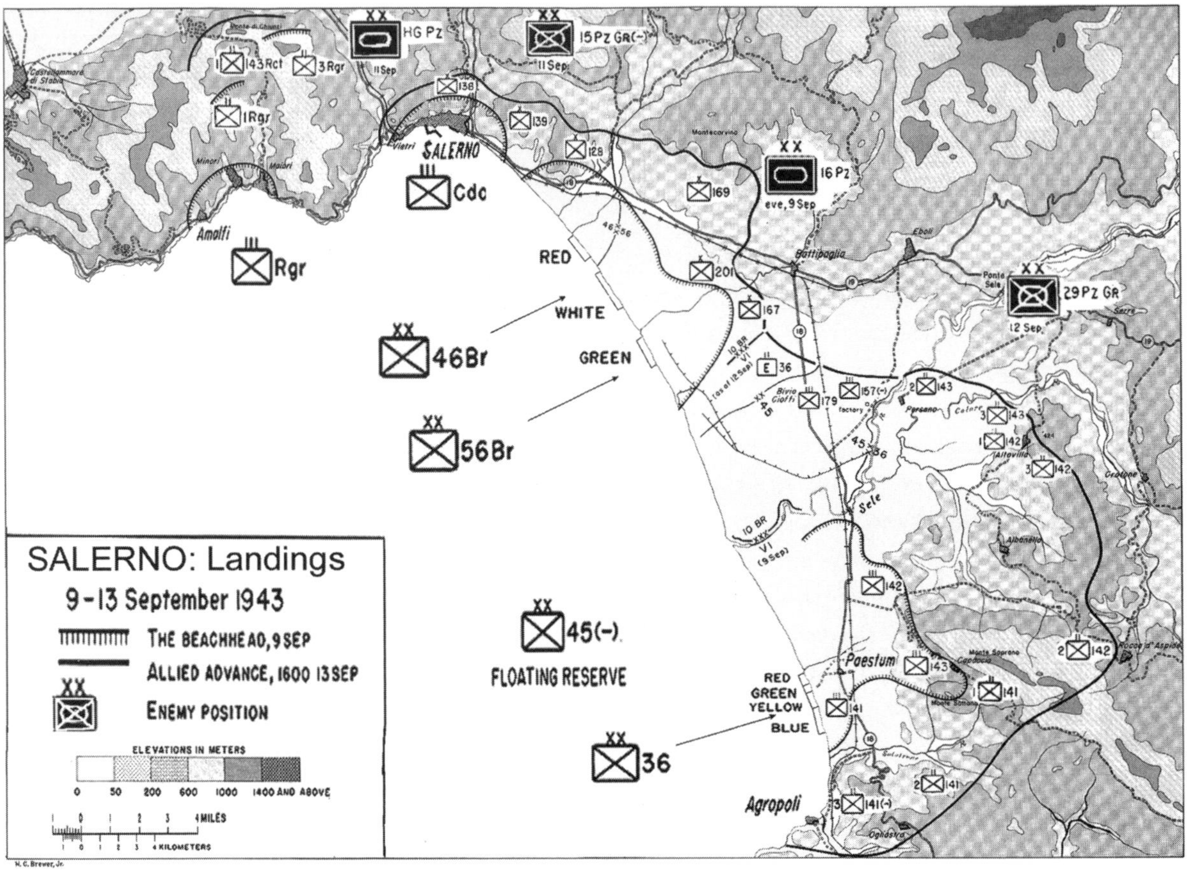

following the same procedures as in past invasions. Unlike the British, the Americans decided to land without artillery support, hoping to surprise the enemy in the dead of night. Unfortunately for the Texans, however, the Germans were on the alert and put up a livelier resistance than the enemy had on previous landings. The American troops that landed on the right ran into a German strongpoint. At about 6:40 A.M., six tanks made it ashore from the LCTs, but four were knocked out by 88s, and then enemy tanks tried to drive the Americans back into the sea. Although few American tanks made it ashore during most of that day, more heavy weapons were landed, and the enemy was eventually routed. The battalions of the 141st and 142nd Infantry finally began pushing inland.

The navy now sent fire control parties ashore. These directed naval gunfire, which began taking out key enemy positions during the morning. This time, the AAF sent P-51s to provide ground support. Late in the day, the Germans dispatched the Hermann Goering Panzer and 29th Panzer Grenadier Divisions to the Salerno front. The battle of the beachhead raged for several days, and the 82nd A/B dropped its troops inside the beachhead as reinforcements. Between September 12 and 14, the Germans launched a major counterattack against the beachhead but failed to smash it. The Americans finally broke out after September 15 and began the slow drive up the Italian peninsula.

The Veterans of Sicily

Before any landings, British and American intelligence had to gather data for the Allied air forces, armies, and navies. The preparation of maps and models greatly improved after Operation Torch, helping ensure the success of Husky. One important source of information was the photo recon units, flying fast and unarmed over enemy territory. The photos they took were used for mapping and target identification. Lt. W. Thomas Barfoot, operations officer of the 12th Photo Squadron, flew his mission out of the major airfield of Maison Blanc Aerodrome, Algiers. Early in 1943, the Germans bombed the field nightly because of the concentration of aircraft here, and many of the airmen ran for cover in the nearby vineyards. The situation changed in the spring, as the Allies gained air superiority. During the Tunisian campaign, Barfoot transferred to the 5th Photo Squadron and flew recon missions until he became group operations officer and later group commander.

I flew missions from North Africa into Italy and over Pantelleria and Sicily. My group organization consisted of P-38 aircraft with the 12th and 5th Squadrons. We had a contingent of French pilots. We flew the F-4 for the greater period of my tour. Towards the end of my tour, we were furnished with the F-5, which was a modified P-38 with hydraulic boost pumps on the ailerons, bigger engines, and larger air-oil scoops.

There were two squadrons in the group plus a French squadron. The French had their own operation entirely, and we assisted them. The HQ was the 3rd Photo Group, under the 90th Wing, with the administration, supply, medics, engineering.

I was in the 5th Squadron [in mid-August] when the strategic people wanted to find out where the enemy battleships were. So I was given the mission out of North Africa as squadron commander to fly to Taranto, photograph the port, and to find visually and with photographs any Italian battleship that was in port.

The *Robert Rowan* explodes off the coast of Gela, Sicily, July 11, 1943. NATIONAL ARCHIVES

I got up there in fine shape and visually saw the battleship with its torpedo net around and took pictures of it and the port. At that point of time, there were four airplanes in the area that I didn't like, so I completed the mission and proceeded home. As an afterthought, they asked if I could take pictures of the Messina Straits—the Germans were being pushed out of Sicily at this point. I was flying at about 20,000 feet, and I was supposed to approach it from the northeast. As I got to within five miles of the straits, looking out of the cockpit, I noticed heavy greenish black puffs of what was flak. I remembered that saying "What you can't see can't hurt you." So at that point, I just went down in my seat and turned my camera on and flew by instruments, because I didn't want to see all that flak. I said this many times to myself and children—that flak was so heavy that I could really, in my mind, get out and walk on it! I returned to North Africa, with the grace of God, without a scratch and the mission completed. I found out it was the heaviest concentration of flak they had seen over Messina so far. That was a typical mission for any pilot.

I know that we could outrun an Me-109 or an Fw-90 if we saw it soon enough. They had a nasty habit of approaching us out of the sun, from above. I have a scarf made of German parachute silk that I picked up and had the parachute shop fix me. The scarf was wrapped around your neck several times and tucked in, because otherwise after a mission, your neck would be scratched up, because when you flew, your head was like a swivel moving around, looking.

Many guys didn't even carry their .45, because when you got strapped in the aircraft with your Mae West, parachute, and flying clothes, the size of the cockpit didn't allow much movement. That .45 and shoulder harness would cause you to come back pretty sore.

There were other types of missions. When we were in North Africa and I was squadron commander, we took on the job of mapping the coast of France from the Spanish border to the Italian border with our cameras in preparation—little did we know—for the invasion of Southern France. When the squadron took that mission, we flew from North Africa into South France. We were flying flight lines, which are straight, ninety miles into the interior; we took five or six of these runs.

The criteria those people gave us were that in order to create these maps from the photos, the airplane could not vary more than 3 degrees of tip or tilt left to right. The altitude we maintained had to be within 300 feet. So flying an airplane straight and level for ninety miles inland, and then making a 180-degree turn and coming back ninety miles, and doing that five or six times—as I look back on it now—was pretty hazardous, because the German radar and antiaircraft guns could pick us up at the altitude and direction we were flying.

Accolades came from the British brigadier in charge of making the maps, since we had not one mission that didn't live up to the criteria established by the engineering people. Subsequently, within six months, maps came out that were accurate, and when the invasion troops got their maps, they were accurate. We mounted a 6-inch and a 12-inch camera, and we had 3-by-6-inch cameras—one vertical and two in the nose of the airplane at oblique angles—that gave the mapmakers all the information they needed. During the debriefing, the intelligence officer would ask us what altitude we flew, if we noticed any tip or tilt or loss or gain of altitude, and where we noticed it. He would make notations on his report for the people making the maps.

We moved from North Africa to Italy shortly after the invasion. We went over by Liberty ship—a small contingent of people. We got there on D+10 after the Salerno invasion. The pilots would fly missions over Italy as requested by the 5th Amy, and the pictures would be developed in North Africa. A courier would come over and deliver the pictures to the army people that wanted them.

Some days, we couldn't fly for the weather. When pilots didn't come back, we didn't know if it was mechanical trouble or if they were shot down or lost to whatever cause. The first year, I think we lost maybe 40 percent of our pilots.

The 505th PIR under Col. James Gavin was the first American unit to land in Sicily, and thus the first to take part in the invasion of Europe. This was the first American regimental combat jump of the war. Lt. Jack Isaacs, at the head of 3rd Platoon, Company G, who had recently been promoted and was still a newlywed, jumped with the regiment. "We had departed New York on

April 29, 1943, bound for Casablanca, arriving on May 10 aboard the *Monterey*." The jump went badly, as the troops were widely scattered. There was one major problem in both Sicily and Italy:

> The heavy weapons such as 60-millimeter mortars and light machine guns had been dropped in bundles. This meant that the mortar man had to find his weapon to be useful. We had also dropped with the M-1 rifle broken down and placed in a canvas container on the man's chest. He had to land, get out of his harness, assemble his weapon, and then defend himself. This had caused unnecessary casualties.

Despite the problems, Isaacs remained with the company through Salerno and Normandy.

Clay Brooks also made his first combat jump in Sicily. He had joined the army in June 1940 and served in the 7th Cavalry, an armored unit. "While I was there, I was still a recruit. Colonel Patton made general and gave all of us a cigar for making general," Brooks recalls. That was the last time he ever saw the general. On the night of his first jump into enemy-controlled territory, he and his comrades went out the door shortly before midnight. "We were supposed to land near a little town named Gela in Sicily. Can't remember the name of the area, but my group of planes landed sixty-five miles from there, where the British were coming in by boat, sixty-five miles away from our drop zone. Our next jump was in Italy."

PFC James R. Richards from Lubbock, Texas, who served in Regimental Supply of the HQ Company, 504th PIR, had volunteered at age twenty-two in May 1942. That fall, after basic training and Parachute School, he was sent to Fort Bragg, where he became a demolitions specialist. He arrived in Casablanca with the 504th PIR on the *George Washington* on May 10, 1943. "We had lots of trouble on our troopship on the way over but landed about eleven days after departure." Once they landed, they traveled across North Africa to the assembly area. He narrowly escaped death on the evening of D+2 when the six C-47s carrying his headquarters and HQ Company ran into a barrage of friendly fire, and one of the planes was shot down. Since he was a subordinate of the S-4, he also worked with the graves registration officer, and the unpleasant duty of collecting and identifying the dead after the battle fell to him.

Richards's comrade in arms, Pvt. Bernard G. Shipton of Smithville Flats, New York, had enlisted in February 1942, a month before turning twenty. After undergoing basic training at Camp Croft, he went on to Fort Benning. He was a mortar man in the 1st Battalion of the 504th PIR.

> We trained at Oujda and at Kairouan, Tunisia. On July 11, 1943, the 1st and 2nd Battalions of the 504th Parachute Infantry jumped at Gela, Sicily.[3] The jump was decimated by friendly fire shooting twenty-three planes out of the sky before the troops were able to jump. Because of this antiaircraft fire, the portion of the two battalions that got through dropped all over the island of Sicily, and the Germans thought that many more parachutists were dropped than there actually were.
>
> After a return trip to Kairouan [thirty-eight days after landing in Sicily], the 504th was reequipped and received replacements to bring it up to strength. The 504th was returned to Sicily, where they trained for future missions. The 504th was finally dropped in Salerno, where it saved the beachhead from being pushed back into the sea. After the beachhead was secured, the

3. The 3rd Battalion jumped on July 9 with the 505th PIR.

American soldiers with civilians on Sicily, July 11, 1943. NATIONAL ARCHIVES

504th boarded LCIs to make a beach landing at Mairo, Italy, then proceeded to the "88 Pass," and then on to Naples.

On the beach, in most amphibious landings, the Rangers would lead the way with the most difficult assignments. Just promoted to first sergeant on June 19, Gino Mercuriali, with Capt. Ralph Colby, led Company D into battle. The sergeant was still suffering from dysentery contracted a couple weeks earlier when he boarded a transport on July 8 for the invasion. The 1st Ranger Battalion was to assault the beaches at Gela, but this time Companies A and B, which had landed first at Arzew, were in the second wave. Companies D, E, F, and the HQ Company were in the first wave, which went ashore at about 3 A.M.

> We encountered stiff opposition on the beach, which was covered with barbed wire and included mines. Despite the fact that the platoon I went in with had two officers, I ended up taking charge of the assault by manually handling new recruits. One of the officers stepped off the ramp of the landing craft and went under it. I never saw him again. The other one chickened and evidently didn't leave the craft, as I never saw him again.
>
> We did well and took many prisoners. Moving on inland toward our defense line,

we encountered a building with an antenna, and I surrounded it with my men. I broke in with a barrage of grenades to capture about five more prisoners. I'm a descendant of parents from Northern Italy, so it was particularly strange for me to see the reaction of the families of many of these men pleading with us to let their men go, as they were mainly Home Guard with Germans commanding them. I did restrain some of our people who wished to shoot some of them.

Some of the companies of the 3rd and 4th Battalions had some rougher times than we did.

On D-Day and D+1, the Rangers of the 1st Battalion in Gela were fighting Italians, in light Renault tanks, from the rooftops with bazookas, demolition charges, and even captured Italian guns. On July 12, from a mountaintop position, Captain Colby directed the 6-inch guns of the light cruiser *Savannah,* which had been supporting the Rangers since the landing and wreaking terrible destruction on enemy formations, against enemy artillery positions several miles inland, neutralizing them before long. (Captain Colby was killed just before the campaign ended.) Back in Gela, Sgt. Marcell Swank, also a veteran of Dieppe, was guarding a bakery when a mob of angry women desperate for food descended on him. Swank held them off by firing a burst from his submachine gun into the air, but the women soon returned to the attack, forcing him and the baker to flee.

A few days later, a patrol from Company E captured the mountain fortress town of Butera. During the cleanup, Mercuriali "experienced again the type of people that can be a part of a great outfit," but "wasn't particularly in agreement with their actions." After the fighting, which involved mainly snipers, was over, he came across a dead German officer and took his pistol. He refrained from removing the German's diamond ring, but another Ranger cut the man's finger off to retrieve the ring. Mercuriali was only a short distance away, administering morphine to a badly wounded Italian soldier.

The 1st Division was usually selected for the toughest missions, and Sicily was no exception. The 16th and 26th Infantry Regiments led the assault east of Gela. Sgt. Theodore Aufort was with the headquarters of the 1st Battalion, 16th Infantry, which landed on Green Beach 2, to the extreme right. The HQ Company included a communications platoon with a message center, radio section, and wire section. Aufort was with the wire section.

My job was strictly infantry communications, to keep telephone service at all costs whenever possible. That was from the battalion headquarters to the line companies. The radio section, I wouldn't say they had it easy, but at times they did, because they couldn't use their radios when radio silence was ordered.

We set up our tents and got ready for the battle of Tunis, which we finished up with the British 8th Army. We went back to Algeria, and there we received a lot of new replacement equipment. Troops had come in from the U.S., and we had quite a few replacements. I got a new jeep driver.

Then we proceeded to Sicily. We landed east of Gela, which was our objective. In that city, after we went through it, we ran out of wire. I started back to Gela and picked up old wire, because we needed it desperately since we couldn't get new wire. The MPs chased us off the road, told us Patton was coming into town and we had to get off the streets. We did, we hid our jeep and saw men as grubby looking as we were. We peeked around the corner and saw Patton coming down and standing up in his tank. They were taking moving pictures of him. A month or so later, we got the *Stars and Stripes* paper and saw Patton capturing Gela, can you believe it? We had a good laugh over that—three days after we pass through, he captures it![4]

A day or two later, a buddy of mine and I were covering a wire line that had gone out. We were in a large ditch about four feet deep, with only our heads and shoulders sticking out of it. My buddy, who was covering me with an M-1 rifle while I was up forward, was maybe twenty-five feet behind me. He called to me to look to the left. Up in a little draw, maybe 500 or 600 yards away, there was a German tank sitting there. I slowly looked at the tank, called back to him without turning around, and said to turn around nonchalantly and start walking the other way. We just barely turned around and started walking back, hoping they wouldn't fire on us or that it might be abandoned—it wasn't. The next thing I knew, my buddy carried me out of the area. I came to, and the bells were ringing for a couple of days after that—it didn't bother me until I got back to England.

Isadore L. Valenti, who enlisted early in 1941, trained as a medic at Fort Meade, not too far from his home in Pennsylvania. He was assigned to the 51st Medical Battalion, which traveled from England to Oran in November. In February 1943, the battalion was assigned to the II Corps in Tunisia. Valenti's fiancée sent him a "Dear John" letter, which he received during the battle of the Kasserine Pass. He was in the 51st Medical Battalion when it sailed for its landing sites at Gela, Sicily. "The night before the invasion, nobody bothered to sleep. Most lay flat on their bunks, eyes closed, but remaining wide awake." The trip to Sicily was quite memorable, as far as Valenti was concerned.

The air was thick and putrid; you could almost cut it with a knife. The latrine floor was soaked from the overflowing urinal because of cigarette butts, and vomit.

Inside, the only empty place in the hold where it was possible to see the card markings from the light of a single bulb, a crap game and two blackjack games were in progress. They had been playing there for hours, and the players seemed to be in a stupor. Even though the stench was unbearable, the card games went on.

Belowdecks, the air reeked of perspiration coupled with the oppressive chlorine and stale urine smell, the stink seeping through from the latrine when someone opened the door.[5]

At about 1 A.M., the sound of the ship engines changed. As Valenti went up on deck to get fresh air and find relief from the stifling atmosphere below decks, the ship came to a stop in the choppy seas. Before long, he was climbing over the side, down the cargo nets, and into the waiting LCVP with the rest of his platoon. Pvt. Joseph K. Wineglaus got tangled in the netting and tumbled into the landing craft. The ride to the beach was rough, and most of the soldiers onboard became seasick. Suddenly, as the beach loomed closer, some German fighters roared above them on a strafing run. The LCVP hit a sandbar and the men had to wade ashore, but not

4. Patton came ashore at Gela the day after Darby's Rangers had taken the town. He set up 7th Army headquarters there, and it is possible that a more impressive entrance was filmed a few days later. On the other hand, Aufort may have confused Gela with another town.

5. The full account of Valenti's experiences can be found in his book *Combat Medic.*

without losing a lot of their brothers in arms and equipment.

From the safety of the beach, Valenti watched an LST explode in flames after it was hit by a German plane. Over the crest of a dune, he ran into troops pulling back from their exposed position to a safer point from which they could observe the advance of enemy tanks. The air observers called in naval gunfire, which stopped the enemy in its tracks. At about 4:30 A.M., enemy aircraft buzzed over the landing beaches. On the outskirts of Gela, a force consisting mostly of rangers had halted an Italian tank contingent sent early by the Italian commander. The 1st Infantry Division, with the help of the ships hovering offshore, turned back the Tigers of the Hermann Goering Division, which showed up in the afternoon. The Germans returned to the attack on the next day, but although they got close, they were driven back once more.

Sgt. Frank Andrews and his friend Verl Pendleton, who were in the headquarters of the 1st Battalion, 7th Infantry, had seen no action after the initial landings of the 3rd Division at Fedhala, Morocco. They had traveled with the division across North Africa and undergone the preinvasion training. In Sicily, their battalion was assigned to Red Beach at Licata, where they got to use LCVPs for the first time in an actual invasion. Although the landing was largely successful, they were caught in crossfire from Italian machine guns on their flanks, an experience they would not soon forget. Nevertheless, there were also lighter moments during the campaign as the division advanced on Palermo and enemy resistance seemed to crack.

> Our objective was first to cut the island in half. One unit would ride the tanks, and the other would walk, and then, on the third day, they would be shuttled forward on trucks. When we got to the north coast, we got instruction not to go into Palermo. There is a steep bluff at the east end of Palermo and quite a cliff overlooking the Mediterranean to the north. This is as far as we went. We were told to hold there. As Patton's tank forces had invaded the western end of the island, which was flat country, the English took the mountains around Mount Etna and that area. Patton's tanks [CCA of the 2nd Armored Division] were supposed to get the glory of taking Palermo, so we held tight.
>
> We had a few prisoners. The division MPs, who had moved to the edge of the town, had taken a villa there and used it for a prison enclosure. Late that afternoon, along towards evening, we were given some prisoners to deliver to this place. It was getting dark, and it was quite a ways down this road that follows this bluff into the east end of the town, and there were people all along who had moved out of town to get away from the bombings. They had dug caves in the side there, and it was a little spooky, because these prisoners needed protection and they were concerned. So it was a better part of the night getting down and finding our way into town. We thought, "Why should we hike back up there only to move into town again when Patton's tanks would be there?"
>
> So we didn't hurry back and kind of broke the rules a bit by wandering into town to look around. What did we spot but a German soldier! He has got a car, and he is going from house to house working on some type of business in this part of town, looting the people. We edged around there and waited for him to get out of the car. We cornered him easy enough and took him prisoner. He didn't speak any English, and we didn't speak much German. He did make it clear to us everything must be according to the "Geneva Conferences," a

Soldiers look at the wreckage of a German plane near Gela, Sicily, July 12, 1943. NATIONAL ARCHIVES

term he kept using. He had sacks full of money, Italian lira. I don't know what he was going to do with it. He kept reaching to us and kept insisting on this "Geneva Conference." My friend from Missouri named Pendleton said, "I think this is one for me to handle." So he gets a sheet of paper and pen and starts going over the car, and he makes out a large receipt for the car and then on the left-hand side of the paper he puts 1,000 for the money. The Germans says, "NO, NO, NO," and motions like a fisherman telling how big a fish he caught. Each time he complains, Pendleton puts a comma and three more zeros, until soon it goes across the paper and the German is smiling. Pendleton puts down some more stuff, signs it, and hands it to me to inspect. He gives the receipt to the German, who folds it and puts it in his pocket. He is smiling like everything as he goes into the prison enclosure. Pendleton had signed it "TOUGH SHIT."

We took his car, drove off, and saw no reason to go back to the outfit. We didn't dare go into town, because Patton's tanks would be there any time. So we headed up the same road, ran into a lot of equipment, and took the first side road off that led back up the hills south of Palermo. The first little town we ran into, it was like out of a storybook. They had town criers. We pulled into town, and somebody stepped out in the street and started hollering. Then someone down the street does the same, and the next thing you know, the whole street is full of people. These criers must have been like policemen, since they seemed to be in charge and they cleared the way for us. We didn't know if we were prisoners or what.

They took us to the mayor's house, and next thing you know, they are digging out wine and everything. We are toasting FDR and everything: "VIVA FDR!" We finally had to get out of there, and out come the town criers, clearing the road for us. We sure laughed about that, but didn't tell anybody about what happened when we got back to the unit. Verl Pendleton was driving, and after we left there, he wanted to see how fast it went and got it up over 100. The next day, it dawned on me it was only kilometers. We ditched the car along the way.

Harold Taylor landed to the east of Licata with the headquarters of the 15th Infantry.

Our movement east was more or less administrative. Much preparation was done in the Tunisia area in preparation for our landing in Sicily. On July 9, 1943, we loaded up onto the landing craft and under the cover of darkness moved out into the Mediterranean, moving ever so close to Malta's coastline. On July 10, 1943, we hit the beach at Licata, Sicily. Daybreak was just upon us. As I hit the beach, I kicked a small object. It was a small Italian prayer book, which I shoved into my shirt pocket and carried until the end of hostilities. I still have it in my possession. At the time we hit the beach, we encountered small-arms fire. With my combat pack on my back, my rifle, and radio equipment, I found myself crawling across the rough terrain as bullets zipped over me. After crawling several hundred feet, we found an area of cover where we could set up communications equipment. A U.S. Army photographer was nearby and took pictures of us. There were large amounts of German and Italian forces on this island. Our division kept nothing in reserve, with all three regiments fighting abreast of each other, taking many casualties. It wasn't long before the 3rd Division entered Palermo; we entered before Patton's tanks and were there before they arrived.[6]

In September 1943, we moved to the mainland of Italy at Salerno to relieve the 36th Division at the beachhead. Not only did we encounter bad weather, but we faced a German panzer division, and for days, we were faced with cold rain, snow, and vehicles bogged down. Vehicles had to be winched out, and mules were brought in.

Pvt. Robert M. Gehlhoff, also in the 15th Infantry, served in the headquarters of the 3rd Battalion after being transferred from his position as a scout in Company I at the end of the African campaign. He was in the S-2 section, which had six to eight men and "operated with carbines, binoculars, telephones, and radio." His section conducted patrols, interrogated prisoners, and manned observation posts.

According to Capt. Harlos V. Hatter, the landings in Sicily were the most successful of the three amphibious operations in which he took part. Hatter, who led a company of the 179th Infantry, 45th Division, ashore north of Scoglitti, was a 1939 ROTC graduate of Oklahoma State University. He had trained with the division at Camp Barkley, Texas, in 1941. The division had moved east and departed from Camp Patrick Henry after amphibious and infantry training in Virginia in May 1943. After landing in North Africa that same month, Captain Hatter's unit engaged in additional amphibious training at

6. The tanks of the 2nd Armored Division finally arrived, but Patton no longer commanded the division. He commanded the 7th Army, which included all American units in Sicily. Most veterans like to assume that Patton was personally in charge of and leading an armored unit long after the African campaign.

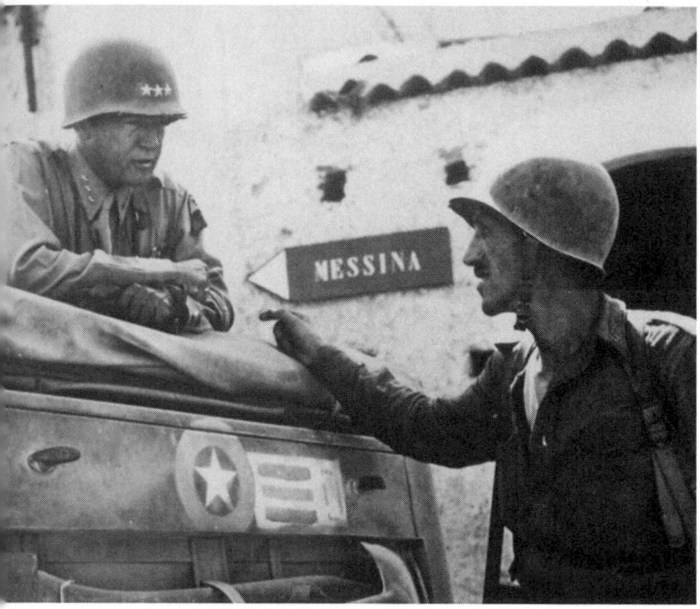

Gen. George S. Patton confers with Lt. Col. Lyle Bernard of the 30th Infantry Regiment near Brolo, Sicily, 1943. NATIONAL ARCHIVES

the beaches of Mostagenem, where "the seas off shore were so rough," he says, "that almost every man in my company was seasick."

Pvt. Ralph W. Fink of Kutztown, Pennsylvania, was drafted in March 1943 at age nineteen. After thirteen weeks of basic infantry training at Camp Wolters, Texas, he was sent to Camp Shanks and put on a ship to North Africa as a replacement. He took the train to Bizerte, where he boarded another ship for Italy, disembarking after the landings in Salerno. When he reached Benevento, he was assigned to Company D, 157th Infantry, 45th Division, and was soon in combat. The worst part of his stay in Italy was "fighting up the Volturno River."[7]

> It came south like a snake. We would cross it and then, a few miles up the road, we would have to cross it again, and so on—always at a horrible cost of men. [Then came] fighting high in the mountains above Venafro, where only mule trains could supply us—always wet and cold. The weather was a demoralizing factor. We really didn't know what was happening except for about ten yards on either side of each of us. In my opinion, that's why men that fought at the same places have entirely different versions of what happened. They know only what happened to them. Life was reduced to just trying to stay alive for a few more minutes.

Ralph Fink remained with the division until the end of the war, and even though he was wounded twice, he always returned to his platoon. In the last year of the war, he reached the rank of platoon sergeant. Like many of the men who fought in Italy, he considered the campaign on the Italian peninsula the toughest American forces fought in the European theater. The Germans, he recalls, "were the enemy, and our misery was blamed directly to them. I hated their guts." Fink was "apprehensive about going back into combat" because it "is only attractive to those who have never experienced it."

In July 1943, Pvt. Otway Burns, Company A, 531st Engineer Shore Regiment, departed for Sicily from Arzew with the invasion force. Burns's account indicates that he landed with the 1st Division on the beaches at Gela.

> I landed on D-Day. I was in a machine-gun squad, and I carried a .50-caliber mount on my back. I had a submachine gun, an M-1 rifle, and a big dagger with brass knuckles. When we were unloading, we had long bayonets strapped around our legs with pieces of rawhide. My bayonet got caught

7. After taking Naples, the Germans had to be cleared from this river just beyond the city. The rains began late in September, and the waters of the Volturno had swollen, aiding the German rear guards in making this a major obstacle. The enemy troops were fighting a delaying action while the Todt Organization was preparing the defenses of the winter line passing through Cassino.

The 478th Amphibian Truck Company and the DUKW

John E. Spires was inducted at Fort Hayes in Columbus, Ohio, in March 7, 1941. From there, in the company of other draftees, he took a train to the Quartermaster Training Center at Camp Lee, Virginia. Spires and his companions were the first class entering the thirteen-week basic training program on the post. He was assigned to Company L, 8th Quartermaster (QM) Training Regiment. The men were assigned according to height, the tallest to the 1st Platoon and the shortest to the 4th Platoon. Unlike in infantry basic training, only half a day was devoted to the typical infantry instruction, which ranged from drill to firing at the rifle range. The remainder of the day was spent on technical training, with instruction for truck drivers, mechanics, and repairmen, among others.

Once he completed his basic training, Spires was assigned to Company A, 201st QM Battalion, at Fort Devens. At the time, there was no overcrowding yet, and the troops were quartered in permanent brick barracks. Surprisingly for a military installation, the meals were excellent, because the cooks were under the guidance of the Army Cooking School, which was on the same post. In August 1941, the battalion took part in maneuvers in Louisiana and the Carolinas. The men learned to handle the gasoline supply for the 2nd Army (Red Army) in Louisiana. In October, the battalion formed a truck convoy to go to North Carolina, where it performed similar functions during the games. The night before the attack on Pearl Harbor, the battalion drove back to Fort Devens. Here it remained in garrison until May 1942, when it moved to Camp Edwards and was assigned to the Engineer Amphibian Command. Company A became part of the 361st QM Battalion, and its commander, Capt. Keith G. Hooker, took over the 362nd QM Battalion. First Lt. David D. Moore, who arrived in June, took over Captain Hooker's command.[8]

The company was sent to Belfast, Northern Ireland, that summer, and then was sent to North Africa after the invasion. It arrived late, causing its assignment to be changed to handling gasoline supply operations for the Base Section in Algeria.

In the spring of 1943, a detachment arrived from the U.S. with amphibian 2½-ton trucks and amphibian jeeps assigned to the 5th Army. They were sent to the brigade, which turned them over to the 361st QM Battalion for training. My company was relieved of its gasoline supply operations, and Company C was relieved of its trucking operations, to learn how to handle DUKWs. A Gasoline Supply Company was authorized 125 enlisted men, compared with 205 enlisted men, for an Amphibian Truck Company, but we had less than 125 enlisted men until our redesignation later as the 478th Amphibian Truck Company. After our companies were trained, the 361st ran a DUKW school

continued

8. David Moore was promoted to captain in December 1942. His unit departed the U.S. so soon in the summer of 1942, he was not able to purchase a new blouse, and could not locate one in Northern Ireland or Scotland so when he was in Africa he was still wearing a Sam Browne Belt. He also could not find a pair of captain's bars, so he used two First Lieutenant bars welded together.

The 478th Amphibian Truck Company and the DUKW *continued*

to train various brigade and army personnel. Captain Kennedy [from Company C] was in active charge of this school, and I ran an advanced training course. Demonstrations of the DUKWs' capabilities and limitations were run for numerous generals and staff officers.

Companies A and C were designated to operate as DUKW companies for the invasion of Sicily. The 361st QM Battalion was designated as part of the 3rd Division Combat Team to support the 36th Combat Engineers in handling the beach operations at Licata, Sicily. Company C was selected for the initial landings, with my company in reserve. The DUKW School was turned over to a detachment from the 5th Army headed by a Captain Sudard, whom we had trained. Company C was brought to strength with the best DUKWs remaining at the school and moved out to Bizerte to join the 36th Engineers. I followed with headquarters and HQ Company, 361st QM Battalion, and a partial complement of DUKWs. My company bivouacked south of Algiers for several days while new DUKWs were being unloaded and serviced in the port of Algiers. We then proceeded to the staging area at Bizerte. We were transported to Sicily aboard LSTs on their first return trip to Sicily.

In the Sicilian campaign, the DUKWs operated as a pool consisting of my DUKWs, those of Company C, and ones that had been used by the 36th Engineers. The harbor at Licata had a draft of only twelve feet, making it necessary to unload the Liberty ships in the open roadstead. Thus it was necessary to use the DUKWs for the duration of the campaign.

The 361st QM Battalion was kept in Sicily when the 36th and 531st Engineer Regiments were ordered back to Africa to prepare for the invasion of Italy. On conclusion of the Sicilian campaign, the 361st was ordered from Licata to Termini Imerse, just east of Palermo. My company was scheduled to be in the first convoy from Sicily in support of the landing at Salerno, but because of the difficulties encountered in securing the beachhead, the 3rd and 45th Divisions were brought to strength in men and equipment and shipped out. Once Naples was taken, there was no further

in the webbing, unloading in the dark, on those nets into the PA boat.[10] Those nets were on the seaward side so they couldn't hit us from shore. My bayonet caught; I turned to look. It was caught in there, and when I let go, the boat dropped away. We had waves about thirty to thirty-five feet, and I fell into a crowd of guys, helmets, and rifles and hurt my back.[11] They tried to put me back on the ship, but I didn't want to

10. PA refers to personnel assault. Burns' assigned boat was PA-26.

11. The waves were more likely three to five feet.

The 478th Amphibian Truck Company and the DUKW *continued*

need for DUKWs, so my company and Company C, 361st QM Battalion, were outfitted with 2½-ton trucks and shipped to Italy, where we operated express convoys for the movement of supplies from the port of Naples to the corps and division dumps. Incidentally, the movement of my company to Italy was aboard a British LST.

During our stay in Italy, the battalion was on detached service with HQ 5th Army. When the 1st Brigade was ordered to return to England, the 5th Army requested our transfer to their command. However, in the absence of War Department approval, we rejoined the brigade aboard the SS *Dickman*, leaving all equipment except our kitchen stoves behind.[9]

In England, the 361st QM Battalion was reorganized, and Company A became the 478th Amphibian Truck Company; Company C, the 479th Amphibian Truck Company; and the HQ Company, the 24th Amphibian Truck Battalion. The 462nd Amphibian Truck Company was attached to the battalion as soon as it arrived from the United States.

The development of the DUKW led to the formation of these amphibian companies. The DUKW (D for the fourth year of the war, or 1942; U for utility; K for front-wheel drive; and W for two rear-drive axles) was created between late April and the beginning of July 1942. It was essentially the army GMC 2½-ton truck with amphibian modifications. After the prototype was demonstrated on July 5, the army ordered 2,000 units and used them first on Guadalcanal. Fifty-five DUKWs were delivered at the training center of Arzew, Algeria, on March 1943. It was not long before they suffered from breakdowns and a lack of mechanics. To remedy the situation, Company C, 361st QM Battalion, which operated specialized training, coached new mechanics, and several DUKW companies were soon formed. One thousand DUKWs in two battalions participated in the invasions of Sicily (one-third were given to the British) and Italy. In Normandy, 2,000 DUKWs were used during the first two months (40 percent operated by the British).

9. Built in 1922 as a passenger ship, the *Peninsula State* was first renamed *President Pierce* and then *President Roosevelt*. The army took it over in 1940 and renamed it the *Joseph T. Dickman*. The navy took possession of it in 1941, listing it as AP-26, and gave it to the Coast Guard to operate. It was redesignated APA 13 in February 1943.

go. A medic gave me a shot of morphine, and I went on in.

I went in and set up our gun on the perimeter of the company. Just as I got set up, the lieutenant came and got me. The truck driver got killed on the landing because he got rolled up on the waves. He put me on a DUKW and told me to go out to the boat about eight miles out and to pick up a net of shells and a net of charges. We weren't supposed to do that, and I said we were supposed to take two nets of charges or shells, but not together. He showed me a gun before I left, said this 105-millimeter was out of ammunition and we had been counterattacked right on the beach, and tanks were coming all around on a big plain nearby. I went out to this boat and yelled up to them to give me a net of charges and shells. They said they couldn't do it. I said the officer told me to bring one of each, so they said OK. I started back and the DUKW started sinking. The pump had clogged up with sand. I had to stop the motor and run to the back of the boat; I was about to sink. I pulled it out, washed it real good, went back and turned it on, and it clicked and went right over. I carried it right in and went to that gun. When I was going over the sand dunes in that DUKW with some other vehicles coming in, three German planes came over the beach strafing. One of them dropped a bomb, and it landed right on an LST in the front elevator. I was on top of the sand dune when I saw this. The other two [aircraft] sped on back toward Naples, I guess. I drove that DUKW for three nights and two days.

During that first night, I got lost in the fog. First thing I heard was one of these speakers or a foghorn challenging me, and I didn't know what it was. I stopped and listened. A guy challenged me and asked me where I was going. I said I was a U.S. Army DUKW trying to find boat number so-and-so. He said, "Hey, you better turn that damn thing around; you are halfway to Africa." I was out on the outer destroyer line, lost in the fog. I turned around, went back, finally found the boat, and carried in another load. I passed out after the third day with malaria. About 90 percent of our outfit caught malaria in Africa or Sicily. I had a 106.5-degree fever. We only had atabrine, which we captured from the Germans.[12] It turned us yellow like jaundice.

When I came back, we spent forty days there. I had to go down every morning and pick up the American paratroopers that were shot down by our own navy. I would go down with German prisoners every morning and pick up the bodies before daylight for morale purposes, because they were bringing in other troops. Then we finished up at Sicily; reloaded at Algiers, where we stayed about a month of two; and then landed in bloody Salerno. I carried in supplies, including food and rations.

The Gilder Troops and Pilots

While Husky was under way, the glider troops and pilots waited in North Africa. Lt. Joe Gault arrived with Company F, 325th Glider Infantry, in early May 1943.

Then we went across Africa in the 40 & 8 boxcars, and we got to Oujda. On the way, the train was so overloaded that at times we had to get off and push. We practiced and trained there and had one glider operation. They would just take you up at the airfield and bring you back to the airfield, because they didn't want to damage those gliders.[13] They cost about $22,000, which nowadays wouldn't be too high—no combat in North Africa, just practice.

We went to Kairouan, Tunisia, in June. They went into Sicily, but the gliders were held in reserve, so the 325th didn't go into Sicily. The paratroopers did; the 504th was

12. Atabrine was a synthetic drug invented by the Germans before the war. Japan's conquests in the Pacific early in the war led the U.S. to turn to not only synthetic rubber, as about 90 percent of the natural rubber supply had been cut off, but also atabrine, because the major sources of quinine had fallen under enemy control.

13. Gault also mentions that this was the last glider practice until the regiment reached England. In addition, he notes that during this time many men in the company suffered badly from dysentery.

shot down by our own navy with the assistant division commander, I believe.[14]

We [the regiment] went into Italy, but I took yellow jaundice at Kairouan, and I was in the hospital at that time. They went by sea, without me, into Italy and then took defensive positions on a mountain, driving the Germans back at Mount San Angela. Then when Naples fell, the regiment went in and policed Naples, and that is where I came in.

Lieutenant Gault left the hospital in Tunisia and rejoined his company when it occupied Naples in October 1943. He believed he was the only man in the regiment who had not yet seen combat. The regiment remained in Naples until late November before it reembarked for the trip to England.

PFC Clinton E. Riddle, a member of the headquarters of Company B, 1st Battalion, 325th Glider Infantry, arrived in Casablanca with his regiment aboard the *Santa Rosa* on the morning of May 10. After the journey to Oujda, he and his comrades set up their pup tents in a large wheat field and began training once more in the oppressive heat.[15] It was here that he experienced his first glider ride, which lasted about fifteen minutes.

On June 22, all of the 325th Glider Infantry loaded in gliders and began a long journey. A storm forced us down at one point, and we had to wait for a tow plane. We had traveled across the Atlas Mountains across Algeria.

On June 25, we arrived near Kairouan, Tunisia, forty miles from Tunis and twelve miles from the nearest village. We lived in pup tents under the trees of an olive orchard. It was very hot, and we continued to train, sometimes at night, because it made it a lot cooler.

Pvt. Roy Humphrey receives blood plasma from PFC Harvey White, Sicily, August 1943. NATIONAL ARCHIVES

Sgt. Harold Owens, Company A, 1st Battalion, 325th Glider Infantry, stayed at Camp Edwards for two weeks before taking the train to State Island and boarding the *Santa Rosa*. As he sailed with his unit from New York, he stood on deck, watching the Statue of Liberty slowly disappear below the horizon. He too remembers traveling by truck from Casablanca to Oujda, not by train. A naïve country boy on his first trip overseas like Riddle, Owens was awestruck by the alien world that surrounded him.

They raised grapes for wine and barley for beer, and that is about all they did in Morocco, except raise goats. It was very

14. It was Brig. Gen. Charles Keerans, the assistant division commander, who went along as an observer.

15. Clinton Riddle says they traveled by truck, whereas Joe Gault recalls that they went by train. It is possible that each of their battalions used a different method or that one of them could be confusing this journey with the later trip to Tunisia. Both men were certain that the paratroopers stayed at Oujda and that the glidermen went on to a smaller site nearby named Marina.

poor. These Arab sheiks had as many wives as they could afford, and the more wives they had, the more work they did for them, so they could get more wives. They would ride around on a little burro, and the men would sit under a shade tree while the women worked all day.

The troops in Owens's and Riddle's units trained mostly at night to escape from the heat of the day. According to Joe Gault, life at Marina was miserable, consisting of "C rations, French cigarettes, dust, winds, and heat," and the men experienced "the worst epidemic of dysentery you can ever imagine, with regular accommodations overrun." The heat was so bad that at times he posted sentries to sound the alarm if any brass approached, while his men rested in the scanty shade of a wadi instead of training. Owens's unit traveled to Tunisia in gliders.

We took off, and instead of circling the field and gaining altitude, they just took off in a beeline. I don't even know if they realized that the Atlas Mountains were there or not, but they acted as if they didn't. Anyhow, a lot of the C-47s flew into the mountains, and some of the gliders cut loose and were able to come down in the valleys and land. We were very fortunate, because we could just barely see the towrope in the thick fog. Our copilot and pilot really did some excellent flying, because when we broke out of the clouds, you could look down and see the mountains. We were up to 15,000 feet, and no oxygen up there and it was very cold. All the gliders were made of something like cheesecloth and windows. There were five gliders in my group as we flew above these mountains, and we finally got up to Constantine, Algeria, and then for some reason got the green light to cut loose. Of course, the glider pilots cut loose, and we went down and landed on the big aerodrome at Constantine.

It was a big installation, a lot of fighters and bombers. We went in and the tow ship took off; they never told us why it did. We stayed there for five days. We had been down on that desert starving to death, so we went into the air force mess hall and ate them out of house and home. Finally they brought five tow ships to pick us up. We took off and went to Kairouan, Tunisia, and rejoined our unit. No one ever told us why they dropped us off at Constantine.

We stayed there getting ready for the invasion of Sicily. We had the gliders all stacked out and everything. When we got ready for the invasion, we loaded them up. At that time, the parachutists jumping into Sicily flew over our navy, and they shot down a lot of our tow ships. They moved us up the coast around Bizerte, and we stayed on the beach for a few days. We moved into Recata, Sicily, in September 1943. There I got the news that my son was born—I had married while at Fort Bragg. We loaded on LCIs, went up the coast to Palermo, and stayed the night, then off for Salerno.

Owens went into Salerno with his regiment and then boarded an LCI to go to Naples. The British LCIs, he complains, were filthy, while the American craft were kept almost immaculate—an opinion no doubt inspired by nationalistic loyalty. In Naples, he saw his first volcano, Vesuvius, and also enjoyed the fresh fruit, but the harbor, in his opinion, was a real mess, littered as it was with sunken ships. When his regiment took over the administration of the city, Owens and a small group of troopers were assigned to guard the city's reservoir. "They had five great vats of water, maybe 40 feet across, 100 feet long, and about 25 feet deep. You could see the water was crystal clear. We had one little hose, and the people would queue up and they would fight, but if we could get them to sing, they would not fight. The rear echelon came in and got things organized."

William Knickerbocker, one of the glider pilots of the 50th Squadron, 314th Group, 52nd Wing, was anxious to see action.

> Only one squadron beat us overseas. We went by way of Casablanca, and the one squadron that beat us there by three or four months came by way of Cairo.
>
> We arrived in Africa in 1943 after the surrender in Tunisia that May. The Germans had not surrendered when we left America. We landed in Casablanca and then we transferred to Bergent, and while there, we were sent to Oujda. The 82nd was there. I am not sure which regiment we worked with.[16] We trained with them for maybe a two-week course of combat training—obstacle course, ground training, but no gliders. We went back to Kairouan, Tunisia.
>
> We got into glider training there. We had those dirt fields where the planes took off and we couldn't see the tow plane because of the dust. We got in extremely valuable training in North Africa, which probably kept most of us alive through the war. Then we went down to the isle of Sejerua, and we spent several weeks there for night training. It was not the first night training, but the most intensive we had. It was 1943 in the summertime. We got in a lot of night training and went back to Kairouan, Tunisia. Then we hung around until after the invasion of Sicily. We were scheduled to go on that mission; we were going on D+1, but the navy shot down all of our ships, so we had no tow planes to get there and the mission was called off.[17] The invasion of Sicily was a British operation near Syracuse, and twenty American glider pilots went on that as instructors for the British on CG-4A.
>
> Then we moved to Sicily and our base Castel Trano, which was on the western plain of Sicily. We stayed there and trained for quite a while, then they started transferring us. I spent quite a bit of time at Gerbenia at the tip of Mount Etna. We trained there quite some time. I got a lot of C-47 time as copilot, flying supplies to British forces. Then we finally got back to our old outfit at Castel Trano. We had been making supply runs all the time to Palermo and North Africa and sometimes to Italy. After eight months in Sicily, we were put on boats and shipped to Scotland in early 1944.

Finally, the 325th Glider Infantry Regiment went into action, not in Sicily, but on the Italian mainland after Operation Avalanche in September 1943. These glider troops would not arrive in gliders, but ships. They did not see another glider until they reached England. As Gault recalls:

> On September 7, we moved by plane to near Gela, Sicily. We left there September 11 and landed [by ship] at Salerno, Italy. We moved from the beach into the mountains just beyond Albanella. The enemy was soon turned back, and we were pulled back to the beach where we had landed, loaded on LCTs, proceeded up the coast, and landed at Red Beach.
>
> We relieved the Rangers on San Angela Mountain. It was called the "Battle above the Clouds." We came down from the mountain and continued battle until the British

16. It was the 325th Gilder Infantry.

17. In actuality, only a few of the planes were shot down. The gliders were actually loaded with the personnel of the division headquarters and ready to go on D+2 when the 15th Army Group canceled all further air movements. They were finally transported in fifty-one aircraft on July 16.

One down, two to go: Cpl. Paul Janesk's jeep—named *Shortstop*—keeps track of Allied progress, Sicily, September 3, 1943. NATIONAL ARCHIVES

> reached us from the coast. We next moved by truck into Naples and set up the city government.

The aircraft and gliders did not fly without their ground support units, which had to be at the airfield once operations started, and which have been all but forgotten by posterity because they did not fight on the front lines. Sgt. James L. Newton, machinist in the 57th Service Squadron, 332nd Service Group, 12th Air Force, was one of the men whose role was just as vital as anyone else in winning the war. He had joined the army in November 1940 at age twenty and served with the 112th Cavalry at Forts Bliss and Clark until June 1941, when he transferred to the Air Corps.

> The 43rd Air Base Group (ABG) formed on January 15, 1941, at Hamilton Field, California. It was composed of the headquarters and HQ Squadron, the 44th Air Base Squadron, and the 57th Material Squadron. Officers and enlisted men were transferred from various squadrons of the 45th Air Base Group at Hamilton Field to the 43rd. On April 18, 1941, the 43rd ABG moved to Portland, Oregon. They were temporarily stationed at Vancouver Barracks, Washington, eight miles away. The 57th Service Squadron was formed as the 57th Material Squadron at Portland Air Base in the spring of 1941. An Air Corps service squadron was made up almost entirely of technicians necessary for the second-echelon maintenance of a tactical fighter or a strategic bomber outfit. The first-echelon maintenance was done by the crews in the bomb group, and that included periodic inspection, changing tires, armament work, and minor repairs. They were supposed to change their engines too, but our mechanics claimed that they waited until the plane came to the service squadron.
>
> As a member, I was an aircraft machinist, with the rank of staff sergeant. The second-echelon maintenance by the service squadron required making new or repairing anything that was broken off an aircraft or otherwise. This included machine work, sheet metal work, welding, electrical, parachute rigging, crash crew, paint shop, carpenter shop, and tech supply, which worked out of two semi trailers in which to stock aircraft parts. The third echelon, I suppose, was the depot group, with heavier and more permanent equipment. It was based at Algiers for a long time and finally moved to Naples [in late 1943 or early 1944].
>
> In the latter part of 1942, the 57th proceeded in two parts to Camp Kilmer, New

Jersey, and left Staten Island by troop convoy to arrive at Casablanca at different times. The second section, of which I was a member, left the U.S. on January 14, 1943, as part of a thirty-six-ship fast troop convoy. I was on the *Santa Rosa,* a converted Caribbean cruiser. The food was rotten. I mostly subsisted on oranges, Fig Newtons, and Hershey candy bars. We had men who volunteered for KP in the officers' mess just to bring leftover sandwiches down to us in the hold. The trip lasted about eleven days and was almost uneventful. There was a bad storm one night. On another night, our ship came very close to colliding with the cruiser. One of us zigged when we should have zagged.

After landing at Casablanca on January 25, 1943, and spending a few nights on the beach, we moved by train to Fez and arrived on February 1. On that field, the 27th Fighter Bomber Group, which the 57th was to service, took delivery of about ninety-five A-36s. On June 14, when the transition was over, we moved up to South Korba at Cape Bon, Tunisia, arriving on June 22. On July 29, we arrived in Gela, Sicily, by LST. On September 5, we departed for San Antonio, near Barcelona, Sicily. After Operation Avalanche, on September 22, we landed on a beach near Battipaglia by LST and moved down to Paestum, below Salerno, near the Temple of Neptune.

Newton's squadron remained in that area for several months, until it moved to another airfield at Pomigliano, near Naples, on January 21, 1944.

Second Lt. Lyle A. Foutz, a copilot on a C-47 with the 47th Troop Carrier (TC) Squadron, 313th TC Group, enlisted at age twenty-one in March 1942 and trained as a pilot. His TC group, formed in 1942, moved to North Africa in April and May 1943 to prepare for Operation Husky. His squadron took the southern way, flying from Florida to Puerto Rico, British Guiana, Brazil (Belem to Natal), Asuncion Island, Liberia, Dakar, and finally Marrakech. At Asuncion, he comments, you could sit at one end of the runway and not be able to see the other.

We arrived the day the North African campaign ended. We landed at Marrakech and then flew to Casablanca and up to Oran. The main ground forces were shipped in. They had the big derricks with which we could lift and change an engine. We could only do minor repairs until they came. We did have a mobile unit we could take off in the aircraft. That included 400-gallon tanks in the fuselage. They were fiberglass. We put in all our personal belongings. You could get eight of them in—that is what they used when they flew nonstop to Hawaii. We had an extreme maximum of about fourteen hours if we were careful with our engines. The normal crew was a pilot, copilot, crew chief, and radioman. The flight leader would carry a navigator.

From Oran back to a French Foreign Legion base called Oujda. We spent a month there and moved to the south of Tunis at a city called Kairouan. We spent one or two months there. From there we moved to Sicily [on August 23], outside of a city in the clouds—forgot the name—and the airport of Trapani. We had already made the Sicilian drop in July and flew to this base in Sicily in August when the island was secure. We flew a transport service then, evacuated the wounded [from Italy] back to the interior sections of Sicily—a hospital at Palermo—or North Africa in August when the island was secure. We spent the winter doing that.

T. Sgt. John W. Birchman signed up right after Pearl Harbor, but he was not inducted until a month later in Wisconsin. He flew with the same pilot, Lt. Fred Fischer, in the same plane, #227 Lady Katy, from West Palm Beach to Europe until the end of the war.

> I had the opportunity—and I enjoyed it very much—to haul the wounded back from Sicily to Algiers. We were then stationed in Algiers. We had fifty-four litters. We brought these people right from the front. The nurses were onboard, treating them until we could get them back to the hospital. I can't tell you how many men I bandaged and helped with parts missing. It was really something. We did this for a good month and a half.
>
> I had an experience I will never forget. We were at the field hospital, ready to load, when the head nurse came out giving orders. She turned to me and said, "John Birchman!" and I said, "Loretta Glen!" She was from my hometown, we went to high school together, and she was in charge of the wounded. We didn't have time to visit, because these people were right from the front, bleeding and everything.

The Coast Guard at War

In addition to its regular duties in the United States, the Coast Guard augmented the American naval forces. It was placed under navy control for better coordination. Coast Guard crews manned the transports *Joseph Dickman, Bayfield,* and *Samuel Chase,* as well as other vessels of various sizes used in amphibious operations.

Coast Guard LCI(L) Flotilla 10 (redesignated Flotilla 4 in England later in the war), consisting of twenty-four LCIs built and commissioned late in 1942 at Orange, Texas, was formed in 1943 and placed under the command of Capt. Myles Imlay.[18] The flotilla was divided into Group 7 under Commander Bresnan and Group 8 under Commander Unger.

Each LCI, 158 feet long, 23 feet beam, and with a 3½-foot draft, was powered by two sets of GM diesel engines that gave it a speed of twelve to fifteen knots. With a crew of twenty-five, it had a capacity of 190 men or 75 tons of cargo. Its armament consisted of four 20-millimeter guns. Instead of ramps, it had two gangways, one on each side of the bow, that lowered when the vessel was beached. The crew dropped an anchor before beaching and pulled the vessel back off the beach with an anchor winch located at the stern.

When Flotilla 10 traveled from Texas to Florida in February 1943, many of its sailors succumbed to seasickness during their rough ride on the flat-bottomed craft. That's when they decided that LCI stood for "lousy civilian idea." The flotilla went on to Norfolk, where it arrived in March. Before sailing for North Africa at the end of the month via Bermuda, its men practiced landing operations. The flotilla arrived at Port Lyautey on April 10, 1943, and proceeded along the African coast to Tunis, stopping at most of the major ports.

The LCIs that took part in the landings on July 9, 1943, in Sicily suffered only light damage from machine guns at Licata. Some of the LCIs moved into the harbor on July 22, when Palermo fell, and later carried troops on flanking operations on the northern coast of Sicily. On September 7, the flotilla's LCIs picked up troops in Tunisia and sailed for the landings at Salerno from Bizerte. Troops of the 36th Division disembarked near Paestum; later, some of the LCIs were sent to evacuate British soldiers.

Leon C. Rodriguez, ship's cook on LCI 323, had joined the Coast Guard when he was twenty years old. After ninety days of training, he was assigned to his LCI in Galveston. He got his sea

18. Flotilla 10 included LCI numbers 83-96, 319-26, and 349-50.

legs during his first week at sea on the flat-bottom boat in rough weather. Since he was the cook, he spent most of his time belowdecks.

> At Bizerte, we had two or three air raids a night. The first time, it seemed like a dream. The searchlights would go on. There was a little town called Ferryville, and when the lights went off, it meant it was an air raid. At night, the aircraft would attack the ships in the harbor, and you would hear the pom-pom guns. We wouldn't fire unless the aircraft was close. One night, a bomb hit one of the LCIs, and I saw when it hit that the LCI just went down like that. We tuned in on Axis Sally, and they would play good music and then report 115,000 tons of Allied shipping sunk at Bizerte, when all that was sunk was the 150-foot-long LCI.
>
> We participated in the invasion of Sicily by landing troops in Licata. We went back and forth to reinforce the troops from the African ports. After that, we went into the Salerno beachhead. We were in the initial landing at Salerno. That is when we were shelled by a German Tiger tank that left a hole in our conning tower. We had landed our troops and were taking on the wounded when this tank started shelling, and luckily, we had only one hole. There were probably seven shells fired at us that day. That night, when we were tied up, an aircraft came over and dropped bombs on us. We had general quarters—the claxon sounded. The bombs landed on both sides of the ship, and that is as close as we came to being sunk.

After its operations in Italy, the LCI flotilla sailed for England, with a stop in Gibraltar that October. It was followed by the divisions and naval units that were to participate in Operation Overlord.

CHAPTER 14

The Buildup in Great Britain

As the chill of approaching winter set in, the American divisions from the sunny Mediterranean front started disembarking in Great Britain during November and early December. The first to arrive was the 1st Infantry Division, which returned to Britain on November 11, 1943, after having participated in the invasions of North Africa and Sicily. The "Big Red One," like the other divisions that followed it, took on replacements after it set foot in England.

One of these replacements, Roger L. Brugger of Toledo, Ohio, had been drafted in March or April 1943. At the end of the fourth week of basic training, he had come down with scarlet fever and was hospitalized. After thirty days of quarantine, he reported for duty and had to start his training all over again in October. Not long after that, he was on his way to New Jersey to embark for overseas duty.

The ship left at dusk, and as we came down the Hudson River, we could see the Statue of Liberty. The next morning, we were in the convoy, which consisted of 150 ships. We had Canadian corvettes and a small aircraft carrier to guard the convoy. We were at sea fifteen days and had submarine scares where we fell out on deck with our life jackets. One of these scares turned out to be whales when they came up between a row of ships.

The ship I was on was a British refrigerator ship built in 1912 to haul meat from Australia to the British Isles. It was my first experience with British cuisine. We were served porridge, herring, and corned beef. We had 200 infantry and 200 artillery replacements with about 20 officers aboard. We arrived at Liverpool, England, on December 4, 1943, and went on to a replacement

Cpl. Carroll Johnson and PFC Carroll Davis work in the machine shop of the 829th Engineer Construction Company near Eye, England, March 1943. NATIONAL ARCHIVES

Private Brugger was assigned to the 16th Infantry, 1st Division. Although he had trained as a mechanic, he became a rifleman because the 1st, like most of the veteran divisions, was short on them.

On November 14, the 2nd Armored Division, relieved from its task of garrisoning Sicily, loaded its men on ships and sailed from the Mediterranean. On November 25, Thanksgiving Day, many of its men, who thought they were returning to the States, were sorely disappointed when they sighted Liverpool instead and moved to Tidworth Barracks. The 9th Infantry Division also landed in England on the same day.

Among the men of the 9th "Varsity" Division who embarked at Palermo, Sicily, was Herbert U. Stern, serving with the 9th Medical Battalion.[2] He made the trip from the Mediterranean to England aboard the former cruise ship *Kungsholm,* now the infamous *Strathnaver,* which broke down as it ferried part of the 101st A/B Division from the United States to England. The trip was largely uneventful, but Stern and many of the other passengers spent most of the time in sick bay, stricken with malaria, jaundice, or influenza. They landed on Thanksgiving night on the Liverpool docks, which showed signs of bomb damage. The following evening, they boarded a train bound for Winchester, around which their camps were located.

The 743rd Tank Battalion and the 70th Tank Battalion, which were to play a key role in the upcoming invasion, arrived in Britain before the end of November 1943. The 743rd came from the States and the battle-scarred 70th from the

2. Later the 9th Division earned the nickname "Hitler's Nemesis."

Floyd West's Odyssey

Floyd West of Portia, Arkansas, volunteered at age twenty-two. He was sworn in on January 27, 1942, and joined up so he could get into the Quartermaster Corps. After being sworn in at Camp Robinson, Arkansas, he took the train for Camp Lee in Virginia, where he trained for eight weeks, four of which he spent in a workshop. Finally, while he was posted at Fort Hamilton in Brooklyn, he volunteered to do odd jobs in New York and spent a great deal of time downtown, a luxury most of the soldiers bound for overseas never got to enjoy.

> It wasn't but a few days until I was called. We got on the trucks, went down to the railway station, loaded on a train, and we were shipped to Boston.

In April 1942, after having spent fewer than three months in the service, two months of those in training, West shipped out on a small ship named the USS *Stratford*.[1] His ship joined a convoy of about fifty-five ships and sailed for Iceland after many alerts and scares. Finally the ship docked at Reykjavik in early May. Floyd describes his first encounter in the Far North:

> I was up on deck and I hollered at a sentry over on shore because we were docked. Iceland has deep sea where a ship can drive right up to the dock and unload. I hollered at this sentry and asked where everyone was, and he said it was midnight, even though the sun was shining. So I went back to my cot and went to sleep. We unloaded the next morning. I was assigned to a quartermaster camp. It was called Camp Whitehorse, north of Reykjavik at a town called Alafos. I began to inquire about

1. The USS *Stratford* was built in 1918 and taken over by the navy in the summer of 1941. It was a small single-stacker with a couple gun tubs for defense. In November 1941, designated AP-41, this transport sailed to Iceland, where it remained until it returned to the United States in March. This transport could carry about 300 troops. Floyd West was on its last voyage to Europe before it moved into the Pacific via the Panama Canal.

Mediterranean. Company A of the 70th, the only company of the battalion to take part in the Tunisian campaign, traveled separately from the rest of the battalion.[3] The battalion headquarters did not sail for North Africa to join the companies until January 1943. After the headquarters' arrival, the battalion trained the French with the M5 light tank (the final version of the M3 Stuart tank) and later trained at Arzew and took part in the Sicilian campaign. "We remained in Sicily until transportation was made available to move us with other troops to England in November," recalls Sgt. Glenn E. Gibson. For T/4 Charles J. Myers from Baltimore, a member of the headquarters, who had been drafted in December 1940 and had been with the battalion when it became the 70th in 1941, the trip from Sicily to England was memorable.

3. The same happened for the North African invasion, when Company A was sent to join the convoy from Great Britain destined to invade Algiers. The other companies of the battalion sailed for Morocco.

Floyd West's Odyssey *continued*

the people that had left me, [the comrades who had sailed before him] and the best information I got was that the ship had been torpedoed, and sunk, and everyone was lost. I spent the next eight months in Camp Whitehorse.

In November 1943, I was put on the ship the *Empress of Russia.* It was manned by a British crew. We spent about six days crossing to the United Kingdom. We were unloaded at Glasgow, Scotland. I was loaded onto a troop transport train, and we went to the 5th Replacement Center between Birmingham and London.

We had not been there long when I was called out because of the fact that I had been experienced in wiring houses before I went into the service, and electricians were needed to finish some wiring at some of the air bases. I was assigned to a company in London, the Electrolite Company, and I had a civilian boss. There were seven of us in this detail, and our highest-ranking man was a staff sergeant—I was a corporal at that time. We were assigned with this civilian group to help them do whatever they saw fit for us to do. Some of my crew wired lights on runways, but my job was wiring barracks and offices. I worked at that and really enjoyed it because I had much freedom and a permanent pass. I could go to London or Birmingham or anywhere I liked, as long as I reported for duty at the work hour the next morning. I could eat anywhere I liked, and I found that the best place to eat was at the U.S. Army mess hall. We would buy fish and chips, and we enjoyed going to the pub, but I never was a drinker.

After spending several months on this assignment, Corporal West returned to the 5th Replacement Center, where he was handed an M-1 carbine and put on a train to Southampton early in June 1944 after the invasion.

On November 11, 1943, we loaded personnel and personal equipment on the USAT *Monterey,* one of the best troop transports in the service. It had been a ship of the Matsun Line before the war and served the Orient. Its speed was in excess of 22 knots. Our ordnance was left in Sicily for shipment to the new war front in Italy.

The convoy that we were to travel with departed Palermo early in the morning of the day we loaded. The *Monterey,* a fast ship considered capable of outrunning U-boats, departed from the same port some ten hours later. By midmorning of the twelfth, we had caught up with the convoy, and the ship assumed her assigned spot in the convoy. We passed through Gibraltar and into the Atlantic and continued sailing in a westerly direction for five days. We were sure that after combat in Africa and Sicily, we were returning to the States. However, upon arising on the eighth day of our trip, the sun rose on the bow of the ship. Sometime during the night, the ship had changed

> course, and we were sailing towards the east. I understand we were within fifteen hours of the Bermuda Islands when the change occurred. Some seven days later, and a few alerts with the sound of depth charges exploding, we docked in Liverpool. We were stationed at Ogbourne St. George, where we finally received the equipment that a medium tank unit should have. In Africa and Sicily, we used light tanks.

By the end of December 1943, most all of the major units that would spearhead the invasion had arrived in Great Britain. On December 9, two key veteran units from the campaigns in the Mediterranean, the 82nd A/B Division and 1st ESB, disembarked. Both had arrived in Africa after the invasion and had performed mostly noncombat service, but both had taken part in the invasions of Sicily and Salerno.

The 82nd A/B Division left behind its 504th PIR, which continued fighting on the Italian front until April 1944, when it rejoined the division in England shortly before the invasion. Except for a handful of volunteers, however, its war-weary veterans sat out the next invasion. The bulk of the 82nd sailed from the Mediterranean in late November. At 6 P.M. on November 19, 1943, PFC Clinton Riddle and his regiment, the 325th Glider Infantry, boarded the APA-90, *James O'Hara,* bound for Belfast, Northern Ireland, in the Naples Harbor. It carried about 2,000 on this trip, which should have been the entire regiment plus some other troops. The ship was not as crowded as the *Santa Rosa,* which had carried about 2,000 men of the regiment to Casablanca months before. The trip to Ireland was delayed several days, because the ship pulled into Oran to await the arrival of the convoy on November 30. The troops arrived in Belfast on December 9. According to Sgt. Harold Owens, the trip was rough until they cleared the Mediterranean.

> They called us out at six o'clock in the morning, but the ships were not going to be ready until ten o'clock. They told us to fall out and reassemble at 9:30 A.M.. The fellows fell out and drank all the *vino* they could. We went down to the harbor and went out to the ship in LCVPs. There were rope ladders on which we climbed up the side of the ship. Some of the fellows were drunk, so we had to push them in and throw in their sea bags. We finally got loaded up.
>
> The German army was a lousy army; they were all full of lice. The lice were so big that they looked a half inch long. We would use their blankets and got the lice off their blankets. We are on this naval transport, and the commander of the ship never had lice on his ship, so they used DDT on everybody. I had run a fever, so I was in the sick bay, but I didn't mind because I had a bathtub.
>
> We stopped in Oran and spent Thanksgiving Day on the ship. We went to the Rock of Gibraltar and we had an air attack and submarine attack going through the strait. We got out to the open sea, and everything was fine then. We landed at Belfast, Northern Ireland, and a lot of the guys were amazed that they spoke English.

Lt. Harold Shebeck of the 325th Glider Infantry was in a special detachment that left ahead of the division. Like many of his men, he fell ill.

> Around the first of November, I began to realize that I was failing physically, losing weight, and very fatigued much of the time. Medical examination could not seem to detect what was wrong. On about November 9, our detachment left on a French ship for Algiers, from where it was expected that

we would eventually be sent to England to prepare for the cross-Channel invasion of Europe now expected in 1944. The rest of the 82nd would follow directly from Italy. During the trip from Sicily to Algiers, I was in sick bay on the ship and was being fed intravenously.

When we landed in Algiers, I was discharged to duty, and our detachment moved to a nearby replacement center. I had now reached the point where it was difficult for me to walk. I was sitting on the floor in a pyramidal tent, leaning against the center pole, when I saw an officer coming down the company street that had been a medical officer in the 325th Glider Regiment but had been transferred out before we left the States. As he came by the tent, I hailed him, and we renewed old acquaintances. He said that he had come overseas as a replacement and expected to be assigned to a unit soon. I told him about my physical condition, and after a quick cursory examination, he said I had hepatitis and I should be hospitalized at once. He told me to have my gear at the head of the company street, and he would have an ambulance there in fifteen minutes. I never saw this man again, but I was always grateful for this chance encounter with him. I felt extremely relieved, because I felt that with hospitalization, I should be able to start regaining my normal physical condition. Little did I realize that it would be nearly four months before I was discharged to duty. Hepatitis was now a serious problem in North Africa and especially among people who had spent time in Sicily.

The ambulance arrived, and I was taken to the 79th Station Hospital, a 500-bed tent hospital a few miles from Algiers. I arrived there on a Sunday early in November and was to remain there till January 1, 1943. With cleaner living conditions, better food, and routine medical care, I began to improve, but a persistent temperature kept me hospitalized. One morning, I woke up and the pillowcase was soaked with blood from a nosebleed that I had during the night. My doctor could not seem to diagnose what was causing my condition, and I finally went before a panel of doctors who questioned and interviewed me. These boards were meeting nearly every day to discuss cases of unusual development. A few days after Christmas, my doctor told me that I was to be evacuated to a general hospital on a hospital train leaving for Oran.

I well remember the scene at the Algiers railroad station the day we left. There must have been about fifteen hospital cars with red crosses painted all over the sides and tops. About half of the patients were litter patients who had been brought by ambulance to the station from various medical facilities around Algiers. The rest were ambulatory patients, as I was, and we were able to take care of ourselves. There were two-tier bunks in each car, and it took two days and one night to cover approximately 225 miles to Oran. I still remember one of the nurses who came into our car with a flashlight during the night and how she had to step gingerly over the couplings of the swaying cars, when one careless step could have meant her death.

There was a large hospital complex near Oran consisting of three general hospitals and two station hospitals, all of which occupied many acres. The general hospitals were 1,000-bed hospitals, and I was sent to the 43rd General Hospital. Italian prisoners were used at this installation as orderlies and general all-around workers. They were pleased to be out of the war and especially enjoyed the amount of food available for them. At this time, these people were referred to as cobelligerents, as the Allies did not refer to them as prisoners after Italy surrendered.

Early in February, my doctor told me that I would have a tonsillectomy, and sometime during the latter part of February, this was accomplished. I had the surgery while sitting in a large wooden chair, which had been made out of various boards.

On February 29, 1944, I was finally discharged from the hospital, and I started the long road through replacement centers to rejoin the 82nd in England. Some units were already en route, and others were in various stages of making the move from Italy. My first move from Algiers was to Mateur, Tunisia, to the 5th Army Replacement Depot. I was the train commander, and the train carried about 350 men and 16 officers. Every troop train had to carry a medical officer. It was now early March, and a day or two before we left, he [the medical officer] had just received his Christmas presents from home, which nearly filled a barracks bag. Practically all the packages were from his wife, and most of them were worthless as far as he was concerned. For instance, she had sent him several pairs of silk red, white, and blue socks. He could really use none of the clothing she sent him, and with each package he opened, he expounded in great detail about the stupidity of his wife. He did not know what to do with all these articles. I told him to sell it to the Arabs. Whenever the train stopped, which was often, it seemed as though there were at least a dozen Arabs clamoring around each car door bartering or trading, usually melons or dates. They seemed to rise up from nowhere. Our medical officer disposed of most of his unwanted presents over the course of many miles, ending up with the equivalent of a few hundred dollars in American money.

After a few weeks at this depot, I received orders to travel back to Algiers to await transportation to England. Around April 1, I boarded an English ship bound for Glasgow, Scotland, which carried about 3,000 passengers who were practically all British. There were a few French troops aboard and possibly 300 Americans, mostly "casuals," like myself, who were traveling independently and were from many different organizations heading for England to rejoin their units, as most had been discharged from hospitals.

There was an ENSA [Entertainments National Service Association] troop aboard, which was the British equivalent of the American USO. This group of entertainers was returning to England after touring British installations all over the world. We were fortunate to have them aboard, as they provided entertainment for us nightly. I roomed in a small cabin with a British naval officer who had been stationed at the British naval base at Alexandria, Egypt, since 1940 and had not had a leave in four years. I remember yet the excitement aboard as we neared Scotland and how I, personally, was so glad to see the green fields after the sand and heat of North Africa. Most of the people aboard were British, and they lined the rails and, with tears in their eyes, sang, "Sailing up the Clyde," a song that appeared familiar to them all. We docked at Greenock on the Clyde River about fifteen miles from the city of Glasgow. An American troop train was at the dock, to which the American troops were directed.

Harold Shebeck reached Great Britain and rejoined his division and regiment less than two months before the cross-Channel invasion.

The 82nd A/B Division received reinforcements a month after it arrived in Northern Ireland. The 507th PIR, formed in July 1942, had transferred to different posts in the States until it finally shipped out for England from New York on December 5, 1943. In January 1944, this regiment and the newly arrived 508th PIR were attached to the 82nd A/B Division. The 508th PIR, created in October 1942 at Camp Blanding, was the last regiment-size airborne unit to leave the United States for Great Britain before the invasion. Before leaving Camp Shanks, its men were allowed into New York City without their wings, insignia, or bloused jump boots to maintain the cloak of secrecy regarding troop movements.

The men of the 507th PIR boarded the USAT *James Parker* and joined a convoy led by the battleship *Texas* and three aircraft carriers. Maj. David Thomas, the 508th's regimental surgeon, who had separated from the 505th PIR in the United States after he broke a leg landing in a tree before the regiment sailed to Africa, was kept busy.

> The *Parker* was a converted cruise ship from the Panama cruise trade. For the officers, it was high-class living, but for the men, it wasn't. They were sleeping in double-decker bunks, and they only got two meals a day. We had one officer, a big fellow named Jack Shannon, who was the most rugged man you ever saw. He got so seasick we had to keep him in fluids intravenously for most of the trip. We also had a kid by the name of Mann; I think his first name was Robert. He got appendicitis, and we had to operate on shipboard. He got killed in Normandy.

After the 507th PIR disembarked in Northern Ireland, it joined up with the 82nd A/B Division. The 101st A/B Division was also augmented by receiving the 501st PIR. The 82nd continued to take on replacements in the months that followed. The experience varied widely for the men, who arrived in Britain unassigned and reported to replacement centers. For Pvt. Richard D. Weese from Madison, Maine, who was nineteen years old when he was drafted on February 25, 1943, the trans-Atlantic crossing was trying.

> In January 1944, I departed Boston, Massachusetts, for England, and it was very cold. We slept on the deck until the mess hall cleared, and then slept in there until 3 A.M. Then back on deck. The ship was overcrowded. We were in a convoy with three destroyer escorts. After eleven days aboard ship, one morning we were dead in the water, the convoy gone and one destroyer with us. By noon we were again moving and arrived in Southampton in the middle of the day.
>
> We boarded a train that took us to a replacement depot near London. I volunteered for the 82nd Airborne while there (one week). Seven of us were approved for transfer to the 82nd at Leicester, to the 325th Glider Infantry. I took glider and parachute training at the Cottesmore Air Base in March and April 1944.

The 82nd and 101st Airborne Divisions trained volunteers in England because there was a shortage of airborne replacements arriving from the States.

PFC James D. Purifoy, who arrived in February, was also a replacement. He had served in the 542nd PIR of the 13th A/B Division until the end of 1943, when it was decided to break up one of the regiment's battalions in order to supply the units already in Great Britain with replacements.

Men of the 1st Tank Group play Santa for local children in England, December 1942. NATIONAL ARCHIVES

We all left as replacements and went on the same ship. After we left Camp Mackall, we went to Fort Meade, Maryland, for three weeks waiting for embarkation, then to Camp Patrick Henry, Virginia, a little camp in the swamps. From there we went to Newport News, Virginia, and boarded a ship in February. It was a British ship built as a Kaiser Liberty ship. The ship had one cannon up front. We sailed from Newport News to Newfoundland, where we were supposed to meet a convoy. We went all the way to Northern Ireland with a small aircraft carrier and three sub chasers.

The meals were terrible, and my quarters were down in the fourth deck. They had something like hammocks of canvas with a metal frame around them. Back then, you could sleep anywhere, so we adapted. They were stacked about four or five high, and you always tried to get on the top. Before we were out of sight of Newport News, I went up on top of the ship. The ship started going up and down, and I threw up. I immediately went back to my bunk. Every time I got out of it, I got sick. I didn't eat very much going over that whole eleven days. Usually for breakfast, they fed us hot dogs and cabbage. They didn't give lunch. I usually skipped dinner because I would get sick. Some of the guys found their way into the food stores, and they came out of there with a lot of crackers, tomato juice, and fruit.[4] They never fed us that on the ship. The guys who took it out would open a big gallon can of fruit cocktail and tomato juice. The stuff they fed us had a lot of grease, and that was bad for seasickness. The crew was used to it.

The waves were as big as mountains. One time we had a sub alert, and the little sub chasers—you could see the smoke boiling out of them—would run around there and drop depth charges. Then we broke down, a propeller or something. I think it took twelve hours to repair. They stayed with us. The aircraft carrier pulled up as close as they could while the sub chasers circled around and around; then we headed on to Northern Ireland.

They put us on some little trains. We stayed in a little camp. We didn't get many sheets in the U.S., because they said they had been sent overseas. Here they gave us a mattress cover, and they told us to get some hay and make a mattress. We used our overcoats for pillows. We were there for twenty-one days. We didn't do anything. Then we crossed on a boat to Scotland and took a train to Newbury, England, to join the 101st.

4. Purifoy's account indicates that although the transports carried stocks of crackers, juice, and fruit, the cooks on the British ships did not serve them to the American enlisted personnel on most voyages.

The 1st ESB, which returned to Great Britain at the same time as the 82nd A/B Division, was short of personnel and did not embark with all its attached units. In some respects, it was a skeleton unit. In England, the brigade took on replacements, reorganized, and acquired some new units.

Newly promoted Capt. David D. Moore returned to England at the head of Company A of the 361st Quartermaster Battalion, redesignated the 478th Amphibian Truck Company in December 1943. They traveled on the APA 13 *Joseph T. Dickman* (AP 26 had been redesignated APA 13 in February 1943), a troop transport manned by the Coast Guard. Colonel Caffee, the commander of the 1st ESB, extracted his unit from Italy against the wishes of the 5th Army commander, who wanted to keep it for future operations. Captain Moore noted that the colonel was displeased by the reorganization of his unit when they reached England.

> On return to England, the battalion was stationed at Budleigh-Salteron, a small resort village on the English Channel, just east of Exmoor in Devon. ETOUSA [European theater of operations, U.S. Army] started to send my company gasoline supply equipment and trucks to Company C. Colonel Caffee almost had a stroke! He informed ETOUSA in no uncertain terms that he had not gone to the trouble to get us out of Italy for those purposes. The upshot of the matter was the War Department changed our designations to reflect our scheduled operations for the invasion. The 361st Quartermaster Battalion was changed as follows:
>
> Hq & Hq Co. became the 24th Amphibian Truck Bn.
>
> Co. A became the 478th Amphibian Truck Co.
>
> Co. C became the 479th Amphibian Truck Co.
>
> In January 1944, these units were moved from the central heated quarters in Budleigh-Salteron to make space for the 4th Division units that had just arrived. We were relocated in a field camp under construction in an abandoned copper mine near St. Austell, Cornwall. We arrived and had to pitch our tents in the middle of a sleet storm!

John A. Perry of Johnstown, Pennsylvania, who was drafted in May 1943, served with the 462nd Amphibian Truck Company. He had completed his basic training at Fort Lee, Virginia, where he was trained as a truck driver in the Quartermaster Corps. When he arrived in England in early 1944 as a replacement, the men in his group were assigned to the 462nd and notified that they would be driving a new type of truck, an amphibian truck called "Duck," the DUKW. His company joined with the 478th and 479th Amphibian Truck Companies to form the 24th Amphibian Truck Battalion of the 1st ESB.

In September 1942, twenty-two-year-old Sgt. Stanley R. Stout from Mount Vernon, Illinois, enlisted in the army. After basic training, he joined the 557th QM Company when it formed at Camp Breckenridge, Kentucky, where the company trained in quartermaster operations and demolitions. Most of the men in the company could not fathom why they had to train in demolitions. When Sergeant Stout and his men arrived in England in August 1943, they continued the training they had started in Kentucky, but with the addition of mine detection this time. The 1st ESB took over control of the company in January 1944.

The 1st ESB and 1116th Engineer Combat Group (later redesignated the 6th ESB), fresh from training in the United States, disembarked in England in December 1943. The 6th and 5th ESBs fell under the command of a larger provisional engineer group, because they were slated

V Mail

To send V mail, the servicemember first wrote his letter on a form. Once mailed, it passed through a censor, who stamped it. Next, the page was photographed and put on microfilm. Then it was shipped by sea to the United States, where copies were made from the microfilm at a fraction of the original size and sent the addressee. Families and friends also used V mail to write to those serving overseas. The following is a letter dated April 4, 1944, that John McBurney sent by V mail to his wife back home in the States:

My Darling;

I have arrived safely after an uneventful trip and am now in Northern Ireland. When you write, please use V-mail, and address me as follows till further notice:

Pfc. John B. McBurney (38487336)
Co. M To Postmaster,
New York, New York

Darling, never in my life have I loved you as much as I do now. Remember that you are my whole life, and keep the home fires burning.

I hope that Donnie and you are all right and happy. I love you both so much. I wish I could have seen you before I left the states. Nine months is a long time, and of course, now it will be longer. Keep your chin up. Baby. I will be back. Kiss Donnie and tell the folks Hello.

All the love in world

to operate on Omaha Beach, while the 1st ESB was destined for Utah Beach.

The 8th "Golden Arrow" Infantry Division, the last major American formation to reach England in 1943, departed from New York on December 5. The 1st and 3rd Battalions of the 13th Regiment sailed on the French liner SS *Athos II,* and the 2nd Battalion on the smaller army transport USAT *Excelsior,* a C-3 type freighter, larger than a Liberty ship (a C-2), that weighed 7,600 tons and could carry more than 2,100 troops. Pvt. John F. Troy was on the *Excelsior.*

> We boarded an army transport on December 5. We were in convoy eleven days. That eleven-day trip was unusually rough! I saw men who were 200-pounders drop 15 or 20 pounds because of seasickness. We arrived in Belfast Harbor on about December 17. We left Belfast for our camp in Enniskellen, Northern Ireland, where we set up at some lord's estate, who turned it over to the U.S. Army. The 34th Division had been there before us and gone on to North Africa. We lived in corrugated tin huts called Nissen huts, one platoon to each hut.

John McBurney from Jennings, Louisiana, was drafted in 1943 and underwent basic training at Camp Adair, Oregon, before he was assigned to the 70th "Trailblazer" Division. He was taught everything he needed to know for warfare in the Pacific. In addition to jungle warfare training, he was instructed in recognition of Japanese aircraft. In due time, he became a mortar squad leader in the weapons platoon. He allowed each of his men to go on leave, putting off his own turn until last. To his chagrin, however, he never got the opportunity to visit his wife and child.

> The lieutenant of our platoon was something of a nut. He and the company

Liberty and Victory Ships

Early in the war, when Great Britain faced Germany with no allies at its side, German U-boats sank merchant ships at an alarming rate. To remedy the shortage of ships thus created, the United States designed a ship that could be built quickly with prefabricated parts. The Maritime Commission, created by Congress in 1936, created the EC-2 (emergency cargo, and the number 2 for medium) type, which became known as the Liberty ship and was dubbed the "Ugly Duckling" by President Franklin D. Roosevelt.

Prefabricated parts for Liberty ships were shipped from all over the country to about a dozen designated shipyards, where they were welded together in a matter of a few months. The first Liberty ship, the SS *Patrick Henry,* took 244 days to complete and was launched on September 27, 1941. Industrialist Henry Kaiser built the first of the Liberty ships and produced one-third of the 2,751 vessels built during the war. Kaiser's shipyards whittled the assembly time down to 72 days. By late 1943, that was further reduced to an average of 42 days.

The Liberty ship was slow, attaining a maximum speed of 11 knots, but it had a range of 17,000 miles and could carry a medium load in its five cargo holds. The ship measured 441 feet long and 57 feet wide and carried a merchant marine crew of thirty-eight to sixty-two men in addition to twenty-one to forty naval personnel, who served as its armed guard and handled communications. These ships were armed with a 4- or 5-inch stern gun, one 3-inch or two 37-millimeter bow guns, and/or six 20-millimeter machine guns to shoot at surfacing U-boats and finish off stragglers.

The faster and larger Victory ship, designated VC-2 type, was designed in 1943 to replace the slow Liberty ship. It took more time to build, with the first one completed in 102 days in February 1944. In June, one was completed in only 59 days. The Victory ship, at 455 feet long and 62 feet wide, was slightly larger than the Liberty ship. It also had five cargo holds and carried 4,555 net tons, compared with the Liberty's 4,380, but it was still classified as a medium-range vessel. Instead of steam engines, the Victory ship had a steam turbine, which gave it a speed of 15 to 17 knots, a significant advantage over the Liberty. Its crew was about the same, typically consisting of sixty-two merchant sailors and twenty-eight naval personnel for the armed guard. The ship's armament included a 5-inch stern gun, a 3-inch bow gun, and up to eight 20-millimeter machine guns. One other advantage over the Liberty was that the Victory was not rigid, so it did not have a tendency to break in half like the Liberty ship. The SS *United Victory* was the first of the type launched on January 12, 1944.

From 1939 until the end of the war, more than 2,700 Liberty, 531 Victory ships, 600 tankers, 500 cargo ships, and 1,000 other types of merchant ships were built in the United States. The *U.S. Army in World War II* series gives the following figures for wartime ship production: 475 standard cargo ships (C-1, C-2), 2,708 Liberty ships, 414 Victory ships, 11 passenger and cargo ships, 678 tanks, 602 minor commercial types, and 682 military types, for a total of 5,570 ships. The Liberty

continued

Liberty and Victory Ships ***continued***

ships represented almost half the total. A standard cargo ship of the C-2 type was estimated at taking a minimum of 113 days to build. The U.S. Maritime Commission, created in 1936, set the standards for rebuilding the merchant fleet and set the categories. The C-1 was the smallest type, with a speed of 14 knots and length of about 413 feet. The C-2 had a speed of 15.5 knots and lengths of up to 469 feet. The army operated 40 of the former and 43 of the latter in March 1945. The C-3 had a speed of 16.5 knots and a length up to 492 feet. The army operated 8 of these as cargo ships and 22 as troopships in March 1945. Two-thirds of the vessels operated by the army were Liberty ships, and 880 of the total 1,285 ships were used for cargo by March 1945.

The enemy sank 200 Liberty ships, and the total number of merchant sailors lost on all types of ships was 9,000. These prefabricated vessels served as cargo and troop transports, and it has been estimated that they carried 70 percent of all the supplies of World War II.

commander were at odds with each other—something to do about a girl or some such. One evening, he told me to keep my mortar squad in and not to fall out for retreat. He said to set our mortar up on the porch of our barracks, which we did. After we had the gun set up, he told me to aim for the captain. I could not believe this and so questioned the order. He said it was an order. I asked if he was sure that it was a direct order. He then insisted that it was and not to worry; he was not going to drop a mortar shell down the tube. I turned to my crew to verify they had heard that it was a direct order, which I had questioned. They answered in the affirmative, and so I said, "Set it up!" When the mortar was ready, and while I was watching like a hawk to be sure he did not indeed have a live round of ammunition, he pulled out the largest firecracker I had ever seen. Just as the bugle was blowing and the flag coming down the staff, he lit the thing, dropped it down the tube, and followed it up with an orange. The thing went off, our aim was good—he must have studied his ballistics correctly. The orange flew out of the mortar and landed right in front of the CO and splattered him good with orange juice.

With juice dripping from his face, the CO stood there at attention until retreat was over, then came charging over to our barracks stoop and yelled, "McBurney, you're up for a court-martial!" I replied, "No, I'm not. I was given an order by a superior officer. I questioned the order, then asked if it was a direct order, and then verified this with my gun crew to be absolutely certain I had heard correctly. The lieutenant also assured me no live ammunition was going to be fired." The CO looked at me like he was going to blow his stack, and then stalked off. That seemed to be the end of the event, but rather than getting my furlough to see my family, and also instead of getting my stripes as squad leader, I was on the next list to ship out as a replacement overseas. I don't remember just when this was; I just remember how angry I was for the way things turned out. Getting the corporal's stripes would have meant more money to be able to send home for my family. I made up my mind then and there that I would never be a squad leader again and would aim for the job of working the OP if given the opportunity. No one wanted this job, and consequently no one bothered you when you were back with the guns.

Thus in late March 1944, McBurney was sent to New York and assigned as a replacement destined for one of the units in Europe. As far as he was concerned, the trans-Atlantic trip was utterly disagreeable. He had missed out on his leave and left for Europe without getting a chance to see his wife and baby. In addition, he was less than impressed with his travel companions.

I would guess that most of these men were replacements and would not be surprised if many of them were goof-offs who had been weeded out of other outfits for some reason or another, or had gotten on someone's shit list as I had done. Before boarding, many of us were conned on the dock by a man representing himself as being authorized to collect money for flowers to be sent to our wives, as we were not able to do so. In fact, after giving him most of our money, none of the flowers reached our wives.

The ship was a veritable stink hole. It was a French vessel, and bunks were stacked five or six high. It appeared I was the only one in my area who did not get seasick, and of course, I kidded all those around me who were green and vomiting all over the place. It is a wonder that this did not get me done in. The moral to this is "always pick out the top bunk on a troopship."

It was a miserable trip. The few times we could go on deck were for exercise. When our time was up, some would manage to find a hiding place in a recess somewhere in order not to have to go back below. The relief of having a little fresh air and sunshine was balanced by the fear caused by all of the imaginary submarine periscopes we thought we saw in the breaking waves. I thought each wave cap was a periscope! We were a stinking mess when we landed in Belfast, as we were allotted only one or two saltwater showers on the trip.

Replacements and New Arrivals of 1944

Replacements for all units continued to flow into England at a higher rate during the first half of 1944, with the arrival of an increasing number of divisions. Pvt. Albert J. Bartelloni, a replacement for the 29th Division, which had been in England since the fall of 1942, had immigrated from Italy to the United States at the age of fourteen months. He received his draft notice at age eighteen, while still in high school, and graduated from an aviation trades school in New York City before going into active service. He was inducted at Queens on July 6, 1943, and as often happened in the army, this potential aviation mechanic was instead sent to infantry training. During basic training at Fort McClellan, Bartelloni received his naturalization papers making him an American citizen so that he could fight for his adoptive country. Not long after basic training, he received his orders for shipment overseas.

I departed from New York Harbor, December 1943, on the cruise ship *Ile de France,* which carried approximately 10,000 to 12,000 troops. We zigzagged across the Atlantic for thirteen days with no escort. I believe this ship could travel at 30 knots, pretty fast, but we had to zigzag, and it took

Soldiers build a steel hut in Northern Ireland, March 1942. NATIONAL ARCHIVES

four times as long to cross the Atlantic. We landed in Firth of Clyde, Scotland, in December 1943. The only problem I had on the trip across was very heavy seas, and I became very seasick till they gave me a small pill, which worked well, to my amazement. The food was terrible, but when you're seasick, all food tastes terrible. One thing that struck me funny is that after we had been on the ocean for two days, they announced we are going to get a short arm inspection!

After landing in Scotland, we took a train to a replacement depot somewhere in England. After four or five days, I was assigned to the 29th Division, 3rd Battalion, 175th Infantry as a scout.

Pvt. John E. McQuaid of Massachusetts went into active service about the same time as Bartelloni.

I joined the army reserve on February 24, 1943, at age seventeen—finished my junior year and was called to active duty in July 1943 at age eighteen. I was sent to Fort Devens, tested etc., and transferred to Camp Wheeler, Macon, Georgia, for basic training and radio operator schooling (Morse code and field radio). It's tough to say, but the radio training was terrible, especially the Morse code—eight hours a day in a booth with dots and dashes. Very few, if any, came out knowing what we were doing. The infantry training was tough but good. That I enjoyed.

When basic finished, we had a pass in review. The general came among the ranks and asked if we thought we were ready for action! All but one yelled, "Yes!"—that one stated the training was not enough to put him into action. He was taken away: we never saw him again. Now we got leave, home with a barracks bagful of pecans—Ha! Ha! Country boy!—then to Fort Meade for more training, until we were sent to Camp Shanks, New York. From there to the docks in New York City—marched aboard the fourth-biggest ship, *Ile de France*—11,000 men and 500 jeeps. This was January 1944—five days to cross the Atlantic—zigzagging all the way. You can't believe how sick most of us were—terrible! We landed in Scotland at the Wall of the Bay Pipes, marched to the train, and transferred to Southern England, Somerset County, to a number of replacements depots in the area.

From there McQuaid was assigned to the 116th Infantry, 29th Division. Neither Bartelloni nor McQuaid recalls the exact dates of departure and arrival; they may well have been on the same ship.

The buildup continued at a fast pace through the winter. The 4th "Breakthrough" Armored and 4th "Ivy" Infantry Divisions disembarked at the end of January. They were followed the next month by the 30th "Old Hickory" Infantry, 5th "Victory," and 6th "Super Sixth" Armored Divisions, which sailed in February and may have been in the largest single troop convoy of the war. In April, the 90th "Tough Hombres" landed, with the 79th "Cross of Lorraine" and 83rd "Thunderbolt" Infantry Divisions close on its heels. All the major elements for the upcoming campaign, as well as many smaller formations, were in position in Great Britain.

The troops that sailed in 1944 had a safer trans-Atlantic journey, as U-boats managed to sink fewer Allied ships. The men of the 4th Division left New York Harbor in the middle of January. The division's 22nd Infantry, 4th Medical, and 44th Field Artillery Battalions boarded the *Capetown Castle.* There were few alarms on the trip beyond the usual gripes about British food and crowded conditions. One of the passengers was PFC William C. Montgomery from Jefferson City, Missouri, who had been drafted in April 1943 at age eighteen and trained as a medical clerk for six months at Camp Barkeley at Abilene, Texas. In October, he went east to join the 4th Division at Camp Gordon Johnson, Florida, as the division was completing amphibious assault training. He was assigned as a litter bearer in Company A, 4th Medical Battalion, as the division moved north to Jackson, South Carolina, and later to Camp Kilmer for embarkation.

We left Camp Kilmer on a train in early January and arrived at what I recognized as a New York Harbor ferry terminal late at night. We filed onto a blacked-out ferry. One of my buddies asked, "Why are we standing in this hall?" Even though we could feel the engines throb and the ferry move, he had never seen such a thing and had no idea we were on a boat.

From the ferry, we went to a New York pier, a gigantic warehouselike building, and to gangplanks leading up to a ship we couldn't see. Red Cross women gave us coffee and doughnuts while we waited to board. They were angels.

Our ship was a large liner called *Capetown Castle,* formerly on the England-South Africa-India run.[5] It was manned by British merchant seamen, some of whom eked out their wages selling baths in otherwise unused

5. The *Capetown Castle* was a British 27,000-ton luxury liner built in 1938 and converted to a troopship in 1940.

passenger bathrooms. I don't remember that any of us took exception to this little racket.

We did, however, resent it at the end of the trip when they sold us postcards and photographs of the *Capetown Castle,* which were promptly confiscated "for security reasons" as we disembarked. We always believed the seamen got them back and sold them again on the next trip.

However, I didn't think they had it easy by any means. Typical of what they had to put up with involved the ship's grand staircase, which wound around an iron-caged elevator shaft in the center of the ship. The staircase was roped off and never used. But every evening, several of the seamen had to slavishly wash and rinse every step all the way down to God knows where. I saw one seaman suffering a loud dressing-down for not washing the staircase properly. I understood he was to be kicked out of the merchant marine and drafted into the army, a severe punishment in those days.

Our living quarters on the *Capetown Castle* had been the grand ballroom. Pipe bunks with canvas slings on rope lashings were built up to the ceiling, perhaps six or seven bunks high. We had to fight with our duffle bags and other gear for sleeping room on the narrow canvas.

During the eleven-day crossing, we were rousted out of the bunks each morning for breakfast, given time to go to the commissary when it was open, and mustered out on deck to stand a good part of the day for "boat drill." I think the real idea was to get us up and out of the incredible crowding, into the fresh air, and onto the broad decks, where discipline was easier to maintain.

Some of our people were so seasick they could not raise their heads and were left in their bunks. The rest of us, when we were at the bunks, played cards or gambled, cleaned weapons, sharpened knives, straightened gear, wrote letters, read, sang, or horsed around.

Among those we bunked with was an infantry I&R platoon, whose lieutenant taught them knife fighting on deck during the day. They kept their blades as sharp as razors. They took great pleasure in finding somebody asleep in his bunk before lights out—just a touch of one of those blades against the rope lacings, and the bunk unraveled instantly, dropping the occupant at least one bunk down.

We had two meals a day, and it took a long time to get each one. We lined up and waited on deck, then sat at long, picnic-style tables in a large room that had hammocks lashed out of the way against the ceiling. The last two men to sit down at the aisle end of the table had to get the food.

This was down one flight of ladderlike steel stairs to a large, hot, steamy galley. The stairs and steel floor were coated with a greasy condensation, so slick and treacherous that the British cooks and helpers propelled us along by grasping both our arms and pushing us like skaters.

The food the two men brought up to feed the twenty or so at their table was in large metal basins—perhaps fish and some kind of potatoes—and a big pitcher of a tepid drink. I thought the drink was a mixture of tea and coffee, with more tea in the mixture in the morning and more coffee in the evening.

The food situation was aggravated for me during the long, long boat drills, because my position on deck was right alongside the skylight looking down into the crew's galley. They had plenty of hot, fresh-looking food, apparently available on demand at any time, and coffee going constantly. I stood on the deck above them and fumed.

One of the Brits told me the way to avoid seasickness was never to stop eating. I couldn't eat much of the awful meals, so I bought a case of gingersnaps from the commissary and ate my way across the Atlantic. I still like gingersnaps.

It was midwinter, and the trip was fairly rough, but we were on a big ship. I remember looking at the destroyers on the edge of the convoy as they bobbed in and out of sight behind huge seas, wondering how you stayed alive on one of those tiny boats.

The roughest time was the final night at the end of the eleven-day trip. We anchored in the Irish Sea, probably waiting for port space somewhere. The ship pitched and rolled around violently. I thought it was going to roll completely over several times. Nobody had fallen out of the bunks during the entire crossing, but they did that night.

The next afternoon, we finally steamed into what turned out to be Liverpool. I was astonished to see the British dockworkers dressed in "everyday" clothes, with overcoats, ties, hats, and street shoes, many of them looking like officer clerks. In the United States, workers doing heavy work like handling ship's lines wore overalls, coveralls, or rough clothing that seemed to me more appropriate.

First Sgt. Vernon Donald Sherwood from White Plains, New York, who had been drafted in March 1941 at age twenty-five, and quickly worked his way through the ranks, also served in the 4th Medical Battalion with PFC Montgomery. "It was a rough trip, and many of our men became seasick," he recalls. The chow was terrible. Among other things, they served us ripe figs for every meal. Some of us were able to buy a decent meal from the crew at a good price. Outside of daily boat drills on the rolling decks, the trip was uneventful. The men spent much of the time in card and dice playing."

The 4th Division's 8th Infantry loaded onto a French liner, the *Franconia,* on January 17 or 18 for an eleven-day trip. According to PFC Harper Coleman, who, like Montgomery, had joined the division at Camp Gordon Johnson, the trip was largely uneventful.

All troops kept belowdecks when leaving the port, except for a few guards. Our company was part of the guard detail. I was on guard, top deck, as we went past the Statue of Liberty. After a short time, ships appeared from all sides.

The meals were typical English. One meal a day, as I recall: mutton, turnips, and hard bread, none of which was very appetizing. Our lieutenant kept us well supplied from the officer's exchange, which kept us from getting too hungry. Except for occasional depth charges, we had no problems, except the food was bad. The crossing was smooth, except for two or three days of rough seas when no one was allowed on deck. There was quite a bit of seasickness, although it never got to me. We learned later that this was one of the largest convoys to cross during the war.

PFC Raymond George Sluder from Asheville, North Carolina, was drafted in October 1942 at age twenty. Like Private Coleman, he was assigned to the 83rd Division at Camp Atterbury, Indiana, for basic training, and then transferred to the 22nd Infantry, 4th Division, in 1943. Here he was trained as a gunner on the 57-millimeter antitank gun and as a bazooka man. According to Sluder, during the crossing of the Atlantic, his unit ran into a severe winter storm, an event his companions apparently had forgotten about. Ralph Brazee from Connecticut, who was drafted a month after Sluder and also went through basic training with the 83rd at Camp Atterbury, was transferred in late November 1943 to the 22nd Infantry and became an antitank gunner. He kept a record of the sea journey with the regiment on the *Capetown Castle.*

> Jan 17, 1944, left Fort Dix late eve. Ferry from New Jersey to boat in N.Y. harbor. Red Cross had coffee and donuts. Departure midnight or later.
>
> We joined a convoy at sea on the 18th. I had a detail to clean up C Deck.
>
> 19th Foggy, I felt woozy.
>
> 20th Rougher still, feel rotten. My bunk (hammock) was third up from deck some place near rear of boat because later on we heard the screw (propeller) as it whirred when out of the water. The food was veal and very greasy so a number of us bought candy bars and ate them instead. The line for food was long and winding around so it took almost an hour for a meal.
>
> 21st Went on deck and felt better.
>
> 22nd Rainy-wet.
>
> 23rd White caps and spray.
>
> 24th Rough.
>
> 25th Rough, but we were able to take a shower-salt water bath.
>
> 26th & 27th Rough. One time while on deck I saw a detail dump these drums of garbage overboard [off stern]—not the drums but their contents.
>
> 28th Sighted land, the Isle of Man.
>
> 29th Docked in Liverpool Harbor. There were turrets sticking up out of the water and a boat had been sunk near entrance to the harbor.
>
> 30th Watched English small cars and taxi and saw a cargo of planes being towed from a carrier.
>
> 31st Disembarked to a train. I missed the volunteers with coffee, donuts and gum altogether.

The 12th Infantry Regiment of the 4th Division boarded the USAT *George Washington.*[6]

> Our entire regiment was loaded on the USS *George Washington* and we sailed on January 17, 1944. Company I was designated as guard company. As XO, I was designated officer of the day every other day, seasick or not.

According to some of the officers, except for a U-boat scare that diverted the convoy, nothing special occurred during the trip. The 4th Division landed in Liverpool with no problems and moved out to its new camps.

Lt. James M. Crutchfield thought he traveled on a Liberty ship from New York at the end of January, but it was actually AP-76, the *Anne Arundel,* a C-3 cargo ship (the largest type) converted to a troopship.[7] His division, the 6th Armored, traveled on several ships; its vehicles and equipment had been shipped in previous convoys over a period of several months.

> My trip was uneventful. I was appointed as provost marshal. We went over in one of the biggest convoys of the war. Our division was on several ships. What made a big impression on me was that the first morning out. I

6. The army transport *George Washington* was a 23,700-ton German passenger ship built in 1908 and taken over by the U.S. Army during World War I. The ship was not converted from coal to oil burning until 1942. As a liner, the ship carried 2,700 passengers, but during the war, it carried between 4,000 and 5,000 soldiers.

7. The *Anne Arundel,* was a 14,400-ton ship completed in 1942. It took part in Operations Torch and Husky.

felt pretty good. Part of my duties was to inspect the ship every day. I started down in the first hold. Everybody was sick, vomiting on the floor. The stench was horrible; it would make anybody sick, including me. By the time I got ten feet into the hold, I was sick, as sick as they were, but I still had to go ahead and inspect the ship. There wasn't much that happened going over except off the coast of Scotland, where we ran into the biggest storm I have ever seen.

We had abandon-ship alerts, but we didn't participate. The first morning out, they sounded the alarm. We didn't know it at the time, but our XO was on the verge of going crazy. We should have known it. He lasted ten days in combat, and we had to ship him out when the psychiatrist that examined him said he had the mind of a two-year-old child. That drill was for the crew only. This guy, the XO, had his field helmet on, his gas mask, his gun, and everything else; he was ready for combat. He had his Mae West vest on, and just as he got to the door, they slammed it on him, and I thought we were going to lose him there. He liked to go crazy. As I said, ten days after combat, he did go crazy.

We had twelve federal prisoners that had been released from the penitentiary. They were under me because I was the provost marshal of the ship. The colonel was the troop commander for the ship. They were going to make soldiers out of them. We had to turn them loose once we were out in international waters. They couldn't go anywhere.

We must have run over a submarine one night. I was in lane seven. This was a huge convoy, probably the largest of the war. That scared the major who later went crazy when we almost ran over it.

Lt. Rodney Mortensen and his battalion were on another ship, a converted luxury liner that made better speed than the Liberty ships.

We had these little corvettes. They were up, down, and sideways and bounced so much it looked like their stacks would scoop up water. Then they would go on the other side of us, where they would refuel, which they had to do periodically all the way across. They had aircraft coming out, long-distance bombers and whatnot, coming out over us all the time. The convoy was so damn big we couldn't see across it or the front of it. We were the last of the troop carrier ships, and outside of us was the screen of destroyers and corvettes.

The first night we left New York, it was snowing so damn hard you couldn't see the Statue of Liberty. It got better outside. One night, this big wave slapped the side of us. Eighteen of us lieutenants in one little room about eight by ten feet, stacked about fourteen inches between your mattress and the next guy. I couldn't turn over if I wanted to. I had to slide out and turn over. A big wave hit the side of the ship, the only incident of the whole trip. It was in the middle of the night, and it was dark. Everybody thought a submarine had popped us—then the sound of the abandon-ship drill.

The first night out, the officer personnel went down in the hold with the troops and stayed there twenty-four hours; we were all together. Then we went up, and you had to force them to come up or some of them would have laid there and just died. So everybody came up and went through the mess line, or at least went up on deck. Some of them got up in the mess line, smelled the food, and Urrrrrrrp!—threw up. That didn't bother me too badly.

American troops training in Northern Ireland. NATIONAL ARCHIVES

After we got between Ireland and England, this big convoy split up, and I don't know how it happened, but our ship went up the Firth of Clyde. We grouped around, and these corvettes were going around until it was light. After light, they pulled the submarine nets, and we started through just at the crack of dawn. We went up there. On both sides, there were corvettes, minesweepers, and ships of that type; both sides were just loaded with them. It was high, and there was a road going in on the left side, about as high as the level of our top deck.

This was a time when the people changed the night crews of various jobs and day crews were going on. There were these three women going along, big tough-looking babes. They looked like they could go bear hunting with a toothpick, and they had on these one-piece coveralls. I don't think they were clerical types, and they weren't the best-looking gals I ever saw. I was standing out there, and the guys started yelling out at them. They were walking almost as fast as the ship was going. There were lots of catcalls back and forth, and they gave as well as they received and they were telling the troops off. More troops and more troops got over there, until pretty soon, this one gal bends over, peels out of her stuff, and moons the crowd. Where she was standing was no further than 100 yards. When she did that, the word got around fast, and all the goddamn men ran over to that side. The ship began to list. They had a hell of a time getting the troops back. They were coming up from all over the ship. This gal, I mean, she was as ugly as nine miles of bad Oklahoma road, but I guess being penned up on that ship for ten days, anything would look pretty good.

The 6th Armored Division departed New York on February 11, 1944, with the 5th Armored Division. The convoy sailed along the coast toward Boston, where it met the transports carrying the 30th Infantry Division the next day. The 30th had departed Boston on three transports. Its engineer battalion, the 105th, had one company on the SS *Brazil,* one on the SS *Argentina,* and one on the *John Ericsson.*[8] Sgt. Charles Benjamin Herndon had enlisted in the Florida National Guard in September 1940 at age twenty-four.[9] He was in the 124th Infantry, 31st Division, and had been inducted into federal service that November with his regiment. When the 124th Infantry was sent to Fort Benning in January 1942, Herndon was assigned to train candidates at OCS. In October 1943, the regiment went to Fort Jackson, where it divided. As a result, Herndon was sent to Camp Atterbury, where he joined the 120th Infantry, 30th Division, in November before the rail trip to Boston.

> I think that we were transported in trucks from Camp Miles Standish to the port of Boston. When we sailed from Boston on February 12, 1944, on the SS *Argentina,* it was snowing. The seas were rough, and there was lots of seasickness. We appeared to have good food on the ship, but I was so seasick I ate only about two meals on the way over. We had some training on ship deck, such as close-order drill.
>
> I observed that our convoy was accompanied by other ships constantly going around protecting us. I think one ship dropped behind for some reason, and a ship lagged back to protect it—maybe a destroyer. Our ship's lookout crew paced back and forth on the decks observing for submarines. Some of the soldiers remained on deck all day for relaxation. Every evening at a certain time, a loudspeaker announced, "Official blackout time, no smoking on deck!" Our convoy arrived in Gournock, near Glasgow, Scotland, on February 22, 1944. We disembarked and got on small boats and went to a train station.

Cpl. Floyd E. Brooks, with the 230th Field Artillery, also traveled on the *Argentina:*

> Saturday, February 12, 1944, was my last day in the States. One of the items for breakfast that morning was hard-boiled eggs. About midway through my egg, I found it had a chick in it that was about a week old. Hard-boiled eggs and I did not get along too good after that. We had a short break in the snow before going to the railroad station. The train ride to Boston took about an hour. The day was cold and gray, with a light snow falling. The battalion stood in formation with our backs to the train and a steel building on the dock. The army band was on one side, playing, and the side of a gray ship could be seen through an open door. Red Cross ladies were passing out coffee and doughnuts.
>
> This was the first time that I had seen an occurrence in the army that looked like some of the war pictures I had seen. Finally an officer mounted a rostrum beside the gangway and began to call the roll. As each man's name was called, he answered, "Here!" put his bag over his shoulder, and started that long walk up the gangplank.
>
> It seemed there were men and equipment everywhere. We finally ended up in

8. The *Argentina* and *Brazil* were USAT ships and supposedly could carry 5,000 to 8,000 troops each.

9. National Archives records state that he enlisted on November 25, 1940, and his occupation was an actor, but these classifications were often vague and not accurate.

the mail and baggage rooms, which were as far down and as far to the rear as it was possible to go. We were on E deck, directly above the propellers. The ammo locker behind each gun was the only thing behind us. I got myself a third bunk in the deck next to the hatchway and cargo hold that went to the main deck. There was a lot of traffic through the area. I had fresh air. In some places, the air was stale. The ship was loaded with the 120th Infantry Combat Team, which included the 230th Field Artillery Battalion, 105th Engineer Battalion's Company C, and 105th Medical Battalion. We were given a coded meal ticket, and that was for two meals a day. We got too much for one meal but not enough to hold to the next. The kitchen fed all day. As soon as breakfast was over for the last unit, supper started for the first unit. A fresh water converter was big enough to handle the water for drinking and tea only. All washing was done in seawater. A guard was stationed at all drinking fountains. We had been told that brushless shaving cream was the only thing that would work in salt water—that was a lie. We did not do any better with anything else.

After the ship was loaded, we had an abandon-ship drill. Some of the men lost their helmets as they went up the ladder. Helmets made a lot of noise as they bounced off the helmets of the men below and the steel walls. I didn't see much of Boston from the deck, and boy, was it snowing! The ship had been a cruise ship in South America. A hole had been cut through the wall, and the mess line passed through this hole and down a stairway of what had been the main dining saloon. The water tanks for washing mess kits were located under the stairwell. The hot steam rising from the boiling seawater wiped out any hunger feelings a person had. It was a typical army mess line. We ate standing up at tables that had sidewalls to keep things from sliding off. We were not permitted on deck when the ship sailed. By the time supper came, I was too sick to go. I didn't feel any better at breakfast. The groundswells outside of Boston Harbor really upset me. At midmorning came the daily abandon-ship drills. I dragged myself up that ladder. After I got a good breath of air topside, I felt so good I stayed on deck most of the day. The deck was still smoke covered. I had no more trouble with seasickness.

On the second day, Captain Bland had us up on the promenade deck to do calisthenics: side jumps, knee bends, and so forth. In two days, the whole ship was doing it.

The big game on the trip over was to try to count the number of ships in convoy. The small corvettes went out of sight and reappeared, and we could never be certain if we counted a ship only once. There were thirty-six ships in the convoy. Our ship had the USS *Nevada* on its right, and it appeared to sit with no roll or pitch. Two aircraft carriers made an appearance. The troop carrier to our left was a converted Liberty ship; it bounced like a cork and appeared it would roll over.

Monday morning, February 21, we saw the sun for the first time since leaving Indiana. The north coast of Ireland was lying low on the horizon to our right. I stood on the deck the whole day and watched the countryside go by. It was one of the most beautiful sights I have ever seen. The sky was a deep blue, the fields a very dark green, and the lighthouses were a pure white.

The ship was too large to tie up, so the anchor was dropped out in the middle of

> the channel. The staircase that we were to go down was at the left corner of the deck. Captain Bland had us walk all the way around the deck to get there. He could have given us an about-face and we would have had less than fifty feet to go. It was stop and go around the deck, set the duffel bag down, pick it up, set it down, pick it up again. By the time we got around that deck, I was too tired to pick myself up. I dragged it down the staircase for six decks. I did manage to pick it up and carry it across the gangway to the ferry that was going to take us to shore. I collapsed when I first found a seat.
>
> We were led a short way to the wharf and had a walk of about 100 yards to the railroad station. We found out later that a man in one of the firing batteries "went over the hill" and walked between the ferry and railroad station.

The other two ships carrying the division landed at Liverpool, and all the units they carried moved by train to their camps near Chichester.

In the month of March, small units, but none division size, crossed the Atlantic. When the *Queen Mary* made a trans-Atlantic trip at the beginning of March, she carried the 978th Field Artillery Battalion. About halfway through the trip, the monotony of the voyage was shattered when the deck gun on the stern opened fire. Pvt. Maynard E. Daggett and his comrades were told to keep belowdecks because there was a submarine in the vicinity. Fortunately, they reached Scotland without mishap. At the end of the same month, Pvt. William Edward Finnigan, a replacement, was on the *Queen Mary* on another of her crossings. He had joined the army reserve on November 12, 1942, as a member of the Signal Corps. At the time, he had been in his senior year at New York State College for Teachers and was required to attend evening meeting on radio theory at the University of Buffalo. He was called to active duty on August 17, 1943, at Fort Dix and sent to Camp Crowder, Missouri, for basic training. Next, he trained in field telephone wire, after which he went to Camp Shanks to embark for Great Britain on March 21, 1944.

> The ship was very overcrowded. My bunk was way down forward, and the pounding noise of the ship in the North Atlantic in winter is something I can't forget. Many were seasick. We lived on the Hershey bars we brought with us. The British cooks "destroyed" the American food. After the war, a coworker who went on the *Mary* as an army officer told me they ate from chinaware with a selection of menu! Nearing the British Isles, we passed fishing vessels and saw a flying boat. I watched a tug close the submarine net after we passed though into the harbor. It was filled with warships. It was soon dark—the beginning of what total blackout would be like for another year.

On March 27, after he disembarked in Greenock, Scotland, Finnigan boarded a train for a replacement center at Oulton Park, near Chester. The camp was crowded with troops from various branches of the army waiting for their assignments. Most joined infantry units, but Finnigan was sent to the 4th Division Signal Company at Tiverton.

Lt. Robert T. Dove, 79th Recon Troop, 79th Infantry Division, who boarded the *Queen Mary* at the same time as Finnigan, got to enjoy much better accommodations than the enlisted men because he was an officer. He was traveling ahead of his division, which followed in April.

> I was one of two from the troop on the division's advance party. New York was lots of fun! Every afternoon and evening was

free time on the town. Four trips to Times Square were enough for me. We saw the Rockettes dance, movies, etc., and Madison Square Garden had basketball play-offs.

We left from Fort Hamilton, New York, and were ferried to the *Queen Mary* and probably left in the early hours of the morning. As I recall, the advance party contained over 500, almost half of them corporals. I was the junior officer of the 250-plus officers and had many varied details with the enlisted ranks. My boss was a division headquarters major who acted as commandant of troops.

March 31, the *Queen Mary* was still gaining speed at first light, and we saw New Jersey vanish as we turned southeast and started zigzagging.[10] At 30 knots, you brace for each turn, and if in bed, you tilt or roll depending upon the way your bunk faces.

Breakfast in the officers' mess was frightening. I got one slice of fried green tomatoes, one plum with very little juice, and a small dinner roll. I wolfed mine down and excused myself with "Our men will riot if treated that way." I bunked and messed with eleven Air Corps pilots. When they found out I was recon [for an] infantry division, they gave me great courtesy and "death-row" glances.

Our enlisted men ate breakfast at 0900 hours. I put the biggest master sergeant first in line and followed him with the four biggest other ranks. I told them to say, "I'm starved," and pause in line till they got the size of serving they could eat comfortably. I stayed between the first two services. The men got a good breakfast. From then on, the senior master sergeant took my job, and we had no complaints. The officers' mess was good from the second morning on.

One night, we all woke up at once. We "zagged" for what seemed like minutes. We figured we did one-eighty or better. We were over an hour before the zigzag returned to normal. We all talked about a German sub, but we never were told a thing. From time to time, we saw smoke over the horizon, but never a smokestack.

We never had lifeboat drill, as 15,000-plus couldn't get out on deck at the same time. The "math majors" figured the lifeboats, fully loaded, would handle 6,500 more or less.

In April, no one stood on the forward deck but the ship's watch. At 30 knots, the windchill was a bit much. Only health nuts and the curious braved the rear decks.

We all woke up in the Irish Sea. The reduced throb of the engines and lack of zigzag was too strange to sleep through. We off-loaded for hours and hours at Greenock, Scotland. It wasn't dark, but it was late in the evening before we left ship for a waiting train. It was still April. The "Gray Ladies" gave us milk and toilet items.

Pvt. John Douglas Gregory from Franklin, Kentucky, was drafted at age nineteen in March 1943. He did not mind being inducted because he could find only odd jobs and was a milk delivery man at the time. After basic training, he spent almost one year training with the 8th Armored Division in Louisiana as part of an armored infantry unit, many of whose men were sent out as replacements.

10. Both Finnigan and a website give March 21 as the departure date, along with a matching arrival date. It is not possible with the information available to determine who is correct, but Dove does state that his recon troop left Boston and arrived in Liverpool on April 17, which would have given the advance party only about twelve days to prepare.

American soldiers and Irish girls at a St. Patrick's Day dance in Northern Ireland, March 1942. NATIONAL ARCHIVES

We got all new clothes and equipment at Fort Meade, Maryland—wool ODs [olive drabs], even wool underwear. One soldier carried four pairs of shoes because he had a shoe size 8E quad. We even had clothing to protect us from poison gas. All this was carried in a duffel bag.

We departed from Boston Harbor in late March 1944. We left Camp Miles Standish, Massachusetts, and boarded the French ship *Liberté*. This was a small ship, and it was rumored we had about 3,600 men onboard. Bunks in the hold were from the floor to the ceiling. Food on this voyage was excellent. Baths were taken in salt water. This left a lot to be desired. We joined a large convoy and moved in a zigzag pattern. We saw no subs, and for that I was thankful. About two days out, we hit a bad storm. The waves went over the deck, and there were very many seasick GIs. I never got sick. We were warned not to toss anything overboard, as this might alert the enemy to us being there. To add to our misery, we got shots from the medics in both arms, and some GIs passed out; some really feared the needle. The water was choppy all the way across—time of the year, I would guess.

Now to a landlubber like me, this ocean was overwhelming—water, water on every side. This voyage took thirteen days. While I slept, someone stole my watch from my arm. This made me very angry. I never found the culprit. As we looked into the water, we wondered what lay ahead. One GI was rumored to have won $2,500 playing poker. I stayed on deck all I could; I found the fresh air tended to keep off sea-

> sickness. We could see other ships in our convoy. I was amazed how the fish swam alongside us.
>
> I had no extra duty; I was one of the lucky ones.
>
> We sighted land, the coast of Scotland. We landed at Glasgow, and here we were put on a train, destination Wales.

After his thirteen-day trip, Gregory and his companions traveled to a tent camp in the Welsh countryside, where the training consisted of hikes, long runs, and sports. Before long, during the month of May, most of the men were assigned to units, except for Gregory, who had severely sprained his ankle as he slid into second base during a baseball game and stayed in the hospital for three weeks, including on June 6, 1944.

On May 12, 1944, the last large convoy transporting a full division before the invasion departed from New York. The troops of the 35th Division sailed on three transports: the 320th Infantry on the USAT *Edmund B. Alexander,* the 134th on the *General A. E. Anderson,* and the 137th on the *Thomas H. Barry.*[11] The advance party had left on the *Queen Elizabeth* on April 20.

Pvt. Robert Lehmann, from New York City was drafted in January 1943 and trained as a signalman to operate the switchboard and lay commo wire. His regiment, the 320th, boarded the *Alexander* during the night—to keep the departure secret, he believes. "But someone did see me leave. My brother was attached to the POE [port of embarkation] detail and was on the pier that night. He knew I was leaving that night and wanted to see me leave. It was a wave of a hand and a silent "So long." He remained at the MP station on pier duty all during the war."

Second Lt. Charles W. Bell, 2nd Platoon leader, Company A, 1st Battalion, 320th Infantry, was also aboard the *Alexander.* This blond-haired, blue-eyed nineteen-year-old from West Texas was in his senior year at Texas A&M when he volunteered late in 1942. Having been a student, he did not even have a Social Security number until he left the army. After more than three years of ROTC, he attended OCS at Fort Benning shortly after basic training and received his commission on November 23, 1943. He was assigned to the 35th Division as a platoon leader, and one year later, he was promoted to company commander. "We moved from Camp Kilmer, New Jersey, to the port by train," he recalls. "The trip to England took thirteen days and was marred by one storm and numerous submarine alerts. We could sometimes see geysers of water erupt from the depth charges. Otherwise, a very boring trip. There was little room to move about in the mass of men, and lots of reading, card games, letter writing, and bull sessions were the main diversions."

According to Dale Kearnes, who was with the 219th Field Artillery, the *Anderson,* on which he traveled, was crowded. But unlike many of his compatriots, he appreciated the British food. "Some of the guys turned green down there, and they wouldn't get up," he says. "They had to carry them on deck. One thing that stands out in my mind is this guy's stinking socks—one guy never changed his socks."

PFC Thomas Heuser, who traveled on the *Anderson* as well, remembers a smoke screen being laid down during a submarine scare, and

11. The *Edmund B. Alexander* was the 21,392-ton German Hamburg liner *Amerika,* built in 1905 and taken over by the United States in World War I. As a troopship, it could carry about 5,150 troops and attained a speed of 17 knots. The *General A. E. Anderson,* AP-111, was built in 1943. It weighed 17,833 tons, transported about 5,200 troops, and could reach 19 knots. The ship was armed with four 5-inch guns. The *Thomas H. Barry,* built in 1930, weighed 11,250 tons, had a speed of 18 knots, and could carry 3,600 troops.

the ship stopping for a few hours sometime during the journey while divers repaired a propeller.

According to Lt. Kenneth Jarvis of the 137th Infantry, the *Barry* was also crammed to the rafters. The men onboard had to do their laundry in their steel helmets. The most serious problem was diarrhea, which generated long lines at the latrines. One of the machines in the galley, which was corroded, turned out to be the source of the infection, and after it was cleaned, the diarrhea stopped. One night, to his astonishment, a ship approached under full lights. "We were, of course, under complete blackout. It got close enough for me to see it was a hospital ship before it turned tail. It was silhouetting the convoy with its lights—too dangerous if there was a sub in the area."

All the troop convoys reached Great Britain safely, the Germans having failed to stop the buildup for the inevitable invasion. As each month passed and the sea-lanes became increasingly secure, more and more troops and war materiel poured into Britain.

A 155-millimeter "Long Tom" and a 75-millimeter howitzer.

CHAPTER 15

The Army Air Force Buildup

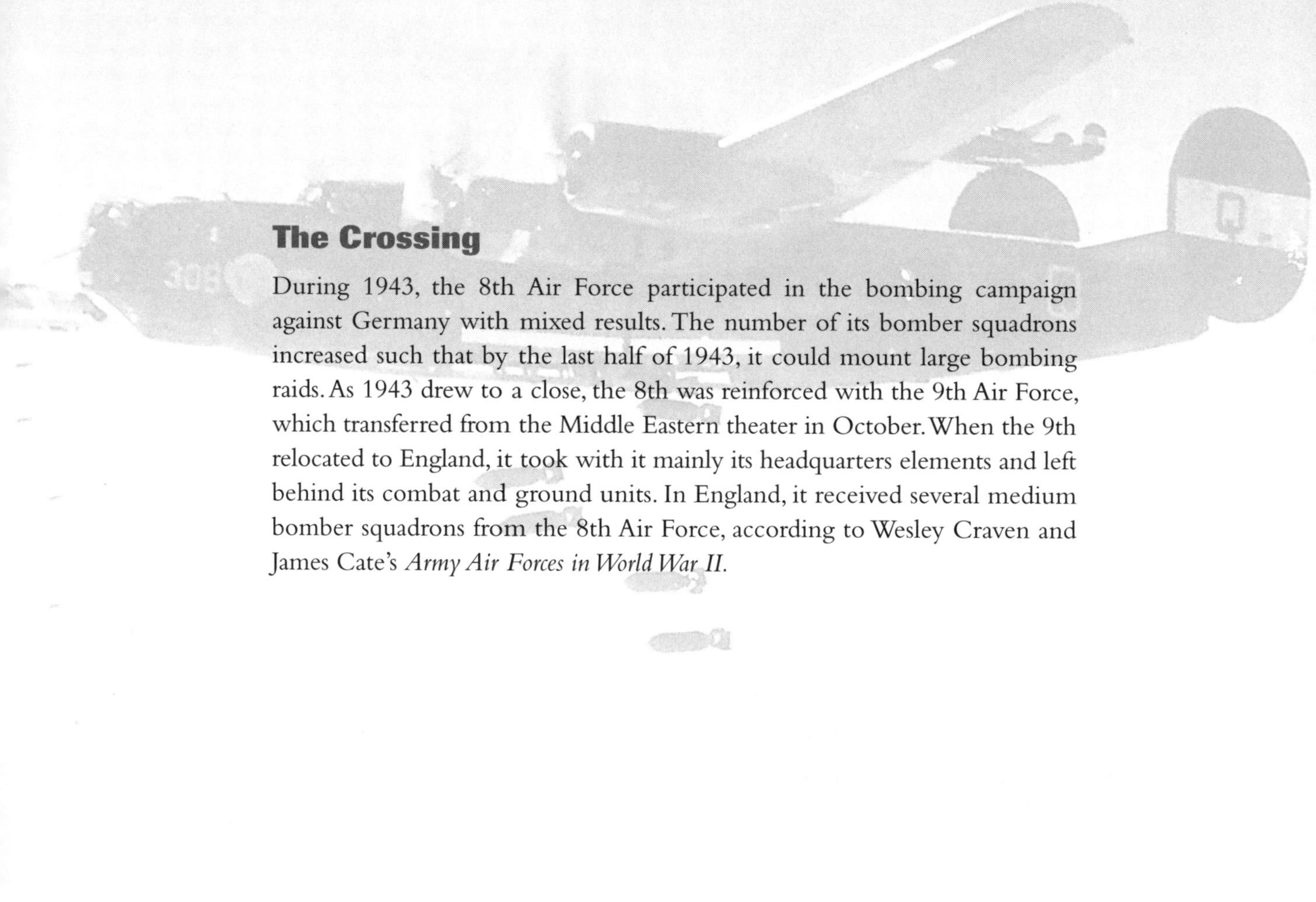

The Crossing

During 1943, the 8th Air Force participated in the bombing campaign against Germany with mixed results. The number of its bomber squadrons increased such that by the last half of 1943, it could mount large bombing raids. As 1943 drew to a close, the 8th was reinforced with the 9th Air Force, which transferred from the Middle Eastern theater in October. When the 9th relocated to England, it took with it mainly its headquarters elements and left behind its combat and ground units. In England, it received several medium bomber squadrons from the 8th Air Force, according to Wesley Craven and James Cate's *Army Air Forces in World War II.*

The 9th Air Force, which became a tactical formation that supported the army's ground operations and preparations for the invasion, took over the Troop Carrier Command and increased in size by absorbing most of the newly arriving medium and light bomber squadrons. The 8th Air Force became the strategic unit controlling most of the heavy bombers in the theater. Each air force had its own fighter command, but the 9th routinely used its fighter squadrons to escort the bomber formations of the 8th. The 9th Air Force also took over responsibility for air defense in England and formed a command that included two army antiaircraft brigades. In addition, during the spring of 1944, the 9th's Engineer Command received several army engineer aviation regiments, which took over the responsibility of improving airfields and following the advancing armies after the invasion. The ranks of the 9th and 8th Air Forces continued to swell as the summer of 1944 approached.

Both new and old squadrons required a constant supply of replacements, to make up for not only the crews lost in combat, but also for those that completed their missions and rotated home. The majority of the 8th Air Force's ground crews and the aircrews that did not fly across the Atlantic traveled to Great Britain between June 1942 and January 1944 mainly on the *Queen Elizabeth* and *Queen Mary* and similar ships. Of the fifty-three ground crew units sent over during that time, forty-two traveled on the *Queens* in fourteen voyages. Meanwhile, most of the aircrews flew their aircraft over, following either the northern or southern route, as did many replacement aircrews. Often, however, regular squadrons and replacement crews left their aircraft when they arrived in England and were reassigned other planes. Aside from trying to send false radio signals, the Germans were unable to hamper the flow of aircraft and the new crews arriving in them. The smaller aircraft, such as the fighters, were transported by sea.

The aircrews that crossed in 1944 traveled along well-established routes, but their trip was not without danger, and every flight was a unique experience. Lt. Jack R. Sargeant of Cincinnati, Ohio, who signed up for the army in June 1942 and became an aviation cadet that November, completed the entire training routine by October 1943. He went to Santa Ana, California, for preflight training, and then began primary training in February 1943, learning to fly the Stearman biplane and other trainers. Next, he went to Bakersfield, where he completed basic flying school on BT-13s. Finally, he went through advanced training in July at Stockton, California, flying the UC-78, or Bamboo Bomber. After he received his wings on October 1, 1943, he reported to Roswell Air Base. He remained there until December 15, when he took the train to Salt Lake City to pick up a crew. Lieutenant Sargeant and his men were housed in a cattle barn on the city fairground. The living conditions were so bad that they were allowed to stay in motels if they maintained beds in the barn. After training in Salt Lake City, Sargeant and his five-man crew, which he called the "Fearless Five," transferred to Dalhart Air Base, Texas, acquiring a navigator. In March, the lieutenant and his men went by train to Kearney, Nebraska, where they picked up a brand new B-17. At this time, the aircrew was issued jungle gear and prepared for an assignment to the South Pacific.

> The night before we were to leave, they brought us all down to change our jungle gear for cold-weather gear. This had a bearing on everybody concerned. The Fearless Five took off last in a loose formation. We were instructed to fly due east, and while we were abeam off Fort Wayne, Indiana, Fort Wayne's control told us where we were going. We had no idea where we were going to land or anything. As it turned out, Fort Wayne radio instructed us to land at an

An 8th Air Force raid on the Focke Wulf plant at Marienburg, Germany, 1943. NATIONAL ARCHIVES

airfield at Manchester, New Hampshire. Our route there took us just south of Chicago, over Toledo, Buffalo, Syracuse, and on to the airfield.

We spent five days waiting for decent weather over the Atlantic. After five days, we got notice to go, and we were sent on to Goose Bay, Labrador. During the five days at the airfield, we were briefed on all other routes, the emergency airfields in case we had trouble, and so forth. We landed at Goose Bay sometime late in the evening of April 12. I can still hear the tower operator instructing us as we were going to land. He commented, "Use caution, braking action is poor!" He was so right! The runway was a sheet of ice, and when I touched the brakes, the airplane just locked up and skidded like crazy. We made it all right. We were advised to spend the night at Goose Bay, leaving the next day for Meeks Field at Reykjavik, Iceland. As a result, I got a room in the hotel there, and at about 1 A.M., they came, woke me, and said to get ready to go.

We went down, checked our aircraft, got our gas, and took off for Reykjavik, Iceland. This was 3 A.M. in the morning, and none of us had ever been over water before in our lives. The cloud cover was so dense that the navigator could not take a shoot with his sextant until just about the time the sun came up in Greenland.

My impression of Greenland—it was like I envisioned the landscape of the moon to be: mountains all around the rim and ice pack in the middle. Shortly after Bluie West 1, which was our alternate, we prayed we could get through there. Our instructions were to go up the canyon, turn left and continue to the blank wall, and turn right and land. There was no going around in Bluie West 1, because there was a blank wall at the other end. You got one shot and that is that. We prayed we could miss that and did.

Shortly after Greenland, we went back into the soup and stayed in the soup all the way to Reykjavik. I homed in on the radio range and made a procedural letdown and landed. It was sort of a nasty gray day, and I guess I made the worst landing I ever made in my life on an airfield. There was a navy patrol boat lined up to take off, so I kept one eye on him and one on the runway. I was on final approach and leveled out a little high, and the airplane dropped in like a lead balloon. We spent the night at Reykjavik. I remember it as a musty, dank spot, and the tents we were in smelled of kerosene to high heaven. That was all the head they had. Base Operations was in a tunnel in the mountain where the water dripped off the walls. We left the next morning, and we were briefed to go to Nutts Corner, Northern Ireland.

Before we left Grener Field, they issued us a new pair of field glasses, which I used for spying submarines for North Atlantic convoys. Each gun had fifty rounds of ammunition in it. What we were to do with fifty rounds of ammunition I have no idea, because those things really spit the lead out. We took off from Meeks Field in Grener. The radio operator with me, who was rather eager, took the long training wire antenna out and contacted Nutts Corner by radio. They assumed we were close to the field and told us to let down to 1,500 feet and make our pattern. He came up from the radio shack and gave me the message. So I let down to 1,500 feet. Little did I know that I had let down to 1,500 feet just past Stronway, Scotland, and it wasn't long before I had two Spitfires on each wing wanting to know what I was doing there. They escorted me quite a ways. I went to Nutts Corner, Ireland, where I had my first experience with a British tower operator, whom I couldn't understand. Finally, after three tries, I got into the flight traffic pattern behind another airplane and landed. We had all our emergency gear, uniforms, etc., stored in the bomb bay. The emergency gear was on the bottom rack, and our flying suits, uniforms, and so forth were just above that, stacked on top. So when he said, "Get out, the airplane is mine," the bombardier salvoed the bomb bay and everything fell out. You have never seen such a mess on a ramp in your life! Anyway, after about three or four hours of clearing up paperwork and turning in the aircraft, we departed by train to Belfast.

I left my binoculars hanging on the backseat of the aircraft, and I presume somebody got themselves a nice set of field glasses. Anyhow, we went by train to Belfast, and my bombardier, being the ranking officer aboard, was voted troop train commander. In Belfast, we boarded a ferry, which took us across to Stranraer, Scotland, where we unloaded and walked up a long, long inclined ramp through the little town to the British army facility where we were to spend a few hours before getting on another train. This was not a troop train. It took us down to Stone, England.

After about four days in Stone, our crew was selected to go to Bovington with quite a few other crews, where we were to undergo aircraft recognition and fire tactics of the enemy, etc. We were there for about two weeks and received our orders to our unit.

Lieutenant Sargeant and his crew were assigned to the 326th Squadron, 92nd Bomb Group, as replacements. A few months before Sargeant made his crossing, CWO William Hart's ground echelon of the 84th Troop Carrier Squadron had arrived on the *Mauritania,* which had raced across the Atlantic unescorted. The men were taken to a new base at Ramsbury, where their air echelon was already posted. When they arrived by truck at night, they experienced some difficulties because the base had no lights yet.

At daylight, we got coordinated and established. It was the winter of 1943-44, and it was icy weather that got pretty chilly. We all had a common mess hall, but each squadron had its own engineering and operation sections on the base. A day or two after we arrived, we were welcomed to the [European] theater by Axis Sally. She named a few of us by name and said she would visit us one of these days. In a few days, we had an air raid, and that sort of spooked us. The bomb shelter was just a trench with piles of dirt. The next alert, we could see the light in the bomb bay; the antiaircraft fired, and it looked like a Christmas tree at nighttime.

Maybe a couple of times a week they came, but they never dropped anything near the base.

Part of the air echelon of the 437th Troop Carrier Group had not yet reached Great Britain when Hart arrived. Lt. William M. Thompson, piloting a C-47, took the southern air route. His squadron, the 85th, had just finished training with the 101st Airborne Division, which had already shipped out about a month or so before Hart and the ground echelon.

We departed January 1944 and went by train out of Pope Field, North Carolina, to Fort Wayne, Indiana. All the pilots and aircrews checked in there, and we picked up brand new C-47s out of the factory. We got one test flight for a functional check and then loaded all our gear. We were there three or four days. Then the whole group of about forty-eight airplanes took off from Fort Wayne in early January 1944, and we flew to Homestead, Florida, and got our orders there. We had sealed orders and took off for the south. Our first stop was Puerto Rico. At this time, I had Elgin Davis as a copilot and Sergeant Mitchell as my crew chief, who was with me throughout the war. My radio operator was Ivan Schwartz, and we received a navigator for the trip.

We flew in a group by squadron in elements of three ships to Puerto Rico. We stayed overnight and took off for Georgetown, British Guiana—a one night stand there, and then to Natal, Brazil, no problems on the way. We flew single ships from Natal to Ascension Island. From Ascension Island, we flew in elements of three to Africa.

We flew to Monrovia, Liberia, and then on to Marrakech, where we stayed overnight. At the next base [possibly Port Lyautey], we stayed four or five days, maybe because of weather. From there we went to England, I think singly. I do remember seeing the lights of Lisbon off to our right. It was a neutral, and it was impressive. Everything was at night on the way there. We arrived in England at about eight or nine in the morning. We landed in Nottingham, England. No trouble coming into England, since we had been briefed well enough and had maps. We refueled, and a B-17 took us to another field after we formed up in a squadron formation. We stayed there a few days, then took off again and went down to Ramsbury Air Base, which became our base.

Hundreds of aircraft followed these routes in 1944, but the Germans, who had their hands full with bombing squadrons flying over German-occupied territory, were unable to stop them. These routes were well beyond the range of German fighter aircraft with the bases available to them. Most of the German fighter squadrons had already been redeployed to protect the homeland, so the skies around the fringes of Axis-occupied Europe were relatively safe during the first half of 1944.

The Allied Bombing Campaign

In May, after the Casablanca Conference of January 1943, the Combined Chiefs of Staff turned their attention to Operation Point Blank, whose aim was to destroy the enemy's means of production. The leaders who met at the conference issued the following directive, stated in Winston Churchill's *Closing the Ring:* "Your primary object will be the progressive destruction and dislocation of the German military, industrial, and economic system and the undermining of the morale of the German people to a point where their capacity for armed resistance is fatally weakened."

Priority targets included U-boat pens and yards, the German aircraft industry, transportation systems, oil production centers, and other industrial targets. In May, after realizing the futility of their effort against the U-boat bases, the planners switched their focus to the German fighter forces and aircraft industry.[1] Throughout the remainder of 1943, the RAF Bomber Command bombed by night and the AAF by day. The British targeted cities and used area bombing, relying on electronic devices to locate them in bad weather. The Americans, on the other hand, attempted precision bombing. In late July 1943, round-the-clock bombing that continued for a week practically destroyed the city of Hamburg. The Allied planes dropped "window" or "chaff," thousands of small metallic strips, to confuse radar-controlled guns. From November 1943 until March 1944, the Bomber Command concentrated its efforts on Berlin. The AAF did not join in the Berlin raids until March 1944. Continued bad winter weather gave the new radar devices, H2S and H2X, a new importance, as they allowed bombing through the clouds.[2] The success of the British bombing strategy is dubious, however, because it did not break German morale.

Gen. Ira C. Eaker, who led the 8th Air Force in 1943, directed the American precision daylight bombing campaign. On October 14, 1943, he undertook a major action that involved a force of more than 320 unescorted bombers, which went deep into enemy territory to attack a center for aircraft production at Schweinfurt. It suffered a loss of 60 aircraft.

In January 1944, Gen. James Doolittle took over the command of the 8th Air Force and Gen. Carl Spaatz the U.S. Strategic Air Forces in Europe. Eisenhower insisted on controlling all air forces in preparation for Overlord, as well as for the duration and in the aftermath of the invasion. In late March, British air marshal Tedder, one of Eisenhower's deputy commanders for SHAEF, pushed through the Transportation Plan, which directed air operations mainly against railroad marshaling yards to choke off all reinforcements to France.

When the weather cleared on February 19, 1944, the 8th Air Force launched Big Week, a series of attacks against the German aircraft industry. The operations staff had selected twelve specific targets related to the production of German aircraft. The aerial assault began on February 20, with the aid of the 15th Air Force operating out of Italy, as described by Craven and Tate. At the end of Big Week, the RAF had lost 141 bombers and the AAF 155.

The Strategic Bombing Survey, which was conducted after the war, determined that the accomplishments of these bombings were diminished by the fact that the Germans had already begun dispersing their industries. It concluded that production of German fighter aircraft at Gotha was up and running seven weeks after the bombings, and the Messerschmitt plant at Augsburg was back in full production after one month. The Regensburg facilities also were back in full production in about four months, according to Craven and Tate. The air commanders argued that if they had not been diverted to Overlord operations, they would have wiped out

1. The U-boat pens had already neared completion by the time they were targeted. They were built with thick concrete roofs (about seven meters or almost eight yards) that could resist any bombs the Allies used until late in the war. The 12,000-pound Tallboy bomb, developed by Barnes Wallis, and the 22,000-pound Grand Slam were effective against these concrete sites. Only the British Lancaster bomber could carry them one at a time, although actually putting the bomb on the target was another problem. When the first Tallboy bombs became available, they destroyed the E-boat pens at Le Havre in June 1944. The Grand Slam was first used in March 1945, but it was less effective against submarine pens, although its shock wave was quite destructive even with a near miss against other targets.

2. Operation Gomorrah began on July 24 and ended on August 3, 1943, with the British arriving at night with more than 700 bombers and the Americans by day with 50 to 70. The British raid the night of July 27 created a devastating firestorm. About 50,000 civilians died, a million were left homeless, and a large part of Hamburg flattened. The operation was the first to employ chaff to confuse the enemy radar. Another first was the H2S radar on British bombers, enabling the pilots of the pathfinder aircraft to have an image of the ground to help mark the target with flares for the bombers that followed.

the German aircraft industry. When D-Day came a few months later, however, the *Luftwaffe* had more aircraft than ever before.

According to Reich Minister of Armaments Albert Speer's memoir, *Inside the Third Reich,* the Allied bombing of Schweinfurt in October 1943 and again in February 1944, during Big Week, could have crippled the German ball-bearing industry and stopped the production not only of aircraft, but also of vehicles. Although these industries were dispersed after these attacks, Speer noted, such industries as engine production could not be moved into woods and caves. Photo recon units recorded the damage inflicted by the bombings, but no proper assessment could be made until after the war.

The next operation, Crossbow, launched in December 1943, received priority second only to Point Blank. It targeted the sites of the new German secret weapons. In the spring of 1943, Allied intelligence had become aware that the Germans were developing the new and vastly destructive V weapons in various places.[3] As a result, in the summer, the Allies organized missions coded Noball that were directed against these sites. On the night of August 17–18, 1943, 596 aircraft of the RAF Bomber Command struck at the research center for the V weapons at Peenemünde on the Baltic. For a loss of 40 aircraft, the German secret-weapons program was set back several weeks.

On December 24, 1943, the 8th Air Force launched all three of its bombardment divisions, a total of 722 aircraft, against the V-weapon sites in the Pas de Calais. This time no aircraft was lost, except in a collision over England. After conducting tests at Eglin Air Base, Florida, the Americans concluded that fighter-bombers and medium- or low-level bombing were best suited for the operation. The British, however, insisted on high-altitude saturation bombing in order to elude the heavy flak defenses the Germans had set up in the Cotentin Peninsula and Pas de Calais area where the V-weapon sites were built. In April 1944, Eisenhower gave Crossbow targets priority once again, because the previously knocked-out concrete sites, known as "ski" sites, had been replaced by simpler installations.[4] This job was assigned to the fighters and medium bombers of the 9th Air Force and the British Mosquito aircraft. By May 1944, the Allies had put out of action more than 100 of the sites and lost over 40 American aircraft. Nevertheless, the Strategic Bombing Survey, which estimated that the bombing delayed the launchings of the V-weapons by up to four months, considered it to have been a worthwhile endeavor.[5]

General Spaatz mistakenly believed that the Transportation Plan would be ineffective and the Germans would recover quickly. In fact, the Germans experienced some difficulty keeping roads and railroads open west of the Seine River, and once the invasion began, the Allied air interdiction campaign proved very successful. In April 1944, the 15th Air Force launched a new campaign against the oil industry at Ploesti, Rumania. On May 12, the 8th Air Force took part in the operations against German oil targets that eventually broke the back of the German war machine. According to Albert Speer, May 12 was "the day the technological war was decided," and although

3. The V, or vengeance, weapons included the V-1 flying bomb, a pilotless bomb launched in the direction of the intended target—usually London—with sufficient fuel to reach it, and the V-2 rocket, a rocket with a warhead. The V-2, unlike the V-1, was so fast it could not be seen or intercepted when it reached the target area. Other V weapons, such as the long-range V-3 high-pressure pump cannon, were not the primary targets of the Noball missions.

4. These sites included assembly buildings with a curved open end to prevent fighters from strafing the inside. The buildings' shape resembled a ski from the air, hence the nickname.

5. Several miles from Calais, a subterranean V-2 rocket base was built in a limestone quarry at Wizernes. The main part of the site where the rockets were to be assembled and rolled out for launching was covered by a 5-meter-thick concrete dome. An RAF bombing raid on June 24 with Tallboy's resulted in so much damage that the site was closed down before it became operational.

German industry still produced everything the military needed, the Allied air operations had seriously affected the flow of armaments. Later in the week, Speer informed Gen. Wilhelm Keitel that the enemy had hit one of Germany's weakest points. Adolf Galland, commander of the *Luftwaffe* fighter units, also declared that the air offensive against the oil targets was threatening to bring about the collapse of his forces. As the oil campaign, an integral part of the Transportation Plan, began to bear fruit, the Allies decided to add bridges to their list of primary targets.

With too many targets to defend, Galland decided to concentrate his fighters over Germany. He pointed out that the Allies had 12,837 aircraft facing him in preparation for the invasion, while the entire *Luftwaffe* consisted of 3,222 aircraft, only 40 percent of which were serviceable. As the Allies established an air umbrella that cleared the path for the invasion, Field Marshal Erwin Rommel worried that they would dominate the battlefield.

While the 8th and 9th Air Forces received an uninterrupted stream of reinforcements from across the Atlantic, they continued with major bombing campaigns during 1943 and 1944. In the Mediterranean theater, the 12th Air Force conducted some long-range operations, including one against Ploesti, but concentrated mainly on supporting the 15th Army Group during the Italian campaign. The 15th was a combined Anglo-American army group that included the U.S. 5th and British 8th Armies and was commanded by British general Harold Alexander.

Sgt. Melvin Frederick Larson, who volunteered in the spring of 1942, thought he had signed up for a position in medical services but ended up in the AAF. He traveled by train from his native Massachusetts to Miami Beach for basic training, and his first assignment was running a small BX at a base in North Carolina. But then he found himself being shipped out to become an aerial gunner, being sent to Lowery Field, Colorado, and Kingman Field, Arizona, for training. By the end of the summer of 1943, he had completed training with the crew of his B-17 in the U.S. Northwest and Utah. In mid-October 1943, without having had a furlough since he had enlisted, he boarded the *Queen Mary* in New York with the rest of his crew. Once he and his comrades reached England, they proceeded to Knettishall to join the 388th Bomb Group, which had arrived only a few months before, during the summer.

> Our crew was assigned to the 560th Bomb Squadron situation one mile west of the Village of Hopton. The officers were assigned quarters that were partitioned into rooms, while we NCOs were assigned to open bay huts arranged so that four crews could occupy a Nissen hut. The 560th Bomb Squadron was located the furthest from the flight line.
>
> Knettishall AAF Base was called Station 136 and was part of the 3rd Bombardment Division of the 8th Air Force. It was a late-design heavy bomber airfield to class A specifications. It had standard 50-yard wide runways, the main runway being 2,000 yards long, and two intersecting runways 1,400 yards each, with an encircling perimeter track. There were fifty hardstands, two T2-type hangars, and full technical services. Mark 11 airfield lighting permitted night flying. The accommodations, largely Nissen huts, were in some dozen dispersed sites to the south of the flying field in the village of Cony Weston and Hopton. The bomb storage dump was situated on the far side of the airfield in a wood near the village of Knettishall.
>
> We were assigned to B-17 number 599 with a crew of ten. We named her Sioux City Queen. Lt. Norman P. Kempton was our pilot, who hailed from Sioux City, Iowa,

B-24s on a mission over Europe. PHOTO COURTESY OF HERBERT BEATTY

and was a full-blooded Sioux. Paul E. Davis was our copilot, from Fayetteville, Arkansas. Lt. Stanley E. Lyntski was our navigator, whose home was Trenton, New Jersey. Lt. Harry McKenna, our original bombardier, was from Charlotte, North Carolina. Our engineer to turret gunner was S. Sgt. Emil Taddeo from Long Island. S. Sgt. Lou Mostardi from Upper Darby, Pennsylvania, was our radio gunner. Our assistant engineer, left waist gunner was S. Sgt. Raymond Evtuch from Chicago. The ball turret gunner was S. Sgt. Harvey Norton from Texas. Tail gunner was S. Sgt. Hamp Nicholson from Wakulla, North Carolina. I was the original right waist gunner for our first four missions. When Lieutenant McKenna, our bombardier, left our crew, I was trained to become a toggalier and flew twenty-six missions in this position.[6]

Anyone who flew combat and said that they were not frightened was a prevaricator. When your aircraft was damaged, you could not get out and walk. You were isolated five miles up in the atmosphere. When I knew we were scheduled to fly a mission the next day, I could never sleep. I would lay awake on my bed listening to the activity on the flight line as the ground crews were readying our aircraft for the mission. It always amazed me how sound travels in the still of the night. Our squadron was over a mile from the flight line, yet at times the sound of voices and machinery sounded as if it was outside of our Nissen hut.

Just about the time I was ready to drop asleep, the door to our hut opened, and the clerk from operations walked down the middle of the bay with a flashlight and clipboard and gently woke up the crew mem-

6. A toggalier was an enlisted man assigned to the bombardier's position, but without a bombsight. His job was to release the bombs as the lead aircraft did. This made it possible to reduce the number of bombardiers, who were not needed in formation bombing, and also put a skilled aerial gunner on the nose gun (or chin gun on a B-17 G), since most officers lacked the gunnery skills of the enlisted men.

bers who were scheduled to fly. He informed you for what time the briefing was scheduled. I quickly got dressed, picked up my shaving kit and towel, and walked to the large building located next to our hut that contained the showers, sinks, and toilets. Then I returned to quarters, secured my personal effects, hopped on my trusty bike, and pumped up to the combat crew mess hall. On the days that a mission was scheduled, the cooks and bakers always provided us with a breakfast of fresh eggs cooked to our specification, bacon, pancakes, and SOS.[7] Moreover, there was always coffee, milk, and all the necessary condiments.

After your hearty meal, you secured your bike and headed for the intelligence briefing room. After stowing the bike, you surrendered all your personal effects: wallet, rings, watches, etc. Your personal effects were carefully placed in a large manila envelope, sealed, and signed. In turn, you were issued two escape kits that snugly fit into the leg pockets of your flying overalls. One kit contained specially made two-sided silk scarves that contained a map of France and Germany, a compass, a survival knife, German and French money, and photos of you taken on your arrival at Knettishall in civilian clothes. These photos were to be turned over to the maquis [French underground guerilla fighters] when they found you, and they would be used to make fake ID cards. The other kit contained such items as penicillin powder, morphine with a hypodermic needle, Halezon tablets to purify the water, a D-ration chocolate bar, Benzedrine tablets for extra energy, and a small first-aid and sewing kit. We also wore a shoulder holster with a .45-caliber pistol and a clip of ammo. The officers were issued a GI wristwatch. Upon our return from the mission, we turned in our escape kits and we were given back our personal items.

After being issued your escape kits, you then checked your parachutes, oxygen masks, and other flying equipment and carefully placed them in your personal parachute bag. You then reported in the briefing room, which was guarded by MPs. I always checked out two parachutes: a backpack and a chest chute. The backpack was a permanent part of the parachute harness, which, when strapped to your body, was securely fastened to your back. The chest chute was a portable chute, which most times you placed near your feet for a quick pickup to snap to your chest harness clips. I did this as a safety precaution, as I knew of some crewmembers who had been blown out of their aircraft, had only a chest chute, and were not able to grab their chute in time to snap it on.

Outside the briefing room, there was always one of the flight surgeons and the Catholic and Protestant chaplains to render medical or spiritual assistance if you required any. The smiling Red Cross girls were also present to serve us with a warm smile, coffee, hot chocolate, and doughnuts. When we returned from our mission, these wonderful people were there to greet us on our safe return.

Inside the briefing room, we sat with our crews on hard wooden benches, waiting for the command "Attention!" which signified that the base commander had arrived. One of the group intelligence officers along with an officer from the Weather Section assisted the CO during the briefing. On the wall

7. Chipped beef on toast, popularly known as "shit on a shingle."

behind the podium was a large map of Europe covered over by a white sheet. When the intelligence officer took over the briefing, he would reveal the map, which showed the target and route into and out of the enemy-occupied territory. We were also briefed on the type of fighter escort, the type and position of the enemy fighters that would intercept our formation, the position of flak batteries, time of takeoff (ETO), estimated time of return (ETR), and positions our aircraft were to fly in the formation.

Following the briefing, we filed outside with our gear and boarded waiting trucks that would take us to our aircraft. The gunners, after they had stowed their flying gear inside the aircraft, would report to the Gunnery Building to check out, meticulously clean, and take the .50-caliber machine guns to the aircraft to be installed into the gun mounts. I would take care of my twin .50s to be installed in the nose turret and also install the two .50s in the navigator's compartment. The aircraft would then be thoroughly inspected outside and inside by the two pilots and the top turret engineer gunner. When all the necessary ground preparations were completed, we usually sat on the ground next to our aircraft, waiting for signal flares from the control tower. A green flare signified the mission was a go, and a red flare indicated that today's mission was scrubbed. In the winter months, we always "commandeered" the ground crew's tent to keep warm as we sat around the potbellied stove.

If the flare was green, each crew member silently boarded our fortress and settled in his respective position. Over the intercom, the pilot informed the men to secure their positions. The pilot and copilot proceeded to follow the procedures outlined in the checklist to start the engines. When the checklist was completed, the pilot opened his window, stuck his head out, and called to the ground crew, "Clear!" "Switches on!" "Starting number one engine!" The ground crew would be positioned with fire extinguishers near each engine. The huge three-bladed propeller slowly began to turn as the engine came to life. Then there was a backfire from the engine, and a huge cloud of black smoke belched from below the engine. This procedure was repeated until all four engines became like giant birds eager to take us up into the sky. The pilot then called out to the ground crew, "Brakes off!" and gently turned our aircraft onto the taxi strip.

Usually there was a long line of waiting 17s positioned on each side of the runway, parked on the taxi strip, awaiting their turn to jockey into position on the runway. A high, piercing sound rent the air each time the brakes of the aircraft were applied during the stop-and-go procedure to get their turn to proceed onto the runway. When our turn came, the pilot positioned us onto the runway and proceeded to apply the brakes. He then commenced to rev the engines to 1,500 rpm and check the generators. Next, he switched on the turbochargers in and out. The propeller controls were moved through various rpm settings to get the controlling oil circulated through the systems. Each engine was then run at high manifold pressure to check each of the two magnetos in turn. Next, the pilot applied a short burst at maximum power. After a final check to see if the turbo supercharges were correctly set for takeoff, the pilot pulled back the controls to idle, and the pilot and copilot completed the rest of the checklist.

When the control tower gave permission to take off, the pilot eased forward the controls of the four Wright cyclone engines until they were roaring. The pilot released the brakes. Vibrating under the 4,800 horsepower, our bomber slowly began to move forward down the runway, gathering speed. During the takeoff run, the copilot called out the ground speed of the aircraft, the pilot eased back on the wheel, and the aircraft slowly began to lift into the air. When we became airborne, the copilot pressed his toes against the brake pedals to stop the spinning wheels and flicked the switch to retract the wheels. Up in the nose section, you would hear a dull thump as the wheels locked into the wheel housing. This was followed by a whirring noise as the gears folded into the housing. The pilot maintained full power as the aircraft continued to gain speed until it reached 140 mph. Then the pilot throttled back to 2,300 rpm for our climb to the prescribed altitude.

When the pilot revved up the four engines, it felt as if the aircraft would shake itself off the runway. I always tuned the intercom to UHF and could hear the control tower give our pilot permission to take off. I sat glued in my seat, situated in the Plexiglas nose of our bomber, watching the runway getting shorter and shorter as we continued to pick up speed. I was always spellbound in our daylight takeoffs, for when you reached the prescribed altitude to form into group formations, there were hundreds of bombers flying about, and different-colored flares lit up the horizon. The color of the flare signified a bomb group's location. The radio was always buzzing with commands and code names. The 388th's code name was Vampire Yellow.

Upon our return back to our base, the aircraft peeled out into a long line for their landing position. Crews with wounded aboard fired a red flare and had priority emergency landing. Medical personnel immediately boarded an ambulance and sped out to the site where the aircraft parked. The wounded were checked over by the flight surgeon, and after temporary bandages were applied, the wounded crewmember was lifted onto a stretcher, placed in the ambulance, and taken to the base hospital. The remaining aircraft made their landing approach, and the pilot taxied the fortress into its designated revetment.

You placed your flying gear in your parachute bag, and the crew was driven back in a waiting truck to the briefing room to be debriefed by an intelligence officer. The flight surgeon visited each crew to ascertain if any medical help was needed. The chaplains were also on hand to offer any spiritual help. When the parachutes and effects were returned, we signed for our personal items. The next step was the combat mess hall, where the cooks and bakers had a sumptuous meal awaiting. We were served steaks done to our request with all the [extras] to make the meal a feast worth remembering. Then back to your squadron area and try to relax and compose yourself for whatever tomorrow would bring. If a crew had been shot down, operations notified the respective squadron. All effects were removed to the squadron orderly room by supply personnel. The personal effects were screened to remove any item that could possibly be an embarrassment to the family when shipped to them.

Unlike most new crews, which were usually given a "milk run," or easy mission of short duration, on their first assignment, Sergeant Larson and his fellow crew members flew right into one of their toughest missions of the war. Their first mission took them over Bremen, Germany, on November 26, 1943. Of the more than 500 bombers that departed from England, only 440 reached the target. "It was cold," Larson recalls, "and my heated suit failed to operate, so I nearly froze my butt off, technically speaking." His squadron was greeted by unusually heavy flak. From his waist gunner position, he could not see the enemy fighters that were viciously attacking parts of the formation before and after it passed through the flak. The planes dropped their bombs and returned to England. Of the forty-one B-17s from the 388th Bomb Group, two were lost and thirty were damaged. After three more missions, Lieutenant McKenna, the bombardier, was transferred to another crew, and Melvin Larson was trained as a toggalier.

> I received a thirty-minute briefing on how to use the bombardier's control panel. A toggalier did the same job as a commissioned bombardier but did not use the Norden bombsight. I was shown the toggle switch that controlled the releasing of the bombs. I was shown how to fuse and defuse the bombs, and how to set the intervalometer that controlled the timing release of the bombs, if they were to be released in either a train release or salvo.[8]

Once the plane was in the air, the bombardier or the toggalier went through the bomb bay, pulled the cotter pins out of the bomb fuses, put the pins with their numbered red tags still attached in the pocket of his A-2 flying jacket, and later handed them to the intelligence officer during the debriefing. If the bombs were not dropped, he reinserted the cotter pins in the noses and tails of the bombs.

On December 30, 1943, Larson flew his first mission as a toggalier. The target was Ludwigshafen, Germany.

> On the IP [Initial Point], which started our bomb run on the target, the PFF [Pathfinder Force] pathfinder aircraft opened their bomb-bay doors and fired a red flare, which signaled that the lead bombardier was working with the Norden bombsight. The rest of the aircraft in the formation then opened their bomb-bay doors. We then set our intervalometer, per instructions at the briefing, and then with our index finger on the toggle switch, we watched the PFF pathfinder aircraft with glued eyeballs. When we saw the first bomb leave the PFF aircraft's bomb bay, the rest of the aircraft released their bombs accordingly. This was known as "pattern bombing," which was how so much destructive ground saturation was accomplished. I was informed that because of the early date of my first toggalier mission, I would have been the first NCO toggalier flying with the 388th Bomb Group.

During this mission, a piece of flak tore a hole in Larson's oxygen hose line. Since his face was dripping with sweat, he quickly changed masks. The aircraft was at 27,000 feet, and the temperature outside was at about 45 degrees below zero. When the pilot climbed down to 10,000 feet and the crew removed their masks, Larson realized that his mask had frozen to his face, giving him a severe case of frostbite. It took a week for the flight surgeon to pry a piece of the mask from his

8. The operator preset the data in the intervalometer, which controlled the dropping of the bombs, so that the desired number would drop at a predetermined interval. During a train release, the instrument controlled the length of time between bomb releases. The toggalier turned the dial to whatever time setting had been predetermined at the briefing, such as one or two seconds. For a salvo, the bomb release switch was flipped.

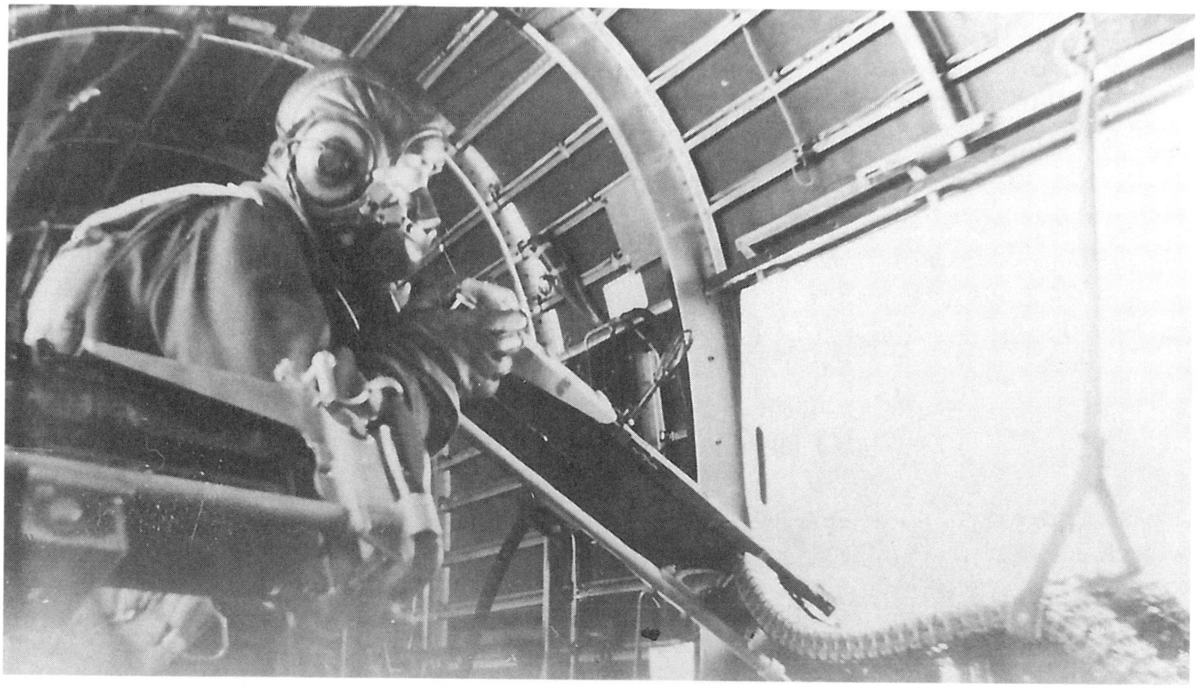

Waist gunner on a B-24 taken with a Brownie camera. PHOTO COURTESY OF HERBERT BEATTY

face, and he was grounded for a month. On January 5, 1944, he was distraught to learn that the aircraft carrying his original crew had failed to return from a bombing mission over Bordeaux, France.[9] As fate would have it, he met his future wife on the evening of the same day.

The ground combat troops envied the life of the airmen, who usually went into battle only a few times a week, returned to their home base after each mission, and enjoyed comforts and luxuries that the dogface in the field could only dream about.[10] After the equivalent of twenty-five to fifty days of combat, depending on the type of aircraft, the pilots and their aircrews were rotated home. The infantrymen, on the other hand, got to go home only if they were badly wounded—the million-dollar wound—no matter how long they had been in combat. What the soldiers on the ground tended to overlook, however, was the unbelievable stress under which the aircrews operated. During a mission, the fear of being shot out of the sky, the possibility of being badly wounded without the ability to obtain immediate medical intervention, and the knowledge that if shot down, they would be helpless and possibly wounded behind enemy lines took a heavy toll on the airmen.[11]

The Medium Bombers

Capt. Frank Gallagher flew as a bombardier on a B-26 Marauder of the 450th Squadron, 322nd Bombardment Group. The 450th Squadron arrived in the United Kingdom in March 1943 (the ground echelon arrived on the *Queen Elizabeth* at the end of November 1942). In the

9. It was the only aircraft lost from the 388th Bomb Group that day. The copilot, Lt. Paul Davis, died when his parachute failed to open. The waist gunners were captured. The remainder of the crew was rescued by the maquis and made it back to England.

10. In World War I, the American soldiers were called doughboys, but this term was largely replaced by GI and usually dogface for the infantryman in World War II.

11. Usually medics were attached to each infantry company, but a wounded GI still might be trapped on the battlefield for hours until he could be evacuated.

summer of 1943, when he and his crewmates were under the 8th Air Force, they flew out of Bury St. Edmund, England. "We started training for low-level stuff in six-ship formations," he recalls. "The pilots got so monotonous we were going down to see which plane could pick up the most grass off the English fields." His crew flew the first B-26 mission, which was also Eubank's first mission, from the United Kingdom on May 14. According to Gallagher, it was "a low-level mission over Ijmagen, Holland."

> All returned badly damaged from there. It was a surprise attack. One aircraft crashed over the field, and the crew bailed out but the pilot did not make it. On May 17, they sent ten ships back to the same area, and the British required them to rise to 1,000 feet and then drop down to the deck over the Channel. That alerted the enemy, and none of the ten came back. Eleven were assigned but one aborted. Eight were knocked down by fighters and AA, and two got to the target and had to ditch in the Channel. After that, we were transferred to the 9th Air Force for medium-altitude bombing.[12]

Lt. Graydon Knox Eubank, whose trans-Atlantic trip with the 449th Squadron had not gone smoothly, joined the group in May, just after the disastrous mission.

> We flew individually from Africa to England. Two aircraft got in trouble off the coast of Spain. Lieutenant Rice was on one engine and went back to Portugal, but crashed off the Spanish coast and some of the crew were rescued. Lieutenant King's plane went down when ice formed on his wing.
>
> We went up to Bury St. Edmunds and landed there. You could tell something was in the air by looking. People were sitting around, and we pulled into our taxi stand and parked. We asked what was wrong, and they said they had shot the entire squadron down yesterday. Out of the whole bunch of sixty-some men, two gunners who got in a rubber raft after ditching were finally picked up.[13] Morale wasn't much.

The group moved to Andrews Field in Braintree on June 12, 1943, and began flying again. Its new field, one of the first to be completed by American army engineers, provided only rough accommodations for the men, some of whom had to live in tents instead of Quonset huts.

> We were bombing marshaling yards. The V-1 rocket didn't come into existence until about December 1943, and then we started bombing them. We were bombing on the lead bombardier after we went to medium altitude, and we didn't take our bombsights on these missions. For the V-1s, we got a briefing of pictures, and it would be just a clump of woods and the coordinates: so far from this town, maybe a railroad track ran down and any sort of visual things you could see, but they were all hidden in little clumps of forests. All we did was bomb the woods, because you couldn't see anything. You would come up to the IP and turn left or right and go in to the site. It was up to the lead bombardier and navigator. You could look out the nose and pick it up ten miles ahead of you, and then you zeroed in with your bombsight and plugged it in, then you got the picture through the bombsight.

12. The transfer of the group to the 9th Air Force did not take place until October 1943.
13. The mission listed fifty-eight men as MIA, and one of the eleven aircraft dispatched had aborted the mission. The lead B-26 was shot down, and two others had a midair collision with an explosion that caused two others to crash. The two men rescued were picked up by a British destroyer.

The Norden bombsight procedure for the medium bombers, which was similar in the heavy bombers, was as follows:

> At preflight before the mission, we would have the altitude, the speed to take into consideration—that is what the sight would work on. The sight magnified everything, and it was electrical. You turned two knobs for control. The sight controlled the B-26. If you turned it too quick or made too big of a correction, it would disrupt the gyro in the bombsight, and you would have to reset it. It was very delicate. With the bomb-bay doors open, you zeroed in, and the bombs were automatically released on that point.
>
> When dropping on the lead bombardier, the pilot keeps it in close. There was a deputy bombardier, and only two bombsights would be carried on the mission. We never lost both bombardiers.

Gallagher and his crewmates did not have another mission until July, because the two low-level missions flown in May proved to be too costly. They spent the time off training for medium-altitude missions. The 323rd Bomb Group also retrained and flew its first mission, a medium-altitude one, on July 16. The 322nd returned to combat missions on August 4, 9, 12, and 16 and lost its first bomber on August 19.

A tour of duty in the AAF in Europe meant different things to different units. For the crews of medium and light bombers, it consisted of fifty to sixty missions, whereas for the crews of heavy bombers, who usually flew longer missions, it was about thirty missions. The air force commander set the number of missions required, and changes were made in 1944.

For Lt. Graydon Eubank, a medium bomber pilot, the tour in Europe began with a ncrve-wracking mishap. On his first mission, probably in September, against a target at St. Omer, France, German flak shattered his windshield, sending a cascade of glass all over him. After that, he flew on the following missions: September 16, airfield at Beaumont Le Roger; September 24, airfield at Beauvais; September 27, Beauvais again; October 2, airfield at St. Omer; and October 3, Amsterdam airport. On October 16, the 322nd Bomb Group transferred to the 9th Air Force, and Eubank flew one mission against French coastal targets on October 21 and two the next day. He flew his first Noball mission against a V-site at Lingheim on December 3. "These Noball attacks were at medium altitude, anywhere from 8,500 to 10,000 feet," he recalls. "We used no oxygen and did no low-level attacks." He flew additional Noball missions on January 4 to Bois Rempré and January 7 to Cherbourg. "At that time, we still did not know what we were hitting; we only knew it was like a construction site," he says. The nature of his targets varied from airfields at St. Omer and Montgit on January 14 and 24 to Noball sites on January 28 and 29 and February 3, 11, and 13. On February 24, he bombed an airfield at Arnhem and flew another Noball mission against the V-1 site at Bois Rempré.

> On these Noball raids, we drew a lot of flak, and from time to time, we drew fighters. We had Spitfires that could go partway and had to return home and would meet us on the return. We had fighter attacks from a group called the "Abbeville Kids" in FW-190s with yellow noses.[14] The flak would always stop when the fighters came in. Later on, we received support from the P-47, and

14. These aircraft were from *Jagdgeschwader 26*. A *Jagdgescwader* was a fighter wing that contained up to four groups *(Jagdgruppen)*, and each of those had three to four squadrons *(Jagdstaffel)* of twelve to sixteen fighters.

> later we didn't need any at all. In March, almost everyday we had a Noball mission, and when we had two missions, we usually hit an airfield in the morning and came back to hit a Noball target in the afternoon. We used a toggalier on these missions. On March 26, the target was the [E-boat] sub pens at Ijmuden, and on April 10, the marshaling yards at Namur with an afternoon mission to the Le Havre gun positions.[15] It was the first time we used chaff, and we didn't get hit. On April 21, on a Noball target at St. Pol, my right engine was shot out by flak. Coming back, we started overheating and began losing altitude but had enough altitude to get to a grass RAF strip called Hokey [spelling unclear]. We landed there. It was such a bad raid that quite a few ships had to go in there. Some belly-landed, and a couple guys were killed on the raid.

Once a yellow-nosed Me-109 came up on Eubank's wing, and the pilot, apparently out of ammunition, looked at him, waved, and peeled off. Like most pilots, Graydon Eubank developed a grudging fondness for his B-26.

> It was a very sturdy and strong aircraft but had a lot of disadvantages. It was difficult to maintain because of the engines. Jimmy Doolittle came down and ran a B-26 out for the guys and showed what it could do. We had an exceptional pilot in Bill Young, who took the plane up and shut down both engines and rolled it. The aircraft had four .50-caliber machine guns on the side, and the bombardier had one in the nose in addition to the machine guns in the rear turrets.
>
> We all slept in huts, and the pilots usually slept together. Once a navigator-bombardier was next to me, but it was a mixup. We would go to bed, and generally we knew the mission for the next day. Wake up at about 4 A.M., breakfast at 5 A.M., briefing at 6 A.M., and takeoff at 7 A.M. Breakfast consisted of Spam, powdered eggs, and brussels sprouts, with a ration of one or two fresh eggs a week. You didn't trust anybody to cook your eggs; you did it yourself. We checked out a flak suit, helmet, parachutes, and all, and then went in and got our briefing. We were informed of the type of formation and aircraft we would fly, the radio frequencies, and how long the fighter escort would be with us.
>
> We got into our trucks, went out to the hardstand, and made our inspection of the aircraft. Everybody has fear, and at about this time the feeling is in your stomach. You go around with the checklist, kicking tires, so to speak, and doing whatever else is necessary. You get on top of your airplane and go back and check your vertical stabilizer, because in training we lost a couple of airplanes because that stabilizer came off. They made some modifications to it to strengthen it. You got in the airplane and all adjusted. Once it was start-engine time, you got the engines running, and the fear was gone. You are a professional, and you've got a job to do.
>
> You take off at about twenty- or thirty-second intervals, and you had to watch for the prop wash. You would make a turn on takeoff and join up at about 12,000 feet. We had as many as thirty-six aircraft on a mission. A box of eighteen each divided into groups of six. We would go out and at a specific point, turn, and we were on our route. At that point, the IP, we had to get ready to

15. The submarine pens were built in Brittany and along the Bay of Biscay in France. Along the French Channel coastline, the only concrete pens built served *Schnellboot* (fast boat), large, fast torpedo boats that the Germans designated as S-boats, but the British called E-boats.

make the bomb run, and you had to stay straight and level. You would go in, and at a specific time, the bomb bay opened. The toggalier had a switch to toggle the bombs out, and the plane would leap in the air when you let out 4,000 to 5,000 pounds of bombs. We kept a tight formation because of fighter attacks.

When you go out on a mission, you told your gunners to test-fire their guns over the Channel. We got a pretty good fighter attack from the tail on one mission. The tail gunner called up and said he couldn't fire because his guns jammed. He hadn't test-fired his guns. What was happening was the gunners didn't want to fire their guns, because they would have to clean them when they got back. We had a lot of fighter attacks in the beginning (1943) and on my last mission (late 1944), a Me-262 jet that was so fast I didn't know what it was.

The Heavy Bombers

Shortly after the devastating bombing of Hamburg, the 8th Air Force flew one of its first deep-penetration missions on August 17, 1943, targeting the Me-109 fighter plants at Regensburg. A diversionary force went against Schweinfurt, the location of an equally important target for the Allies: most of Germany's ball-bearing industry. The Regensburg mission required the aircraft to fly on to the Mediterranean. This was Sgt. Bonnie Skloss's sixth mission as a gunner in the 388th Bomb Group.

They woke us up at about four o'clock in the morning, and we were told to take an overnight change of clothes and our canteens. We didn't know what was happening. In the briefing room, I saw the picture on the wall. We were to go all the way to Africa.

What really stands out in my mind is that when we were past the target, we didn't get any opposition at all. I saw the Swiss Alps looking out the window at those mountains while eating dinner, a can of Spam or something. Everything was crisp with the dry air up there. When we hit the Mediterranean, we felt safe from the fighters. We may have gotten a few holes over Regensburg, but we weren't attacked by fighters, although I guess some of the boys were.[16]

We landed in Algiers and stayed a whole week. We pumped that B-17 full of gas with a little hand pump, and we slept under the wing every night. I think five or so planes ditched. Out of all the planes that went there, I think only ten or so were flyable and could come back home, because the rest had to be repaired. We made our return trip along the western coast of France, and we had a target coming back. When we hit the target, Bordeaux, we got in a rainstorm where the whole group just dispersed, and from there to England, we were on our own. We ran out of fuel and hit the first airfield we saw, refueled, and made it back by sundown.[17]

Several months later, during Big Week, the new campaign between February 20 and 25, 1944, to cripple the German aircraft industry, Lt. David C. Burton's squadron of the 15th Air Force flew northward over the Alps. It was February 23, a day of rest for the 8th Air Force in England. Burton's squadron flew out of San Pancrazio, located in the "heel" of the Italian "boot."

16. Of 146 aircraft dispatched, 26 did not return.
17. On August 26, 1943, 85 aircraft took off from North Africa, which was about 70 percent of those that had made it there.

A B-17 on a mission. PHOTO COURTESY OF BONNIE SKLOSS

This was my crew's seventh combat mission, and our group of four squadrons put up about 50 planes for this mission. We were joined by about 150 other B-24s that were carrying thousands of high-explosive and incendiary bombs to one of the main factories for Me-109s in Regensburg, Germany. The Germans protected these fighter factories with everything they had at their disposal.

We were on the bomb run when our number 3 engine was hit by shrapnel from an antiaircraft shell that exploded near the copilot's side of the plane. I pushed on more power to the remaining three engines in order to stay with the formation on the bomb run. A bomber with one engine feathered and lagging behind the formation always attracted enemy fighters. Our three engines responded, but then I noticed the number 1 prop governor was failing, and the prop started to "run away," or overspeed. It had to be feathered before the engine froze up, and it couldn't be feathered.

It was no decision-making time, [as we were] losing altitude and expecting to become an easy target for the enemy fighters. If we bailed out into the enemy-held snow-covered mountains below, we might not survive anyway. Another option was to throw out everything that was loose in the plane, including guns. This last option was the one we selected. We set about making the last two Pratt and Whitneys take us as far as they could before they failed. Lady Luck was with us, because by the time we could no longer stay close to the formation, the enemy fighters had left the area.

The two 1,200-horsepower, R-1830 Pratt and Whitney engines were now being "sacrificed" for the few minutes of flying time. To keep from losing too much altitude and flying speed, we turned up the supercharger, and when the engines would get too hot, we would cut back on the power and let them cool off. We wondered how long these engines could take this abuse.

Switzerland was another option, but we would be interned. The entire crew wanted to try to get back to home base. Over the next couple of hours, the engines responded every time we applied full power to them. The plane was becoming lighter because of the large amount of fuel we were burning, so we were still at about 6,000 feet altitude by the time we reached the Adriatic coast. We radioed Air-Sea Rescue, because we knew if one engine quit, we would ditch the plane in the sea. [The crew opted to continue passing two Air-Sea Rescue boats and even other airfields, until they reached their own.]

Since there was no radio contact with the tower at our base, and we knew that we didn't have the luxury of making more than one approach, we flew over the base at about 1,500 feet, firing red flares and hoping they would see that we had two engines feathered. The tower did recognize our plight. We had to crank down our landing gear and flaps by hand, because we had lost our hydraulic pressure when the number 3 engine was hit. Bob Mellinger, the tail gunner, continued to fire red flares, letting other ships know we were in trouble, and I pulled back the throttles as we turned on the base leg. All the crew took crash-landing positions, in case we came in short. With half flaps, the B-24 glided just as other planes had done, and as we turned into the final approach, I called, "Full flaps! We've got it made! Thank God for Pratt and Whitney!" Everyone let out a "Yah-hoo!" when the landing gear settled on the runway.

The 15th Air Force flew most of its missions over Italy and the Balkans. On March 30, 1944, Lieutenant Burton flew a mission over the marshaling yards of Sofia, Bulgaria, as part of the overall plan to cut off oil shipments.

Our Allied fighter escort left us two hours before, when they reached their fuel limit, and the enemy Me-109s and FW-190s moved in to take their toll of the slow-flying bombers. Significant openings began to appear in our formations as one plane after another was attacked, caught fire, or lost an engine and had to drop out.

It wasn't long before black clouds of death were bursting all around us as the antiaircraft shells sought us out.

As we turned on the IP, tail gunner Sgt. Bob Mellinger called on the intercom, "Hey, Skipper! Tail gunner here! There's another formation of B-24s about 1,000 feet above us. Goddamn! They all just opened their bomb-bay doors!" I glanced up through the Plexiglas overhead and saw a group of B-24s that had taken a shortcut across the IP and were heading for the same assigned target. I called back on the intercom, "Pilot to tail! They are bound to see us and pull away. Keep an eye on them and let me know what they are doing. We have about eight minutes to the target."

In the meantime, I switched to the assigned command radio frequency and broke radio silence with "Red leader! Red leader! This is B flight leader. We have a formation of B-24s directly over us with bomb-bay doors open and following our bomb run! Let's turn and get the hell out of their way! Over!"

Burton's attempts to contact the formation leader failed, but he remained in formation, hoping the group above would see them.

Copilot Shuman yelled, "Here they come!" I glanced up. Ten 500-pound high-explosive bombs were dropping right in front of us. To the right and left, there were two more strings of ten 500-pound bombs. When they reached about 500 feet above us, we could see the yellow tags of the arming devices fly off, indicating that the bombs were fully armed and that they would explode at the slightest touch. I had about two and a half seconds to decide before we collided with them. With more of a reflex action than a decision, I kicked the right rudder all the way and pushed forward and right on the control wheel. The great, bulky four-engine bomber responded immediately and rolled right into a vertical dive, heading for the ground 22,000 feet below. Copilot Shuman grabbed for the control wheel, thinking I had been hit by shrapnel from the flak, but I waved him off.

As our B-24 headed straight for the mountains below, I could see the bombs floating down beside us less than 200 feet away. The plane gradually pulled away from the danger of falling bombs, and my attention was turned to saving the crew and plane. I punched the bailout button. With the bailout bell ringing in their ears, the crew members tried to leave the supposedly doomed plane. The centrifugal force of the plane in the violent maneuver held their bodies where they were, and they couldn't move. Sgt. Herb Graham in the top turret, Al Kurzontikowski in the ball turret, and Sgt. Bill Furney in the nose turret could not lift themselves from their tight quarters. Tail gunner Sgt. Bob Mellinger managed to fall backwards out of his tail turret only because he never closed its doors. Our flight engineer, Sgt. Ed Steiner, was in the open bomb bay, standing on a six-inch catwalk between the bomb racks, ready to take pictures of the bomb hits on the target. When the plane rolled, he was pressed between the bomb racks and he couldn't move. His parachute was ten feet away on the flight deck. Bombardier Lt. Dan Delaney was looking through his bombsight, and when the plane rolled, he saw blue sky through his scope. He threw the salvo toggle switch, releasing the ten high-explosive bombs, but they rolled around inside the bomb bay before dropping out. Navigator Lt. Hugh Banta was at his cramped desk in the nose compartment, and when the plane rolled, he pulled the emergency nose wheel door opener and clipped on his chest chute. Sgt. John Knol was standing at the .50-caliber machine gun in the waist window. When he tried to lean over and pick up his chest chute, he was pinned to the floor and he couldn't move because of centrifugal force.

The plane continued to pick up speed in the dive and was vibrating badly as the wind whistled and roared past the rivets and corners of the plane's fuselage. The aluminum skin on the upper surface of the wing rippled like water on a lake. My right hand reached for the elevator trim tab and started turning it slowly, trying to gently bring the plane out of the dive. The plane began to respond to the controls. I had the feeling we were going to make it. I shut off the bailout switch and yelled on the intercom, "Pilot to crew! Don't bail out!"

Every one of the crew had been trying to get to an escape hatch, but not one of the crew bailed out. It certainly wasn't because they didn't try. We stayed low to the ground to avoid radar and keep hidden from the enemy fighters attacking the rest of our formation 20,000 feet above us.

I called on the command radio, "I don't know where the rest of you guys are, but I'm down here in a valley and I'm heading for home! Did you see that? Those sons of bitches really did bomb us!" I didn't expect a reply, but a voice came in loud and clear on the radio. "Yeah, we know! We're right behind you! Wait for us!"

It was Lt. Bob Hunter, who had been flying formation on my right wing. When I rolled to the right, he had to do the same, and a string of bombs came between us, just missing both planes by a few feet. He did a nice job of flying to avoid a midair collision. This was Lieutenant Hunter's first mission, and after we were back at base, he lamented, "Hell, combat is going to be worse than I thought. Not only do the Jerries shoot at us, but our own damn planes bomb us!" He told me why he and four other planes followed me down. It was because they had been told to follow the leader of the formation "no matter what."

Lt. William Denham, with the 730th Squadron, 452nd Bomb Group, got to England at the beginning of 1944 and flew a few practice missions. The normal procedure in his unit was to have an experienced pilot take the crew on a mission. On his first mission, which he recalls as having taken place on February 14, 1944, Denham asked, "Where is my old hand?" and they replied, "We ain't got any; go ahead and just follow those people there!"[18] He followed the command. The mission turned out to be a Noball target. "From that mission, I was able to judge the concentration of flak and their accuracy," says Denham. "On the rest of the missions after that, I never saw more flak, nor so close."

T. Sgt. William F. French, a radio operator on a B-17 who was also in the 452nd Bomb Group, but the 729th Squadron, flew his missions from January until mid-June 1944. On his fourth mission, his aircraft was so badly shot up that it had to be replaced. "I had a little radio compartment," he recalls, "which was a little room right behind the bomb-bay compartment and just over the edge of the wing. It was about six by six, enough for one man and the radio equipment. I had one flexible .50-caliber machine gun out of the hatch. I used it, especially on Poznan, several times. It had a limited arc of fire compared to the waist guns. I could get it out quite a ways and up, of course."

The mission over Poznan, Poland, took place on April 11, 1944. Technical Sergeant French's baptism of fire had taken place earlier in January over Romilly, France, where the flak gunners showed their mettle with uncanny precision. French's group flew several nerve-wracking missions over Germany, and then a fourteen-hour mission to Poznan. After their fighter escort left them over Denmark, they had to shake off German fighters that came in strong before they reached their target, which to their disappointment was blanketed in clouds. Consequently, they turned their attention to a secondary target in northern Germany. On that day, the 3rd Bombardment Division lost 33 B-17s.

Lt. Robert Walsh, a bombardier in a B-17 with the 524th Squadron, 379th Bomb Group, had been flying missions since early December 1943. His first mission had been to Emden. On one of the missions in 1944, either the mission to the sub pens at Kiel on January 5 or the one to Ludwigshaven on January 7, Walsh's crew flew in a B-17F instead of the G model assigned to the other crews. His plane ran out of fuel while

18. Denham may be mistaken about the date. It may have been February 13, since that mission to the V-sites in the Pas de Calais was the only one flown by his group until about February 17.

the pilot was looking for the airfield, which was clouded over, and a Spitfire had to guide it in as the third engine shut down because of the lack of fuel. On February 4, his birthday, Walsh flew his eighth mission against the marshaling yards at Frankfurt. His birthday present from the German antiaircraft gunners was a piece of flak that hit Walsh's leather helmet and then dropped to the floor. It had come through the plane's plastic observation nose, and it was spent by the time it hit him. On March 18, Walsh's target was an aviation industrial site at Oberhaffenpaffenhofen. General Morley's lead aircraft took 113 holes from flak, and Walsh's 11. Of the 284 B-17s in the 1st Bombardment Division, 102 were damaged and 8 shot down. Even though the next day should have been a "milk run" to the V-2 site at Wizernes, once again the losses were heavy, as 74 of the 117 participating B-17s were damaged and 1 was downed.[19]

After arriving in England, Sgt. Alvin Anderson's crew was assigned to the 379th Bombardment Group. After some additional training, the crew started flying combat missions in February 1944, just at the end of Big Week. When they were not battling in the skies over Europe, Anderson and his crewmates fought the conditions at their base in Kimbolton.

> We had three crews in a metal Quonset hut, and the officers had their own hut. In this hut, there was a stove that burned coal or coke. You couldn't get much heat out of coke. We had a person who was a good pole-vaulter; he would vault over the wall where they kept the fuel and throw the coal over to us. Consequently, we had more coal than coke, and we had a good fire in our barracks.
>
> Of course, you get over there and your food is substantial. Dehydrated eggs . . . They found a farmer who would sell us eggs on the black market. It cost us $1 per egg or $12 a dozen. One night, we chipped in $35 to a fellow. He took off on his bicycle and came back with three dozen eggs, but just before he got to the barracks, he had a wreck, and we had three dozen scrambled eggs in the musette bag that couldn't be eaten. That ended our buying eggs for a while.

The hassles of garrison life paled in comparison with the difficulties Anderson and his crewmates faced in the air, however. The crew was broken up and sent to fly a few missions with other, more experienced crews, a routine procedure in this group. For his first mission, Anderson found an opening for a waist gunner, but since he was a top turret gunner, he had to get permission from the commander. On February 24, he departed on a mission over Schweinfurt, during which 11 of the 238 B-17s were downed and 160 damaged.

> My partner on the other side of the plane was firing at a fighter that was fairly low below us. His ammunition wouldn't feed, so I had to feed the ammunition to him. About that time, something went ping, and there was daylight up there towards the radio room that shouldn't have been there. I now knew what flak was. By the time we had reached the target area, I had counted over 10 B-17s that I could see going down myself. Well, that was 100 men. After being through that and coming back, you began to realize what combat was. If you made

19. The 379th Bomb Group proved to be the leader in bombing effectiveness for the 8th Air Force in 1944 and 1945. At the same time, it had the highest rate of venereal disease (VD) in the 1st Bombardment Division, and all its members had to attend a VD lecture each month in the fall of 1944.

five or six missions, you were a veteran, and everybody looked up to you.

The next day, Anderson flew a mission to Augsburg. Again, losses were high: Of the 196 B-17s that reached the target, 13 were lost and 172 damaged. In early March, Anderson's crew reassembled, but a few days later, on March 6, he flew on another aircraft that needed an engineer for that day. It was a flight of almost 800 bombers heading for Berlin and its vicinity. Once again, the flak was heavy.

On this day, when we came close to Berlin, the smoke on the flak bursts was so thick that you could not see the squadron that went ahead of you, but you went on. They went to open our bomb-bay doors, but they wouldn't open electrically. While the bombardier and the pilot had an emergency release they could use, I knew from their conversation on the intercom that they were in trouble at this time. I had gotten out of my turret, and I still remember seeing in my mind Lieutenant Ramberger, the pilot. He had to hold his release. He stood right straight up, pulled it, and this released the bombs, which fell right through the bomb-bay door. While it opened automatically that way, to get it to close, you had to crank it down by hand. Then they would engage, and you had to crank them back up. This was my job. I always carried my crank underneath the turret, where it would be handy if I needed it. Well, it was my fault too; I never checked it before we took off. They kept it back in the radio room [in this aircraft]. This meant that you had to walk the catwalk—and if I remember correctly, this catwalk could not have been more than twelve inches wide—back across the open bomb-bay doors to the radio room, open the door, go inside, and get the crank. I couldn't wear a parachute and get through the center supports of the bomb bay. I had to pick up an oxygen bottle and walk around with it, holding on where I could. I got out there and had to hold on to the stanchion to open the radio room door, so I had to let loose of my oxygen bottle, and it rolled out through the bomb bay. I got the crank and stuck it in my jacket, took another bottle of oxygen, and repeated the steps back to the front. I lay down, cranked those screws down, engaged them, and cranked them back up. The only thing you could see from the ground was flashes of red from the antiaircraft guns. Well, we got back all right ourselves, but a lot of them didn't make it back that day. We lost over 700 men.[20]

Sgt. Melvin Larson, a toggalier in the 388th Bomb Group, also flew on the Berlin mission that day.

Flying over the English Channel, I could see bombers stretched out for miles ahead of our formation. Our group continued on towards Berlin, and so far, it had been unopposed. We were going to have to face a powerful flak defense that lay ahead, protecting Berlin. We could hear over the VHF bombers that had already bombed their targets telling us that the flak over Berlin was thick.

Our fighter escort improved, and twenty-five P-51 Mustangs had caught up with the formation. [We were] flying close

20. Anderson's bomb division, the 1st, put 248 B-17s over Berlin and lost 18, with another 72 aircraft damaged, suffering almost 200 casualties, including 184 MIA. The 2nd and 3rd Bomb Divisions sent in 424 B-17s and B-24s to targets around Berlin and lost 51 bombers plus 175 damaged and 502 airmen MIA.

Col. Francis "Gabby" Gabreski in his P-47 escorting Melvin Larson's badly shot-up B-17 back from a raid on Berlin, March 6, 1944. PHOTO COURTESY OF MELVIN LARSON

behind this formation that was presently under deadly attacks by German fighters. We could see this conflict. Eight B-17s were shot down; three of these bombers were destroyed in midair collisions with German fighters. Several more fortresses had to leave the formation because of severe battle damage. We lost four "little friends," and twenty-one German fighters were destroyed.

Then all seemed calm for a while as we flew towards Berlin. The waist gunners were busy throwing out chaff, which were metal strips of tin foil. However, the chaff today was not as effective as it was supposed to be. Berlin was saturated with heavy flak guns. As we neared Berlin, it looked as if the whole city was covered with a thick, black cloud that kept discharging huge, red fireballs of death-dealing shrapnel. This ugly shroud of death was waiting for us. I had never seen flak so thick. The bombers ahead of the formation seemed engulfed in the black cloud as they flew into the exploding flak area. The formation leader failed to find a clear target on the south side of Berlin. We continued to fly across the most heavily defended part of the city. Finally, after what seemed an eternity, the group leader leveled out, and we commenced our bomb run.

The 388th Bomb Group dropped its bombs over the Wittenburg area of Berlin. I called out over the intercom, "Bombs away!" The flak was now getting closer and increasing in intensity. When our bombs were released, we felt our aircraft leap upwards, for we were now 6,000 pounds lighter. I observed the aircraft flying on either side of us being hit by flak, and I could see large, ragged holes appearing on their wings and fuselage. You could hear the flak bouncing off the roof of our aircraft that sounded like hailstones hitting on a metal roof. Abruptly, the death-dealing flak stopped.

[On the return trip from Berlin,] the tail gunner called to me over the intercom and asked what the time was and how long would it be before we reached the English Channel. I had just informed him that it was 2:40 P.M., when, from both sides of our formation, it looked like a black swarm of angry hornets were about to attack us. The attack on our group was by over thirty FW-190s. At first they flew alongside of our formation, out of range of our .50-caliber machine guns. Then they flew ahead of us, turned across our flight path, and proceeded to attack us from 11 to 1 o'clock positions, so close that we could only spot every second or third attacker. These attacks were almost suicidal, as they came at us rolling, firing, and diving away as they pressed their attacks as if they intended to ram our aircraft. White and gray parachutes began to fill the sky as crew members abandoned their crippled aircraft. I saw a body curled into a ball position falling towards our aircraft and thought that it was going to collide with one of our propellers. Miraculously, the body fell under our bomber. Our ball-turret gunner also saw the falling body and reported that after the body passed below our aircraft, he saw a gray parachute (German) open.

A B-17 in front and off to our right was hit by fighters, and two engines caught on fire. I observed the crew starting to bail out of their doomed aircraft, but I did not get a chance to count how many left, as my attention had to be diverted to a FW-190 that started to attack our aircraft at 12 o'clock level. For what seemed an eternity, the German fighter pilot and I were both blasting away at each other. My chin-turret twin .50s were spitting out lead, and I could see that I was on target. Just when I was certain that he was going to ram us head-on, the fighter dived under our aircraft so close that I could see the pilot pushing his control stick forward. I did not know if the fighter was damaged or the pilot wounded.

Another FW-190 started to attack us, and during this confrontation, our aircraft shuddered when 20-millimeter shells were finding their mark. I heard Lt. Mike Soldato, our pilot, order the two inboard engines to be feathered. Number 2 engine stopped, and the propeller slowly turned inwards into its feathered position. However, number 3 propeller began to windmill, which caused the nose section to vibrate so that it was almost impossible for the navigator and me to hold our firing stations. Mike dove our aircraft straight down, and at the same time, the two FW-190 fighters kept up their relentless attacks on our Fortress. They were determined to put us out of action forever. Mike leveled our aircraft off at 10,000 feet after we had been in a steep dive from 25,000 feet. During this breathtaking dive, I was glued to my seat by inertia and found it was impossible to move. After Lieutenant Soldato leveled our bomber, the windmilling propeller slowly moved itself into a feathered position. The two FW-190s still continued their attacks on our damaged bomber, but our gunners were doing a commendable job in making the enemy pilots more cautious.

We had now reached the outskirts of Drummer. Just when we thought we would have to bail out of our Fortress, an angel came flying out of the sun. Our savior was a P-47 Thunderbolt fighter, which took off in hot pursuit after our now fleeing adversaries. A cheer went up from our crew, and I uttered a silent prayer of gratitude to our Savior for sending our angel. A few minutes later, our angel returned but remained off at a safe distance to be out of range of our guns. Our angel called Mike on UHF and requested that he have his crew stow their guns, since he wanted to fly alongside our aircraft; he was going to escort us back to our base. When Mike asked our angel who he was, the answer came back, "Just call me Gabby." I observed the code marking HV-Y on the side of the fighter and the tail number 16385. It dawned on me that we were being honored by having the most decorated fighter pilot in the 8th Air Force, Maj. Francis "Gabby" Gabreski, escorting us back to our base.

While Mike taxied our crippled bomber to our revetment, Major Gabreski made another approach and landed. The news that Major Gabreski was escorting us back to Knettishall spread rapidly. Most of the individuals gathering were officers who wanted to meet such a distinguished fighter pilot. He had received permission to buzz the field before he took off for his own base. On his second pass, as he neared the end of the runway, he put the nose of his P-47 straight up and, after a couple of barrel rolls, straightened out and disappeared over the horizon.

Becoming an Aerial Gunner

Byron Criswell Cook was drafted in November 1942 and was given a ground support position. After being stationed in England, he left his relatively safe position to volunteer for duty as an aerial gunner.

The chairman of the draft board was my grandmother, Minnie Cook! She also drafted my younger brothers, Robert, an air force cartographer with a fighter group, and William, who was a paratrooper and was later killed in Luzon. It must have been very emotional for her. My father was an officer in the air force [Air Service]; he was a World War I pilot who flew Neuports and Spads in France and then reenlisted in World War II on a nonflying status. My sister was an army nurse, so all immediate members of my family were in the military service at one time.

At the time that I was drafted, I was working in the chemical laboratory of Alcoa, where we were running tests on aluminum and magnesium alloys used in the manufacture of military airplanes. Little did I realize that I would eventually be flying in one! After being drafted, I received my Chemical Warfare Service (CWS) Basic Training at Camp Sibert near Gadsden, Alabama. To the best of my knowledge, it was part of the Army Chemical Corps. I was first sent to Fort George Wright in Spokane, Washington. After a short stint there, I was put on detached service to the air force at Reno, Nevada, and then to the CWS at Dyersburg Air Base in Tennessee. I was then put on a train for Camp Kilmer, New Jersey, on October 12, 1943, and as we left, I handed a card out the window so someone would mail it to my wife, which they did.

After a few days in Camp Kilmer, I boarded the British ship *Orion,* which had a diverse group of troops on it. I don't recall any particular units, but there were no navy personnel or marines to my knowledge. We were in a troopship convoy, which included a couple of ships that had been modified to make them "junior" type aircraft carriers. They had RAF airplanes on deck, but I never saw any of them take off or land. We encountered rough weather going over, and everyone was sick and throwing up. It was overcrowded, and men were sleeping on the decks and the stairway landings. I slept on top of barracks bags that were piled in the ship's mess hall. As long as I stayed horizontal, I didn't get nauseous. The mutton that we had every day didn't exactly help! We disembarked at Greenock, Scotland, and I was then transferred to Altrincham, England, near Manchester, before being assigned to the 388th Heavy Bombardment Group.

I was assigned to the Chemical Warfare Company there, which meant assisting the Armament Company in loading bombs onto B-17s. After serving several months in that capacity at the bomber base, I received an opportunity to volunteer as an aircrew member. Quite a few combat crew members had been lost or wounded, and since replacements had failed to arrive from the States, an emergency call was sent out for volunteers. I had been denied training as an air cadet or air gunner previously, due to a color-blindness defect, but this ban was waived due to the urgency of the replacement gunner situation.

Seventy volunteers were interviewed, and of these, twenty were selected for training. I was chosen, and I received a week of concentrated schooling from the base gunnery officer. We were then sent to an RAF gunnery school located at King's Lynn on the North Sea. We received a week of instruction and of actual firing before returning to another week of schooling back at the 388th Group base.

About this time, a fresh group of gunnery replacements arrived from the States, so only nine of the original class of volunteers were retained for further schooling. Four of us were assigned to combat crews as waist gunners, three as ball turret gunners, and two as air photographers. I was placed in the waist gunner group. Of this group of nine, only two were fortunate enough to survive and complete their combat tour—one of the photographers, Victor LaBruad, and myself.

Cook maintained a diary of his experiences as a waist gunner on B-17 of the 388th Heavy Bombardment Group. The following excerpts come from his diary.

March 13, 1944. Preparation for First Mission—Calais

I was awakened about 0500 hours and told to get breakfast and then report for briefing with Pohl's crew. I was too excited to eat much, but choked a little down and then went to my locker and got out my flying togs. I inquired around, amongst the crewmembers, as to the whereabouts of Pohl's crew, and a short, homely, little Irishman named Bleem spoke up and identified himself as Pohl's engineer. He introduced me to Carney, the ball-turret gunner, Babicky, the tail-gunner, and Hay, the right-waist. I told Bleem that this was my first mission, and he replied that it was also number one for the crew as a unit, although the co-pilot, Etter, and Bob Hay (right-waist) had flown previous missions with other crews. Marksoh, the left-waist gunner that I was replacing, had been shot down on his first mission while serving as a replacement in another crew. Hay had had such a narrow squeak that it was almost two weeks before he could speak normally. We dressed and then went into the General Briefing Room to get the dope on the forthcoming mission. There was a large blackboard set up in nose of the front corners of the room and all the pilots were seated on benches near it, busily copying the diagram of their positions in the formation, which it revealed. The rest of the room contained benches that were being rapidly filled with EMs and bombardiers. The intelligence officer that was to do the briefing was standing by a curtain-shrouded map, the pointer in his hand restlessly tapping the floor as he waited for the room to fill up. The benches were filled and several men were lounging against the sidewalls or standing at the rear. The group wasn't quiet, but speaking in hushed and terse phrases, as location of the target was anxiously awaited. The roll call was taken and, after it was ascertained that all crews were present, the briefing officer drew open the curtain covering the map. Loud cheers went up as the target was revealed to be Calais, France. A short mission counted just the same as a long one as far as credit went towards a complete tour of duty. . . . The S-2 officer went through his briefing on the locations of flak guns, the MPI [Mean Point of Impact—for the bombardiers], the location of check-points, the places where the various fighter groups were to make rendezvous with us, where the bomb-run would commence, where evasive action would commence, the places where fighter opposition could be expected, etc., illustrating his words with thrusts of his pointer. The path of the bombers was marked with pieces of red ribbon fastened down with varicolored pins. The briefing over, the group broke up; the radio-operators to receive further instructions on code words, signals, etc.; the bombardiers to get further target-study; and the navigators to be additionally briefed on check-points. The rest of us lined up at the supply room to draw our electrically heated suits and our parachutes. We then climbed aboard a truck, which circled the perimeter, dropping off the crews at their previously assigned planes. The "Forts" were identified by the last three digits of their serial number, but of course, all of them had had titles or names affectionately bestowed upon them by their crews. Our regularly assigned ship was 851, with the name "Little Boy Blue" painted on her in bright yellow color. After we had dropped off our equipment at the ground crew's tent, we went over to the Armament Hut, drew our guns, and checked and oiled them. We then climbed aboard an Ordnance bomb-carrier, carried our guns back to the ship, commenced to install them. It was still black as pitch and most of the guns had to be installed by the Braille system. Carney had an extension light running from a small gasoline generator [called a putt-putt] for his ball-turret gun installation, but the rest of us found that you can't hold a flashlight and use both hands at the same time. Funny, how different a gun seems to be constructed, when it can't be seen! The drills we used to have in assembling and fieldstripping the .50 caliber, while blindfolded, really paid off!

After the guns were installed, we went into the ground crew's tent to await the crewmembers who hadn't yet shown up from their briefings. We jawed with the ground crew, but they very carefully refrained from asking where we were going and we just as carefully avoided any talk that might prove dangerous to the success of the mission. Of course, they could pretty well guess the probable length of the mission by the amount of gasoline that was loaded into the plane. The type of target could sometimes be guessed, as well, by the type of bombs carried.

Lt. Young, the navigator, entered the tent, was introduced to the ground crew and me, looked at his watch, and suggested that we get prepared. Pohl and Owen climbed in the ship and commenced their routine check of all the instruments and controls. Young and Hervatine swung up into the nose from their nose door, while the rest of us entered through the waist door and commenced pulling our heated suits over our flying suits. Hay showed me how to plug the extension cord from the suit into the rheostat controlling the heat. He also helped me adjust my oxygen mask, and I must confess that I was plenty apprehensive about my ability to make it function properly since I had had no previous experience with one. I was pretty well keyed-up by this time, and checked and rechecked all my equipment. I had a sheepskin jacket and pants in a canvas bag for use in the event of failure of my electrically heated suit. Also, contained in the bag were my leather shoes, which had been removed in favor of fleece-lined boots. My flak helmet and flak suit were propped up behind the ammunition feed box and my parachute and chute-harness were back near the tail wheel assembly awaiting take-off time to be donned.

There came a series of rapidly ascending whines as the self-starters kicked the engines over and, one after the other, they commenced to come to life with ear shattering roars—a hundred air hammers pounding at once. I pulled my chute harness on and Hay and I adjusted each other's leg and shoulder straps, aided by sign language. To hear each other's voices in the thundering din was out of the question.

Bob Hay went up into the radio room to recheck Galson's guns, which Engineer Bleem had installed, but hadn't had time to give the routine going-over. Then the waist door was forced open and Galson, returning from the radio-operator's briefing and fighting the prop-wash battering against the door, forced his way inside. He made a couple of quick, circular motions with his hands, as though he was washing them, and then went on up through the fuselage toward the nose. Owen cut the engines and they all came back through the radio room into the waist. "What's up?" I asked. "Mission scrubbed. Bad weather closing in!" It was quite a let down, but I didn't mind too much. Now I knew the routine to be accomplished before take-off.

March 15. First Mission—Brunswick (7 Hours) [Target industrial area] . . . Campbell . . . was assigned to us as pilot this trip. . . . The roar stepped up to a high crescendo and the ship strained and quivered, impatient at the leash. Then the brakes were released, inertia slammed me hard against a bulkhead, and the fortress roared down the runway, between the rows of red and green lights. The ground zipped past in rapidly increasing streaks of speed and then dropped away altogether as the plane lifted up through the ground mists and into the clear air above the end of the runway.

We swung around in a broad sweeping turn and headed for our first assembly point, climbing as we went. Through my open waist window, I could barely make out the running lights of other fortresses making their way toward their assigned locations. From time to time, identification flare signals would arch from the groups of planes forming up. Each Group would fly around a previously determined radio beacon at a given altitude. Combinations of colors would aid the planes taking their places in the formations. These identification signals looked very much like Roman candles, but they were shot from a large pistol in groups of two. The engineers on the lead planes [were] assigned to this job.

As we gained altitude towards the spot that we were to join the Group formation, the temperature dropped lower and lower. I had to keep setting the rheostat on my heated suit until finally the pointer was over as far as it would go. Still it grew colder. Pohl [Campbell?] called out, "Twelve Thousand Feet, better get your oxygen masks on!" After a little difficulty, I got mine

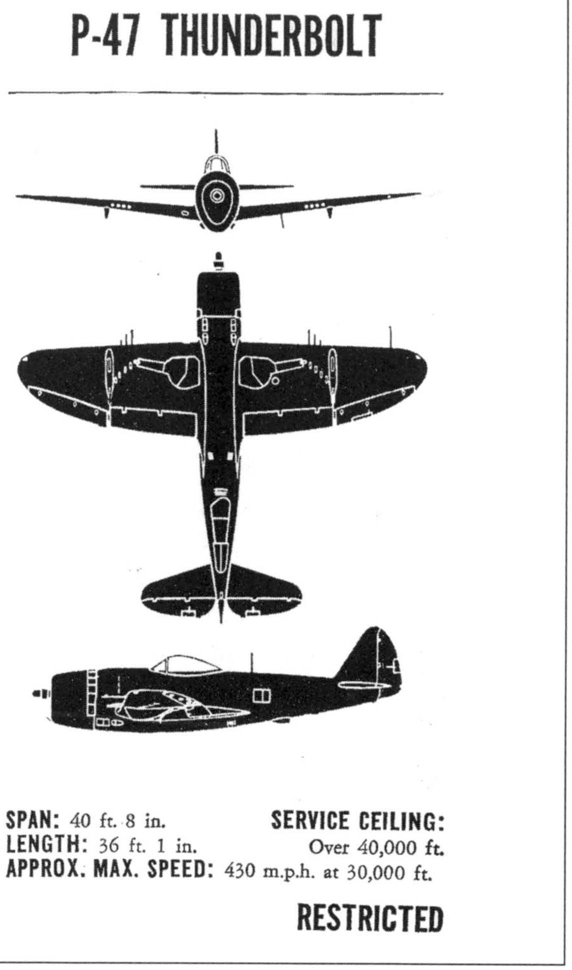

P-47 THUNDERBOLT
SPAN: 40 ft. 8 in.
LENGTH: 36 ft. 1 in.
APPROX. MAX. SPEED: 430 m.p.h. at 30,000 ft.
SERVICE CEILING: Over 40,000 ft.
RESTRICTED

Profiles of the P-47 Thunderbolt. ARMY/NAVY RECOGNITION MANUAL

snapped onto my helmet. The air was cold and thin at this altitude and the effort of any little exertion was magnified tenfold. I pushed the other end of my oxygen tube into the plug and made sure that the white rubber valve on the indicator was fluttering properly. I also turned on the heating element that kept the recoil mechanism of the gun from freezing up.

The pilot, Campbell, kept the navigator busy checking our location as we climbed on through the dawn toward our rendezvous point. Hervatine spotted the flares of the 388th Group and we swung over in a half circle to intercept them. When we caught them, we took our place in the squadron while the whole group circled around the beacon waiting for the stragglers to drop into place. Then, at the previously determined time, we set out for the rendezvous point on the coast where we were to join up with other groups to form the wing formation. By this time, we had reached 15,000 feet.

At the coast, our Group swung into position in the 45th Combat Wing and headed out over the English Channel. Here we fell into position in the bomber stream of the 3rd Bomb Division, now flying level at 18,000 feet. The temperature was about forty degrees below zero! Ice kept forming in the outlet valve of my mask and I had to keep taking my gloves off in order to unsnap the mask from the helmet. I was forced to pinch the rubber to crack the ice loose, and by the time that was accomplished, my hands were almost numb from the bitter cold. . . .

. . . Before long Campbell's voice came over the intercom, ordering us to get our flak suits and helmets on. The French coast was coming up! I got up close to the waist window and, squinting against the propwash streaming in, I could see the white flecked Channel, a long buff-colored line of cliffs extending into the purplish haze and the crazy quilt pattern of green and brown that was enemy-occupied France!

. . . The flak suit was sort of a bulletproof vest made up of overlapping plates of titanium steel sewn up in a canvas vest. The helmet was a sort of inverted soup bowl made of steel and leather and it was intended to be fastened over the regular flying helmet. . . .

As we passed in over the coast, I was hanging on my gun intensely searching the sky for signs of enemy fighters. None was to be seen, but in short order several small black puffs of smoke appeared some distance to the left of the formation. Hervy called out, "Flak ahead, about eleven o'clock!" By standing up next to the window and forcing my head out into the prop-wash, I could just see the flak puffs ahead, that Hervy was reporting, so I pushed my intercom button on my gun and reported some shots that I had seen directly opposite to the left, as "Flak at nine o'clock!" . . . Several more puffs appeared off to the left, but we were evidently too far out of range for them. Now we were getting up into the barrage ahead that Hervy had called out and it was a pretty good one. However, I wasn't experienced enough to realize it—Thank Gawd! I was fascinated with the sight and kept my eyes glued to the window, watching the oily-looking dirty puffs mushrooming out near by. The close ones had a sort of whooshing, crrummp that sounded like they were just under us. Now and then came the sharp "Ping" of metal ripping through the ship, but none seemed to do any appreciable damage.

I was so engrossed in the Jerry's efforts with the flak guns that Carney's "Fighters at four o'clock, low!" rudely jarred me into the realization that I wasn't keeping on the alert for enemy fighters. Four "peashooters" crossed behind, under our tail, and appeared off the left wing. They were close enough to identify easily as our escorting Spitfires. As if by magic, two more and then a group of four just seemed to appear out of nowhere. One minute the sky was empty, and the next minute we had a swarm of "little friends." It took me some time before I learned how to look for the minute specks against earth, cloud, and sky. Our escorting "Spits" were flying faster than the much slower cruising speed of the bombers, so they wove in and out of the bomber stream—now under it, now ahead, now off, investigating a nearby cloud mass.

After some little time, the "Spits" vanished and we flew on alone. An hour passed by before Babicky called out, "Fighters at five o'clock!" These proved to be our own P-47 Thunderbolts, on time at the rendezvous checkpoint. They sped around, through the vapor trails streaming back from the bombers, until their gas got fairly low, and then turned tail for home.

It was very difficult to shake off the lethargy produced by the constant roar of the engines, the steady vibration of the whole ship, and the early hour of arising. . . .

Two hours passed by before navigator Young prepared us for the approach of the bomb run. Campbell notified us, over the intercom that evasive action would soon start. We were now approaching the target located in the city of Brunswick, and, as we drew nearer, we passed in over a low-lying blanket of clouds that covered everything to the east. Still no sign of Jerry fighters, but the flak guns were coming to life and kicking up quite a heavy barrage. Fortunately, we weren't visible to the gunners, so aiming was done by means of radar. It didn't prove to be too accurate, but there was plenty of it. The formation commenced its weaving evasive action, then swung hard to the left and headed "down the alley" on the bomb run. This is the most difficult time. Now we are flying on a straight and level path, leading directly to the target and the bombardier is lining up his bombsight, driftmeter, and setting his toggle switches. There can be no dodging or turning to avoid enemy fire, and well he knows it! The gunners on the ground have ample time to set their aiming devices, for their targets are flying a straight course. . . . The flak is . . . very concentrated. We bored on through it and then the big ship "ballooned" up, suddenly freed of its restraining bomb load. Someone called out "Bombs away!" and all around us the other ships were releasing their finned eggs, tilting up on one wing, and sliding hard around to the left as the whole Division swung into evasive action again. The results of our efforts were not visible for we had bombed through the cloud cover by means of PFF [radar]. The lead plane of each Wing was so equipped, the other ships toggling off their loads when his bombs were seen to fall. The lead planes also dropped smoke bombs, which served as markers to following Groups.

Campbell called Hervy on the intercom and asked him if the bomb bay doors were closed—the ship was dragging. The answer was, "No, they didn't close, I'm working with the lever." Five minutes passed and they still were open, acting as a huge brake. Engineer Bleem tried to kick them loose, but no success. We were back in the flak again and Campbell sounded worried. Ten more minutes passed and still the doors were open. . . . Campbell called Radio Operator Galson and told him to tell Bleem to give up on closing them. "I'll boost the engines and we'll make out all right. We might need you in a hurry, back at your gun positions!" . . . A couple of rather nervous hours passed by before the welcome sight of our protective Thunderbolts took some of the pressure off.

Campbell had now pulled our ship out of its scheduled position in the Group formation and was flying in the "Tail-end Charley" position at the rear of the Group. Formation flying proved rather difficult due to the sluggish control caused by the open bomb bay doors. It was with great relief that I heard Hervatine announce that he could see the French coastline dead ahead, but we soon found out that the action wasn't over yet! We were too far south of scheduled course and we were passing over Ijmuiden, Holland—a lovely target for the Kraut flak guns. They sure had a wild party—beat the group up badly, but none of our ships were going down. The shell bursts were hitting smack in the middle of the bomber stream and plenty of damage was being done. I could hear bursts all around our ship and see several, right at the wingtips. The ship bucked once, and then commenced to vibrate. We'd caught a hit on our #1 engine and it lost too much oil to enable the pilot to feather it. The slowly spinning prop was setting up ragged vibration, and the other three engines were now running rough. Campbell cut our airspeed and we were dropping rapidly back from the Group. . . . Campbell kept calling us on the intercom, to reassure us that we should make the English coast O.K. About halfway across, the big Fort began to vibrate so badly that Carney came up out of the ball turret like a streak. The whole crew hastily donned parachutes, but "Little Boy Blue" was staying up, although shaking pretty badly. . . . The terrific vibration abruptly stopped. The prop had frozen up due to the lack of oil and the wind milling ceased. It was with great relief that we passed in over the English coast and hobbled back to base. The Group was still circling the field in the regulation traffic pattern, peeling off one by one for their landings; so we cut in ahead of them and let down for our approach. Campbell landed it a little roughly, but not badly considering the conditions.

March 18. Second Mission—Munich-Augsburg (10 hours)
. . . The clouds near this target were scattered and broken. . . . The enemy gunners were . . . accurate and they really poured it on. The

flak was the heaviest I had ever seen and intensely accurate. They knocked a couple of our B-17's out of the formation during the bomb run and during our evasive action immediately following, I observed several more of the fortresses from our Wing pull out and head toward Switzerland.[21] Bombers from other Groups following were going down. Quite a few were damaged too badly to stand a chance of making it back to England. . . . Our ship was riddled with holes in the wings and tail . . . no vital damage.

March 27. Fifth Mission—Bordeaux/Merignac (9 hours) [Target airfield]
We reported for briefing at 0800. A groan went up when the target was announced as Bordeaux, for it meant another long haul. . . .

This mission still remains clear in my mind, for it was the first I had been on where we were flying in sunlight nearly all the way. For some reason, France nearly always seemed friendlier to us, for it nearly always appeared to be sunny. On the other hand, the forbidding appearance of Germany was probably largely due to the darker appearing landscape caused by cloudiness. . . .

The mission went along smoothly enough, with fighter rendezvous made on schedule at the specified points. Thunderbolts furnished the escort. We ran into occasional heavy barrage, but not too much damage seemed to be done. I still watched the bursts. . . .

It was during a period of comparative inactivity that I saw my first Fort go down. What caused it will probably never be known, although I think that some of the control cables on the big ship must have snapped, evidently weakened by flak damage from one of our earlier barrages. Anyway, the Fortress, named "Big Red," suddenly swung wide through the formation, narrowly missing several ships, and commenced to spiral slowly downward. I could see the waist door fly off, released from its emergency hinges, and the crew bail out. One after another, the chutes blossomed open until six were counted. Pohl commented on the irony of the situation, for the crew going down into enemy country was on its last—the twenty-fifth—mission. (I learned later that there had been a fire in the Radio Room and that six of the crewmembers survived the war in German prison camps.)

As we turned into the bomb run near the city, the flak picked up in intensity and accuracy and was one of the worst barrages we would experience. We got holes through every position of the ship, with the tail being the most severely damaged. Babicky was very fortunate in escaping unscathed, for the tail sections were badly riddled, and the vertical stabilizer had a section shot completely out of it. I was watching the bursts near us when I became aware of a bright flash within a couple of inches from my head. My first thought was that a shell had gone off in the waist, but on investigation, it turned out to be the sun glinting through a flak hole that had suddenly appeared next to my face. Bleem also reported a close call. We dropped our eggs visually with excellent results. . . .

April 11. Ninth Mission—Rostock/Krepinki (11 hours) [Targets of opportunity]
. . . The ragged clouds thickened up over the North Sea and built up into solid cover over the Danish Peninsula. Just past Denmark, we

21. Four B-17s and twelve B-24s from different groups and missions did make it to Switzerland.

emerged into clear air between two layers of mushrooming clouds. The overcast was at a height of approximately 40,000 feet, while the undercast was around 10,000 feet. . . . At this point, our escorting P-38s turned back for home and we were met by P-51 Mustangs. . . . The 51s escorted us until their fuel ran low, then they set out for home. We were supposed to connect up with more escorting Mustangs, but they failed to put in an appearance. We later learned that they had run into a brawl with the Krauts and they were forced to drop their tanks before reaching us.

[Soon after] . . . A group of mixed Me-109s and FWs commenced circling our Wing. There was about fifteen of them in all, most of which were painted jet black. Several more groups of fighters joined them and they looked our formation over pretty well. Then they left us and proceeded up to the leading Wing of our Division. Here, a group of about twenty commenced an attack on them, while the bulk of the fighters headed back to our trailing wing. Here they commenced to circle it while looking for weaknesses.

Off to our right, the First Division was already under attack by enemy fighters, but my attention was on the Wing to the rear. . . .

While a band of approximately fifty fighters was encircling the hapless bombers, one of the Krauts detached himself from the group and from a six o'clock position, low, climbed up through the bomber formation, twisting and turning as he flew between the big ships. Once he had successfully braved the hail of .50 caliber bullets from the outside of the bomber formation, he was safe within the cluster for the gunners on the inside had to hold their fire to prevent hitting their own planes.

I could plainly see the flashing of his guns and the tiny puffs of smoke from them as he climbed. One of the big Forts suddenly pitched downward and pieces of wing and fuselage tore off as she plummeted. I reported it on the intercom. I observed only two chutes blossom out, although more of the crew might have escaped from it after she passed out of sight in the undercast. . . . Two or three at a time, a group of about twenty pursued the same tactics: knocking down about five B-17s. The bombers shot down two of their fighter planes.

About this time, we passed in over land, near Stettin, and heavy flak was being thrown up. The German fighters attacked through their own anti-aircraft fire, being very aggressive in their tactics. Several groups of twin-engined fighters joined in the melee, firing 20-mm cannon and then closing with .50-caliber machine gun fire. . . . There must have been over seventy enemy fighter planes in the near vicinity, most of which were participating in the attack on our rear Wing. Many damaged forts were dropping behind the formation and it was to these cripples that the twin-engine Junkers-88s and Me-110s were pressing their attacks.

One fort in particular I noticed put up a terrific struggle. It was knocked out of its formation just after they dropped their bombs, and it attempted to continue on up to ours. Two Me-109s and a Ju-88 took out after it in pursuit but the B-17 shot down the two single-engine fighters and put a good fight against the slowing closing Ju-88, before spinning down in smoke herself.

. . . They were waiting for us and threw up lots of flak, including ground rockets. We entered the bomb run while the fighter opposition became more frantic. . . . The air was full of swarming fighters and bombers and everywhere the barrage of flak was bursting as the gain air battle raged. Our Wings divided to hit their individual targets. The cloud cover broke somewhat under us and the target was hit visually. We pulled hard over to the left to rejoin the other two Wings, and as we did so, we were bounced by a band of FW-190s.

. . . Most of the attacks were made from the nose and the closing speed must have been in the neighborhood of 400 miles per hour. I could see fighters flashing past my window so I opened up on the more distant ones. Some of them climbed around in a sweeping circle, after passing through and returned for another nose attack. Some dove or continued to the rear to hit the Wing behind us.

From the waist position, I could only get in wide deflection shots without much chance of success, but the nose gunners were getting in some deadly licks. Hervatine shot an FW down into the water and Babicky saw it hit. Carney also knocked one down from his ball turret position. . . . Bleem was firing long bursts from the top turret, but Hay was unable to do much since he was on the formation side.

. . . At least five Forts were knocked down out of our Wing. At one time, I saw three bombers and two fighters spinning down into the water and the air was full of chutes. It had formerly been the belief that enemy fighters preferred to fight only over land, but these carried the brawl well out over the bay before heading back for land. . . . The waist of our ship was littered with expended shells and the intercom was busy with excited account of the attacks.

. . . It was with greatest of relief, that we identified . . . our "little friends," the P-51s! . . . Many Forts were straggling back behind the Division, and some were forced to ditch in the North Sea.

. . . At interrogation, we learned that we had lost sixty-four of our bombers. It had been my first real air battle and I must truthfully say that I learned the meaning of fear and respect for the German fighter plane. . . .

April 13. Tenth Mission—Augsburg (9 Hours) [Aviation industry]

. . . About fifty of the Jerries appeared and commenced their deadly passes at the bombers. They were joined by thirty or more. . . . Bombers and fighters alike were spinning down out of control, many of them in flames. Our Group was engaged by a mixed assortment of Me-109s and FW-190s, and we staged quite a brawl! The ship in front of us went down, but I was too busy firing to see if anyone got out of it. A Messerschmidt whipped past my waist window and blew up. Two more of the forts in the Division went down, but I saw three German fighter planes . . . go down . . . .

While the fight was raging at its height, our silver colored P-51s appeared and tore into the battle. The Germans had to give up their attacks . . . we didn't get much further action until nearing the Belgian border.

Here "bandits" were again reported in the vicinity, at a time when no escorting P-shooters were around. A lone FW-190 bounced us from the rear, attacking behind the protecting obscurity of a cloudbank. The Fort, trailing behind the Group was shot down and then "Little Boy Blue". . . was given attention. 20-mm bursts flickered around us, several of them passing completely through without effect, but a third burst inside the waist—just in front of the tail-wheel assembly. There was a loud crack, with a shocking concussion effect and then

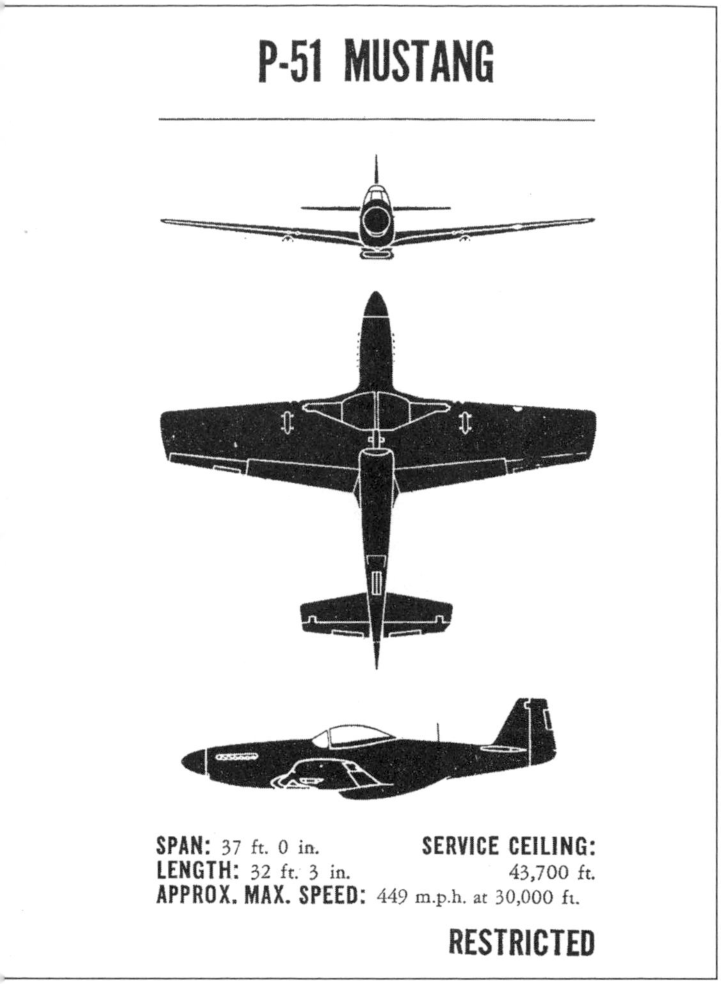

P-51 MUSTANG
SPAN: 37 ft. 0 in.
LENGTH: 32 ft. 3 in.
APPROX. MAX. SPEED: 449 m.p.h. at 30,000 ft.
SERVICE CEILING: 43,700 ft.
RESTRICTED

Profiles of the P-51 Mustang. ARMY/NAVY RECOGNITION MANUAL

the whistle of oxygen escaping from the ruptured lines. The ship jerked, and I could hear the pilot's conversation about the failure of the aileron controls. I tried to call them, but my intercom mike wasn't working. They were unaware of the explosion in the rear and they were trying to regain control of the ship. The German fighter pulled away and took off for other parts, fortunately for us!

Meanwhile, the oxygen had been almost completely exhausted from the ruptured line, and I was forced to remove my tube from that connection and place it in one of the large, portable oxygen bottles.

I could feel a tingling in my leg and thought that I must have been hit, so I dropped the pants to my heated suit, in order to apply first aid.

It was very difficult to move, for the waist was a juggle of oxygen tubing, intercom and heating element wires, cords from suits, and snapped control wires. The waist had been riddled with the tiny holes of high velocity shrapnel, and the whole ship was off kilter as the pilots attempted to trim it.

In the midst of all this confusion, several enemy fighters again hit our Group formation, and I had to fire my gun with one hand, while supporting the oxygen bottle with the other. The comic touch was present, for my pants were at half-mast! In between bursts of gunfire, I succeeded in getting a bandage over the wound, the pants back up, and a parachute snapped onto the harness. In the meantime, the pilots got the ship back under control and we made the trip back O.K. after weathering the usual flak barrage at the coast.

I told Pohl that I wasn't hit badly enough to make an emergency landing, so we dropped into the usual landing pattern. Four or five of our ships were shooting red flares, so they made rush landings ahead of the Group. Bleem put up some red ones while we were taxiing around the perimeter and the ambulance met us in front of the Operations Hut. I was transferred aboard, taken to the Group First-Aid section, and then transferred to the 65th General Hospital. We lost 36 bombers on this mission.

Cook missed four missions with his crew and returned on May 7 for the mission to Berlin.

Lt. Douglas McArthur and his crew departed from Grenier Field in Manchester, New Hampshire, on April 1, 1944. They landed at snow-blanketed Goose Bay in Labrador, and the proceeded to Meeks Field, Iceland, on April 5. The next day, they flew through bad weather to

Nutts Corner in Northern Ireland. Barely one hour before landing, at 12,000 feet altitude, their plane got iced up, but fortunately, "there were still deicing boots on the wings and deicing fluid for the propellers.[22] They only removed the wing boots before going into combat to reduce weight." The group with which McArthur flew left fifty-four Flying Fortresses in Ireland to be refitted for combat. The men took the train to Larne, where they transferred to a boat bound for Stranraer, Scotland. From there they took a train to Stone, England, where McArthur and his crew were assigned to the 561st Squadron, 388th Bomb Group, Station 136, at Knettishall on April 13. McArthur and the other officers of his crew were quartered in a Quonset hut christened "Sackmore on the Heath," which held a total of four crews, or sixteen officers.

> The first pilot from this barracks out on a mission today was killed by a 25-millimeter cannon shell, and I was given his bed—was this going to be a bad or good omen?! Most of the fellows were superstitious.
>
> Short period of training after we arrived. But before flying any combat missions, our copilot, Stamos O. Zades, got hurt while trying to operate the top gun turret and ended up in the hospital for a couple of months. So I had to work with new (fill-in) copilots—some good and some not so good.
>
> I made first lieutenant shortly after arriving at the 388th. Our first combat mission was flown on April 27, 1944, a short two weeks after arriving at the 388th base, ready or not! We were all supposed to wear flak vests—especially on bad missions—but in addition, to protect the pilot's and copilot's backs, there was a half-inch-thick steel plate added right behind their seats. Also, the first thing I looked for after getting in the plane was a piece of loose armor plate under the seat cushion, to be sure it hadn't been stolen—this piece of plate saved my life on one mission.
>
> The new crews *did not* get the new bombers that we flew over from the States. Until we proved how our luck was going to be, we got the oldest beat-up planes on the base. Many new crews were shot down or otherwise lost on their first or second mission. After getting five or six missions, you became "old-timers" and started getting some of the newer planes. One of the big differences between the older and newer planes was that the old planes had hydraulic superchargers and prop pitch controls (very difficult to keep synchronized at high altitude), whereas the newer planes were electrically controlled and very easy to keep things synchronized. In addition, the newer planes [B-17Gs] had a chin gun turret.

McArthur's second mission on April 29 was no "milk run," but a trip to Berlin. Of the 218 B-17s from his divisions, 28 went down that day, and half of the others had some damage. (The total losses from the three bombardment divisions that day were 63 bombers.) McArthur and his crew had arrived at a time when the number of required missions to complete a tour was changed from twenty-five to thirty-five to compensate for a shortage of crews or possibly because of a surplus of aircraft. Some, such as Sgt. Alvin Anderson, who arrived before the change in required missions went into effect, were required to complete thirty missions.

22. Deicing boots were rubber strips on the leading edge of an airfoil activated by air pressure to break up ice. At the base of the leading edge of the propeller blades, another rubber strip with a fluid containing alcohol sprayed over the blades to prevent ice from forming.

CHAPTER 16

The War in Italy

The Italian Campaign

Although the Allies encountered stiff enemy resistance when they landed at Salerno, they prevailed yet again thanks to the intervention of their air and naval powers, which foiled once more the German attempts to launch a decisive counterattack by massing their armored forces. Nonetheless, the Germans took advantage of the rugged terrain of the Apennines, which ran the length of the Italian boot, and conducted a successful delaying action that held back the advance of the American 5th Army on the west coast and the British 8th Army on the east coast.[1] Destroyed bridges and blocked defiles slowed the Allies. Naples fell late in late September, but not before the Germans had wrecked its port facilities and other parts of its infrastructure. This was only a warning to the Allies of things to come. Surprisingly, U.S. Army and other Allied engineers put the port back in operation before the end of October, and before long, it reached greater capacity than it had before the war. As the Allies pushed forward in October, autumn rains turned many roads into mud. The German rear guard put up a heavy resistance along the Volturno River as it fell back to the newly created Gustav or Winter Line, where the monastery of Cassino would play a prominent role in 1944. The Germans built numerous bunkers and deployed countless booby traps and mines, frustrating the Allies.

The 82nd A/B Division, minus one regiment, was withdrawn in mid-November, while the 3rd, 36th, and 45th Infantry and 1st Armored Divisions remained with the British forces to engage in difficult mountain warfare until the summer of 1944. The advance in Italy, no longer "a walk in the sun," turned into a stalemate in the bitter winter cold and rain.[2] In December, the 5th Army stood in front of Monte Cassino on the Gustav Line, and General Clark, the army commander, and his subordinates prepared an outflanking amphibious movement.

Fred Majdalany's *Battle of Cassino* and G. A. Shepperd's *Italian Campaign 1943–45* provide a good overview. The Germans had three months to build the Winter Line, whose defenses included damming the Rapido River and flooding the valley. They fortified the town of Cassino, hid tanks in some large buildings, and built bunkers inside others. The II Corps was to assault this line on January 17, 1944, and the VI Corps was to land at Anzio on January 22 in Operation Shingle. The British X Corps opened the offensive on January 17 with an assault on the left flank, along the Garigliano River. At the same time, the French Expeditionary Corps advanced on the 5th Army's right flank, east of Cassino. A few days later, the 36th Division, II Corps, had the honor, or misfortune, of breaching the Rapido River north and south of the fortified ruins of San Angelo in a nighttime crossing and advancing into the Liri Valley. Both the British and French assaults succeeded, but without sufficient reserves, they were stopped by German reinforcements. The 36th Division attacked at the place where the Germans had erected in-depth defenses that included new semimobile pillboxes, tank turrets mounted in concrete positions, and other types of fortifications bolstered with plenty of minefields, booby traps, and barbed wire. The whole complex was under observation from Monte Cassino. The 34th Division, II Corps, was to launch an attack on the town of Cassino.

The II Corps, in the center of the 5th Army front, was to cross the Rapido, a sixty-foot-wide river with steep banks averaging nine feet in depth.[3] The Germans had dammed the river and flooded certain areas, mainly on their side, creating a marshy obstacle. The assaulting force had to haul its boats up to the river at night and follow marked paths through minefields. To make things worse, many of the collapsible boats capsized. The 36th Division launched its assault on the night of January 21, only to be badly beaten back after three days. The engineers built footbridges, an eight-ton bridge, and tried to put up a Bailey bridge, but the Germans soon brought these structures down. With most of the assault boats gone, and having lost 1,700 men, the survivors struggled back across the Rapido.

The Germans, who were fully committed to the Winter Line, were taken by surprise when the Allies launched a major predawn landing at Anzio, far behind the battlefront, on January 22. On the first day, 36,000 men and 3,000 vehicles came ashore. The VI Corps, under Gen. John P. Lucas, included the British 1st Division and commando units, three Ranger battalions, the 3rd

1. When General Eisenhower departed for England to take over at SHAEF, the Mediterranean theater came under the command of British field marshal Maitland Wilson, who was replaced by Gen. Harold Alexander, also commander of the 15th Army Group responsible for the Italian campaign. The Italian campaign was largely under the direction of the British, with the 5th Army and 15th Air Force the only major U.S. commands.

2. *A Walk in the Sun* was the title of a 1945 film depicting the American citizen-soldiers serving as infantrymen during the Italian campaign at the time of the landings at Salerno. Italy was an infantryman's war, and instead of being a second front, it became a backwater of the war on an international scale, with American, British, Canadian, New Zealander, Indian, Polish, French, and Brazilian infantry divisions taking part.

3. Clifford Peek's regimental history, *Five Years, Five Countries, Five Campaigns with the 141st Infantry Regiment,* puts the river at forty-five feet wide and up to twelve feet deep.

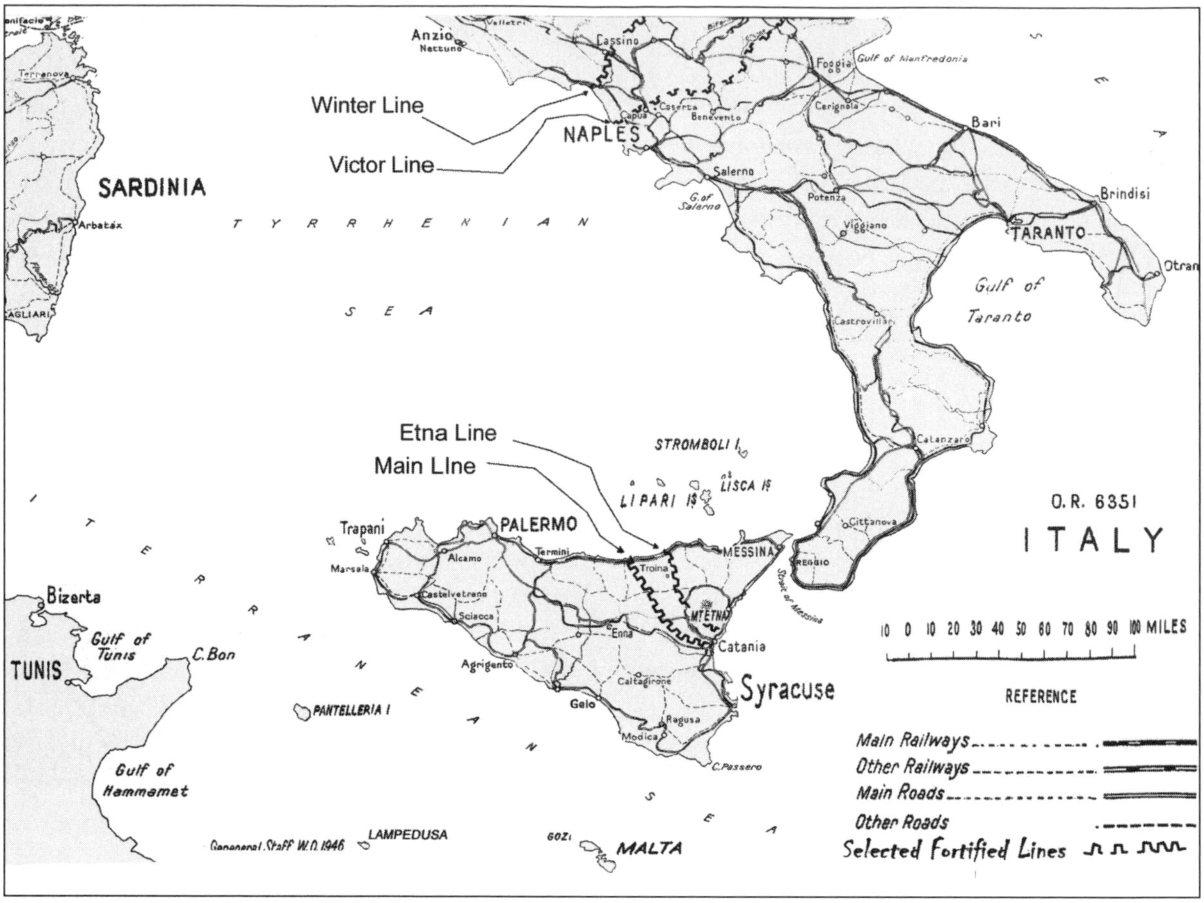

Division, 504th PIR, 45th Division, and 1st Armored Division. Although he met little opposition, General Lucas failed to capitalize on his success by not advancing rapidly out of the beachhead toward the Alban Hills and collapsing the German Winter Line. The Germans took advantage of the delay to rush troops from other fronts to Anzio, bottling up the Allied forces for months. The first battle of Cassino, which began with the 34th Division's assault, bogged down in early February. The division and the rest of the II Corps were pulled back and replaced with the New Zealand Corps, which also failed to advance. Three more battles had to be fought at Cassino before the stalemate ended, the VI Corps broke out of Anzio, and Cassino and the Gustav Line fell in May 1944.

Into the Italian Mainland with the 3rd Division

Pvt. Louis G. Sumien from Oceanside, New York, was drafted on February 8, 1943, and went through basic training at Camp Wheeler, Georgia. Late in the spring, he transferred to Camp Shenango, where "each day names would be called, and they shipped out without ever getting a pass home, he recalls," he recalls.

> One day, my name was called out. We had all of our equipment, including gas mask and a B bag full of impregnated clothing, looking somewhat powdered orange and stinking to high heaven; it included even socks. I could imagine that all of this clothing could have been put on for a gas attack,

Supply area with jerry cans filled with gasoline, Italy, 1943.

providing we had two days' notice—it was ridiculous. Most of the men went to San Francisco (AP) for shipment to the Aleutian Islands. I, on the other hand, was sent to Camp Patrick Henry, Virginia, and then to Newport News, where I boarded what once had been a luxury line, the *Pasteur,* a French ship with an English crew.[4] Encumbered with my heavy equipment, minus rifle, but swaying along under my A and B bags, I boarded my assigned spot, E-3 starboard.

Our compartment was small; the propeller shaft ran through, and bilge water sloshed beneath. It was hot and it stank with a combination of steam, urine, and sweat. We were told that in case of a submarine attack, the trapdoor above the steps leading down would be shut tight.

Once in a while, an orderly called down a name, and a soldier, with or without his equipment, was ushered out. To my amazement, my name was called, and I was ushered up to A deck. Somehow they found out that I could run a motion picture projector (had done so in New York's Broadway), and I was asked if I could figure out the ship's equipment.[5] It was a French ship, and on my card, or record, was also the fact that I spoke French, and the instructions were written in French. I worked the equipment (American made) for five days, accompanied by a member of the crew, a fireman who liked his liquor and carried it

4. The *Pasteur* was a new French liner completed in August 1939. The 29,253-ton liner had a speed of up to 22 knots and could carry 1,700 passengers, but as a troopship it took up to 4,490 men. The ship, according to some accounts, was armed with a couple of 5-inch guns (and possibly a 6-inch gun). In the summer of 1940, the ship carried the French gold reserve to Canada as France surrendered and the British took over the ship. Like the *Queens,* the *Pasteur* did not sail in convoy.

5. After leaving the army, Sumien began a career in the film industry.

along in case it was needed during a sub attack for courage. I ran Bogart's *High Sierra, Last of Kin, Strike Up the Band,* and others, even during a submarine attack, which the ship, traveling alone, soon lost. We could hear everything vibrating in its speed. I might also add that I lived in the booth for five days, oiling the equipment.

We landed in Casablanca around September 1943, and I joined Company L, 7th Infantry, 3rd Division, the day before Thanksgiving [November 20], 1943, on the Cassino front. The company was bivouacked in a muddy area at the base of Mount Della Costa called Bajae Latina. The area was covered with mud everywhere. A latticework of planks hastily nailed together formed paths near the mess hall (facetiously called so, as it was nothing but a pyramidal tent where the cook had his equipment: upright, rectangular gas stoves). It was raining as we stood on line for chow. All cowpath roads leading up to the area were sunken, giving the jeeps a rocked and swaying time getting anywhere. The whole company was grouped in pyramidal tents.

The fighting on the Volturno River and the battle for Venafro left Pvt. Verl Pendleton and Sgt. Frank Andrews, 1st Battalion HQ, 7th Infantry, with unpleasant memories. Pendleton lost a good friend during these operations. The only positive thing he remembers is the friendliness of the Italians in the area. One evening, when the battalion stopped for the night and the soldiers were told to dig in, Pendleton and Andrews walked back to a nearby village they had passed earlier. The villagers welcomed them with open arms, even allowing the men to sleep in their beds with muddy boots on. Shortly before Thanksgiving, Sergeant Andrews almost qualified for the Purple Heart.

We pushed as far north as we could to the Cassino Line. When we pulled up to the last position we were to occupy, it was cold and rainy. The medics had a house behind a hill where they thought it was safe to have a fire. They were taking the guys in and giving them a blanket while their clothes dried out. Anyway, I came by and was in there. A little guy from New Jersey with quite an accent was getting these guys to strip down, and he was yelling to me, "Hey Sarge, you got a hole in your ass!" I got dried out, and a day or so later he came back with some papers to fill out. By that time, the humor of it struck me. I laughed at him [and did not sign the papers] and never got my Purple Heart. I was glad I did not, because I could just see people asking me where I got hit and if they could see the scar.

Private Sumien arrived on November 20, only a few days after the division had withdrawn from the fighting around Venafro after fifty-nine days of "Mountains and Mud," according to Gen. Lucian Truscott in his memoir *Command Missions.* Sumien was one of the numerous replacements that took the place of soldiers lost in battle or to illness. At the end of December, the division, which was supposed to have crossed the Rapido with the 36th, was sent to the Naples area to practice for Operation Shingle.

Pvt. Robert Lee Zahradka from Illinois, who was with the 3rd Division, had been drafted in January 1943. After basic, he had trained for service with a tank destroyer unit at Fort Hood. In May, he passed through Camp Shenango en route for Hampton Roads, where he boarded the former liner *America,* which had been renamed the *West Point* and served as a troopship during the war. He left the ship at Casablanca five days later. Zahradka stayed at Camp Lyautey for a week before he went by truck to Bizerte with a group

The Battle of San Pietro

In the advance up Route 6 toward Monte Cassino, the 36th Division encountered the enemy defending the picturesque town of San Pietro on the slopes of Mount Sammurco. At the beginning of December 1943, the 142nd Infantry with the 1st SSF had cleared the Germans from Mounts Camino and Maggiore. The heavy fighting took place as it began to rain on the troops, who had little or no shelter and a difficult line of communication through the mountainous terrain.

According to the official history *Fifth Army at the Winter Line,* San Pietro was at the core of an advance position of the Winter Line and a key observation position. The defenses consisted of bunkers deployed in depth. These bunkers were made from triple layers of logs and earthen cover. They were impervious to fighter-bomber attacks and protected by minefields laden with S-mines. German artillery was ready to zero in on any American troops that actually reached their outpost line. On December 8, the 3rd Ranger Battalion and the 1st Battalion of the 143rd Infantry advanced to clear the Mount Sammurco area. This would leave San Pietro exposed and thus force the Germans to pull back. They took the key heights by December 11 and held on despite fierce German counterattacks during the next few days that caused heavy casualties for both sides. Meanwhile, two battalions of the 143rd that had advanced on San Pietro on December 8 had been held in check after close fighting failed to drive the Germans from their bunkers. The assault was renewed on December 15, with the San Pietro being outflanked on both sides as the 36th Division pushed along the high ground. The 143rd attempted to attack the town again, hoping to bring supporting tanks up the slopes. But the terrain was too difficult and the plan failed. The 141st Infantry attempted to cross the valley south of the town on December 15 and the next day, but it failed each time under withering enemy fire. Finally, the town was outflanked, and the Germans had to pull back their troops.

The battle of San Pietro became the subject of an award-winning film produced in 1945, which some considered to take an anti-war view. On April 9, 1944, Sgt. Newton H. Fulbright, a correspondent for *Yank,* reported on the German counterattack on the last day of the battle.

> With the Fifth Army in Italy—A hero is a damn fool, as any soldier in the front-line Infantry will tell you; a reckless guy can die in a minute in the shellfire in the Bowling Alley (G.I. name for the narrow twisting valley through which threads Highway 6, the principal road from Naples to Rome). Yet once in a while a guy gets to be a sort of hero and lives to fight again. There were heroes like that in our push on San Pietro. . . .
>
> The night my outfit piled over a mountain ridge to open the drive we lost so many men under concentrated mortar and artillery fire in the first few hours that we were literally stunned.
>
> We dug in to hold what we had. Our position was precarious. We were seriously strained for manpower to outpost our positions facing the enemy on an indefinite front, extending from barren towering rocks on our right to the open shell-plowed valley below us on the left.

continued

The Battle of San Pietro ***continued***

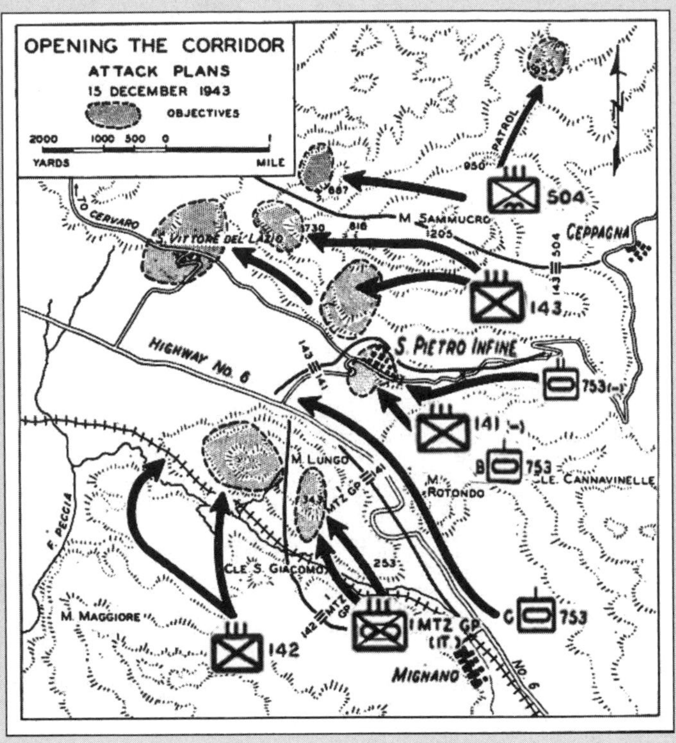

U.S. ARMY

. . . I dived out of the CP and began threading my way up the hill, amid the crash of shells, toward the positions. Added to the noise was the cry of the wounded, thrashing and stumbling in the dark, pleading for help to get them to the aid station. The plight of the wounded is always a strain on the nerves of the unwounded soldier. He wants to help; his instinct is to stop and give aid. But he hasn't time; he must keep going.

At that moment I heard our 81s begin firing. I recognized the voice of a soldier in the dark who was calling for a medic. I went up to him. "I've been hit," he said. "They got me in the back with a hand grenade. They crawled up to a wall and tossed it right into my foxhole. It blew me out." Fully a dozen walking wounded had come up. It was only a little way to the aid station. We started out. I gave support to my friend. . . . One of his legs was dragging. "I think they got me in the kidney," he said.

The counterattack was definitely over by 2300 hours. . . .

We sat there for the next few days nervously feeling the Jerry out, blasting away with our artillery and being blasted in turn by his. We renewed the attack supported this time by tanks. The sound and fury was terrific. . . .

Then the Jerry attacked, it came about dark on the tenth day. I was sitting in the company CP [command post] when the German machine guns began chattering down the road. "Counterattack!" There was no need for anyone to shout the warning. Already soldiers were dashing to shooting positions on the double; telephones and radios were busy calling down artillery fire.

For the troops in Italy, this article only described the everyday routine. This gave the green troops waiting to take part in Operation Overlord some idea of what to expect when they met the enemy.

of other replacements. Soon after that, he went to Sicily, but instead of being assigned to a tank destroyer unit, he "was given a rifle and a berth" in Company M, 26th Infantry, 1st Division. When that campaign ended, he was transferred to Company D, 7th Infantry, 3rd Division, as a radioman." He stayed with the 7th Infantry from Salerno to the campaign against Venafro.

> I was in the message center, which consisted of two runners from each company and two from battalion headquarters. The message center sergeant and a T/5 made up the balance of about twelve men. We traveled with the battalion headquarters, to be close at hand for delivery of messages for the companies. We had two encoding machines, one a simple handheld letter-substituting unit, which they claimed could be read by the other side in about ten minutes, and a heavier machine, about four pounds, that broke the message into five-letter groups, which they said would take upwards of an hour or so to read! My specific duties were to make runs to the company headquarters, and later on, after I had transferred to battalion as a battalion runner, to make runs to regiment, motor pool, medics, etc.

For Sgt. Harold Taylor, headquarters, 15th Infantry, the advance toward the Rapido in December was one of the most miserable moments of his life.

> I went for a period of more than thirty days without my clothing off. Oftentimes wet and muddy, it was left to dry on my body. The number of American lives lost was high. I can remember a caravan of stretchers that stretched for blocks, winding its way down the mountainside, with GIs that had sacrificed their lives so that democracy could prevail. At the clearing at the bottom of the mountain, the dead soldiers' belongings were removed and tagged, as well as the bodies after they were put in bags and stacked like cordwood until they could be moved to a burial site. After the main resistance dwindled to sniper fire, we were relieved by other units and moved to the staging area near Naples.
>
> By the time we reached full strength, the Anzio operation came into focus. At first we met sporadic resistance. Our job was to establish a beachhead. We dug in and camouflaged our weapons and positions. During the weeks [months] we spent at Anzio, we went through a daily bombardment of artillery and mortar fire.

Initiation into Hell

Lt. Carl Strom, who had departed the United States on October 5, 1943, had an uneventful two-week trip to Oran on a troop transport, which was part of a large convoy.

> We arrived at the Straits of Gibraltar on October 21 and went through single file with a French battleship and destroyers leading the way. On the evening of October 22, we arrived in Oran and disembarked the following morning. We were trucked to Camp Canastel, about ten miles from Oran, and were assigned to pyramidal tents with dirt floors. We did not have cots but bunks with wooden frames with ropes, instead of canvas, on the sides and ends to hold the mattresses. There were about 1,000 officers and some 10,000 enlisted men awaiting shipment to Italy. We were part of Mark Clark's 5th Army.
>
> It wasn't long before they had us in school again, leadership and battle training, navigation problems with trucks, and continuing classes in many other related sub-

jects. We were able to go to Oran and see the sights. On November 14, we packed our gear and boarded trucks for a transfer several miles inland to a British-run Commando Training Camp. The British instructors really put us through the paces. Hand-to-hand fighting, infiltrating enemy positions, more tactical use of weapons, and even one session where we had to cross a river on a rope with our rifles strung over our backs. This was extremely dangerous, as the riverbed was full of large rocks, and if you fell, you were almost certain to be injured. Only one man fell, but was only injured slightly. After a very tough and instructive week, we returned to Camp Canastel.

On December 6, we boarded a former British passenger liner that also had British troops aboard for Italy. We sailed without escort. We had many questions about each other's training, weapons, and related subjects. Passing Sicily, we finally spotted the Isle of Capri and Mount Vesuvius in the distance. Arriving in Naples Harbor, we saw many sunken ships the Germans had left in an attempt to deny us use of the harbor. Along the waterfront, there were bombed-out buildings.

We disembarked and boarded trucks for a huge Replacement Center at a former racetrack just outside of Naples. There were hundreds of men here awaiting assignment. We were assigned to two-man pup tents with blankets but slept on the ground. As we were about fifty miles from the front, we could hear the big guns firing to the north. While here, we experienced some wild, windy, and rainy weather. At one point, our tent blew down and all our gear got thoroughly soaked. We had no duties or training, just had to be present each morning in case we had received an assignment. We spent a lot of time in Naples sightseeing, going to the movies, and visiting the Red Cross Center, where we could write letters, read, and generally relax, or at the officers' club, where we could listen to good music and buy drinks. I spent Christmas Day at the Red Cross, which had special treats for us.

On December 31, 1943, I was notified that I was assigned to the 36th Infantry Division, which was in the vicinity of San Pietro. My feeling was that finally I was part of a unit, and I was through with the many schools I had attended. Oh, how wrong can one be! On arriving at the division, we brand new second lieutenants were to attend a one-week Mountain Fighting School. This made sense, as at no time had I received any training in mountain combat tactics. Brigadier General Wilbur, assistant division commander, conducted the school, and what we learned stood us in good stead. Mountain fighting is very different—much tougher, more rigorous and demanding than in most terrain. For one thing, you often cannot see what is ahead of you, and you can't dig foxholes in solid rock.

Finally, after a very tough week, I was assigned, along with three other new second lieutenants, to Company B, 141st Infantry Regiment. They had just been pulled out of the line after several weeks of hard fighting and had suffered many casualties. The company commander, executive officer, and the weapons platoon commander were the only officers left from when the unit had gone into combat at Mount Lungo and San Pietro in November. At least 50 percent of the men were also replacements from this Texas National Guard division, and most of the new men were not Texans, nor was I. I was assigned command of the 3rd Platoon. We met the men in our units and began immediate training. This was not so much to teach us what both enlisted men and officers already knew, but to get to know each other and to get used to working together. All of the NCOs were battle experienced. After about a week, we moved up and took over positions held by the 34th Division behind Mount Trocchio. We arrived at the village of Santa Lucia, perhaps a dozen houses situated behind Mount Trocchio, which overlooked the Rapido River, Cassino, and the Liri Valley.

The Germans had retreated to fixed positions in the mountains and Liri Valley behind the Rapido and Garigliano Rivers. They had about three months to prepare defensive positions. On January 21, the 36th Division was ordered to attack across the Rapido River, just upstream from the village of Sant'Angelo.[6] B Company was chosen to lead the attack for the 1st Battalion.

The night before the assault, the platoon leaders of the company met and cut cards. Strom pulled the low card, which meant that his platoon would lead the assault.

The attempt was a disaster. While I was up ahead with my runner and an engineer guide, who was to show us the way through the minefields, my platoon was wiped out by German artillery fire.[7] The company commander was killed, and the executive officer and weapons platoon leader were wounded before crossing. This left the company with three new second lieutenants to continue the attack. We crossed the river, but I had no platoon left and was an extra officer. When daylight came, we were pinned down, losing men from artillery, machine-gun, and rifle fire all day. When darkness finally came, we pulled back the remnants of the company that was still across the river and returned to Santa Lucia. There was only one other officer and about thirty enlisted men left in the company. Of my entire platoon, only a runner and I were not KIA or WIA.

On January 25, I was called to battalion headquarters and ordered to take command of C Company, which was outposted in the sunken road area where my platoon had been wiped out. When I arrived there, I received a call telling me a Red Cross party was on its way to our position, and I was to take them to the site of our river crossing to meet with a German officer there. I was to arrange a six-hour truce with them, from noon to 6 P.M., for both sides to pick up wounded and dead. Soon a group of about five, bearing a large Red Cross flag, led by one of our chaplains, arrived, and I led them down to the river. A German officer and a sergeant crossed the Rapido to our side in a rubber boat. One of the sergeants of C Company spoke German, and I had taken him along as my interpreter. The German sergeant spoke English, so the German officer and I were able to arrange the truce. Having had several men killed on the German side of the river, I requested to be allowed to go over to that side to recover our wounded and dead. The German officer was very adamant that we each only clear our sides of the river and that we transport our dead and wounded to each other. Of course, there were no German casualties on our side of the river. We recovered only two

6. The 141st Infantry was to attack north of the ruined town of Sant'Angelo, where the ruins had been fortified by the Germans, and the 143rd Infantry would hit to the south with the 142nd Infantry in reserve.

7. The engineer guide was to help lead the way through the German minefields, using lanes marked with white tape on the friendly side of the river. German artillery fire destroyed many of the markers and also created additional casualties.

wounded and about twenty-five dead.[8] On return from the river, I was ordered to return to B Company.

The following day, we moved to a defensive position in front of Mount Trocchio along the Rapido, where we remained for a few days until relieved by a combat engineer unit. We then moved to the right, east of the town of Cassino, and across the river, where the 34th Division had crossed shortly after our initial attempt. I now had command of B Company, which had been built up to about forty men, and we received two new second lieutenants, all of the other officers either having been killed, wounded, or on sick leave. Climbing by a mule trail, we reached a position, at about 1,600 feet elevation, on Snakeshead Ridge, where we relieved Company E of the 34th Division, consisting of twelve men led by a PFC. They were doing a great job, which speaks well of the training of our troops. For a week, we sat on the ridge in cold, mostly snowy, and rainy weather, trying to oust the Germans. Since it was primarily solid rock, we could not dig shelters and survived by piling rocks around our positions, what the British called "sangers." The famous Benedictine Abbey was in full view on top of Monte Cassino, about half a mile away.

On February 11, the 1st and 3rd Battalions of the 141st Infantry were combined, the 1st Battalion with ten officers and sixty-six men who had survived the Rapido assault, and the 3rd Battalion with its remaining twelve officers and ninety-four men. Captains were put in charge of each battalion. This combined force took over from the few 34th Division troops holding the Snakeshead Ridge. To do this, they had to cross the Rapido, this time on the bridgehead secured by the 34th Division. The 34th Division had crossed the Rapido and established this key bridgehead, taking the Snakeshead Ridge, which was to the north and west of Monte Cassino, almost to the rear of it. Even when it was reinforced with the 36th Division, the 34th did not have strength to smash the well-prepared positions of the Gustav Line. Once the 141st Regiment occupied this position, it was counterattacked by the Germans from Hill 593. Although it managed to beat them back in close fighting, it was unable to drive them from Hill 593. Supplies had to be brought by mules over deteriorating trails, according to Peek. On February 14, the British relieved the two badly depleted 34th and 36th Divisions on the bridgehead.

According to Carl Strom, the casualties sustained were due not only to German artillery and mortar fire, but also to trench foot, caused by the cold and wet conditions. This made "the men's feet red and sore, and soon they could not walk. There was no way we could keep warm and dry." Finally, Strom and his men took up positions on a spur of Mount Castellone called Phantom Ridge, which was relatively quiet. "Night patrols were sent out every night, and I led four. Fortunately, I only lost two men." The company was built back up to about twenty men and was supplied with blankets, dry socks, rations, and even copies of *Stars & Stripes.* On one sunny afternoon in February, "a huge fleet of bombers came over and leveled the Abbey." Although "we could not see the Abbey," says Strom, "the smoke from the bombs rose several hundred feet in the air."

Reuben D. Parker of Murray, Kentucky, reached the 36th Division in much the same way as Strom. He was drafted on July 31, 1941, and graduated as a lieutenant from OCS in March 1942. His first assignment to the 80th Division lasted until August 1943, when he was sent first to Oran, and then to a replacement depot near

8. Peek's regimental history gives three wounded and fifty dead.

Naples. "On January 27, 1944, during the crossing of the Rapido River," Parker recalls, "the replacement depot was practically cleaned out. Each of us went to each battalion of the 141st, and I wound up in Company E as XO and became the CO by August 1944."

Martin Tully from Chicago ended up in the 36th Division the same way. He was thirty-two years old when he enlisted in May 1942; went through basic training at Camp Walters, Texas; and completed OCS just before Christmas. Next, he traveled by train to the infantry replacement training center at Fort Meade. "A special draft was sent from the 36th Division. They wanted some shave tails, and being one of the older second lieutenants, I was volunteered by the colonel and sent to North Africa. Subsequently, I was assigned to Company B, 141st Infantry, while in North Africa before the invasion of Salerno."

Lieutenant Tully remained with Company B through Salerno and during the assault across the Rapido. He was next to his commander, behind Lieutenant Strom's platoon, when an enemy shell exploded, wounding him and killing his superior. Lieutenant Arnold took over his platoon and passed by Strom, whose platoon had been wiped out before reaching the river. Tully was sent to the rear lines to recuperate for many weeks before he was deemed fit to return to his regiment and take command of Company A.

Cpl. Arthur J. Zalud, drafted in February 1942, also went through basic at Camp Walters before he was sent to a replacement depot at Shenango, Pennsylvania. When he reached North Africa shortly after the Salerno landings, he was assigned to the 36th Division and took part in the first battle of Cassino as a member of Service Battery for the 155-millimeter gun battalion. I was one of their replacements after the invasion. Most of the fellows with me were sent as infantry, and how I wound up with the artillery is beyond me; that was how the army operated. I was very for-

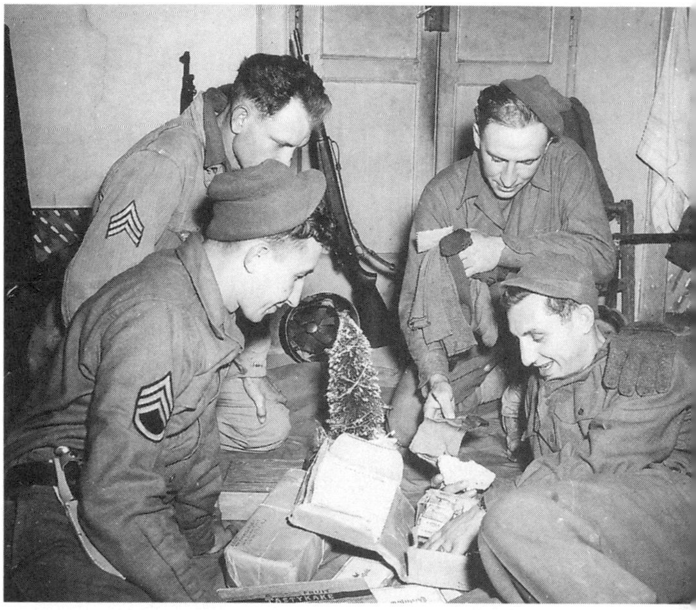

American soldiers open Christmas packages from home in Italy, December 1943. The Tastykake box indicates a recipient likely hailed from the greater Philadelphia area. NATIONAL ARCHIVES

tunate, because most of the fellows I was shipped over with were killed in Italy."

On February 27, the 88th Division relieved the 36th, which was trucked to the rear. Strom was stationed at a rest camp at Caserta, where, to his elation, he took his first bath in two months and received an issue of clean clothes.

> We were quartered in the former stables of the king's palace, very clean and comfortable, with cots and Italian civilians to keep the place clean. I thought, "This is going to be great!" until I found I had charge of seventy-one enlisted men who were also there on leave. Nevertheless, it was a great relief to get out of harm's way for a few days.
>
> Returning to B Company on March 2, we went through retraining and orientation. We received three new second lieutenants and a large number of replacements to build the company back up to combat strength. I was promoted to first lieutenant and made executive officer.

Ranger Mercuriali Goes Home

Ranger Gino Mercuriali, whom his fellow Rangers nicknamed "Big Mercy," was one of the original members of the 1st Ranger Battalion when it formed in Great Britain in 1942. He took part in the commando raid on Dieppe, the 1st Rangers' assault landing in Arzew in November 1942, the Tunisian campaign, the landings at the beaches of Gela in July, and the Sicilian campaign. On September 7, 1943, he boarded another ship to participate in the 1st Rangers' third invasion. At the time, he was still suffering from the aftereffects of dysentery and malaria, he would later learn. Nevertheless, he stayed with the battalion through the mountains of Italy. On October 19, 1943, he received a battlefield commission.

> The life in the mountains [was harsh] in the severe cold rain, meager food supply at times, and the need to ration our water supply or replenish it while dangerously close to German troops.
>
> Late in the campaign, the diarrhea and added frozen feet took their toll on me during patrols. I felt I lost confidence trying to walk on stubs I couldn't feel, and the loss of weight and energy, so that I left the command and was hospitalized by the battalion doctor. I was sent back to Africa for rest and rehabilitation and thus I missed the Anzio beachhead. This left me with some guilty feelings after learning of some of my men being killed. I particularly felt guilty when I learned of my platoon sergeant, Sgt. Lester Harrington, a good man and friend, having been killed soon after I left.

In February 1944, after the 1st, 3rd, and 4th Ranger Battalions had been decimated while attempting to infiltrate enemy lines at Cisterna in the Anzio beachhead, Mercuriali returned to Company D. The remnants of the battalion were pulled out of the line and sent to run the 5th Army School of Scouting and Patrolling, where Lieutenant Mercuriali served as an instructor. On April 7, 1944, he returned to the United States with the 4th Ranger Battalion. He was given various assignments, mainly as an instructor, until the end of the war.

Carl Strom, like many of his fellow veterans of the 36th Division, never forgave Mark Clark for the misguided attempted crossing of the Rapido and the first battle of Cassino. Many accused Clark of "showboating" for publicity, like Patton and Montgomery. There is no doubt that their judgment was tinted by their nightmarish experiences. In fact, Clark alone was not responsible for the failure, because the army group and politicians imposed many demands on the 5th Army without providing it sufficient support.

Anzio

Operation Shingle might have been considered a brilliant move, if Gen. Lucian Truscott had aggressively pushed inland after landing virtually unopposed. In December, General Clark expressed the belief that even if the Allies didn't advance, the Germans in the Winter Line would withdraw before such a threat. He turned out to be wrong. Even as the 5th Army, British Corps, and French Corps offensive was launched on January 17, the 36th Division was smashed on the Rapido on January 22, 1943. At about 1 A.M. on

January 22, the naval rocket craft let loose on the landing sites at Anzio, and at 2 A.M., commando and Ranger units—the British 1st and U.S. 3rd Divisions—stormed ashore. The landings were virtually unopposed.

According to Pvt. Louis Sumien, after a month near the front, the 3rd Division had spent Christmas far behind the lines, training and going on hikes until it conducted amphibious training only a few days before the actual landings. "The company moved to an area about ten miles northeast of Naples called Piano di Quattro, where at least the ground was dry." Here the amphibious training began. Although most of the troops were unaware that the practice landings had not gone well, General Truscott was seriously concerned. Fortunately, the actual landings were successful, but the operation degenerated into "four months of combat, with short rest periods, on flat land, with the Krauts in the Lepini Hills along Cisterna di Littoria looking down our necks." On March 22, 1944, Sumien wrote home:

> Dear Mom and Pop,
>
> Well, on our 60th day at the front things are still nice and quiet.[9] It's like Sunday morning around 49th Street. I'm sitting outside my foxhole writing this letter. This morning the Germans shot over some propaganda leaflets about "The Girl You Left Behind." They are supposed to break the morale of the soldiers by saying that their girls are going out with other men. But the boys are thanking the Germans for some nice pin-up girls.
>
> Your loving son, Louis

Although casualties were light the first day, Pvt. Robert L. Zahradka, Company D, 7th Infantry, had the misfortune of being one of them. He had plenty of time to recover and rejoin his unit, however, as General Lucas failed to advance, the Germans sealed off the bridgehead, and there was no breakout until May.

A 240-millimeter howitzer of the 697th Field Artillery Battalion in the area of Mignana, January 1944. NATIONAL ARCHIVES

John B. Shirley of Costa Mesa, California, one of the numerous replacements for the 3rd Division, had been drafted on March 5, 1943. After completing basic training on the West Coast, he was eventually sent east, where he boarded a Liberty ship at Camp Pickett, Virginia. He noticed "125 replacements aboard that had been escorted to the ship under guard by MPs," and that "they were being paroled from stockades." These men were a streetwise, tough lot from East Coast big-city backstreets.

> We sailed out of Hampton Roads in March 1943 and joined a very large convoy of about 120 ships. We took twenty-two days to cross the Atlantic.[10] I was seasick for seven

9. Sumien apparently was trying to avoid problems with the censor.

10. It appears that actually, the ship joined a convoy that had departed New York on March 3 and arrived at Casablanca on March 18.

days and never very comfortable. We ate only boiled food, standing at narrow high tables. The hole we slept in was impossible with odors, etc. We had numerous drills and many submarine alerts, but never came under attack. We spent one night offshore at Casablanca and left our convoy, sailing for Palermo, where the wheat we were carrying was off-loaded. The infantry rēplacements were put on trucks and driven to Messina. We crossed the straits on a ferry, and they boarded electric trains for a trip up the boot of Italy to a replacement depot near Caserta, about twenty miles from the Cassino front. On the way, thirteen of the Italian-speaking men from the stockades went AWOL when the train stopped at a station. Several of them melted into the crowds, and that was repeated at several stations. I stayed here for a week and was assigned to the 3rd Division at Anzio. We were trucked to Naples, and we boarded an LST that took us to Anzio.

T/5 James R. Richards was assigned as a truck driver to regimental supply for the 504th PIR, which stayed behind when the 82nd A/B Division departed for England. The regiment was involved in holding the right flank along the Mussolini Canal and sent constant patrols to infiltrate enemy lines. The paratroopers' fierce fighting spirit earned them the sobriquet of the "Devils in Baggy Pants" among the Germans. In the spring, Richards was wounded in his right leg, but his injury did not require hospitalization. Finally, in March, his regiment was pulled out of the line and loaded onto the *Capetown Castle* for a trip to England.

On June 27, 1944, weeks after the breakout, Sumien wrote home about his experiences at the Anzio beachhead.

Lt. Ralph J. Yates is now our company commander, but now it is Captain Yates. I guess that you'd be interested in knowing what goes on in this company of ours. Well, it's just like one big happy family. For instance, we had one soldier with us, up on the line, who was from another company, but he said he liked going around inspecting the front line positions, riding around on a bicycle. This was Anzio where the Krauts were breathing down our necks. We were in position where, during the daytime we couldn't stick our heads up, out of the foxholes without it being knocked off by an 88-artillery shell. We were told that our positions were in a terrible condition, smelling of something awful. So this is what they sent us from the rear area: five big (immense) wooden boxes like the size of a large refrigerator and rectangle. Two large round holes had been cut into their tops. We were to set these five refrigerator type boxes along our position and use them as TOILETS. Remember, we couldn't even stick our heads out of the foxholes, let alone our asses. We were supposed to dig five large and deep holes and place the boxes over it. I guess it was figured that our front line position would smell better, if whenever we had to go to the toilet we could use these boxes, sit on top and over the holes, directly in front of the enemy, who upon noticing this would be too dumfounded to shoot at. . . . Another thing, if shot at, we could always jump in one of the round holes! The boys crawled out in the middle of the night and moved these five toilets out into no-man's land, figuring, perhaps, that the Krauts would like to use them when we weren't. So, the next morning, these five boxes stood spread out in no-man's land in front of the company, along with a long wooden pole near each with a roll of toilet paper fluttering in the breeze with us all aiming our rifles at them eagerly waiting for some

Patrols: An Infantryman's View

Rifleman John B. Shirley, Company I, 15th Infantry, 3rd Division, describes one of the company's most common activities, whether on the defensive or the offensive: the patrol.

> "Never volunteer," was sound advice, but it was patrol duty most GIs would rather avoid if possible. Patrolling meant a variety of activities, all dangerous.
>
> Flank patrols scout the terrain adjacent to the main body's route of march. Keeping up can be very difficult, as the main body usually moves on improved roads, and the patrol is working its way through forests, meadows, scrub, etc.
>
> Contact patrols are usually a few men working their way back and forth between two adjacent defensive positions that have some separation between them. If the distance is very great, the patrol's activity is very important in scouting possible enemy penetration or activity.
>
> The most common patrol is for intelligence gathering. Patrols are charged with certain terrain to scout. They are often asked to bring back a prisoner, or occasionally asked to find a ford to cross a river. They must learn as much as possible about enemy positions and activity. Such patrols avoid detection and combat if possible.
>
> A combat patrol is usually platoon size or larger, often reinforced with light machine guns and mortar squads. The objective is often to capture territory, or at least engage the enemy in a firefight to determine the opponent's position and strength.
>
> The longer one is in combat, the more patrols one experiences. As a member of I Company, 15th Infantry, I had my share. Once, in Italy, I led my one-third-strength platoon for eighteen hours, patrolling over very hilly terrain, looking for Germans that were harassing an Italian village south of Artena near Highway 6.[11] My company command was a little surprised and disappointed we did not make contact with the enemy. It didn't bother us that we missed seeing the dreaded German infantrymen that fought so effectively in Italy. Eighteen hours is a long time to be scared.

11. After a few months of combat in the Anzio beachhead, Shirley rose to the rank of sergeant. This patrol took place in May at about the time of the breakout.

unsuspecting German officer to go take a crap. "Vas ist das? Ya! Camouflaged positions?" Instead, they spent a fortune in artillery destroying them. "Mein Gott!"

Louis Sumien found among his papers the following poem, whose origin he does not know. It was written shortly before the fall of Rome in May 1944.

> Thirteen months we have been here now,
> Sweating out lines for GI chow,
> Watching bombs fall out of the sky,
> Praying that death would pass us by.

The 370th Infantry Regiment moves through Prato, Italy, April 1945. NATIONAL ARCHIVES

We've made all the beachheads that had to
be made,
Then waited for months before we got paid.
We've had our share of African crud,
And have slogged around in Italian mud.

We've swatted mosquitoes and flies as well,
Just living a life of physical hell.
We've slept on bare ground and not on a cot,
Washed our clothes when they started to rot.

Bambinos have chiseled our cigarette butts,
And begged us for food to fill up their guts.
We've never blundered, we've surely played
ball
So grant our request when we've captured
Rome,
For God's sake General, "SEND US HOME."

Just before the breakout from the Anzio beachhead in May 1944, Sgt. Frank Andrews of the 7th Infantry became operations sergeant in the 1st Battalion. He felt rather fortunate, because his job, which involved taking care of maps, kept him behind the lines at a time when his regiment was taking heavy losses from constant bombardment.

> We had a lot of replacements and a lot of new personnel. We lost our first sergeant, so in being one of the few old-timers left in the outfit, I wound up with that job. That was the first time I got into administration work and got away from the tactical aspects of it. It had its advantages, but it was entirely new to me and completely different from what I was involved with before. It gave me a better chance to know the people around me rather than being tied up in my own little line of work. It was more of a human relations job.
>
> The push on Rome and the fall of the city ended our campaign in Italy. We stayed there and pitched pup tents in one of the beautiful parks in downtown Rome and stayed a few days before pulling back to Pozzuoli, a suburb of Naples.

Capt. Kenneth P. Stemmons of Kansas City, Missouri, who had joined the army in March 1942, commanded Company B, 157th Infantry, in the 45th Infantry Division, which also occupied the Anzio bridgehead. He served with the division from Sicily to Anzio. Like most of his fellow soldiers, he did his best to make do with what he had.

> In the infantry, anything and everything you owned you had to carry on your person, day and night, rain and shine, freezing and hot. I don't know of any rifleman that carried a

Sledding into Battle

To facilitate a rapid armored breakthrough, Gen. John "Iron Mike" O'Daniel, commander of the 3rd Infantry Division, came up with a brilliant idea. If the infantry could maintain a low profile, it could accompany tank units and remove obstacles or strongpoints that tanks could not neutralize. The infantry faced many pitfalls in such a situation, however. Riding on tanks and walking upright exposed the infantrymen to enemy small arms, and following in armored personnel carriers confined them and could hinder their deployment whenever the advancing force met resistance. The general concluded that the best position of the infantrymen was to lie flat on their bellies, presenting a minimal target, as long as they could keep up with the tanks. This could be done if the Sherman tanks towed sleds on which the soldiers lay flat, from which they would be able to deploy quickly whenever they were needed.

The army secretly produced 360 sleds at a site near Capua during the first two weeks of May. The sleds were made with a $\frac{3}{16}$-inch steel plate, which General Truscott called half of an aircraft wing tank. This contraption was enough to protect the soldiers from antipersonnel mines. The tank, however, had no protection against antitank mines, which were often planted in a minefield of antipersonnel mines. This could leave the entire squad trapped in a minefield.

Each tank towed two rows of six sleds each. A steel rod attached to each pair of sleds kept the two rows from banging against each other. Each of the division's regiments sent over sixty men to form five squads that trained at a site beyond the view of the enemy in the Anzio beachhead. Nineteen-year-old John Shirley was among these soldiers. In his memoir *I Remember: Stories of a Combat Infantryman,* he wrote:

> There were very few volunteers. . . . A Company Commander ordered to give up a sergeant and a few men for such an unusual and untried assignment is not going to send his best men. I was untested in battle and was one of two sergeants detailed from "I" Company along with four privates. [We] ate and lived with [our] company, and, every morning for about three weeks, marched off to a special training area. Everyone on the beachhead lived in dugouts because German artillery could cover the entire beachhead. Our sled team could train with relative safety in the rear areas, because giant smoke-fog generators laid down huge smoke screens . . . to obscure the vision of . . . artillery observers.
>
> Occasionally, shells interrupted the training and once, a man near me was hit with a small shell fragment. . . . The sled teams had several weapons not generally assigned to infantry. One man was trained to use a flame-thrower; another carried a . . . "bangalore torpedo" to blow up barbed wire obstacles; another carried "satchel charges" . . . to be placed against a bunker or building. . . . Most of us turned in our M-1 rifles for Thompson sub-machine guns, and we carried extra hand grenades.

Apparently the training was not as secret as the Allies hoped, because Axis Sally announced on the radio that if the Americans tried using these sled teams, they would be annihilated. Finally the training drew to an end, and the breakout began late in May. Before they went into action, Shirley and his teammates were prepped.

continued

Our team was assembled in a house near the front. The men waited inside, and the tanks and sleds were camouflaged . . . nearby. . . . I heard the ungodly sounds of battle growing in intensity. . . . If the assault companies were successful, perhaps we wouldn't be called.

Several hours after the attack started, a radio message called us to battle. . . . We were waved towards our sleds without a word about our objective. . . . I, as assistant squad leader, didn't have the slightest idea what we were expected to attack.

We lay on our stomachs, head down, in our sleds, and moved onto the road and towards the front. We couldn't see a thing with our heads down, and with German artillery shells landing nearby, there wasn't much inclination to look over the edge of the sled. After a short distance on the road, the tanks made a left turn into an open field. In what only seemed like a minute or two, the tanks turned right and stopped. The squad leader yelled to get out and move forward. We had stopped in a flat field of grain. . . . As I climbed out of the sled . . . bursts of German machine gun bullets were chopping into the stalks of wheat only inches above my head.

While he lay on his stomach near his sled, Shirley noticed in front of him some partially buried objects about eighteen inches apart and exposed by the recent rains. There was also one right next to his foot. On closer inspection, he realized they were wooden antipersonnel "Schu" mines. Shirley was probably referring to the Schutzenmine 42, which consisted of a small plywood box with a few metal parts. He and his squad were pinned down by incoming artillery and could not see each other in the tall grain stalks. Shirley crawled for about sixty feet under a hail of bullets, carefully avoiding the mines, until he reached a deep antitank ditch. When he jumped in the ditch for cover, he discovered the remnants of his 3rd Battalion, including his company. Apparently his battle sled team had been called in behind his pinned-down battalion to help relieve the situation, but it never reached the ditch. Their objective was a fortified enemy position. The lieutenant leading the sled team gathered about half a dozen men from the team, including Shirley, and led them out to penetrate the enemy defenses. The lieutenant and one of Shirley's comrades nicknamed "Flash," who took the lead, were felled. After a fierce battle, Shirley and his surviving comrades reached the enemy position and captured about thirty German soldiers. Thus, although the sleds turned out to be a resounding disappointment, Shirley survived his first battle and lived to fight another day.

camera from home. Lots of German soldiers had cameras, so you simply took their cameras, shot what was left on the roll of film, removed the film, and the rear-area supply or admin clerk would trade the German souvenir camera to the Air Corps or navy personnel for food or candy. Most hospitals and signal companies had the capability of processing the film. You had to give a German souvenir to them for services rendered. I have a hundred or so pictures taken with probably twenty different cameras.

The oldest trick in the army was to tell a new soldier taken to a hospital that you were a censor, and then take his camera or other German souvenir. A soldier that fell for that was not too swift. Lots of rear-area soldiers had cameras because they had a place to keep and carry them.

Captain Stemmons got a comrade to take a photo of him in a foxhole dug under a road with a fence behind it in the Anzio area. A short time after the photo was taken, German artillery blew the fence and everything in its immediate vicinity to smithereens.

Stemmons also recalls some of their other needs: "During the winter, we needed good combat suits, gloves, and winter shoepacks; rear noncombat units had winter equipment. At all times, good rifle scopes were hard to get and keep. The small squad gas stoves were in super short supply. Time is very important in combat, and during the night, a watch will be handed down from one soldier to the next. Any kind of knife was always needed."

In May 1944, the 5th Army smashed the Gustav Line after its VI Corps broke out of Anzio. On June 5, Rome fell to the Allies, and PFC Ralph Fink, Company D, 157th Infantry, 45th Division, rejoiced when his division finally pulled out of line. At Anzio, "every inch of the beachhead was vulnerable to artillery fire, and the Germans loved to lay it in." The division had spent almost ten months in constant combat—first in Sicily, then in the mountains of Southern Italy, and finally on the exposed beachhead of Anzio. Its exhausted troops went into bivouac near Naples, where they were joined by the men of the 3rd and 36th Divisions. In Naples, "we were kept busy, but I think things were low key," says Fink. "This period was a time of renewal. Replacements were brought in to get all companies up to strength; equipment was repaired or replaced as needed. The previous months had taken a huge toll in KIA, illness, trench foot, and battle fatigue. Many of us had, and still have, guilt feelings because we somehow survived and so many other good men didn't."

Japanese-American soldiers of the 442nd Regiment run for cover in Levine, Italy, April 1945. NATIONAL ARCHIVES

While the army slogged it out in the mountains and mud of Italy, the AAF did its best to assist. As its strength grew, the 15th Air Force became an increasingly important factor in the campaign. In February, it reduced to rubble the Abbey of Monte Cassino, even though the Germans were not there. After the bombing, the Germans moved in. In March, the 15th Air Force launched Operation Strangle, whose objectives were to interdict the enemy line of communications and prevent the Germans from reinforcing, shifting, and supplying their forces at Anzio and on the Gustav Line.

Supporting the Troops

Logistical support is critical to keeping a military force in action, and it involved many types of units during World War II. The navy escorted convoys laden with vital supplies across the

Atlantic and Mediterranean. The needed munitions and supplies they unloaded had to be moved to the troops, and for this, the Quartermaster and Transportation Corps ran truck convoys.[12] The Military Railway Service (MRS) restored the railways behind the advancing Allied armies and made it possible to maintain critical logistical support, which included everything from munitions and troop trains to hospital trains. After the North African campaign, Sgt. Keith Wilson, who served as a conductor on a train crew of the 727th Railway Operation Battalion (ROB), enjoyed a brief respite from his duties.

> They put us in a rest camp in Tunisia, and from there we went into Sicily and ran the railroads all over the island.
>
> There was a big tunnel there where we stopped one day to take water and found an engineer group. I asked what they were doing, and they told me they were checking for land mines. I told them we had been running trains through for two weeks.
>
> After we finished the [Sicilian] campaign, the 36th Division had 150 trucks they had to have in Italy, so they assigned us as truck drivers to take them out to Italy. We drove through the toe of Italy, crossed the straits at Reggio Calabria, and went up to Salerno, where we were split up again. We went from Salerno to Naples, which was where our headquarters was.

During the winter stalemate on the Gustav Line in front of Cassino, the 727th ROB worked the port area of Naples, from where it ran about thirty trains a day up to the front and back. MPs were assigned to the trains, and the crews were armed with .45-caliber pistols and rifles to prevent looting.

> On some trains, we had antiaircraft, but more so in Africa, where we had AA outfits. Usually the AA weapons were mounted in the middle of the train on an armored car. We received American diesels that had been with the 8th (British) Army when we got to Italy. They were armor plated.
>
> After Anzio, we went north to Rome and then ran trains up to Leghorn. The main port for Rome was Civitavecchia, and we operated out of there.

"We never lost a single man through enemy action," declares with pride Sgt. Fred Buffington, also of Company C, 727th ROB, even though in Naples they endured forty-five days of bombing. Keith Wilson never forgot the air attacks on that city because he "used to get the shakes when it got dark in Naples." According to his comrade Buffington, "The port was bathed in light every night, and in the day it was bathed in smoke."

Air Intelligence

Capt. Elmer D. Richardson of Oak Grove, Missouri, was assigned to the 5th Photo Recon Squadron, 3rd Photo Group, 90th Photo Recon Wing, in the Mediterranean theater. His group provided the AAF, army mapping units, and army G-2 and S-2 sections with intelligence needed prior to bombing missions. Richardson had attended the Photo Interpretation School at Harrisburg, Pennsylvania, set up especially to support Elliott Roosevelt and his photo operations in the Mediterranean.[13] He departed Hampton Roads on the *Empress of Scotland,* one of the fast liners

12. Many of the quartermaster and transportation companies were African American units, since the political and military leadership refused to allow these Americans to service in more than a handful of combat units because of prejudice.

13. Roosevelt, the president's son, commanded the 90th Recon Wing until he was sent to England in 1944.

that traveled unescorted, and landed in Casablanca in November 1943. From there he went by train to Tunisia and by a British LST to Naples, where he arrived in mid-December 1943. Next, he was sent to the headquarters at San Severa, where he attended another school for photo interpretation run by the British. Finally, he replaced Maj. Byron Stevens as S-2 with the 5th Photo Recon when the major was promoted to group intelligence officer.

> My job was S-2 [intelligence]. We had F-4, F-2, and P-38 photo recon aircraft, which mounted 6-inch, 24-inch, and 40-inch cameras. The mission of the squadron was supporting the 12th Air Force, which had medium bombers, B-25s, and A-20 aircraft. The job was taking pictures of all the bridges that were cut and lines of transportation supporting the German Army in Italy. Just before the invasion of South France, they had photographed all of the gun positions in the area where they were going to make the landing.
>
> The headquarters [of which Richardson was part] was with the 90th Photo Recon Wing, located at San Severa, Italy. The squadron had twelve aircraft with our own maintenance section and radio section, so we were self-contained and could move out to any location and operate.
>
> The 5th Photo Group out of Bari supported the heavy bomber and the 3rd Group supported the mediums and the 5th Army. The 5th Squadron was supporting the 12th Air Force and charged with keep all lines of transportation broken.

In 1944, Maj. Thomas Barfoot joined the 3rd Photo Recon Group, which had lost two pilots shortly before he arrived in Italy from North Africa. "One of them went down when he dived and the FW-190 could dive faster than his P-38. The operations officer always told the pilots, if you got into trouble, you were supposed to go into a slight dive and then a gradual climb, because the P-38 could outclimb anything the Germans had."

Captain Richardson took part in preparing the operations.

> At Intelligence Office, we would get an Allied tactical bomb plan with the targets they would like to bomb in the morning by courier. I would plot them on the map, and we would have from 120 to 200 targets that had to be covered. On a typical mission, the photo recon aircraft would take from 15 to 20 targets. You couldn't group them too much together, because if the aircraft were in one area too long, they could vector their fighters up to intercept it. We let the pilot determine the way he would fly. When he got back, he would draw an overlay showing which way he had been going over the target. That was sent with the film over to the photo lab and the photo interpreter.
>
> The operations officer would explain the mission. I would brief them on why we needed the photos and the location of safe areas in case they were shot down, and also let them know if the navy had a chance to get them. This happened to Red Willis, one of our pilots shot down. He remembered the safe areas I pointed out. He went down in the area of Genoa, walked back, and returned about four months later with the help of the Partisans. They took him in. He had a pair of British escape boots, which were tall boots that were cut off at the top part so they didn't look like military boots. He said he had to have them resoled three times. Donovan's OSS got us information on Northern Italy, but most of our information came for the 12th Air Force to our squadron.

In 1944, missions were flown in the Adriatic to help prepare for a possible invasion. "It was a serious proposition," says Richardson, "but I think the 5th Group did that."

According to Major Barfoot, part of Operation Strangle required new methods of detecting the manner in which the Germans were moving supplies and troops into Central Italy.

> The other aspect of photo recon is your night photo recon. We got a request from the 5th Air Force that the Germans were bringing supplies and personnel from Northern Italy into Central Italy, north of Rome, and they couldn't figure out how they were doing it. We figured it must be at night, and we can't photograph it at night. The wing had a B-25 that was rigged up for night photo missions. We got the B-25 into Corsica, and a young lad named Spencer, who has now passed on, and I flew this night mission over the Po Valley. It was maybe five months before the invasion [of Southern France], but I can't remember when. We had a navigator in the nose who was the photographer. We were loaded with six phosphorous bombs and the camera had a photoelectric cell, and the bombs were fused to ignite at about 2,000 feet. So when the bomb ignited, the camera shutter opened and took pictures. We flew down the Po River and at intervals dropped the bombs. We expended the six bombs and hoped the camera worked. We came back, and they got the pictures and interpreted them.
>
> What the Germans were doing was, during the day, they had pontoons which were up against the bank of the river upstream attached to the banks and camouflaged. At night, they cut them loose, floated them down the river, attached them to the other side, and in the darkness the convoys crossed. In these pictures we took, they had eight bridges. There were convoys lined up on the bridges and backed up for at least four to six miles—trucks and everything. Needless to say, within twenty-four hours, they had destroyed the banks of the Po River, and from that time on, there was nothing more than a trickle of supplies coming over the river.

Maj. Barfoot flew no further night missions, but the 5th Recon Group, which supported the heavy bombers, continued to do so. According to Captain Richardson, the 3rd Recon Group continued similar missions after the invasion of Southern France, during the fall of 1944.

> We had night missions flown out of Pisa. The B-25 had the flash bomb, which was the magnesium bomb that flashed. We had an A-20 that had a strobe light. The strobe light popped off and on at intervals. The B-25 flew at about 5,000 feet, and the A-20 flew at a much lower level. They could only take three to four pictures, because they were dead ducks if they took any longer—they had to get off the track. When these missions were flown, we had photo interpreters standing by, and the film was developed in rapid order. Then we called in the P-61 night fighters, Black Widows, and they went up there and knocked out those pontoons and bridges.
>
> This happened over a period of several days. The Germans were very creative; they had a lot of good engineers. There was one bridge up there where we thought the rail span was down. Every daylight picture we took it was down, and we couldn't possibly see how they were getting stuff through there. We got information through the Rat Line—the underground up north—that the Germans were taking this railroad trestle by

Service Troops in Action in the Mediterranean Theater

In Italy, it seemed as if it were a makeshift war and only a secondary front as the buildup for Normandy began. Sgt. Burtt Evans, another correspondent for *Yank,* wrote an article on April 30, 1944, about S. Sgt. Vance B. Luten of Quincy, Florida, who was "an Aerial Traffic Cop."

> An advanced Air base in Italy—From his control window high in the operations tower, unshaven S/Sgt. Vance B. Luten trains his binoculars on a smoking bomber that just joined the fighters and transports circling this field, the nearest big field to the front.
>
> The B-24 is full of flak holes, with two props feathered, one engine shot out and another smoking badly, no brakes and the hydraulic system out of commission. . . . Sgt. Luten can't tell all that at a glance, but the Liberator is obviously crippled. [Luten orders the runway cleared for a crash landing.]
>
> Seconds later the bomber pilot makes a downwind landing, tilts the nose forward and finally grinds to a stop 10 feet short of the end of the runway.
>
> The meat wagon rolls up to do its grisly duty. Jerry has accounted for all the casualties; the nose gunner is dead and two men wounded. No one has been hurt in the landing.
>
> Up in the control tower a relieved Sgt. Luten turns his glasses away and returns to the job of playing aerial traffic cop.
>
> Planes take off or land at this base on an average of one every 50 seconds, which probably makes it the most active single runway field currently operating. . . .
>
> From the control tower before the runway, the sergeant—or one of the four other Air Service Command operators who work in shifts—must keep tabs on everything in the air and on the ground, identifying planes with binoculars, flashing red "Stop" or green "Go Ahead" signals with his reflector gun, nursing each plane to a correct landing by radio and then guiding it to a dispersal area. . . .
>
> When the fighter squadrons moved to a field as close to the front as possible, Luten and the service squadron go right with them. They have set up base operations in all possible places, in the air, on the ground, even underground. In Sicily they operated underground from a B-25 turret planted in a cave on the side of a hill. Shortly after the invasion of Italy, their "tower" was a trailer with a tarpaulin thrown over it.
>
> It isn't unusual for some of these fighter fields to operate in front of the Artillery, but on occasion—just after the invasion of Italy—the boys were busy setting up shop when a runner arrived with news that they were ahead of the Infantry. They had started to operate on a field that actually hadn't been captured yet. . . .
>
> Mix-ups like that happened in the African campaign, too. One morning two Jerry pilots flew into the traffic pattern over the field where Luten and his boys were set up, landed as nice as you please and stepped out of the plane into the arms of some GIs.

> train, hauling it back up to the Po River at nighttime, putting it into position, and running stuff across. They had another system, which we initially thought was an oil pipeline, but it was a cable that ran across there. Melvin Lloyd took those pictures; they came back and said that it was a pipeline. Here was a station where they do the transfer and so forth.

The German position in Northern Italy was more secure than in France after the Normandy invasion, and that allowed them more time and opportunities to be creative.

The Ships Arrive in Britain

As troops engaged in intensive preinvasion training in England, the navy was called upon to provide ships for amphibious exercises. The U.S. Navy shifted the required vessels from the Mediterranean and America to England relatively quickly. The smaller landing craft, a critical element of the upcoming invasion, were in high demand, albeit short supply. New landing craft had to be shipped from the United States to add to the number of those being built in British yards.

One of the largest landing craft units to arrive in England was the Coast Guard LCI Flotilla, a veteran of the Sicilian invasion and the landings at Salerno. It departed Italy during the first part of October 1943 and slowly steamed west, making only about 15 knots per hour. John L. Gatton of Louisville, Kentucky, the chief quartermaster on LCI 96, says the stopover at Gibraltar proved to be memorable.

> I have vivid memories of Gibraltar, because we had a larger casualty rate there than in the previous landings in the Mediterranean. It seems as though some of our crewmembers got a little firewater and they wanted to take on the British Navy and the Royal Marines. In fact, one guy had to offer a toast at one of the local establishments. He wanted to drink a toast to the British 8th Army, and then he had to add the additional information, "Run rabbit, run, Dunkirk!" With that, all hell broke loose.
>
> There were a large number of capital units there. We had American cruisers and LSTs. The place was loaded with monkeys, and the monkeys were loaded with fleas, so you didn't want to bring one aboard as a pet.

Only half of the men had liberty in Gibraltar, and many of them took advantage of the opportunity to get involved in brawls. To the commanders' relief, the flotilla left the rock on October 23, sailing in four columns. The danger from U-boats was relatively negligible, because the landing craft's shallow draft made them less susceptible to torpedoes. Lt. Ed Fabian of California was part of the little armada.

> When we left Gibraltar, we went west, and we knew we were heading for England, or at least I did. We had to make a very wide detour around the Bay of Biscay because of the submarine pens that were in St. Nazaire and that area on the coast of France. I would imagine we were 500 miles out at sea during the detour, until we arrived at the west of England in Falmouth. One of the worries we had all of the time was that we were traveling without escort. We didn't sight any submarines. We had air cover from bases in England.

Boatswain Mate 2/C Elmer E. Carmichael was struck by one incident during the trip.

> We were picked up by one German recon plane. I watched it, and I would say it was

four engines; it was big and was strictly observation. He stayed out of range, and we watched him a long time. He completely circled our flotilla and then left. We thought maybe we would be in for problems. We carried two racks of depth charges and four 20-millimeter antiaircraft guns. We were not attacked in any way, and the trip was uneventful, except for the one German recon plane.

For CMM (Chief Machinist's Mate) Ralph Gault from Chicago, who had joined the Coast Guard in 1941 at age twenty-four, seen service on antisubmarine patrols in American waters, and been transferred to LCI 88 just before it left the Mediterranean, the trip to England was more harrowing. "We were due west of the Brest submarine pens and I blew an engine," he recalls. "The flotilla pulled alongside one by one to give us parts and whatever, but we had to drop back while the flotilla went on ahead. We had the pressure of this plane overhead, observing us, and we did not really expect to get there. I was down in the engine room busy as a cat."

Once they reached England, all the ships went into dry dock, where they underwent repairs and their barnacles were scraped off. The flotilla's LCIs docked at several British ports. Cmdr. Joseph A. Bresnan of Montgomery, Alabama, set up his headquarters at Greenway House, Agatha Christie's summer house on the Dart River near Dartmouth. He enjoyed very much his stay at the famous writer's residence as he prepared his ships for the upcoming invasion. Early in 1944, after undergoing the necessary repairs, the flotilla's LCIs took part in training exercises.

Not all the American navy's landing craft left for England. Only 68 of the 90 LSTs stationed in Italy were to sail there. On October 24, however, Eisenhower informed the Combined Chiefs of Staff that those 68 LSTs would remain in the Mediterranean for several additional weeks. Their stay was eventually extended until January 5, 1944, so they could take part in Operation Shingle. Of the 201 LCTs in the Mediterranean, 129 were to sail for England, and the remainder was to operate the Messina Ferry, support the 8th Army, and work the ports. The planners had to juggle the landing craft, some of which had to be repaired, to have enough for the invasion. In the final count, 84 LSTs, 90 LCIs, and 60 LCTs were available for the Anzio landings, but according to Samuel Eliot Morison in *Sicily-Salerno-Anzio,* about 71 LSTs, 94 LCIs, and 79 LCTs took part in the operation. In February, according to the same source, 33 LSTs were ordered to sail for England, and 36 were held and refitted for the landings in Southern France. LSTs and all other types of landing craft were a valuable commodity but in short supply for Operation Overlord and the other invasions.

Many of the LSTs that arrived in England from the United States and the Mediterranean also carried LCTs on their deck. Shortly after their overhaul, the landing craft were engaged in landing exercises, providing much-needed experience for the crews fresh from training at the Amphibious Operations Center at Solomons Island in Maryland. Before 1944, no American force of this size or this well equipped had graced the British Isles with its presence. Such an expeditionary force could not have been maintained if the lines of communication had not been secured and the U-boat threat eliminated between 1942 and the first half of 1943.

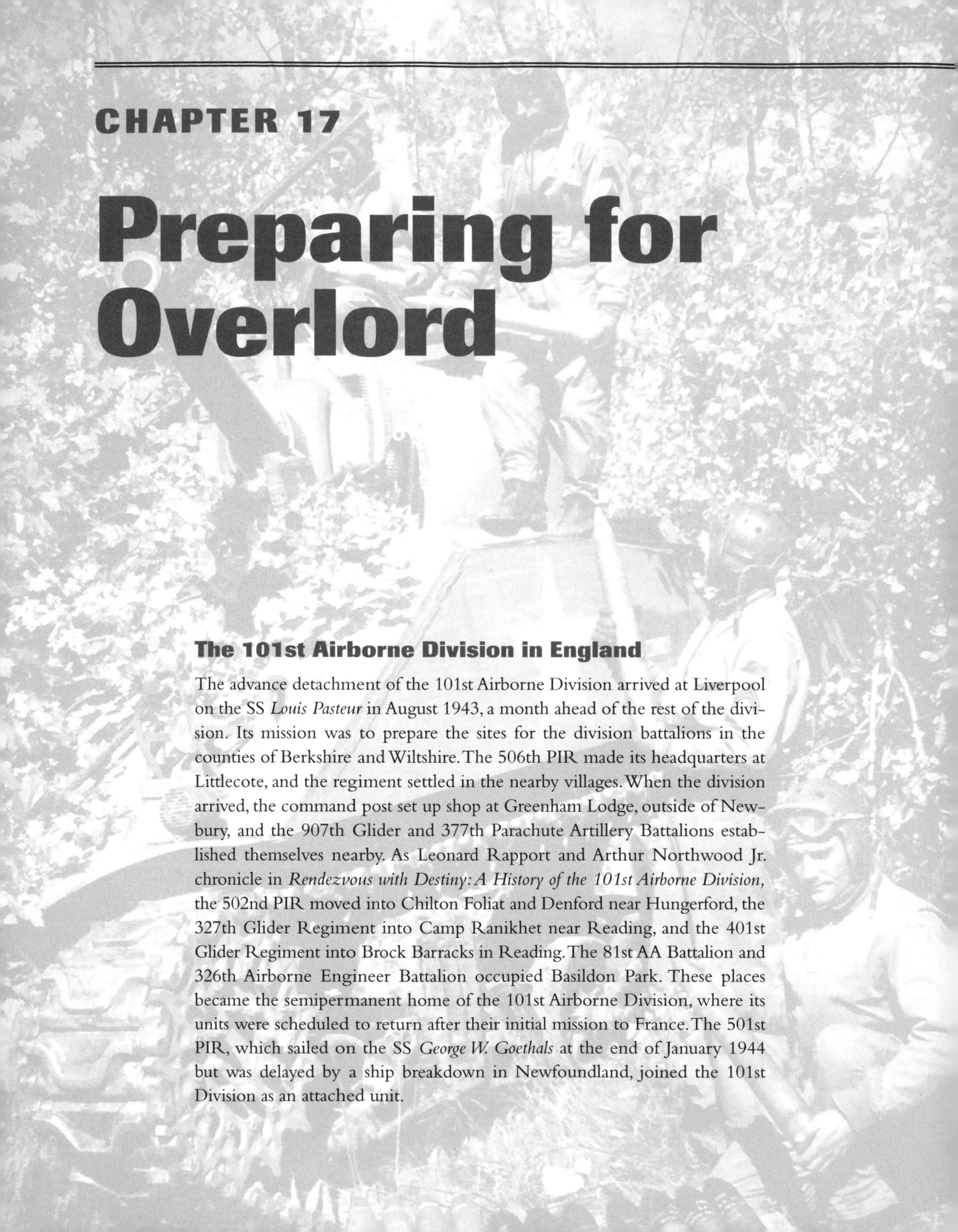

CHAPTER 17

Preparing for Overlord

The 101st Airborne Division in England

The advance detachment of the 101st Airborne Division arrived at Liverpool on the SS *Louis Pasteur* in August 1943, a month ahead of the rest of the division. Its mission was to prepare the sites for the division battalions in the counties of Berkshire and Wiltshire. The 506th PIR made its headquarters at Littlecote, and the regiment settled in the nearby villages. When the division arrived, the command post set up shop at Greenham Lodge, outside of Newbury, and the 907th Glider and 377th Parachute Artillery Battalions established themselves nearby. As Leonard Rapport and Arthur Northwood Jr. chronicle in *Rendezvous with Destiny: A History of the 101st Airborne Division,* the 502nd PIR moved into Chilton Foliat and Denford near Hungerford, the 327th Glider Regiment into Camp Ranikhet near Reading, and the 401st Glider Regiment into Brock Barracks in Reading. The 81st AA Battalion and 326th Airborne Engineer Battalion occupied Basildon Park. These places became the semipermanent home of the 101st Airborne Division, where its units were scheduled to return after their initial mission to France. The 501st PIR, which sailed on the SS *George W. Goethals* at the end of January 1944 but was delayed by a ship breakdown in Newfoundland, joined the 101st Division as an attached unit.

In the fall of 1943, Pvt. Harold Martino, 401st Glider Infantry, wrote home about his new home at Reading and his first day at the new camp.

> [There was] the rattle of mess kits and the familiar cry, "Chow!" It didn't take any time at all for me to find my mess kit and run for the line that was already forming. After the usual G.I. meal, I returned to the barracks to find that I was late for another important formation, "Mail Call." It had been a long time since we had any mail due to our unusually long voyage. . . .
>
> There was a huge pile of mail, the mail had beaten us over, and every day was piling up, Uncle Sam takes good care of his mail—piles and piles of letters from worried mothers and sweethearts. My reward was much more than I expected. I received in the neighborhood of 75 to 80 letters. Overjoyed and thrilled to death, I took my pile to the privacy of my bunk with tearful eyes to read news of home. Here I was, all settled in England, waiting for that day when we would be called upon to do our part in this worldwide conflict. . . .
>
> The days in Reading, England, and the London vicinity, were to become my most enjoyable days of my army career. . . . Brock Barracks, the home of the Royal Berkshire Regiment of the Boer War, now the home of the 401st Gliders, began to look more like a college campus than an army camp. Its ancient two-story red brick buildings, velvet green recreation field, and macadam parade ground, centered by a huge wreath covered memorial of the "Royal Berks" was completely enclosed by a red brick wall 12 feet high, whose only entrance was a huge wrought iron double gate, which was posted by two full dressed sentries twenty-four hours daily.
>
> After the inevitable two weeks quarantine, which always follows when setting up a new camp, I with a six-hour pass, companion, and heart full of anxiety passed through the main gates in quest of soldiers' solitary pastime—"Women and drink," which later we were pleased to discover there was an abundance of both.
>
> With darkness came "blackout." This was my first experience in a wartime city totally blackened out, and I was amazed at the apparent ease the war-hardened civilians could swiftly move about, while I was constantly running into telephone poles and feeling absolutely silly making apologies to poles and fireplugs for my stupidity while groping through the darkness. I don't know how I could ever get used to this inky darkness filled with hundreds of people walking briskly and by some divine miracle preventing head-on collisions, but I guess after four years of it one could become accustomed to it.
>
> As night grew on and the pubs closed, people on the streets became noticeably scarce. As we were groping our way towards the barracks we were startled by a dim flash light in our faces and a friendly tap on the shoulder by a Bobby who said, "It's best you'd be hurrying back to the barracks mates. Jerries due any minute you know, on his way to London and the blighter may drop a couple here if he sees us stirring about."

As Martino and his comrades hurried back to camp, the shrill sound of the air-raid siren rent the air and they broke into a run, reaching the barracks only a few minutes before some planes droned past on their way toward London. When the "All clear" sounded an hour later, Martino breathed a sigh of relief; he had survived his first air raid.

> Soon we knew just when to expect them and began to take it as casually as the natives. Although no bombs were ever dropped on Reading, the town bore scars of earlier raids. . . .
>
> The weeks that followed were spent in issuing of new equipment and salvaging worn-out clothing and equipment in preparation for the rigid training program that was promised us. . . .
>
> Weeks of training and lengthy field problems followed. . . . Training problems involving airborne tactics and even sea borne operations took us over the greater part of the British Isles.

Private Martino went on to describe his first pass to London.

> Passes were now being issued for London, which was only 40 miles from the base. . . . A mixture of thrill and excitement surged through me when I learned I was to receive a London pass. The following day was spent in that "Pre-pass Ritual," borrowing money, shining boots, pressing uniforms, and asking veterans of London passes what to see, where to go, was there plenty of drink—how are the women???
>
> Fortified with money, information, neatly pressed uniforms, and a forty-eight-hour pass, my buddy and I boarded the train headed for the forty-five-minute ride. When we pulled into Paddington Street Station, London, I was both thrilled and disappointed. Thrilled that I was at last in the world-renowned London, and disappointed in not seeing it a mass of charred rubble as I expected. The first stop was the Red Cross Club for a bed and meal. The club was set up in what had been a hotel when England knew only of "Yankee Soldiers" through what they had read. The Red Cross clubs, of which there were many throughout the London area, offered food, bedding, relaxation, entertainment, and historical tours for the GIs at reasonable prices.
>
> London: Famous for its Big Ben, Buckingham Palace, London Bridge, and other historical sites . . . attracted sight seeing parties led and narrated by a proud native lecturer [who] could always be seen at any time leading huge throngs of soldiers, armed to the teeth with cameras and guide books. . . .
>
> London: Equally famous "Piccadilly Circus, . . ." world-famous for its prostitutes, black market, dance halls, thugs, thieves, and murderers, ironically enough, was completely untouched by the destruction of the war and attracted thousands of Allied soldiers in quest of thrills, excitement, and temporary escape from the war.
>
> With darkness in Piccadilly, came the hustle and bustle of humans, drunken soldiers singing, taxi cabs honking their weird horns and groping their way through the inky blackness, the laughter of girls in doorways and alleys (where the "Piccadilly Commandos"—prostitutes—usually propositioned their prospective customers), the whisper of a beggar begging the price of a drink, the nudge of the ever present pickpockets, and his weak excuse when caught, and the ghostly appearance of the MPs in their white helmets, white leggings, gloves, and night stick . . . there you have London. . . .
>
> We wormed and pushed our way through the crowded streets and by some miracle found ourselves in a brightly lighted dance hall luxuriously furnished and attended by uniformed girls. The dance hall was filled to overflowing capacity with soldiers, sailors, marines, and WACs of every allied nation. The orchestra was good and sounded surprisingly American. The English girls were very

good dancers and very plentiful, ranging in all ages and types and could execute very well all the intricate steps of American "jitterbug dancing."

The crowd was gay and noisy, a huge mass of uniformed men and women, to the rhythms of the orchestra the crowd seemed to sway and bob in one solid mass. It would require all the military strategy of a supreme commander to attempt even to dance so with this thought in mind, we left to continue our tour of London.

PFC Ray Hood, 2nd Battalion, 502nd PIR, moved with his regiment to a small village called Hungerford in Berkshire, England, about sixty-five miles west of London. The large country estate of Denford consisted of a big two- or three-story manor nestled in a bucolic setting of emerald lawns, shrubbery, and good-sized oak trees. The enlisted men's Quonset huts, orderly rooms, a dispensary, showers, and latrines were scattered throughout the grounds. One of the larger huts served as the mess hall and recreation room, where the men could buy British beer and watch an occasional movie. The officers were billeted in the manor house, which also held the various battalion offices. An old wooden building, formerly a stable, served as the battalion supply room. A large grass-covered cricket field among the oaks served as a playing field and the battalion's marching grounds.

One of the major problems for the troops was taking care of their laundry, but they quickly solved it by making arrangements with local housewives to provide the much-needed service. Whenever the laundress for Hood's platoon had to pick up or deliver the laundry, she brought along her ten-year-old daughter, Ivy, who won the tough paratroopers' hearts by singing to them. The soldiers took to spoiling the little girl with gifts of candy, chewing gum, toothpaste, cigarettes, soap, and razor blades—all items that were hard to find in England. Little Ivy later grew up to become the mayor of Hungerford.

The new home of Maj. X. B. Cox's 81st A/B AA Battalion in Britain was at Basildon, on a 600-acre estate with a ninety-one-room manor house enclosed by a stone wall. The enlisted men lived in Quonset huts in the wooded area, while the battalion offices and officers' quarters were in the manor house. No other units were stationed nearby, and discipline problems were few. The battalion continued its rigorous training, which included marching, physical fitness, map reading, weaponry, orientation on the enemy, aircraft identification, and instruction on loading and unloading gliders. The training operations took place at several sites, including St. Agnes, Nottingham. "On or about March 20th, 1944," Cox recalls, "I was informed that Lt. Col. W. C. Scoggins was being transferred because of night blindness. The change of command took place on the twenty-fifth. At the time I was told of the transfer, I was giving a briefing of all the invasion plans except for the date, which was easy to figure out within a few days."

During October and November, the 101st A/B Division began intensive training, which included fifteen- to twenty-five-mile hikes, hand-to-hand combat, gas warfare, and mastery of German weapons, with emphasis on the use of automatic weapons. According to Rapport and Northwood *Rendezvous with Destiny,* practice jumps involved company- and battalion-size units, and the glidermen trained with the British Horsa gliders. Several specialized schools, including one for pathfinders, were established. Everyone trained with the bazooka.

For most of the American soldiers stationed in Britain in 1943–44, the winter months were particularly trying, because they were not used to the rain and cold. Ray Hood and his comrades of the 502nd PIR did their best to adapt to the cli-

Division Paymaster

Few men in the 101st A/B Division headquarters had it in their power to raise the men's morale as much as the paymaster, Lt. Col. William P. Machemehl, who arrived in Britain late with the 502nd PIR. "We landed at a port in Great Britain," he says. "Our commanding general wanted the troops paid before we left the U.S., but we didn't have a chance to transfer the payrolls, and there was some delay in locating the field safes with payrolls and U.S. money. We arrived in the dark, but luckily they were located, and the next day I transferred payrolls to a finance officer in England."

The Finance Section of the division headquarters consisted of a finance officer, an assistant finance officer (a captain), and twenty enlisted men. Several men handled the officers' pay, and most worked with the enlisted men's pay by computing amounts due and converting the amounts into foreign currencies. The Finance Section also prepared change lists showing the numbers of coins of different denominations needed to pay each payroll. To Machemehl's amazement, the weight of the coinage in England was so perfectly balanced that the banks were able to weigh any quantity of coins of the same denomination to determine the value of the total.

Each company's clerks typed a payroll and sent it to the Finance Office. Division headquarters appointed an officer in each company as a class A agent, whose job it was to pick up his payroll and a bag of money. The class A agent paid his men, redlined those who were not paid, and made sure each man signed the payroll. He also redlined money returned to the Finance Office. The officers had to prepare their own pay vouchers, received a check signed by the finance officer, and mailed it to their bank or to a designated address. Form no. 29 was used to make allotments that were distributed by the finance officer, U.S. Army, Washington, D.C.

The finance officer and his assistant supervised all the office work, counting of the money that was kept in locked field safes, travel preparations, and other expense vouchers.

mate, but their stratagems were sometimes puzzling, if not shocking, to the Britons.

> We regularly used condoms to keep water off the muzzles of our rifles, carbines, and submachine guns. They were ideal for the job—very effective—but when we hiked through villages and towns, these "field expedients," as we called them, attracted shocked stares and muttered comments. We were ordered to stop using the things, and thenceforth, we all carried our weapons slung muzzle down. When we went into combat, of course, a different attitude prevailed—back came the field expedients.

The Veterans Arrive

As the newly trained combat divisions arrived from the States, the seasoned veterans from the Mediterranean also came back to Britain. The men of the 2nd Armored, 1st and 9th Infantry, and 82nd A/B Divisions no longer felt the excitement of impending adventure; they had left their innocence behind, in the sands of North Africa and the hills of Sicily and Italy. The British Isles offered them a respite from war, a chance to lick their wounds, and an opportunity to take on replacements. Many of them were disappointed because rumors of a pending return to the States turned out to be unfounded. The green divisions and reinforcements showed more determination and eagerness to end the training and get at the enemy than the veterans. Long after the war, many of the men of the 1st Division, "Big Red One," admitted that they were tired and not really keen about playing at war exercises. The battle-weary veterans of "The Varsity," the 9th Division, did their best to prepare their replacements for the battle ahead. The "All American" paratroopers of the 82nd A/B had mixed feelings about the upcoming operation, because even though their experiences in Sicily and Italy had been tough, they had been in combat for only a short time. Many of them were still eager for battle. The glider men of the division, on the other hand, had engaged in combat but had yet to enter the field of battle in their "flying coffins."

The troopers of the veteran divisions that had established their reputation in combat soon came to realize that they were expected to play a prominent role in the upcoming invasion. The presence of Eisenhower, fiery-tempered George Patton, and British field marshal Montgomery in Britain indicated to them that the main Allied force in the West was about to come into existence. Some of the seasoned NCOs, like Sgt. Ted Aufort of the 1st Division, were fully of aware of the role propaganda played to boost the images of the Allied leaders, such as Patton.

The 82nd Airborne Division Arrives

After it left the 504th PIR behind in Italy, the 82nd Airborne Division sailed for Northern Ireland, reaching Belfast in early December 1943. The 325th Glider Infantry Regiment disembarked on December 9 and moved to Portglenone. PFC Clinton Riddle realized how safe he was when he was able to sleep without his pants on for the first time since April 26, 1943.

Riddle and his friend Owens soon found out that life away from the front lines was not necessarily devoid of new experiences. During their infantry training in Ireland, they discovered to their consternation that when they stomped down hard on the ground, water oozed out; when they tried to dig a foxhole more than a foot deep, they created a well. Lt. Joe Gault complained that the rations were rather skimpy, especially when it came to the small luxuries that made life bearable. The men received only one Coca-Cola and one ration of cigarettes a week.[1]

The 2nd Battalion of the 325th was scattered all over Northern Ireland. Companies E and F bivouacked on an old farm with a huge two-story farmhouse, whose bottom floor served as the mess hall and upper floor as the residence for the officers. The enlisted men lived in Quonset huts. Gault commanded Company F now, but he was not promoted to captain until a few months later. Capt. Bob Dickerson of Company E was the senior officer and thus the camp commander, but he delegated some of his responsibilities to Gault, notably his meetings with Major Swenson, the battalion commander. Whenever the major was expected, Dickerson posted guards to warn him of his arrival. As soon as the major's vehicle

---

1. The tobacco companies and the military made sure that most GIs were well supplied with cigarettes, resulting in many nonsmokers becoming smokers. Many troops became addicted and sorely felt any shortage. In combat, they found that cigarettes were included in C and K rations.

was spotted, Dickerson left the camp, and Gault had to escort the commanding officer. With only about eight hours or less of daylight in the winter, Gault took his company on only short marches before daybreak, and then began training in infantry tactics.

During their free time, the GIs downed large quantities of Irish beer and whiskey. One of Captain Gault's best squad leaders, Robert C. McCarthy, who was of Irish ancestry, particularly enjoyed his stay by overindulging in good cheer on weekends and was unfit for duty on Mondays. One Monday, when Major Swenson came to inspect the camp, he found McCarthy just rolling out of bed and ordered Gault to court-martial him. McCarthy was broken to the rank of private, but Gault, who respected the man's abilities, ordered his company to treat him with the rank and privileges of a sergeant.

Gault's company received about ten replacements, not all of whom were model soldiers. Among the replacements that came to Company F was an eighteen-year-old lieutenant who proved unable to handle the veterans in his platoon and had to be replaced in Normandy. Another was a sergeant whose clothes were wrinkled and wouldn't shave. "He was disobedient to a point, but not enough to get in real trouble." Still, "although he was a bad influence, when he got into combat he was a holy terror; that was our business."

On December 28, 1943, the 508th PIR sailed from New York on the USAT *James Parker.*[2] When the 508th PIR arrived in Northern Ireland in January, it was attached to the 82nd A/B Division and moved to Port Stewart. Maj. David Thomas, who had sailed with the 508th PIR, discovered that his old regiment, the 505th PIR, had just arrived there from the Mediterranean. He sent some of his medical NCOs to work with the 505th at Port Rush so they could learn from the veterans' experiences. As he and his men took up training, the major discovered to his dismay that the terrain got muddier the higher up a mountain they went.

Also in December, a group of replacements taken from the 541st PIR left the States on the liner *Mariposa* and reached Northern Ireland sometime around January 1, 1944. [3] The small contingent, which included Sgt. Edward Jeziorski, traveled from Belfast to Port Rush to join the 507th PIR. Jeziorski had joined the 44th Division of the New Jersey National Guard in April 1940 and attended Parachute School with the 541st PIR in the spring of 1943. After checking in at a replacement center in Ireland, he was assigned to Company C of the 507th PIR, but he was reduced to the rank of private because the regiment had its full complement of NCOs.

> After three years as a noncom, it was back to step one. Morale was no problem. I knew that sooner or later, I would get this rank back. I was made a machine gunner in the 2nd Squad, 2nd Platoon. It was just a matter of doing a job, and I really liked this outfit.
>
> While in the Port Rush area, we participated in one live ammo field problem plus all the other regular things, the running around and whatnot. I admit here that on many an evening, with the Bushmill's Distillery operating in Coleraine, something like fourteen miles further inland from us, on more than one occasion a couple of us would go on over to the distillery, and the guards there would give us each a bottle to take back—AWOL but fun. Even though it wasn't a hospitable climate at that time of

2. The former SS *Panama* was built in 1939, taken over by the army in 1941 and renamed the *James Parker,* and turned into a troopship that carried up to 2,300 troops. It had a speed of 18 knots and mounted a 4-inch gun.

3. The *Mariposa* was an 18,152-ton liner taken over by the U.S. Navy in 1941 as a troop transport. It had a speed of 20 knots and could carry 4,272 troops.

> the year—very, very cold—we had the goodwill of the distillers on our side, and they made things just a little bit more endurable.

Pvt. Dick Johnson, with the 507th PIR, also participated in practice jumps in Northern Ireland.

> We went into a tent city and set up camp there. There we were to practice our jumping, night jumping, and a lot of exercise to get us back in physical shape. After three or four day jumps, we started making night jumps and found that the winds were too much in Ireland to jump at night. We were landing in farmhouses and farmers' fields. A lot of these villagers weren't told the Americans were going to land that particular night, and a lot of boys were out there under siege by the farmers standing there with pitchforks trying to defend their farms. Consequently, the higher-ups decided this was a bad deal, so we were taken from Belfast by ship to Nottingham, England.

When the 82nd Airborne Division was ordered to England in early February, the 325th sailed aboard the Dutch ship *Cempo* to Liverpool. From there the glider men were driven to a tent camp in Leicester, which they reached at 6 P.M. on February 15.

> We were stationed at Camp March Hare near Leicester and the village of Scroptoft. On April 7, four days of field problems, including glider rides for the guys. I was on guard at the airport near Newbury; we slept on cots in the big hangar. The glider ride was on April 9; the rest of the month we spent in regular infantry drill.
>
> I was trained to use every weapon in the company at my request. I was given an M-1 to carry most of the time. I was the first man to train on the bazooka when we got one in the company. The first one was just one long stovepipe, and later they came in two pieces to make it easier to jump with or carry into the gliders.

The camp near Leicester, which was near a beautiful golf course, was a particular treat for Lieutenant Gray, Sgt. Harold Owens's superior and a professional golfer. One day, to Owens's amusement, Gray had a near apoplexy when he read in the newspaper that the winner of a recent golf tournament was a man he had regularly beat in the past.

The diet mainstays in Owens's unit consisted of orange marmalade and sausages made of soybean meal. Owens learned quickly that if one did not develop a taste for fish and chips, he would not find a decent meal. "It was just like being in the U.S.," with all the shortages, he says. As for training, "we did little except for mock-ups as far as glider training, loading, and unloading. They did have a night drop of paratroopers into the golf course area; they dropped quite a few troopers into our camping area, and we were out guiding them down with flashlights."

Capt. Harold Shebeck, who had been left behind in a hospital in North Africa, rejoined the 325th in Great Britain. When he stepped off the ship in Scotland, he was put in command of a troop train.

> In due time, we were under way, although we did not know our destination. The train commander was responsible for loading the train and for the troops while en route. The train had no sooner left the port than I discovered that none of the service records of the men had been put aboard. This was a serious matter, which could have resulted in a complete administrative foul-up for over 300 men. I asked the conductor where the

Illustrated guide to German phrases from the April 30, 1944, issue of *Yank*.

train was headed and he said to Bristol. It was a very fast train, which would make only two stops en route, one at Carlisle just inside the English border and the second at Sheffield. I told him the situation, and when we got to Carlisle, I hopped off the train to contact the American authorities at the port about the problem. Every large railroad station in England had an American rail transportation officer stationed at the depot whose job it was to facilitate movement of American troops. I contacted the RTO in the Carlisle station, who telephoned the port, and I learned that the oversight had already been recognized and the records would be on the way.

Arriving at Bristol, we were directed to a large brick complex, which had been the famous Muller's Orphanage in peacetime. In a sociology class in college, I had read a lot about this place. Of course, the children had long since been removed to the country, and the place had been taken over by the American army. The first night we were there, I experienced my one and only air raid in England. The people had to file down into the cellars of the building, a large and cavernous-looking structure.

Within a day or two of arriving in Bristol, I was on my way to Leicester, in the Midlands, where the 325th was stationed. Now I was assigned as assistant regimental supply officer, as my previous job as special services officer had been taken over by someone else in my long absence.

Our supply system for the regiment operated out of the S-4 Section and worked closely with the Service Company. Trucks from the Service Company were dispatched daily to the division supply dumps, and supplies were obtained and delivered to the various companies of the regiment. Rations were requisitioned in accordance with the daily strength reports of the companies. Men needing various kinds of clothing or other individual GI supplies, shoes, etc., made their needs known, and these requisitions were then consolidated in the S-4 Section and forwarded to division. Eventually the items came back to the requisitioning companies. Ammunition, when needed for the firing range for instance, was requisitioned through S-4, and this particular item was handled by the regimental ammunition sergeant.

One would have to live through those times and personally feel the excitement to realize what a momentous event was approaching. England is a small country, and every available vacant piece of land in the country was jam-packed with supply depots, repair shops, ammunition dumps, truck and tank parks, 1,000 locomotives, 20,000 railroad cars, jeeps, trucks, and ambulances, 124,000 hospital beds, and literally thousands of other types of supplies and equipment too numerous to mention. Imagine the airfields all over England on which nothing could be parked except the 10,000 planes, fighters, and bombers, as well as hundreds of transport aircraft. Foodstuffs alone amounted to thousands of tons, and total tonnage of all stacked supplies amounted to six million.

Maj. David Thomas was a regimental surgeon stationed in the English Midlands with the 508th PIR.

> We were garrisoned in tents with a few Nissen huts for latrines and honey buckets—we didn't have flush toilets. We were there from March until the invasion. During this time, we had more advanced divisional training to include divisional night jumps and things of that nature. In Ireland, we were in Quonset huts, while in England, we had the regular pyramidal squad tents with a center pole and bunks all around the edge, and heated by a small potbellied stove with a chimney through the top of the tent and heated with coal. While we were in Ireland, the coal was terrible; it was slate, peat moss, and peat, and we had a hell of a time getting enough fire to get a good meal. We did better in England. The officers, we had two or three men to a tent, and the enlisted men had more than that. They set up in platoons and company streets. We were in garrison in Sherwood Forest, but we never did see Little John or the rest of them!
>
> I remember the exercise when we had this division-sized jump at night. It was dark as a chimney. We had a fair number of injured, because you just could not see where the ground was, and you were lucky if you didn't get hurt. I accumulated a bunch of these injured and had a light on because you can't set fractures very well without light. By this time, Jimmy Gavin was a brigadier general. He comes along and says, "You know this is supposed to be a lights-out proposition!" and I said, "I will tell you I am a hell of a doctor, but I can't set bones without seeing what I am doing." So he just went on his way.
>
> A strange thing happened; there was this one guy we could not account for. We

didn't find him until the third day after the jump. What he had done was land in this little copse of trees. We were using camouflaged parachutes, and it settled in all over him. What he had was a malfunction. He died on landing because his chute never opened. I took his gloves. By this time, they had the sweet smell of death on them. I laundered them carefully until they got all that out of them. I took them into Normandy. I figured those gloves could not be that unlucky twice.

The way we handled the medics was that after we got them, we trained for what they had to know: how to stop blood, how to splint a fracture, how to apply a dressing, how to give a shot of morphine, how to evacuate a guy, and that kind of stuff. Then we sent the company medics out to their companies. They didn't live together with the other medics. The platoon medic would live with the platoon he would serve with in combat. The way I ran my aid stations in garrison, if a guy wanted to go on sick call, he had to get by the platoon medic. If the platoon medic could not handle it, he would send him up to the battalion aid station. If the battalion aid station couldn't handle it and thought he had to go to the hospital, they would send him over to regimental aid. Anybody that my doctors out in the battalion wanted to send to the hospital, they sent to regiment, and then I would look them over. If I decided they needed to go to the hospital, we would ship them over. This way, the platoon medic got to know everybody in the platoon, and he got knitted into the outfit.

I had a detachment with three platoons. We had three battalion medical sections with two doctors, four enlisted men per rifle company, with one per platoon and one per company headquarters. We had some medics in the battalion aid stations with the two doctors, and we had a jeep, a couple of ambulances for the regimental aid station. We had three battalions with six doctors, two per battalion, and at regimental level two doctors and one dentist. The doctors were all lieutenants or captains except for the regimental surgeon—I was a major. We also had one dentist, but he was captured in Normandy, and we never did get a replacement for him for the rest of the war.

We used the dentist, John Thurncoast, as another doctor. We were not filling teeth on the front lines. In garrison, he was invaluable to us. He was a hard-working guy. He had these hand-pumped drills. Old Jimmy Ternane, his dental technician, kept pumping on that damn thing, and he filled teeth until he was blue in the face.

I also had one Medical Service Corps type whom I used as my registrar. He kept the books on who got evacuated.

Problems other than the shortages of luxury items and German air raids also developed in the American military camps. Resentment grew among American soldiers of African descent who served in segregated units, performed mostly menial duties, and had no opportunity to show their mettle on the battlefield. In addition, friction developed between white and black American soldiers who vied for the same entertainment and women when they were off duty. Some black soldiers told the girls that all the paratroopers were Chicago gangsters, which could have led to a serious confrontation if their officers had not intervened.

Lt. Jack Isaacs of Company G, 505th PIR, a veteran of the Mediterranean campaigns, moved from Italy to the town of Quarn in Northern Ireland with his battalion.

Our training intensified with small unit, company, and battalion field problems and several practice drops being made in this area. One resulted in a midair collision, which killed Lieutenant Gulick from G Company and Captain Rice from D Company. This was on a drop in which only one man dropped from each plane so that the pattern could be studied and corrections could be made in navigation.

At this time, we received replacements of men and equipment lost in the Mediterranean because we took many casualties in that campaign. We received more company officers, and as I was not the ranking first lieutenant, I was relieved as XO and returned to the 3rd Platoon. Other officers at the time were Capt. Willard Follmer, the company commander; Capt. Ivan F. Wood, the XO; 1st Lt. Travis Ormand; 1st Lt. Bill Mastrangel; and myself, as platoon leader. My assistant platoon leader was 2nd Lt. Robert Ringwald.

PFC Raymond Gonzalez of Company C, 505th PIR, who was drafted at age twenty in 1942, was sent to Fort Custer for induction. The son of a coal miner and a Native American woman from Indian Territory, he was born in Oklahoma and raised in Detroit. After he was inducted, he volunteered for the paratroopers. At Quarn, he experimented with a device one of his superiors had invented.

For about half the time we were there, we had patrols, we read compass, and more or less kept busy in drills and problems. Around March, it was just muggy; we had one night jump. I was in radar and on one jump carried telephone wire and different things.

Somebody up in the high command decided he had an idea. He had about three broom handles and put sleeves on the end of them. In one of them, he had a can—a tomato can, or whatever. You shoved this flashlight in there, turned it on, and assembled these two sticks on each sleeve. The thing was maybe nine or ten feet high, and you stuck it in the ground. When you stuck it in the ground at night, the men jumping would look at this light and think it was a house or church or something with a light, and they would assemble to the right or left of it. Whoever invented this brought it to radar and wanted somebody to try it to see how it worked on a practice jump in England. They asked me if I wanted to try it, and I agreed. These three- or five-foot-long sections I stuck just like my rifle, in between my rifle and shoulder blades. My rifle hung to the right of my shoulder, and that made them stick straight up in line with my head. When I went to jump, they had a C-54 instead of the usual C-47. The doors are a lot shorter on it, so when I went out of the door, the stick got caught on top of the door and I couldn't get out. Finally they gave me a shove, and that made me tumble head over heels instead of going off the right way.

When I hit the ground, the thing was broken into pieces, and I never did assemble the thing because they were broken in half and the sleeves were all gone. The shock on hitting the ground broke the thing in about a half dozen pieces, and I couldn't get it together. They asked what happened to this thing, and I said, "This goddamn thing won't work!" I said, "Here it is!" and gave it to him in pieces. I said, "In the first place, it hits the top of the door, and in the second place, the shock when the parachute opened up caused me to almost lose it. When I hit the ground, I hit backwards, and it broke into several pieces." The guy said that he would have to think of something else. I said, "When you do, can you appoint somebody else? I don't want to jump with the damn thing!"

Gonzalez's first experience upon arriving in Great Britain had been even more harrowing. He had gone to Britain as a replacement. After landing in Glasgow, he had shipped to Birmingham.

In Birmingham, you stayed in compounds like barracks, and right next to the street there was a fence only about four foot high. There were holes in the fence, and you could walk across the street, get a beer, and talk to girls or do whatever you wanted. As a matter of fact, a lot of English girls snuck in that fence to meet the boys in the barracks separately. I got caught one night out of the compound, and I was sent to the detention center at Litchfield. In Litchfield, I imagine they sent the British hard-core soldier, because I know that is where they used to hang the British soldiers. They were on one side, and we were on the other. We hardly ever saw a British convict.

This Lieutenant Colonel Kilian was the head of the compound there and the MPs. In fact, I didn't know his name until over forty years later. I knew he was a high-ranking officer and that he was sort of like not all there! He was more like a Patton, a show-off. If he could have got a half a dozen pistols stuck around him chrome plated and all that, he would have done it. If he could have designed his own helmet with a big point and blood all over it, he would have—that is the way I took him for. He was either a drinker or taking morphine, because morphine was easy to get in those days from the first-aid kits. His eyes always seemed like they were glassy. He would hardly ever look at you, but if you saw his eyes, they were all glassy. He didn't look you straight in the eyes. It was more like he would look down on his desk and raise his eyes; he would not raise his head, he would raise his eyes and look at you—sort of like embarrassed. When I was there the second time [Gonzalez got in trouble again], I thought he must have been embarrassed because he hadn't seen combat or he hadn't had the opportunity because they gave him this shitty job.

When I was there the first time, somebody had just told me he had killed a prisoner by hitting him with the butt of a rifle across the mouth or neck or something. They said that his men, like the corporals or sergeants, were the same way and would do anything. I can't believe a guy like that could actually command an American soldier to mutilate these prisoners. I've got to say, when I was in Litchfield Prison, I was warned to just play it cool and do what you had to. I was a disciplined soldier and just minded my business. I would just sit in that cell. There were six of us, or four of us sometimes, and all we did was sit-ups, push-ups, and chin-ups. We used to do chin-ups by grabbing the bars on the window. That window must have been about two foot wide and three foot long. When you chinned up, you could look out into the compound. We would see how long we could stand there, and then come down and the other guy would do it. One time I was chinning up, and I saw this lieutenant walking across the compound. The church bells rang, and I said, "Here comes this 'Ding Dong.'" We all called him "Ding Dong," but of course, not to his face. I imagine other fellows in other cells called him different names. I guess fellows thought "Ding Dong" was the perfect name because he was kind of dingy, or at least to me he was. We did do work in prison, either work on KP for the whole prison, mop all the cells, mop the shithouses, mop everything, police the area, all the grounds, or paint stones. We were glad when we got things to do, because we were out of the cell and could do something.

Most of the time, we sat in there, and guys picked up butts and smoked, and they'd take cigarettes and break them down to get all the tobacco. They had English and American cigarettes, and they mixed the tobacco. They would go to the shithouse and roll the toilet paper to make the cigarette, and take about two puffs and put it away because they did not want the smoke smell in the cell. I didn't smoke or drink then, because I was a boxer and I didn't believe in it.

One time I was in the office when they brought in a soldier who I guess had been drinking. He put both hands on the desk, and the MP that was there took his rifle, hit him across the back, and knocked him to the floor. I didn't say anything. They would take a rifle and actually swing it as hard as they could and hit you in the mouth or skull. If you put your hands up, you knew you were going to have a broken hand or a broken shoulder. If he knocked you out, he was glad, and if you bent down to help the guy, they would say, "Leave him alone!" or "You are going to get the same thing!" It was something to see—you had to be there to believe man's inhumanity to man. When I was there the first time, somebody said he had killed a man by beating him with a rifle. When I was there the second time, they said he killed three or four. So I really don't know. I know a few were hit in the mouth when they were in an outer room. They never came back, because they took them to a hospital or put them in a different room, and I guess they suffered there. A lot of broken bones, eyes knocked out, hands broken, I guess.

I was there three or four weeks when one day they came and kicked me out. I went to the barracks, got my bags with all my uniforms, got in a truck, and they sent me to Glasgow, Scotland, and from there over to Ireland, where I hooked up with the 82nd Airborne.

After two combat jumps, Gonzalez was wounded at Bastogne in December 1944 and sent to a hospital in England. When he was released from the hospital, he received a pass before he returned to his unit. He was picked up by the MPs for staying out too long with his girlfriend, which made him AWOL. He was sent again to Litchfield, to find that Colonel Kilian (court-martialed after the war and fined $500) and "Ding Dong" were still there.

His two visits to Litchfield notwithstanding, Gonzalez distinguished himself in battle. A citation he received on November 30, 1944, reads in part:

> The First Platoon of Company "C," 505th Parachute Infantry Regiment, was caught between heavy enemy machine gun fire from both flanks while moving through the woods after having been relieved. Under such conditions, the platoon was unable to remain and fight and had to withdraw. Upon reaching a comparatively safe position, Private First Class GONZALES [the army always misspelled his name] dropped his equipment and declared that he was going to return to the area and bring back the wounded. With total disregard for his own personal safety, he made two trips through severe enemy machine gun and

> sniper fire and carried wounded men back to safety. Private First Class GONZALES' deeds were beyond the call of duty and saved two comrades from death or capture.

The citation, signed by James M. Gavin, awarded Gonzalez the Silver Star for this action during Operation Market Garden on September 24, 1944, about one mile from Reithorst, Holland.

Pvt. Paul E. Pachowka of Coatesville, Pennsylvania, arrived in England with the 507th PIR from Northern Ireland. He volunteered for Pathfinder training and made six night jumps outside the North Witham Airdrome. "I was assigned to a radar group, and it was with this group of men that I had all my training, which took about six weeks." His unit consisted of nineteen men.

The 101st Airborne Division in Training

Major Cox took over the 81st AA Battalion in March 1944, when things were beginning to get busy. Capt. Robert Jackson took Batteries D, E, and F to Western Sitlomere to be attached to the VII Corps and train for amphibious operations. After these batteries completed their training with Exercise Tiger, they were the first units slated to set up antiaircraft protection for Utah Beach. They arrived fifteen minutes after H-Hour with the 8th Infantry, 4th Division.

On March 25, Major Cox received British 6-pounders to replace his 57-millimeter antitank guns. Although these weapons were well suited to glider operations, his men had to make minor adjustments in their loading procedure. Cox and his antitank batteries continued to train with the gliders.

In the meantime, the paratroopers made a number of practice jumps. According to Rapport and Northwood in *Rendezvous with Destiny,* not long after the division's arrival in Britain, a jump school run by Col. Robert Sink was established at Chilton Foliat to qualify replacements. Practice drops took place late in 1943 before winter set in and resumed during the spring of 1944. That year, the 101st A/B also took part in some practice amphibious exercises. These were barely memorable for the enlisted men, who were driven to the drop zones and jumped out of the backs of $2\frac{1}{2}$-ton trucks.

Sgt. William Gammon of the 377th Parachute Field Artillery Battalion volunteered for Pathfinder training.

> I made several jumps in the Pathfinders. I think we made at least six jumps with the battery, although I might be confusing some of these with the Pathfinder exercises. Our Pathfinder group had two planes, and we would jump with a Eureka [radar] set and set up lights. We trained out of Newbury, where we had our barracks and officers. We had two teams and we put out panels. We had about nine men on a team; one jumped with a Eureka set, and then we had the panels and our security. We had a light that flashed a strong beam to the lead plane. The plane carried a Rebecca set. The Eureka set was 32 pounds, and it was a long console, which the man carried on his hip and leg. Jim Dietrich jumped with it because he was the most muscular. The panels were as if you put on a DZ with a T for direction. The light beam came with a backpack battery, and you would flash a code to the lead plane. We had some machine guns for security. There was no backup set. It was hoped one of the two teams might make it. Lt. Grady Hensley had the other team, but he was killed in Normandy. During training, we carried loaded weapons all the time, because it was supposed to be secret equipment.

We jumped out of Canterbury one night on a Friday, and I was an assistant under Lt. Robert Smith of El Paso. I turned an ankle on the jump, but since I had great plans for going to London the next day, I didn't mention it and I marched into camp. The next day, I couldn't get out of my bunk, and Lieutenant Smith was a bit disturbed for my not letting him know. He told me there was an ambulance out there at the drop zone for that purpose.

According to PFC Robert Flory, 1st Battalion, 506th PIR, one of the most important activities his regiment practiced in England was assembling quickly after a drop.

Normally we jumped in twelve-man squads, and your position in the plane determined the way you would walk. The first five men walked in the reverse direction from the flight, the last five walked in the direction of the flight, and the two in the middle stayed where they were as the rallying point. This was important, because these planes flew at about 100 to 110 mph. We ended up being able to jump eighteen men in twelve seconds.

PFC Jim Purifoy, 2nd Battalion, 501st PIR, arrived in Britain as a replacement in January 1944, and he was assigned to the S-2 Section of the battalion headquarters under Lt. Bill Sefton and Sergeant Darnek. There were only about ten men in the section, including three—Privates Fisher, Tantello, and Burrows—who had come from the 13th A/B Division with Purifoy.

We just went on patrols. When we were not advancing, we set up observation and listening posts. The lieutenant or sergeant went on all the patrols. We were trained specifically for patrols. We usually manned two two-man outposts for twenty-four hours a day. We shot an azimuth when we saw artillery fire and timed the number of seconds and recorded it on a log.

Patrols were usually three men, although sometimes as many as five. The lieutenant alternated who went on patrol, but it was usually him or the sergeant with two men.

When we joined the section, they took us on field trips and showed us what to do. We used the compass and practiced navigation day and night over and over again. Every man had to be able to read the map and compass well. In England, we made

The 377th Parachute Field Artillery Battalion

The 377th had four guns to a battery, a number that increased to six later in Holland. It had three firing batteries—A, B, and C—each of which consisted of 75-millimeter pack howitzers. Battery D was the supply and service unit.

At full strength, a battery numbered about 120 to 130 men. Each battery included a wire section, an instrument section, a gun section, and truck drivers. Each firing battery also had a machine-gun section. The gun section consisted of ten men: chief of section; gunner corporal; number one man, who opened the breech and fired; number two man, who loaded the gun; number three man, who took the round from the number four man after he had set the fuse (fuse quick or time delay) and charge on the round. The other four men shifted the gun's box trail, carried the ammunition, and served in other functions as required. The gun section also had two machine guns that were attached from the battery's machine-gun section.

two night jumps; two or three of us were assigned to each company in the battalion with a radio to contact each other and report back to battalion headquarters.

They also found a little town in England much like the one we were to secure in France. We were assigned a certain route for each company to take.

PFC Ray Hood, HQ Company, 2nd Battalion, 502nd PIR, served as a radio operator.

During the six months or so that we trained in England, emphasis was placed on small unit tactics, street and night fighting, and physical conditioning. We made three jumps in England. Two of these were daylight, one at night. One jump included all three parachute infantry regiments, but only the command and communications personnel participated—these were command post exercises (CPX).

The entire division participated in large-scale military field problems in Southern England on two different occasions. These exercises took place near the cities called Torquay and Bournemouth.

The division's code name was "Kangaroo," and each regiment was given a code name beginning with the letter K. The 502nd PIR was called "Kickoff." Identification between units of the division was simplified by painting emblems on each side of every man's helmet. The symbol for the 502nd was a two-inch white heart (each unit used playing-card and other symbols). The 1st Battalion had a small white dash to the right of the heart, 2nd Battalion had a dash beneath the heart, and 3rd Battalion's dash, of course, was on the left. Other regiments had clubs, hearts, diamonds, etc. The three battalions in each regiment were known as red white, and blue. Thus the 2nd Battalion, 502nd PIR, would be called "Kickoff White." Officers had a vertical, white four-inch bar painted on the backs of their helmets. NCOs had a horizontal bar.

The SCR-300 was dependable for more than five miles. It was carried in a special harness on the operator's back, and a handset was used for communications. It was a voice radio—no Morse code. I carried one of the damn things all over Europe, and it was an excellent piece of equipment. The thirty-five pounds it weighed could get a tad heavy, however, in addition to full field equipment. The communications platoon also carried and strung wire to establish communications by phone. Both sound-powered phones and crank-'em-up leather-cased phones, called EE-8s, were used. No switchboard was ever used in a combat situation; such use was not considered practical. Wiremen, whose job was to maintain wire communications, also acted as runner-messengers, and these men earned their pay. The Germans knew very well what they were doing and were always ready to devote a little time to livening up the runners' days—when I call them runners, I am not stretching the truth.

We had a CW (Morse code) radio called an SCR-694. This little jewel weighed more than forty pounds. The hand-cranked generator weighed another twenty-five, including handles with which to turn it. The wooden tripod, complete with a seat for the cranker on which the generator rested while being cranked, was cumbersome and heavy. From the time we started field exercises in the States and realized just how maneuverable we had to be, it was obvious that this contraption was useless. A top-notch Morse operator can send and receive no more than twenty-five words per minute. That's not nearly fast enough, and the whole rig was a waste of time, money, and vast amounts of energy. We never once used it in a combat situation.

We also had a device called, if I remember correctly, the M-1 converter, a coding machine. It weighed about fifteen pounds. Encoding a message as long as this paragraph took about twenty minutes. We were hardly ever in a spot that allowed twenty minutes for such shenanigans. The converter was never used. Our messages were delivered by voice—radio or telephone—our use of slang and argot and our own brand of verbal shorthand combined to make our messages indecipherable to any stranger, let alone someone who did not learn American (not English—American!) as his first language.

Eisenhower and SHAEF Planning

Capt. Harry C. Butcher, General Eisenhower's naval aide, kept a diary of his years with the supreme commander of Allied forces, published as *My Three Years with Eisenhower.* The following description of Eisenhower's activities is based on Captain Butcher's writings.

General Eisenhower assumed command of the Allied Expeditionary Force on January 16, 1944, before the final plans for Overlord were worked out. The operation covered the planning for the first ninety days of the operation. The code name Neptune was assigned to the actual landing in France, including preliminary movements. The 29th Division completed Exercise Duck before the details of the Overlord landing were finalized.

British general Fredrick E. Morgan relinquished his role as chief of staff to the supreme Allied commander (COSSAC) to General Eisenhower, who took over the planning of the cross-Channel invasion. Until then, the entire operation had been under the aegis of Britain. Gen. Bernard Montgomery headed the 21st British Army Group, which controlled all ground forces for the operation; Adm. Bertram Ramsay was in charge of all Allied naval forces for the operation; and Air Marshal Trafford Leigh-Mallory commanded all Allied air forces.

When Eisenhower met with the three British commanders on January 21, 1944, he informed them that he wanted to increase the invasion force from three to five divisions and expand the landing area. He planned to use two airborne divisions in the Cotentin Peninsula. Leigh-Mallory opposed these plans, warning of looming disaster and potential losses of more than 75 percent in such an operation, but Montgomery supported Eisenhower's view. According to Butcher, the Allies agreed to send one British airborne division to seize the bridges over the Orne and Dives Rivers near Caen rather than attempt to take the city. As a result, two additional assault divisions, one American and one British, had to prepare for the invasion. The mission of the 29th Division had not changed significantly, except that it would no longer be supporting a two-division British force landing near Caen. In addition, to meet the requirements of Eisenhower's new plan, it was necessary to prepare another division for amphibious operations. The task fell to the 4th Division, which, although green, was fresh and well trained. The 1st ESB, a combat-hardened unit, was shifted from supporting the 29th Division to backing up the 4th when Exercise Fox started.

Gen. Jacob Devers, head of ETOUSA headquarters in England, had a disagreement with Gen. George Marshall over command structure and general headquarters for American ground forces in England during 1943. The animosity between the two men was exacerbated when Marshall ordered the activation of the 1st U.S. Army Group headquarters in England in October 1943. According to Albert Norman's *Operation Overlord,* when Gen. Omar Bradley took over command of the new army group, Devers refused to cooperate in staffing the new army group, and he was sent to the Mediterranean upon Eisenhower's return to England.

In January 1944, Eisenhower demanded control over all Allied air forces in England for the duration of the campaign. On January 23, it appeared that General Patton would be brought to Great Britain. Four days later, Eisenhower visited the British 79th Armored Division, with its unusual assortment of tanks known as "Funnies." He was treated to a demonstration of the special tanks in action and was most impressed by the swimming duplex-drive (DD) tanks. He even climbed into one and tried to steer it, says Butcher.

During a discussion on February 9, Captain Butcher became aware for the first time of the artificial harbors, known as Mulberry, that the Allies planned to use. Of the 113 required steel breakwaters, or Bombardon units, 73 apparently were ready by April 18, and the huge concrete caissons, or Phoenixes, were scheduled for completion by April 21. Additional important components for the invasion were causeways that would lead from the offshore unloading piers that required 13,000 pontoons. The time needed to gather and build the components for the artificial harbors indicates that even if Eisenhower had not changed the original landing plan, no invasion could have taken place before late May. Since neither the original nor the new plan for Neptune offered a chance of rapidly securing a port, the Mulberry artificial harbors had to be ready before the invasion. The optimal moon and tide conditions for Operation Overlord, which were not determined until some time after January 1944, limited the number of days when a landing was feasible.

The year before Eisenhower arrived, the British commanders had taken certain emergency measures, and the 29th and 101st A/B Divisions were prepared to implement them. These measures, called the Rankin series of plans, included plans A, B, and C. Plan A called for a quick landing in France if the German sufficiently weakened their forces in Western Europe to reinforce those on the Russian front. Plan B was to be implemented if the Germans withdrew from France. Finally, plan C would be put into operation in case Germany collapsed altogether, according to Gordon A. Harrison in *Cross Channel Attack.* In all three cases, the small American force and all available British forces were to seize the major ports in France so that an Allied occupation could proceed. The 29th Division was expected to land in France and secure a port quickly; the 101st A/B was slated to drop outside of Le Havre and secure it. The 101st A/B G-2 was even provided with a map indicating the position of demolition charges in the harbor of Le Havre. Few men in any of the American units were familiar with, or even knew of, the plans, but they were there and prepared for this contingency. The initial tactical plan for Neptune was ready on February 1, 1944, but modifications continued until mid-May. The amphibious exercises had a good deal of influence on these changes.

During the winter months, a problem developed concerning the plan known as Anvil, later renamed Dragoon, which called for a small-scale landing in Southern France about the same time as Neptune. The British, primarily Churchill and Montgomery, did not want to implement it, although the Americans did. As a result, it remained in the planning stages, and its date was pushed back to August because of a scarcity of the necessary landing craft.

On February 14, Eisenhower was formally appointed as the supreme commander, and SHAEF came into existence. He set the target date of May 31, 1944, for Neptune. On February 17, his intelligence committee reported that the Germans would most likely not use poison gas to stop the invasion. The assault troops and follow-up units received impregnated uniforms to wear for the invasion. The next day, the British Admiralty notified Eisenhower that the requirements for Overlord had been revised. The British proposed using five battleships or monitors, eighteen cruisers, seventy-eight destroyers, and eighty-eight old destroyers, frigates, and corvettes, in addition to hundreds of smaller vessels. Although Eisenhower agreed with their projections, he did not like the fact that all the warships would be British, according to Butcher.

On February 24, Eisenhower, Tedder, Montgomery, and Bradley boarded a private train in London to inspect the British 51st Division and American 2nd and 3rd Armored Divisions in order to keep up the troops' morale.

For the landing, the British 21st Army Group under Montgomery was to control the Canadian 1st Army and British 2nd Army on the beaches of Juno, Gold, and Sword, as well as the 1st U.S. Army on Utah and Omaha Beaches. Sixty days later, Gen. Courtney Hodges took over the 1st U.S. Army, leaving Gen. Omar Bradley free to activate the 12th U.S. Army Group, which included the 1st U.S. Army and Patton's 3rd U.S. Army. The British ground forces were to be supported by the British 2nd Tactical Air Force, while the Americans would receive tactical support from the 9th Air Force. Eisenhower demanded and received control of the British Bomber Command and the U.S. 8th Air Force for Overlord.

On March 18, Eisenhower received information about his advanced command post at Southwick, a few miles north of Portsmouth. An estimate of U.S. forces in England by the end of May indicated that there would be thirteen infantry, six armored, and two airborne divisions; five armored groups; and two Ranger battalions. The British would field ten infantry, five armored, and two airborne divisions; ten armored brigades; eight commandos units; and one infantry brigade. This was about the equivalent of about forty divisions, not even close to the German intelligence estimate of at least sixty-five divisions.

Security was a key concern at SHAEF. One careless soldier nearly succeeded in doing what all the German agents had been unable to do. A package was intercepted in Chicago by postal officials because it was coming apart. It contained information revealing the strength, locations, equipment, and tentative date for Neptune. The soldier, who was supposed to have sent the package to the War Department, had addressed it to his sister instead, presumably because he had been worrying about her failing health. There was no indication that anyone other than ten postal employees in Chicago had an opportunity to examine it, according to Butcher. This was the most serious breach in security to take place before the landings.

On March 30, Eisenhower, who exercised control over the Allied bombing campaign, decided to go with the Transportation Plan instead of the Oil Plan in an attempt to cripple the enemy's ability to move and support its forces when the invasion came. Two days later, on April 1, Eisenhower resumed his inspection of the divisions earmarked for the invasion. As he visited with the troops, he shivered in his overcoat, which offered him little protection against the damp and cold weather, and by the time he got back to headquarters, he was nursing a bad cold. A mixed bag of news awaited him on his return. To his relief, the documents discovered in the Chicago post office had not been compromised. On the other hand, he learned that the enemy had the ability to launch a secret weapon against troop concentrations, but the threat was too limited to require the removal of the assault forces to an area west of Southampton.

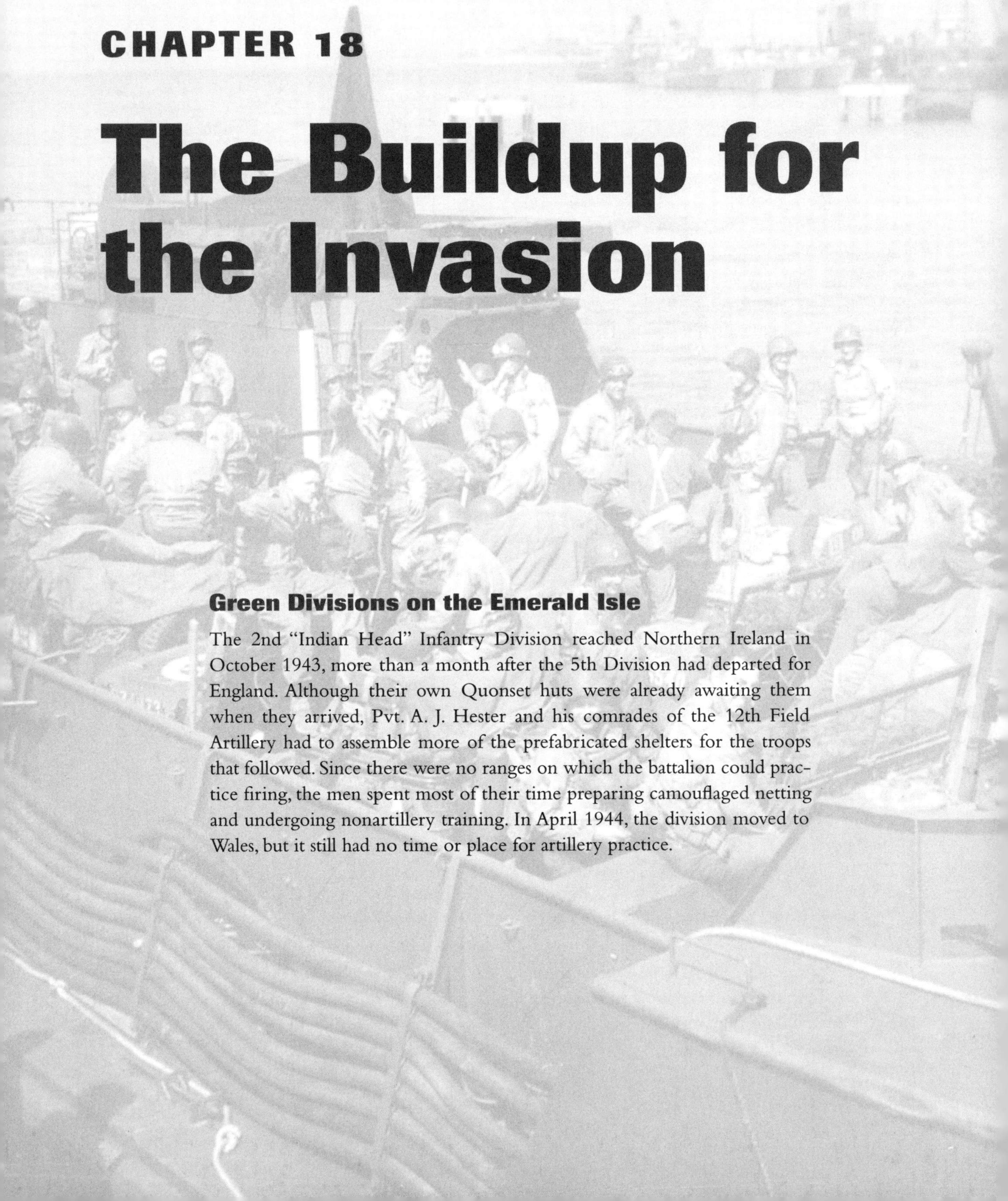

CHAPTER 18

The Buildup for the Invasion

Green Divisions on the Emerald Isle

The 2nd "Indian Head" Infantry Division reached Northern Ireland in October 1943, more than a month after the 5th Division had departed for England. Although their own Quonset huts were already awaiting them when they arrived, Pvt. A. J. Hester and his comrades of the 12th Field Artillery had to assemble more of the prefabricated shelters for the troops that followed. Since there were no ranges on which the battalion could practice firing, the men spent most of their time preparing camouflaged netting and undergoing nonartillery training. In April 1944, the division moved to Wales, but it still had no time or place for artillery practice.

The 8th "Golden Arrow" as well as the 2nd and 5th Divisions arrived in Northern Ireland at the end of 1943, overcrowding this little corner of the United Kingdom. The 8th Division was scattered over a thirty-mile radius. The 121st Regiment billeted at Shadow Camp in Fintona (later at Bally-Northland in Dungannon) and Ashbrooke-Colebrooke, the estate of Sir Basil Brooks; the 13th and 28th Regiments at Ely Lodge and the Drumcose estate in Enniskillen; and the 13th Regiment near the border with the Republic of Ireland. In Northern Ireland, the men of the 13th were exposed to an unexpected kind of war when the Irish Republican Army (IRA) attacked a constabulary station nearby. The men in Pvt. John Troy's battalion, however, had more pressing concerns on their minds and did not let the terrorist attack worry them too much.

> On New Years Day 1944, we had a turkey dinner, but when we went back to our huts, we all had that sick feeling; we ended up outside throwing up, then shitting. Most of us couldn't make it to the latrine, for there was only one latrine for a company, and it only had nine or ten coal buckets in which to shit. If I had a camera then, I could have had pictures of almost 200 men with their pants down suffering from spoiled turkey. The medics brought medicine in gallon jars. They said the whole battalion [2nd Battalion] was sick, so that's near 1,000 men. The next day, we had to take our shovels, go out, and cover all that "heave and shit." Even if our huts are no longer there, I could still find it today.

The 8th Division continued its infantry training, which included firing weapons, night marches, and even some amphibious exercises in small boats, but its men never glimpsed a tank. Pvt. John McBurney, who arrived at Ely Lodge as a replacement in April 1944, was struck by the unrelentingly gray skies and emerald fields of Northern Ireland.

> I was assigned to Company D, a heavy-weapons company. We did much practice firing in various training missions. Every time we fired our mortars, the base plate sank several inches in the ground, due to the peat soil and eternal rain of the area. We then got claims from local farmers, allegedly for the lambs that were aborted due to the reaction of the mother sheep to the noise of the explosions. Though we were told many such payments were made, I personally never saw any such thing happen.
>
> Our mess hall menu was different every day. At least the name of the main course meat was different, but each, not surprisingly, smelled and tasted like old mutton.
>
> I went into the town of Enniskillen on several occasions, but there wasn't much to do except buy and eat "fish and chips," which were greasy and not too good. I learned to like the warm black beer, but we did not seem to be welcome in the pubs. The local patrons were very clannish and seemed to dislike outsiders. The girls appeared to value the company of the American soldiers, though.
>
> I enjoyed the exquisite countryside, the narrow roads with the rock fences on each side, the trees, and especially the green of the grass and shrubs. The thatched roofs of the cottages were very interesting to me, with the clay chimney pots sticking out the top. It seemed like I was hungry all of the time and would occasionally dig up a rutabaga from a nearby field, peel and eat it. I did this even though we were warned not to do it, as we could get dysentery from the human fertilizer used by the local farmers.

The 4th "Ivy" Infantry Division Arrives

The 4th Division arrived in Britain from the States during January 1944. It was slated, together with the 1st and 29th Divisions, to lead the assault on D-Day. A Regular army division, it was a green unit like the 29th Division and was scheduled to be the first to land on Utah Beach. As the 4th Division disembarked in England, preparations were already under way for major invasion exercises, and some of the units had already trained at the amphibious centers in England.

Capt. John E. Galvin, regimental adjutant of the 8th Infantry, traveled with the advance party of officers from each battalion and Col. Carleton McNeilly. According to Galvin, the small group left from Fort Hamilton, New York, for Greenoch, Scotland, onboard the *Queen Elizabeth* on January 2, 1944.[1] The men reached Scotland about five days later and continued on to Huntington, England, to select places to quarter their units. There they stayed at an English barracks, where a room marked "Off Limits" held all the information pertaining to the 8th Infantry and its projected role in the upcoming invasion of France after the arrival of the unit in Britain.

The 12th Infantry Regiment departed from New York on the USS *George Washington* on January 17, disembarking at Liverpool and boarding a train on January 30. First Lt. Thomas Cortright's Company I settled at Budleigh Salterton, "a beautiful town right on the Channel." The trip south was not without excitement for Cortright's men. The train engine struck a coal car protruding from a siding onto the main line. The engine and first car derailed and rolled over, killing the engineer. Lieutenant Cortright, who was in the second car, survived the mishap, and there were no other fatalities. His company took up quarters in about seven houses in Budleigh.

> We formed each morning in front of the town hall. Of course, there were no autos or traffic to worry about. From there we went to our training for the day at the surrounding Dartmoor, which was great for training, and we did plenty of it. We had maneuvers some days and some nights. We had driver training and learned how to waterproof the vehicles as well as how to use the inflatable life tubes and the gas masks. In late February, along with others, I went to Assault School for two weeks.
>
> One night, after cruising the bars till closing time, another officer and I were sitting in a restaurant on the town square having a sandwich, when we noticed crowd noise outside, so we stepped out and saw perhaps the biggest fight in history. There must have been three battalions going at it. I looked at Cushman and said, "Well, I guess we better break this up!" We stepped out into it. Somebody promptly hit me, I hit back, and when I realized what I had done, I slipped into a jeep between two of my very large friends. The MPs were there by then, and this sergeant went around with one of the MPs looking for the officer that had hit him, but they never recognized lucky me.
>
> On returning to the unit, the battalion was put on the USS *Bayfield,* and we made an assault landing up the Firth of Clyde in Scotland. I saw my first casualty there when a P-39 dipped too close to the waves and cartwheeled in.

Pvt. Dalton H. Coffin of Ashland, Maine, was drafted in July 1942 at age twenty-two and became a member of the I&R Platoon of HQ Company, 1st Battalion, 12th Infantry Regiment. He traveled to Britain in a convoy of more than

1. No travel data for the *Queen Elizabeth* is available in standard references for late December and early January, but it seems more likely that the advance party departed between December 20 and 26, 1943.

100 ships. As usual, the food was terrible, and he could not wait for the sea voyage to end. Although Coffin's battalion departed at the same time as Cortright's, its final destination in Britain was different. "We were stationed at Higher Barracks, a former girls' school, in Exeter. Other units of the 4th Division were scattered about the countryside. Our training in England was on the water—on the River Clyde in Scotland and at Slapton Sands in Southeast England. Our platoon, the I&R, was made up of six jeep teams of approximately twenty-five men."

Pvt. Francis R. Steel, inducted in December 1941 at Jefferson Barracks, Missouri, served with Company K, 3rd Battalion, 12th Infantry. He was stationed at Exmouth. On weekends, he and his comrades scaled the fence of their compound to go into town and have a good time. Their battalion also took part in a practice landing in Scotland.

The 8th Infantry of the 4th Infantry Division crossed the Atlantic on the HMS *Franconia* and arrived at Liverpool with the rest of the division. Sgt. Vincent A. Angeloni from Butler, Pennsylvania, who had been drafted in June 1941, was greatly relieved to reach his destination after having been cooped up belowdecks for most of the trip with his comrades. To his great chagrin, however, he could not leave the ship right away, because his battalion, being the last one to disembark, had to clean the entire ship. Finally Angeloni and his comrades were allowed to board a train bound for Seaton by the Sea, near Exeter, where life took on a decided turn for the better.

> We moved into a bunch of Quonset huts. Being in the headquarters of 2nd Battalion, you get a little bit more favoritism. One day Colonel McNeilly, who was working in headquarters, said to get a piece of paper and pen, we were going up to this old hotel—I think it was called the Palladium or something like that. We went up; it was abandoned, but it was still in pretty good shape. We were going through the rooms, and on the second floor was a room that looked out over town square and over the water. The colonel said, "What do you think?" I was only a poor little sergeant, so I said, "Boy, that is pretty!" He said, "I want you to put your name in there and pick two more people." Later on, the first sergeant came after me because he wanted to have it. I said, "Gee, Colonel McNeilly said I could have it."

Sgt. Irving A. Bradbury Jr. from Maine, drafted in February 1942, was a radio operator in Company D.

> The 2nd Battalion was commanded by Col. Carleton McNeilly. He had also been over there in the advance party picking out the area for different organizations. He had this craving to get his battalion alone, because like all leaders, he said his battalion never gets credit for what they do; they are lumped into the regiment. So he took us to a little town called Creeky [Bradbury's spelling], down on the water by the River Exe in Devon. We put some sandbag gun emplacements in the sand on the beach. We had a regular guard mounted there twenty-four hours a day by rotating by companies in the battalion. We had orders to get any German planes that made the big U-turn and were driven out of London by the Home Guard. We did get some planes in that area turning back to France. One night, a Home Guard in combination with an American shot down a Junkers 88 in our area. We were called out late in the night to look for survivors. To my knowledge, only one little overgrown eighteen-year-old German *Luftwaffe* officer was captured. He was taken to the Seaton constabulary

lockup, and the next day he was picked up by regimental MPs.

S. Sgt. Murphy J. Chustz and Cpl. Charles Bergeron, both from Livonia, Louisiana, had worked as farmhands in the South before they enlisted together in Montgomery, Alabama, in January 1940 and requested postings in the field artillery. Bergeron was in Battery A of the 42nd Field Artillery Battalion, which used M7 self-propelled guns, and Chustz was in Battery B. When they arrived at their unit's base, Camp Broomhill, it was night, all the lights were out, and it was the darkest place they had ever seen. Bergeron kept blundering into foxholes in the dark and fell so hard he feared he had broken his back. As soon as their unit settled in, it began training. "We were given regular training using fire control instruments and running surveys," Bergeron says. "My section's job was to locate gun positions by survey, setting up the guns for firing, and establishing communications with battalion headquarters."

Sgt. William "Porky" Youmans from Passaic, New Jersey, drafted in November 1942, sailed on the HMS *Mauritania* to Britain at the end of February. His ship docked into Liverpool after lying offshore for two days, waiting for the tide. Once they reached land, Youmans and his travel companions took a train to the vicinity of Exeter, where they reported to the Service Company. Youmans, who was appointed as the supply sergeant, had to stay in Huntington whenever his unit went out on maneuvers for several days, because the entire supply unit was not scheduled to participate in the invasion and was to continue functioning in England.

S. Sgt. William Conrad, 2nd Battalion, 8th Infantry, also traveled on the *Mauritania.*

> We were in quarantine and placed in a staging area for preparation to shipping out [January]. While there, about 2,000 of us got food poisoning. They sent us to the hospital for treatment. We were kept there a week to ten days, then put in special quarters for observation and reassignment. In about a month, we were alerted, put on the English ship *Mauritania,* crossed the Atlantic in about four days, and then waited for the change of tide at Liverpool for a couple of days. We joined the company at Exeter. There we did beach training, hill climbing, and various maneuvers.

Pvt. William C. Montgomery was a nineteen-year-old litter bearer with the division's 4th Medical Battalion, Company A.

> My entire company—reinforced to about 120 from the normal 90 or so—was comfortably housed in one wing of a country mansion, Widworthy Court, Honiton, Devon.
>
> The husband, son, and daughter of the family, which owned Widworthy Court in 1944, were in the navy, we were told. The wife, her sister or companion, and one or two servants lived in the other wing of the house. We kept strictly apart from each other.
>
> The front rooms of the mansion, which looked out over a formal garden to the meadows beyond, joined the two wings. These front rooms were our dayroom and company headquarters downstairs, and the officers' quarters upstairs.
>
> The rest of the high-ceilinged rooms in "our" wing, upstairs and down, were our quarters. Most rooms had a small coke grate and a number of two-by-four-and-chickenwire double bunks. The mattresses were the large cloth covers that go *over* the hard-sided cases for bass violins. These covers were stuffed with straw.

Our principal complaints were about the impossibility of staying warm with the coke grates and about the food. Our company kitchen had been set up in what had once been a stable, then a garage, facing the inner courtyard at the rear of the mansion. Our cooks were supplied with what seemed an endless stream of mutton, with which they never learned to cope. With that, the powdered eggs, the lack of milk and butter, and their limited cooking skills, we felt sorely tried. That is, until we tried to buy a meal in Honiton, or Taunton, or Plymouth.

One bright spot was a pub in the tiny village about a half mile from Widworthy Court. It was complete with walk-in fireplace and friendly atmosphere. Hard liquor was only available occasionally, and seldom to us, but we learned that the beer was strong and the cider lethal.

On a larger training scale, we accompanied elements of the 8th Regiment for assault training in stormy dune country along the sea in the northwest of England. We lived in Quonset huts briefly and stood duty as medics in foxholes while the infantry attacked dummy pillboxes with live ammunition.

There were some casualties—an infantryman didn't throw his hand grenade far enough, somebody in a mortar crew dropped a shell down the tube backwards—but they were limited.

No major landing operation could succeed without the U.S. Army Engineers and British Royal Engineers. They had the equipment for building and repairing roads, bridges, and ports. In addition, they devised techniques for breaching beach obstacles, minefields, and other barriers. The American engineer units, which arrived in England in 1943, lacked the necessary training for upcoming invasion and had to learn the techniques for camouflaging, planting and removal of mines and booby traps, using the British-designed Bailey bridges, and other skills. The units that had trained in port construction and repairs in the States had to become familiar with the equipment used in Europe. According to Alfred Beck et al. in *The Corps of Engineers: The War against Germany,* the topographic engineers, who, with the aid of modern aerial photography, produced the best maps available for planning and operational use, were among the best-trained engineer units.

The American engineers trained at the School of Military Engineering in Ripon, Waterproofing School at Sudbury, British Railway Bridging School at King's Newton, Engineer Training Center at Porthcawl (Wales), Engineer School at Wallingford, and Marine Pipeline Training Center on the Isle of Wight. The Assault Training Center, under Col. Paul W. Thompson, was set up at Ilfracombe in April 1943. The colonel's staff studied the French coastline and concluded that the Germans could use no more than one platoon to defend every 2,000 to 2,500 yards of shoreline.[2] Next, Thompson's men tried to replicate the enemy's defenses as closely as they could on the beaches near Ilfracombe. The complete mockup, which was not finished until March 1944, included almost every type of obstacle the Allied soldiers might encounter: Belgian gates, element C, the more famous concrete dragon's teeth, wire obstacles, and bunkers. In addition, according to Beck et al., rope nets were installed so the troops could practice loading into dummy landing craft before actually going out to sea.

2. This was not a realistic estimate, except along areas of rugged coastline not suitable for a large invasion force. Every section of coastline that could be assaulted by a substantial invasion force had no less than a company-size force for each mile of beach, and usually more than that.

Experiences of the 29th "Blue and Gray" Division

Sgt. Walter Condon, Company C, 121st Engineer Battalion, 29th Division, endured the long hikes of more than twenty miles through the English countryside that became part of the weekly infantry training. Rumors circulated throughout the camp that the troops in North Africa had not been able to lug their loads and that General Gerhardt, division commander, did not want his own division to be shamed in a like manner. It sounded logical at the time but was not true. Condon, unlike others in his division, enjoyed the move to the windswept moors of Cornwall and Devon, particularly the pleasant resort towns of Torquay and Paignton.

> We were stationed on top of the hill in Paignton in what were tourist cabins sitting on stilts. It wasn't bad; we could walk down into town every night and get fish and chips without the fish. Many times all they had was the chips. They had nice beaches at Paignton, but it was all covered with barbed wire against invasion. We would go to various towns like Plymouth and Weymouth.
>
> We would go out on various types of landing craft and land at Slapton Sands, which was about twenty-five miles south of Paignton and just below the Dart River. In one of our night exercises on the Dart River, we were loading on pontoon boats across the river, which was a tidal river. When the tide went out, the river would fall at an extremely high rate. As we were out in the pontoon boats one night, several swamped, and a great many men drowned because they could not swim. There was a panic in that river in the middle of the night.

S. Sgt. William Lewis had arrived in Britain from the United States from his assignment at Fort Ritchie and was allowed to pick his assignment. He chose to serve with the AT Platoon, HQ Company, 1st Battalion, 116th Infantry, 29th Division.

> For months, we went down every week, loaded on landing craft, went out to sea, came back in, and landed at Slapton Sands or one of those places that looked like Omaha Beach. We had antitank guns, and they always made it in there, never lost a one—in practice. We would land and never get machine-gunned there or anything; it was pretty nice compared to what came in June. During the landing, there were explosions from TNT charges, but we all knew it was not going to hurt us. We took the gun up to a position and protected the perimeter against armor assault. We just came along and went right where we were supposed to go. Of course, there was nobody to keep us from going there. So we went up there and set up our four guns. Sometimes the truck picked up the gun and we walked back to camp.
>
> The terrain of the area resembled Normandy. They had hedgerows in England, but we were never instructed about how to handle them. We never learned a cockeyed thing about blowing up hedgerows. They were very similar to the French ones and had sunken roads, but they were not as big. They never mentioned the possibility that the enemy might defend those hedgerows.
>
> When we finished the problem, they held a big critique as to what we did right or wrong. Then we went marching back up to Ivybridge and cleaned up our gear. After the exercise, we walked back to camp.
>
> On Sunday, we cleaned up our gear and started hauling our butts back down there. On Monday or Tuesday, we did the same thing.

> We did a lot of marching and practiced setting up our antitank guns. We had very little firing practice and maybe went to the firing range twice. The rest of the time, we dragged the gun around, dug holes, found locations for the best fields of fire—just the things you do with an antitank gun.

First Sgt. Ernest Lee, who went to Britain with his friend Lewis, was placed in the I&R Platoon, HQ Company, 175th Infantry, 29th Division.

> We came in early in the morning. We were out at night in the Channel, and we came in on a practice landing almost identical to the way that we came in on Omaha Beach. They had obstacles, and they also had simulated mines blowing up. They simulated some of the action we would normally run into on a landing beach, but it was a formality of logistics of getting the ships ashore with the men, working with the navy primarily, and practicing on a beach similar to the one in Normandy.
>
> They used similar-type tetrahedrons, but they were just there to give the troops an idea of what they looked like. In some areas, they tried to simulate the defense with artillery firing over our heads to give us some actual type of feeling of combat. Actually, it was really good, getting that many boats together to come in as waves, then land, then exit. We formed up in boat teams, and we worked and practiced the same way we actually tried to land during the invasion. Each company had its own assigned boat teams.
>
> They had to evacuate several miles of beach and several villages of English people, but they were very cooperative. Slapton Sands was used for practice, and it was sealed off so you could not get in or out of it.

Second Lt. Charlie Adalaus Miller of Baton Rouge, Louisiana, commanded the 1st Platoon of Company I, 3rd Battalion, 115th Infantry, 29th Division. Drafted during his final year of college, he had been married for only a few weeks and he was unhappy about the fact that he had seen his wife for a mere two weeks during his fourteen months of training in the United States. He left the States in 1942, only two months after graduating from OCS and being assigned to the 29th Division. His disappointments notwithstanding, he took the final training exercises before D-Day very seriously.

> In this training exercise, all weapons to be used in the invasion were to be used. As my platoon approached an objective, we were behind the attacking units. We looked up and to the right. A flight of three bombers came toward us. We thought they would circle and bomb the objective, which was 1,000 yards to the front, but the bomb-bay doors opened, and the bombs came raining down. It looked as if it was a direct hit. Luckily, the bombs were of the phosphorous type, not high explosive. One bomb hit ten steps from us (I stepped it off). The phosphorus splashed over me and others were burned—none seriously. Training with live ammo was dangerous but necessary.

After the 29th Provisional Ranger Battalion was disbanded, Sgt. John Slaughter returned to his old unit. Oblivious to the rain and cold, his captain, Schilling, led the company on grueling marches through marshes and across windswept moors. When they were not marching, the troops continued to hone other skills, such as "loading and unloading dummy landing craft, exiting in columns of threes; peeling off left, center, and right, then quickly moving into a perimeter of defense. Crawling under barbed wire with live machine-gun grazing fire just inches overhead

Troops, including members of the 1st Infantry Division, begin to assemble for D-Day. NATIONAL ARCHIVES

and live explosions, strategically placed, detonating all around lent realism to these exercises."

The 1st "Big Red One" Division in Great Britain

Sgt. John B. Ellery had been with the 16th Infantry, 1st Division, from North Africa through Sicily. He had been trained in several different skills and wanted to transfer back to the 509th PIR in Italy, or at least to an airborne unit in England. But the 1st Division, which had lost a substantial number of its contingent and was taking on replacements, was not about to let go of an experienced veteran. Thus Ellery remained with the 16th Infantry, which was billeted at Lyme Regis, a town that enchanted him. His regiment began to practice beach landings. Unlike many of the other men, Ellery could see no resemblance between the practice site and the real thing in Normandy.

Raymond Voight, another veteran of the Mediterranean who returned to England with the 1st Division, was not impressed with the training, like many of his comrades.

> We trained by climbing down the ships as a regular invasion, then wading through the water, and standing around all day listening to these Stateside people tell us how to probe for mines. It was soaking wet all day, and it was foggy and miserable over there. There's not much sunshine to speak of, and this did not make a lot of real sense to me, and to the captain who was a combat veteran, as were most of the troops. I was a combat veteran, so this didn't go over too big.
>
> We were supposed to go onto the beach as a team. Now this is ridiculous. They sent in a few riflemen. I was a BAR man. For this assault, I became a demolition man. I had to wrap dynamite charges on a board; I had a six-foot pole, and detonators in my pocket, and I was supposed to go after the riflemen. My ammunition carrier, now the BAR man for the assault, was supposed to go up and pepper away at the pillbox, try to close it, and then I was to run up and try to blast open the window. Then the bazooka man would fire in, and the flamethrower would crawl up and shoot the flame in. So when we got finished there, three or four days, and we were going back to Bridgeport, where we were stationed, the captain turned around and told us all before we got in the trucks, "You know, when we hit the beach, it's every man for himself."

The 17th Base Post Office

The 17th Base Post Office (BPO) formed under Col. A. J. Harkins, who returned with a number of enlisted men from the 8th BPO from Egypt in March 1944. They had served in Cairo for fourteen months in what they called a "soldier's paradise." They traveled by ship, the British-manned French SS *Cuba*, to Italy and then Algiers.4 There they were put on a Liberty ship for a two-week trip back to the United States, living on C rations. The Atlantic crossing in stormy winter weather made this the most trying experience the mailmen had since arriving in Egypt in early 1943.

Meanwhile, the men from the 4th BPO at Pomona, California, handled the mail for the armored troops at the Desert Training Center in 1943. From this group, a cadre was selected to form the new 17th BPO in January 1944. They soon boarded a train, with low priority, for a ten-day stay at Fort Bragg. Next, the unit departed for Fort Dix to continue their training. In a month, the strength of the unit grew from 75 to 456 men. The training day began with reveille, followed by roll call, with some of the men returning from overnight stays at nearby homes. Then came breakfast, with the traditional immersion of the mess kit into boiling water, and some additional time was spent policing the area. This was followed by exercise time and a little marching. The official activation of the 17th BPO took place in March, when Colonel Harkins finally arrived.

Later in the morning, the men watched orientation films in a large theater and continued training. One of the training courses included three days of fire tending, and another was dedicated to poisonous gas, with the men being exposed to tear gas in an enclosed chamber. They also had rifle training. The postal clerks continued with infantry training, including hikes and obstacles courses.

Finally, in April 1944, the men of the 17th BPO embarked on the overcrowded *Île de France,* landing at Greenock, Scotland. From there they proceeded south to their quarters at the 10th Replacement Depot in Litchfield, where they were to assist the 1st BPO. The men who did not assist the 1st BPO were assigned to construction details to build a camp for the 17th BPO. On April 28, the 17th BPO moved to Pheasey Farms near Birmingham. Of the men in this unit, 68 percent had postal experience, and 50 percent were age thirty or older.

On May 8, Detachments A and B, numbering about 100 men each, were activated. Detachment A was attached to the 1st Army, and Detachment B to the Advance Section Communication Zone. A few days later, Detachment C, with more than 200 men, was activated. These detachments were slated to cross the Channel after the invasion to handle the distribution of mail, but Detachment A did not embark until July 25. Detachment B came ashore on July 3 at Omaha Beach and was split into three groups—one operating near Omaha Beach, another near Utah Beach, and the third at Cherbourg—working fourteen to sixteen hours a day to get the mail through. According to James R. Brady in *Invasion B.P.O.: A History of the 17th Base Post Office,* few buildings were available, so their operations were largely done in the open, as the combat troops, only a few miles away, needed the morale-boosting mail. Until August, these were the only mailmen in the beachhead.

4. The *Cuba* was an 11,420-ton luxury liner turned into a troopship. Just a few weeks before the war ended it was sunk by a U-oat off Portsmouth.

The Buildup

The 3rd "Spearhead" Armored Division was the first unit of this type to arrive in Britain to prepare for the invasion after the departure of the 1st "Old Ironsides" Armored Division for North Africa in 1942. It arrived in mid-September 1943, aboard the *Capetown Castle* and *John Erickson,* the latter of which returned to Canada to pick up the stranded units of the 101st A/B Division, whose ship had broken down. Most of the division was quartered in Wiltshire, England, and its headquarters was set up at Bruton, Somerset. It was assigned first to the V Corps, and in November to Gen. Joe Collins's VII Corps. According to Frank Millner in his history, *Spearhead in the West 1941–1945: The Third Armored Division,* the division drew new weapons in England and continued training while maneuvers took place on the Salisbury Plain.

The 2nd "Hell on Wheels" Armored Division returned to England in November 1943, leaving its vehicles in Sicily. Its men took up quarters at Tidworth and received new equipment. After several weeks of drawing equipment, the division began its training program. The 2nd was the only American armored division in England with combat experience, but its men continued to train to prepare for the big tank battles that might take place in Northern France.[3]

After it arrived in England in November, the 430th Anti-Aircraft Artillery (Automatic Weapons) Battalion waited in Hogton for its equipment. Pvt. Edward Trennert gripes about the terrible coffee he and his comrades were served. Next, the unit moved to another American air base, which it protected for several weeks. After that, the battalion was sent to Warrington to set up its 40-millimeter antiaircraft guns to protect a base repair depot. For Trennert and most of his comrades, it was their first Christmas away from home, and many of them were homesick, but American Red Cross girls bearing a gift for each of them brightened their day. Trennert received a khaki scarf, his only Christmas present, which he cherished for the rest of his life. On January 21, 1944, the unit began antitank training at Minehead, antiaircraft training at Blandford, and mountain warfare training at Brixham Hills. PFC Fred Bewersdorf escaped the grueling routine by spending most of the time playing basketball in interservice games as part of a program to boost morale.

The 9th "Varsity" Division returned from the Mediterranean in late November 1943. According to Sgt. Herbert U. Stern, the training was routine for the veterans, and occasionally some of the experienced men from various units gave classes to the newly arrived troops.

> I was a member of Company D, 9th Medical Battalion. The battalion was made up of Companies A, B, C, and D and a headquarters unit. Companies A through C were ambulance companies, and Company D was a traveling emergency hospital, which also had drivers to treat emergencies as well as walking wounded who were sent on to field hospitals for processing.
>
> I had been assigned to spend one week in London to attend a British Intelligence School, where I learned how to interpret

3. The armored division (TO) for 1942 consisted of two tank regiments (three battalions each) and one armored infantry regiment (three battalions). After the North African campaign, this was revised. The division's regiments were replaced by three combat combats, similar to brigade headquarters, that received the battalions they needed for their missions. The division's size was reduced from six tank battalions to three, and the three armored infantry battalions remained. This was true for all the armored divisions except the 1st, 2nd, and 3rd, which were in England and Italy at the time of the new TO late in 1943. These three divisions retained their regiments and all six tank battalions and remained "heavy" armored divisions.

enemy documents and interrogation techniques.

While in England, our unit was stationed on a small estate four miles outside of Winchester. It consisted of barns, a main building, stables, and Nissen huts; all the facilities were used for housing. A great deal of freedom existed. After 5 P.M., many units were able to go to local pubs and restaurants, and attend organized dances at units of the British Women's Auxiliary Navy and Army. Curfews and regulations common to rest area situations existed. The months in England were pleasant, and many of us became friends with local families.

A steady stream of replacements arrived in Britain on the convoys. Among them was nineteen-year-old Pvt. Sam L. Burns, who had been drafted late in May 1943 and landed at Liverpool in late December on the troopship *Edmund B. Alexander.* It was a rough voyage, during which eleven men were lost at sea. At Liverpool, Burns boarded a train for the replacement center at Yoevill, where he remained for several days. He was then sent to the 9th Division at Winchester and from there to Barton Stacy, where he joined the 2nd Battalion, 39th Infantry Regiment. In February, his battalion went on maneuvers for two weeks, and then returned to continue the conditioning marches and infantry training throughout the spring. Like many of his comrades, he had a hard time getting used to the damp climate of England. His mood was not improved by the cold showers he had to take in the garrison area. The only bright spot of his stay in England was a trip to London he took during a rare seven-day leave.

PFC Ernest J. Botella arrived a few weeks after Sam Burns as a replacement aboard the *Edmund B. Alexander.*[5] From Olive Bridge, New York, Botella, was the son of Spanish immigrants from Barcelona. He enlisted on February 1, 1943, and went to Camp Croft for basic. He and several comrades were held over for OCS. In the end, however, he did not get to attend OCS, and after a period of almost four months, he was given leave and then sent to Camp Miles Standish to ship out to Europe. He recalls his ship being part of a convoy of about thirty-five vessels escorted by ten destroyers or destroyer escorts. The sea voyage was hard on him, as he suffered from seasickness for the ten days the trip lasted.

We landed at Liverpool, England. It took about three hours from the time we docked for the group I was with to debark. As we went down a gangplank, a British army band was playing. The British version of the Red Cross was handing out coffee and doughnuts. We just walked out, boarded trucks, and started moving. The whole procedure from gangplank to truck was about five minutes. We drank the coffee on the fly.

We went to an area known as Litchfield. It was a replacement depot and the location of the army detention center. We were briefed that if we goofed up, we could figure on ending up in the army detention barracks. Litchfield was supposedly full of deserters, AWOL, and black marketeers. We were cautioned about keeping our noses clean and not being in there with them. The CO of Litchfield had a reputation for a sadistic streak.

From the depot, the largest part of us was assigned to the 9th Division, and we convoyed out. We went to an old British army base with cold stone buildings and little

5. It is possible that both embarked at the same time and one of them is mistaken about the date, but no source exists to confirm this. It is a fact, however, that they both departed from Camp Miles Standish on the same ship, whether or not it was on a different date.

heat. English-style latrines with nothing to sit on, just pads you stood on and squatted.[6] Most of us never had seen anything like that before, and it took a little getting used to. Later we found out that they were pretty prevalent throughout England.

I would say that most of the men on the transport went there—2,000 to 3,000 men. It was run by Americans; I don't recall seeing indigenous personnel. There were at least 1,000 of us who went to the 9th Division. We went in a truck convoy to the 9th Division area, which was about fourteen miles east of Winchester in a little town called Aldershot, if I remember correctly. By the time we got to headquarters, they had already made assignments. So it was just a case of going from division headquarters directly to the company you were assigned to.

There were three of us who took basic together, were held over and went overseas together, and ended up being assigned to the same squad and platoon.

The first company the three of us were assigned to—the other two were Donald Blish and Oliver Blumberg—we ended up being assigned to E Company of 2nd Battalion of the 47th Infantry, which was a rifle company. I know I am still alive because we had a conscientious squad leader, but I don't remember his name. One of the first things he asked us was what type of basic we had. We all had heavy-weapons training and we were in a rifle company, but this wasn't going to cut it. He said we would be dead the first time we went out, because we had no background for our type of operation. This man went through the platoon sergeant, platoon leader, company commander, and finally got the battalion commander, who was Lieutenant Colonel Johnson. The end result was that all of us with the heavy-weapons training that were assigned to rifle companies were reassigned to heavy-weapons companies. This is how I ended up in H Company, and I am grateful to that individual who started this. He was three or four years older than we were, and he was a veteran of Africa and Sicily. He had been around.

In the 1st Platoon of H Company, the squads were designated as the 1st, 2nd, 3rd, and 4th. I was in 1st Squad, 1st Section, 1st Platoon. I started as an ammo bearer and probably number five down the line. There was one older man between the number three man and me. Blumberg and Blish were right behind me. We carried an M-1 and switched to a carbine before the invasion. The number one and number two were armed with .45-caliber pistols.

It was late January, with snow on the ground, and colder than hell. We had extensive field training between January and May. I am grateful for the training, although we bitched like hell then. We were mixed in with veterans that knew their way around, so we had an advantage over green divisions that went into Normandy. We had firing with all the weapons to which we were exposed. We were cross-trained—machine gunners fired mortars and vice versa.

When firing the 81-millimeter mortar, the first thing you learn is to drop your head down when you drop that round down the barrel. The number one mortar man is responsible for aiming of the mortar based on fire directions from the section leader. The number two drops the rounds in

6. These were also called Italian-style toilets.

after he pulls off the excess increments based on instructions of the section leader.[7] Number three makes sure number two doesn't run out of ammo. The platoon is the same size as the sections and squads of the machine-gun platoon.

My platoon leader, Lieutenant Zesser—a man from Chicago who was about four years older than me and about my height (tall)—realized I was the only one who could keep step with him, so I graduated from ammo bearer to platoon guide. Eventually I was platoon runner. We were both about the same height and build, and sometimes people would confuse us, although I didn't shave that much.

7. Charges were attached to the mortar rounds. The number of charges kept on each round depended on the desired range.

ACKNOWLEDGMENTS

It took the accounts of more than 200 veterans to put this project together. There are too many veterans to list here, but all are listed with their unit in the bibliography (found in volume 3). Here we would simply like to acknowledge some of those who provided additional materials, such as memoirs or books, and gave permission to quote from them. Some veterans, like Larry Knecht and Peter Trioli, even conducted interviews for us early in the 1990s. In addition, we would like to thank the staff at NARA for helping us locate records.

Special thanks go to John "Slim" Stokes, our reader, who spent many hours correcting errors in the manuscript and helping locate veterans with whom we had lost contact during the past fifteen years. We apologize for anyone we may have forgotten to mention.

Sadly, since we began this project in 1989, many of the veterans who contributed their accounts have passed away. It took until 2007 to find a publisher interested in this book, and by that time, many of the contributors had either forgotten about us or assumed the book would never be done. Some, like Robert Dove and Ray Hood, remained in contact and waited patiently, but passed away in the last few years. We regret that they and many other contributors will never see the final product, but we hope that their families and descendants will take the time to read their accounts.

The following is a partial list of those who made contributions to this volume:

Lt. Col. John A. Allison (veteran), who provided a copy of his memoirs.

Steven E. Anders, Ph.D., Command Historian, U.S. Army Quartermaster Center at Fort Lee, who provided information on army rations.

Mark Bando, who provided data on the 101st Airborne Division and gave us additional contacts.

Sidney Berger (veteran), who provided a copy of his manuscript.

Raus Blondo (veteran), who provided a copy of the 112th Engineer Combat Battalion history.

Byron Cook (veterans), who provided a copy of his manuscript *Little Boy Blue*.

X. B. Cox (veteran), who provided a copy of his memoirs.

Gerard M. Devlin, who provided contacts and additional information on airborne operations not included in his books.

Barbara Donnelly, Reference Librarian at the Naval War College, who provided reference material on naval training.

Col. Robert Dove (veteran), who provided his 79th Recon diary.

Eugene E. Eckstam, who provided additional material on Operation Tiger.

Don Garrigues (veteran), who provided a copy of his unpublished memoir *From the Delphus to Destiny* and documents on the 551st Parachute Infantry Battalion.

Ray B. Hood (veteran), who provided a copy of his memoirs in addition to other material, including a piece of his parachute.

Wardell Hopper (veteran), who provided a copy of the history of the 741st Tank Battalion.

Jack Ilfrey (veteran), who provided a copy of part of the 20th Fighter Group's unit history as well as association newsletters.

Larry Knecht (veteran), who provided additional material and contacts for the 4th Division.

Allan L. Langdon (veteran), who provided a copy of his manuscript.

Rev. Melvin Larson (veteran), who provided new details for this book and another project.

William Lewis (veteran), who was always in contact with additional information for this and other projects.

Bernard Lowry, who helped locate sites in England referred to by veterans (who often could not properly spell the names) and clarifyed many details.

Harold Martino (veteran), who provided a copy of his unpublished manuscript.

Ray Merriam, who contacted veterans and provided copies of now-rare books.

Col. Don Patton, who located former veterans.

Henry Phillips (veteran), who provided a copy of his book *Heavy Weapons.*

Col. Sherman Pratt (veteran), who provided material from his book, *Autobahn to Berchtesgaden.*

Murray Pulver (veteran), who provided a copy of his book, *The Longest Year.*

Leon J. Renicker, who provided a copy of the 137th Infantry Regiment's combat history.

Gordon Rottman, who providing details on various items of equipment and special units.

Harold Schebeck (veteran), who provided a copy of his memoirs.

Charles Scheffel, who provided a copy of materials about the 1st Battalion, 39th Infantry Regiment, 9th Infantry Division, including memoirs and a report on the German attack at Avranche.

John Shirley (veteran), who provided a copy of his book, *I Remember*, as well as other details.

J. R. Slaughter (veteran), who provided a copy his early manuscript concerning veterans of the 29th Division.

J. B. Smith (veteran), who provided organization information for the of 463rd AAA AW Battalion.

John Stokes, who read this manuscript and helped with research on veterans.

Carl Strom (veteran), who providing additional information.

Lee Unterborn, who helped with general research and loaned books.

Isadore Valenti (veteran), who provided sections from his book, *Combat Medic.*

John Votaw at the 1st Infantry Division Museum at Cantigny, Chicago, who provided veterans' accounts and contacts plus information on the 1st Division.

Andrew Woods at the McCormick Research Center of the 1st Infantry Division Museum, who provided information on training and on General Mason.

INDEX